Western Society: A Brief History

WESTERN SOCIETY:
A Brief History

VOLUME I:
From Antiquity to the Enlightenment

John P. McKay
University of Illinois at Urbana-Champaign

Bennett D. Hill
Late of *Georgetown University*

John Buckler
University of Illinois at Urbana-Champaign

Clare Haru Crowston
University of Illinois at Urbana-Champaign

Merry E. Wiesner-Hanks
University of Wisconsin–Milwaukee

Bedford/St. Martin's
Boston   New York

For Bedford/St. Martin's

Publisher for History: Mary Dougherty
Director of Development for History: Jane Knetzger
Executive Editor for History: Traci Mueller
Senior Production Editor: Rosemary R. Jaffe
Senior Production Supervisor: Joe Ford
Executive Marketing Manager: Jenna Bookin Barry
Associate Editor for History: Lynn Sternberger
Production Assistants: David Ayers and Lidia MacDonald-Carr
Copyeditor: Peggy Flanagan
Text Design: Cia Boynton
Photo Research: Carole Frohlich
Indexer: Jake Kawatski
Cover Design: Donna Lee Dennison
Cover Art: Anonymous, fifteenth century, *Market Scene* (detail with vendors and women). Late fifteenth-century fresco, Castello d'Issogne, Italy. Scala/Art Resource.
Cartography: Charlotte Miller/GeoNova
Composition: NK Graphics
Printing and Binding: RR Donnelley and Sons

President: Joan E. Feinberg
Editorial Director: Denise B. Wydra
Director of Marketing: Karen R. Soeltz
Director of Editing, Design, and Production: Marcia Cohen
Assistant Director of Editing, Design, and Production: Elise S. Kaiser
Managing Editor: Elizabeth M. Schaaf

Library of Congress Control Number: 2008928070

Manufactured in the United States of America.
4   3   2   1   0   9
f   e   d   c   b   a

For information, write: Bedford/St. Martin's, 75 Arlington Street, Boston, MA 02116
(617-399-4000)

ISBN-10: 0–312–68299–9 ISBN-13: 978–0–312–68299–6 (combined edition)
ISBN-10: 0–312–68300–6 ISBN-13: 978–0–312–68300–9 (Vol. I)
ISBN-10: 0–312–68301–4 ISBN-13: 978–0–312–68301–6 (Vol. II)

Preface

The first edition of *A History of Western Society* grew out of our desire to infuse new life into the study of Western civilization. We knew that historians were using imaginative questions and innovative research to open up vast new areas of historical interest and knowledge. We also recognized that these advances had dramatically affected the subject of European economic, cultural, and, especially, social history, while new scholarship and fresh interpretations were also revitalizing the study of the traditional mainstream of political, diplomatic, and religious developments. Our goal was to write a textbook that reflected these dynamic changes, and we have been gratified by the tremendous response to this book on the part of both instructors and students.

This version of the textbook—*Western Society: A Brief History*—reflects the same goals and approach of its full-length counterpart. But its brevity addresses the needs of a growing number of instructors whose students need a less comprehensive text, either because of increased supplemental reading in the course or because their students benefit from less detail in order to grasp key developments. It also suits courses that cover the entire history of Western civilization in one semester. Finally, its lower price makes it an affordable alternative to larger texts, and the retention of a particularly strong illustration and map program and a full program of pedagogical support make the book a particularly good value.

In developing *Western Society: A Brief History*, we shortened our full-length narrative by thirty percent. We began by judiciously reducing coverage of subjects of secondary importance. We also condensed and combined thematically related sections and aimed throughout the text to tighten our exposition while working hard to retain our topical balance, up-to-date scholarship, and lively, accessible writing style. The result, we believe, is a concise edition that preserves the narrative flow, balance, and power of the full-length work.

Central Themes and Approach

It was our conviction, based on considerable experience introducing large numbers of students to the broad sweep of Western civilization, that a book in which social history was the core element could excite readers and inspire a renewed interest in history. Therefore we incorporated recent research by social historians as we sought to re-create the life of ordinary people in appealing human terms. At the same time, we were determined to give great economic, political, cultural, and intellectual developments the attention they unquestionably deserve. We wanted to give individual readers a balanced, integrated perspective so that they could pursue—on their own or in the classroom—those themes and questions that they found particularly exciting and significant.

In an effort to realize fully the potential of our innovative yet balanced approach, we made many changes, large and small, in the editions that followed the original publication of *A History of Western Society*. In particular, we approached the history of the West as part of the history of the world, devoting more attention throughout the book to Europe's interactions with other cultures and societies. Too, we took advantage of the exciting recent scholarship on women's and gender history to provide even fuller discussion of the role of gender in the shaping of human experience. Producing this briefer edition gave us the opportunity to bring even more clarity and focus to our core themes and approach.

Pedagogy and Features

We know from our own teaching that students need and welcome help in assimilating information and acquiring critical-thinking skills. Thus we retained the class-tested learning and teaching aids of the parent text while adding more such features. Each chapter opens by posing four or five historical questions keyed to its main sections in a clearly defined *chapter preview* that accompanies the chapter introduction. The relevant questions appear at the start of the chapter's main sections, all of which conclude with a *section review* that encapsulates the material presented and provides an answer to the question. Then a carefully crafted *chapter review* at the close of each chapter reprises the chapter questions and summary answers.

In other measures to promote clarity and comprehension, bolded *key terms* in the text are defined in the margin next to their appearance and repeated at the end of the chapter, and confidence-building *phonetic spellings* are located directly after terms that readers are likely to find hard to pronounce. *Chapter chronologies* alert students to the major developments discussed in the chapter and *topic-specific chronologies* appear at key points throughout the book.

We are particularly proud of the illustrative component of our work, its *art and map programs*. Over 340 illustrations, many of them in full color and all contemporaneous with the subject matter—reveal to today's visually attuned students how the past speaks in pictures as well as in words. Recognizing students' difficulties with geography, we also offer over 65 full-color maps and the popular *"Mapping the Past"* chapter feature, which provides questions that encourage students' close investigation of one map in each chapter, often with prompts to compare it to other maps in order to appreciate change over time. Substantive captions for all our illustrations help students to make the most of these informative materials.

We are proud as well of the biographical and primary-source special features that appear in each chapter to spotlight our focus on social history. These were so well received by readers of the full-length edition that we determined to keep them in our concise account.

Each chapter features *"Individuals in Society,"* an illustrated biographical essay of a woman, man, or group intended to extend the chapter narrative while showing students the similarities and differences between these former lives and their own. This special feature evidences our focus on people, both famous and obscure, and we believe that student readers will empathize with these human beings as they themselves seek to define their own identities. Examples include Bithus, a typical Roman soldier (Chapter 6), the German abbess and mystic Hildegard of Bingen (Chapter 10), freed slave and abolitionist Olaudah Equiano (Chapter 19), and Tariq Ramadan, the controversial European-Muslim intellectual (Chapter 31). "Questions for Analysis" guide students' consideration of the historical significance of these figures. For a complete list of the individuals highlighted, see page xxv.

Each chapter also includes a one- or two-page feature titled *"Listening to the Past,"* chosen to extend and illuminate a major historical issue raised in the chapter through the presentation of a single original source or several voices on the subject. Each "Listening to the Past" selection opens with a problem-setting introduction and closes with "Questions for Analysis" that invite students to evaluate the evidence as historians would. Selected for their interest and importance and carefully fitted into their historical context, these sources, we hope, do indeed allow students to "listen to the past" and to observe how history has been shaped by individual men and women, some of them great aristocrats, others ordinary folk. Sources include Gilgamesh's quest for immortality (Chapter 1), an Arab view of the Crusades (Chapter 9), parliamentary testimony of young British mine workers (Chapter 22), and Simone de Beauvoir's critique of marriage (Chapter 30). A full list of these features appears on page xxv.

The complete volume presents eight photo essays entitled *"Images in Society."* Each consists of a short narrative with questions, accompanied by several pictures. The goal of the feature is to encourage students to think critically: to view and compare visual illustrations and draw conclusions about the societies and cultures that produced those objects. Thus, in Chapter 1 appears the discovery of the "Iceman," the frozen remains of an unknown herdsman. "The Roman Villa at Chedworth" in Britain mirrors Roman provincial culture (Chapter 6). The essay "From Romanesque to Gothic" treats the architectural shift in medieval church building and aims to show how the Gothic cathedral reflected the ideals and values of medieval society (Chapter 11). "Art in the Reformation" (Chapter 14) examines both the Protestant and Catholic views of religious art. Chapter 17 presents the way monarchs displayed their authority visually in "Absolutist Palace Building." Moving to modern times, the focus in Chapter 19 changes to "London: The Remaking of a Great City," which depicts how Londoners rebuilt their city after a great catastrophe. "Class and Gender Boundaries in Women's Fashion, 1850–1914" studies women's clothing in relationship to women's evolving position in society and gender relations (Chapter 24). Finally, "Pablo Picasso and Modern Art" looks at some of Picasso's greatest paintings to gain insight into his principles and the modernist revolution in art (Chapter 28).

Supplements

To aid in the teaching and learning processes, a wide array of print and electronic supplements for students and instructors accompanies *Western Society: A Brief History*. Some of the materials are available for the first time with our new publisher, Bedford/St. Martin's. For more information on popular value packages and available materials, please visit bedfordstmartins.com/mckaywestbrief/catalog or contact your local Bedford/ St. Martin's representative.

For Students

Print Resources

The Bedford Series in History and Culture.   Over 100 titles in this highly praised series combine first-rate scholarship, historical narrative, and important primary documents for undergraduate courses. Each book is brief, inexpensive, and focuses on a specific topic or period. Package discounts are available.

Rand McNally Atlas of Western Civilization.   This collection of over fifty full-color maps highlights social, political, and cross-cultural change and interaction from classical Greece and Rome to the post-industrial Western world. Each map is thoroughly indexed for fast reference.

The Bedford Glossary for European History.   This handy supplement for the survey course gives students historically contextualized definitions for hundreds of terms—from Abbasids to Zionism—that students will encounter in lectures, reading, and exams. Available free when packaged with the text.

Trade Books.   Titles published by sister companies Farrar, Straus and Giroux; Henry Holt and Company; Hill and Wang; Picador; St. Martin's Press; and Palgrave are available at a 50 percent discount when packaged with Bedford/St. Martin's textbooks. For more information, visit bedfordstmartins.com/tradeup.

New Media Resources

WESTERN SOCIETY: A BRIEF HISTORY e-Book.   This electronic version of *Western Society: A Brief History* offers students unmatched value—the complete text of the print book, with easy-to-use highlighting, searching, and note-taking tools, at a significantly reduced price.

Online Study Guide at bedfordstmartins.com/mckaywestbrief.   The popular Online Study Guide for *Western Society: A Brief History* is a free and uniquely personalized learning tool to help students master themes and information presented in the textbook and improve their critical-thinking skills. Assessment quizzes let students evaluate their comprehension, a flashcard activity tests students' knowledge of key terms, and learning objectives help students focus on key points of each chapter. Instructors can monitor students' progress through the online Quiz Gradebook or receive e-mail updates.

Benjamin, A Student's Online Guide to History Reference Sources **at bedfordstmartins .com/mckaywestbrief.**   This Web site provides links to history-related databases, indexes, and journals, plus contact information for state, provincial, local, and professional history organizations.

The Bedford Bibliographer **at bedfordstmartins.com/mckaywestbrief.**   *The Bedford Bibliographer*, a simple but powerful Web-based tool, assists students with the process of collecting sources and generates bibliographies in four commonly used documentation styles.

The Bedford Research Room **at bedfordstmartins.com/mckaywestbrief.**   *The Research Room*, drawn from Mike Palmquist's *The Bedford Researcher*, offers a wealth of resources— including interactive tutorials, research activities, student writing samples, and links to hundreds of other places online—to support students in courses across the disciplines. The site also offers instructors a library of helpful instructional tools.

Diana Hacker's Research and Documentation Online **at bedfordstmartins.com/ mckaywestbrief.**   This Web site provides clear advice on how to integrate primary and secondary sources into research papers, how to cite sources correctly, and how to format in MLA, APA, *Chicago*, or CBE style.

The St. Martin's Tutorial on Avoiding Plagiarism **at bedfordstmartins.com/ mckaywestbrief.**   This online tutorial reviews the consequences of plagiarism and explains what sources to acknowledge, how to keep good notes, how to organize research, and how to integrate sources appropriately. The tutorial includes exercises to help students practice integrating sources and recognizing acceptable summaries.

For Instructors
Print Resources

Instructor's Resource Manual.   This helpful manual offers both first-time and experienced teachers a wealth of tools for structuring and customizing Western civilization history courses of different sizes. For each chapter in the textbook, the manual includes a set of instructional objectives; a chapter outline; lecture suggestions; suggestions on using primary sources in the classroom; a list of classroom activities; a suggested map activity; an audiovisual bibliography; a list of internet resources; and an annotated list of suggested reading.

New Media Resources

Instructor's Resource CD-ROM.   This disc provides instructors with ready-made and customizable PowerPoint multimedia presentations built around chapter outlines, maps, figures, and selected images from the textbook, plus jpeg versions of all maps, figures, and selected images suitable for printing onto transparency acetates. Also included are chapter questions formatted in PowerPoint for use with i>clicker, a classroom response system, as well as outline maps.

Computerized Test Bank.   This test bank CD-ROM offers instructors a flexible and powerful tool for test generation and test management. The test bank offers key term identification, essay questions, multiple choice questions with page references and feed-back, map questions that refer to maps in the text, and a sample final exam. Instructors can customize quizzes, add or edit both questions and answers, and export questions and answers into a variety of formats, including WebCT and Blackboard.

Book Companion Site at bedfordstmartins.com/mckaywestbrief.   The companion Web site gathers all the electronic resources for the text, including the Online Study Guide and related Quiz Gradebook, at a single Web address. Convenient links to PowerPoint chapter outlines and maps, an online version of the Instructor's Resource Manual, the digital libraries at Make History, and PowerPoint chapter questions for i>clicker, a classroom response system, are also available from this site.

***Make History* at bedfordstmartins.com/mckaywestbrief.**   Comprising the content of Bedford/St. Martin's acclaimed online libraries—*Map Central*, the Bedford History Image Library, DocLinks, and HistoryLinks—*Make History* provides one-stop access to relevant digital content including maps, images, documents, and Web links. Students and instructors alike can search this free, easy-to-use database by keyword, topic, date, or specific chapter of *Western Society: A Brief History*. Instructors can create collections of content and post their collections to the Web to share with students.

Content for Course Management Systems.   A variety of student and instructor re-sources developed for this textbook are ready to use in course management systems such as WebCT, Blackboard, and other platforms. This e-content includes nearly all of the offerings from the book's Online Study Guide as well as the book's test bank.

Videos and Multimedia.   A wide assortment of videos and multimedia CD-ROMs on various topics in European history is available to qualified adopters.

Acknowledgments

It is a pleasure to thank the many instructors who read and critiqued the manuscript for the ninth edition of the parent text, from which this version is derived:

Hugh Agnew, George Washington University
Melanie Bailey, Centenary College of Louisiana
Rachael Ball, Ohio State University
Eugene Boia, Cleveland State University
Robert Brown, State University of New York, Finger Lakes Community College
Richard Eichman, Sauk Valley Community College
David Fisher, Texas Technical University
Wayne Hanley, West Chester University of Pennsylvania
Michael Leggiere, Louisiana State University, Shreveport
John Mauer, Tri-County Technical College
Nick Miller, Boise State University
Wyatt Moulds, Jones County Junior College
Elsa Rapp, Montgomery County Community College
Anne Rodrick, Wofford College
Sonia Sorrell, Pepperdine University
Lee Shai Weissbach, University of Louisville

It is also a pleasure to thank our many editors for their efforts on this edition. To Carol Newman and Rosemary Jaffe, who guided production, and to Tonya Lobato, our development editor, we express our special appreciation. And we thank Carole Frohlich for her contributions in photo research and selection as well as Doug McGetchin of Florida Atlantic University and Cynthia Ward for their editorial contributions.

Many of our colleagues at the University of Illinois and the University of Wisconsin–Milwaukee continue to provide information and stimulation, often without even knowing it. We thank them for it. In addition, John McKay thanks JoAnn McKay for her unfailing support and encouragement. John Buckler thanks Professor Jack Cargill for his advice on topics in Chapter 2. He also thanks Professor Nicholas Yalouris, former General Inspector of Antiquities, for his kind permission to publish the mosaic from Elis, Greece in Chapter 3. He is likewise grateful to Dr. Amy C. Smith, Curator of the Ure Museum of Archaeology of the University of Reading, for her permission to publish the vase also in Chapter 3. His sincerest thanks go also to Professor Paul Cartledge of Clare College, Cambridge University, for his kind permission to publish his photograph of the statue of Leonidas in Chapter 3. Clare Crowston thanks Ali Banihashem, Max Edelson, Tara Fallon, John Lynn, Dana Rabin, and John Randolph. Merry Wiesner-Hanks thanks Jeffrey Merrick, Carlos Galvao-Sobrinho, and Gwynne Kennedy.

Each of us has benefited from the criticism of his or her coauthors, although each of us assumes responsibility for what he or she has written. Originally, John Buckler wrote the first six chapters; Bennett Hill continued the narrative through Chapter 16; and John McKay wrote Chapters 17 through 31. Beginning with the ninth edition of the parent text and continuing with this brief edition, Merry Wiesner-Hanks assumed primary responsibility for Chapters 7 through 14, and Clare Crowston took responsibility for Chapters 15 through 21.

Finally, we continue to welcome the many comments and suggestions that have come from our readers, for they have helped us greatly in this ongoing endeavor.

J. P. M.   J. B.   C. H. C.   M. E. W.

Brief Contents

Contents

13
European Society in the Age of the Renaissance, 1350–1550 307

14
Reformations and Religious Wars, 1500–1600 337

17
Absolutism in Central and Eastern Europe to 1740
432

Maps, Figures, and Tables

Features

About the Authors

John P. McKay Born in St. Louis, John P. McKay received his B.A. from Wesleyan University (1961), his M.A. from the Fletcher School of Law and Diplomacy (1962), and his Ph.D. from the University of California, Berkeley (1968). He began teaching history at the University of Illinois in 1966 and became a Professor there in 1976. John won the Herbert Baxter Adams Prize for his book *Pioneers for Profit: Foreign Entrepreneurship and Russian Industrialization, 1885–1913* (1970). He has also written *Tramways and Trolleys: The Rise of Urban Mass Transport in Europe* (1976) and has translated Jules Michelet's *The People* (1973). His research has been supported by fellowships from the Ford Foundation, the Guggenheim Foundation, the National Endowment for the Humanities, and IREX. He has written well over a hundred articles, book chapters, and reviews, which have appeared in numerous publications, including *The American Historical Review, Business History Review, The Journal of Economic History*, and *Slavic Review*. He contributed extensively to C. Stewart and P. Fritzsche, eds., *Imagining the Twentieth Century* (1997).

Bennett D. Hill A native of Philadelphia, Bennett D. Hill earned an A.B. from Princeton (1956) and advanced degrees from Harvard (A.M., 1958) and Princeton (Ph.D., 1963). He taught history at the University of Illinois, where he was department chair from 1978 to 1981. He published *English Cistercian Monasteries and Their Patrons in the Twelfth Century* (1968), *Church and State in the Middle Ages* (1970), and articles in *Analecta Cisterciensia, The New Catholic Encyclopaedia, The American Benedictine Review*, and *The Dictionary of the Middle Ages*. His reviews appeared in *The American Historical Review, Speculum, The Historian*, the *Journal of World History*, and *Library Journal*. He was one of the contributing editors to *The Encyclopedia of World History* (2001). He was a Fellow of the American Council of Learned Societies and served on the editorial board of *The American Benedictine Review*, on committees of the National Endowment for the Humanities, and as vice president of the American Catholic Historical Association (1995–1996). A Benedictine monk of St. Anselm's Abbey in Washington, D.C., he was also a Visiting Professor at Georgetown University.

John Buckler Born in Louisville, Kentucky, John Buckler received his Ph.D. from Harvard University in 1973. In 1980 Harvard University Press published his *Theban Hegemony, 371–362* B.C. He published *Philip II and the Sacred War* (Leiden 1989) and also edited *BOIOTIKA: Vorträge vom 5. Internationalen Böotien-Kolloquium* (Munich 1989). In 2003 he published *Aegean Greece in the Fourth Century* B.C. In the following year appeared his editions of W. M. Leake, *Travels in the Morea* (three volumes), and Leake's *Peloponnesiaca*. Cambridge University Press published his *Central Greece and the Politics of Power in the Fourth Century*, edited by Hans Beck, in 2008.

Clare Haru Crowston Born in Cambridge, Massachusetts, and raised in Toronto, Clare Haru Crowston received her B.A. in 1985 from McGill University and her Ph.D. in 1996 from Cornell University. Since 1996, she has taught at the University of Illinois, where she has served as associate chair and Director of Graduate Studies, and is currently Associate Professor of history. She is the author of *Fabricating Women: The Seamstresses of Old Regime France, 1675–1791* (Duke University Press, 2001), which won two awards, the Berkshire Prize and the Hagley Prize. She edited two special issues of the *Journal of Women's History* (vol. 18, nos. 3 and 4) and has published numerous articles and reviews in journals such as *Annales: Histoire, Sciences Sociales, French Historical Studies, Gender and History*, and the *Journal of Economic History*. Her research has been supported with grants from the National Endowment for the Humanities, the Mellon Foundation, and the Bourse Châteaubriand of the French government. She is a past president of the Society for French Historical Studies and a former chair of the Pinkney Prize Committee.

Merry E. Wiesner-Hanks   Having grown up in Minneapolis, Merry E. Wiesner-Hanks received her B.A. from Grinnell College in 1973 (as well as an honorary doctorate some years later), and her Ph.D. from the University of Wisconsin–Madison in 1979. She taught first at Augustana College in Illinois, and since 1985 at the University of Wisconsin–Milwaukee, where she is currently UWM Distinguished Professor in the department of history. She is the co-editor of the *Sixteenth Century Journal* and the author or editor of nineteen books and many articles that have appeared in English, German, Italian, Spanish, and Chinese. These include *Early Modern Europe, 1450–1789* (Cambridge, 2006), *Women and Gender in Early Modern Europe* (Cambridge, 3d ed., 2008), and *Gender in History* (Blackwell, 2001). She currently serves as the Chief Reader for Advanced Placement World History and has also written a number of source books for use in the college classroom, including *Discovering the Western Past* (Houghton Mifflin, 6th ed, 2007) and *Discovering the Global Past* (Houghton Mifflin, 3d. ed., 2006), and a book for young adults, *An Age of Voyages, 1350–1600* (Oxford 2005).

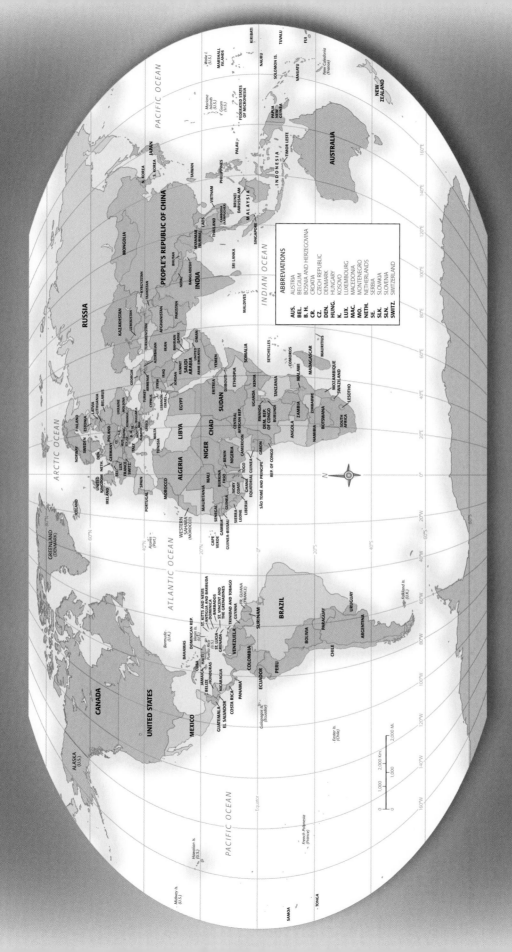

Western Society: A Brief History

CHAPTER 1
Origins
ca. 400,000–1100 B.C.E.

Chapter Preview

From Caves to Towns
How did early peoples evolve from bands of hunter-gatherers to settled farming communities?

Mesopotamian Civilization
How did the Sumerians create a complex society in the arid climate of Mesopotamia?

The Spread of Mesopotamian Culture
How did the Babylonians unite Mesopotamia politically and culturally and spread that culture to the broader world?

Egypt, the Land of the Pharaohs (3100–1200 B.C.E.)
How did Egypt's geography contribute to the rise of a unique culture, and what was the role of the pharoah in this society?

The Hittites and the End of an Era (ca. 1640–1100 B.C.E.)
How did the Hittites rise to power, and how did they facilitate the exchange of ideas throughout the Near East? How did the Egyptian and Mesopotamian cultures survive the fall of empires?

INDIVIDUALS IN SOCIETY: Nefertiti, the "Perfect Woman"

IMAGES IN SOCIETY: The Iceman

LISTENING TO THE PAST: A Quest for Immortality

Osiris. Egyptian lord of life and death, powerful and serene, here depicted in his full regalia. (G. Dagli-Orti/The Art Archive)

The civilization and cultures of the modern Western world, like great rivers, have many sources. Peoples in western Europe developed numerous communities uniquely their own but also sharing some common features. They mastered such diverse subjects as astronomy, mathematics, geometry, trigonometry, engineering, religious practices, and social organization. Yet the earliest of these peoples did not record their learning and lore in systems of writing. Their lives and customs are consequently largely lost to us.

Other early peoples confronted many of the same basic challenges as those in Europe. They also made progress, but they took the important step of recording their experiences in writing. The most enduring innovations occurred in the ancient Near East, a region that includes the lands bordering the Mediterranean's eastern shore, the Arabian peninsula, parts of northeastern Africa, and perhaps above all, Mesopotamia, the area of modern Iraq. Fundamental to the development of Western civilization and culture was the invention of writing by the Sumerians, which allowed knowledge of the past to be preserved. It also facilitated the spread and accumulation of learning, science, and literature. Ancient Near Eastern civilizations also produced the first written law codes, as well as religious concepts that still permeate daily life.

From Caves to Towns

How did early peoples evolve from bands of hunter-gatherers to settled farming communities?

Virtually every day brings startling news about the path of human evolution. We now know that by about 400,000 B.C.E. early peoples were making primitive stone tools, which has led historians to refer to this time as the **Paleolithic** (pay-lee-oh-LITH-ik) **period.** During this period, which lasted until about 7000 B.C.E., people survived as gatherers and hunters, usually dwelling in caves or temporary shelters. These **nomads** (NO-madz) led roaming lives, always in search of new food sources. (See the feature "Images in Society: The Iceman.")

Settled communities began to emerge in the **Neolithic** (nee-oh-LITH-ik) **period,** usually dated between 7000 and 3000 B.C.E. The term *Neolithic* stems from the new stone tools that came into use at that time. People used these tools to manage crops and animals, leading to fundamental changes in civilization.

Sustained agriculture made possible a stable and secure life. With this settled routine came the evolution of towns and eventually of cities. Neolithic farmers usually raised more food than they could consume, so their surpluses permitted larger, healthier populations. Population growth in turn created an even greater reliance on settled farming, as only systematic agriculture could sustain the increased numbers of people. Since surpluses of food could also be bartered for other commodities, the Neolithic era witnessed the beginnings of the large-scale exchange of goods. Neolithic farmers also improved their tools and agricultural techniques. They domesticated bigger, stronger animals to work for them, invented the plow, and developed new mutations of seeds. By 3000 B.C.E. they had invented the wheel. Agricultural surpluses also made possible the division of labor. It freed some people to become artisans who made tools, pottery vessels, woven baskets, clothing, and jewelry. In short, life became more complex yet also more comfortable for many.

These developments generally led to the further evolution of towns and a whole new way of life. People not necessarily related to one another created rudimentary

Paleolithic period The time between 400,000 and 7000 B.C.E., when early peoples began making primitive stone tools, survived by hunting and gathering, and dwelled in temporary shelters.

nomads Homeless, independent people who lead roaming lives, always in search of pasturage for their flocks.

Neolithic period The period between 7000 and 3000 B.C.E. that serves as the dividing line between anthropology and history; the term itself refers to the new stone tools that came into use at this time.

governments that transcended the family. These governments, led by a recognized central authority, made decisions that channeled the shared wisdom, physical energy, and resources of the whole population toward a common goal. These societies made their decisions according to custom, the generally accepted norms of traditional conduct. Here was the beginning of law. Towns also meant life in individual houses or groups of them, which led to greater personal independence. People erected public buildings and religious monuments, evidence of their growing wealth and communal cooperation. Some of these groups also protected their possessions and themselves by raising walls.

A mute but engaging glimpse of a particular Neolithic society can be seen today in southern England. Between 4700 and 2000 B.C.E. arose the Stonehenge (STOHN-henj) people, named after the famous stone circle on Salisbury (SAWLZ-ber-ee) Plain. Though named after a single spot, this culture spread throughout Great Britain, Ireland, and Brittany in France. Stonehenge and neighboring sites reveal the existence of prosperous, well-organized, and centrally led communities that were able to pool material and human resources in order to raise the circles. Stonehenge indicates an intellectual world that encompassed astronomy, the environment, and religion. The circle is oriented toward the midwinter sunset and the midsummer sunrise. It thus marked the clocklike celestial change of the seasons. This silent evidence proves the existence of a society prosperous enough to endure over long periods during which lore about heaven and earth could be passed along to successive generations. It also demonstrates that these communities considered themselves members of a wider world that they shared with the deities of nature and the broader universe.

Section Review

- Human communities evolved from bands of hunter-gatherers in the Paleolithic period (until 7000 B.C.E.) to stable farming communities in the Neolithic period (7000–3000 B.C.E.).

- Neolithic innovations included stone tools, the wheel, large-scale exchange of goods, and greater complexity, including division of labor.

- Agricultural surpluses allowed the evolution of towns, government, and law.

- Prosperous, well-organized communities led to the contruction of sophisticated sites such as Stonehenge.

Mesopotamian Civilization

How did the Sumerians create a complex society in the arid climate of Mesopotamia?

The origins of Western civilization are generally traced to an area that is today not seen as part of the West: Mesopotamia (mes-oh-puh-TAY-mee-uh), the Greek name for the land between the Euphrates (you-FRAY-teez) and Tigris (TIE-gris) Rivers. There the arid climate confronted the peoples with the hard problem of farming with scant water supplies. Farmers learned to irrigate their land and later to drain it to prevent the buildup of salt in the soil. **Irrigation** on a large scale, like

irrigation The solution to the problem of arid climates and scant water supplies, a system of watering land and draining to prevent buildup of salt in the soil.

building stone circles in Western Europe, demanded organized group effort. That in turn underscored the need for strong central authority to direct it. This corporate spirit led to governments in which individuals subordinated some of their particular concerns to broader interests. These factors made urban life possible in a demanding environment. By about 3000 B.C.E. the Sumerians (SOO-mehr-ee-uhnz), whose origins are mysterious, established a number of cities in the southernmost part of Mesopotamia, which became known as Sumer (see Map 1.1). The fundamental innovation of the Sumerians was the creation of writing, which evolved from a tool for recording business transactions to the means of promoting and preserving cultural ideas.

MAPPING THE PAST

MAP 1.1   Spread of Cultures in the Ancient Near East

This map depicts the area of ancient Mesopotamia and Egypt, a region often called the "cradle of civilization." Map 1.2 on page 14 shows the balance of power that later extended far beyond the regions depicted in Map 1.1. **[1]** Does this expansion indicate why Mesopotamia and Egypt earned the title of "cradle"? **[2]** What geographical features of this region naturally suggest the direction in which civilization spread? **[3]** Why did the first cultures of Mesopotamia spread farther than the culture of Egypt spread?

CHRONOLOGY

3200 B.C.E.	Development of wheeled transport and invention of cuneiform writing
ca. 3200–2200 B.C.E.	Sumerian and Akkadian domination in Mesopotamia
ca. 3100 B.C.E.	Invention of Egyptian hieroglyphic writing
3100–ca. 1333 B.C.E.	Evolution of Egyptian polytheism and belief in personal immortality
3000–1000 B.C.E.	Origins and development of religion in Mesopotamia
ca. 2700–1000 B.C.E.	Arrival of Indo-European peoples in western Asia and Europe
ca. 2660–1640 B.C.E.	Old and Middle Kingdoms in Egypt
ca. 2600–1200 B.C.E.	Expansion of Mesopotamian trade with neighbors
ca. 2000–1595 B.C.E.	Babylonian empire in Mesopotamia
ca. 1790 B.C.E.	*Epic of Gilgamesh* and Hammurabi's law code
ca. 1600–1200 B.C.E.	Hittite power in Anatolia
ca. 1570–1075 B.C.E.	New Kingdom in Egypt
ca. 1400 B.C.E.	Development of Phoenician alphabet
ca. 1300–1100 B.C.E.	Increased use of iron in western Asia

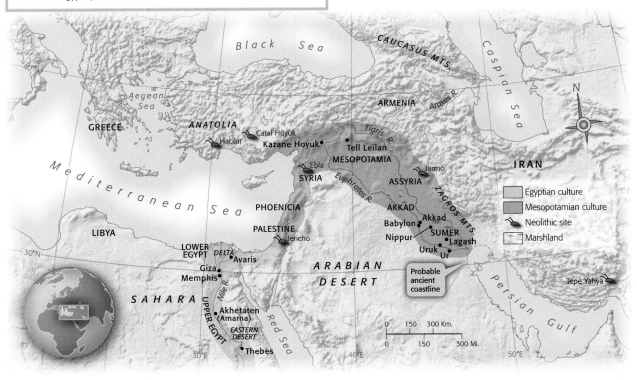

Images in Society

The Iceman

On September 19, 1991, two German vacationers climbing in the Italian Alps came upon one of the most remarkable finds in European history: a corpse lying face-down and covered in ice (Image 1). They had stumbled on a mystery that still intrigues archaeologists and many others in the scientific world. After chiseling the body out of the ice, various specialists examined the man. Having died 5,300 years ago, he is the earliest and best-preserved corpse from the Neolithic period (Image 2).

The skin of most corpses found in glaciers appears white and waxy, but the skin of the Iceman, as he is generally known, was brown and dry. Forces of nature had so desiccated the body that it became mummified: the body, including the internal organs, was perfectly preserved. The Iceman's less perishable possessions also survived, so scientists were able to examine him almost as though he had died recently.

The Iceman was quite fit, was between twenty-five and thirty-five years of age, and stood about five feet two

IMAGE 2 The Face of the Iceman (Rex USA)

inches tall. The bluish tinge of his teeth showed that he had enjoyed a diet of milled grain, perhaps millet—and also showed that he came from an environment where

IMAGE 1 The Discovery of the Iceman (Paul Hanny)

crops were grown. He wore an unlined robe of animal skins that he had stitched together with careful needlework, using thread made of grass, which he probably had made for himself. Over his robe he wore a cape of grass, very much like capes worn by shepherds in this region as late as the early twentieth century (even as late as the Second World War German soldiers stuffed straw into their boots to withstand the fierce Russian cold). The Iceman also wore a furry cap.

The equipment discovered with the Iceman demonstrates his mastery of several technologies. He carried a hefty copper ax (a sign of stoneworking), but he seems to have relied chiefly on archery. In his quiver were numerous wooden arrow shafts and two finished arrows, all indicating a great deal of knowledge and ingenuity (Image 3). The arrows had flint heads (another sign of stoneworking), and feathers were attached with a resin-like glue to the ends of the shafts. These simple facts convey much information about the technological knowledge of this mysterious man. He knew how to work stone, he knew the value of feathers to direct the arrows, and he was fully aware of the basics of ballistics. He chose for his bow the wood of the yew, some of the best wood in central Europe. Yet yew trees do not grow everywhere, so the use of yew wood proves that the Iceman had thoroughly explored his environment. He carried his necessary supplies in a primitive rucksack that he had made.

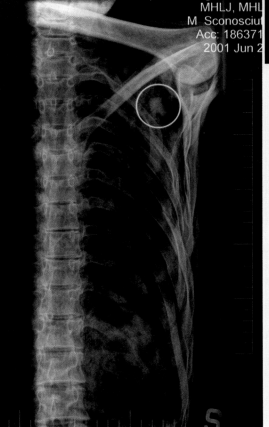

IMAGE 4 X-ray of the Iceman's Shoulder (South Tyrol Museum of Archaeology/AP Images)

One last mystery surrounds the Iceman. When his body was first discovered, scholars assumed that he was a hapless traveler overtaken by a fierce snowstorm. But a recent autopsy found an arrowhead lodged under his left shoulder (Image 4). The Iceman was not alone on his last day. Someone accompanied him, someone who shot him from below and behind. The Iceman is the victim in the first murder mystery of Western history.

Given this information, can you picture the circumstances of the Iceman's discovery (Image 1)? What was he doing there? From Image 2 can you imagine how nature preserved his remains? From the picture of his arrows (Image 3) can you conclude anything about the Iceman's self-reliance? From Image 4 comes the evidence for the cause of his death. Does it necessarily prove that Neolithic society was as violent as ours?

IMAGE 3 The Iceman's Quiver (S.N.S./Sipa Press)

MEANING	PICTOGRAPH	IDEOGRAM	PHONETIC SIGN
A Star			
B Woman			
C Mountain			
D Slave woman			
E Water In			

FIGURE 1.1　Sumerian Writing

(*Source:* From S. N. Kramer, *The Sumerians: Their History, Culture and Character,* 1963. Reprinted by permission of the publisher, the University of Chicago Press.)

cuneiform　Sumerian form of writing (from the Latin term for "wedge-shaped"); used to describe the strokes of the stylus.

The Invention of Writing and the First Schools

The origins of writing probably go back to the ninth millennium B.C.E., when Near Eastern peoples used clay tokens as counters for record keeping. By the fourth millennium people had realized that drawing pictures of the tokens on clay was simpler than making tokens (see Figure 1.1). This breakthrough in turn suggested that more information could be conveyed by adding pictures of still other objects, resulting in a complex system of *pictographs*. These pictographs were the forerunners of a Sumerian form of writing known as **cuneiform** (kyoo-NEE-uh-form), from the Latin term for "wedge-shaped," used to describe the strokes of the stylus.

The next step was to simplify the system. Instead of drawing pictures, the scribe made *ideograms:* conventionalized signs that were generally understood to represent ideas. The sign for star could also be used to indicate heaven, sky, or even god. The real breakthrough came when the scribe learned to use signs to represent sounds. For instance, the scribe drew two parallel wavy lines to indicate the word *a* or "water" (line E). Besides water, the word *a* in Sumerian also meant "in." The word *in* expresses a relationship that is very difficult to represent pictorially. Instead of trying to invent a sign to mean "in," some clever scribe used the sign for water because the two words sounded alike. This phonetic use of signs made possible the combining of signs to convey abstract ideas.

The Sumerian system of writing was so complicated that only professional scribes mastered it after many years of study. By 2500 B.C.E. scribal schools flourished throughout Sumer. Most students came from wealthy families and were male. Each school had a master, teachers, and monitors. Discipline was strict, and students were caned for sloppy work and misbehavior. One graduate of a scribal school had few fond memories of the joy of learning:

> My headmaster read my tablet, said:
> "There is something missing," caned me.
> . . . .
> The fellow in charge of silence said:
> "Why did you talk without permission," caned me.
> The fellow in charge of the assembly said:
> "Why did you stand at ease without permission," caned me.[1]

Although Mesopotamian education was primarily intended to produce scribes for administrative work, schools were also centers of culture and scholarship.

Mesopotamian Thought and Religion

The building of cities, palaces, temples, and canals demanded practical knowledge of geometry and trigonometry. The Mesopotamians made significant advances in mathematics using a numerical system based on units of sixty, ten, and six. They also developed the concept of place value—that the value of a number depends on where it stands in relation to other numbers.

Mesopotamian medicine was a combination of magic, prescriptions, and surgery. Mesopotamians believed that demons and evil spirits caused sickness and that magic spells and prescriptions could drive them out. Over time, some prescriptions were found to work and thus were true medicines. In this slow but empirical fashion medicine grew from superstition to an early form of rational treatment.

The Sumerians originated many religious beliefs, and their successors added to them. The Mesopotamians were **polytheists** (POL-eh-thee-ists), that is, they believed that many gods run the world. However, they did not consider all gods and goddesses equal. Some deities had very important jobs, taking care of music, law, sex, and victory, while others had lesser tasks, overseeing leatherworking and basketweaving.

polytheism The worship of several gods; this was the tradition of Egyptian religion.

Mesopotamian gods were powerful and immortal and could make themselves invisible. Otherwise, Mesopotamian gods and goddesses were very human: they celebrated with food and drink, and they raised families. They enjoyed their own "Garden of Eden," a green and fertile place. They could be irritable, vindictive, and irresponsible. The motives of the gods were not always clear. In times of affliction one could only pray and offer sacrifices to appease them.

Encouraged and directed by the traditional priesthood, which was dedicated to understanding the ways of the gods, the people erected shrines in the center of each city and then built their houses around them. The best way to honor the gods was to make the shrine as grand and as impressive as possible, for gods who had a splendid temple might think twice about sending floods to destroy the city.

Ziggurat
The ziggurat is a stepped tower that dominated the landscape of the Sumerian city. Surrounded by a walled enclosure, it stood as a monument to the gods. Monumental stairs led to the top, where sacrifices were offered for the welfare of the community. (Corbis)

The Mesopotamians had many myths to account for the creation of the universe. According to one Sumerian myth (echoed in Genesis, the first book of the Bible), only the primeval sea existed at first. The sea produced heaven and earth, which were united. Heaven and earth gave birth to Enlil, who separated them and made possible the creation of the other gods. These myths are the earliest known attempts to answer the question "How did it all begin?"

In addition to myths, the Sumerians produced the first epic poem, the *Epic of Gilgamesh* (GIL-guh-mesh), which evolved as a reworking of at least five earlier myths. An epic poem is a narration of the achievements, labors, and sometimes the failures of heroes that embodies a people's or a nation's conception of its own past. The Sumerian epic recounts the wanderings of Gilgamesh—the semihistorical king of Uruk (OO-rook)—and his companion Enkidu (EN-kee-doo). It shows the Sumerians grappling with such enduring questions as life and death, humankind and deity, and immortality. (See the feature "Listening to the Past: A Quest for Immortality" on pages 22–23.)

nobles The top level of Sumerian society; consisted of the king and his family, the chief priests, and high palace officials.

clients Free men and women who were dependent on the nobility; in return for their labor they received small plots of land to work for themselves.

patriarchal Societies in which most power is held by older adult men, especially those from the elite groups.

Section Review

- Early hunters created a stable life by relying on sustained agriculture that in turn led to the creation of villages and small towns.

- The Mesopotamian civilization of Sumer used irrigation and created a centrally organized urban society.

- Sumerian scribes, trained in schools where they were subject to corporal punishment, used wedge-shaped cuneiform writing to represent words and ideas phonetically.

- Sumerians developed mathematics, medicine, and their polytheistic religion, building temples to appease their hierarchical pantheon.

- The Sumerians produced the first epic poem, the *Epic of Gilgamesh*, about the wanderings of a king and his companion Enkidu.

- Sumerian society was patriarchal and divided between nobles, slaves, clients, and commoners.

Sumerian Social and Gender Divisions

Sumerian society was a complex arrangement of freedom and dependence, and its members were divided into four categories: nobles, slaves, clients, and commoners. **Nobles** consisted of the king and his family, the chief priests, and high palace officials. Generally, the king rose to power as a war leader elected by the citizenry; he established a regular army, trained it, and led it into battle. The might of the king and the frequency of warfare quickly made him the supreme figure in the city, and kingship soon became hereditary. The symbol of royal status was the palace, which rivaled the temple in grandeur.

The king and the lesser nobility held extensive tracts of land that were, like the estates of the temple, worked by slaves and clients. Slaves were prisoners of war, convicts, and debtors. While they were subject to whatever treatment their owners might mete out, they could engage in trade, make profits, and even buy their freedom. **Clients** were free men and women who were dependent on the nobility. In return for their labor, the clients received small plots of land to work for themselves. Although this arrangement assured the clients a livelihood, the land they worked remained the possession of the nobility or the temple. Commoners were free and could own land in their own right. Male commoners had a voice in the political affairs of the city and full protection under the law.

Each of these social categories included both men and women, but their experiences were not the same, for Sumerian society made clear distinctions based on gender. Sumerian society—and all Western societies that followed, until very recently—was **patriarchal** (PAY-tree-AR-kal), that is, most power was held by older adult men, especially those from the elite groups. Boys became the normal inheritors of family land. Women could sometimes inherit if there were no sons in a family, but they did not gain the political rights that came with land ownership for men.

The states that developed in the ancient Middle East, beginning with Sumer, further heightened gender distinctions. Laws governing sexual relations and marriage practices set up a very unequal relationship between spouses. Women were required to be virgins on marriage and were strictly punished for adultery; sexual relations outside of marriage on the part of husbands were not considered adultery. Religious concepts heightened gender distinctions. In some places heavenly hierarchies came to reflect those on earth, with a single male god, who was viewed as the primary creator of life, dominating the religious pantheon.

The Spread of Mesopotamian Culture

How did the Babylonians unite Mesopotamia politically and culturally and spread that culture to the broader world?

The Sumerians established the basic social, economic, and intellectual patterns of Mesopotamia, but the Semites (SEH-mites) played a large part in spreading Sumerian culture far beyond the boundaries of Mesopotamia. The interaction of the Sumerians and Semites, in fact, gives one of the very first glimpses of a phenomenon that can still be seen today. History provides abundant evidence of peoples of different origins coming together, usually on the borders of an established culture. The outcome in these instances was the evolution of a new culture that consisted of two or more old parts. Although the older culture almost invariably looked on the newcomers as inferior, the new just as invariably contributed something valuable to the old. So it was in 2331 B.C.E. The Semitic chieftain Sargon conquered Sumer and created a new empire. The symbol of his triumph was a new capital, the city of Akkad (AH-kahd). Sargon, the first "world conqueror," led his armies to the Mediterranean Sea. Although his empire lasted only a few generations, it spread Mesopotamian culture throughout the Fertile Crescent, the belt of rich farmland that extends from Mesopotamia in the east up through Syria in the north and down to Egypt in the west (see Map 1.1).

The Triumph of Babylon

Although the empire of Sargon (SAHR-gone) was extensive, it was short-lived. It was left to the Babylonians to unite Mesopotamia politically and culturally. The Babylonians were Amorites (AM-uh-rites), a Semitic people who had migrated from Arabia and settled on the site of Babylon along the middle Euphrates, where that river runs close to the Tigris. Babylon enjoyed an excellent geographical position and was ideally suited to be the capital of Mesopotamia. It dominated trade on the Tigris and Euphrates Rivers: all commerce to and from Sumer and Akkad had to pass by its walls. It also looked beyond Mesopotamia. Babylonian merchants followed the Tigris north to Assyria (uh-SEER-ee-uh) and Anatolia. The Euphrates led merchants to Syria, Palestine, and the Mediterranean. The city grew to be great because of its commercial importance and soundly based power.

Babylon's king Hammurabi (ham-moo-RAH-bee) (r. 1792–1750 B.C.E.) set out to do three things: make Babylon secure, unify Mesopotamia, and win for the Babylonians a place in Mesopotamian civilization. The first two he accomplished by conquering Assyria in the north and Sumer and Akkad in the south. Then he turned to his third goal.

Politically, Hammurabi joined in his kingship the Semitic concept of the tribal chieftain and the Sumerian idea of urban kingship. Culturally, he encouraged the spread of myths that explained how the Babylonian god Marduk (MAHR-dook) had been elected king of the gods by the other Mesopotamian deities, thus making Babylon the religious center of Mesopotamia. Through Hammurabi's genius the Babylonians made their own contribution to Mesopotamian culture—a culture vibrant enough to maintain its identity while assimilating new influences. Hammurabi's conquests and the activity of Babylonian merchants spread this enriched culture north to Anatolia and west to Syria and Palestine.

law code A proclamation issued by the Babylonian king Hammurabi to establish law and justice in the language of the land, thereby prompting the welfare of the people; it inflicted harsh punishments, but despite its severity, was pervaded with a spirit of justice and sense of responsibility.

Life Under Hammurabi

One of Hammurabi's most memorable accomplishments was the proclamation of a **law code** that offers a wealth of information about daily life in Mesopotamia. Hammurabi's was not the first law code in Mesopotamia; indeed, the earliest goes back to about 2100 B.C.E. Like earlier lawgivers, Hammurabi proclaimed that he issued his laws on divine authority "to establish law and justice in the language of the land, thereby promoting the welfare of the people."

The Code of Hammurabi has two striking characteristics. First, the law differed according to the social status and gender of the offender. Nobles were not punished as harshly as commoners, nor commoners as harshly as slaves. Certain actions that were crimes for women were not crimes for men. Second, the code demanded that the punishment fit the crime. It called for "an eye for an eye, and a tooth for a tooth," at least among equals. However, a noble who destroyed the eye of a commoner or slave could pay a fine instead of losing his own eye. Otherwise, as long as criminal and victim shared the same social status, the victim could demand exact vengeance.

Hammurabi's code began with legal procedure. There were no public prosecutors or district attorneys, so individuals brought their own complaints before the court. Each side had to produce written documents or witnesses to support its case. For example, in cases of murder, the accuser had to prove the defendant guilty; any accuser who failed to do so was put to death. This strict law was designed to prevent people from lodging groundless charges.

Because farming was essential to Mesopotamian life, Hammurabi's code dealt extensively with agriculture. Farmers who rented land were required to keep the irrigation canals and ditches in good repair. Otherwise the land would be subject to floods and the owners would face crippling losses. Any tenant whose neglect of the canals resulted in damaged crops had to bear all the expense of the lost crops. Those tenants who could not pay the costs were forced into slavery.

Consumer protection is not a modern idea; it goes back to Hammurabi's day. Merchants had to guarantee the quality of their goods and services. A boatman who lost the owner's boat or sank someone else's boat replaced it and its cargo. House builders guaranteed their work with their lives. A merchant who tried to increase the interest rate on a loan forfeited the entire amount.

Hammurabi gave careful attention to marriage and the family. As elsewhere in the Near East, marriage had aspects of a business agreement. The prospective groom or his father offered the prospective bride's father a bridal gift, usually money. If the man and his bridal gift were acceptable, the father provided his daughter with a dowry. After marriage the dowry belonged to the woman (although the husband normally administered it) and was a means of protecting her rights and status. Once the two men agreed on financial matters, they drew up a contract; no marriage was considered legal without one. Fathers often contracted marriages

Law Code of Hammurabi

Hammurabi ordered his code to be inscribed on a stone pillar and set up in public. At the top of the pillar Hammurabi is depicted receiving the scepter of authority from the god Shamash. (Hirmer Verlag München)

while their children were still young, and once contracted, the children were considered to be wed even if they did not yet live together. The husband had virtually absolute power over his household. He could even sell his wife and children into slavery to pay debts. Any son who struck his father could have his hand cut off. A father was free to adopt children and include them in his will. Artisans sometimes adopted children to teach them the family trade.

Law codes, preoccupied as they are with the problems of society, provide a bleak view of things. Other documents give a happier glimpse of life. Although marriage was primarily an arrangement between families, evidence of romantic love survives in Mesopotamian poetry. Countless wills and testaments show that husbands habitually left their estates to their wives, who in turn willed the property to their children. Hammurabi's code restricted married women from commercial pursuits, but financial documents prove that many women engaged in business without hindrance. Some carried on the family business, while others became wealthy landowners in their own right. Mesopotamians found their lives lightened by holidays and religious festivals. Traveling merchants brought news of the outside world and swapped marvelous tales. In all, the Mesopotamians enjoyed a vibrant and creative culture that left its mark on the entire Near East.

Egypt, the Land of the Pharaohs (3100–1200 B.C.E.)

How did Egypt's geography contribute to the rise of a unique culture, and what was the role of the pharoah in this society?

The Greek historian and traveler Herodotus (heh-ROD-uh-tuhs) in the fifth century B.C.E. called Egypt the "gift of the Nile." No other single geographical factor had such a fundamental and profound impact on the shaping of Egyptian life, society, and history as the Nile (see Map 1.2). Unlike the rivers of Mesopotamia, it rarely brought death and destruction by devastating entire cities. The Egyptians never feared the relatively tame Nile in the way the Mesopotamians feared the Tigris. Instead, they sang its praises:

> Hail to thee, O Nile, that issues from the earth and comes to keep Egypt alive! . . .
> He that waters the meadows which Re [Ra] created,
> He that makes to drink the desert . . .
> He who makes barley and brings emmer [wheat] into being . . .
> He who brings grass into being for the cattle . . .
> He who makes every beloved tree to grow . . .
> O Nile, verdant art thou, who makest man and cattle to live.[2]

In the mind of the Egyptians, the Nile was the supreme renewer of the land. Each September the Nile floods its valley, transforming it into a huge area of marsh or lagoon. By the end of November the water retreats, leaving behind a thin covering of fertile mud ready to be planted with crops. Farmers were able to produce an annual agricultural surplus, which in turn sustained a growing and prosperous population. The Nile also unified Egypt. The river was the region's principal highway, promoting communication throughout the valley.

Egypt's natural resources made it nearly self-sufficient. Besides the fertility of its soil, Egypt possessed enormous quantities of stone, which served as the raw material of architecture and sculpture. Abundant clay was available for pottery, as was gold for jewelry and ornaments. The raw materials that Egypt lacked were

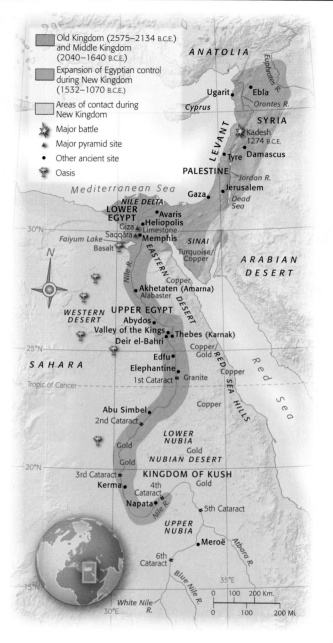

MAP 1.2   Ancient Egypt
Geography and natural resources provided Egypt with centuries of peace and abundance.

close at hand. The Egyptians could obtain copper from Sinai (SIGH-nigh) and timber from Lebanon (LEB-uh-non). They had little cause to look to the outside world for their essential needs, a fact that helps explain the insular quality of early Egyptian life.

The God-King of Egypt

The Nile divided ancient Egypt into two entities— Upper Egypt, the upstream valley in the south, and Lower Egypt, the land of the delta where the Nile branches into smaller waterways and then empties into the Mediterranean Sea. The Egyptians told of a great king, Menes (MEH-neez), who united Upper and Lower Egypt into a single kingdom around 3100 B.C.E. Thereafter the Egyptians divided their history into dynasties, or families of kings; modern historians organize it into periods (see page 15). The political unification of Egypt ushered in the period known as the Old Kingdom (2660–2180 B.C.E.), an era remarkable for prosperity, artistic flowering, and the evolution of religious beliefs.

In religion, the Egyptians were polytheists, like the Mesopotamians. They developed complex, often contradictory, ideas of their gods that reflected the world around them. The most powerful of these gods were Amon (AH-muhn), a primeval sky-god, and Ra, the sun-god. Amon created the entire cosmos by his thoughts. He caused the Nile to flood and the northern wind to blow. The Egyptians considered Ra (ra) the creator of life. He commanded the sky, earth, and underworld. This giver of life could also take it without warning. The obvious similarities between Amon and Ra eventually led the Egyptians to combine them into one god, **Amon-Ra.** Yet the Egyptians never fashioned a formal theology to resolve these differences. Instead they worshiped these gods as different aspects of the same celestial phenomena.

The Egyptians likewise developed views of an afterlife that reflected the world around them. The dry air of Egypt preserves much that would decay in other climates. Thus there was a sense of permanence about Egypt: the past was never far from the present. The dependable rhythm of the seasons also shaped the fate of the dead, for, unchanged, they regulated the afterlife, which continued in accordance with the same regularity. The Egyptian *Book of the Dead* explained that the god Osiris (oh-SIGH-ris), king of the dead, weighed each person's heart to determine if he or she had lived justly enough to deserve everlasting life. After death the soul left the body to become part of the divine. It entered gladly through the gate of heaven and remained in the presence of Aton (AHT-on) (a sun-god) and the stars.

Amon-Ra An Egyptian god, consisting of Amon, a primeval sky-god, and Ra, the sun-god.

Book of the Dead An Egyptian book that preserved their ideas about death and the afterlife; it explains that after death the soul leaves the body to become part of the divine.

Ra and Horus
The god Ra appears on the left in a form associated with Horus, the falcon-god. The red circle over Ra's head identifies him as the sun-god. In this scene Ra also assumes characteristics of Osiris, god of the underworld. He stands in judgment of the dead woman on the right. She meets the god with respect but without fear, as he will guide her safely to a celestial heaven. (Egyptian Museum, Cairo)

The focal point of religious and political life in the Old Kingdom was the **pharaoh** (FAY-roh), who commanded the wealth, resources, and people of all Egypt. The pharaoh's power was such that the Egyptians considered him to be the falcon-god Horus in human form, a living god on earth, who became one with Osiris after death. The queen was associated with the goddess Isis (EYE-sis), wife of Osiris, and both the queen and the goddess were viewed as protectors. The pharaoh was not simply the mediator between the gods and the Egyptian people. Above all, he was the power that achieved the integration between gods and human beings, between nature and society, that ensured peace and prosperity for the land of the Nile. The pharaoh was thus a guarantee to his people, a pledge that the gods of Egypt (strikingly unlike those of Mesopotamia) cared for their people.

The pharoah's surroundings had to be worthy of a god. Just as he occupied a great house in life, so he reposed in a great **pyramid** (PIR-uh-mid) after death. The massive tomb contained all the things needed by the pharaoh in his afterlife. The walls of the burial chamber were inscribed with religious texts and spells relating to the pharaoh's journeys after death. After burial the entrance was blocked and concealed to ensure his undisturbed peace. To this day the great

pharaoh The leader of religious and political life in the Old Kingdom, he commanded the wealth, resources, and people of Egypt.

pyramid The burial place of pharaohs, it was a massive tomb that contained all things needed for the afterlife; also symbolized the king's power and his connection with the sun-god.

Periods of Egyptian History

Period	Dates	Significant Events
Archaic	3100–2660 B.C.E.	Unification of Egypt
Old Kingdom	2660–2180 B.C.E.	Construction of the pyramids
First Intermediate	2180–2080 B.C.E.	Political chaos
Middle Kingdom	2080–1640 B.C.E.	Recovery and political stability
Second Intermediate	1640–1570 B.C.E.	Hyksos "invasion"
New Kingdom	1570–1075 B.C.E.	Creation of an Egyptian empire; Akhenaten's religious policy

King Menkaure and Queen
The pharaoh and his wife represent all the magnificence, serenity, and grandeur of Egypt. (Old Kingdom, Dynasty 4, reign of Mycerinus, 2532–2510 B.C.; Greywacke; H x W x D: 54¹¹/₁₆ x 22⅜ x 21⁵/₁₆ in. (139 x 57 x 54 cm). Harvard University–Museum of Fine Arts Expedition, 11.1738. Museum of Fine Arts, Boston)

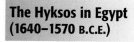

Hyksos Called Rulers of the Uplands by the Egyptians, these people began to settle in the Nile Delta shortly after 1800 B.C.E.

pyramids at Giza near Cairo bear silent but magnificent testimony to the god-kings of Egypt.

The Pharaoh's People

Because the common folk stood at the bottom of the social and economic scale, they were always at the mercy of grasping officials. The arrival of the tax collector was never a happy occasion. One Egyptian scribe described the worst that could happen:

> And now the scribe lands on the river-bank and is about to register the harvest-tax. The janitors carry staves and the Nubians rods of palm, and they say, Hand over the corn, though there is none. The cultivator is beaten all over, he is bound and thrown into a well, soused and dipped head downwards. His wife has been bound in his presence and his children are in fetters.[3]

That was an extreme situation. Nonetheless, taxes might amount to 20 percent of the harvest, and tax collection could be brutal.

Egyptian society seems to have been a curious mixture of freedom and constraint. Slavery did not become widespread until the New Kingdom (1570–1075 B.C.E.). There was neither a caste system nor a color bar, and humble people could rise to the highest positions if they possessed talent. On the other hand, most ordinary folk could not easily leave the land of their own free will. Peasants were also subject to forced labor, including work on the pyramids and canals. Young men were drafted into the pharaoh's army, which served both as a fighting force and as a labor corps.

The vision of thousands of people straining to build the pyramids brings to the modern mind a distasteful picture of absolute power. Indeed, the Egyptian view of life and society is alien to those raised with modern concepts of individual freedom and human rights. To ancient Egyptians the pharaoh embodied justice and order—harmony among human beings, nature, and the divine. If the pharaoh was weak or allowed anyone to challenge his unique position, he opened the way to chaos. Twice in Egyptian history the pharaoh failed to maintain rigid centralization. During those two eras, known as the First and Second Intermediate Periods, Egypt was exposed to civil war and invasion. Yet the monarchy survived, and in each period a strong pharaoh arose to crush the rebels or expel the invaders and restore order.

The Hyksos in Egypt (1640–1570 B.C.E.)

While Egyptian civilization flourished behind its bulwark of sand and sea, momentous changes were taking place in the ancient Near East. These changes involved enormous and remarkable movements, especially of peoples who spoke Semitic tongues. The original home of the Semites was perhaps the Arabian peninsula. Some tribes moved into northern Mesopotamia, others into Syria and Palestine, and still others into Egypt. Shortly after 1800 B.C.E. people whom the Egyptians called **Hyksos,** which means "Rulers of the Uplands," began to settle in the Nile Delta. The movements of the Hyksos were part of a larger pattern of migration of peoples during this period. The Hyksos arrived in such numbers that they were able to take political control, creating a capital city at Avaris in the northeastern Nile Delta.

Although the Egyptians portrayed the Hyksos as a conquering horde, their entry into the delta was generally peaceful. The Hyksos brought with them the method of making bronze and casting it into tools and weapons. They thereby brought Egypt fully into the **Bronze Age** culture of the Mediterranean world, a culture in which the production and use of bronze implements became basic to society. Bronze tools were sharper and more durable than the copper tools they replaced. The Hyksos' use of bronze armor and weapons revolutionized Egyptian warfare, as did their use of chariots and stronger bows. Yet the newcomers also absorbed Egyptian culture. The Hyksos came to worship Egyptian gods and modeled their monarchy on the pharaonic system.

The New Kingdom: Revival and Empire (1570–1075 B.C.E.)

The pharaohs of the Eighteenth Dynasty arose to challenge the Hyksos. These pharaohs pushed the Hyksos out of the Nile Delta, subdued Nubia in the south, and conquered Palestine and parts of Syria in the northeast. In this way, Egyptian warrior-pharaohs inaugurated the New Kingdom—a period in Egyptian history characterized by enormous wealth and conscious imperialism. During this period, probably for the first time, widespread slavery became a feature of Egyptian life. The pharaoh's armies returned home leading hordes of slaves who constituted a new labor force for imperial building projects.

One pharoah of this period, Akhenaten (ah-keh-NAT-en) (r. 1367–1350 B.C.E.), was more concerned with religion than with conquest. Nefertiti (nef-uhr-TEE-tee), his wife and queen, encouraged his religious bent. (See the feature "Individuals in Society: Nefertiti, the 'Perfect Woman.'") The precise nature of Akhenaten's religious beliefs remains debatable. Most historians, however, agree that Akhenaten and Nefertiti were **monotheists** (mon-oh-THEE-ists); that is, they believed that the sun-god Aton, whom they worshiped, was universal, the only god. They considered all other Egyptian gods and goddesses frauds and disregarded their worship. Yet Akhenaten's monotheism, imposed from above and accompanied by intolerance and persecution, failed to find a place among the people and did not endure beyond his reign.

The Hittites and the End of an Era (ca. 1640–1100 B.C.E.)

How did the Hittites rise to power, and how did they facilitate the exchange of ideas throughout the Near East? How did the Egyptian and Mesopotamian cultures survive the fall of empires?

Like the Mesopotamians and the Egyptians before them, the Hittites (HIT-ites) introduced a new element into the development of the ancient Near East. The Hittites were the first Indo-Europeans to become broadly important throughout the region. The term **Indo-European** refers to a large family of languages that includes English, most of the languages of modern Europe, including Greek and Latin, and languages as far afield as Persian and Sanskrit, spoken in ancient Turkey and India. They left a lasting imprint on the Near East before the empires of the whole region suffered the shock of new peoples and widespread disruption.

Bronze Age The period in which the production and use of bronze implements became basic to society; bronze made farming more efficient and revolutionized warfare.

monotheism The belief in one god; when applied to Egypt it means that only Aton among the traditional Egyptian deities was god.

Indo-European A large family of languages that includes English, most of the languages of modern Europe, Greek, Latin, Persian, and Sanskrit, the sacred tongue of ancient India.

Individuals in Society

Nefertiti, the "Perfect Woman"

Egyptians understood the pharaoh to be the living embodiment of the god Horus, the source of law and morality, and the mediator between gods and humans. His connection with the divine stretched to members of his family, so that his siblings and children were also viewed as in some ways divine. Because of this, a pharaoh often took his sister or half-sister as one of his wives. This concentrated divine blood set the pharaonic family apart from those of other Egyptians (who did not marry close relatives), and allowed the pharaohs to imitate the gods, who in Egyptian mythology often married their siblings. A pharaoh chose one of his wives to be the "Great Royal Wife," or principal queen. Often this was a relative, though sometimes it was one of the foreign princesses who married pharaohs to establish political alliances.

Nefertiti, queen of Egypt (Bildarchiv Preussischer Kulturbesitz/Art Resource, NY)

The familial connection with the divine allowed a handful of women to rule in their own right in Egypt's long history. We know the names of four female pharaohs, the most famous being Hatshepsut (hat-SHEP-soot) (ruled 1479–1458 B.C.E.). She was the sister and wife of Thutmose II and, after he died, served as regent for her young stepson Thutmose III, who was actually the son of another woman. Hatshepsut sent trading expeditions and sponsored artists and architects, ushering in a period of artistic creativity and economic prosperity. She built one of the world's great buildings, an elaborate terraced temple at Deir el Bahri, which eventually served as her tomb. Hatshepsut's status as a powerful female ruler was difficult for Egyptians to conceptualize, and she is often depicted in male dress or with a false beard, thus looking more like the male rulers who were the norm. After her death, Thutmose III tried to destroy all evidence that she had ever ruled, smashing statues and scratching her name off inscriptions, perhaps because of personal animosity and per-

haps because he wanted to erase the fact that a woman had once been pharaoh. Only within the last decades have historians and archaeologists begun to (literally) piece together her story.

Though female pharaohs were very rare, many royal women had power through their position as "Great Royal Wives." The most famous of these was Nefertiti, the wife of Akhenaten. Her name means "the perfect (or beautiful) woman has come," and inscriptions also give her many other titles. Nefertiti used her position to spread the new religion of the sun-god Aton. Together she and Akhenaten built a new palace at Akhetaten, the present Amarna, away from the old centers of power. There they developed the cult of Aton to the exclusion of the traditional deities. Nearly the only literary survival of their religious belief is the "Hymn to Aton," which declares Aton to be the only god. It describes Nefertiti as "the great royal consort whom he! Akhenaten! Loves, the mistress of the Two Lands! Upper and Lower Egypt!"

Nefertiti is often shown the same size as her husband, and in some inscriptions she is performing religious rituals that would normally have been done only by the pharaoh. The exact details of her power are hard to determine, however. An older theory held that her husband removed her from power, though there is also speculation that she may have ruled secretly in her own right after his death. Her tomb has long since disappeared, though in 2003 an enormous controversy developed over her possible remains. There is no controversy that the bust shown above, now in a Berlin museum, represents Nefertiti, nor that it has become an icon of female beauty since it was first discovered in the early twentieth century.

Questions for Analysis

1. Why might it have been difficult for Egyptians to accept a female ruler?

2. What opportunities do hereditary monarchies such as that of ancient Egypt provide for women? How does this fit with gender hierarchies in which men are understood as superior?

The Coming of the Hittites (ca. 1640–1200 B.C.E.)

During the nineteenth century B.C.E. the native kingdoms in Anatolia engaged in suicidal warfare that left most of the area's once-flourishing towns in ashes and rubble. In this climate of exhaustion the Hittite king, Hattusilis I, led his army to victory against neighboring kingdoms.

The Hittites, like the Egyptians of the New Kingdom, produced an energetic and able line of kings who built a powerful empire. Perhaps their major contribution was the introduction of iron in the form of weapons and tools. Around 1300 B.C.E. the Hittites stopped the Egyptian army of Rameses II at the Battle of Kadesh in Syria. Having fought each other to a standstill, the Hittites and Egyptians first made peace, then an alliance. Alliance was followed by friendship, and friendship by active cooperation between the two greatest powers of the early Near East.

The Hittites and Egyptians next included the Babylonians in their diplomacy. All three empires developed an official etiquette in which they treated one another as "brothers," using this gendered familial term to indicate their connection. These alliances facilitated the exchange of ideas throughout the Near East. Furthermore, the Hittites passed much knowledge and lore from the Near East to the newly arrived Greeks in Europe. The details of Hittite contact with the Greeks are unknown, but enough literary themes and physical objects exist to prove the connection.

Hittite Solar Disc
This cult standard represents Hittite concepts of fertility and prosperity. (A standard is a flag or emblematic object raised on a pole.) The circle surrounding the animals is the sun, beneath which stands a stag flanked by two bulls. Stylized bull's horns spread from the base of the disc. The symbol is also one of might and protection from outside harm. (Museum of Anatolian Civilizations, Ankara)

Sea Peoples Invaders who destroyed the Egyptian empires in the late 13th century; they are otherwise unidentifiable because they went their own ways after their attacks on Egypt.

The Fall of Empires and the Survival of Cultures (ca. 1200 B.C.E.)

The Battle of Kadesh ushered in a period of peace and stability in the Near East that lasted until the thirteenth century B.C.E. Then, however, foreign invaders destroyed both the Hittite and the Egyptian empires. The most famous of these marauders, called the **Sea Peoples** by the Egyptians, launched a series of stunning attacks that brought down the Hittites and drove the Egyptians back to the Nile Delta.

The Egyptians took the lead in the recovery by establishing commercial contact with their new neighbors. With the exchange of goods went ideas. Both sides shared practical concepts of shipbuilding, metal technology, and methods of trade that allowed merchants to transact business over long distances. They began to establish and recognize recently created borders, which helped define them geographically and politically. When the worst was over, the Egyptians made contact with the Semitic peoples of Palestine and Syria, whom they found living in small walled towns. Farther north in the land soon to be named Phoenicia (fi-NEE-sha), they also encountered a people who combined sophisticated seafaring with urban life.

The situation in northern Syria reflected life in the south. Small cities in all these places were mercantile centers, rich not only in manufactured goods, but also in agricultural produce, textiles, and metals. The cities flourished under royal families that shared power and dealt jointly in foreign affairs. These northerners relied heavily on their Mesopotamian heritage. While adopting Babylonian writing to communicate with their more distant neighbors to the east, they also adapted it to write their own north Semitic language. At the same time they welcomed the knowledge of Mesopotamian literature, mathematics, and culture. They worshiped both their own and Mesopotamian deities. Yet the cultural exchange remained a mixture of adoption, adaptation, contrast, and finally balance, as the two cultures came to understand and appreciate each other.

A pattern emerged in Palestine, Syria, and Anatolia. In these areas native cultures established themselves during the prehistoric period. Upon coming into contact with the Egyptian and Mesopotamian civilizations, they adopted many aspects of these cultures, adapting them to their own traditional customs. Yet they also contributed to the advance of Egyptian and Mesopotamian cultures by introducing new technologies and religious ideas. The result was the emergence of a huge group of communities stretching from Egypt in the south to Anatolia in the north and from the Levant in the west to Mesopotamia in the east. Each enjoyed its own individual character, while at the same time sharing many common features with its neighbors.

Section Review

- The iron-wielding Hittites were the first Indo-Europeans to become important in the Near East.

- The Hittites at first fought the Egyptians, such as at the Battle of Kadesh, but then they made peace and included the Babylonians in their fraternal alliance, easing the flow of ideas throughout the three empires and the region.

- The Sea Peoples disturbed this peace, resulting in the downfall of the Hittites and the withdrawal of Egyptians to the Nile Delta.

- The Phoenicians combined sophisticated seafaring with urban life.

- A huge group of communities across the Near East maintained local character while also sharing and helping to develop further common cultural elements from Egypt and Mesopotamia.

Chapter Review

How did early peoples evolve from bands of hunter-gatherers to settled farming communities? (page 3)

For thousands of years Paleolithic peoples moved from place to place in search of food. Only in the Neolithic era—with the invention of new stone tools, a reliance on sustained agriculture, and the domestication of animals—did people begin to live in permanent locations. These villages evolved into towns, where people began to create new social bonds and political organizations. Stonehenge is one example of the collective effort and imagination of a Neolithic community.

Key Terms
Paleolithic period (p. 3)
nomads (p. 3)
Neolithic period (p. 3)

How did the Sumerians create a complex society in the arid climate of Mesopotamia? (page 4)

The earliest area where these developments led to genuine urban societies is Mesopotamia. Here the Sumerians and then other Mesopotamians developed writing, which enabled their culture to be passed on to others. Their religious beliefs reflected a pessimistic view of the world in which the gods could bring destruction without concern for human life. The great Sumerian poem, the *Epic of Gilgamesh*, shows them grappling with questions of life and death that are still of importance today. The beginnings of patriarchy and social class inequalities can also be seen in their culture.

How did the Babylonians unite Mesopotamia politically and culturally and spread that culture to the broader world? (page 11)

The Sumerians established the basic social, economic, and intellectual patterns of Mesopotamia, but the Semites played a large part in spreading Mesopotamian culture to the broader world through both conquest and commercial exchange. First the Akkadians and then the Babylonians came to power in the region. Under Hammurabi, the Babylonians were able to unify Mesopotamia politically and culturally. The law code of Hammurabi illustrates the king's intentions to regulate the lives of his people and promote social harmony.

How did Egypt's geography contribute to the rise of a unique culture, and what was the role of the pharoah in this society? (page 13)

Around the same time in Egypt, the fertile Nile valley and other natural resources contributed to the rise of a wealthy and insular culture. The Egyptians too developed their own writing system and religious beliefs, and they undertook monumental building projects that required sophisticated organizational and intellectual skills. Under the strong central leadership of the pharaoh, Egyptian life was stable and predictable. The Hyksos brought Bronze Age culture to the Egyptians when they settled the Nile Delta.

How did the Hittites rise to power, and how did they facilitate the exchange of ideas throughout the Near East? How did the Egyptian and Mesopotamian cultures survive the fall of empires? (page 17)

Finally, the Hittites, an Indo-European people, entered the Near East from the north. Distant ancestors of the modern folk of Europe and the Americas, the Hittites introduced iron tools and weapons to the region. Along with the Egyptians and then the Babylonians, they developed an alliance that facilitated the exchange of goods and ideas throughout the Near East. Near East peoples received hard knocks from hostile invaders beginning around the thirteenth century B.C.E., but key social, economic, and cultural patterns survived to enrich future generations.

irrigation (p. 4)
cuneiform (p. 8)
polytheism (p. 9)
nobles (p. 10)
clients (p. 10)
patriarchal (p. 10)
law code (p. 12)
Amon-Ra (p. 14)
Book of the Dead (p. 14)
pharaoh (p. 15)
pyramid (p. 15)
Hyksos (p. 16)
Bronze Age (p. 17)
monotheism (p. 17)
Indo-European (p. 17)
Sea Peoples (p. 20)

Notes

1. Quoted in S. N. Kramer, *The Sumerians: Their History, Culture and Character*, 1963. Reprinted by permission of the publisher, the University of Chicago Press. John Buckler is the translator of all uncited quotations from a foreign language in Chapters 1–6.
2. J. B. Pritchard, ed., *Ancient Near Eastern Texts*, 3d ed. (Princeton, N.J.: Princeton University Press, 1969), p. 372. Hereafter called ANET.
3. Quoted in A. H. Gardiner, "Ramesside Texts Relating to the Taxation and Transport of Corn," *Journal of Egyptian Archaeology* 27 (1941): 19–20.

To assess your mastery of this chapter, go to **bedfordstmartins.com/mckaywestbrief**

A Quest for Immortality

The human desire to escape death and achieve immortality is one of the oldest wishes of all peoples. The Sumerian Epic of Gilgamesh *is the earliest recorded treatment of this topic. The oldest elements of the epic go back at least to the third millennium B.C.E. According to tradition, Gilgamesh was a king of Uruk whom the Sumerians, Babylonians, and Assyrians considered a hero-king and a god. In the story Gilgamesh and his friend Enkidu set out to attain immortality and join the ranks of the gods. They attempt to do so by performing wondrous feats against fearsome agents of the gods, who are determined to thwart them.*

During their quest Enkidu dies. Gilgamesh, more determined than ever to become immortal, begins seeking anyone who might tell him how to do so. His journey involves the effort not only to escape from death but also to reach an understanding of the meaning of life. Along the way he meets Siduri, the wise and good-natured goddess of wine, who gives him the following advice.

Gilgamesh, where are you hurrying to? You will never find that life for which you are looking. When the gods created man they allotted to him death, but life they retained in their own keeping. As for you, Gilgamesh, fill your belly with good things; day and night, night and day, dance and be merry, feast and rejoice. Let your clothes be fresh, bathe yourself in water, cherish the little child that holds your hand, and make your wife happy in your embrace; for this too is the lot of man.

Ignoring Siduri's advice, Gilgamesh continues his journey, until he finds Utnapishtim [oot-nuh-PISH-tim], a mortal whom the gods so favored that they put him in an eternal paradise. Gilgamesh puts to Utnapishtim the question that is the reason for his quest.

Oh, father Utnapishtim, you who have entered the assembly of the gods, I wish to question you concerning the living and the dead, how shall I find the life for which I am searching?

Utnapishtim said, "There is no permanence. Do we build a house to stand forever, do we seal a contract to hold for all time? Do brothers divide an inheritance to keep forever, does the flood-time of rivers endure? . . . What is there between the master and the servant when both have fulfilled their doom? When the Anunnaki [the gods of the underworld], the judges, come together, and Mammetun [the goddess of fate], the mother of destinies, come together they decree the fates of men. Life and death they allot but the day of death they do not disclose.

Utnapishtim then tells Gilgamesh of a time when gods decided to send a great flood to destroy the Sumerians, who had angered the great god Enlil.

Gilgamesh, from decorative panel of a lyre unearthed at Ur.
(The University Museum, University of Pennsylvania, neg. T4-108)

The god Ea, however, intervened and commanded Utnapishtim to build a boat big enough to hold his family, various artisans, and all animals in order to survive the flood that was to come. Enlil was infuriated by the Sumerians' survival, and Ea rebuked him. Then Enlil relented and blessed Utnapishtim with eternal paradise. After telling the story, Utnapishtim foretells Gilgamesh's fate.

O Gilgamesh, this was the meaning of your dream [of immortality]. You were given the kingship, such was your destiny, everlasting life was not your destiny. Because of this do not be sad at heart, do not be grieved or oppressed; he [Enlil] has given you power to bind and to loose, to be the darkness and the light of mankind. He has given you unexampled supremacy over the people, victory in battle from which no fugitive returns, in forays and assaults from which there is no going back. But do not abuse this power, deal justly with your servants in the palace, deal justly before the face of the Sun."

Questions for Analysis

1. What does the *Epic of Gilgamesh* reveal about Sumerian attitudes toward the gods and human beings?

2. At the end of his quest, did Gilgamesh achieve immortality? If so, what was the nature of that immortality?

3. What does the epic tell us about Sumerian views of the nature of human life? Where do human beings fit into the cosmic world?

Source: From *The Epic of Gilgamesh*, translated and with an introduction by N. K. Sanders (Penguin Classics, 1960; Third Edition, 1972). Copyright © N. K. Sanders, 1960, 1964, 1972. Reproduced by permission of Penguin Books Ltd.

CHAPTER 2

Small Kingdoms and Mighty Empires in the Near East

ca. 1100–513 B.C.E.

Chapter Preview

Disruption and Diffusion
How did the Nubians, Kush, and Phoenicians respond to the power vacuum in Egypt and the western Near East?

The Children of Israel
How did the Hebrew state evolve, and what were the unique elements of Hebrew religious thought?

Assyria, the Military Monarchy
What enabled the Assyrians to conquer their neighbors, and how did their aggression finally cause their undoing?

The Empire of the Persian Kings
How did the Persians rise to power and maintain control over their extensive empire? What were the central concepts of their religion, Zoroastrianism?

INDIVIDUALS IN SOCIETY: Wen-Amon

LISTENING TO THE PAST: The Covenant Between Yahweh and the Hebrews

Reconstruction of the "Ishtar Gate," Babylon, early sixth century B.C.E. Located in the Berlin Museum. (Bildarchiv Preussischer Kulturbesitz/Art Resource, NY)

The migratory invasions that brought down the Hittites and stunned the Egyptians in the late thirteenth century B.C. ushered in a new era in the ancient Near East. In the absence of powerful empires, the Phoenicians, Hebrews, and many other peoples carved out small independent kingdoms until the Near East was a patchwork of small states. During this period Hebrew culture and religion evolved under the influence of urbanism, kings, and prophets.

In the ninth century B.C.E. this jumble of small states gave way to an empire that for the first time embraced the entire Near East. Yet the very ferocity of the Assyrian Empire led to its downfall only two hundred years later. In 550 B.C.E. the Persians and Medes (**meeds**), who had migrated into Iran, created a "world empire" stretching from Anatolia in the west to the Indus Valley in the east. For over two hundred years the Persians gave the ancient Near East peace and stability.

Disruption and Diffusion

How did the Nubians, Kush, and Phoenicians respond to the power vacuum in Egypt and the western Near East?

The fall of empires was a time of both massive political disruption and cultural diffusion. In Africa, the decline of Egyptian power energized the kingdoms of Nubia and Kush, who adopted elements of Egyptian culture as they rose to power

Nubian Pyramids

The Nubians adopted many aspects of Egyptian culture and customs. The pyramids shown here are not as magnificent as their Egyptian predecessors, but they served the same purpose of honoring the dead king. Their core was constructed of bricks, which were then covered with stone blocks. At the doors of the pyramids stood monumental gates to the interiors of the tombs. (Michael Yamashita)

Individuals in Society

Wen-Amon

Wen-Amon, an official of the temple of Amon-Ra at Karnak in Egypt, personally experienced the weakening of Egypt's power on a trip to Byblos in Phoenicia sometime in the eleventh century B.C.E. His mission was to obtain lumber for Amon-Ra's ceremonial barge. Wen-Amon's detailed account of his experiences comes in the form of an official report to the chief priest of the temple.

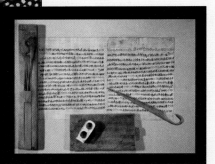

The essentials of Egyptian writing: a sheet of papyrus, a stylus or pen, an ink well. (*Réunion des Musées Nationaux/Art Resource, NY*)

Entrusted with silver to pay for the lumber, Wen-Amon set out on his voyage. He docked at Dor, in modern Israel, which was independent of the pharaoh, but the local prince received him graciously. While his ship was at anchor, one of Wen-Amon's own sailors vanished with the silver. Wen-Amon immediately reported the robbery to the prince and demanded that he investigate the theft. The prince flatly told Wen-Amon that he did not care whether Wen-Amon and the others were important men and that the matter was not his problem. No earlier foreign prince would have dared speak to a high Egyptian official in such terms.

Although rebuffed, Wen-Amon found a ship from Byblos and robbed it of an equivalent amount of silver. When he left Dor and entered the harbor of Byblos, the prince there, who had learned of the theft, ordered him to leave. For twenty-nine days there was an impasse. Finally the two men met and a heated argument ensued. Not until Wen-Amon reminded the prince of the god Amon's power did the prince agree to the sale of the timber.

After the timber was loaded aboard his ship, Wen-Amon saw eleven enemy ships entering the harbor. They anchored, and those in charge reported to the prince of Byblos that they had come for the Egyptians. The prince refused to hand them over, saying that he would never arrest a messenger of Amon-Ra. He agreed, however, to send Wen-Amon away first and allow the enemy ships to pursue the Egyptians. Stormy seas blew the Egyptian ship into Hittite territory. When Wen-Amon landed there, Queen Heteb granted him protection and asylum.

The papyrus breaks off at this point, but it is obvious that Wen-Amon weathered his various storms to return safely to Egypt. The document illustrates the presumption of power by Wen-Amon and his bluster at the lack of respect shown him. It also shows how Egypt's neighbors no longer feared Egyptian power. Finally, it illustrates the impact of Egyptian culture and religion on the peoples living along the coast of the Levant. Although Egyptian political power was in eclipse, its gods were respected.

Questions for Analysis

1. What do Wen-Amon's experiences tell us about political conditions in the eastern Mediterranean?
2. Since Wen-Amon could no longer depend on the majesty of Egypt for respect, how did he fulfill his duty?

in the region. The Phoenicians also thrived with the absence of pressure from the Egyptians and Hittites, using their independence to develop a trade network that spread Mesopotamian culture along the Mediterranean.

ca. 1100–653 B.C.E.	Third Intermediate Period in Egypt
ca. 1100–400 B.C.E.	Era of the prophets in Israel
ca. 1025–925 B.C.E.	United Hebrew kingdom
950–730 B.C.E.	Movement of new peoples into Egypt
ca. 950–500 B.C.E.	Beginning of the Hebrew Bible
ca. 900–612 B.C.E.	Assyrian Empire
ca. 900–550 B.C.E.	Phoenician seafaring and trading in the Mediterranean
ca. 710–550 B.C.E.	Creation of the Persian Empire
ca. 600–500 B.C.E.	Spread of Zoroastrianism
586–538 B.C.E.	Babylonian Captivity of the Hebrews
ca. 550–513 B.C.E.	Expansion of Persian trade from western Asia to India

The End of Egyptian Power

The long wars against the Sea Peoples impoverished Egypt, weakening its power in the region and at home. The four hundred years of political fragmentation are known as the Third Intermediate Period (eleventh–seventh centuries B.C.E.). (See the feature "Individuals in Society: Wen-Amon.")

In southern Egypt, the pharaoh's decline opened the way to the Nubians, who extended their authority northward throughout the Nile Valley. Nubian kings and aristocrats embraced Egyptian culture wholesale, repeating a Near Eastern phenomenon: new peoples conquered old centers of political and military power but were assimilated into the older culture.

Another independent African state, the kingdom of Kush, grew up during the period of Egyptian weakness. The Kushites worshiped Egyptian gods and used Egyptian hieroglyphs (high-ruh-GLIFS). In the eighth century B.C.E. their king, Piankhy, swept north from their capital at Nepata in the region of modern Sudan, extending his conquests all the way to the Nile Delta. Egypt enjoyed a brief period of peace, but reunification of the realm did not lead to a new Egyptian empire.

The Rise of Phoenicia

The fall of the Hittite Empire and Egypt's collapse created a vacuum of power in the western Near East that allowed for the rise of numerous small states. The Phoenicians, who had long inhabited several cities along the coast of modern Lebanon, used their new freedom to become the seaborne merchants of their broad world. With the Greeks, one of their early customers, they traded their popular purple and blue textiles, from which originated their Greek name, Phoenicians, meaning the "Purple People."

Their growing success inspired new ventures, and the Phoenicians began to manufacture other goods for export, such as metal tools, weapons, and cooking ware. They also expanded their trade routes, first to Egypt, then along the coast of North Africa, eventually to the far western Mediterranean and beyond, to the Atlantic Ocean. Although the Phoenicians did not found colonies, they planted trading posts and small farming communities along the way. Their trading post in Carthage prospered to become a leading city in the western Mediterranean. Through these ventures the Phoenicians peacefully spread Mesopotamian customs to less urbanized peoples.

The Phoenicians' overwhelming cultural achievement was the development of an alphabet: they, unlike other literate peoples, used one letter to designate one sound, a system that vastly simplified writing and reading. The Greeks modified this alphabet and then used it to write their own language.

Section Review

- Long wars against the Sea Peoples impoverished Egypt, leading to the Third Intermediate Period (11th–7th c. B.C.E.) of political fragmentation.

- In southern Egypt the Nubians and the Kushites gained strength as the pharaohs declined.

- In the western Near East the Phoenicians became skilled merchants, manufactured goods for export, and spread their customs peacefully to other peoples.

- The name Phoenician, Greek for the "Purple People," reflected the rich textiles they traded.

- The most remarkable cultural achievement of the Phoenicians was their development of an alphabet using one letter for each sound, vastly simplifying writing.

Phoenician Ships

These small ships seem too frail to breast the waves. Yet Phoenician mariners routinely sailed them, loaded with their cargoes, to the far ports of the Mediterranean. (British Museum/Michael Holford)

The Children of Israel

How did the Hebrew state evolve, and what were the unique elements of Hebrew religious thought?

South of Phoenicia arose a small kingdom, the land of the ancient Israelites or Hebrews. Virtually the only source for much of their history is the Bible, a religious document that contains many myths and legends as well as historical material.

The Evolution of the Jewish State

According to Hebrew tradition, the patriarch Abraham led his people from Mesopotamia in the second millennium B.C.E. Together with other seminomadic peoples, they probably migrated into the Nile Delta seeking good land. According to the Bible the Egyptians enslaved them. One group, however, under the leadership of Moses (**MOH-zis**), left Egypt in what the Hebrews remembered as the Exodus. From Egypt they wandered in the Sinai Peninsula until they settled in Palestine in the thirteenth century B.C.E.

Once in Palestine, the greatest danger to the Hebrews came from the neighboring Philistines (**FIL-uh-steens**), whose superior technology and military organization at first made them invincible. In Saul (ca. 1000 B.C.E.), a farmer of the tribe of Benjamin, the Hebrews found a champion and a spirited leader. In the biblical account Saul led attacks on the Philistines, often without success. Yet in the meantime he established a monarchy over the twelve Hebrew tribes.

Saul's work was carried on by David of Bethlehem, who pushed back the Philistines. To give his kingdom a capital, he captured the city of Jerusalem, which he enlarged, fortified, and made the religious and political center of his realm. His work in consolidating the monarchy and enlarging the kingdom paved the way for his son Solomon.

The Golden Calf
According to the Hebrew Bible, Moses descended from Mount Sinai, where he had received the Ten Commandments, to find the Hebrews worshiping a golden calf, which was against Yahweh's laws. In July 1990 an American archaeological team found this model of a gilded calf inside a pot. The figurine, which dates to about 1550 B.C.E., is strong evidence for the existence of the cult represented by the calf in Palestine. (Courtesy of the Leon Levy Expedition to Ashkelon. Photo: Carl Andrews)

Solomon (ca. 965–925 B.C.E.) applied his energies to creating a nation. He began by dividing the kingdom into twelve territorial districts cutting across the old tribal borders. To bring his kingdom up to the level of its more sophisticated neighbors, he set about a building program that encompassed cities, palaces, fortresses, and roads. The most symbolic of these projects was the Temple of Jerusalem, which became the home of the Ark of the Covenant, the cherished chest that contained the holiest of Hebrew religious articles. The temple in Jerusalem was intended to be the religious heart of the kingdom and the symbol of Hebrew unity.

At Solomon's death, his kingdom broke into two political halves (see Map 2.1). The northern part became Israel, with its capital at Samaria. The southern half was Judah, and Jerusalem remained its center. With political division went a religious rift: Israel, the northern kingdom, established rival sanctuaries for gods other than **Yahweh** (YAH-way).

Eventually, the northern kingdom of Israel was wiped out by the Assyrians, but the southern kingdom of Judah survived numerous calamities until the Babylonians crushed it in 587 B.C.E. The survivors were sent into exile in Babylonia, a period commonly known as the **Babylonian Captivity.** In 538 B.C.E. the Persian king Cyrus (SIGH-russ) the Great permitted some forty thousand exiles to return to Jerusalem. During and especially after the Babylonian Captivity, the exiles redefined their beliefs and practices and thus established what they believed was the law of Yahweh. Those who lived by these precepts can be called Jews.

Yahweh A god, who in Medieval Latin became Jehovah, that appeared to Moses on Mount Sinai and made a covenant with the Hebrews.

Babylonian Captivity A period of time in 587 B.C.E. when the survivors of a Babylonian attack on the southern kingdom of Judah were sent into exile in Babylonia.

MAP 2.1   Small Kingdoms of the Near East
This map illustrates the political fragmentation of the Near East after the great wave of invasions that occurred during the thirteenth century B.C.E.

SYRIA
Sidon
Damascus
PHOENICIA
Tyre
Mt. Hermon
Litani R.
Akzib
Lake Huleh
Akko
Sea of Galilee
Mt. Carmel
Megiddo
Ramoth Gilead
Mediterranean Sea
ISRAEL
Samaria
Shechem
PLAIN OF SHARON
Joppa
Jordan R.
AMMON
32°N
PHILISTINES
Jericho
Jerusalem
Mt. Nebo
Ashkelon
Bethlehem
Gaza
Lachish
Hebron
Dead Sea
JUDAH
Beersheba
MOAB
NEGEV DESERT
EDOM
ca. 800 B.C.E.
Kingdom of Israel
Kingdom of Judah
SINAI
0   30   60 Km.
0   30   60 Mi.
30°N
Ezion-geber
34°E   Gulf of Aqaba
36°E

Covenant A formal agreement between Yahweh and the Hebrew people that if the Hebrews worshiped Yahweh as their only god, he would consider them his chosen people and protect them from their enemies.

Section Review

- The main source of information for the Hebrews comes from the Bible, a religious document containing myths and legends in addition to history verifiable through other sources.

- King Saul defended the Israelites against the Philistines, and King David founded Jerusalem.

- King Solomon built the Temple of Jerusalem and created a sophisticated nation through an ambitious building program.

- At Solomon's death, the kingdom split into Israel in the north, which the Assyrians wiped out, and Judah in the south.

- The Babylonians crushed Judah in 587 B.C.E., the beginning of the Babylonian Captivity, which lasted until 538 B.C.E.

- Those who followed god Yahweh's law became known as Jews.

- The Hebrews' religion was unique because they knew what Yahweh expected and that if they followed his commandments and lived an ethical life they would be protected.

Elements of Jewish Religion

According to the Bible, the god Yahweh appeared to Moses on Mount Sinai. There Yahweh made a contract with the Hebrews, known as the **Covenant.** If they worshiped Yahweh as their only god, he would consider them his chosen people and protect them from their enemies. As the chosen people, the Hebrews' chief duty was to maintain the worship of Yahweh as he demanded. That worship was embodied in the Ten Commandments, which forbade the Hebrews to steal, murder, lie, or commit adultery. The Covenant was a constant force in Hebrew life (see the feature "Listening to the Past: The Covenant Between Yahweh and the Hebrews" on page 37).

The uniqueness of the Hebrews' religion can be seen by comparing the essence of Hebrew monotheism with the religious outlook of the Mesopotamians. Whereas the Mesopotamians considered their gods capricious, the Hebrews knew what Yahweh expected. The Hebrews believed that their god would protect them and make them prosper if they obeyed his commandments. The Mesopotamians thought human beings insignificant compared to the gods, so insignificant that the gods might even be indifferent to them. The Hebrews, too, considered themselves puny in comparison with Yahweh. Yet they were Yahweh's chosen people, whom he had promised never to abandon. Finally, though the Mesopotamians believed that the gods generally preferred good to evil, their religion did not demand ethical conduct. The Hebrews could please their god only by living up to high moral standards as well as by worshiping him.

Religious leaders were important in Judaism, but not as important as the written texts they interpreted; these texts came to be regarded as the word of Yahweh and thus had a status other writings did not. The most important task for observant Jews was to study religious texts, an activity limited to men until the twentieth century. Women were obliged to provide for men's physical needs so that they could study, which often meant that Jewish women were more active economically than their contemporaries of other religions. Women's religious rituals tended to center on the home, while men's centered on the temple. The reverence for a particular text or group of texts was passed down from Judaism to the other Western monotheistic religions that grew from it, Christianity and Islam.

Assyria, the Military Monarchy

What enabled the Assyrians to conquer their neighbors, and how did their aggression finally cause their undoing?

Small kingdoms like those of the Phoenicians and the Hebrews could exist only in the absence of a major power. The beginning of the ninth century B.C.E. saw the rise of such a power: the Assyrians of northern Mesopotamia, whose chief capital was at Nineveh (NIN-uh-vuh) on the Tigris River. The Assyrians were a Semitic-speaking people heavily influenced by the Mesopotamian culture of Babylon to the south. Living in an open, exposed land, the Assyrians experienced frequent and devastating attacks by the tribes to their north and east and by the Babylonians to the south. The constant threat to survival promoted Assyrian political cohesion and military might, and they evolved into one of the most warlike societies in history. Yet they were also a mercantile people who had long pursued commerce with their neighbors to the north and south.

The Power of Assyria

For over two hundred years the Assyrians labored to dominate the Near East. In 859 B.C.E. the new Assyrian king, Shalmaneser (shal-muh-NEE-zer), unleashed the first of a long series of attacks on the peoples of Syria and Palestine.

Under the warrior-kings Tiglath-pileser III (TIG-lath-pih-LEE-zuhr) (774–727 B.C.E.) and Sargon II (r. 721–705 B.C.E.), the Assyrians stepped up their attacks on Anatolia, Syria, and Palestine. The kingdom of Israel and many other states fell; others, like the kingdom of Judah, became subservient to the warriors from the Tigris. In 717 to 716 B.C.E., Sargon led his army in a sweeping attack along the Philistine coast, where he defeated the pharaoh. Sargon also lashed out at Assyria's traditional enemies to the north and then turned south against a renewed threat in Babylonia. By means of almost constant warfare, Tiglath-pileser III and Sargon II carved out an Assyrian empire that stretched from east and north of the Tigris River to central Egypt (see Map 2.2).

Although it was renowned for gruesome displays of violence, Assyria's success was actually due to its sophisticated military machine. Infantrymen were armed with spears and swords and protected by helmet and armor. Archers charged the enemy on horseback and in chariots. Other heavily armored archers served as a primitive field artillery, sweeping the enemy's walls of defenders so that others could storm the defenses. Slingers also served as artillery in pitched battles.

MAPPING THE PAST

MAP 2.2   The Assyrian and Persian Empires

Compare this map showing the extent of the Assyrian and Persian Empires with Map 2.1 on page 29, which shows the earliest political extent of the Eastern states. **[1]** What do these maps tell us about the growth of political power? **[2]** What new areas have opened to the old cultures? **[3]** What do the two maps suggest about the shift of power and the spread of civilization in the ancient Near East?

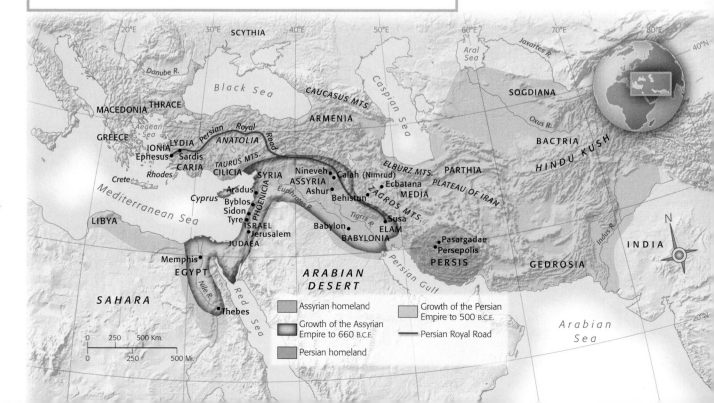

Section Review

- Assyrian monarchs Tiglath-pileser III and Sargon II attacked Anatolia, Syria, and Palestine, destroying the Kingdom of Israel and occupying Judah and Egypt.

- Assyria rose to power at the beginning of the 9th c. B.C.E. because of its superior military technology, including heavily armored archers and siege machinery.

- Assyrian artists used a series of pictures to show progression of a story—an idea later adopted by the Persians along with Assyrian military tactics. The Assyrians depicted their military campaigns in continuous friezes and monumental sculpted figures.

- Babylon won independence from Assyria in 626 B.C.E., and the Assyrians disappeared from history until the modern era.

The Assyrians' military genius extended to siege machinery and techniques, including excavation to undermine city walls and battering rams to knock down walls and gates. Never before in the Near East had anyone applied such technical knowledge to warfare. The Assyrians even invented the concept of a corps of engineers, who bridged rivers with pontoons or provided soldiers with inflatable skins for swimming. And the Assyrians knew how to coordinate their efforts, both in open battle and in siege warfare.

Assyrian Culture

In the seventh century B.C.E. Assyrian power seemed firmly established. Yet the downfall of Assyria was swift and complete. Babylon finally won its independence in 626 B.C.E. and joined forces with a newly aggressive people, the Medes, an Indo-European-speaking folk from Iran. Together the Babylonians and the Medes destroyed the Assyrian Empire in 612 B.C.E., paving the way for the rise of the Persians. The Hebrew prophet Nahum (**NEY-hum**) spoke for many when he asked: "Nineveh is laid waste: who will bemoan her?"[1]

Their cities destroyed and their power shattered, the Assyrians disappeared from history, remembered only as a cruel people of the Old Testament. Two hundred years later, when the Greek adventurer and historian Xenophon (**ZEN-uh-fuhn**) passed by the ruins of Nineveh, he marveled at the extent of the former city but knew nothing of the Assyrians. The glory of their empire was forgotten until modern

Royal Lion Hunt
This wall painting from the seventh century B.C.E. depicts the Assyrian king frightening a lion, a typical representation of the energy and artistic brilliance of Assyrian artists. The lion hunt signified the king as the protector of society, not simply as a sportsman. (Louvre/Réunion des Musées Nationaux/Art Resource, NY)

archaelogy brought the Assyrians out of obscurity. Among the treasures unearthed in recent centuries were monumental sculpted figures—huge winged bulls, human-headed lions, and sphinxes—as well as brilliantly sculpted friezes. Assyrian artists had hit on the idea of portraying a series of episodes in a continuous frieze, so that the viewer could follow the progress of a military campaign from the time the army marched out until the enemy was conquered. These techniques influenced Persian artists, who adapted them to gentler scenes. In fact, many Assyrian innovations, military and political as well as artistic, were taken over by the Persians.

The Empire of the Persian Kings

How did the Persians rise to power and maintain control over their extensive empire? What were the central concepts of their religion, Zoroastrianism?

Like the Hittites before them, the Iranians were Indo-Europeans from central Europe and southern Russia. They migrated into the land known in ancient times as Persia and today as Iran. From Persia would come one of the greatest empires of antiquity, one that encompassed scores of peoples and cultures.

The Land of the Medes and Persians The Iranians who entered Persia around 1000 B.C.E. were nomads who migrated with their flocks and herds. They were also horse breeders, and the horse gave them a decisive military advantage over the prehistoric peoples of Iran. These centuries of immigration saw constant cultural interchange between conquering newcomers and conquered natives.

Persian Charioteers

Here are two Persians riding in a chariot pulled by four horses. The chariot is simple in construction but elegant in ornamentation. The harness of the horses is worked in elaborate and accurate detail. This chariot was used for ceremonial purposes, not for warfare. (Courtesy of the Trustees of the British Museum)

The Royal Palace at Persepolis
King Darius began and King Xerxes finished building a grand palace worthy of the glory of the Persian Empire. Pictured here is the monumental audience hall, where the king dealt with ministers of state and foreign envoys. (George Holton/Photo Researchers)

Two groups of Iranians gradually began coalescing into larger units: the Persians and the Medes. The Medes united under one king around 710 B.C.E. and then extended their control over the Persians to the south. In 612 B.C.E. they joined the Babylonians to overthrow the Assyrian Empire. With the rise of the Medes, the balance of power in the Near East shifted for the first time east of Mesopotamia.

The Rise of the Persian Empire (550–540 B.C.E.)

In 550 B.C.E. Cyrus the Great (r. 559–530 B.C.E.), king of the Persians and one of the most remarkable statesmen of antiquity, conquered the Medes. Cyrus's conquest of the Medes resulted not in slavery and slaughter but in the union of the Iranian peoples. Having united Iran, Cyrus set out to achieve two goals. First, he wanted to win control of the West and thus of the terminal ports of the great trade routes that crossed Iran and Anatolia. Second, he strove to secure eastern Iran from the pressure of nomadic invaders.

In a series of major campaigns, Cyrus achieved his goals. He swept into Anatolia, easily overthrowing the young kingdom of Lydia (LID-ee-uh). His generals subdued the Greek cities along the coast of Anatolia, thus gaining him important ports on the Mediterranean. From Lydia, Cyrus marched to the far eastern corners of Iran and conquered the regions of Parthia (PAHR-thee-uh) and Bactria (BAK-tree-uh). The Babylonians welcomed him as a liberator when his soldiers moved into their kingdom.

With these victories, Cyrus demonstrated to the world his benevolence as well as his military might. He spared the life of Croesus (KREE-suhs), the conquered king of Lydia, to serve him as friend and adviser. He allowed the Greeks to live according to their customs, thus making possible the spread of Greek culture. Cyrus's humanity likewise extended to the Jews, whom he found enslaved in Babylonia. He returned their sacred objects to them and allowed them to return to Jerusalem and rebuild the temple.

Cyrus's successors Darius (duh-RIE-uhs) (r. 521–486 B.C.E.) and Xerxes (ZERK-sees) (r. 486–464 B.C.E.) rounded out the Persian conquest of the ancient Near East. Within thirty-seven years (550–513 B.C.E.) the Persians transformed themselves from a subject people to the rulers of an empire that included Anatolia, Egypt, Mesopotamia, Iran, and western India. They had created a **world empire** encompassing all the oldest and most honored kingdoms and peoples of the ancient Near East. Never before had this region been united in one such vast political organization (see Map 2.2).

The Persians knew how to preserve the peace. Unlike the Assyrians, they did not resort to royal terrorism to maintain order. Instead, the Persians built an efficient administrative system to govern the empire, based in the capital city of Persepolis (per-SEP-uh-lis), near modern Schiras, Iran. From Persepolis they sent directions to the provinces and received reports back from their officials. To do so they maintained a sophisticated system of roads linking the empire. The main highway, the famous **Royal Road,** spanned some 1,677 miles (see Map 2.2). Other roads branched out to link all parts of the empire from the coast of Asia Minor to the valley of the Indus River. This system of communications enabled Persian kings to keep in close touch with their subjects and officials. They were thereby able to make the concepts of right, justice, and good government a practical reality.

world empire All of the oldest and most honored kingdoms and peoples of the ancient Near East that were united under the Persian political organization.

Royal Road The main highway created by the Persians; it spanned 1,677 miles from Greece to Iran.

Zoroastrianism A religion teaching that Ahura Mazda, god of good and light, fought continuously with Ahriman, god of evil and dark, with Ahura Mazda ultimately winning.

Thus Spake Zarathustra

Around 600 B.C.E. a preacher named Zarathustra (zar-uh-THUH-struh)—Zoroaster (zo-ro-ASS-ter), as he is better known—introduced new spiritual concepts to the people of Iran. Zoroaster taught that life is a constant battleground for the two opposing forces of good and evil. The Iranian god Ahuramazda (ah-HOOR-uh-MAZZ-duh) embodied good and truth but was opposed by Ahriman (AH-ree-mahn), a hateful spirit who stood for evil and lies. Ahuramazda and Ahriman were locked together in a cosmic battle for the human race, a battle that stretched over thousands of years.

Zoroaster emphasized the individual's responsibility to choose between good and evil. He taught that people possessed the free will to decide between Ahuramazda and Ahriman and that they must rely on their own conscience to guide them through life. Their decisions were crucial, Zoroaster warned, for there would be a time of reckoning. The victorious Ahuramazda, like the Egyptian god Osiris, would preside over a last judgment to determine each person's eternal fate. Those who had lived according to good and truth would enter a divine kingdom. Liars and the wicked, denied this blessed immortality, would be condemned to eternal pain, darkness, and punishment. Thus Zoroaster preached a last judgment that led to a heaven or a hell.

Zoroaster's teachings converted Darius, who did not, however, try to impose them on others. Under the protection of the Persian kings, **Zoroastrianism** (zo-ro-ASS-tree-uh-niz-uhm) won converts throughout Iran. It survived the fall of the Persian Empire to influence liberal Judaism, Christianity, and early Islam. Good behavior in the world, even though unrecognized at the time, would receive

Section Review

- Iranians (Medes and Persians) were Indo-European nomads who entered Persia around 1000 B.C.E. and joined the Babylonians to overthrow the Assyrians in 612 B.C.E.

- Cyrus the Great formed the Persian Empire in 550 B.C.E., subduing important Greek port cities on the coast of Anatolia, yet allowing the Greeks to live according to their customs.

- Persian successors Darius and Xerxes built an efficient administrative system that included the Royal Road.

- About 600 B.C.E. a sage named Zarathustra (Zoroaster) taught that a cosmic battle was occurring between the good god Ahuramazda and the evil spirit Ahriman, and individuals would be subjected to eternal heaven or hell through a last judgment by Ahuramazda.

- Darius adopted Zarathustra's religion of Zoroastrianism, and it in turn influenced Judaism, Christianity, and Islam.

ample reward in the hereafter. Evil, no matter how powerful in life, would be punished after death. In some form or another, Zoroastrian concepts still pervade the major religions of the West and every part of the world touched by Islam.

Chapter Review

How did the Nubians, Kush, and Phoenicians respond to the power vacuum in Egypt and the western Near East? (page 25)

During the centuries following the Sea Peoples' invasions, the African kingdoms of the Nubians and the Kush filled the power vacuum in Egypt and adopted elements of Egyptian culture such as hieroglyphs and pyramids. In Anatolia, the Phoenicians in particular took advantage of the fall of the Hittites and the weakness of Egyptian power to spread commodities and ideas through trade.

How did the Hebrew state evolve, and what were the unique elements of Hebrew religious thought? (page 28)

Another group to benefit from the absence of a major power in the region were the Hebrews, who created a small kingdom in Palestine. Their kingdom was short-lived, but their religious beliefs and written codes of law and custom proved to be long lasting. Judaism, their monotheistic religion, continues as a vibrant faith today and was an important source for Christianity and Islam.

What enabled the Assyrians to conquer their neighbors, and how did their aggression finally cause their undoing? (page 30)

In this world rose the Assyrians, another Semitic people who had lived on its periphery. The Assyrians' superior military organization enabled them to conquer many small kingdoms, but they also created many enemies who ultimately joined to defeat them. Assyrian artists, however, were innovators whose ideas were adapted by the Persians.

How did the Persians rise to power and maintain control over their extensive empire? What were the central concepts of their religion, Zoroastrianism? (page 33)

The Persians assimilated the best of the civilizations that they found around them. Through conquest that was mild compared with that of the Assyrians, they broadened the geographical horizons of the ancient world. Their empire looked west to the Greeks and east to the peoples of the Indus Valley, and they gave the Near East a long period of peace. The Persians, whose empire far surpassed the Assyrians', had a farsighted conception of empire. Though as conquerors they willingly used force to accomplish their ends, they preferred to depend on diplomacy to rule. They usually respected their subjects and allowed them to practice their native customs and religions. Thus the Persians gave the Near East both political unity and cultural diversity. Through their religion, Zoroastrianism, they also introduced the concept of life as a battleground between good and evil.

Key Terms

Yahweh (p. 29)

Babylonian Captivity (p. 29)

Covenant (p. 30)

world empire (p. 35)

Royal Road (p. 35)

Zoroastrianism (p. 35)

Note

1. Nahum 3:7.

To assess your mastery of this chapter, go to **bedfordstmartins.com/mckaywestbrief**

Listening to the Past

The Covenant Between Yahweh and the Hebrews

As we mentioned in this chapter, the Hebrew Bible is not a document that we may accept as literal truth, but it does tell us a great deal about the people who created it. From the following passages we may discern what the Hebrews thought about their own past and religion.

The background of the excerpt is a political crisis that has some archaeological support. The king of the Ammonites had threatened to destroy the Hebrews, and word of the threat was sent among the Hebrew tribes. Saul came forth as a leader and rallied the men of Israel and Judah to fight the aggressors, and his army overwhelmed the Ammonites. The elders of the tribes had previously chosen judges to lead the community only in times of crisis. However, the Hebrews demanded that a kingship be established. They turned to Samuel, the last of the judges, who anointed Saul as the first Hebrew king. In this excerpt Samuel reminds the Hebrews of their obligation to honor the Covenant and recognize Yahweh as their true king.

Now therefore behold the king whom you have chosen, and whom you have desired! and behold, the Lord has set a king over you. If you will fear the Lord, and serve him, and obey his voice, and not rebel against the commandment of the Lord, then shall both you and also the king who reigns over you continue following the Lord your God: But if you will not obey the voice of the Lord, but rebel against the commandment of the Lord, then shall the hand of the Lord be against you, as it was against your fathers. Now therefore stand and see this great thing, which the Lord will do before your eyes. Is it not wheat harvest today? I will call to the Lord, and he shall send thunder and rain; that you may perceive and see that your wickedness is great, which you have done in the sight of the Lord, in asking you a king. So Samuel called to the Lord; and the Lord sent thunder and rain that

day: and all the people greatly feared the Lord and Samuel. And all the people said to Samuel, pray for your servants to the Lord your God, so that we will not die: for we have added to all of our sins this evil, to ask us for a king. And Samuel said to the people, Fear not: you have done all this wickedness; yet turn not aside from following the Lord, but serve the Lord with all your heart; And do not turn aside; for then should you go after vain things, which cannot profit nor deliver; for they are vain. For the Lord will not forsake his people for his great name's sake: because it pleases the Lord to make you his people. Moreover, as for me, God forbid that I should sin against the Lord in ceasing to pray for you: but I will teach you the good and the right way: Only fear the Lord, and serve him in truth with all your heart: for consider how great things he has done for you. But if you shall still act wickedly, you will be consumed, both you and your king.

Questions for Analysis

1. What was Samuel's attitude toward kingship?
2. What were the duties of the Hebrews toward Yahweh?
3. Might those duties conflict with those toward the secular king? If so, in what ways, and how might the Hebrews avoid the conflict?

Source: 1 Samuel 11:1–15; 12:1–7, 13–25. Abridged and adapted from *The Holy Bible*, King James Version.

Ark of the Covenant, depicted in a relief from Capernaum Synagogue, second century C.E.
(Ancient Art & Architecture Collection)

CHAPTER **3**

Classical Greece

ca. 1650–338 B.C.E.

Chapter Preview

Hellas: The Land
When the Greeks arrived in Hellas, how did they adapt themselves to their new landscape?

The Polis
After the Greeks had established the polis, in which they lived their political and social lives, how did they shape it into its several historical forms?

The Archaic Age (800–500 B.C.E.)
What major developments mark the Archaic Greek period in terms of spread of culture and the growth of cities?

The Classical Period (500–338 B.C.E.)
How did the Greeks develop their literature, philosophy, religion, and art, and how did war affect this intellectual and social process?

The Final Act (404–338 B.C.E.)
How did the Greek city-states meet political and military challenges, and how did Macedonia become dominant?

INDIVIDUALS IN SOCIETY: Aspasia

LISTENING TO THE PAST: The Great Plague at Athens, 430 B.C.E.

Dionysos at sea. Dionysos here symbolizes the Greek sense of exploration, independence, and love of life. (Bildarchiv Preussischer Kulturbesitz/Art Resource, NY)

The people of ancient Greece developed a culture that fundamentally shaped Western civilization. They were the first to explore most of the questions that continue to concern Western thinkers to this day. Going beyond myth-making, the Greeks strove to understand the world in logical, rational terms. The result was the birth of philosophy and science—subjects that were as important to most Greek thinkers as religion. The concept of politics evolved through Greek philosophy. Greek contributions to the arts and literature were equally profound.

The history of the Greeks is divided into two broad periods: the **Hellenic** (HELL-len-nic) **period** (the subject of this chapter), roughly the time between the arrival of the Greeks (approximately 2000 B.C.E.) and the victory over Greece in 338 B.C.E. by Philip of Macedon (mas-ee-DOHN); and the **Hellenistic** (hel-uh-NIS-tik) **period** (the subject of Chapter 4), the age beginning with the remarkable reign of Philip's son, Alexander the Great (336–323 B.C.E.), and ending with the Roman conquest of the Hellenistic East (200–146 B.C.E.).

Hellenic period The time between the arrival of the Greeks (approximately 2000 B.C.E.) and the victory of Greece in 338 B.C.E. by Philip of Macedon.

Hellenistic period The new culture that arose when Alexander overthrew the Persian Empire and began spreading Hellenism, Greek culture, language, thought, and way of life as far as India. It is called Hellenistic to distinguish it from the Hellenic period.

Hellas: The Land

When the Greeks arrived in Hellas, how did they adapt themselves to their new landscape?

Hellas, as the Greeks still call their land, encompassed the Greek peninsula, the islands of the Aegean (ah-GEE-uhn) Sea, and the lands bordering the Aegean, an area known as the **Aegean basin** (see Map 3.1). The Aegean basin included Ionia (eye-OH-nee-uh), on the coast of modern Turkey. The Greek peninsula consisted of various regions with distinctive geographical features. In the north and center were Thessaly (THES-uh-lee) and Boeotia (bee-OH-shuh), regions containing good farmland that helped sustain a strong population capable of fielding a formidable cavalry and infantry. Immediately to the south of Boeotia was Attica (AT-eh-kah), an area of thin soil but home to the olive and the vine. Its harbors looked to the Aegean, which invited its inhabitants, the Athenians, to concentrate on maritime commerce. Still farther south was the Peloponnesus (PELL-eh-puh-neze-us), a patchwork of high mountains and small plains that divided the area into several regions.

Aegean basin The territory surrounding Greece proper, including the Aegean Sea and Greek islands.

The geographical fragmentation of Greece encouraged political fragmentation. Furthermore, communications were extraordinarily poor. Rocky tracks were far more common than roads, which were seldom paved. These conditions prohibited the growth of a great empire like those of the Near East.

The Minoans and Mycenaeans (ca. 2000–ca. 1100 B.C.E.)

The origins of Greek civilization are complicated, obscure, and diverse. Neolithic peoples had already built prosperous communities in the Aegean, but not until about 2000 B.C.E. did they establish firm contact with one another. By then artisans had discovered how to make bronze, which gave these Stone Age groups more efficient tools and weapons. Some Cretan (KREE-tan) farmers and fishermen began to trade their surpluses with their neighbors. The central position of Crete (kreet) in the eastern Mediterranean made it a crucial link in this trade. The Cretans voyaged to Egypt, Asia Minor (the lands from the coast of Anatolia to the Euphrates River), other islands, and mainland Greece. They thereby played a vital part in creating an Aegean economy that brought them all into close contact. These favorable circumstances produced the vibrant **Minoan** culture on Crete, named after the mythical King Minos.

Minoan A flourishing and vibrant culture on Crete around 1650 B.C.E., named after King Minos. The symbol of their culture was the palace and its surrounding buildings, the most important one being Cnossus.

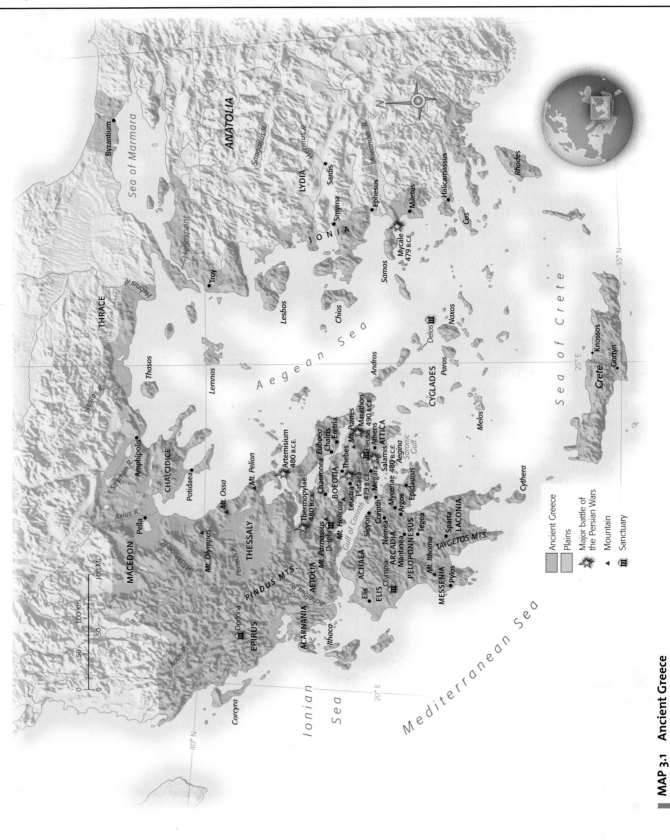

MAP 3.1 Ancient Greece

In antiquity, the home of the Greeks included the islands of the Aegean and the western shore of Asia Minor as well as the Greek peninsula itself.

Although the Minoans created a script now called Linear A, very little of it can be read with any certainty. However, archaeology and art offer some glimpses of life on the island. The palace was the political and economic center of its society. About 1650 B.C.E. Crete was dotted with them, but the palace at Cnossus (NOSS-suhs) towered above all others in importance. Few specifics are known about Minoan life except that at its head stood a king and his nobles. Minoan society was wealthy and, to judge by the absence of fortifications on the island, relatively peaceful. Minoan artistic remains, including frescoes and figurines, show women as well as men leading religious activities, watching entertainment, and engaging in athletic competitions such as leaping over a bull. We do not know if these represent daily life or mythological scenes, but many scholars see fewer restrictions on women than elsewhere in the ancient world.

Greek-speaking peoples arrived in the peninsula around 2000 B.C.E. They came gradually as individual groups who spoke various dialects of the same language. Despite these dialects, the Greeks considered themselves a related folk. By about 1650 B.C.E. one group had founded a powerful kingdom at Mycenae (my-SEE-nee), while others spread elsewhere in Greece. They merged with native inhabitants, and from that union emerged the society that modern scholars call **Mycenaean** (my-suh-NEE-uhn), after the most famous site of this new culture.

Early Mycenaean Greeks established cities at Thebes (theebz), Athens (ATH-ins), and elsewhere. As in Crete, the political unit was the kingdom. The king and his warrior aristocracy stood at the top of society. The seat and symbol of the king's power and wealth was his palace, which was also the economic center of the kingdom. Within its walls royal artisans fashioned jewelry and rich ornaments, made and decorated fine pottery, forged weapons, prepared hides and wool for clothing, and manufactured the other goods needed by the king and his retainers. Palace scribes kept records of taxes and the king's possessions in Greek with a script known as Linear B, which was derived from Minoan Linear A. The Mycenaean economy was marked by an extensive division of labor, all tightly controlled from the palace. At the bottom of the social scale were male and female slaves, who were normally owned by the king and aristocrats but who also worked for ordinary people.

Contacts between the Minoans and Mycenaeans were originally peaceful, and Minoan culture flooded the Greek mainland. But around 1450 B.C.E. the Mycenaeans attacked Crete, destroying many Minoan palaces and taking possession of the grand palace at Cnossus. For about the next fifty years, the Mycenaeans ruled much of the island until a further wave of violence left Cnossus in ashes.

Whatever the explanation of these events, Mycenaean kingdoms in Greece benefited from the fall of Cnossus, quickly expanding commercially throughout the Aegean. Palaces became grander, and citadels were often protected by mammoth stone walls. Prosperity, however, did not bring peace, and between 1300 and 1000 B.C.E. kingdom after kingdom suffered attack and destruction. Although later Greeks accused the Dorians (DOR-ee-ahns) of overthrowing the Mycenaean kingdoms, these centers undoubtedly fell because of mutual discord. The fall of the Mycenaean kingdoms ushered in a period of such poverty and disruption that historians usually call it the "Dark Age" of Greece (ca. 1100–800 B.C.E.). Even

ca. 1650–1000 B.C.E.	Arrival of the Mycenaean Greeks in Europe
ca. 1100–800 B.C.E.	Evolution of the polis; Greek migrations within the Aegean basin; poems of Homer and Hesiod
ca. 800–500 B.C.E.	Rise of Sparta and Athens; flowering of lyric poetry
776 B.C.E.	Founding of the Olympic games
ca. 750–550 B.C.E.	Greek colonization of the Mediterranean
ca. 700–500 B.C.E.	Concentration of landed wealth
ca. 640 B.C.E.	Use of coinage in western Asia
ca. 525–362 B.C.E.	Birth and development of tragedy, historical writing, and philosophy; spread of monumental architecture
499–479 B.C.E.	Persian wars
431–404 B.C.E.	Peloponnesian War
404–338 B.C.E.	Spartan and Theban hegemonies; success of Philip of Macedon

Mycenaean A society created from a union between native inhabitants and the powerful group centered at Mycenae; it was named after the most famous site of this new culture.

literacy, which was not widespread in any case, was a casualty of the chaos. None-theless, Greece remained Greek; nothing essential was swept away. Greek religious cults remained vital to the people, and basic elements of social organization continued to function effectively. It was a time of change and challenge, but not of utter collapse.

The disruption of Mycenaean societies caused the widespread movement of Greek peoples. They dispersed beyond mainland Greece farther south to Crete and in greater strength across the Aegean to the shores of Asia Minor. They arrived during a time when traditional states and empires had collapsed. Economic hardship was common, and various groups wandered for years. Yet by the end of the Dark Age, the Greeks had spread their culture throughout the Aegean basin.

Homer, Hesiod, Gods, and Heroes (1100–800 B.C.E.)

The Greeks, unlike the Hebrews, had no sacred book that chronicled their past. Instead they had the poems of Homer and Hesiod (HES-ee-uhd) to describe a legendary Heroic Age when gods and heroes still walked the earth. In terms of pure history these works contain scraps of information about the Bronze Age, much about the early Dark Age, and some about the poets' own era.

Homer's *Iliad* recounts an expedition of Mycenaeans, whom Homer called "Achaeans" (ah-KEY-uhns), to besiege the city of Troy in Asia Minor. The war was incited, as Homer tells it, by the Trojan prince Paris's abduction of the beautiful Helen, wife of a Mycenaean king. The heart of the *Iliad*, however, concerns the quarrel between Agamemnon, leader of the Mycenaean force, and his greatest

The Hellenic Period

Period	Significant Events	Major Writers
Bronze Age	Arrival of the Greeks in Greece	
2000–1100 B.C.E.	Rise and fall of the Mycenaean kingdoms	
Dark Age	Greek migrations within the Aegean basin	Homer
1100–800 B.C.E.	Social and political recovery	Hesiod
	Evolution of the polis	
	Rebirth of literacy	
Archaic Age	Rise of Sparta and Athens	
800–500 B.C.E.	Colonization of the Mediterranean basin	Sappho
	Flowering of lyric poetry	Solon
	Development of philosophy and science in Ionia	Anaximander Heraclitus
Classical Period	Persian wars	Herodotus
500–338 B.C.E.	Growth of the Athenian Empire	Thucydides
	Peloponnesian War	Aeschylus
	Rise of drama and historical writing	Sophocles
	Flowering of Greek philosophy	Euripides
	Spartan and Theban hegemonies	Aristophanes
	Conquest of Greece by Philip of Macedon	Plato Aristotle

warrior Achilles (uh-KIL-eez), who refuses to fight when Agamemnon wounds his pride. The *Odyssey* (OD-uh-see) narrates Odysseus's (oh-DIS-ee-uhs) long journey home from Troy; while quick-witted, his pride is also the source of his misfortunes.

Both of Homer's epics portray engaging but flawed characters who are larger than life and yet typically human. Homer was also strikingly successful in depicting the great gods, who generally sit on Mount Olympus (oh-LIM-puhs) and watch the fighting at Troy like spectators at a baseball game, although they sometimes participate in the action. Homer's deities are reminiscent of Mesopotamian gods and goddesses. Hardly a decorous lot, the Olympians are raucous, petty, deceitful, and splendid. In short, they are human.

Hesiod, who lived somewhat later than Homer, made the gods the focus of his epic poem, the *Theogony* (thee-OG-uh-nee). Hesiod was influenced by Mesopotamian myths, which the Hittites had adopted and spread to the Aegean. Like the Hebrews, Hesiod envisaged his cosmogony—his account of the way the universe developed—in moral and gendered terms. Originally the primary deity was an earth goddess, Gaia (GAY-yah), but through a series of incestuous relationships and generational conflicts, Zeus (zooss) emerged triumphant. He established a moral order with himself at the head, ending the chaotic female-dominated system. In *Theogony* and others of his works, Hesiod attributes all human problems to the first woman, Pandora (pan-DOHR-uh), whose curiosity led her to open the container in which pain, war, and other evils had been enclosed.

The Polis

After the Greeks had established the polis, in which they lived their political and social lives, how did they shape it into its several historical forms?

After the upheavals that ended the Mycenaean period and the slow recovery of prosperity during the Dark Age, the Greeks developed the **polis** (PAU-lis). The term *polis* is generally interpreted as "city-state," although the word is basically untranslatable. While "city-state" does not capture how integral the countryside was to the community, it is at least a term generally understood and accepted.

The polis was far more than a political institution. Above all it was a community of citizens whose customs comprised the laws of the polis. Even though the physical, religious, and political form of the polis varied from place to place, it was the very badge of Greekness.

Origins of the Polis

Recent archaeological expeditions and careful study have done much to clarify the origins of the polis. Even during the late Mycenaean period, towns had grown up around palaces. These towns and even smaller villages performed basically local functions. The first was to administer the ordinary political affairs of the community. The village also served a religious purpose in that no matter how small, each had its local cult to its own deity. The exchange of daily goods made these towns and villages economically important, if only on a small scale. These settlements also developed a social system that was particularly their own. They likewise had their own views of the social worth and status of their inhabitants and the nature of their public responsibilities. In short, they relied on custom and mutual agreement to direct their ordinary affairs.

Section Review

- The vibrant Minoans from their palace at Cnossus in Crete, using Linear A writing, ruled an artistic society, including relatively liberated women, without needing fortifications.

- Mycenaean Greeks, who used Linear B writing and owned slaves, attacked Crete and seized Cnossus about 1450 B.C.E. before building grand palaces protected with mammoth stone walls.

- The chaotic, illiterate Dark Age of Greece (1100–800 B.C.E.) led to the spread of Greek peoples and culture throughout the Aegean basin.

- The Greek epic poet Homer created the *Illiad* and *Odyssey* about the Trojan war, depicting heroes and powerful but flawed gods.

- Hesiod's misogynist *Theogony* depicts the sky god Zeus's triumph over the earth goddess Gaia, and attributes all human problems to the first woman, Pandora.

polis Generally interpreted as city-state, it was the basic political and institutional unit of Greece.

When fully developed, each polis normally shared a surprisingly large number of features with other poleis. Physically a polis was a society of people who lived in a city (*asty*) and cultivated the surrounding countryside (*chora*). The city's water supply came from public fountains, springs, and cisterns. By the fifth century B.C.E. the city was generally surrounded by a wall. The city contained a point, usually elevated, called the **acropolis** (ah-KROP-uh-lis) and a public square or market-place called the **agora** (AG-er-uh). On the acropolis, which in the early period was a place of refuge, stood the temples, altars, public monuments, and various dedications to the gods of the polis. The agora was originally the place where the warrior assembly met, but it became the political center of the polis. In the agora were porticoes, shops, and public buildings and courts.

The countryside was essential to the economy of the polis and provided food to sustain the entire population. But it was also home to sanctuaries for the deities of the polis and the site of important religious rites. The sacred buildings, shrines, and altars were the physical symbols of a polis, uniting country and city dwellers. The religious dedications in them were the possessions not only of the gods but also of the polis, reflecting its power and prestige.

The average polis did not have a standing army. Instead it relied on its citizens for protection. Very rich citizens often served as cavalry, which was, however, never as important as the heavily armed infantry, or **hoplites** (HOP-lites). These were the backbone of the army. Hoplites wore metal helmets and body armor, carried heavy, round shields, and armed themselves with spears and swords. They provided their own equipment and were basically amateurs. In some instances the citizens of a polis hired mercenaries to fight their battles. Mercenaries were expensive, untrustworthy, and willing to defect to a higher bidder. Even worse, they sometimes seized control over the polis that had hired them.

acropolis An elevated point within a city on which stood temples, altars, public monuments, and various dedications to the gods of the polis.

agora A public square or marketplace that was a political center of Greece.

hoplites The heavily armed infantry that were the backbone of the Greek army.

monarchy Derived from the Greek for the rule of one man, it was a type of Greek government in which a king represented the community.

tyranny Rule by a tyrant, a man who used his wealth to gain a political following that could take over the existing government.

Governing Structures

Greek city-states had several different types of government. **Monarchy,** rule by a king, was prevalent during the Mycenaean period but afterwards declined. While Sparta (SPAHR-tuh) boasted of two kings, they were only part of a more broadly based constitution. During fully developed historical times Greek states were either democracies or oligarchies. Sporadic periods of violent political and social upheaval often led to a third type of government—tyranny. **Tyranny** was rule by one man who had seized power by unconstitutional means, generally by using his wealth to win a political following that toppled the existing legal government.

The Delphic Oracle

The Marmaria, the sanctuary of Athena, is seen here against the backdrop of the mountains that surround the sanctuary of Apollo. Around the oracle clustered many temples to various deities, shrines, and other sacred buildings, all of them in a remote mountainous area especially chosen by Apollo to be his home and the place where he answered the supplications of the faithful. (John Buckler)

Only democracy and oligarchy (OLL-ih-gahr-key) played lasting, broad roles in Greek political life, and these two forms flourished across Greece well into later years. In principle, **democracy** meant that all people, without respect to birth or wealth, administered the workings of government. In reality, Greek democracy meant the rule of citizens, not "the people" as a whole, and citizenship was drastically limited. In Athens and in other democracies, only free adult men who had lived in the polis a long time were citizens. Women, foreigners, slaves, and others had no rights. The 10 to 20 percent of the population who were citizens generally shared equally in the determination of policy and the administration of government. Along with military service, citizenship provided men with an opportunity to bond with one another, and it became an important component in Greek ideas of masculinity.

democracy A type of Greek government in which all citizens, without regard to birth or wealth, administered the workings of government; it translates as the power of the people.

Most Greek states actually preferred oligarchy to democracy as their form of government. **Oligarchy,** which literally means "the rule of the few," was government by a small group of wealthy citizens. Oligarchy generally gave its whole population—leaders and people alike—stable government and freedom to prosper. Men could advance politically by earning enough wealth to qualify for the right to vote for officials and to hold office. Although the wealthy governed the city, they officially endorsed social mobility for capable men and application of the law equally to everyone. Corinthian oligarchs also listened to the will of the citizens, a major factor in their long success.

oligarchy The rule of a few; a type of Greek government in which a small group of wealthy citizens, not necessarily of aristocratic birth, ruled.

Oligarchy evolved into federalism first in the region of Boetia, where the oligarchy of Thebes united with neighboring oligarchies to form the "Boeotian Confederacy." **Federalism** in Greece meant a system of government in which individual city-states joined to create one general government. The Boeotian Confederacy of oligarchic city-states proved so successful that elsewhere in Greece other states followed its example. It was particularly popular and widespread later in the Hellenistic period.

federalism One of two political concepts created by Greeks in the fourth century B.C.E. in an attempt to prevent war. It uses the idea that security can be gained through numbers. Greek leagues would band together and marshal their resources to defend themselves from outside interference.

During the classical period (500–338 B.C.E.), however, despite the allure of federalism, the citizens of the vast majority of city-states were determined to remain autonomous. The very integration of the polis proved to be one of its basic weaknesses. The political result, as earlier in Sumer, was almost constant warfare. The polis could dominate, but unlike earlier and later empires, it could not incorporate.

The Archaic Age (800–500 B.C.E.)

What major developments mark the Archaic Greek period in terms of spread of culture and the growth of cities?

The Archaic (ahr-KAY-ik) Age was one of the most vibrant periods of Greek history, an era of extraordinary expansion geographically, artistically, and politically. Greeks ventured as far east as the Black Sea and as far west as Spain. With the rebirth of literacy, this period also witnessed a tremendous literary flowering. Politically these were the years when Sparta and Athens—the two poles of the Greek experience—rose to prominence.

Overseas Expansion

During the years 1100–800 B.C.E. the Greeks not only recovered from the breakdown of the Mycenaean world but also grew in wealth and numbers. This new prosperity brought new problems. The increase in population meant that many families had very little land or none at all. Land hunger and the resulting social and political tensions drove many Greek men and women to seek new homes outside of Greece. Other factors, largely intangible, played their part as well: the desire for a new start, a love of excitement and adventure, and natural curiosity about what lay beyond the horizon.

From about 750 to 550 B.C.E., Greeks from the mainland and Asia Minor traveled throughout the Mediterranean and even into the Atlantic Ocean in their quest for new land. They sailed in the greatest numbers to Sicily and southern Italy, where there was ample space for expansion.

Colonization changed the entire Greek world, both at home and abroad. In economic terms it created a much larger market for the exchange of agricultural and manufactured goods. From the east, especially from the northern coast of the Black Sea, came wheat in a volume beyond the capacity of Greek soil. In return flowed Greek wine and olive oil, which could not be produced in the harsher climate of the north. Greek-manufactured goods, notably rich jewelry and fine pottery, circulated from southern Russia to Spain. During this same period the Greeks adopted the custom of minting coins, a custom they apparently imported from Lydia. At first coinage was of little economic importance, and only later did it replace the common practice of barter. In the barter system one person simply exchanges one good for another without the use of money. Thus Greek culture and economics, fertilized by the influences of other societies, spread throughout the Mediterranean basin.

Colonization presented the polis with a huge challenge, for it required organization and planning on an unprecedented scale. The colonizing city, called the **metropolis,** or mother city, first decided where to establish the colony, how to transport colonists to the site, and who would sail. Then the metropolis collected and stored the supplies that the colonists would need both to feed themselves and

metropolis The colonizing or "mother" city, responsible for deciding where to establish the colony.

Mosaic Portrait of Sappho
The Greek letters in the upper left corner identify this idealized portrait as that of Sappho (SAF-oh), a poet of the Archaic period. Sappho's verse expressed the intensely personal side of life, including erotic love. She was bisexual, and her name become linked with female homosexual love. The English word *lesbian* is derived from her island home of Lesbos (LEZ-bos). (Museum of Sparta/Archaeological Receipts Fund)

to plant their first crop. Once the colonists landed, their leader laid out the new polis, selected the sites of temples and public buildings, and established the government. Then he surrendered power. The colony was thereafter independent of the metropolis. For the Greeks, colonization had two important aspects. First, it demanded that the polis assume a much greater public function than ever before, thus strengthening the city-state's institutional position. Second, colonization spread the polis and its values far beyond the shores of Greece. Even more important, colonization on this scale had a profound impact on the course of Western civilization. It meant that the prevailing culture of the Mediterranean basin would be Greek.

The Growth of Sparta

During the Archaic period the Spartans expanded the boundaries of their polis and made it the leading power in Greece. Like other Greeks, the Spartans faced the problems of overpopulation and land hunger. Unlike other Greeks, the Spartans solved these problems by conquest, not by colonization. To gain more land, the Spartans set out in about 735 B.C.E. to conquer Messenia (muh-SEE-nee-uh), a rich, fertile region in the southwestern Peloponnesus. This conflict, the First Messenian War, lasted for twenty years and ended in a Spartan triumph. The Spartans appropriated Messenian land and turned the Messenians into **helots** (HELL-uts), or state serfs who worked the land.

In about 650 B.C.E. Spartan exploitation and oppression of the Messenian helots led to a helot revolt so massive and stubborn that it became known as the Second Messenian War. The Spartan poet Tyrtaeus, a contemporary of these events, vividly portrays the ferocity of the fighting:

helots   State serfs who worked the land.

For it is a shameful thing indeed
When with the foremost fighters
An elder falling in front of the young men
Lies outstretched,
Having white hair and grey beard,
Breathing forth his stout soul in the dust,
Holding in his hands his genitals
stained with blood.[1]

It took the full might of the Spartan people, aristocrat and commoner alike, to win the Second Messenian War. After the victory non-noblemen, who had done much of the fighting, demanded rights equal to those of the nobility. The agitation of these non-nobles disrupted society until the aristocrats agreed to erase political distinctions among Spartan warriors. An oligarchy of five *ephors* (EF-fors), or over-seers, held the real executive power, while two kings and twenty-eight elders delib-erated on foreign and domestic matters.

Every Spartan citizen owed primary allegiance to the polis. Once Spartan boys reached the age of seven, they were enrolled in separate companies with other boys their age. They lived in this **homosocial** (same-sex) setting for much of their lives. They slept outside on reed mats and underwent rugged training until age twenty-four, when they became frontline soldiers. For the rest of their lives, Spar-tan men kept themselves prepared for combat. Their military training never ceased, and the older men were expected to be models of endurance, frugality, and sturdiness to the younger men. In battle Spartans were supposed to stand and die rather than retreat. An anecdote frequently repeated about one Spartan mother sums up Spartan military values. As her son was setting off to battle, the mother handed him his shield and advised him to come back either victorious, carrying the shield, or dead, being carried on it.

In this militaristic atmosphere, citizen women were remarkably free. The Spartan leadership viewed maternal health as important for the bearing of strong children and thus encouraged women to participate in athletics and to eat well. With men in military service most of their lives, citizen women owned property and ran the household; they were not physically restricted or secluded. Marriage often began with a trial marriage period to make sure the couple could have chil-dren, with divorce and remarriage the normal course if they were unsuccessful. Men saw their wives only rarely when they sneaked out of camp, and their most meaningful relations were same-sex ones. Spartan military leaders viewed such relationships as militarily advantageous, judging that men would fight more fiercely in defense of close comrades and lovers. Close links among men thus contributed to Spartan dedication to the state and understanding of civic virtue, which were admired throughout the Greek world.

homosocial Same-sex setting in which Spartan boys lived for much of their lives.

The Evolution of Athens

Like Sparta, Athens faced pressing social and economic problems during the Archaic period, but the Athenian response was far different from that of the Spartans. Instead of creating an oligarchy, the Athenians extended to all citizens the right and duty of governing the polis. Indeed, the Athenian democracy was one of the most thoroughgoing in Greece.

The late seventh century B.C.E. was for Athens a time of turmoil, the causes of which are virtually unknown. In 621 B.C.E. Draco (DRAY-koh), an Athenian aristo-crat, doubtless under pressure from the peasants, published the first law code of the Athenian polis. His code was thought harsh, but it nonetheless embodied the ideal that the law belonged to the citizens. Nevertheless, the aristocracy still governed Athens oppressively and by the early sixth century B.C.E. the situation was explosive. The aristocrats owned the best land, met in an assembly to govern the polis, and interpreted the law. Noble landowners were forcing small farmers into economic dependence. Many families were sold into slavery; others were exiled and their land was pledged to the rich.

One person who recognized these problems clearly was the poet Solon (SOH-luhn), himself an aristocrat. Solon recited his poems in the Athenian agora, where anyone there could hear his call for justice and fairness and his condemnation of aristocratic greed and dishonesty. The aristocrats realized that Solon was no crazed revolutionary, and the common people trusted him. Around 594 B.C.E. the nobles elected him *archon* (AHR-kon), chief magistrate of the Athenian polis, and gave him extraordinary power to reform the state.

Solon immediately freed all people enslaved for debt, recalled all exiles, canceled all debts on land, and made enslavement for debt illegal. Solon allowed even the poorest men into the old aristocratic assembly, where they could take part in the election of magistrates.

Although Solon's reforms solved some immediate problems, they did not bring peace to Athens. Some aristocrats attempted to make themselves tyrants, while others banded together to oppose them. In 546 B.C.E. Pisistratus (pie-SIS-tra-tus), an exiled aristocrat, returned to Athens, defeated his opponents, and became tyrant. Pisistratus reduced the power of the aristocracy while supporting the common people. Under his rule Athens prospered, and his building program began to transform the city into one of the splendors of Greece. His reign as tyrant promoted the growth of democratic ideas by arousing rudimentary feelings of equality in many Athenian men.

Democracy took shape in Athens under the leadership of Cleisthenes (KLAHYS-thuh-neez), a prominent aristocrat who won the support of lower-status men to emerge triumphant in 508 B.C.E. Cleisthenes created the **deme** (deem), a local unit that kept the roll of citizens, or *demos*, within its jurisdiction.

The democracy functioned on the idea that all full citizens were sovereign. Yet not all citizens could take time from work to participate in government. Therefore, they delegated their power to other citizens by creating various offices meant to run the democracy. The most prestigious of them was the board of ten archons who were charged with handling legal and military matters. Six of them oversaw the Athenian legal system. They presided over courts, fixed dates for trials, and ensured that the laws of Athens were consistent. They were all elected for one year. After leaving office they entered the *Areopagus* (ar-ee-OP-uh-gus), a select council of ex-archons who handled cases involving homicide, wounding, and arson.

Legislation was in the hands of two bodies, the **boule** (BOO-lee), or council, composed of five hundred members, and the **ecclesia** (ee-KLEE-zhee-uh), the assembly of all citizens. The boule, separate from the Areopagus, was perhaps the major institution of the democracy. By supervising the various committees of government and proposing bills to the assembly, it guided Athenian political life. It received foreign envoys and forwarded treaties to the assembly for ratification. It oversaw the granting of state contracts and was responsible for receiving many revenues. It held the democracy together. Nonetheless, the ecclesia had the final word. Every citizen could express his opinion on any subject on the agenda, and a simple majority vote was needed to pass or reject a bill.

Athenian democracy was to prove an inspiring ideal in Western civilization. It demonstrated that a large group of people, not just a few, could efficiently run the affairs of state. Because citizens could speak their minds, they did not have to resort

deme　A local unit that served as the basis of Cleisthenes' political system.

boule　Part of a larger legislative body (with the ecclesia), it is a council composed of five hundred members.

ecclesia　An assembly of all citizens that serves as the other legislative body with the boule.

Section Review

- The Greek growth in population and wealth led to overseas colonization throughout the Mediterranean basin.

- The colonizing city, the metropolis, spread Greek culture by determining the sites of colonies.

- Sparta was a militaristic society involved in both the First and Second Messenian wars, making the Messenians into helots (slaves).

- Spartan males lived in a homosocial setting for most of their lives, contributing to their dedication to the state and allowing their women much economic freedom.

- Draco made harsh laws and Solon reformed Athens, leading to tyrannical rule before Cleisthenes established democracy through the *deme*.

- Citizens ruled democratically in Athens through *archons* (legal and military), the *Areopagus* (former archons), the *boule* (council of five hundred), and *ecclesia* (assembly of all citizens).

to rebellion or conspiracy to express their desires. Like all democracies in ancient Greece, however, Athenian democracy was limited. Slaves, women, recent migrants, and foreigners could not be citizens; their opinions about political issues were not taken into account or recorded.

The Classical Period (500–338 B.C.E.)

How did the Greeks develop their literature, philosophy, religion, and art, and how did war affect this intellectual and social process?

In the years 500 to 338 B.C.E., Greek civilization reached its highest peak in politics, thought, and art. In this period the Greeks beat back the armies of the Persian Empire. Then, turning their spears against one another, they destroyed their own political system in a century of warfare. Some thoughtful Greeks felt prompted to record and analyze these momentous events. Herodotus (ca. 485–425 B.C.E.), from Asia Minor, traveled the Greek world to piece together the course of the Persian wars. Although he consulted documents when he could find them, he relied largely on the memories of the participants, making him the first oral historian as well as the "father of history." Next came Thucydides (thoo-SID-ih-dees) (ca. 460–ca. 399 B.C.E.), whose account of the Peloponnesian (PELL-eh-puh-neze-an) War remains a classic of Western literature. Unlike Herodotus, he was often a participant in the events that he described.

This era also saw the flowering of philosophy, as thinkers in Ionia and on the Greek mainland began to ponder the nature and meaning of the universe and human experience. The Greeks invented drama, and the Athenian tragedians Aeschylus (ES-kuh-luhs), Sophocles (SOF-uh-kleez), and Euripides (yoo-RIP-eh-deez) explored themes that still inspire audiences today. Greek architects reached the zenith of their art and created buildings whose very ruins still inspire awe. Because Greek intellectual and artistic efforts attained their fullest and finest expression in these years, this age is called the "classical period." Few periods in the history of Western society can match it in sheer dynamism and achievement.

Leonidas at Thermopylae

This heroic statue symbolizes the sacrifice of King Leonidas at the battle. Together with his Spartans, the Thespians, and the Thebans, he heroically died to stop the Persians at the pass of Thermopylae. (Professor Paul Cartledge)

The Persian Wars (499–479 B.C.E.)

One of the hallmarks of the classical period was warfare. In 499 B.C.E. the Ionian Greeks, with the feeble help of Athens, rebelled against the Persian Empire. In 490 B.C.E. the Persians struck back at Athens but were beaten off at the Battle of Marathon, on a small plain in Attica. This victory taught the Greeks that they could defeat the Persians and successfully defend their homeland. It also prompted the Persians to try again. In 480 B.C.E. the Persian king Xerxes led a mighty invasion force into Greece. In the face of this emergency, many of the Greeks united and pooled their resources to resist the invaders. The Spartans provided the overall leadership and commanded the Greek armies. The Athenians, led by the wily Themistocles (thuh-MIS-tuh-kleez), provided the heart of the naval forces. After an initial defeat at the battle of Thermopylae (thuhr-MOP-uh-lee), the Greek military repelled the Persians at sea and on land.

The significance of these Greek victories is nearly incalculable. By defeating the Persians, the Greeks ensured that they would not be taken over by a monarchy, which they increasingly viewed as un-Greek. The decisive victories meant that Greek political forms and intellectual concepts would be handed down to later societies.

Growth of the Athenian Empire (478–431 B.C.E.)

The defeat of the Persians created a power vacuum in the Aegean, and the Athenians took advantage of this situation. The Athenians and their allies formed the **Delian** (DAY-lee-un) **League**, a grand naval alliance aimed at liberating Ionia from Persian rule. Athenians provided most of the warships and crews and determined how many ships or how much money each member of the league should contribute to the allied effort.

Delian League A grand naval alliance aimed at liberating Ionia from Persian rule created by the Athenians and led by Aristides.

The Athenians, supported by the Delian League and led by the young aristocrat Cimon (SIGH-muhn), carried the war against Persia. But Athenian success had a sinister side. While the Athenians drove the Persians out of the Aegean, they also became increasingly imperialistic. Athens began reducing its allies to the status of subjects. Tribute was often collected by force, and the Athenians placed the economic resources of the Delian League under tighter and tighter control. Dissident governments were put down, and Athenian ideas of freedom and democracy did not extend to the citizens of other cities.

Athens justified its conduct by its successful leadership. In about 467 B.C.E. Cimon defeated a new and huge Persian force at the Battle of the Eurymedon River in Asia Minor, once again removing the shadow of Persia from the Aegean. But as the threat from Persia waned and the Athenians treated their allies more harshly, major allies such as Thasos (THAH-saws) revolted (ca. 465 B.C.E.), requiring the Delian League to use its forces against its own members.

The expansion of Athenian power and the aggressiveness of Athenian rule also alarmed Sparta and its allies. While relations between Athens and Sparta cooled, Pericles (PER-eh-kleez) (ca. 494–429 B.C.E.) became the leading statesman in Athens. Like the democracy he led, Pericles, an aristocrat of solid intellectual ability, was aggressive and imperialistic. At last, in 459 B.C.E. Sparta and Athens went to war over conflicts between Athens and some of Sparta's allies. Though the Athenians conquered Boeotia (bee-OH-shuh), Megara (MEG-er-uh), and Aegina (ee-JAY-nuh) in the early stages of the war, they met defeat in Egypt and later in Boeotia. The war ended in 445 B.C.E. with no serious damage to either side and nothing settled. But this war divided the Greek world between the two great powers.

Athens continued its severe policies toward its subject allies and also battled Corinth, one of Sparta's leading supporters (see Map 3.2). Pericles also escalated the tension in the region by excluding Megara from trade with the Athenian empire as punishment for alleged sacrilege. In response the Spartans convened a meeting of their allies, whose complaints of Athenian aggression ended with a demand that Athens be stopped. Reluctantly the Spartans agreed to declare war.

The Peloponnesian War (431–404 B.C.E.)

At the outbreak of this conflict, the Peloponnesian War, the Spartan ambassador Melesippus warned the Athenians: "This day will be the beginning of great evil for the Greeks." Indeed, the Peloponnesian War lasted a generation and brought

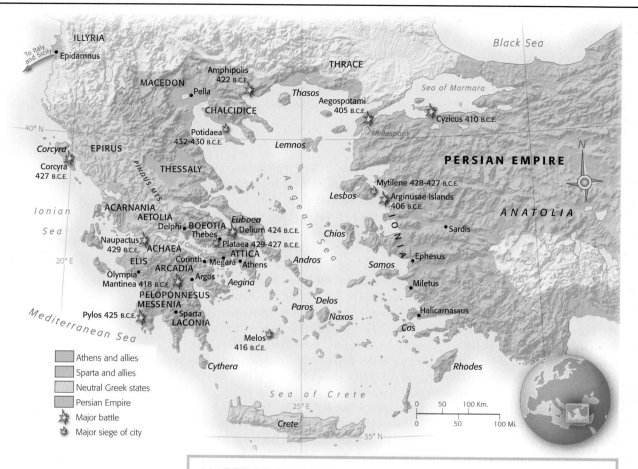

MAPPING THE PAST

MAP 3.2   The Peloponnesian War

This map shows the alignment of states during the Peloponnesian War. **[1]** What does Map 3.2 tell us about the balance of power during the Peloponnesian War? Which states led the others? **[2]** Are the leading states in Map 3.2 still the leaders in the next century?

in its wake fearful plagues, famine, civil wars, widespread destruction, and huge loss of life.

After a Theban attack on the nearby polis of Plataea (pluh-TEE-uh), the Peloponnesian War began in earnest. In the next seven years, the army of Sparta and its Peloponnesian allies invaded Attica five times. The Athenians stood behind their walls, but in 430 B.C.E. the cramped conditions nurtured a plague that killed huge numbers, eventually claiming Pericles himself. (See the feature "Listening to the Past: The Great Plague at Athens, 430 B.C.E." on page 64.) Under a new leader, Cleon (KLEE-on), the Athenians counterattacked and defeated the Spartans at Pylos (PIE-lohs), yet the Spartans responded by widening the war. Only after ten years of death, destruction, and stalemate did Sparta and Athens agree to the Peace of Nicias (NISH-ee-uhs) in 421 B.C.E.

The Peace of Nicias resulted in a cold war. But even cold war can bring horror and misery. Such was the case when in 416 B.C.E. the Athenians sent a fleet to the neutral island of Melos with an ultimatum: the Melians could surrender or perish. The motives of the Athenians were frankly and brutally imperialistic. The Melians resisted. The Athenians conquered them, killed the men of military age, and sold the women and children into slavery.

The cold war grew hotter, thanks to the ambitions of Alcibiades (al-suh-BAHY-uh-dees) (ca. 450–404 B.C.E.), an aristocrat, a kinsman of Pericles, and a student of the philosopher Socrates (SOK-ruh-teez). Alcibiades convinced the Athenians to attack Syracuse, the leading polis in Sicily. Ultimately the people of Syracuse prevailed, as Thucydides wrote: "[Athenian] infantry, fleet, and everything else were utterly destroyed, and out of many few returned home."[2]

The disaster in Sicily ushered in the final phase of the war, which was marked by three major developments: the renewal of war between Athens and Sparta, Persia's intervention in the war, and the revolt of many Athenian subjects. The year 413 B.C.E. saw Sparta's declaration of war against Athens and widespread revolt within the Athenian Empire. Yet Sparta still lacked a navy, the only instrument that could take advantage of the unrest of Athens's subjects, most of whom lived either on islands or in Ionia. The sly Alcibiades, now working for Sparta, provided a solution: the Persians would build a fleet for Sparta, and Sparta would give Ionia back to Persia. Now equipped with a fleet, the Spartans challenged the Athenians in the Aegean, the result being a long roll of inconclusive naval battles.

The strain of war prompted the Athenians in 407 B.C.E. to recall Alcibiades from exile. He cheerfully double-crossed the Spartans and Persians, but even he could not restore Athenian fortunes. In 405 B.C.E. Athens met its match in the Spartan commander Lysander, who destroyed the last Athenian fleet and block-aded Athens until it was starved into submission. After twenty-seven years the Peloponnesian War was over, and the evils prophesied by the Spartan ambassador Melesippus in 431 B.C.E. had come true.

Athenian Arts in the Age of Pericles

In the last half of the fifth century B.C.E., Pericles turned Athens into the showplace of Greece. He appropriated Delian League funds to pay for a huge building program, planning temples and other buildings to honor Athena (uh-THEE-nuh), the patron goddess of the city, and to display to all Greeks the glory of the Athenian polis. The main site of these projects was the acropolis, and the largest monument was the Parthenon (PAHR-thuh-non), a temple to Athena.

In many ways the Athenian Acropolis is the epitome of Greek art and its spirit. Although the buildings were dedicated to the gods and most of the sculptures portray gods, these works nonetheless express the Greek fascination with the human form. In the Parthenon sculptures it is visually impossible to distinguish the men and women from the gods and goddesses. The Acropolis also exhibits the rational side of Greek art. Greek artists portrayed action in a balanced and restrained fashion, capturing the noblest aspects of human beings: their reason and dignity.

Other aspects of Athenian cultural life were also rooted in the life of the polis. The development of drama was tied to the religious festivals of the city. The polis sponsored the production of plays and required that wealthy citizens pay the expenses of their production. Many plays were highly controversial, but they were neither suppressed nor censored.

The Athenian dramatists were the first artists in Western society to examine such basic questions as the rights of the individual, the demands of society on the individual, and the nature of good and evil. Conflict is a central element in Athenian drama.

In his trilogy of plays, *The Oresteia* (ohr-e-STEE-uh), Aeschylus (525–456 B.C.E.) deals with the themes of betrayal, murder, and reconciliation, urging that

The Acropolis of Athens

These buildings embody the noblest spirit of Greek architecture. From the entrance the visitors walk through the Propylaea, a ceremonial gateway. Ahead opens the grand view of the Parthenon, still noble in ruins. To the left stands another temple, the Erectheum, the whole a monument to Athens itself.   (Courtesy, Sotiris Toumbis Editions)

reason and justice be applied to resolve fundamental conflicts. The final play concludes with a prayer that civil dissension never be allowed to destroy the city and that the life of the city be one of harmony and grace.

Sophocles (496–406 B.C.E.) also dealt with matters personal and political. In *Antigone* (an-TIG-uh-nee) he highlights conflicts between divine and human law and comments on the gender order in Greek society. Antigone defies Creon, her uncle and king, to follow divinely established rules and bury her brother against Creon's decree. Creon rages that she is not above the laws he has established, and that if he does not punish her she will be more man than he is. Antigone escapes her punishment by committing suicide.

Perhaps his most famous plays are *Oedipus* (ED-uh-puhs) *the King* and its sequel, *Oedipus at Colonus. Oedipus the King* is the tragic story of a man doomed by the gods to kill his father and marry his mother. Try as he might to avoid his fate, Oedipus's every action brings him closer to its fulfillment. When at last he realizes that he has carried out the decree of the gods, Oedipus blinds himself and flees into exile. In *Oedipus at Colonus* Sophocles dramatizes the last days of the broken king, whose patient suffering and piety win him an exalted position. In the end the gods honor him for his virtue. These stories are renowned for their psychological depth and wrenching emotions.

With Euripides (ca. 480–406 B.C.E.), drama entered a new, in many ways more personal, phase. To him the gods were far less important than human beings. The essence of Euripides' tragedy is the flawed character—men and women who bring disaster on themselves and their loved ones because their passions overwhelm reason. Although Euripides' plays were less popular in his lifetime than were those of Aeschylus and Sophocles, his work was to have a significant impact on Roman drama.

Writers of comedy treated the affairs of the polis and its leading politicians bawdily and often coarsely. Even so, their plays also were performed at religious festivals. Best known are the comedies of Aristophanes (ar-uh-STOFF-uh-neze) (ca. 445–386 B.C.E.), an ardent lover of his city and a merciless critic of cranks and quacks. He lampooned eminent generals, at times depicting them as morons. He commented snidely on Pericles, poked fun at Socrates, and hooted at Euripides. Through satire, he too commented on human conduct and values.

Daily Life in Periclean Athens

The Athenian house was rather simple. It consisted of a series of rooms opening onto a central courtyard that contained the well, an altar, and a washbasin. Larger houses often had a room at the front where the men of the family ate and entertained guests, and a women's quarter at the back. If the family lived in the country, the stalls of the animals faced the courtyard. Country dwellers kept oxen for plowing, pigs for slaughtering, sheep for wool, goats for cheese, and mules and donkeys for transportation. Even in the city chickens and perhaps a goat or two roamed the courtyard together with dogs and cats.

In the city a man might support himself as a craftsman—a potter, bronzesmith, sailmaker, or tanner—or he could contract with the polis to work on public buildings, such as the Parthenon. Certain crafts, including spinning and weaving, were generally done by women. Men and women without skills worked as paid laborers but competed with slaves for work. Slaves were usually foreigners whose native language was not Greek. Citizens and slaves were paid the same amount for their work.

Woman Grinding Grain
Here a woman takes the grain raised on the family farm and grinds it by hand in a mill. She needed few tools to turn the grain into flour. (National Archaeological Museum, Athens/Archaeological Receipts Fund)

Gender

The social condition of Athenian women has been the subject of much debate. One of the difficulties is the fragmentary nature of the evidence. Women appear frequently in literature and art, often in idealized roles, but seldom in historical contexts of a wider and more realistic nature (see the feature "Individuals in Society: Aspasia"). This is due in part to the fact that most Greek historians of the time recounted primarily the political, diplomatic, and military events of the day, events in which women seldom played a notable part. Yet that does not mean that women were totally invisible in the life of the polis. It indicates instead that ancient sources provide only a glimpse of how women affected the society in which they lived. Athenian men believed that men and women should be segregated and that women should not appear in public, but the reality was less limiting then the ideal.

The status of a free woman of the citizen class was strictly protected by law. Only her children, not those of foreigners or slaves, could be citizens. She was in

Greek Courtship

Here two young lovers embrace. With one arm around his girl and the other holding a wine vessel, he draws his girl nearer. With a smile she seems more interested in her music, for with her right thumb she turns the boy down. (Erich Lessing/Art Resource, NY)

charge of the household and the family's possessions, yet the law protected her primarily to protect her husband's interests. Raping a free woman was a lesser crime than seducing her, because seduction involved the winning of her affections. This law was concerned not with the husband's feelings but with ensuring that he need not doubt the legitimacy of his children.

A citizen woman's main functions were to have and raise children. Childbirth could be dangerous for both mother and infant, so pregnant women often made sacrifices or visited temples to ask help from the gods. Demeter (di-MEE-ter) and Artemis (AHR-tuh-mis) were particularly favored. In practical terms, citizen women relied on their friends, relatives, and midwives to assist in the delivery. Greek physicians did not concern themselves with obstetrical care.

Citizen women never appeared in court or in the public political assemblies that were the heart of Athenian democracy, though they did attend public festivals, ceremonies, and funerals. They took part in annual processions to honor the goddess Athena and in harvest festivals honoring the goddess Demeter, who protected the city's crops. In a few cases, women were priestesses in the cults of various goddesses. Priestesses prayed in public on behalf of the city and, like priests, were paid for their services. The most prominent priestess was at Delphi (DEL-fye), near Athens, where the god Apollo (ah-POL-oh) was understood to give messages about the future. The priestess at the oracle at Delphi interpreted these prophecies, and people came from all over Greece and beyond to hear them.

Greek Religion

Greek religion is extremely difficult for modern people to understand, largely because of the great differences between Greek and modern cultures. In the first place, it is not even easy to talk about "Greek religion," since the Greeks had no uniform faith or creed. Although the Greeks usually worshiped the same deities—Zeus, Hera (HEER-uh), Apollo, Athena, and others—the cults of these gods and goddesses varied from polis to polis. The Greeks had no sacred books such as the Bible, and Greek religion was often a matter more of ritual than of belief. Nor did cults impose an ethical code of conduct. Greeks did not have to follow any particular rule of life, practice certain virtues, or even live decent lives in order to participate. Unlike the Egyptians and Hebrews, the Greeks lacked a priesthood as the modern world understands the term. In Greece priests and priestesses existed to care for temples and sacred property and to conduct the proper rituals, but not to make religious rules or doctrines, much less to enforce them. In short, there existed in Greece no central ecclesiastical authority and no organized creed.

The most important members of the Greek pantheon were Zeus, the king of the gods, and his consort, Hera. Although they were the mightiest and most honored of the deities who lived on Mount Olympus, their divine children were closer

Individuals in Society

Aspasia

Aspasia (a-SPEY-shuh) was born in the Greek city of Miletus and came to Athens in about 445 B.C.E. She moved in a society in which the greatest glory for women was to be "least talked about by men, either for excellence or blame" (Thucydides 2.46). This ideal became the reality for most Athenian women, whose names and actions never became part of "history." It was not true, however, for Aspasia, who is easily one of the most intriguing women in ancient history. Once in Athens, Aspasia may have become a *hetaira* (hi-TAHYR-uh), which literally means "companion." The duties of a hetaira varied. She accompanied men at dinners and drinking parties, where their wives would not have been welcome, and also served as a sexual partner. The major attractions of a successful hetaira included beauty, intelligent conversation, and proper etiquette. In return she was paid for her services. No contemporary sources specifically say that Aspasia was a hetaira, but she may have been.

Contemporary sources do make clear that Aspasia enjoyed a rare opportunity to influence the men who shaped the political life of Athens. The Roman biographer Plutarch reports that she enjoyed the company of the most famous men in Athens. In one of Plato's dialogues, Socrates claims that she taught him the art of public speaking. The story is probably not true, but it points to her public reputation.

Aspasia was introduced to Pericles, who was either already divorced from his wife or divorced her soon afterward. Because Aspasia was not an Athenian citizen, she and Pericles could not marry, but they did have a son, also named Pericles. When Pericles' sons by his wife died in an epidemic, Pericles pressured the Athenian citizenship to let his son by Aspasia become a citizen. Sons of noncitizen women were normally barred from citizenship (a law Pericles himself had introduced), but the law was waived in this case.

Pericles was powerful enough to get his way, though he could not halt criticism and ridicule. Not only had he let himself get attached to a foreign woman, but he was more devoted to her than Athenians felt was appropriate for an adult man. Even Athens's greatest statesman was expected to follow the proper gender order in his personal relationships.

Idealized portrait of Aspasia. (Alinari/Art Resource, NY)

Pericles died shortly after his son became a citizen, and Aspasia disappears from the historical record. We can celebrate her achievements, but we do not know what motivated her. A funeral speech attributed to her is included in one of Plato's dialogues, but whether these were her actual words we will never know.

Questions for Analysis

1. How did Aspasia's position as a foreigner in Athens shape her opportunities?

2. In what ways does her story support and in what ways does it contradict the general picture of gender roles in Athenian society?

Sacrificial Scene
Much of Greek religion was simple and festive, as this scene demonstrates. The participants include women and boys dressed in their finest clothes and crowned with garlands. Musicians add to the festivities. Only the sheep will not enjoy the ceremony. (National Archaeological Museum, Athens/Archaeological Receipts Fund)

to ordinary people. Apollo was especially popular. He represented the epitome of youth, beauty, benevolence, and athletic skill. He was also the god of music and culture and in many ways symbolized the best of Greek culture. His sister Athena, who patronized women's crafts such as weaving, was also a warrior-goddess and had been born from the head of Zeus without a mother. Best known for her cult at Athens, to which she gave her name, she was highly revered throughout Greece, even in Sparta, which eventually became a fierce enemy of Athens. Besides the Olympian gods, each polis had its own minor deities, each with his or her own local cult.

Though Greek religion in general was individual or related to the polis, the Greeks also shared some Pan-Hellenic festivals, the chief of which were held at Olympia in honor of Zeus and at Delphi in honor of Apollo. The festivities at Olympia included the famous athletic contests that have inspired the modern Olympic games. Held every four years, they attracted visitors from all over the Greek world and lasted well into Christian times. The Pythian (PITH-ee-uhn) games at Delphi were also held every four years, but these contests included musical and literary contests. Both the Olympic and the Pythian games were unifying factors in Greek life.

The Flowering of Philosophy

The myths and epics of the Mesopotamians are ample testimony that speculation about the origin of the universe and of humans did not begin with the Greeks. The signal achievement of the Greeks was the willingness of some to treat these questions in rational rather than mythological terms. Although Greek philosophy did not fully flower until the classical period, Ionian thinkers had already begun in the Archaic period to ask what the universe was made of. These men are called the

Pre-Socratics, for their work preceded the philosophical revolution begun by the Athenian, Socrates. Though they were keen observers, the Pre-Socratics rarely undertook deliberate experimentation. Instead, they took individual facts and wove them into general theories. Despite appearances, they believed the universe was actually simple and subject to natural laws. Drawing on their observations, they speculated about the basic building blocks of the universe.

The first of the Pre-Socratics, Thales (THEY-leez) (ca. 600 B.C.E.), learned mathematics and astronomy from the Babylonians and geometry from the Egyptians. Yet there was an immense and fundamental difference between Near Eastern thought and the philosophy of Thales. The Near Eastern peoples considered such events as eclipses to be evil omens. Thales viewed them as natural phenomena that could be explained in natural terms. In short, he asked why things happened. He believed the basic element of the universe to be water. Although he was wrong, the way in which he had asked the question was momentous: it was the beginning of the scientific method.

Thales' follower Anaximander (un-nak-suh-MAN-der) (d. ca. 547 B.C.E.) continued his work. He theorized that the basic element of the universe is the "boundless" or "endless"—something infinite and indestructible. In his view the earth floats in a void, held in balance by its distance from everything else in the universe. Heraclitus (her-uh-KLAHY-tuhs) (ca. 500 B.C.E.), however, declared the primal element to be fire. He also declared that the universe was eternal yet changed constantly. An outgrowth of this line of speculation was the theory of Democritus (di-MOK-reh-tuhs) (b. ca. 460 B.C.E.) that the universe was made up of invisible, indestructible atoms. The culmination of Pre-Socratic thought was the theory that four simple substances made up the universe: fire, air, earth, and water.

A Greek God

Few pieces of Greek art better illustrate the conception of the gods as greatly superior forms of human beings than this magnificent statue, over six feet ten inches in height. Here the god, who may be either Poseidon or Zeus, is portrayed as powerful and perfect but human in form. (National Archaeological Museum, Athens/Archaeological Receipts Fund)

Hippocrates (hi-POK-ruh-teez) (second quarter of the fifth century B.C.E.), the father of medicine, contributed ideas about the workings of the body based on empirical knowledge rather than magic. The human body, he declared, contained four humors, or fluids: blood, phlegm, black bile, and yellow bile. In a healthy body the four humors were in perfect balance; too much or too little of any particular humor caused illness.

The teachings of the revolutionary thinker Socrates (ca. 470–399 B.C.E.) are known to us largely through the writings of his student Plato (PLAY-toh), whose dialogues show Socrates engaged in probing discourse with others. Socrates' approach was to start with a philosophical problem and to narrow the matter to its essentials. He did so by continuous questioning rather than lecturing, a process known as the Socratic dialogue. Socrates thought that through the pursuit of wisdom, human beings could approach the supreme good and thus find true happiness. Yet in 399 B.C.E. Socrates was brought to trial, convicted, and executed on charges of corrupting the youth of the city and introducing new gods.

Section Review

- The Greek victories over the Persians at Marathon (490 B.C.E.) and against Xerxes (480 B.C.E.) meant the survival and spread of Greek political and intellectual ideas.

- After driving out the Persians, Athens became increasingly imperialistic, treating their allies harshly, leading to war between Sparta and Athens.

- The Peloponnesian war brought widespread destruction to both Sparta and Athens and was only won when Sparta, with the aid of the Persian navy, finally defeated Athens.

- The Athenian Acropolis exhibited Greek art portraying the noble side of humans and sponsored the production of plays dealing with a variety of themes from drama to comedy and satire.

- Greek women ideally lived a segregated, private life, although some women had important public roles as priestesses, for example at the Delphic oracle.

- Although Greek religion lacked scriptures, ethics, or a priesthood, Greeks worshipped gods and celebrated festivals such as the Olympic games, which unified Greeks culturally.

- Greek philosophers included the Pre-Socratics Thales (water), Anaximander (void), Heraclitus (change), and Democritus (atoms); Hippocrates and his four humors for medicine; and Socrates, Plato, and Aristotle.

Plato (427–347 B.C.E.) carried on his master's search for truth, founding a philosophical school, the Academy. Plato believed that the ideal polis could exist only when its citizens were well educated. He developed the theory that there are two worlds: the impermanent, changing world of appearance that we know through our senses, and the eternal, unchanging realm of "forms" that constitute the essence of true reality. Only the mind can perceive eternal forms. The intellectual journey consists of moving from the realm of appearances to the realm of forms.

Aristotle (ar-ih-STAH-tahl) (384–322 B.C.E.) disagreed with Plato's idea of a separate, supernatural reality and believed that genuine knowledge is derived through close examination of the natural world. He believed that the universe operated according to principles and laws that could be discovered through scientific reasoning. Aristotle argued that everything and everyone has an inner potential or purpose that they are meant to fulfill.

The philosophies of Plato and Aristotle both viewed women as inferior beings. Plato associated women with the body and emotions and men with the superior faculties of mind and reason. Aristotle thought that women's primary purpose was to bear children. Athenian philosophers thus reflected the patriarchy of their society, while also pushing beyond the magical thinking of previous generations. Both the breadth of their vision and its limitations are their legacies to Western civilization.

The Final Act (404–338 B.C.E.)

How did the Greek city-states meet political and military challenges, and how did Macedonia become dominant?

The turbulent period from 404 to 338 B.C.E. is sometimes mistakenly seen as a period of failure and decline. It was instead a vibrant era in which Plato and Aristotle thought and wrote, one in which literature, oratory, and historical writing flourished. The architects of the fourth century B.C.E. designed and built some of the finest buildings of the classical period, and engineering made great strides. If the fourth century was a period of decline, this was so only in politics. The Peloponnesian War and its aftermath proved that the polis had reached the limits of its success as an effective political institution. The attempts of various city-states to dominate the others led only to incessant warfare. The polis system was committing suicide.

The Greeks of the fourth century B.C.E. experimented seriously with two political concepts in the hope of preventing war. First was the **Common Peace**, the idea that the states of Greece, whether large or small, should live together in peace and freedom, each enjoying its own laws and customs. In 386 B.C.E. this concept was a vital part of a peace treaty with the Persian Empire, in which the Greeks and Persians pledged themselves to live in harmony.

Federalism, the second concept to become prominent, already had a long history in some parts of Greece (see page 45). Strictly speaking, the new impetus toward federalism was intended more to gain security through numbers than to

Common Peace One of two political concepts created by Greeks in the fourth century B.C.E. in an attempt to prevent war. It was the idea that the states of Greece should live together in peace and freedom, each enjoying its own laws and customs.

prevent war. In the fourth century B.C.E. at least ten other federations of states either came into being or were revitalized. Federalism never led to a United States of Greece, but the concept held great importance not only for fourth-century Greeks but also for the Hellenistic period and beyond. In 1787, when the Founding Fathers met in Philadelphia to frame the Constitution of the United States, they studied Greek federalism very seriously in the hope that the Greek past could help guide the American future.

The Struggle for Hegemony

The chief states, Sparta, Athens, and Thebes, each tried to create a **hegemony** (heh-JEM-uh-nee), that is, a political ascendancy over other states, even though they sometimes paid lip service to the ideals of the Common Peace. In every instance, the ambition, jealousy, pride, and fear of the major powers doomed the effort to achieve genuine peace.

hegemony A political ascendancy over other states.

When the Spartans defeated Athens in 404 B.C.E., they used their victory to build an empire instead of ensuring the freedom of all Greeks. Their decision brought the Spartans into conflict with their own allies and with Persia, which now demanded the return of Ionia to its control (see page 39). From 400 to 386 B.C.E. the Spartans fought the Persians for Ionia, a conflict that eventually engulfed Greece itself. After years of stalemate the Spartans made peace with Persia and their Greek enemies. The result was the first formal Common Peace, the King's Peace of 386 B.C.E., which cost Sparta its empire but not its position of ascendancy in Greece.

Not content with Sparta's hegemony of Greece, Agesilaos (ah-gis-il-A-us) betrayed the very concept of the Common Peace to punish cities that had opposed Sparta during the war. He treacherously ordered Thebes to be seized and even condoned an unwarranted and unsuccessful attack on Athens. Agesilaos had gone too far. Even though it appeared that his naked use of force had made Sparta supreme in Greece, his imperialism was soon to lead to Sparta's downfall at the hands of the Thebans, the very people whom he sought to tyrannize.

After routing the once-invincible Spartans from Thebes, the Theban leader Epaminondas (ee-pam-uh-NON-duhs) eliminated Sparta as a major power through a series of invasions. He concluded alliances with many Peloponnesian states but made no effort to dominate them, instead fostering federalism in Greece. He also threw his support behind the Common Peace. Although he made Thebes the leader of Greece from 371 to 362 B.C.E., other city-states and leagues were bound to Thebes only by voluntary alliances. By his insistence on the liberty of the Greeks, Epaminondas, more than any other person in Greek history, successfully blended the three concepts of hegemony, federalism, and the Common Peace. His death at the Battle of Mantinea in 362 B.C.E. put an end to his efforts, but not to these three political ideals.

Statue of Eirene

The Athenians erected this statue of Eirene (Peace) holding Ploutos (Wealth) in her left arm. Athens had seen only war for some fifty-six years, and the statue celebrated the Common Peace of 375 B.C.E. The bitter irony of this poignant scene is that the treaty lasted scarcely a year. (Glyptothek, Munich/Studio Koppermann)

Philip and the Macedonian Ascendancy

While the Greek states exhausted one another in endless conflicts, a new and unlikely power rose in Macedonia to the north. The land of Macedonia, extensive and generally fertile, nurtured a numerous and hardy population. Yet Macedonia was often internally divided and distracted by foreign opportunists. Nevertheless, under a strong king Macedonia was a power to be reckoned with, and in 359 B.C.E. such a king ascended the throne. Philip II fully understood the strengths and needs of the Macedonians, whose devotion he won virtually on the day that he became king.

The young Philip, already a master of diplomacy and warfare after years spent in Thebes, quickly saw Athens as the principal threat to Macedonia. Once he had secured the borders of Macedonia against barbarian invaders, he launched a series of military operations in the northwestern Aegean. Not only did he win rich territory, but he also slowly pushed the Athenians out of the region. Macedonian warriors gained a reputation for fierceness, as one comic playwright from Athens suggests:

> Do you know that your battle will be with men
> Who dine on sharpened swords,
> And gulp burning firebrands for wine?
> Then immediately after dinner the slave
> Brings us dessert—Cretan arrows
> Or pieces of broken spears.
> We have shields and breastplates for
> Cushions and at our feet slings and arrows,
> And we are crowned with catapults.[3]

These dire predictions and the progress of Philip's military operations at last had their effect. In 338 B.C.E. the armies of Thebes and Athens met Philip's veterans at the Boeotian city of Chaeronea. There on one summer's day Philip's army won a hard-fought victory that gave him command of Greece and put an end to classical Greek freedom. Because the Greeks could not coexist peacefully, they fell to an invader. Yet Philip was wise enough to retain much of what the fourth-century Greeks had achieved. Not opposed to the concepts of peace and federalism, he sponsored a new Common Peace in which all of Greece, except Sparta, was united in one political body under his leadership. Philip thus used the concepts of hegemony, the Common Peace, and federalism as tools of Macedonian domination. The ironic result was the end of the age of classical Greece.

Section Review

- Greeks of the fourth century B.C.E. experimented with the Common Peace and federalism to gain peace and security.

- Sparta, Athens, and Thebes each tried to achieve hegemony (political control) over all of Greece.

- Spartan King Agesilaos used Spartan power to terrorize Athens and Thebes, leading to Sparta's downfall by the Thebans.

- The Theban leader Epaminondas (371–362 B.C.E.) successfully blended hegemony, federalism, and the Common Peace.

- Philip II of Macedon militarily threatened Athens from the north beginning in 359 B.C.E.

Chapter Review

When the Greeks arrived in Hellas, how did they adapt themselves to their new landscape? (page 39)

The Greeks entered a land of mountains and small plains, which led them to establish small communities. Sometimes these small communities were joined together in kingdoms, most prominently the Minoan kingdom on the island of Crete and the Mycenaean kingdom on the mainland. Minoans and Mycenaeans used written records, and the fall of these kingdoms led writing to disappear for centuries, a period known as the Greek Dark Age (1100–800 B.C.E.).

Key Terms

Hellenic period (p. 39)

Hellenistic period (p. 39)

Aegean basin (p. 39)

Minoan (p. 39)

After the Greeks had established the polis, in which they lived their political and social lives, how did they shape it into its several historical forms? (page 43)

Even though kingdoms collapsed, Greek culture continued to spread, and more independent communities were formed. Such a community, called a polis, developed social and political institutions. Some were democracies, in which government was shared among all citizens, which meant adult free men. Other Greeks established smaller governing bodies of citizens, called oligarchs, which directed the political affairs of all.

What major developments mark the Archaic Greek period in terms of spread of culture and the growth of cities? (page 46)

During the Archaic Age (800–500 B.C.E.) Greeks colonized much of the Mediterranean, establishing cities in Asia Minor, southern Italy, Sicily, and southern France. This brought them into contact with many other peoples, and also spread Greek culture widely. During this period Sparta and Athens became the most important poleis.

How did the Greeks develop their literature, philosophy, religion, and art, and how did war affect this intellectual and social process? (page 50)

Sparta and Athens joined together to fight the Persian Empire, but later turned against one another in the Peloponnesian War (431–404 B.C.E.). During this time of warfare, Athenian leaders turned their city into an architectural showplace, supporting the creation of buildings and statues that are still prized. Playwrights presented tragedies and comedies that dealt with basic issues of life. Life for the men in Athens who were citizens revolved around public political assemblies, while for women it revolved around the household. Athenian thinkers regarded women as inferior and did not think they should have a public role. Both women and men took part in ceremonies honoring gods and goddesses, though some men, most prominently the philosophers Plato and Aristotle, developed ideas about the universe and the place of humans in it that did not involve the gods.

How did the Greek city-states meet political and military challenges, and how did Macedonia become dominant? (page 60)

The Greeks destroyed a good deal of their flourishing world in a series of wars. Despite their political advances, they never really learned how to routinely live peacefully with one another. Their disunity allowed for the rise of Macedonia under the leadership of King Philip II, a brilliant military leader.

Notes

John Buckler is the translator of all uncited quotations from a foreign language in Chapters 1–6.

1. J. M. Edmonds, *Greek Elegy and Iambus* (Cambridge, Mass.: Harvard University Press, 1931), I.70, frag. 10.
2. Thucydides, *History of the Peloponnesian War* 7.87.6.
3. J. M. Edmonds, *The Fragments of Attic Comedy* (Leiden: E. J. Brill, 1971), 2.366–2.369, Mnesimachos frag. 7.

To assess your mastery of this chapter, go to **bedfordstmartins.com/mckaywestbrief**

Listening to the Past

The Great Plague at Athens, 430 B.C.E.

In 430 B.C.E. many of the people of Attica sought refuge in Athens to escape the Spartan invasion. The overcrowding of people, the lack of proper sanitation, and the scarcity of clean water made the population vulnerable to virulent disease, and indeed a severe plague swept the city. The great historian Thucydides lived in Athens at the time and contracted the disease himself. He was one of the fortunate people who survived the ordeal. For most people, however, the disease proved fatal. Thucydides left a vivid description of the nature of the plague and of people's reaction to it.

The most terrible thing of all was the despair into which people fell when they realized that they had caught the plague. Terrible, too, was the sight of people dying like sheep through having caught the disease as a result of nursing others. This indeed caused more deaths than anything else. For when people were afraid to visit the sick, then they died with no one to look after them. Indeed, there were many houses in which all the inhabitants perished through lack of attention. When, on the other hand, they did visit the sick, they lost their own lives, and this was particularly true of those who made it a point of honor to act properly. Such people felt ashamed to think of their own safety and went into their friends' houses at times when even the members of the household were so overwhelmed by the weight of their calamities that they had actually given up the usual practice of making laments for the dead. . . .

A factor that made matters much worse than they were already was the removal of people from the country into the city, and this particularly affected the newcomers. There were no houses for them, and, living as they did during the hot season in badly ventilated huts, they died like flies. The bodies of the dying were heaped one on top of the other, and half-dead creatures could be seen staggering about in the streets or flocking around the fountains in their desire for water.

The catastrophe was so overwhelming that people, not knowing what would happen next to them, became indifferent to every rule of religion and law. Athens owed to the plague the beginnings of a state of unprecedented lawlessness. People now began openly to venture on acts of self-indulgence which before then they used to keep in the dark. Thus they resolved to spend their money quickly and to spend it on pleasure, since money and life alike seemed equally ephemeral. As for what is called honor, no one showed himself willing to abide by its laws, so doubtful was it whether one would survive to enjoy the name for it. It was generally agreed that what was both honorable and valuable was the pleasure of the moment and everything that might conceivably contribute to that pleasure. No fear of god or law of man had a restraining influence. As for the gods, it seemed to be the same thing whether one worshiped them or not, when one saw the good and the bad dying indiscriminately. As for offenses against human law, no one expected to be punished. Instead, everyone felt that already a far heavier sentence had been passed on him and was hanging over him, and that before the time for its execution arrived, it was only natural to get some pleasure out of life.

This, then, was the calamity that fell upon Athens, and the times were hard indeed, with people dying inside the city and the land outside being laid waste.

Questions for Analysis

1. What does this account of the plague say about human nature when put in an extreme crisis?
2. Does popular religion offer any solace during such a catastrophe?
3. How did public laws and customs cope with such a disaster?

Source: From *The History of the Peloponnesian War* by Thucydides, translated by Rex Warner, with an introduction and notes by M. I. Finley (Penguin Classics 1954; Revised edition 1972). Translation copyright © Rex Warner, 1954. Introduction and Appendices copyright © M. I. Finley, 1972. Reproduced by permission of Penguin Books Ltd. and Curtis Brown Group Ltd., London on behalf of the Estate of Rex Warner.

Coin depicting the god Asclepius, represented by a snake, putting an end to urban plague. (Bibliothèque nationale de France)

CHAPTER 4

The Hellenistic World

336–146 B.C.E.

Tetrapylon of Aphrodisias. This monumental gate celebrates the beautiful and rich city of Aphrodisias in modern Turkey. (John Buckler)

Chapter Preview

Alexander and the Great Crusade
Why did Alexander launch his massive attack on the Persian Empire? How extensive were his conquests?

Alexander's Legacy
What happened to Alexander's empire after his death? What was his political and cultural legacy?

The Spread of Hellenism
What effect did Greek migration have on Greek and native peoples?

The Economic Scope of the Hellenistic World
What effects did East-West trade have on ordinary peoples during the Hellenistic period?

Hellenistic Intellectual Advances
What is the intellectual legacy of the Hellenistic period?

INDIVIDUALS IN SOCIETY: Archimedes and the Practical Application of Science

LISTENING TO THE PAST: Alexander and the Brotherhood of Man

Two years after his conquest of Greece, Philip of Macedon fell victim to an assassin's dagger. Philip's twenty-year-old son, historically known as Alexander the Great (r. 336–323 B.C.E.), assumed the Macedonian throne. This young man, one of the most remarkable personalities of Western civilization, was to have a profound impact on history. By overthrowing the Persian Empire and by spreading *Hellenism*—Greek culture, language, thought, and way of life—as far as India, Alexander was instrumental in creating a new era, traditionally called **Hellenistic** to distinguish it from the Hellenic. As a result of Alexander's exploits, the individualistic and energetic culture of the Greeks came into intimate contact with the venerable older cultures of the Near East.

Hellenistic The new culture that arose when Alexander overthrew the Persian Empire and began spreading Hellenism, Greek culture, language, thought, and way of life as far as India. It is called Hellenistic to distinguish it from the Hellenic period.

Alexander and the Great Crusade

Why did Alexander launch his massive attack on the Persian Empire? How extensive were his conquests?

In 336 B.C.E. Alexander inherited not only Philip's crown but also his policies. After his victory at Chaeronea (ker-uh-NEE-uh), Philip had organized the states of Greece into a huge league under his leadership and announced to the Greeks his plan to lead them and his Macedonians against the Persian Empire. Fully intending to carry out Philip's designs, Alexander proclaimed to the Greek world that the invasion of Persia was to be a great crusade, a mighty act of revenge for the Persian invasion of Greece in 480 B.C.E. It would also be the means by which Alexander would create an empire of his own in the East.

Despite his youth, Alexander was well prepared to lead the attack. Philip had groomed his son to become king and had given him the best education possible.

Alexander at the Battle of Issus
At left, Alexander the Great, bareheaded and wearing a breastplate, charges King Darius of Persia, who is standing in a chariot. The moment marks the turning point of the battle, as Darius turns to flee from the attack. (National Museum, Naples/Alinari/Art Resource, NY)

In 334 B.C.E. Alexander led an army of Macedonians and Greeks into Asia Minor. With him went a staff of philosophers and poets, scientists whose job it was to map the country and study strange animals and plants, and the historian Callisthenes (kuh-LIS-thuh-neez), who was to write an account of the campaign. Alexander intended not only a military campaign but also an expedition of discovery.

In the next three years Alexander won three major battles at the Granicus (gran-UH-kuhs) River, Issus (IS-uhs), and Gaugamela (GAW-guh-mee-luh). As Map 4.1 shows, these battle sites stand almost as road signs marking his march to the East. When Alexander reached Egypt, he quickly seized the land, honored the priestly class, and was proclaimed pharaoh, the legitimate ruler of the country. He next marched to the oasis of Siwah, west of the Nile Valley, to consult the famous oracle of Zeus-Amon. No one will ever know what the priest told him, but henceforth Alexander considered himself the son of Zeus. Next he marched into western Asia, where at Gaugamela he defeated the Persian army. After this victory the principal Persian capital of Persepolis easily fell to him. There he performed a symbolic act of retribution by

340–262 B.C.E.	Rise of Epicurean and Stoic philosophies
336–24 B.C.E.	Alexander's "Great Crusade"
330–200 B.C.E.	Establishment of new Hellenistic cities
326–146 B.C.E.	Spread of Hellenistic commerce from the western Mediterranean to India
323–301 B.C.E.	Wars of Alexander's successors; establishment of the Hellenistic monarchies
310–212 B.C.E.	Scientific developments in mathematics, astronomy, and physics
305–146 B.C.E.	Growth of mystery religions
301–146 B.C.E.	Flourishing of the Hellenistic monarchies

MAP 4.1 Alexander's Conquests

This map shows the course of Alexander's invasion of the Persian Empire and the speed of his progress. More important than the great success of his military campaigns was his founding of Hellenistic cities in the East.

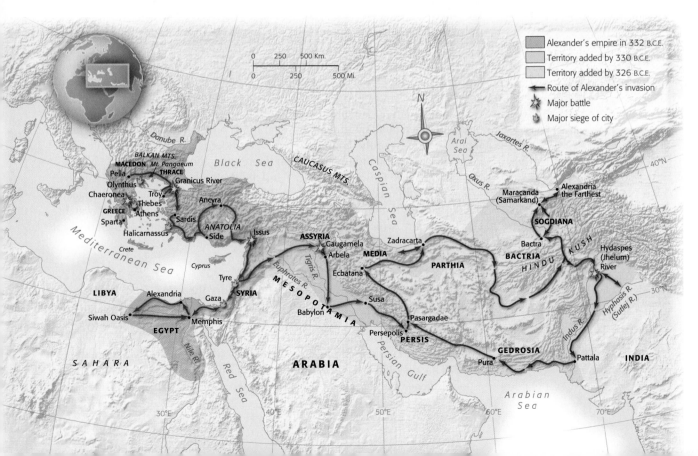

- Alexander set out to conquer Persia as an act of revenge at the beginning of his own empire.

- Alexander used his campaign as a method of study as well as war, bringing along scientists and philosophers to document the adventure.

- After conquering Egypt, Alexander honored the priests who proclaimed him pharaoh, then he consulted the oracle of Zeus-Amon, and from then on considered himself the son of Zeus.

- Alexander defeated the Persians at the battle of Gaugamela and then captured the Persian capital Persepolis, pursuing the Persian king to his death, and capturing the last capital of Ecbatana.

- Alexander next conquered Bactria and entered India, where his troops mutinied and refused to go farther; in retaliation, Alexander waged needless wars along the Arabian Sea and marched them home through the Gedrosian Desert.

- Alexander died in 323 B.C.E. in Babylon.

burning the buildings of Xerxes, the invader of Greece. In 330 B.C.E. he took Ecbatana (ek-BAT-un-uh), the last Persian capital, and pursued the Persian king to his death.

The Persian Empire had fallen, and the war of revenge was over, but Alexander had no intention of stopping. He dismissed his Greek troops but permitted many of them to serve on as mercenaries. Alexander then began his personal odyssey. With his Macedonian soldiers and Greek mercenaries, he set out to conquer the rest of Asia. He plunged deeper into the East, into lands completely unknown to the Greek world. It took his soldiers four additional years to conquer Bactria and the easternmost parts of the now-defunct Persian Empire, but still Alexander was determined to continue his march.

In 326 B.C.E. Alexander crossed the Indus River and entered India. There, too, he saw hard fighting, and finally at the Hyphasis (HIF-ah-sis) River his troops refused to go farther. Alexander was enraged by the mutiny, for he believed he was near the end of the world. Nonetheless, the army stood firm, and Alexander relented. Still eager to explore the limits of the world, Alexander turned south to the Arabian Sea. Though the tribes in the area did not oppose him, he waged a bloody, ruthless, and unnecessary war against them. After reaching the Arabian Sea and turning west, he led his army through the grim Gedrosian Desert. The army suffered fearfully, and many soldiers died along the way; nonetheless, in 324 B.C.E. Alexander reached his camp at Susa. The great crusade was over, and Alexander himself died the next year in Babylon.

Alexander's Legacy

What happened to Alexander's empire after his death? What was his political and cultural legacy?

Alexander so quickly became a legend during his lifetime that he still seems superhuman. That alone makes a reasoned interpretation of him very difficult. Some historians have seen him as a high-minded philosopher, and none can deny that he possessed genuine intellectual gifts. Others, however, have portrayed him as a bloody-minded autocrat, more interested in his own ambition than in any philosophical concept of the common good. Alexander is the perfect example of the need for the historian to use care when interpreting the known facts. (See the feature "Listening to the Past: Alexander and the Brotherhood of Man," on page 84.) What is not disputed is that Alexander was instrumental in changing the face of politics and culture in the eastern Mediterranean. His campaign swept away the Persian Empire, which had ruled for over two hundred years, and opened the East to the tide of Hellenism.

The Political Legacy

In 323 B.C.E. Alexander the Great died at the age of thirty-two. The main question at his death was whether his vast empire could be held together. Although he fathered a successor while in Bactria, his son was an infant at Alexander's death. The child was too young to assume the duties of kingship and was cruelly murdered. That meant that Alexander's empire was a prize for the taking by the strongest of his generals. Within a week of Alexander's death a round of fighting began

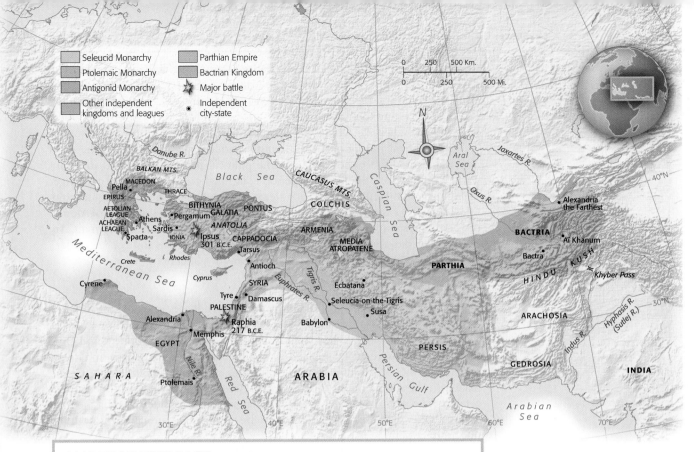

that was to continue for forty years. No single Macedonian general was able to re-place Alexander as emperor of his entire domain. In effect, the strongest divided it among themselves. By 263 B.C.E. three officers had split the empire into large monarchies (see Map 4.2). Antigonus Gonatas became king of Macedonia and established the Antigonid (an-TIG-uh-nid) dynasty, which ruled until the Roman conquest in 168 B.C.E. Ptolemy (TAWL-uh-mee) made himself king of Egypt, and his descendants, the Ptolemies, assumed the powers and position of pharaohs. Seleucus (sih-LOO-sus), founder of the Seleucid (sih-LOO-sid) dynasty, carved out a kingdom that stretched from the coast of Asia Minor to India. In 263 B.C.E. Eumenes (yoo-MEN-eez), the Greek ruler of Pergamum (PUR-guh-mum), a city in western Asia Minor, won his independence from the Seleucids and created the Pergamene monarchy. Though the Seleucid kings soon lost control of their east-ernmost provinces, Greek influence in this area did not wane. In modern Turke-stan (tur-kuh-STAN) and Afghanistan (af-GAN-uh-stan) another line of Greek kings established the kingdom of Bactria and even managed to spread their power and culture into northern India.

The political face of Greece itself changed during the Hellenistic period. The day of the polis was over; in its place rose leagues of city-states. The two most powerful and extensive were the Aetolian (ee-TOH-lee-uhn) League in western and central Greece and the Achaean (a-KEY-an) League in the Peloponnesus. Once-powerful city-states like Athens and Sparta sank to the level of third-rate powers.

The political history of the Hellenistic period was dominated by the great monarchies and the Greek leagues. The political fragmentation and incessant warfare that marked the Hellenic period continued on an even wider and larger scale during the Hellenistic period. Never did the Hellenistic world achieve political stability or lasting peace. Hellenistic kings never forgot the vision of Alexander's empire, spanning Europe and Asia, secure under the rule of one man. Try though they did, they were never able to re-create it. In this respect Alexander's legacy fell not to his generals but to the Romans of a later era.

The Cultural Legacy

As Alexander waded ever deeper into the East, distance alone presented him with a serious problem: how was he to retain contact with the Greek world behind him? Communications were vital, for he drew supplies and reinforcements from Greece and Macedonia. His solution was to plant cities and military colonies in strategic places. In these settlements Alexander left Greek mercenaries and Macedonian veterans who were no longer up to active campaigning. Besides keeping the road open to the West, these settlements served the purpose of dominating the countryside around them.

Their military significance apart, Alexander's cities and colonies became powerful instruments in the spread of Hellenism throughout the East. His successors

The Great Altar of Pergamum

A new Hellenistic city needed splendid art and architecture to prove its worth in Greek eyes. The king of Pergamum ordered the construction of this monumental altar, now in Berlin. The scenes depict the mythical victory of the Greek gods over the Giants, who symbolize non-Greeks. The altar served the propaganda purpose of celebrating the victory of Hellenism over the East. (Bildarchiv Preussischer Kulturbesitz/Art Resource, NY)

continued his policy by luring Greek colonists to their realms. For seventy-five years after Alexander's death, Greek immigrants poured into the East. At least 250 new Hellenistic colonies were established. The Mediterranean world had seen no comparable movement of peoples since the Archaic Age (see page 46), when wave after wave of Greeks had turned the Mediterranean basin into a Greek-speaking region.

The overall result of Alexander's settlements and those of his successors was the spread of Hellenism as far east as India. Throughout the Hellenistic period, Greeks and Easterners became familiar with and adapted themselves to each other's customs, religion, and way of life. Although Greek culture did not completely conquer the East, it gave the East a vehicle of expression that linked it to the West. Hellenism became a common bond among the East, peninsular Greece, and the western Mediterranean. This pre-existing cultural bond was later to prove supremely valuable to Rome—itself heavily influenced by Hellenism—in its efforts to impose a comparable political unity on the Western world.

The Spread of Hellenism

What effect did Greek migration have on Greek and native peoples?

When the Greeks and Macedonians entered Asia Minor, Egypt, and the more remote East, they encountered civilizations older than their own. In some ways the Eastern cultures were more advanced than the Greek, in others less so. Thus this third great tide of Greek migration differed from preceding waves, which had spread over land that was uninhabited or inhabited by less-developed peoples.

What did the Hellenistic monarchies offer Greek immigrants politically and materially? More broadly, how did Hellenism and the cultures of the East affect one another? What did the meeting of East and West entail for the history of the world?

Cities and Kingdoms

One of the major developments of these new kingdoms was the resurgence of monarchy, which had many repercussions. For most Greeks, monarchs were something out of the heroic past, something found in Homer's *Iliad* but not in daily life. Furthermore, most Hellenistic kingdoms embraced numerous different peoples who had little in common. Hellenistic kings thus needed a new political concept to unite them. One solution was the creation of a ruler cult that linked the king's authority with that of the gods. Thus, royal power had divine approval and was meant to create a political and religious bond between the kings and their subjects. These deified kings were not considered gods as mighty as Zeus or Apollo, and the new ruler cults probably made little religious impact on those ruled. Nonetheless, the ruler cult was an easily understandable symbol of unity within the kingdom.

Hellenistic kingship was hereditary, which gave women who were members of royal families more power than any women in democracies, in which citizenship was limited to men. Wives of kings and queen mothers had influence over their husbands and sons, and a few women ruled in their own right when there was no male heir.

Hellenistic monarchs continued the policy of establishing cities throughout their kingdoms in order to entice Greeks to immigrate. They gave their cities all

The Main Street of Pergamum
No matter where in old Greece they had come from, all Greeks would immediately feel at home walking along this main street in Pergamum. They would all see familiar sights. To the left is the top of the theater where they could watch the plays of the great dramatists, climb farther to the temple, and admire the fortifications on the right. (Faith Cimok, Turkey)

sovereign An independent, autonomous state run by its citizens, free of any outside power or restraint.

the external trappings of a polis. Each had an assembly of citizens, a council to prepare legislation, and a board of magistrates to conduct the city's political business. Yet, however similar to the Greek polis they appeared, these cities could not engage in diplomatic dealings, make treaties, pursue their own foreign policy, or wage their own wars. The Greek polis was by definition **sovereign** (SOV-er-in)— an independent, autonomous state run by its citizens, free of any outside power or restraint. Hellenistic kings, however, refused to grant sovereignty to their cities. In effect, these kings willingly built cities but refused to build a polis.

A new Hellenistic city differed from a Greek polis in other ways as well. The Greek polis had one body of law and one set of customs. In the Hellenistic city Greeks represented an elite citizen class. Natives and non-Greek foreigners who lived in Hellenistic cities usually possessed lesser rights than Greeks and often had their own laws. In some instances this disparity spurred natives to assimilate Greek culture in order to rise politically and socially. Yet the Hellenistic city was not homogeneous and could not spark the intensity of feeling that marked the polis.

Though Hellenistic kings never built a true polis, that does not mean that their urban policy failed. Rather, the Hellenistic city was to remain the basic social and political unit throughout the Hellenistic world until the sixth century C.E. Cities were the chief agents of Hellenization, and their influence spread far beyond their walls. These cities formed a broader cultural network in which Greek language, customs, and values flourished. Roman rule in the Hellenistic world would later be based on this urban culture, which facilitated the rise and spread of Christianity. In broad terms, Hellenistic cities were remarkably successful.

Men and Women in Hellenistic Monarchies

If the Hellenistic kings failed to satisfy the Greeks' political yearnings, they nonetheless succeeded in giving them unequaled economic and social opportunities. The ruling dynasties of the Hellenistic world were Macedonian, and Greeks filled all important political, military, and diplomatic positions. They constituted an upper class that sustained Hellenism in the East. Besides building Greek cities, Hellenistic kings offered Greeks land and money as lures to further immigration.

The opening of the East offered ambitious Greeks opportunities for well-paying jobs and economic success. Some talented Greek men entered a professional corps of Greek administrators. Greeks and Macedonians also found ready employment in the armies and navies of the Hellenistic monarchies. Greeks were able to dominate other professions as well. The kingdoms and cities recruited Greek writers and artists to create Greek works on Asian soil. Architects, engineers, and skilled craftsmen found their services in great demand because of the building policies of the Hellenistic monarchs.

Increased physical and social mobility benefited some women as well as men. More women learned to read than before, and they engaged in occupations in which literacy was beneficial, including care of the sick. During the Hellenistic period some women took part in commercial transactions. They still lived under legal handicaps; in Egypt, for example, a Greek woman needed a male guardian to buy, sell, or lease land, to borrow money, and to represent her in other transactions. Yet often such a guardian was present only to fulfill the letter of the law. The woman was the real agent and handled the business being transacted.

As long as Greeks continued to replenish their professional ranks, the kingdoms remained strong. In the process they drew an immense amount of talent from the Greek peninsula, draining the vitality of the Greek homeland. However, the Hellenistic monarchies could not keep recruiting Greeks forever, in spite of their wealth and willingness to spend lavishly. In time the huge surge of immigration slowed greatly. Even then the Hellenistic monarchs were reluctant to recruit Easterners to fill posts normally held by Greeks. The result was at first the stagnation of the Hellenistic world and finally, after 202 B.C.E., its collapse in the face of the young and vigorous Roman republic.

Marital Advice

This small terra-cotta sculpture is generally seen as a mother advising her daughter, a new bride. Such intimate scenes of ordinary people were popular in the Hellenistic world, in contrast to the idealized statues of gods and goddesses of the classical period.
(British Museum/Michael Holford)

Greeks and Easterners

Because they understood themselves to be "the West," Greeks generally referred to Egypt and what we now call the Near East collectively as "the East." Many historians have continued that usage, seeing the Hellenistic period as a time when Greek and "Eastern" cultures blended to some degree. Eastern civilizations were older than Greek, and the Greeks were a minority outside of Greece. Hellenistic monarchies were remarkably successful in at least partially Hellenizing Easterners and spreading a uniform culture throughout the East, a culture to which Rome eventually fell heir. The prevailing institutions, laws, and language of the East became Greek. Indeed, the Near East had seen nothing comparable since the days when Mesopotamian culture had spread throughout the area.

Yet the spread of Greek culture was wider than it was deep. At best it was a veneer, thicker in some places than in others. Hellenistic kingdoms were never entirely unified in language, customs, and thought. Greek culture took firmest hold along the shores of the Mediterranean, but farther east, in Persia and Bactria, it was less strong. The principal reason for this curious phenomenon is that Greek culture generally did not extend far beyond the reaches of the cities. Many urban residents adopted the aspects of Hellenism that they found useful, but others in the countryside generally did not embrace it wholly.

Cultural Blending
Ptolemy V, a Macedonian by birth and the Hellenistic king of Egypt, dedicated this stone to the Egyptian sacred bull of the Egyptian god Ptah. Nothing here is Greek or Macedonian, a sign that the conquered had, in some religious and ceremonial ways, won over their conquerors. (Egyptian Museum, Cairo)

For non-Greeks the prime advantage of Greek culture was its very pervasiveness. The Greek language became the common speech of Egypt and the Near East. It was also the speech of commerce: anyone who wanted to compete in business had to learn it. As early as the third century B.C.E. some Greek cities were giving citizenship to Hellenized natives.

The vast majority of Hellenized Easterners, however, took only the externals of Greek culture while retaining the essentials of their own ways of life. Though Greeks and Easterners adapted to each other's ways, there was never a true fusion of cultures. Nonetheless, each found useful things in the civilization of the other, and the two fertilized each other. This fertilization, this mingling of Greek and Eastern elements, is what makes Hellenistic culture unique and distinctive.

Hellenism and the Jews

A prime illustration of cultural mingling is the impact of Greek culture on the Jews. At first, Jews in Hellenistic cities were treated as resident aliens. As they grew more numerous, they received permission to form a political corporation, which gave them a great deal of autonomy. They obeyed the king's commands, but there was virtually no royal interference with the Jewish religion. Indeed, the Greeks were typically reluctant to tamper with anyone's religion. Antiochus III (an-TIE-uh-kuhs) (ca. 242–187 B.C.E.), for instance, recognized that most Jews had become loyal subjects, and he went so far as to deny any uninvited foreigner permission to enter the temple at Jerusalem. Only the Seleucid king Antiochus Epiphanes (175–ca. 164 B.C.E.) tried to suppress the Jewish religion in Judaea. He did so not because he hated the Jews (who were a small part of his kingdom), but because he was trying to unify his realm culturally to meet the threat of Rome. To the Jews he extended the same policy that he applied to all subjects. Apart from this instance, Hellenistic Jews suffered no official religious persecution. Some Jews were given the right to become full citizens of Hellenistic cities, but few exercised that right. Citizenship would have allowed them to vote in the assembly and serve as magistrates, but it would also have obliged them to worship the gods of the city—a practice few Jews chose to follow.

Jews living in Hellenistic cities often embraced a good deal of Hellenism. So many Jews learned Greek, especially in Alexandria, that the Old Testament was translated into Greek, and services in the synagogue came to be conducted in Greek. Jews often took Greek names, used Greek political forms, adopted Greek practice by forming their own trade associations, put inscriptions on graves as the Greeks did, and much else. Yet no matter how much of Greek culture or its externals Jews borrowed, they normally remained attached to their religion.

Section Review

- To create unity, Hellenistic kings established remarkably successful cities with the governmental structure of a Greek polis, although they refused to grant them sovereignty and Greeks had more rights than natives and non-Greek foreigners.

- Hellenistic cities formed a broad cultural network upon which the Romans later based their rule.

- The Hellenistic monarchs offered economic and social opportunities to Greeks and benefited women through increased literacy and economic opportunities.

- Greek became the language of commerce in the East, and although a true blending of cultures did not happen, the intermingling of Greek and Eastern cultures makes Hellenistic culture unique.

- Jews in Hellenistic cities generally had religious freedom and many learned Greek but most refused citizenship so they could practice their own religion and not be required to worship the gods of the city.

The Economic Scope of the Hellenistic World

What effects did East-West trade have on ordinary peoples during the Hellenistic period?

Alexander's conquest of the Persian Empire not only changed the political face of the ancient world but also brought the East fully into the sphere of Greek economics. Yet the Hellenistic period did not see a revolution in the way people lived and worked. The material demands of Hellenistic society remained as simple as those of Athenian society in the fifth century B.C.E. Clothes and furniture were essentially unchanged, as were household goods, tools, and jewelry. The real achievement of Alexander and his successors was linking East and West in a broad commercial network. The spread of Greeks throughout the Near East and Egypt created new markets and stimulated trade. The economic unity of the Hellenistic world, like its cultural bonds, would later prove valuable to the Romans.

Alexander's conquest of the Persian Empire had immediate effects on trade. In the Persian capitals Alexander had found vast sums of gold, silver, and other treasure. This wealth financed the building of roads and the development of harbors as well as the creation of new cities. Whole new markets opened to Greek merchants, who eagerly took advantage of the new opportunities. In bazaars, ports, and trading centers Greeks learned of Eastern customs and traditions while spreading knowledge of their own culture.

The Seleucid and Ptolemaic dynasties traded as far afield as India, Arabia, and sub-Saharan Africa. Overland trade with India and Arabia was conducted by caravan and was largely in the hands of Easterners. Once the goods reached the Hellenistic monarchies, Greek merchants took a hand in the trade.

Essential to the caravan trade from the Mediterranean to Afghanistan and India was the southern route through Arabia. The desert of Arabia may seem at first unlikely and inhospitable terrain for a line of commerce, but to the east of it lies the plateau of Iran, from which trade routes stretched to the south and still farther east to China. Commerce from the East arrived at Egypt and the excellent harbors of Palestine, Phoenicia, and Syria. From these ports goods flowed to Greece, Italy, and Spain. The backbone of this caravan trade was the camel, a splendid beast of burden that could endure the harsh heat and aridity of the caravan routes.

Over the caravan routes traveled luxury goods that were light, rare, and expensive. In time these luxury items became more of a necessity than a luxury. In part this development was the result of an increased volume of trade. In the prosperity of the period more people could afford to buy gold, silver,

Harbor and Warehouse at Delos
During the Hellenistic period Delos became a thriving center of trade. Shown here is the row of warehouses at water's edge. From Delos, cargoes were shipped to virtually every part of the Mediterranean. (SuperStock)

Great Silk Road The name of the major route for the silk trade.

ivory, precious stones, spices, and a host of other easily transportable goods. Perhaps the most prominent goods in terms of volume were tea and silk. Indeed, the trade in silk gave the major route its name, the **Great Silk Road.** In return the Greeks and Macedonians sent east manufactured goods, especially metal weapons, cloth, wine, and olive oil. Although these caravan routes can trace their origins to earlier times, they became far more prominent in the Hellenistic period. Business customs developed and became standardized, so that merchants from different nationalities communicated in a way understandable to all of them.

More economically important than this exotic trade were commercial dealings in essential commodities like raw materials, grain, and industrial products. The Hellenistic monarchies usually raised enough grain for their own needs as well as a surplus for export. For the cities of Greece and the Aegean this trade in grain was essential, because many of them could not grow enough. Fortunately for them, abundant wheat supplies were available nearby in Egypt and in the Crimea (cry-MEE-ah) in southern Russia.

The Greek cities paid for their grain by exporting olive oil and wine. Another significant commodity was fish, which for export was either salted, pickled, or dried. This trade was doubly important because fish provided poor people with an essential element of their diet. Of raw materials, wood was high in demand.

Most trade in bulk commodities was seaborne, and the Hellenistic merchant ship was the workhorse of the day. The merchant ship had a broad beam and relied on sails for propulsion. It was far more seaworthy than the Hellenistic warship, which was long, narrow, and built for speed. A small crew of experienced sailors could handle the merchant vessel easily. Maritime trade provided opportunities for workers in other industries and trades: sailors, shipbuilders, dockworkers, accountants, teamsters, and pirates. Piracy was always a factor in the Hellenistic world and remained so until Rome extended its power throughout the East.

Throughout the Mediterranean world slaves were almost always in demand as well. Only the Ptolemies discouraged both the trade and slavery itself, and they did so only for economic reasons. Their system had no room for slaves, who would only have competed with free labor. Otherwise slave labor was to be found in the cities and temples of the Hellenistic world, in the factories and fields, and in the homes of wealthier people.

Section Review

- The Hellenistic period did not change the way people lived and worked but was successful in uniting the East and West economically, creating a broad commercial network.
- Alexander used the wealth he captured to build roads, cities, and harbors, opening new markets in which Greek merchants could trade.
- The caravan trade routes carried luxury goods, especially tea and silk, across the southern desert by camel from as far east as China.
- Commercial trade in essential commodities was economically more important than trade in luxury goods for Hellenistic cities.
- Hellenistic merchant ships carried bulk commodities and provided opportunities for workers in other industries, including pirates.
- Slave labor was common throughout the Mediterranean except in Egypt, where it would have competed with free labor.

Hellenistic Intellectual Advances

What is the intellectual legacy of the Hellenistic period?

The peoples of the Hellenistic era took the ideas and ideals of the classical Greeks and advanced them to new heights. Their achievements created the intellectual and religious atmosphere that deeply influenced Roman thinking and eventually the religious thought of liberal Judaism and early Christianity. Far from being stagnant, this was a period of vigorous growth, especially in the areas of philosophy, science, and medicine.

Religion in the Hellenistic World

In religion the most significant new ideas were developed outside Greece. At first the Hellenistic period saw the spread of Greek religious cults throughout the Near East and Egypt. When Hellenistic kings founded cities, they also built temples and established new cults and priesthoods for the old Olympian gods.

Greek cults sponsored literary, musical, and athletic contests, which were staged in beautiful surroundings among impressive Greek buildings. On the whole, however, the civic cults were primarily concerned with ritual and neither appealed to religious emotions nor embraced matters such as sin and redemption. Although the new civic cults were lavish in pomp and display, they could not satisfy deep religious feelings or spiritual yearnings. Greeks increasingly sought solace from other sources. Some turned to philosophy as a guide to life, while others turned to superstition, magic, or astrology. Still others might shrug and speak of **Tyche** (TIE-kee), which meant "Fate" or "Chance" or "Doom"—a capricious and sometimes malevolent force.

Beginning in the second century B.C.E., some individuals were increasingly attracted to new **mystery religions,** so called because they featured a body of ritual not to be divulged to anyone not initiated into the cult. These new mystery cults incorporated aspects of both Greek and Eastern religions and had broad appeal for people who yearned for personal immortality. Since the Greeks were already familiar with old mystery cults, such as the Eleusinian (el-yoo-SIN-ee-uhn) mysteries in Attica, the new cults did not strike them as alien. Familiar, too, was the concept of preparation for an initiation. Devotees of the Greek Eleusinian mysteries and other such cults had to prepare themselves mentally and physically before entering the gods' presence. Thus the mystery cults fit well with Greek usage.

The new religions enjoyed one tremendous advantage over the old Greek mystery cults. Whereas old Greek mysteries were tied to particular places, such as Eleusis (ee-LOO-sis), the new religions spread throughout the Hellenistic world.

Tyche Fate or chance or doom; a capricious and sometimes malevolent force.

mystery religions Bodies of ritual not to be divulged to anyone not initiated into the cult. They incorporated aspects of both Greek and Eastern religions and had broad appeal for both Greeks and Easterners who yearned for personal immortality.

Hellenistic Mystery Cult
The scene depicts part of the ritual of initiation into the cult of Dionysus. The young woman here has just completed the ritual. She now dances in joy as the official with the sacred staff looks on. (Scala/Art Resource, NY)

People did not have to undertake long and expensive pilgrimages just to become members of the religion. In that sense the mystery religions came to the people, for temples of the new deities sprang up wherever Greeks lived.

The mystery religions all claimed to save their adherents from the worst that fate could do and promised life for the soul after death. They all had a single concept in common: the belief that by the rites of initiation devotees became united with a god, usually male, who had himself died and risen from the dead. The sacrifice of the god and his victory over death saved the devotee from eternal death. Similarly, all mystery religions demanded a period of preparation in which the convert strove to become holy, that is, to live by the religion's precepts. Once aspirants had prepared themselves, they went through an initiation in which they learned the secrets of the religion. The initiation was usually a ritual of great emotional intensity, symbolizing the entry into a new life.

The mystery religions that took the Hellenistic world by storm were the Egyptian cults of Serapis (si-REY-pis) and Isis. Serapis, who was invented by King Ptolemy, was believed to be the judge of souls, who rewarded virtuous and righteous people with eternal life.

The cult of Isis enjoyed even wider appeal than that of Serapis. Isis, wife of Osiris, was believed to have conquered Tyche and promised to save any mortal who came to her. She became the most important goddess of the Hellenistic world, and her worship was very popular among women. Her priests claimed that she had bestowed on humanity the gift of civilization and founded law and literature. She was the goddess of marriage, conception, and childbirth, and like Serapis she promised to save the souls of her believers.

Mystery religions took care of the big things in life, but many people resorted to ordinary magic for daily matters. When a cat walked across their path, they stopped until someone else had passed by them. Or they could throw three rocks across the road. People often purified their houses to protect them from Hecate (HEK-uh-tee), a sinister goddess associated with magic and witchcraft. Many people had dreams that only seers and augurs (AW-gers) could interpret. Some of these things are familiar today because some old fears are still alive.

Philosophy and the People

During the Hellenistic period, philosophy reached out to touch the lives of more men and women than ever before. Two significant philosophies caught the minds and hearts of contemporary Greeks and some Easterners, as well as some later Romans. The first was **Epicureanism** (ep-ee-kyoo-REE-uh-niz-uhm), a practical philosophy of serenity in an often tumultuous world. Epicurus (ep-ee-KYOOR-uhs) (340–270 B.C.E.) taught that the principal good of human life is pleasure, which he defined as the absence of pain. He was not advocating drunken revels or sexual dissipation, which he thought actually caused pain. Instead, Epicurus concluded that any violent emotion is undesirable and advocated mild self-discipline. Even poverty he considered good, as long as people had enough food, clothing, and shelter. Epicurus also taught that individuals can most easily attain peace and serenity by ignoring the outside world and looking into their personal feelings and reactions. His followers ignored politics and issues, for they led to tumult, which would disturb the soul.

Opposed to the passivity of the Epicureans, Zeno (ZEE-noh) (335–262 B.C.E.), a philosopher from Citium in Cyprus, advanced a different concept of human beings and the universe. Zeno first came to Athens to form his own school, the Stoa, named after the building where he preferred to teach. **Stoicism** (STOH-uh-siz-uhm)

Epicureanism A practical philosophy founded by Epicurus, it argued that the principal good of human life is pleasure.

Stoicism The most popular of Hellenistic philosophies, it considered nature an expression of divine will; people could be happy only when living in accordance with nature.

became the most popular Hellenistic philosophy and the one that later captured the mind of Rome. To the Stoics the important question was not whether they achieved anything, but whether they lived virtuous lives. In that way they could triumph over Tyche, for Tyche could destroy achievements but not the nobility of their lives.

Zeno and his followers considered nature an expression of divine will; in their view, people could be happy only when living in accordance with nature. They stressed the unity of man and the universe, stating that all men were brothers and were obliged to help one another. The Stoics' most significant practical achievement was the creation of the concept of **natural law.** The Stoics concluded that as all men were brothers, partook of divine reason, and were in harmony with the universe, one law—a part of the natural order of life—governed them all. The Stoic concept of a universal state governed by natural law is one of the finest heirlooms the Hellenistic world passed on to Rome. The Stoic concept of natural law, of one law for all people, became a valuable tool when the Romans began to deal with many different peoples with different laws. The ideal of the universal state gave the Romans a rationale for extending their empire to the farthest reaches of the world. The obligation of individuals to their fellows served the citizens of the Roman Empire as the philosophical justification for doing their duty. In this respect, too, the real fruit of Hellenism was to ripen only under the cultivation of Rome.

natural law A Stoic concept that as all men were brothers, partook of divine reason, and were in harmony with the universe, one law—a part of the natural order of life—governed them all.

Hellenistic Science

Hellenistic culture achieved its greatest triumphs in the area of science. The most notable of the Hellenistic astronomers was Aristarchus (ar-uh-STAHR-kuhs) of Samos (ca. 310–230 B.C.E.), who was educated in Aristotle's school. Aristarchus concluded that the sun is far larger than the earth and that the stars are enormously distant from the earth. He argued against Aristotle's view that the earth was the center of the universe. Instead, Aristarchus propounded the **heliocentric** (he-lee-oh-CENT-rik) **theory**—that the earth and planets revolve around the sun. His work is all the more impressive because he lacked even a rudimentary telescope. Aristarchus had only the human eye and brain, but they were more than enough.

Unfortunately, Aristarchus's theories did not persuade the ancient world. In the second century C.E. Claudius Ptolemy, a mathematician and astronomer in Alexandria, accepted Aristotle's theory of the earth as the center of the universe, and this view prevailed for fourteen hundred years. Aristarchus's heliocentric theory lay dormant until resurrected in the sixteenth century by the brilliant Polish astronomer Nicolaus Copernicus (koh-PUR-ni-kuhs).

In geometry Euclid (YOO-klid) (ca. 300 B.C.E.), a mathematician who lived in Alexandria, compiled a valuable textbook of existing knowledge. His book *The Elements of Geometry* has exerted immense influence on Western civilization, for it rapidly became the standard introduction to geometry. Generations of students, from the Hellenistic period to the present, have learned the essentials of geometry from it.

The greatest thinker of the Hellenistic period was Archimedes (ahr-kuh-MEE-deez) (ca. 287–212 B.C.E.), a native of Syracuse. (See the feature "Individuals in Society: Archimedes and the Practical Application of Science.") His mathematical research, covering many fields, was his greatest contribution to Western thought. In his book *On Plane Equilibriums* Archimedes dealt for the first time with the basic principles of mechanics, including the principle of the lever. He once said that if he were given a lever and a suitable place to stand, he could move the world. With his treatise *On Floating Bodies* he founded the science of hydrostatics.

heliocentric theory The theory of Aristarchus that the earth and planets revolve around the sun.

Individuals in Society

Archimedes and the Practical Application of Science

Throughout the ages generals have besieged cities to force them to surrender. Between 213 and 211 B.C.E. the Roman general Marcellus laid close siege to the strongly walled city of Syracuse, the home of the scientist Archimedes. Hiero, king of Syracuse and friend of Archimedes, turned to him for help. Archimedes used his knowledge of mechanics to create engines that could fire objects at the enemy.

Archimedes, however, began to ply his engines, and shot against the land forces of the attackers all sorts of missiles and immense masses of stones, which came down with incredible din and speed. Nothing whatever could ward off their weight, but they knocked down in heaps those who stood in their way, and threw their ranks into confusion. At the same time huge beams were suddenly projected over the [Roman] ships from the walls [of Syracuse], which sank some of them with great weights plunging down from on high. Others were seized at the prow by iron claws, or beaks like the beaks of cranes, drawn straight up into the air, and then plunged stern first into the depths, or were turned round and round by means of enginery within the city, and dashed upon the steep cliffs that jutted out beneath the wall of the city, with great destruction of the fighting men on board, who perished in the wrecks. Frequently, too, a ship would be lifted out of the water into mid-air, whirled here and there as it hung there, a dreadful spectacle, until its crew had been thrown out and hurled in all directions. Then it would fall empty upon the walls, or slip away from the clutch that had held it.

Then in a council of war the Romans decided to come up under the walls while it was still night. . . . When, therefore, they came under the walls, thinking themselves unnoticed, once more they encountered a great storm of missiles. Huge stones came tumbling down upon them almost perpendicularly, and the wall shot out arrows at them from every point. They therefore retired. And here again, when they were some distance off, missiles darted forth and fell upon them as they were going away, and there was a great slaughter among them. Many of their ships, too, were dashed together, and they could not retaliate in any way upon their foes. For Archimedes had built most of his engines close behind the wall, and the Romans seemed to be fighting against the gods, now that countless mischiefs were poured out upon them from an invisible source.

At last the Romans became so fearful that whenever they saw a bit of rope or a stick of timber projecting a little over the wall. "There it is," they shouted, "Archimedes is training some engine upon us." They then turned their backs and fled. Seeing this, Marcellus desisted from all the fighting and assault, and thenceforth depended on a long siege.

For all his genius, Archimedes did not survive the siege. His deeds of war done, he returned to his thinking and his mathematical problems, even with the siege still in the background. When Syracuse was betrayed to the Romans, soldiers streamed in, spreading slaughter and destruction throughout the city. A Roman soldier came upon Archimedes in his study and killed him outright, thus ending the life of one of the world's greatest thinkers.

Questions for Analysis

1. How did Archimedes' engines repulse the Roman attacks?
2. What effect did his weapons have on the Roman attackers?
3. What is the irony of Archimedes' death?

Source: Reprinted by permission of the publishers and the Trustees of the Loeb Classical Library from *Plutarch: Volume V*, Loeb Classical Library Volume 87, translated by B. Perrin, pp. 475–477, Cambridge, Mass.: Harvard University Press, 1917. The Loeb Classical Library® is a registered trademark of the President and Fellows of Harvard College.

Archimedes' mill. A slave turns a large cylinder fitted with blades to form a screw that draws water from a well. (Courtesy, Soprintendenza Archeologica di Pompei. Photo: Dr. Penelope M. Allison)

He concluded that whenever a solid floats in a liquid, the weight of the solid is equal to the weight of the liquid displaced. He made his discovery when he stepped into a bath. He noticed that the weight of his body displaced a volume of water equal to it. He immediately ran outside shouting "Eureka, eureka" (I have found it, I have found it).[1]

Archimedes was willing to share his work with others, among them Eratosthenes (er-uh-TOS-thuh-neez) (285–ca. 204 B.C.E.), who was librarian of the enormous royal library in Alexandria, Egypt. Eratosthenes used mathematics to further the geographical studies for which he is most famous. He calculated the circumference of the earth geometrically, estimating it as about 24,675 miles. He was not wrong by much: the earth is actually 24,860 miles in circumference. Eratosthenes also concluded that the earth was a spherical globe and that the land was surrounded by ocean.

Using geographical information gained by Alexander the Great's scientists, Eratosthenes tried to fit the East into Greek geographical knowledge. Although for some reason he ignored the western Mediterranean and Europe, he declared that a ship could sail from Spain either around Africa to India or directly westward to India. Not until the great days of Western exploration did sailors such as Vasco da Gama and Magellan actually prove Eratosthenes' theories.

Catapult

This model shows a catapult as its crew would have seen it in action. The arrow was loaded on the long horizontal beam, its point fitting into the housing. There the torsion spring under great pressure released the arrow at the target, which could be some 400 yards away. (Courtesy, Noel Kavan)

For all of its speculation, Hellenistic science made an inestimable, if grim, contribution to practical life. The Greeks and Macedonians applied theories of mechanics to build siege machines, thus revolutionizing the art of warfare. The catapult became the first and most widely used artillery piece. The earliest catapults could shoot only large arrows and small stones. By the time Alexander the Great besieged Tyre in 332 B.C.E., his catapults threw stones big enough to knock down city walls. Generals soon realized that they could also hurl burning bundles over the walls to start fires in the city. To approach enemy town walls safely, engineers built siege towers, large wooden structures that served as artillery platforms, and put them on wheels so that soldiers could roll them up to the wall. Once there, archers stationed on top of them swept the enemy's ramparts with arrows, while other soldiers manning catapults added missile fire. To aid the siege towers, generals added battering rams that brought down large portions of walls. If these new engines made waging war more efficient, they also added to the misery of the people. War was no longer confined to the battlefield and fought between soldiers. It had come to embrace the whole population.

Hellenistic Medicine

The study of medicine flourished during the Hellenistic period, and Hellenistic physicians carried the work of Hippocrates into new areas. Herophilus, who lived in the first half of the third century B.C.E., approached the study of medicine in a systematic, scientific fashion: he dissected dead bodies and measured what he observed. He discovered the nervous system and concluded that two types of

An Unsuccessful Delivery

This funeral stele depicts a mother who has perhaps lost her own life as well as her baby's. Childbirth was the leading cause of death for adult women in antiquity, though funeral steles showing this are quite rare. Another of the few that do show death in childbirth bears the heartbreaking words attributed to the mother by her grieving family: "All my labor could not bring the child forth; he lies in my womb, among the dead." (National Archaeological Museum, Athens/Archaeological Receipts Fund)

Section Review

- Greek religious cults were based on ritual and did not satisfy deeper religious feelings, causing many Greeks to turn to philosophy, astrology, magic, and mystery cults to guide their lives.

- The mystery cults such as the Eleusinian mysteries and the Egyptian cults of Serapis and Isis held broad appeal and promised life after death for those who passed their emotionally intense rituals and adhered to their religious precepts.

- Epicureanism taught individuals to attain peace by seeking pleasure and ignoring the outside world while Stoicism maintained that one achieved happiness by living a dutiful, virtuous life according to universal nature.

- Many significant advances were made in science including the heliocentric theory, geometry, and the basic principles of mechanics, hydrostatics, and using mathematics in geographical studies.

- Advances in science revolutionized warfare with the introduction of the catapult, siege towers, and battering rams.

- The study of medicine led to a greater understanding of the human body through dissection as well as the use of drugs and medicine to treat illnesses, but the popularity of quacks who claimed to cure illness through magic and potions hindered these advances.

nerves, motor and sensory, existed. Herophilus also studied the brain, which he considered the center of intelligence, and discerned the cerebrum (suh-REE-bruhm) and cerebellum (ser-uh-BEL-uhm). His other work dealt with the liver, lungs, and uterus.

In about 280 B.C.E. Philinus and Serapion, pupils of Herophilus, concentrated on the observation and cure of illnesses rather than focussing on dissection. They also laid heavier stress on the use of drugs and medicine to treat illnesses. Heraclides of Tarentum (tuh-REN-tuhm) (perhaps first century B.C.E.) carried on this tradition and discovered the benefits of opium and worked with other drugs that relieved pain.

The Hellenistic world was also plagued by people who claimed to cure illnesses through incantations and magic. Their potions included such concoctions as blood from the ear of an ass mixed with water to cure fever, or the liver of a cat killed when the moon was waning and preserved in salt. Quacks damaged the reputation of dedicated doctors who intelligently tried to heal and alleviate pain. The medical abuses that arose in the Hellenistic period were so flagrant that the Romans, who later entered the Hellenistic world, developed an intense distrust of physicians and also considered the study of Hellenistic medicine beneath the dignity of a Roman. Nonetheless, the work of men like Herophilus and Serapion made valuable contributions to the knowledge of medicine, and the fruits of their work were preserved and handed on to the West.

Chapter Review

| Why did Alexander launch his massive attack on the Persian Empire? How extensive were his conquests? (page 66)

| Although Alexander may not originally have intended to march all the way to the Indus Valley, he gained so much territory that he saw every reason to continue as far as possible. It was an almost foolhardy adventure, but it permanently changed the face of world history.

| What happened to Alexander's empire after his death? What was his political and cultural legacy? (page 68)

| Alexander's legacy proved of essential importance to the future of the West. He brought the vital civilization of the Greeks into intimate contact with the older cultures of the East. He and his successors established cities and encouraged a third great wave of Greek migration.

| What effect did Greek migration have on Greek and native peoples? (page 71)

| In the Aegean and Near East the fusion of Greek and Eastern cultures laid the social, intellectual, and cultural foundations on which the Romans would later build. In the heart of the old Persian empire, Hellenism was only another new influence that was absorbed by older ways of thought and life. Yet overall, in the exchange of ideas and the opportunity for different cultures to learn about one another, a new cosmopolitan society evolved.

| What effects did East-West trade have on ordinary peoples during the Hellenistic period? (page 75)

| For ordinary men and women, the greatest practical boon of the Hellenistic adventure was economic. Trade connected the world on a routine basis. Economics brought people together just as surely as it brought them goods. By the end of the Hellenistic period, the ancient world had become far broader and more economically intricate than ever before.

| What is the intellectual legacy of the Hellenistic period? (page 76)

| Hellenistic achievements included intellectual advances as well as trade connections. Mystery religions, such as the worship of the goddess Isis, provided many people with answers to their questions about the meaning of life, while others turned to practical philosophies such as Stoicism for ethical guidance. Mathematicians and scientists developed theoretical knowledge and applied this to practical problems in geography, mechanics, and weaponry. Physicians also approached medicine in a systematic fashion, though many people relied on magic and folk cures for treatment of illness. People of the Hellenistic period not only built on the achievements of their predecessors, but they also produced one of the most creative intellectual eras of classical antiquity.

Key Terms

Hellenistic (p. 66)
sovereign (p. 72)
Great Silk Road (p. 76)
Tyche (p. 77)
mystery religions (p. 77)
Epicureanism (p. 78)
Stoicism (p. 78)
natural law (p. 79)
heliocentric theory (p. 79)

Note

1. Vitruvius, *On Architecture* 9 Preface, 10.

To assess your mastery of this chapter, go to **bedfordstmartins.com/mckaywestbrief**

Listening to the Past

Alexander and the Brotherhood of Man

At one point in his crusade, Alexander found himself confronted with a huge mutiny by his Macedonian veterans. He ordered the most vocal of the rebels to be executed and reminded the others of the glory they had achieved in battle and the shame they would endure at home if they returned as deserters. He then refused to see any of the Macedonians and turned over command of the brigades to the Persians. Alexander's words of reconciliation at the conclusion of this episode have been interpreted as an expression of his desire to establish a "brotherhood of man." Readers can determine for themselves whether Alexander attempted to introduce a new philosophical ideal or whether he harbored his own political motives for political cooperation.

[The Macedonian soldiers] declared they would not retire from the gates either day or night, unless Alexander would take some pity upon them. When he was informed of this, he came out without delay; and seeing them lying on the ground in humble guise, and hearing most of them lamenting with loud voice, tears began to flow also from his own eyes. He made an effort to say something to them, but they continued their importunate entreaties. At length one of them, Callines by name, a man conspicuous both for his age and because he was a captain of the Companion cavalry, spoke as follows, "O king, what grieves the Macedonians is that you have already made some of the Persians kinsmen to yourself, and that Persians are called Alexander's kinsmen, and have the honour of saluting you with a kiss; whereas none of the Macedonians have as yet enjoyed this honour." Then Alexander interrupting him, said, "But all of you without exception I consider my kinsmen, and so from this time I shall call you." When he had said this, Callines advanced and saluted him with a kiss, and so did all those who wished to salute him. Then they took up their weapons and returned to the camp, shouting and singing a song of thanksgiving. After this Alexander offered sacrifice to the gods to whom it was his custom to sacrifice, and gave a public banquet, over which he himself presided, with the Macedonians sitting around him; and next to them the Persians; after whom came the men of the other nations, preferred in honour for their personal rank or for some meritorious action. The king and his guests drew wine from the same bowl and poured out the same libations, both the Grecian prophets and the Magians commencing the ceremony. He prayed for other blessings, and especially that harmony and community of rule might exist between the Macedonians and Persians.

Questions for Analysis

1. What was the purpose of the banquet?
2. Were all of the guests treated equally?
3. What did Alexander gain from bringing together the Macedonians and Persians?

Source: From *The Greek Historians* by Francis R. B. Godolphin. Copyright © 1942 and renewed 1970 by Random House, Inc. Used by permission of Random House, Inc.

This gilded case for a bow and arrows indicates that Alexander's success came at the price of blood. These vigorous scenes portray more military conflict than philosophical compassion. (Archaeological Museum Salonica/Dagli Orti/The Art Archive)

CHAPTER 5

The Rise of Rome

ca. 750–44 B.C.E.

The Roman Forum. (Josephine Powell Photography, Courtesy of Special Collections, Fine Arts Library, Harvard College Library)

Chapter Preview

Like the Persians under Cyrus and the Greeks under Alexander, the Romans managed to conquer vast territories in less than a century. Their achievement lay in their ability to incorporate conquered peoples into the Roman system. Unlike the Greeks, who refused to share citizenship, the Romans extended their citizenship first to the Italians and later to the peoples of the provinces. With that citizenship went Roman government and law. Rome created a world state that embraced the entire Mediterranean area and extended northward.

Nor was Rome's achievement limited to the ancient world. Rome's law, language, and administrative practices shaped later developments in Europe and beyond. London, Paris, Vienna, and many other modern European cities began as Roman colonies or military camps. When the Founding Fathers created the American republic, they looked to Rome as a model. On the darker side, Napoleon and Mussolini paid their own tribute to Rome by aping its forms. All were acknowledging admiration for the Roman achievement.

Roman history is usually divided into two periods: the republic, the age in which Rome grew from a small city-state to ruler of an empire, and the empire, the period when the republican constitution gave way to constitutional monarchy. The republic is the focus of this chapter.

The Etruscans and Rome

How did the Etruscans shape early Roman history?

While the Greeks pursued their destiny in the East, the Etruscans (eh-TRUS-kuns) and Romans entered the peninsula of Italy. The arrival of the Etruscans in the region of Etruria can reasonably be dated to about 750 B.C.E. The Romans settled farther south in Latium. Located at an easy crossing point on the Tiber (TIE-ber) River, Rome stood astride the main avenue of communication between northern and southern Italy. Its seven hills were defensive and safe from the floods of the Tiber. (See Map 5.1.)

The Etruscans and the Roman Settlement of Italy (ca. 750–509 B.C.E.)

The Etruscans established permanent settlements that evolved into the first Italian cities, which resembled the Greek city-states in political organization. Their influence spread over the surrounding countryside, which they farmed but also mined, as it contained rich mineral resources. From an early period the Etruscans began to trade natural products, especially iron, with their Greek neighbors on the Mediterranean in exchange for luxury goods. They thereby built a rich cultural life that became the foundation of civilization throughout Italy. In the process they touched a small collection of villages subsequently called Rome.

The Romans had settled in Italy by the eighth century B.C.E. According to one legend, Romulus and Remus founded the city in 753 B.C.E., Romulus making his home on the Palatine Hill, while Remus chose the Aventine (see inset of Map 5.1). Under Etruscan influence the Romans prospered, spreading over all of Rome's seven hills.

From 753 to 509 B.C.E. a line of Etruscan kings ruled the city and introduced many customs. The Romans adopted the Etruscan alphabet, which the Etruscans themselves had adopted from the Greeks. The Romans later handed on this alphabet to medieval Europe and from there to the modern Western world. Even the **toga** (TOH-guh), the white woolen robe worn by citizens, came from the Etruscans.

Under the Etruscans Rome enjoyed contacts with the larger Mediterranean world, while the city continued to grow. In the years 575 to 550 B.C.E. temples and public buildings began to grace the city. The **forum** ceased to be a cemetery and began its history as a public meeting place, similar to the Greek agora. Trade in metalwork became common, and wealthier Romans began to import fine Greek vases. The Etruscans had found Rome a collection of villages and made it a city.

750–31 B.C.E.	Beginning of the economic growth of Rome
750–133 B.C.E.	Traditional founding of Rome; evolution of the Roman state
509–290 B.C.E.	Roman conquest of Italy
499–186 B.C.E.	Introduction of Greek deities
ca. 494–287 B.C.E.	Struggle of the Orders
264–133 B.C.E.	Punic Wars and the conquest of the East
262 B.C.E.	Growth of large estates
239–159 B.C.E.	Rise of Latin Literature
88–31 B.C.E.	Civil war
86–35 B.C.E.	Birth of historical and political writing

The Roman Conquest of Italy (509–290 B.C.E.)

Legend has it that the republic was formed when the son of the Etruscan king raped Lucretia (loo-KREE-shuh), a virtuous Roman woman, and the people rose up in anger. The republic was actually founded in the years after 509, when the Romans fought numerous wars with their neighbors on the Italian peninsula. Not until roughly a century after the founding of the republic did the Romans drive the Etruscans entirely out of Latium (LA-cee-um). Early on, the Romans learned the value of alliances, and the Latin towns around them provided them with a large reservoir of manpower. These alliances involved the Romans in still other wars and took them farther afield in the Italian peninsula.

Around 390 B.C.E. the Romans suffered a major setback when a new people, the Celts—or **Gauls** (gawls), as the Romans called them—swept aside a Roman army and sacked Rome. More intent on loot than on land, they agreed to abandon Rome in return for a thousand pounds of gold. In the century that followed, the Romans rebuilt their city and

toga The white woolen robe worn by citizens.

forum A public meeting place; a development parallel to that of the Greek agora.

Gauls The Celts, people who swept aside a Roman army and sacked Rome around 390 B.C.E.

Sarcophagus of Lartie Seianti

The woman portrayed on this lavish sarcophagus is the noble Etruscan Lartie Seianti. Although the sarcophagus is her place of burial, she is portrayed as in life, comfortable and at rest. The influence of Greek art on Etruscan is apparent in almost every feature of the sarcophagus. (Archaeological Museum, Florence/Nimatallah/Art Resource, NY)

recouped their losses. They brought Latium and their Latin allies fully under their control and conquered Etruria. In 343 B.C.E. they grappled with the Samnites in a series of bitter wars for the possession of Campania (**kam-PAY-nee-uh**) and southern Italy (see Map 5.1). The Samnites were a formidable enemy, but the superior military organization and manpower of the Romans won out in the end. Although Rome had yet to subdue the whole peninsula, for the first time in history it stood unchallenged.

The Romans spread their religious cults, mythology, and drama throughout Italy. They did not force their beliefs on others, but they did welcome their neighbors to religious places of assembly. The Romans and Italians grew closer by the mutual understanding of and participation in religious rites.

With many of their oldest allies, such as the Latin cities, the Romans shared full Roman citizenship. In other instances they granted citizenship without the **franchise**,

franchise The right to vote or hold Roman offices.

MAP 5.1   Italy and the City of Rome

The geographical configuration of the Italian peninsula shows how Rome stood astride north-south communication routes and how the state that united Italy stood poised to move into Sicily and northern Africa.

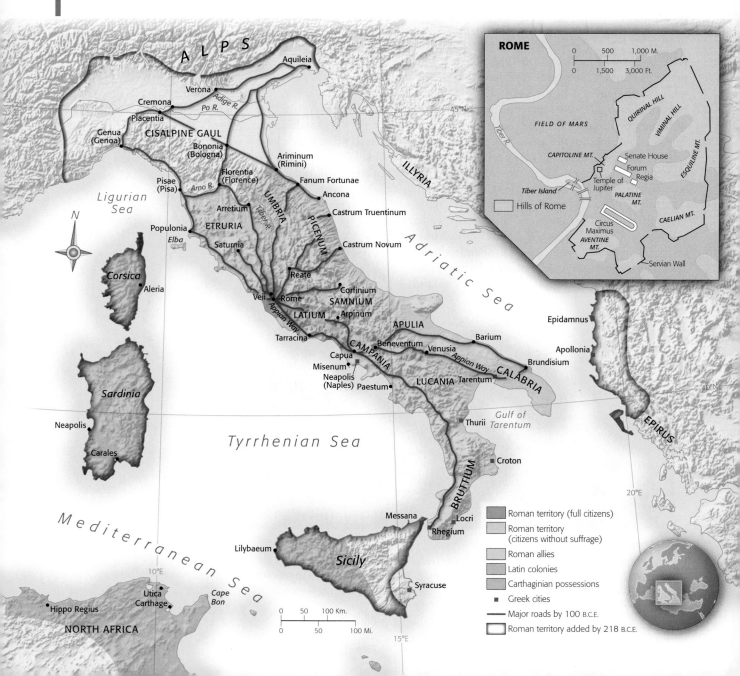

that is, without the right to vote or hold Roman offices. These allies were subject to Roman taxes and calls for military service but ran their own local affairs. The Latin allies were able to acquire full Roman citizenship by moving to Rome.

The Roman roads, many of which were in use as late as the medieval period, allowed for the flow of communication, trade, and armies from the capital to outlying areas. They were the tangible sinews of unity.

The Roman Republic

What was the nature of the Roman republic?

The Romans summed up their political existence in a single phrase: *senatus populusque Romanum*, "the Roman senate and people." This sentiment reflects the republican ideal of shared government rather than concentrated power within a monarchy. Abbreviated as "SPQR," the letters became a shorthand way of saying "Rome." The beliefs, customs, and laws of the republic—its unwritten constitution— evolved over centuries to meet the demands of the governed.

The Roman State

In the early republic social divisions determined the shape of politics. Political power was in the hands of the aristocracy—the **patricians** (puh-TREESH-uhns), who were wealthy landowners. Patrician families formed clans, as did aristocrats in early Greece. Patrician men dominated the affairs of state, provided military leadership in time of war, and monopolized knowledge of law and legal procedure. The common people of Rome, the **plebeians** (plee-BEE-ahns), were free citizens with a voice in politics, but they could not hold high political office or marry into patrician families. While some plebeian merchants rivaled the patricians in wealth, most were poor artisans, small farmers, and landless urban dwellers.

The chief magistrates of the republic were the two **consuls**, elected for one-year terms. At first the consulship was open only to patrician men. The consuls commanded the army in battle, administered state business, and supervised financial affairs. When the consuls were away from Rome, *praetors* (PRAY-ters) could act in their place. Otherwise, the praetors dealt primarily with the administration of justice.

After the age of overseas conquest, the Romans divided the Mediterranean area into provinces governed by ex-consuls and ex-praetors. Because of their experience in Roman politics, they were well suited to administer the affairs of the provincials and to fit Roman law and custom into new contexts.

Other officials included *quaestors* (KWEH-ster), who took charge of the public treasury and prosecuted criminals in the popular courts; *censors*, whose many responsibilities included the supervision of public morals, the power to determine who lawfully could sit in the senate, the registration of citizens, and the leasing of public contracts; and the *aediles* (AY-dials), who supervised the streets and markets and presided over public festivals.

Perhaps the greatest institution of the republic was the **senate**, which had originated under the Etruscans as a council of noble elders who advised the king. During the republic the senate advised the consuls and other magistrates. Because the senate sat year after year, while magistrates changed annually, it provided stability and experienced counsel. Technically, the senate could not pass legislation; it could only offer its advice. But increasingly, because of the senate's prestige, its advice came to have the force of law.

patricians The aristocracy; wealthy landowners who held political power.

plebeians The common people of Rome who had few of the patricians' advantages.

consuls The two chief Roman magistrates.

senate Originating under the Etruscans, it was a council of noble elders who advised the king.

natural law A universal law that could be applied to all people and societies.

Struggle of the Orders A great social conflict that developed between patricians and plebeians; the plebeians wanted real political representation and safeguards against patrician domination.

tribunes The people whom plebeians were able to elect; tribunes would in turn protect the plebeians from the arbitrary conduct of patrician magistrates.

paterfamilias A term that means far more than merely father, it indicates the oldest, dominant male of the family, one who held nearly absolute power over the lives of his family as long as he lived.

Section Review

- The Roman political ideal was *"Senatus populusque Romanum"* or *"SPQR"* ("the Roman senate and people"), which meant they valued shared government over a monarchy.

- In the early republic, political power was in the hands of wealthy men—patricians—who were elected for one-year terms as consuls, while the plebeians (the common people) were free but could not hold high office or marry into patrician families.

- The senate advised the consuls and other magistrates, providing stability, and while initially it could not pass legislation, due to its reputation its advice later came to have the force of law.

- The development of Roman law, added to by assemblies and interpreted by praetors, included the adoption of the law of equity and the concept of "natural law," which provided equal justice for all involved.

- The Struggle of the Orders was a conflict between the plebeians and the patricians, during which the plebeians went on strike and won the right to elect their own officials (tribunes), to hold one of the two annual consul positions, and to legal equality.

- The paterfamilias was the male head of the family and held absolute power over the lives of his wife and children as long as he lived.

The Romans created several assemblies, through which men elected magistrates and passed legislation. The *comitia centuriata* (kuh-MISH-ee-uh cent-ur-EE-ah-tah) was a popular assembly organized by *centuries*, which were both military companies and political voting blocs. The patricians possessed the majority of centuries and could easily outvote the plebeians. In 471 B.C.E. plebeian men won the right to meet in an assembly of their own, the *concilium plebis*, and to pass ordinances.

One of the most important achievements of the Romans was their development of a body of law. Roman assemblies added to the law, and praetors interpreted it. The spirit of the law aimed at protecting the property, lives, and reputations of citizens, and redressing wrongs. As the Romans came into more frequent contact with foreigners, the praetors adopted aspects of other legal systems and resorted to the law of equity—what they thought was right and just to all parties. By the time of the late republic, Roman jurists were reaching decisions on the basis of the Stoic concept of **natural law,** a universal law that could be applied to all societies.

Social Conflict in Rome

The inequality between plebeians and patricians led to a conflict known as the **Struggle of the Orders.** Rather than using violence to achieve their goals, the plebeians leveraged their power as a group. The patricians also responded peacefully, ultimately resorting to a practical compromise.

The first showdown between plebeians and patricians came, according to tradition, in 494 B.C.E. To force the patricians to grant concessions, the plebeians literally walked out of Rome and refused to serve in the army. The plebeians' general strike worked, and the patricians made important concessions. They allowed patricians and plebeians to marry one another. They recognized the right of plebeians to elect their own officials, the **tribunes** (trib-YOONS), who could bring plebeian grievances to the senate for resolution. And they gave up their legal monopoly, publishing the law and legal procedures so that plebeians could also argue cases in court.

Further reforms followed after a ten-year battle. Wealthy plebeians wanted the opportunity to provide political leadership for the state. They demanded that the patricians allow them access to all the magistracies of the state. If they could hold the consulship, they could also sit in the senate and advise on policy. They won the right to one of the two annual consul positions. Though decisive, this victory did not automatically end the Struggle of the Orders. That happened only in 287 B.C.E. with the passage of a law that gave the resolutions of the concilium plebis the force of law for patricians and plebeians alike.

The compromise established a new nobility shared by wealthy plebeians and patricians. They were both groups of aristocrats who had simply agreed to share the great offices of power within the republic. This would lead not to major political reform but to an extension of aristocratic rule.

The Struggle of the Orders made all male citizens equal before the law, but a man's independence was limited by the power that the male head of the family, termed the **paterfamilias** (pat-er-fuh-MEE-lee-uhs), had over him. This was also true for all women, who even as adults were always under the legal guardianship of some man. The paterfamilias held nearly absolute power over the lives of his wife and children as long as he lived. He could legally kill his wife for adultery, or divorce her at will. He could kill his children or sell them into slavery. Until the paterfamilias died, his sons could not even own property.

Roman Expansion

How did the Romans take control of the Mediterranean world?

Once the Romans had settled their internal affairs, they turned their attention outward. As seen earlier, they had already come to terms with the Italic peoples in Latium. Only later did Rome achieve primacy over its Latin allies, partly because of successful diplomacy and partly because of overwhelming military power. In 282 B.C.E. Rome expanded even farther in Italy and extended its power across the sea to Sicily, Corsica (KAWR-si-kuh), and Sardinia (sahr-DIN-ee-uh).

Italy Becomes Roman

In only twenty years, from 282 to 262 B.C.E., the Romans established a string of colonies throughout Italy, some of them populated by Romans and others by Latins. Those living closest to Rome were incorporated into the Roman state. They enjoyed the full franchise and citizenship that the Romans themselves possessed. Those Italians who lived farther afield were bound by treaty with the Romans and were considered allies. Although they received lesser rights of active citizenship, the allies retained their right of local self-government. Through these contacts— social, political, and legal—Rome and the rest of Italy began to share similar views of their common welfare.

Overseas Conquest (282–146 B.C.E.)

In 282 B.C.E., when the Romans had reached southern Italy, they embarked upon a series of wars that left them the rulers of the Mediterranean world (see Map 5.2). These wars became fiercer and were fought on a larger scale than those in Italy. Though the Romans sometimes declared war reluctantly, they nonetheless felt the need to dominate, to eliminate any state that could threaten them. Yet they did not map out grandiose strategies for world conquest but rather responded to situations as they arose.

The Samnite wars had drawn the Romans into the political world of southern Italy. In 282 B.C.E., alarmed by the powerful newcomer, the Greek city of Tarentum (tuh-REN-tuhm) in southern Italy called for help from Pyrrhus (PEER-uhs), king of Epirus (eh-PAHY-ruhs) in western Greece. A relative of Alexander the Great and an excellent general, Pyrrhus won two furious battles but suffered heavy casualties—thus the phrase **Pyrrhic victory** for a victory involving severe losses. Against Pyrrhus's army the Romans threw new legions, and in the end manpower proved decisive. In 275 B.C.E. the Romans drove Pyrrhus from Italy and extended their sway over southern Italy. They then needed to secure the island of Sicily (SIS-uh-lee) in order to block the northward expansion of Carthage (KAHR-thij).

Pyrrhic victory A phrase for a victory involving severe losses, stemming from the victories of Pyrrhus, which were won despite major casualties.

The Punic Wars and Beyond (264–133 B.C.E.)

By 264 B.C.E. Carthage was the unrivaled power of the western Mediterranean. It had created and defended a mercantile empire that stretched from western Sicily to beyond Gibraltar. The battle for Sicily set the stage for the **First Punic** (PYOO-nik) **War** between Rome and Carthage, two powers expanding into the same area. The First Punic War lasted for twenty-three years (264–241 B.C.E.). The Romans quickly learned that they could not conquer Sicily

First Punic War A war between Rome and Carthage that lasted 23 years.

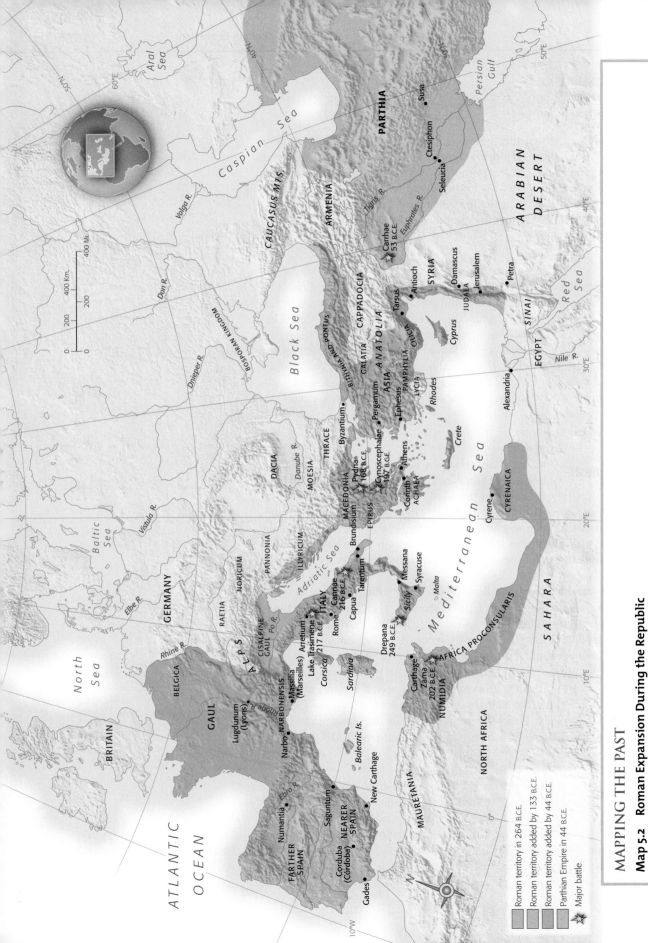

MAPPING THE PAST

Map 5.2 Roman Expansion During the Republic

Previous maps have shown that the Greeks and Macedonians concentrated their energies on opening the East. This map indicates that Rome for the first time looked to the West. **[1]** What does this say about the expansion of Roman power in the Mediterranean? **[2]** What does this foreshadow for the subsequent development of Europe?

Roman territory in 264 B.C.E.

Roman territory added by 133 B.C.E.

Roman territory added by 44 B.C.E.

Parthian Empire in 44 B.C.E.

Major battle

unless they controlled the sea, and so they built a navy. They fought seven major naval battles with the Carthaginians, won six, and finally wore them down. In 241 B.C.E. the Romans took possession of Sicily, which became their first real province.

The peace treaty between the two powers brought no peace, in part because in 238 B.C.E. the Romans took advantage of Carthaginian weakness to seize the islands of Sardinia and Corsica. Unable to resist the Roman move, Carthage looked to Spain to recoup its fortune. In 237 B.C.E. Hamilcar led an army to Spain in order to turn it into Carthaginian territory. With him he took his nineteen-year-old son, Hannibal, but not before he had led Hannibal to an altar and made him swear forever to be an enemy to Rome. In the following years Hamilcar and his son-in-law Hasdrubal (HAS-droo-buhl) rebuilt Carthaginian power. Rome responded in two ways: first, the Romans made a treaty with Hasdrubal in which the Ebro River of Spain formed the boundary between Carthaginian and Roman interests, and second, the Romans began to extend their own influence in Spain.

In 221 B.C.E. the young Hannibal became Carthaginian commander in Spain. When Hannibal laid siege to Saguntum (suh-GOON-tum), which lay within the sphere of Carthaginian interest, the Romans declared war, claiming that Carthage had attacked a friendly city. So began the **Second Punic War.** In 218 B.C.E. Hannibal struck first by marching more than a thousand miles over the Alps into Italy. Once there, he defeated one Roman army at the Battle of Trebia and later another at the Battle of Lake Trasimene. Hannibal won his greatest victory at the Battle of Cannae (KAN-ee), in which he inflicted some forty thousand casualties on the Romans. He then spread devastation throughout Italy, and a number of cities in central and southern Italy rebelled against Rome. Yet Hannibal failed to crush Rome's iron circle of Latium, Etruria, and Samnium. The wisdom of Rome's political policy of extending citizenship to its allies showed itself in these dark hours. And Rome fought back.

In 210 B.C.E. Rome found its answer to Hannibal in the young commander Scipio, later better known as Scipio Africanus. Scipio copied Hannibal's methods of mobile warfare, streamlining the legions by making their components capable of independent action and introducing new weapons. In the following years, Scipio operated in Spain, which in 207 B.C.E. he wrested from the Carthaginians. Also in 207 B.C.E. the Romans sealed Hannibal's fate in Italy. At the Battle of Metaurus, the Romans destroyed a major Carthaginian army coming to reinforce Hannibal. Scipio then struck directly at Carthage itself, prompting the Carthaginians to recall Hannibal from Italy to defend the homeland.

In 202 B.C.E., near the town of Zama (see Map 5.2), Scipio defeated Hannibal in one of the world's truly decisive battles. Scipio's victory meant that the world of the western Mediterranean would henceforth be Roman. The Second Punic War contained the seeds of still other wars. Unabated fear of Carthage led to the Third

Triumphal Column of Caius Duilius

This curious monument celebrates Rome's naval victory, in the First Punic War. In the battle Caius Duilius (KEY-uhs doo-ILL-ee-us) destroyed fifty Carthaginian ships. He then celebrated his success by erecting this column, which portrays the prows of the enemy ships projecting from the column.
(Alinari/Art Resource, NY)

Second Punic War A war fought between Carthage, led by the young Hannibal, and Rome. By the end of the war in 202 B.C.E., Rome was victorious, ensuring that Roman heritage would pass on to the Western world.

Section Review

- Romans established colonies throughout Italy; they incorporated those closest into the Roman state, granting full citizenship, while Italians who lived farther away were considered allies and allowed the right to local self-government.

- The Romans wanted to be free of any state that could threaten them; instead of looking for conquests they acted defensively, such as against Pyrrhus, the Greek king of Epirus, whose army defeated the Romans in several battles, but suffered such losses that the Romans eventually succeeded in driving it out of Italy.

- The First Punic War between Carthage and Rome over control of Sicily became a battle of the sea, which the Romans finally won, gaining Sicily.

- The peace treaty with Carthage did not last and during the Second Punic War, the Carthaginians under Hannibal defeated Rome's legions at Cannae and devastated much of Italy, but were ultimately unable to conquer Rome's power in Latium, Etruria, and Samnium.

- The Roman Scipio Africanus defeated the Carthaginians by attacking Spain and enemy armies in Italy and then Hannibal's army at Zama, while an unnecessary Third Punic War destroyed Carthage and years later Scipio's son Scipio Aemilianus conquered Spain.

- The Romans fought the Macedonians because they had made an alliance with Hannibal and by 133 B.C.E. the Hellenistic kingdoms, Pergamum, and Ptolemaic Egypt fell to Rome.

Punic War, a needless, unjust, and savage conflict that ended in 146 B.C.E. when Scipio Aemilianus (SKIP-ee-oh AY-mil-ee-an-us), grandson of Scipio Africanus, destroyed the old hated rival.

During the war with Hannibal, the Romans had invaded Spain, a peninsula rich in material resources and the home of fierce warriors. When the Roman legions tried to reduce the Spanish tribes, they met with bloody and determined resistance. Not until 133 B.C.E., after years of brutal and ruthless warfare, did Scipio Aemilianus finally conquer Spain.

Rome Turns East (211–133 B.C.E.)

During the Second Punic War, King Philip V of Macedonia made an alliance with Hannibal against Rome. Despite the mortal struggle in the West, the Romans found the strength to turn eastward to settle accounts. Their first significant victory against the Macedonians came in 197 B.C.E. Piece by piece the Hellenistic kingdoms and city-states fell to Rome, first Sparta, then the Seleucid kingdom, the Achaean League, the Macedonian kingdom, and finally, in 133 B.C.E., Pergamum and the Ptolemic kingdom of Egypt.

Old Values and Greek Culture

How did Roman society change during the age of expansion?

Rome had conquered the Mediterranean world, but some Romans considered that victory a misfortune. The historian Sallust (86–34 B.C.E.), writing from hindsight, complained that the acquisition of an empire was the beginning of Rome's troubles: "The Romans had easily borne labor, danger, uncertainty, and hardship. To them leisure, riches—otherwise desirable—proved to be burdens and torments. So at first money, then desire for power grew great. These things were a sort of cause of all evils."[1]

Indeed, in the second century B.C.E. the Romans learned that they could not return to what they fondly considered a simple life. They were world rulers. They had to change their institutions, social patterns, and way of thinking to meet the new era. But in the end Rome triumphed here just as it had on the battlefield, for out of the turmoil of change would come the *pax Romana*—"Roman peace."

How did the Romans of the day meet these challenges? How did they lead their lives and cope with these momentous changes? Obviously there are as many answers to these questions as there were Romans. Yet two men represent the major trends of the second century B.C.E. Cato the Elder shared the mentality of those who longed for the good old days and idealized the traditional agrarian way of life. Scipio Aemilianus led those who embraced the new urban life, with its eager acceptance of Greek culture.

Cato and the Traditional Ideal

Marcus Cato (MAHR-kuhs KAY-toh) (234–149 B.C.E.) was born a plebeian, but his talent and energy carried him to Rome's highest offices. He created an image of himself as the bearer of "traditional" Roman virtues. His description of his life is partly invented, but its details reflect the way many Romans actually lived.

Because of his political aspirations, Cato often walked to the marketplace of the nearby town and defended anyone who wished his help. He received no fees for these services, but in return Cato's clients gave him their political support or their votes whenever he asked for them. This practice of a patron offering his protection in return for support from a client is know as clientage. The notion of clientage was a particularly Roman custom that helped men of lower social status advance themselves and advance the careers of their patrons.

Cato was married, as were almost all Roman citizens. Grooms were generally somewhat older than their brides, who often married in their early teens. There were two types of marriage in Rome, one of which put the woman under control of her husband's family and one of which kept her under her father's control. Each had advantages and disadvantages for women.

Women could inherit property under Roman law, though they generally received a smaller portion of any family inheritance than their brothers did. A woman's inheritance usually came as a dowry on marriage. By the time of Cato, both men and women could initiate divorce. Women appear to have gained greater control over their dowries, perhaps in response to the fact that Rome's military conquests meant that many husbands were away for long periods of time and women needed some say over family finances.

Until the age of seven, children were under their mother's care. During this time the matron began to educate her daughters in the management of the household. After the age of seven, sons—and in many wealthy households daughters too—began to receive formal education. Formal education for wealthy children

Temple of Mater Matuta
This round temple was dedicated to Mater Matuta (**MAY-ter ma-TWO-tah**), a very old Roman mother goddess. Its shape and architectural ornamentation indicate Hellenistic influence. (Vanni/Art Resource, NY)

was generally in the hands of tutors, who were often Greek slaves. By the late republic, there were also a few schools.

The agricultural year followed the sun and the stars—the farmer's calendar. The main money crops, at least for rich soils, were wheat and flax. Forage crops included clover, vetch, and alfalfa. Prosperous farmers like Cato raised olive trees chiefly for the oil. They also raised grapevines for the production of wine. Cato and his neighbors harvested their cereal crops in summer and their grapes in autumn.

An influx of slaves resulted from Rome's wars and conquests. Races were not enslaved because the Romans thought them inferior. The black African slave was treated no worse—and no better—than the Spaniard. For the talented slave the Romans always held out the hope of eventual freedom. **Manumission**—the freeing of individual slaves by their masters—became so common that it was limited by law.

manumission The freeing of individual slaves by their masters.

For Cato and most other Romans, religion played an important part in life. Originally the Romans thought of the gods as invisible, shapeless natural forces. Only through Etruscan and Greek influence did Roman deities take on human form. Jupiter, the sky-god, and his wife Juno became equivalent to the Greek Zeus and Hera. The gods of the Romans were stern, powerful, and aloof. But as long as the Romans honored the cults of their gods, they could expect divine favor. The shrine of the goddess Vesta (**VES-tuh**), for example, was tended by six so-called vestal virgins, chosen from patrician families. Roman military losses were sometimes blamed on inattention by the vestal virgins, a link between female honor and the Roman state.

Along with the great gods the Romans believed in spirits who haunted fields, forests, crossroads, and even the home itself. Some of these deities were hostile; only magic could ward them off. The spirits of the dead, like ghosts in modern horror films, frequented places where they had lived. They too had to be placated but were ordinarily benign. (See the feature "Listening to the Past: A Magic Charm" on pages 105–106.)

Scipio Aemilianus: Greek Culture and Urban Life

The old-fashioned ideals that Cato represented came into conflict with a new urban culture that reflected Hellenistic influences. The spoils of war went to build baths, theaters, and other places of amusement, and Romans and Italian townspeople began to spend more of their time in leisure pursuits. The poet Horace (**HAWR-iss**)

African Acrobat

Conquest and prosperity brought exotic pleasure to Rome. Every feature of this sculpture is exotic. The young African woman and her daring gymnastic pose would catch anyone's attention. And to add to the spice of her act, she performs using a live crocodile as her platform. Americans would have loved it. (Courtesy of the Trustees of the British Museum)

(64–8 B.C.E.) summed it up well: "Captive Greece captured her rough conqueror and introduced the arts into rustic Latium."

One of the most avid devotees of Hellenism and the new was Scipio Aemilianus, the destroyer of Carthage. Scipio realized that broad and worldly views had to replace the old Roman narrowness. Rome was no longer a small city on the Tiber; it was the capital of the world. Scipio broke with the past in the conduct of his political career, choosing a more personal style of politics, one that reflected his own views and looked unflinchingly at the broader problems that the success of Rome brought to its people. Perhaps more than anyone else of his day, Scipio represented the new Roman—imperial, cultured, and independent.

In his education and interests, too, Scipio broke with the past. As a boy he had received the traditional Roman training in Latin and the law. He mastered the fundamentals of rhetoric and learned how to throw the javelin, fight in armor, and ride a horse. But later Scipio also learned Greek and promoted the spread of Hellenism in Roman society. He became the center of the Scipionic (SKIP-ee-ohn-ik) Circle, a small group of Greek and Roman artists, philosophers, historians, and poets. Conservatives like Cato tried to stem the rising tide of Hellenism, but men like Scipio carried the day and helped make the heritage of Greece an abiding factor in Roman life.

The new Hellenism profoundly stimulated the growth and development of Roman art. Soldiers returned from the Hellenistic East with Greek paintings and sculpture to grace Roman temples, public buildings, and private homes. Roman artists copied many aspects of Greek art, but their emphasis on realistic portraiture carried on a native tradition.

Roman Table Manners
This mosaic is a floor that can never be swept clean. It whimsically suggests what a dining room floor looked like after a lavish dinner and also tells something about the menu: a chicken head, a wishbone, and remains of various seafood, vegetables, and fruit are easily recognizable. (Museo Gregoriano Profano, Vatican Museums/Scala/Art Resource, NY)

In literature, the Greek influence was also strong. Fabius Pictor (FAY-bee-us PIK-ter) (second half of the third century B.C.E.), a senator, wrote the first history of Rome in Greek. Other Romans translated Greek classics into Latin. Still others, such as the poet Ennius (EN-ee-us) (239–169 B.C.E.), the father of Latin poetry, adapted many of Euripides' tragedies for the Roman stage. The Roman dramatist Terence (ca. 195–159 B.C.E.), a member of the Scipionic Circle, wrote comedies of refinement and grace that owed their essentials to Greek models. In contrast, Plautus (PLAW-tus) (ca. 254–184 B.C.E.) brought a bawdy humor to his reworkings of Greek plays.

During the second century B.C.E. the Greek custom of bathing also became a Roman passion. Large buildings containing pools and gymnasia went up in great numbers, and the baths became an essential part of the Roman city. They became even more elaborate several centuries later. Architects built intricate systems of aqueducts to supply the bathing establishments with water. Bathing establishments were more than just places to take a bath. They also contained snack bars and halls where people chatted and read and even libraries and lecture halls. The baths were socially important places where men and women went to see and be seen. Social climbers tried to talk to the right people and wangle invitations to dinner; politicians took advantage of the occasion to discuss the affairs of the day; marriages were negotiated by wealthy fathers. Prostitutes added to the attraction of many baths. These women might be slaves, members of the lower classes, or actresses and entertainers who needed more income.

Did Hellenism and new social customs corrupt the Romans? Perhaps the best answer is this: the Roman state and the empire it ruled continued to exist for six more centuries. Rome did not collapse; the state continued to prosper. The golden age of literature was still before it. The high tide of its prosperity still lay in the future.

The Late Republic (133–31 B.C.E.)

What were the main problems and achievements of the late republic?

The wars of conquest created serious problems for the Romans, some of the most pressing of which were political. The republican constitution had suited the needs of a simple city-state but was inadequate to meet the requirements of Rome's new position in international affairs. Officials had to be appointed to govern the provinces and administer the law. These officials and administrative organs had to find places in the constitution. Armies had to be provided for defense, and a system of tax collection had to be created.

Other political problems were equally serious. During the wars Roman generals commanded huge numbers of troops for long periods of time. These men of great power and prestige were on the point of becoming too mighty for the state to control. Although Rome's Italian allies had borne much of the burden of the fighting, they received fewer rewards than did Roman officers and soldiers. Italians began to agitate for full Roman citizenship, including the right to vote. In addition, the armies became weaker as a result of a complex shift in land ownership.

These problems, complex and explosive, largely account for the turmoil of the closing years of the republic. This period produced some of Rome's most famous figures: the Gracchi (GRAK-hi), Marius, Sulla (SUHL-uh), Cicero, Pompey (POM-pee), and Julius Caesar (JOOL-yuhs SEE-zar), among others. In one way or another, each of these men attempted to solve Rome's problems. Yet personal ambition often clashed with patriotism to create political tension throughout the period.

Unrest in Rome and Italy

Hannibal's operations and the warfare in Italy had left the countryside a shambles. The prolonged fighting had also drawn untold numbers of Roman and Italian men away from their farms for long periods. The families of these soldiers could not keep the land under full cultivation.

When the legionaries returned to their farms in Italy, they encountered an appalling situation. All too often their farms looked like the farms of people they had conquered. Two courses of action were open to them. They could rebuild as their forefathers had done, or they could take advantage of a new alternative and sell their holdings to wealthy investors who bought up small farms to create huge estates, which the Romans called **latifundia** (lat-uh-FUHN-dee-uh).

Selling their land appealed to the veterans for a variety of reasons. Many veterans had tasted the rich city life of the Hellenistic states and were reluctant to settle down to a dull life on the farm. Often their farms were so badly damaged that rebuilding hardly seemed worthwhile. Besides, it was hard to make big profits from small farms.

Most veterans migrated to the cities, especially to Rome. Although some found work, most did not. Industry and small manufacturing were generally in the hands of slaves. Even when work was available, slave labor kept the wages of free men low. Instead of a new start, veterans and their families encountered slum conditions.

This trend held ominous consequences for the strength of Rome's armies. The Romans had always believed that only landowners should serve in the army, for only they had something to fight for. Once the war veterans sold their land, they became ineligible for further military service. The landless ex-legionaries wanted a new start, and they were willing to support any leader who would provide it.

One man who recognized the plight of Rome's peasant farmers and urban poor was an aristocrat, Tiberius Gracchus (tie-BEER-ee-uhs GRAK-uhs) (163–133 B.C.E.). Appalled by what he saw, Tiberius scolded his countrymen about the legionaries: "[N]ot a man of them has an hereditary altar, not one of all these many Romans an ancestral tomb, but they fight and die to support others in luxury, and though they are styled masters of the world, they have not a single clod of earth that is their own."[2]

After his election as tribune in 133 B.C.E., Tiberius proposed that public land be given to the poor in small lots. Although his reform enjoyed the support of some very distinguished and popular aristocrats, it angered those who had usurped large tracts of public land for their own use. They had no desire to give any of it back, so they bitterly resisted Tiberius's efforts. This was to be expected, yet he made additional problems for himself. He introduced his land bill in the concilium plebis without consulting the senate. When King Attalus III left the kingdom of Pergamum to the Romans in his will, Tiberius had the money appropriated to finance his reforms—another slap at the senate. A large body of senators, led by the *pontifex maximus* (the chief priest), decided to kill Tiberius in cold blood. It was a black day in Roman history. The very people who directed the affairs of state and administered the law had taken the law into their own hands. The death of Tiberius was the beginning of an era of political violence. In the end that violence would bring down the republic.

Although Tiberius was dead, his land bill became law. Furthermore, Tiberius's brother Gaius Gracchus (GEY-uhs GRAK-uhs) (153–121 B.C.E.) also became tribune and demanded even more extensive reform than had his brother. To help the urban poor Gaius pushed legislation to provide them with cheap grain for bread. He defended his brother's land law and proposed that Rome send many of its poor and propertyless people out to form colonies in southern Italy. Gaius even went so far as to urge that all Italians be granted full rights of Roman citizenship.

latifundia Huge Roman estates created by buying up several small farms.

This measure provoked a storm of opposition, and it was not passed in Gaius's lifetime. Had the senate listened to Gaius, it could have prevented a later bloody conflict known as the Social War (91–88 B.C.E.). Yet like his brother Tiberius, Gaius aroused a great deal of personal opposition. To many he seemed too radical; political opponents considered him belligerent and headstrong. When Gaius failed in 121 B.C.E. to win the tribunate for the third time, he feared for his life. In desperation he armed his staunchest supporters, whereupon the senate ordered the consul Opimius to restore order. Opimius did so by having Gaius killed, along with three thousand of his supporters who opposed the senate's order. Once again the cause of reform had met with violence.

The death of Gaius brought little peace, and trouble came from two sources: the outbreak of new wars in the Mediterranean basin and further political unrest in Rome. For five years, the Roman legions made little headway against the rebellious North African kingdom of Jugurtha (**joo-GUR-thuh**). Then in 107 B.C.E. Gaius Marius (**GEY-uhs MAIR-ee-uhs**), an Italian new man (a politician not from the traditional Roman aristocracy), became consul. Marius's values were those of the military camp. He took the unusual but not wholly unprecedented step of recruiting an army by permitting landless men to serve in the legions. In 106 B.C.E. Marius and his new army handily defeated Jugurtha.

An unexpected war broke out in the following year when two groups of German peoples moved into Gaul and later into northern Italy. After the Germans had defeated Roman armies sent to repel them, Marius was again elected consul, even though he was legally ineligible. From 104 to 100 B.C.E. Marius annually held the consulship, putting unprecedented power into a Roman commander's hands.

Before engaging the Germans, Marius encouraged enlistments by promising his volunteers land after the war. Poor and landless veterans flocked to him, and together they conquered the Germans by 101 B.C.E. When Marius proposed a bill to grant land to his veterans, the senate refused to act, in effect turning its back on the soldiers of Rome. It was a disastrous mistake. Henceforth the legionaries expected the commanders—not the senate or the state—to protect their interests.

Another strong general, Sulla, was elected to consul in 88 B.C.E. after putting down the Italian allies in the Social War. While Sulla was away from Rome fighting the last of the rebels, factions agitating on behalf of Marius had him deposed from his consulship. He immediately marched on Rome and restored order, but it was an ominous sign of the deterioration of Roman politics and political ideals. Order restored, Sulla in 88 B.C.E. led an army to Asia Minor where Roman rule was being challenged. In Sulla's absence, rioting and political violence again exploded in Rome. Marius and his supporters marched on Rome and launched a reign of terror.

Although Marius died shortly after his return to power, his supporters continued to hold Rome. Sulla returned in 82 B.C.E., and after a brief but intense civil war, he entered Rome and ordered a ruthless butchery of his opponents. He also proclaimed himself dictator. He launched many political and judicial reforms, including strengthening the senate while weakening the tribunate, and he voluntarily abdicated his dictatorship in 79 B.C.E. Yet Sulla the political reformer proved far less influential than Sulla the successful general and dictator. Civil war was to be the constant lot of Rome for the next fifty years, until the republican constitution gave way to the empire of Augustus (**aw-GUHS-tuhs**) in 27 B.C.E. (See the feature "Individuals in Society: Quintus Sertorius (**KWIN-tuhs ser-TAWR-ee-uhs**).")

One figure who stands apart from the struggles of the late Republic is Cicero (106–43 B.C.E.), a practical politician whose greatest legacy to the Roman world

Individuals in Society

Quintus Sertorius

Quintus Sertorius (126–73 B.C.E.), son of a prominent Italian family, stands as an example of a Roman leader caught up in the political and military upheavals of the day. He became a rebel against Rome while bringing Roman influences to the province of Spain. Sertorius launched his public career in Rome, where he mastered Roman law and became a gifted military officer. When two barbarian tribes invaded Gaul in 105 B.C.E., he fought so effectively that his ability and valor brought him to the attention of senior Roman military commanders. These events honed his martial skills and acquainted him with the new peoples gradually entering western Europe.

Sertorius's success in Gaul led him in 97 B.C.E. to higher command in Spain. From that time until his death, his destiny and Spain's would be intertwined. He, like Marius, Sulla, and other notable men, was swept up in this vast and chaotic episode in republican history. He chose the wrong side and upon defeat fled to Spain, where he worked to establish his own independent authority.

A surprising accident put another tool of authority into Sertorius's hands. As the story goes, one of his soldiers, while hunting, encountered a white fawn and presented it to Sertorius. Sertorius declared that the animal was the gift of Diana whose attributes included the gifts of wisdom and prophecy. This divine endorsement enhanced his authority among the Spaniards.

The Roman civil war soon reached Spain. Sertorius's reputation and exploits persuaded many Spaniards to invite him to lead them against the Romans. As commander, he trained Spanish troops in Roman military tactics. His army's success prompted many Romans to switch sides. Even some senators left Rome to join him. Welcoming them with honor, he got them involved in the civil government that he introduced. Sertorius mod-

eled his Spanish state along Roman civil lines but under his leadership. Spain had never seen so many military, cultural, and civil developments in such a short time.

The Romans to whom he had bestowed a home began to insult, punish, and abuse the Spaniards while doing everything possible to thwart Sertorius's plans. Then they rebelled against him, hoping either to topple him and reign in his place or to return the province to Roman rule. Finally, with a treachery that matched that of the conspirators against Caesar, some Romans who were still considered loyal assassinated Sertorius at a banquet in 73 B.C.E. Roman generals from the East easily took control of Spain.

Death and defeat did not erase Sertorius's achievements in Spain. He introduced the region to Greco-Roman culture. He gave the land and its peoples a civil government that united them. He turned their tribal hordes into an army along Roman lines. He paved the way for peaceful Spanish inclusion into the quickly evolving Roman Empire.

This statue of Quintus Sertorius still bears testimony to Rome's respect for his efforts to unite Romans and Spaniards.
(Courtesy, Luca Bonacina)

Questions for Analysis

1. How did Sertorius create a state in Spain?
2. What was his legacy to Spain, Rome, and Western civilization in general?

and to Western civilization is his mass of political and oratorical writings. Yet Cicero commanded no legions, and only legions commanded respect.

First Triumvirate A political alliance between Caesar, Crassus, and Pompey in which they agreed to advance one another's interests.

Section Review

- The Roman countryside suffered greatly from the prolonged fighting and much of the farmland was in shambles, so returning legionaries often sold their farms to wealthy investors who created huge estates called latifundia.

- Tiberius Gracchus and later his brother Gaius sought land reform for the poor but aristocrats and the senate opposed them vigorously, eventually having them both killed.

- Gaius Marius became consul and gained power by allowing non-landowners into the army and promising them land after the war, but when the senate did not approve this plan, the legionaries turned their allegiance to their commanders, not the senate or state, for protection.

- In the following years, another general, Sulla, was elected consul and fought against Marius for control of Rome, proclaimed himself dictator and introduced many political and judicial reforms before voluntarily abdicating his dictatorship in 79 B.C.E.

- Sulla's political heirs were Pompey, Crassus, and Julius Caesar who formed the First Triumvirate and agreed to help each other, but following Crassus' death Pompey and Caesar suspected each other of treason and fought a bloody civil war.

- Caesar allied with Egypt's Cleopatra, defeating Pompey's forces, and made himself dictator before his assassination, which left his grandnephew Octavian (later called Augustus) and two lieutenants, Marc Antony and Lepidus, to form the Second Triumvirate, avenging Caesar.

- Octavian (Augustus) defeated Antony and Cleopatra in the naval battle of Actium (31 B.C.E.), after which the couple committed suicide, leaving Augustus to rule the entire Roman world.

Civil War

Sulla's real political heirs were Pompey and Julius Caesar, with at least Caesar realizing that the days of the old republican constitution were numbered. Pompey, a man of boundless ambition, began his career as one of Sulla's lieutenants. After his army put down a rebellion in Spain, he himself threatened to rebel unless the senate allowed him to run for consul. He and another ambitious politician, Crassus (KRAS-uhs), pooled political resources, and both won the consulship. They dominated Roman politics until the rise of Julius Caesar, who became consul in 59 B.C.E. Together the three concluded a political alliance, the **First Triumvirate** (try-UHM-ver-it), in which they agreed to advance one another's interests.

The man who cast the longest shadow over these troubled years was Julius Caesar (100–44 B.C.E.). Born of a noble family, he received an excellent education, which he furthered by studying in Greece with some of the most eminent teachers of the day. Caesar was a superb orator, and his affable personality and wit made him popular. Caesar launched his military career in Spain, where his courage won the respect and affection of his troops.

In 58 B.C.E. Caesar became governor of Cisalpine Gaul (sis-AL-pine gawl), or modern northern Italy. By 50 B.C.E. he had conquered all of Gaul, or modern France. By 49 B.C.E. the First Triumvirate had fallen apart. Crassus had died in battle, and Caesar and Pompey, each suspecting the other of treachery, came to blows. The result was a long and bloody civil war that raged from Spain across northern Africa to Egypt.

Egypt, meanwhile, was embroiled in a battle for control between brother and sister, Ptolemy XIII and Cleopatra (klee-uh-PA-truh) VII (69–30 B.C.E.). Cleopatra first allied herself with Pompey but then switched her alliance to Caesar. The two became lovers as well as allies, and she bore him a son. She returned to Rome with Caesar, but was hated by the Roman people as a symbol of the immoral East.

Although Pompey enjoyed the official support of the government, Caesar finally defeated Pompey's forces in 45 B.C.E. He had overthrown the republic and made himself dictator.

Julius Caesar was not merely another victorious general. He was determined to make basic reforms, even at the expense of the old constitution. He extended citizenship to many of the provincials who had supported him. He also founded at least twenty colonies, most of which were located in Gaul, Spain, and North Africa, in part to cope with

Julius Caesar

In this bust, the sculptor portrays Caesar as a man of power and intensity. It is a study of determination and an excellent example of Roman portraiture. (Museo Archeologico Nazionale Naples/Scala/Art Resource, NY)

Rome's burgeoning population. These colonies were important agents in spreading Roman culture in the western Mediterranean.

In 44 B.C.E. a group of conspirators assassinated Caesar and set off another round of civil war. Caesar had named his eighteen-year-old grandnephew, Octavian (ok-TAY-vee-uhn)—or Augustus, as he is better known to history—as his heir. Augustus joined forces with two of Caesar's lieutenants, Marc Antony and Lepidus (LEP-ee-dus), in a pact known as the **Second Triumvirate,** and together they hunted down and defeated Caesar's murderers. In the process, however, Augustus and Antony came into conflict.

In 41 B.C.E. Antony met Cleopatra, who had returned to Egypt after Julius Caesar's assassination. Though Antony was already married to Augustus's sister Octavia, he became Cleopatra's lover. Antony repudiated Octavia, married Cleopatra, and changed his will to favor his children by Cleopatra. Romans turned against Antony as a traitor and a weakling, and in 31 B.C.E. Augustus defeated the army and navy of Cleopatra and Antony at the battle of Actium in Greece. The two committed suicide. This victory put an end to an age of civil war that had lasted since the days of Sulla.

Second Triumvirate A pact between Augustus and two of Caesar's lieutenants, Marc Antony and Lepidus; together they hunted down and defeated Caesar's murderers.

Chapter Review

How did the Etruscans shape early Roman history? (page 86)

The land of Italy proved kinder to the Romans and their neighbors than did the peninsula of Hellas to the Greeks. The newcomers settled comfortably on the seven hills of Rome by the banks of the Tiber River. They came into contact with the Etruscans, who had settled in Italy before their arrival. Separate villages soon merged into one city, creating a single community. Under the governance of the more politically and socially advanced Etruscans, the Romans fully entered the wider world around them.

What was the nature of the Roman republic? (page 89)

Once established, the Romans created an advanced and flexible political constitution of their own. Their society fell into two principal groups: the aristocratic patricians who led the community and the commoners (plebeians) who made up the rest of the citizenry and filled the ranks of the army. The conflict between these two basic social groups resulted in the Struggle of the Orders, which led to greater rights for the plebeians.

How did the Romans take control of the Mediterranean world? (page 91)

From these beginnings the Romans spread their power and influence through the rest of Italy. Beginning as conquerors, the Romans learned to use alliances and political agreements to unite their efforts with those of other Italian communities to create a common policy. They put this association on a formal political basis to create a government shared by Romans and non-Romans. Looking beyond Italy, the Romans fought three hard wars with the Carthaginians, their Punic neighbors in North Africa. In the process they included the Greeks of southern Italy in their growing empire. As these wars spread to western Europe, the Romans won control of Spain and Gaul (modern France). Further warfare next took them eastward into the Hellenistic world. Conquest followed conquest to create the nucleus of the Roman Empire.

Key Terms
toga (p. 87)
forum (p. 87)
Gauls (p. 87)
franchise (p. 88)
patricians (p. 89)
plebeians (p. 89)
consuls (p. 89)
senate (p. 89)
natural law (p. 90)
Struggle of the Orders (p. 90)
tribunes (p. 90)
paterfamilias (p. 90)
Pyrrhic victory (p. 91)
First Punic War (p. 91)
Second Punic War (p. 93)
manumission (p. 96)
latifundia (p. 99)
First Triumvirate (p. 102)
Second Triumvirate (p. 103)

How did Roman society change during the age of expansion? (page 94)

These tumultuous events fundamentally reshaped Roman society. Though some Romans longed for what they saw as simpler times, many were dazzled by Hellenistic sophistication and ways of life. They learned to appreciate the arts and intellectual pursuits of the older Greek and Eastern cultures. They joined fully the broad cultural world of the Mediterranean, all the while making their own contribution.

What were the main problems and achievements of the late republic? (page 98)

In some ways the Romans had moved too far and too fast from their small beginnings. Their empire had become too big for them to manage easily. Their constitution and political institutions could no longer adequately cope with the burdens and pressures that imperial life brought. After a series of bloody civil wars, the general Octavian, soon to be more generally known as Augustus, restored order and forever changed the nature of Roman life and government.

Notes

1. Sallust, *War with Catiline* 10.1–3. John Buckler is the translator of all uncited quotations from a foreign language in Chapters 1–6.
2. Plutarch, *Life of Tiberius Gracchus* 9.5–6.

To assess your mastery of this chapter, go to **bedfordstmartins.com/mckaywestbrief**

Listening to the Past

A Magic Charm

The pursuit of love has one of the oldest histories in the world. When their own efforts failed, lovers of the past might turn to magic to win the hearts of the beloved. The following text of a love charm comes from a papyrus found in Egypt and dates from the period of the Roman Empire. The applicant, in this case a man, asks the spirits of the underworld to assist him.

Take wax [or clay] from a potter's wheel and form two figures, one male and one female. Make the male one look like Ares in arms, holding a sword in his left hand and pointing it at her right collarbone. Her arms must be (tied) behind her back, and she must kneel. Fasten the magical substance on her head or neck. On the figure of the woman you want to attract write as follows. On the head: ISEE IAO ITHI OUNE BRIDO LOTHION NEBOUTOSOUALETH. On the right ear: OUER MECHAN. On the left: LIBABA OIMATHOTHO. On the face: AMOUNABREO. On the right eye: ORORMOTHIO AETH. On the right arm: ENE PSA ENESGAPH. On the other: MELCHIOU MELCHIEDA. On the hands: MELCHAMELCHOU AEL. On the breast write the name, on her mother's side, of the woman you want to attract. On the heart: BALAMIN THOOUTH. Under the abdomen: AOBES AOBAR. On her sexual organs: BLICHIANEOI OUOIA. On her buttocks: PISSADARA. On the sole of the right foot: ELO. On the other: ELOAIOE. Take thirteen bronze needles and stick one in the brain and say: "I am piercing your brain, NN." Stick two in the ears, two in the eyes, one in the mouth, two in the midriff, one in the hands, two in the genital organs, two in the soles, saying each time: "I am piercing such and such a member of NN, so that she may remember me, NN alone." Take a lead tablet and write on it the same formula and recite it. Tie the lead leaf [i.e., the lead tablet] to the two creatures with thread from the loom after making three hundred sixty-five knots, saying, as you have learned: "Abrasax, hold her fast." As the sun is setting, you must place it near the tomb of a person who has died an untimely or a violent death, along with the flowers of the season.

The formula to be written and recited: "I am handing over this binding spell to you, gods of the underworld, HYESEMIGADON and KORE PEERSEPHONE ERESCHIGAL and ADONIS, the BARBARITHA, chthonic HERMES THOOUTH PHOKENTAZEPSEU AERCHTHATOUMI SONKTAI KALBANACHAMRE and to mighty ANUBIS PSIRINTH who has the keys to the realm of Hades, to gods and daemons of the underworld, to men and women who have died before their time, to young men and women, from year to year, from month to month, from day to day, from hour to hour. I adjure all the daemons in this place to assist this daemon. Arouse yourself for me, whoever you are, male or female, and enter every place, every neighborhood, every house, and attract and bind,

Amulet of Abrasax, the demon with the head of a cock, the body of a Roman soldier, feet of snakes, and whip in the right hand. This amulet protected against other demons.
(Kelsey Museum of Archaeology, University of Michigan, KM 26054)

attract NN, daughter of NN, whose magical substance you have. Make NN, daughter of NN be in love with me. Let her not have sexual intercourse with another man, . . . let her not have pleasure with another man, only with me, NN, so that she, NN, is unable to drink or eat, to love, to be strong, to be healthy, to enjoy sleep, NN without me. . . . Yes, drag her, NN, by her hair, by her heart, by her soul to me, NN, every hour of life [or: eternity], night and day, until she comes to me, NN, and let her, NN, remain inseparable from me. Do this, bind her for all the time of my life and force her, NN, to be my, NN, servant, and let her not flutter away from me for even one hour of life [or: eter-nity]. If you accomplish this for me, I will let you rest at once.

Questions for Analysis

1. How does this magical charm invoke the help of the gods?

2. Does the woman he seeks favor him, or is she reluctant?

3. Is the charm to entice love or to force submission?

CHAPTER 6

The Pax Romana

31 B.C.E.–450 C.E.

Hadrian's Wall. (Sandro Vannini/Corbis)

Chapter Preview

Augustus's Settlement (31 B.C.E–14 C.E.)
How did Augustus transform the Roman Empire?

The Coming of Christianity
Why did Christianity, originally a minor local religion, sweep across the Roman world to change it fundamentally?

Augustus's Successors
How did Augustus's successors build on his foundation to enhance Roman power and stability?

Life in the "Golden Age"
What was life like in the city of Rome in the "golden age," and what was it like in the provinces?

Rome in Disarray and Recovery (177–450 C.E.)
What factors led Rome into political and economic chaos, and how and to what extent did it recover?

INDIVIDUALS IN SOCIETY: Bithus, a Typical Roman Soldier

IMAGES IN SOCIETY: The Roman Villa at Chedworth

LISTENING TO THE PAST: Rome Extends Its Citizenship

H{ad the Romans conquered the entire Mediterranean world only to turn it into their battlefield? Would they, like the Greeks before them, become their own worst enemies, destroying one another and wasting their strength until they perished? At Julius Caesar's death in 44 B.C.E., it must have seemed so to many. Yet finally, in 31 B.C.E., Augustus restored peace to a tortured world, and with peace came prosperity, new hope, and a new vision of Rome's destiny. The Roman poet Virgil (**VUR-juhl**) expressed this vision most nobly:

> You, Roman, remember—these are your arts:
> To rule nations, and to impose the ways of peace,
> To spare the humble and to wear down the proud.[1]

pax Romana A period during the first and second centuries C.E. of security, order, harmony, flourishing culture, and expanding economy.

Augustus created the structure that the modern world calls the "Roman Empire." For the first and second centuries C.E., the lot of the Mediterranean world was the Roman peace—the **pax Romana** (**paks ro-MAN-ah**), a period of security, order, harmony, flourishing culture, and expanding economy and territory. By the third century C.E., Rome and its culture had left an indelible mark on the ages to come.

Augustus's Settlement (31 B.C.E.–14 C.E.)
How did Augustus transform the Roman Empire?

When Augustus put an end to the civil wars that had raged since 88 B.C.E., he faced monumental problems of reconstruction. The first problem facing him was to rebuild the constitution and the organs of government. Next he had to demobilize much of the army yet maintain enough soldiers to protect the European frontiers. Augustus was highly successful in meeting these challenges. His gift of peace to a war-torn world ushered in the Golden Age of Latin literature.

The Principate and the Restored Republic

In an inscription known as the *Res Gestae* (The Deeds of Augustus), Augustus claimed that he had restored the republic after regaining the peace:

> In my sixth and seventh consulships [28–27 B.C.E.], I had ended the civil war, having obtained through universal consent total control of affairs. I transferred the Republic from my power to the authority of the Roman people and the senate. . . . After that time I stood before all in rank, but I had power no greater than those who were my colleagues in any magistracy.[2]

constitutional monarchy A monarchy in which the power of the ruler is restricted by the constitution and the laws of the nation.

princeps A title meaning "First Citizen" that later came to mean "prince," in the sense of a sovereign ruler.

principate Position of the emperor resulting fom the combination of his consular and tribunician powers.

He took the title of *princeps civitatis* (**prin-SEPS civ-ee-TAT-is**), "First Citizen of the State," a title that carried no power but that indicated that he was the most distinguished of all Roman citizens. Yet despite his claims, Augustus had not restored the republic. He had created a **constitutional monarchy**, something completely new in Roman history. The title **princeps**, "First Citizen," came to mean in Rome, as it does today, "prince" in the sense of a sovereign ruler. The period of the First Citizen came to be known as the **principate.**

Augustus's genius was to gather power while operating within the structure of the republic. As consul he had no more constitutional and legal power than his fellow consul. Yet in addition to the consulship Augustus had many other magistracies, which his fellow consul did not. Constitutionally, his ascendancy within the state stemmed from the number of magistracies he held and the power granted him by the senate. At first he held the consulship annually; then the senate voted him proconsular power on a regular basis. The senate also voted him the "full power of the tribunes," which gave him the right to call the senate into session, present legislation to the people, and defend their rights. He held either high office or the powers of chief magistrate year in and year out. No other magistrate could do the same. In 12 B.C.E. he became *pontifex maximus* (PAHN-tih-fex MAX-ih-muhs), the chief priest of the state. By assuming this position of great honor, Augustus also became chief religious official.

The main source of Augustus's power was his position as commander of the Roman army. He made a momentous change in the army by turning it into Rome's first permanent, professional force. Soldiers received standard training under career officers who advanced in rank according to experience, ability, and valor. Augustus controlled the deployment of troops and paid their wages, bonuses, and retirement benefits. His title **imperator** (im-puh-RAH-ter), with which Rome customarily honored a general after a major victory, came to mean "emperor" in the modern sense of the term. The army was loyal to the imperator but not necessarily the state.

This arrangement worked well at first, but by the third century C.E. the army would make and break emperors at will. Nonetheless, it is a measure of Augustus's success that his settlement survived as long as it did.

27 B.C.E.–68 C.E.	Julio-Claudian emperors; expansion into northern and western Europe; growth and stability of trade in the empire
17 B.C.E.–17 C.E.	Flowering of Latin literature
ca. 3 B.C.E.–29 C.E.	Life of Jesus
ca. 30–312 C.E.	Spread of Christianity
41–54 C.E.	Creation of the imperial bureaucracy
60–120 C.E.	Composition of the New Testament
69–96 C.E.	Consolidation of the European frontiers
96–180 C.E.	"Golden age" of prosperity and huge expansion of trade
96–180 C.E.	"Five good emperors"; increasing barbarian menace on the frontiers
193–284 C.E.	Military monarchy; extension of citizenship to all free men
278–337 C.E.	Steady spread of administration, government, and law from Britain to Syria
284–337 C.E.	Inflation and decline of trade and industry; transition to the Middle Ages in the West and the Byzantine Empire in the East
337 C.E.	Baptism of Constantine

Roman Expansion into Northern and Western Europe

Augustus initially used the army to expand the Roman Empire into northern and western Europe (see Map 6.1). First he completed the conquest of Spain. In Gaul, he founded twelve new towns, and the Roman road system linked new settlements with one another and with Italy. But the German frontier, along the Rhine River, was the scene of hard fighting. Roman legions advanced to the Elbe River, and the area north of the Main River and west of the Elbe was on the point of becoming Roman. But in 9 C.E. Augustus's general Varus lost some twenty thousand troops at the Battle of the Teutoburger (two-TO-burg-er) Forest. Thereafter the Rhine remained the Roman frontier.

Meanwhile Roman legions penetrated the area of modern Austria, southern Bavaria, and western Hungary. The regions of modern Serbia, Bulgaria, and Romania fell. Within this area the legionaries built fortified camps linked by roads, and settlements grew up around the camps. Traders began to frequent the frontier and to traffic with the native peoples, who adopted those aspects of Roman culture that fit in with their own way of life. Eventually provincial towns were granted Roman citizenship if they embraced Roman culture and government and were important to the Roman economy. (See the feature "Listening to the Past: Rome Extends Its Citizenship" on pages 131–132.)

On the other hand, the arrival of the Romans often provoked resistance from tribes of peoples who were not Greco-Roman. Romans generally referred to such

imperator A title that usually honored a general after a major victory, it came to mean "emperor."

Augustus as Imperator

Here Augustus, dressed in breastplate and uniform, emphasizes the imperial majesty of Rome and his role as imperator. The figures on his breastplate represent the restoration of peace, one of Augustus's greatest accomplishments and certainly one that he frequently stressed. (Erich Lessing/Art Resource, NY)

barbarians Tribes of people who were not Greco-Roman and who simply wanted to be left alone.

people as **barbarians,** a word derived from a Greek word for those who did not speak Greek. The Romans maintained peaceful relations with the barbarians whenever possible, but their legions remained on the frontier to repel hostile barbarians.

Literary Flowering and Social Changes

Augustus and many of his friends actively encouraged poets and writers, and indeed the period has become known as the golden age of Latin literature. Roman poets and prose writers celebrated the dignity of humanity and the range of its accomplishments. They stressed the physical and emotional joys of a comfortable, peaceful life. Their works were elegant in style and intellectual in conception.

Rome's greatest poet was Virgil (0–19 B.C.E.), a sensitive man who delighted in simple things. Virgil left in his *Georgics* a charming picture of life in the Italian countryside during a period of peace. His masterpiece is the *Aeneid* (uh-NEE-id), an epic poem that is the Latin equivalent of the Greek *Iliad* and *Odyssey*. Virgil's account of the founding of Rome and the early years of the city gave final form to the legend of Aeneas, a Trojan hero who escaped to Italy at the fall of Troy. The legend of Aeneas (ah-NEE-uhs) was a third story about the founding of Rome, along with those of Romulus and the rape of Lucretia (see page 87). As Virgil told it, Aeneas became the lover of Dido (DIE-doh), the widowed queen of Carthage, but left her because his destiny called him to found Rome. She committed suicide, and their relationship eventually became the cause of the Punic Wars. In leaving Dido, an "Eastern" queen, Aeneas put the good of the state ahead of marriage or pleasure; the parallels between this story and the real events involving Antony and Cleopatra were not lost on Virgil's audience. This fit well with Augustus's aims; he had encouraged Virgil to write the *Aeneid* and made sure it was published immediately after Virgil died.

The poet Ovid (OV-id) [43 B.C.E.–17? C.E.] shared Virgil's views of the simple pleasures of life and also celebrated the popular culture of the day. In his *Fasti* (FAS-tee) (ca. 8 C.E.) he explains the ordinary festivals of the Roman year, and his work offers modern readers a rare glimpse of Roman life and religion.

The historian Livy (LIV-ee) (59 B.C.E.–17 C.E.) approved of Augustus's efforts to restore republican virtues. Livy's 142-book history of Rome, titled simply *Ab Urbe Condita* (*From the Founding of the City*), began with the legend of Aeneas and ended with the reign of Augustus. His theme of the republic's greatness complemented Augustus's program of restoring the republic.

The poet Horace (65–8 B.C.E.) rose from humble beginnings as the son of an ex-slave to friendship with Augustus. He loved Greek literature and finished his

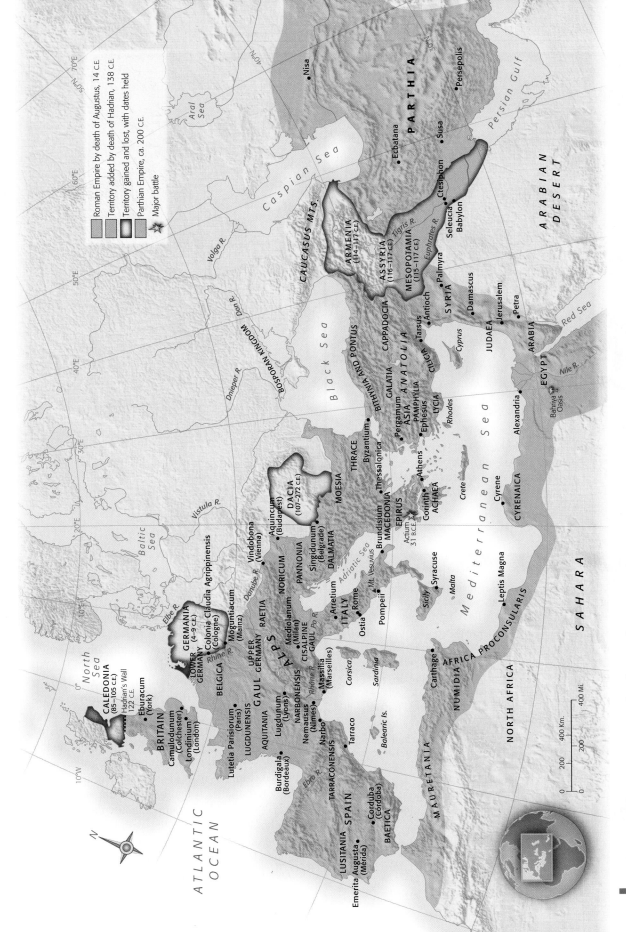

MAP 6.1   Roman Expansion Under the Empire

Following Roman expansion during the republic, Augustus added vast tracts of Europe to the Roman Empire, which the emperor Hadrian later enlarged by assuming control over parts of central Europe, the Near East, and North Africa.

Legend:

- Roman Empire by death of Augustus, 14 C.E.
- Territory added by death of Hadrian, 138 C.E.
- Territory gained and lost, with dates held
- Parthian Empire, ca. 200 C.E.
- ★ Major battle

Scale: 0   200   400 Km. / 0   200   400 Mi.

Ara Pacis

This scene from the Ara Pacis, the Altar of Peace erected in Rome by Augustus, celebrates Augustus's restoration of peace and imperial family values. On this side, Mother Earth is depicted with twin babies on her lap, framed by nymphs representing land and sea. The sheep and the cow are both agricultural and sacrificial animals. Other sides of the altar show Romulus and Remus (another set of twins) and Augustus and his wife Livia in traditional Roman clothing. (Scala/Art Resource, NY)

Section Review

- Augustus rebuilt the government to restore the republic and gained power by holding many magistracies and eventually becoming *"pontifex maximus,"* the chief priest of the state and the chief religious official.

- Augustus's real power came as commander of the Roman army, which he controlled as imperator (emperor) and made into a professional organization with standard training wages and advancement opportunities.

- The army completed the conquest of Spain and Gaul but was turned back at the Rhine on the German frontier; next they took Serbia, Bulgaria, and Romania, linking settlements with roads and trading with the natives.

- The golden age of literature celebrated humanity, peace, and comfort as Rome's greatest poet Virgil told the story of the founding of Rome in his epic, the *Aeneid.*

- Augustus promoted marriage and childbearing by releasing women from male guardianship if they gave birth to a certain number of children, by declaring adultery a crime, and by setting up his own family as a model.

- Augustus solved the problem of a legal successor by sharing his powers and wealth with his adopted son, Tiberius; the senate requested that Tiberius be the next ruler of the principate.

education in Athens. After Augustus's victory he returned to Rome and became Virgil's friend. Horace happily turned his pen to celebrating Rome and Augustus.

Concern with morality and traditional Roman virtues was a matter for law as well as literature. Augustus promoted marriage and childbearing through legal changes that released free women and freedwomen (female slaves who had been freed) from male guardianship if they had given birth to a certain number of children. Men and women who were unmarried or had no children were restricted in the inheritance of property. Adultery, defined as sex with a married woman or a woman under male guardianship, was made a crime, not simply the private family matter it had been. In imperial propaganda, Augustus had his own family depicted as a model of traditional morality, with his wife Livia at his side dressed in conservative and somewhat old-fashioned clothing rather than the more daring Greek styles of the time.

The solidity of Augustus's work became obvious at his death in 14 C.E. Since the principate was not technically an office, Augustus could not legally hand it to a successor. Augustus recognized this problem and long before his death had found a way to solve it. He shared his consular and tribunician powers with his adopted son, Tiberius, thus grooming him for the principate. In his will Augustus left most of his vast fortune to Tiberius, and the senate formally requested Tiberius to assume the burdens of the principate. Formalities apart, Augustus had succeeded in creating a dynasty.

The Coming of Christianity

Why did Christianity, originally a minor local religion, sweep across the Roman world to change it fundamentally?

During the reign of the emperor Tiberius (14–37 C.E.), in the Roman province created out of the Jewish kingdom of Judah, Jesus of Nazareth preached, attracted a following, and was executed on the order of the Roman prefect Pontius Pilate. Much contemporary scholarship has attempted to understand who Jesus was and what he meant by his teachings. Views vary widely. Some see him as a visionary and a teacher, others as a magician and a prophet, and still others as a rebel and a revolutionary. The search for the historical Jesus is complicated by many factors. One is the difference between history and faith. History relies on proof for its conclusions; faith depends on belief. Thus, whether Jesus is divine or not is not an issue to be decided by historians. Their role is to understand him in his religious, cultural, social, and historical context.

Unrest in Judaea

The civil wars that destroyed the Roman republic had extended as far as Judaea in the eastern Mediterranean. Jewish leaders took sides in the conflict, and Judaea suffered its share of violence and looting. Although Augustus restored stability, his appointed king for Judaea, Herod (r. 37–4 B.C.E.), was hated by the Jews. Upon Herod's death, the Jews revolted, and Herod's successor waged almost constant war against the rebels. Added to the horrors of this war were years of famine and plague.

Among the Jews two movements spread. First was the rise of the Zealots (ZEL-uhts), extremists who fought to rid Judaea of the Romans. The second movement was the growth of militant **apocalypticism**—the belief that the coming of the **Messiah** (mi-SIGH-uh) was near. The Messiah would destroy the Roman legions, and all the kingdoms that had ruled Israel, and then inaugurate a period of happiness and plenty for the Jews.

The pagan world of Rome is also part of the story of early Christianity. The term **pagans** (PAY-gans) refers to all those who believed in the Greco-Roman gods. Paganism at the time of Jesus' birth can be broadly divided into three spheres: the official state religion of Rome, the traditional Roman cults of hearth and countryside, and the new mystery religions that flowed from the Hellenistic East (see Chapter 4). The mystery religions gave their adherents what neither the state religion nor traditional cults could—the promise of immortality. Yet the mystery religions were by nature exclusive, and none was truly international, open to everyone.

apocalypticism The belief that the coming of the Messiah was near.

Messiah The savior of Israel.

pagans All those who believed in the Greco-Roman gods.

The Life and Teachings of Jesus

Into this climate of Jewish Messianic hope and Roman religious yearning came Jesus of Nazareth (ca. 3 B.C.E.– 29 C.E.). He was raised in Galilee, stronghold of the Zealots. The principal evidence for the life and deeds of Jesus are the four Gospels of the New Testament. These Gospels—the word means "good news"—are records of his teachings and religious doctrines with certain details of his life. The earliest Gospels were written some seventy-five years after his death, and there are discrepancies among the four accounts. These differences indicate that early Christians had a diversity of beliefs about Jesus' nature and purpose. Only slowly, as the Christian church became an institution, were lines drawn more clearly between what was considered correct teaching and what was considered incorrect, or **heresy** (HER-uh-see).

heresy Incorrect teachings within the Christian church.

Despite this diversity, there were certain things about Jesus' teachings that almost all the sources agree on: he preached of a heavenly kingdom, one of eternal happiness in a life after death. His teachings were essentially Jewish. His orthodoxy enabled him to preach in the synagogue and the temple. His major deviation from orthodoxy was his insistence that he taught in his own name, not in the name of Yahweh. Was he then the Messiah? A small band of followers thought so, and Jesus claimed that he was. Yet Jesus had his own conception of the Messiah. He would establish a spiritual kingdom, not an earthly one.

The prefect Pontius Pilate knew little of Jesus' teachings. His concern was maintaining peace and order. The crowds following Jesus at the time of the Passover, a highly emotional time in the Jewish year, alarmed Pilate, who faced a volatile situation. Some Jews believed that Jesus was the long-awaited Messiah, which triggered Roman concerns about rebellion; others hated and feared Jesus and wanted to be rid of him. To avert riot and bloodshed, Pilate condemned Jesus to death and had his soldiers carry out the sentence.

On the third day after Jesus' crucifixion, some of his followers claimed that he had risen from the dead. For the earliest Christians and for generations to come, the resurrection of Jesus became a central element of faith: he had triumphed over death, and his resurrection promised all Christians immortality.

The Spread of Christianity

The memory of Jesus and his teachings survived and flourished. Believers in his divinity met in small assemblies or congregations, often in one another's homes, to discuss the meaning of Jesus' message. These earliest Christians defined their faith to fit the life of Jesus into an orthodox Jewish context. Only later did these congregations evolve into what can be called a church with a formal organization and set of beliefs.

The catalyst in the spread of Jesus' teachings and the formation of the Christian church was Paul of Tarsus, a Hellenized Jew who was comfortable in both the Roman and Jewish worlds. He had begun by persecuting the new sect, but on the road to Damascus he was converted to belief in Jesus. He was the single most important figure responsible for changing Christianity from a Jewish sect into a separate religion. He urged the Jews to include **Gentiles** (JEN-tie-uhls) (non-Jews) in the faith. His was the first universal message of Christianity.

Gentiles A term for non-Jews. Paul helped spread Christianity by not distinguishing between Jews and Gentiles.

Many early Christian converts were women, who seem to have come particularly from the Greco-Roman middle classes. Paul greeted male and female converts by name in his letters and noted that women provided financial support for his activities. Missionaries and others spreading the Christian message worked

The Catacombs of Rome
The early Christians used underground crypts and rock chambers to bury their dead. The bodies were placed in these galleries and then sealed up. The catacombs became places of pilgrimage, and in this way the dead continued to be united with the living. (Catacombe di Priscilla, Rome/Scala/Art Resource, NY)

through families and friendship networks. The growing Christian communities in various cities of the Roman Empire had different ideas about many things, including the proper gender roles for believers. Some communities favored giving women a larger role, while others were more restrictive (see page 120).

Christianity might have remained just another sect had it not reached Rome, the capital of the Western world. Rome proved to be a dramatic step in the spread of Christianity for different reasons. First, Jesus had told his followers to spread his word throughout the world, thus making his teachings universal. The pagan Romans also considered their secular empire universal, and early Christians there combined these two concepts of **universalism.** Secular Rome provided another advantage to Christianity. If all roads led to Rome, they also led outward to the provinces of central and western Europe. The very stability and extent of the Roman Empire enabled early Christians easily to spread their faith southward to Africa and northward into Europe and across the channel to Britain.

The **catacombs,** underground cemeteries for Christian burial, testify to the vitality of the new religion and Rome's toleration of it. Although many people today think of the catacombs as secret meeting places of oppressed Christians, they were actually huge public structures along the Via Appia, one of Rome's proudest lanes. The development of Christian art can be traced on their walls, with pagan and Christian motifs on early tombs, and biblical scenes on later ones.

universalism The result of the combination of the two concepts: first, Jesus told his followers to spread his word throughout the world, thus making his teachings universal, and second, the pagan Romans also considered their secular empire universal.

catacombs Huge public underground cemeteries found along Via Appia in Rome.

The Appeal of Christianity

Christianity offered its adherents the promise of salvation. Christians believed that Jesus had defeated evil and that he would reward his followers with eternal life after death. Christianity also offered the possibility of forgiveness. Human nature was weak, and even the best Christians would fall into sin. But Jesus loved sinners and forgave those who repented.

Christianity was also attractive because it gave the Roman world a cause. Instead of passivity, Christianity stressed the ideal of striving for a goal. By spreading the word of Christ, Christians played their part in God's plan for the triumph of Christianity on earth. The Christian was not discouraged by temporary setbacks, believing Christianity to be invincible.

Christianity also gave its devotees a sense of community. Believers met regularly to celebrate the Eucharist (**YOO-kuh-rist**), the Lord's Supper. Each individual community was in turn a member of a greater community. And that community, according to Christian Scripture, was indestructible, for Jesus had promised, "the gates of hell shall not prevail against it."[3]

Augustus's Successors

How did Augustus's successors build on his foundation to enhance Roman power and stability?

Augustus's success in creating solid political institutions was tested by the dynasty he created, the Julio-Claudians, who schemed against one another trying to win and hold power. This situation allowed a military commander, Vespasian (**ve-SPEY-zhuhn**), to claim the throne and establish a new dynasty, the Flavians. The Flavians were followed by the "Good Emperors," who were successful militarily and politically.

The Julio-Claudians and the Flavians

For fifty years after Augustus's death the dynasty that he established—known as the Julio-Claudians because they were all members of the Julian and Claudian clans—provided the emperors of Rome. Some of the Julio-Claudians, such as Tiberius and Claudius, were sound rulers and able administrators. Others, including Caligula and Nero, were weak and frivolous men. The story of the Julio-Claudians involves adultery, bigamy, murder, incest, sexual promiscuity, forced suicide, and a host of other ills, as emperors and empresses sought to win and hold power. Nonetheless, during their reigns the empire largely prospered.

Augustus's creation of an imperial bodyguard known as the Praetorians (**pray-TOR-ee-ahns**) had repercussions for his successors. In 41 C.E. the Praetorians murdered Caligula and forced the senate to ratify their choice of Claudius as emperor. It was a story repeated frequently. During the first three centuries of the empire, the Praetorian Guard all too often murdered emperors they were supposed to protect and saluted emperors of their own choosing.

Claudius was murdered by his fourth wife to allow her son by a previous marriage, Nero, to become emperor. In 68 C.E. Nero's inept rule led to military rebellion and his suicide, thus opening the way to widespread disruption. In 69 C.E., the "Year of the Four Emperors," four men claimed the position of emperor. Roman armies in Gaul, on the Rhine, and in the East marched on Rome to make their commanders emperor. Vespasian, commander of the eastern armies, emerged triumphant.

Vespasian did not solve the problem of the army in politics. To prevent usurpers from claiming the throne, Vespasian designated his sons Titus and Domitian as his successors. By establishing the Flavian dynasty (named after his clan), Vespasian openly turned the principate into a monarchy. He also expanded the emperor's power by increasing the size of the professional bureaucracy Claudius had created.

Roman History After Augustus

Period	Important Emperors	Significant Events
Julio-Claudians 27 B.C.E.–68 C.E.	Augustus, 27 B.C.E.–14 C.E.	Augustan settlement
	Tiberius, 14–37	Beginning of the principate
	Caligula, 37–41	Birth and death of Jesus
	Claudius, 41–54	Expansion into northern and western Europe
	Nero, 54–68	Creation of the imperial bureaucracy
Year of the Four Emperors 69	Nero	Civil war
	Galba	Major breakdown of the concept of the principate
	Otho	
	Vitellius	
Flavians 69–96	Vespasian, 69–79	Growing trend toward the concept of monarchy
	Titus, 79–81	Defense and further consolidation of the European frontiers
	Domitian, 81–96	
Antonines 96–180	Nerva, 96–98	The "golden age"—the era of the "five good emperors"
	Trajan, 98–117	Economic prosperity
	Hadrian, 117–138	Trade and growth of cities in northern Europe
	Antoninus Pius, 138–161	Beginning of barbarian menace on the frontiers
	Marcus Aurelius, 161–180	
	Commodus, 180–192	
Severi 193–235	Septimius Severus, 193–211	Military monarchy
	Caracalla, 198–217	All free men within the empire given Roman citizenship
	Elagabalus, 218–222	
	Severus Alexander, 222–235	
"Barracks Emperors" 235–284	Twenty-two emperors in forty-nine years	Civil war
		Breakdown of the empire
		Barbarian invasions
		Severe economic decline
Tetrarchy 284–337	Diocletian, 284–305	Political recovery
	Constantine, 306–337	Autocracy
		Legalization of Christianity
		Transition to the Middle Ages in the West
		Birth of the Byzantine Empire in the East

He is also known for sending a Roman army to put down revolts in Judaea, which led to the destruction of Jerusalem and the enslavement of the Jewish survivors.

The Flavians carried on Augustus's work on the frontiers. Domitian, the last of the Flavians, won additional territory in Germany and consolidated it in two new provinces. He defeated barbarian tribes on the Danube (DAN-yoob) frontier and strengthened that area as well. Even so, Domitian was one of the most hated of Roman emperors because of his cruelty, and he fell victim to an assassin's dagger.

The Emperor Marcus Aurelius

This equestrian statue, with the emperor greeting his people, represents both the majesty and the peaceful intentions of this emperor and philosopher—one of the five good emperors. Equestrian statues present an image of idealized masculinity, but most portray their subjects as fierce and warlike, not with a hand raised in peace as Marcus Aurelius's hand is here. (Tibor Bognar/Alamy)

Nevertheless, the Flavians had kept the legions in line. Their work paved the way for the Antonine dynasty and the era of the "five good emperors."

The Age of the "Five Good Emperors" (96–180 C.E.)

The **five good emperors**—Nerva, Trajan (TREY-juhn), Hadrian (HEY-dree-uhn), Antoninus Pius, and Marcus Aurelius—ruled the empire wisely, fairly, and humanely. Yet the nature of their rule was considerably different from what it had been under Augustus.

Augustus had claimed that his influence arose from the collection of offices the senate had bestowed on him and that he was merely the First Citizen. Under the Flavians the principate became a full-blown monarchy, and by the time of the Antonines the principate was an office with definite rights, powers, and prerogatives. While the five good emperors were not power-hungry autocrats, they were absolute kings all the same. They needed vast powers and the help of professional bureaucrats in order to run the empire efficiently. Later rulers would use this same power in a despotic fashion.

The Roman army had also changed since Augustus's time. Under the Flavian emperors the frontiers became firmly fixed, except for a brief period under Trajan, who attempted to expand the empire. No longer a conquering force, the army concentrated on defending what had already been won. Forts and watch stations guarded the borders. Outside the forts the Romans built a system of roads that allowed the forts to be quickly supplied and reinforced in times of trouble. The army had evolved from a mobile unit into a garrison force, with legions guarding specific areas for long periods.

The personnel of the legions was changing, too. Italy could no longer supply all the recruits needed for the army. Increasingly, only the officers came from Italy and from the more Romanized provinces. The legionaries were mostly drawn from the provinces closest to the frontiers. In the third century C.E. this shift would result in an army indifferent to Rome and its traditions. In the age of the five good emperors, however, the army was still a source of economic stability and a Romanizing agent. (See the feature "Individuals in Society: Bithus, a Typical Roman Soldier.")

> **five good emperors** The name for the five emperors who ruled the empire wisely, fairly, and humanely. They created a period of peace and prosperity.

Section Review

- For fifty years after Augustus, the Julio-Claudian dynasty included able rulers, such as Tiberius and Claudius, and inept rulers, such as Caligula and Nero.

- During the Julio-Claudian dynasty, the Praetorians, the imperial bodyguard of Augustus, often murdered emperors and then established successors of their own choosing.

- During the "Year of the Four Emperors" Vespasian finally claimed the throne and openly changed the principate into a monarchy, expanding the emperor's power while his heirs the Flavians continued expansion on the frontiers.

- The "Five Good Emperors" Nerva, Trajan, Hadrian, Antoninus Pius, and Marcus Aurelius ruled fairly but were still kings with vast powers using the aid of professional bureaucrats to rule.

- Under the Flavians, the Roman army changed its role from mobile expansion unit to garrison force, protecting the borders, using forts, and building roads for rapid movement of supplies and reinforcements.

Individuals in Society

Bithus, a Typical Roman Soldier

Few people think of soldiers as missionaries of culture, but they often are. They expose others to their own traditions, habits, and ways of thinking while at the same time they gain an understanding of other cultures that they can bring home. This was true of the soldiers of the Roman Empire. The empire was so vast even by modern standards that soldiers were recruited from all parts of it to serve in distant places. A soldier from Syria might find himself keeping watch on Hadrian's Wall in Britain. He brought with him the ideas and habits of his birthplace and soon realized that others lived life differently. Yet they all lived in the same empire. Despite their ethnic differences, they were united by many commonly shared beliefs and opinions.

Historical records offer us a glimpse into the life of the infantryman Bithus, who was typical of many who served in the legions. Born in Thrace, the region of modern northeastern Greece, his military life took him to Syria, where he spent most of his career. There he met others from as far west as Gaul and Spain, from West Africa, and from the modern Middle East. This experience gave him an idea of the size of the empire. It also taught him about life in other areas.

Unlike many other cohorts who were shifted periodically, Bithus saw service in one theater. While in the army, he raised a family, much like soldiers today. The children of soldiers like Bithus often themselves joined the army, which thereby became a fruitful source of its own recruitment. After twenty-five years of duty, Bithus received his reward on November 7, 88. Upon mustering out of the army he received the grant of Roman citizenship for himself and his family. In his civilian life the veteran enjoyed a social status that granted him honor and privileges accorded only to Romans. From his military records there is no reason to conclude that Bithus had even seen Rome, but because of his service to it, he became as much a Roman as anyone born near the Tiber.

The example of Bithus is important because it is typical of thousands of others who voluntarily supported the empire. In the process they learned about the nature of the empire and something about how it worked. They also exchanged experiences with other soldiers and the local population and this helped shape a sense that the empire was a human as well as a political unit.

Idealized statue of
a Roman soldier.
(Deutsches Archaeologisches
Institut, Rome)

Questions for Analysis

1. What did Bithus gain from his twenty-five years of service in the Roman army?

2. What effect did soldiers such as Bithus have on the various parts of the Roman Empire where they served, both in their way of seeing new cultures and in their way of sharing new experiences?

Source: Corpus Inscriptionum Latinarum, vol. 16 (Berlin: G. Reimer, 1882), no. 35.

Life in the "Golden Age"

What was life like in the city of Rome in the "golden age," and what was it like in the provinces?

The years of peace and prosperity under the five good emperors are considered by many to represent the "golden age" of Rome. Life in the capital city was significantly different from that in the provinces of northern and western Europe, and the Romans went to no great lengths to spread their culture. Yet roads and secure sea-lanes linked the empire in one vast web, with men and women traveling and migrating more often than they had in earlier eras (see Map 6.2). Through this network of commerce and communication, greater Europe entered the economic and cultural life of the Mediterranean world.

Imperial Rome

Rome was truly an extraordinary city, especially by ancient standards. It was also enormous, with a population somewhere between 500,000 and 750,000. Although it could boast of stately palaces, noble buildings, and beautiful residential areas, most people lived in jerrybuilt apartment houses. Fire and crime were perennial problems, even after Augustus created fire and urban police forces. Streets were narrow and drainage was inadequate. During the republic sanitation had been a common problem. Numerous inscriptions record prohibitions against dumping human refuse and even cadavers on the grounds of sanctuaries and cemeteries. Under the empire this situation improved. By comparison with medieval and early modern European cities, Rome was a healthy enough place to live.

Rome was such a huge city that the surrounding countryside could not feed it. Because of shortages and high prices, the emperor, following republican practice, provided the citizen population with free grain for bread and, later, oil and wine. By feeding the citizenry the emperor prevented bread riots. For those who were not citizens, the emperor provided grain at low prices. By furnishing free bread he eliminated shortages.

The emperor and other wealthy citizens also entertained the Roman populace, often at vast expense. The most popular forms of public entertainment were gladiatorial (glad-ee-uh-TAWR-ee-uhl) contests and chariot racing. Many **gladiators** (glad-ee-ay-TAWRS) were criminals under a death sentence. These convicts were given no defensive weapons and stood little real chance of survival. Other criminals were sentenced to fight in the arena as fully armed gladiators. Some gladiators were the slaves of gladiatorial trainers; others were prisoners of war. Still others were free men who volunteered for the arena. Even women at times engaged in gladiatorial combat. Some Romans protested gladiatorial fighting, but the emperors recognized the political value of such spectacles, and most Romans appear to have enjoyed them. Christian authors generally opposed gladiatorial and animal combat, but this did not lead to immediate bans.

The Romans were even more addicted to chariot racing than to gladiatorial shows. Under the empire four permanent teams competed against one another. Each had its own color—red, white, green, or blue. Two-horse and four-horse chariots ran a course of seven laps, about five miles. One charioteer, Gaius Appuleius Diocles, raced for twenty-four years. During that time he drove 4,257 starts and won 1,462 of them. His admirers honored him with an inscription that proclaimed him champion of all charioteers.

gladiators Criminals and convicts who were sentenced to be slaughtered in the arena as public entertainment.

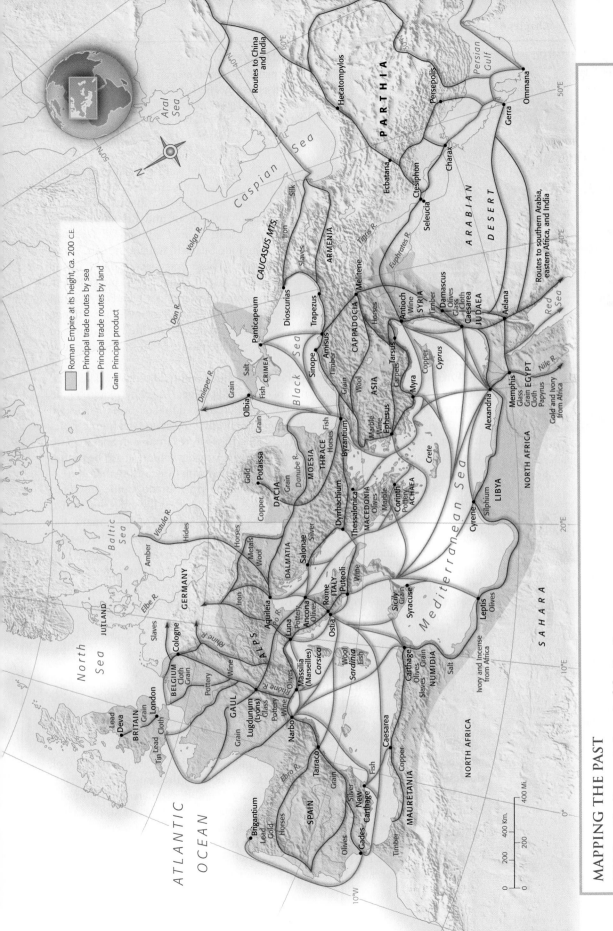

MAPPING THE PAST

MAP 6.2   The Economic Aspect of the Pax Romana

This map gives a good idea of trade routes and the economic expansion of the Roman Empire at its height. Map 11.1 on page 254 is a similar map that shows trade in roughly the same area nearly a millennium later. Examine both maps and answer the following questions: **[1]** To what extent did Roman trade routes influence later European trade routes? **[2]** What similarities and differences do you see in trade in the Mediterranean during these two periods?

Gladiatorial Games
Though hardly games, the contests were vastly popular among the Romans. Gladiators were usually slaves, but successful ones could gain their freedom. The fighting was hard but fair, and the gladiators shown here look equally matched. (Interfoto Pressebildagentur/Alamy)

villa A country estate, which was the primary unit of organized political life.

Rome and the Provinces

The rural population throughout the empire left few records, yet the inscriptions that remain point to a melding of indigenous and Roman cultures. This melding can be seen in the evolution of Romance languages, which include Spanish, Italian, French, Portuguese, and Romanian. These languages evolved in the provinces where people used Latin for legal and state religious purposes, eventually leading to a blending of Latin and their native tongues. The process of cultural exchange was at first more urban than rural, but the importance of cities and towns to the life of the wider countryside ensured that its effects spread far afield.

On the frontiers of the empire, the city was not as central to society. The **villa**, a country estate, was the primary unit of organized political life. This pattern of life differed from that of the Mediterranean, but it prefigured that of the early Middle Ages. The same was true in Britain, where the normal social and economic structures were farms and agricultural villages. (See the feature "Images in Society: The Roman Villa at Chedworth" on pages 124–125.) Very few cities were to be found, and many native Britons were largely unacquainted with Greco-Roman culture.

Across eastern Europe the pattern was much the same. In the Alpine provinces north of Italy, Romans and native Celts came into contact in the cities, but native cultures flourished in the countryside. In Illyria (eh-LEER-ee-uh) and Dalmatia, the regions of modern Albania and the former Yugoslavia (yoo-gah-SLAH-vee-uh), the native population never widely embraced either Roman culture or urban life. Similarly, the Roman soldiers who increasingly settled parts of these lands made little effort to Romanize the natives, and there was less intermarriage than in Celtic areas. To a certain extent, however, Romanization occurred simply because these peoples lived in such close proximity.

Section Review

- Roads and secure sea-lanes connected Rome to the empire, encouraging increased travel and migration, and fostering Roman economic and cultural life.

- Rome was an enormous city with both noble buildings and run-down apartments that boasted a fire and police force.

- The emperor provided free grain to the population to prevent riots and entertained the public with gladiator fights and chariot races.

- The Romance languages, Spanish, Italian, French, Portuguese, and Romanian, are proof of a melding of cultures, with Latin blending with the native tongues.

- Romanization in the countryside was less profound than in the cities.

Rome in Disarray and Recovery (177–450 C.E.)

What factors led Rome into political and economic chaos, and how and to what extent did it recover?

The long years of peace and prosperity abruptly gave way to a convulsed period of domestic upheaval and foreign invasion. Law yielded to the sword. Only the political mechanisms of the empire—its bureaucrats and its ordinary lower officials, protected by loyal soldiers—staved off internal collapse and foreign invasion. Peace came with the ascension of Diocletian (die-uh-KLEE-shuhn) to emperor in 284.

Once Diocletian had ended the period of turmoil, succeeding emperors confronted the work of repairing the damage. Yet the Roman world, like Humpty Dumpty, could not quite be put back together again.

Civil Wars and Foreign Invasions in the Third Century

After the death of Marcus Aurelius, the last of the five good emperors, misrule by his successors led to a long and intense spasm of fighting. More than twenty different emperors ascended the throne in the forty-nine years between 235 and 284. So many military commanders ruled that the middle of the third century has become known as the age of the **barracks emperors.** The Augustan principate had become a military monarchy, and that monarchy was nakedly autocratic.

Preoccupied with creating and destroying emperors, the army left gaping holes in the border defenses. Taking advantage of the weakness, bands of Goths devastated the Balkans as far south as Greece and down into Asia Minor. The Alamanni (al-uh-MAN-eye), a Germanic people, swept across the Danube. At one point they reached Milan in Italy before being beaten back. Meanwhile, the Franks, still another Germanic folk, invaded eastern and central Gaul and northeastern Spain. Saxons from Scandinavia sailed into the English Channel in search of loot. In the east the Sassanids (suh-SAH-nidz) overran Mesopotamia.

barracks emperors The name of the period in the middle of the third century when many military commanders ruled.

Reconstruction Under Diocletian and Constantine (284–337 C.E.)

At the close of the third century C.E. the emperor Diocletian (r. 284–305) put an end to the period of turmoil. Repairing the damage done in the third century was the major work of the emperor Constantine (r. 306–337) in the fourth. But the price was high.

augustus A title that became synonymous with emperor, it was given by Diocletian to a colleague along with the rule of the western part of the empire.

Tetrarchy A system by which four men rule the empire.

Under Diocletian, the princeps became *dominus*—"lord." The emperor claimed that he was "the elect of god"—that he ruled because of divine favor. To underline the emperor's exalted position, Diocletian and Constantine adopted the gaudy court ceremonies and trappings of the Persian Empire. People entering the emperor's presence prostrated themselves before him and kissed the hem of his robes.

Diocletian recognized that the empire had become too great for one man to handle and divided it into a western and an eastern half (see Map 6.3). Diocletian assumed direct control of the eastern part; he gave the rule of the western part to a colleague, along with the title **augustus,** which had become synonymous with emperor. Diocletian and his fellow augustus further delegated power by appointing two men to assist them. Each man was given the title of *caesar* to indicate his exalted rank. Although this system is known as the **Tetrarchy** (TEE-trahrk-ee) because four men ruled the empire, Diocletian was clearly the senior partner and final source of authority.

Each half of the empire was further split into two prefectures, each governed by a prefect responsible to an augustus. Diocletian reduced the power of the old provincial governors by dividing

Diocletian's Tetrarchy

The emperor Diocletian's attempt to reform the Roman Empire by dividing rule among four men is represented in this piece of sculpture. Here the four tetrarchs demonstrate their solidarity by clasping one another on the shoulder. Nonetheless each man has his other hand on his sword—a gesture that proved prophetic when Diocletian's reign ended and another struggle for power began. (Alinari/Art Resource, NY)

The Roman Villa at Chedworth

On the European borders of the Roman Empire, the villa was often as important as the town. Indeed, villas sometimes assumed many of the functions of towns. They were economic and social centers from which landlords directed the life of the surrounding countryside. The villa at Chedworth in Roman Britain provides an excellent example. The ordinary villa included a large courtyard with barns, gardens, storehouses, and buildings for processing agricultural products and manufacturing goods. The villa also included the comfortable living quarters of the owner and his family. These structures included the usual bedrooms and baths. A small temple or shrine often provided a center for religious devotions. Quarters for servants and slaves were nearby but set apart from the great houses. Equally important were the other buildings that served domestic and light industrial needs. The villa, then, was essentially a small, self-contained community. Yet it was not necessarily isolated. The villa at Chedworth was connected by roads and rivers to other similar neighboring villas. The whole picture depicts a society that, though rural, was nonetheless cultured, comfortable, and in touch with the wider world. A good analogy is the American southern plantation before the Civil War. Like many of these villas, Chedworth survived the demise of the Roman Empire. They all remained to play a crucial role in preserving Greco-Roman civilization in northern Europe.

What did a Roman villa look like, and how can archaeological remains define and explain its functioning? Since few ancient structures remain intact, many must obviously be reconstructed from excavations. Image 1 is the archaeological ground plan of Chedworth. At first it seems to show only a series of foundations. Yet a closer look reveals its design. The large buildings marked 3, 5a, and 5 are the remains of the manorial houses. Rooms 10

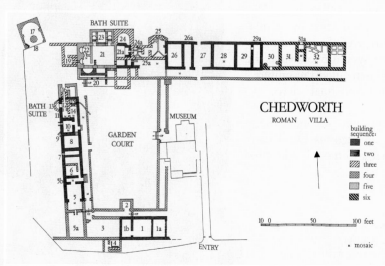

IMAGE 1 Ground Plan of the Roman Villa at Chedworth (From R. Goodburn, *The Roman Villa, Chedworth.* Reproduced with permission.)

IMAGE 2 Archaeological Reconstruction of the Villa (Courtesy, Professor Albert Schachter)

IMAGE 3 Aerial View of Chedworth (Courtesy of West Air Photography)

IMAGE 4 A View of the Site Today (John Buckler)

through 25a are the bath structures. Number 17 is a small temple. Buildings on the northern side, numbers 26–32, were domestic quarters.

Two questions immediately arise. How do we know what these buildings looked like, and how do we know how they functioned? By analyzing the physical remains and the building techniques of the site, archaeologists and architects have made a patient reconstruction of the entire villa (see Image 2). Artifacts found in the structures reveal their functions. The most obvious example is the elaborate bath complex of numbers 19–25a. Image 3 gives an aerial view of the villa, and Image 4 provides an excellent cameo of the western wing of the villa.

From this information can you determine from the ground plan (Image 1) and the reconstruction (Image 2) what the villa actually looked like? From Image 3, an aerial view of Chedworth, together with Images 1 and 2, can you locate the landlord's houses, the temple, and the domestic buildings? Now using these three images, can you identify the buildings in Image 4? Lastly, from this material can you imagine the functions of the villa in its environmental and cultural context?

MAP 6.3 The Roman World Divided

Under Diocletian, the Roman Empire was first divided into a western and an eastern half, a development that foreshadowed the medieval division between the Latin West and the Byzantine East.

dioceses Small administrative units that were governed by a prefect responsible to an augustus.

provinces into smaller units. He organized the prefectures into small administrative units called **dioceses** (DIE-uh-seez), which were in turn subdivided into small provinces. Provincial governors were also deprived of their military power, leaving them only civil and administrative duties.

Diocletian's political reforms were a momentous step. The Tetrarchy soon failed, but his division of the empire into two parts became permanent. Constantine and later emperors tried hard but unsuccessfully to keep the empire together. Throughout the fourth century C.E. the eastern and the western sections drifted apart. In later centuries the western part witnessed the fall of Roman government and the rise of Germanic kingdoms, while the eastern empire evolved into the Byzantine Empire.

Economic, social, and religious problems confronted Diocletian and Constantine. They needed additional revenues to support the army and the imperial court, yet the wars and invasions had struck a serious blow to Roman agriculture. Christianity had become too strong either to ignore or to crush. How Diocletian,

Constantine, and their successors responded to these problems influenced later developments.

Inflation and Taxes

The empire was less capable of recovery than in earlier times. Wars and invasions had disrupted normal commerce and the means of production. Mines were exhausted in the attempt to supply much-needed ores, especially gold and silver. In the cities, markets were disrupted, and travel became dangerous. Merchant and artisan families rapidly left devastated regions. The barracks emperors had dealt with economic hardship by cutting the silver content of coins until money was virtually worthless. The immediate result was crippling inflation throughout the empire.

Diocletian's attempt to curb inflation illustrates the methods of absolute monarchy. In a move unprecedented in Roman history, he issued an edict that fixed maximum prices and wages throughout the empire. The emperors dealt with the tax system just as strictly and inflexibly. Taxes became payable in kind, that is, in goods or produce instead of money. All those involved in the growing, preparation, and transportation of food and other essentials were locked into their professions. A baker or shipper could not go into any other business, and his son took up the trade at his death. In this period of severe depression many localities could not pay their taxes. In such cases local tax collectors, who were also locked into service, had to make up the difference from their own funds. This system soon wiped out a whole class of moderately wealthy people.

The Decline of Small Farms

Because of worsening conditions during the third century C.E., many free tenant farmers and their families were killed, fled the land to escape the barbarians, or abandoned farms ravaged in the fighting. Consequently, large tracts of land lay deserted. Great landlords with ample resources began at once to reclaim as much of this land as they could. The huge estates that resulted, called villas, were self-sufficient. Because they often produced more than they consumed, they successfully competed with the declining cities by selling their surplus in the countryside. They became islands of stability in an unsettled world.

The rural residents who remained on the land were exposed to the raids of barbarians or brigands and to the tyranny of imperial officials. In return for the protection and security landlords could offer, the small landholders gave over their lands and their freedom. They could no longer decide to move elsewhere. Henceforth they and their families worked their patrons' land, not their own. Free men and women were becoming what would later be called serfs.

The Acceptance of Christianity

The Roman attitude toward Christianity evolved as well during the period of empire. A splendid analysis of the different phases in the relationship between official Rome and Christianity has come from the eminent Italian scholar Marta Sordi.[4] At first many pagans genuinely misunderstood Christian practices and rites. They thought that such secret rites as the Lord's Supper, at which Christians said that they ate and drank the body and blood of Jesus, were acts of cannibalism. Pagans thought that Christianity was one of the worst of the mystery cults, with immoral and indecent rituals. They also feared that the gods would withdraw their favor from the Roman Empire because of the Christian insistence that the pagan gods either didn't exist or were evil spirits.

There were some cases of pagan persecution of the Christians, including some executions in Rome ordered by the Emperor Nero, but with few exceptions they were local and sporadic in nature. The Christians exaggerated the degree of pagan hostility toward them, and although there were some martyrs, most of the gory stories about the martyrs are fictitious. No constant persecution of Christians occurred.

As time went on, pagan hostility decreased. Pagans realized that Christians were not working to overthrow the state and that Jesus was no rival of Caesar. The emperor Trajan forbade his governors to hunt down Christians. Trajan admitted that he thought Christianity an abomination, but he preferred to leave Christians in peace.

The stress of the third century, however, seemed to some emperors the punishment of the gods. Although the Christians depicted the emperor Diocletian as a fiend, he persecuted them in the hope that gods would restore their blessings on Rome. Yet even these persecutions were never very widespread or long-lived. By the late third century, pagans had become used to Christianity. Constantine recognized Christianity as a legitimate religion and himself died a Christian in 33. Constantine's acceptance of Christianity can be seen as the pagans' alliance with the strongest god of them all.

In time the Christian triumph would be complete. In 380 the emperor Theodosius (thee-uh-DOH-shee-uhs) made Christianity the official religion of the Roman Empire. At that point Christians began to persecute the pagans for their beliefs. History had come full circle.

The Construction of Constantinople

The triumph of Christianity was not the only event that made Constantine's reign a turning point in Roman history. Constantine took the bold step of building a new capital for the empire. Constantinople, the New Rome, was constructed on the site of Byzantium, an old Greek city on the Bosporus. Throughout the third century emperors had found Rome and the West hard to defend. The eastern part of the empire was more easily defensible and escaped the worst of the barbarian devastation. It was wealthy and its urban life still vibrant. Moreover, Christianity was more widespread in the East than in the West, and the city of Constantinople was intended to be a Christian center.

From the Classical World to Late Antiquity

The two-faced Roman god Janus, who represented transitions, well symbolizes this period. A great deal of the past remained through these years of change. People still lived under the authority of the emperors and the guidance of Roman law. They communicated with one another as usual, in Latin throughout the West and Greek in the East. Greco-Roman art, architecture, and literature surrounded them.

Yet changes were also under way. Government had evolved from the SPQR of the past to the Christian monarchy of the new age. The empire itself split into East and West, and the latter became the home of barbarians who built a different world on classical foundations. Greek philosophy was replaced by theology, as thinkers tried earnestly to understand Jesus' message.

Through all these changes the lives of ordinary men and women did not change dramatically. They farmed, worked in cities, and hoped for the best for their families. They took new ideas, blended them with old, and created new cultural forms. Gradually the classical world gave way to a vibrant new intellectual, spiritual, and political life.

Section Review

- Following Marcus Aurelius's death, the empire was so preoccupied with military commanders vying for rule that foreign invaders took advantage and swept in on several fronts.

- Diocletian, and later Constantine, ended the turmoil, dividing the empire into a western and eastern half with an augustus and two caesars to rule each half, a system known as the Tetrarchy.

- Because of war, the empire was drained of resources so Diocletian fixed prices and wages and taxes were payable in kind, but this severe system soon wiped out the moderately wealthy.

- As small-scale farming became increasingly dangerous, wealthy landlords bought up the land and offered small tracts of land and protection to the farmers in exchange for their freedom.

- Christians exaggerated stories about martyrs, and although pagans at first misunderstood Christian rites, fearing it was the cause of the empire's troubles, pagans eventually grew used to Christianity and in 380 emperor Theodosius made it the official religion of the Roman Empire.

- Constantine built a new capital, Constantinople, on the site of Byzantium on the Bosporus, intending it to be a Christian center in the wealthier East while abandoning Rome and the western half of the empire to the barbarians.

Chapter Review

How did Augustus transform the Roman Empire? (page 108)

Once Augustus had restored order, he made it endure by remodeling the Roman government. The old constitution of the city-state gave way to the government of an empire. Although Augustus tried to save as much of the old as possible, he necessarily created a virtually new and much expanded system of rule. Furthermore, he made it endure.

Why did Christianity, originally a minor local religion, sweep across the Roman world to change it fundamentally? (page 113)

Christianity triumphed because it offered salvation to all people, men and women, regardless of their nationality, race, or social status.

How did Augustus's successors build on his foundation to enhance Roman power and stability? (page 116)

As life settled down under this calming order, a small event with universal repercussions occurred in remote Judaea. There a young Jew named Jesus taught a new religion,

Key Terms

pax Romana (p. 108)

constitutional monarchy (p. 108)

princeps (p. 108)

principate (p. 108)

imperator (p. 109)

barbarians (p. 110)

apocalypticism (p. 113)

Messiah (p. 113)

pagans (p. 113)

heresy (p. 114)

Gentiles (p. 114)

universalism (p. 115)

(continued)

promising salvation to all who embraced it. Although Roman officials executed him, this new religion did not die. Instead it spread across the East, then to Rome, and by the end of the period throughout the empire.

What was life like in the city of Rome in the "golden age," and what was it like in the provinces? (page 120)

Augustus's success in creating solid political institutions was tested by the dynasty he created, the Julio-Claudians. The fifty years during which they ruled Rome saw emperors and empresses trying to win and hold power through multiple political marriages, murder, and other tactics. In 70 C.E., Vespasian, a military commander, established a new dynasty, the Flavians, who restored some stability in Rome and expanded the empire. The Flavians were followed by a series of effective emperors, later called the "Five Good Emperors," who created a more effective bureaucracy and larger army to govern the huge Roman Empire.

What factors led Rome into political and economic chaos, and how and to what extent did it recover? (page 122)

For many Romans these were rich and happy years. Much of the population enjoyed sufficient leisure time, which many spent pursuing literature and art. Others preferred watching spectacular games including gladiatorial contests and chariot races. In the ever-expanding provinces, Roman and native cultures combined, and products and peoples moved more easily across huge areas.

The good times fell into disarray when a series of weak emperors, many of them backed by soldiers they had commanded, fought for the throne. To worsen matters, barbarians on the frontiers took advantage of these internal troubles to invade, plunder, and destroy. These factors brought Rome near collapse. With the end apparently at hand, two stern and gifted emperors, Diocletian and Constantine, restored order and breathed fresh life into the economic and social order. By the end of this period, Christianity had made such gains that it was recognized as the official religion of the empire. By the end of Constantine's reign the Roman Empire was politically divided and religiously changing. Still, many aspects of Greco-Roman culture remained strong.

Notes

1. Virgil, *Aeneid* 6.851–6.853. John Buckler is the translator of all uncited quotations from a foreign language in Chapters 1–6.
2. Augustus, *Res Gestae* 6.34.
3. Matthew 16:18.
4. See Marta Sordi, *The Christians and the Roman Empire* (London: Croom Helm, 1986).

To assess your mastery of this chapter, go to **bedfordstmartins.com/mckaywestbrief**

Listening to the Past

Rome Extends Its Citizenship

One of the most dramatic achievements of the pax Romana was the extension of citizenship throughout the Roman Empire. Citizenship gave people advantages in judicial procedures, property transmission, and commercial relations. Male citizens could vote, and both female and male citizens passed citizenship on to their children.

Yet various emperors went even further by viewing Rome not only as a territorial but also as a political concept. In their eyes Rome was a place and an idea. Not every Roman agreed with these cosmopolitan views. The emperor Claudius (r. 41–54) took the first major step in this direction by allowing Romanized Gauls to sit in the senate. He was roundly criticized by some Romans, but in the damaged stone inscription that follows, he presents his own defense.

Surely both my great-uncle, the deified Augustus, and my uncle, Tiberius Caesar, were following a new practice when they desired that all the flowers of the colonies and the municipalities everywhere—that is, the better class and the wealthy men—should sit in this senate house. You ask me: Is not an Italian senator preferable to a provincial? I shall reveal to you in detail my views on this matter when I come to obtain approval for this part of my censorship [a magistracy that determined who was eligible for citizenship and public offices]. But I think that not even provincials ought to be excluded, provided that they can add distinction to this senate house.

Look at that most distinguished and most flourishing colony of Vienna [the modern Vienne in France], how long a time already it is that it has furnished senators to this house! From that colony comes that ornament of the equestrian order—and there are few to equal

him—Lucius Vestinus, whom I cherish most intimately and whom at this very time I employ in my affairs. And it is my desire that his children may enjoy the first step in the priesthoods, so as to advance afterwards, as they grow older, to further honors in their rank. . . .

All these distinguished youths whom I gaze upon will no more give us cause for regret if they become senators than does my friend Persicus, a man of most noble ancestry, have cause for regret when he reads among the portraits of his ancestors the name Allobrogicus. But if you agree that these things are so, what more do you want, when I point out to you this single fact, that the territory beyond the boundaries of Narbonese Gaul already sends you senators, since we have men of our order from Lyons and have no cause for regret. It is indeed with hesitation, members of the senate, that I have gone outside the borders of the provinces with which you are accustomed and familiar, but I must now plead openly the cause of Gallia Comata [a region in modern France]. And if anyone, in this connection, has in mind that these people engaged the deified Julius in war for ten years, let him set against that the unshakable loyalty and obedience of a hundred years, tested to the full in many of our crises. When my father Drusus was subduing Germany, it was they who by their tranquility afforded him a safe and securely peaceful rear, even at a time when he had been summoned away to the war from the task of organizing the census which was still new and unaccustomed to the Gauls. How difficult such an operation

Provocatio, the right of appeal, was considered a fundamental element of Roman citizenship. (Courtesy of the Trustees of the British Museum)

is for us at this precise moment we are learning all too well from experience, even though the survey is aimed at nothing more than an official record of our resources. [The rest of the inscription is lost.]

Questions for Analysis

1. What was the basic justification underlying Claudius's decision to allow Gallic nobles to sit in the senate? Did he see them as debasing the quality of the senate?

2. What do his words tell us about the changing nature of the Roman Empire?

Source: Slightly adapted and abbreviated from *Roman Civilization*, 2 volumes, Third Edition. Volume 1 by N. Lewis and M. Reinhold. Copyright © 1966 Columbia University Press. Reprinted with permission of the publisher.

CHAPTER 7

Late Antiquity

350–600

Hagia Sophia (AH-yah SOH-fee-uh) ("Holy Wisdom"), built by
the Emperor Justinian in the sixth century, was the largest Christian
cathedral in the world for a thousand years. After Constantinople
was conquered by the Ottoman Turks in 1453, it became a mosque,
and today is a museum. (Editore Sadea Editore)

Chapter Preview

The Byzantine Empire
How was the Byzantine Empire able to
survive for so long, and what were its
most important achievements?

The Growth of the Christian Church
What factors enabled the Christian
church to expand and thrive?

Christian Ideas and Practices
How did Christian thinkers adapt Greco-
Roman ideas to Christian theology?

Christian Missionaries and Conversion
What techniques did missionaries
develop to convert barbarian peoples
to Christianity?

Migrating Peoples
What were some of the causes of the
barbarian migrations and how did they
affect the regions of Europe?

Barbarian Society
What patterns of social, political, and
economic life characterized barbarian
society?

INDIVIDUALS IN SOCIETY: Theodora
of Constantinople

LISTENING TO THE PAST: The Conversion of Clovis

133

From the third century onward, the Western Roman Empire slowly disintegrated. The last Roman emperor in the West, Romulus Augustus, was deposed by the Ostrogothic (OS-truh-goth-ic) chieftain Odoacer in 476, but much of the empire had already come under the rule of various barbarian tribes well before this. Scholars have long seen this era as one of the great turning points in Western history, a time when the ancient world was transformed into the very different medieval world. During the past several decades, however, scholars have shifted their focus to continuities as well as changes, and what is now usually termed "late antiquity" has been recognized as a period of creativity and adaptation, not simply of decline and fall.

The two main agents of continuity were the Eastern Roman (or Byzantine) Empire and the Christian church. The Byzantine Empire lasted until 1453, a thousand years longer than the Western Roman Empire, and preserved and transmitted much of ancient law, philosophy, and institutions. Missionaries and church officials spread Christianity within and far beyond the borders of the Roman Empire, transforming a small sect into the most important and wealthiest institution in Europe. The main agents of change in late antiquity were the barbarian groups migrating into the Roman Empire. They brought different social, political, and economic structures with them, but as they encountered Roman culture and became Christian, their own ways of doing things were also transformed.

The Byzantine Empire

How was the Byzantine Empire able to survive for so long, and what were its most important achievements?

Constantine had tried to maintain the unity of the Roman Empire, but during the fifth and sixth centuries the Western and Eastern halves drifted apart. From Constantinople, Eastern Roman emperors worked to hold the empire together and to reconquer at least some of the West from barbarian tribes. Justinian (r. 527–565) waged long wars against the Ostrogoths and temporarily regained Italy and North Africa, but the costs were high. Justinian's wars exhausted the resources of the state, destroyed Italy's economy, and killed a large part of Italy's population. Weakened, Italy fell easily to another Germanic tribe, the Lombards, shortly after Justinian's death. In the late sixth century, the territory of the Western Roman Empire came once again under Germanic sway.

However, the Roman Empire continued in the East. The Eastern Roman or Byzantine Empire (see Map 7.1) preserved the forms, institutions, and traditions of the old Roman Empire, and its people even called themselves Romans. Most important, however, is the role of Byzantium as preserver of the wisdom of the ancient world. Byzantium protected the intellectual heritage of Greco-Roman civilization and then passed it on to the rest of Europe.

Sources of Byzantine Strength

While the Western parts of the Roman Empire gradually succumbed to Germanic invaders, the Eastern Roman or Byzantine Empire survived waves of attacks. In 559 a force of Huns and Slavs reached the gates of Constantinople, and in 583 the Avars (AH-varz), a mounted Mongol people, also threatened the capital. Between 572 and 630 the Sasanid (suh-SAH-nid) Persians put pressure on the Byzantine

Empire, and only two years after the Persians were repelled, Arab forces began their own assaults (see Chapter 8).

Why didn't one or a combination of these enemies capture Constantinople as the Germans had taken Rome? First, the Byzantine Empire enjoyed strong military leadership. General Priskos (d. 612) skillfully led Byzantine armies to a decisive victory over the Avars in 601. Then, after a long war, the emperor Heraclius I (her-uh-KLY-uhs) (r. 610–641) crushed the Persians at Nineveh in Iraq. Second, the capital city was well fortified. Massive triple walls, built by Constantine and Theodosius II (408–450) and kept in good repair, protected Constantinople from sea invasion. Within the walls huge cisterns provided water, and vast gardens and grazing areas supplied vegetables and meat so that the defending people could hold out far longer than the besieging army. Attacking Constantinople by land posed greater geographical and logistical problems than a seventh- or eighth-century army could solve. The site was not absolutely impregnable—as the Venetians demonstrated in 1204 and the Ottoman Turks in 1453 (see pages 211 and 374)—but it was almost so. For centuries, the Byzantine Empire served as a bulwark for the West, protecting it against invasions from the East.

312	Constantine legalizes Christianity in Roman Empire
340–419	Life of Saint Jerome; creation of the Vulgate
354–430	Life of Saint Augustine
380	Theodosius makes Christianity official religion of Roman Empire
385–461	Life of Saint Patrick
481–511	Reign of Clovis
527–565	Reign of Justinian
529	*The Rule of Saint Benedict*
542–560	"Justinian plague"

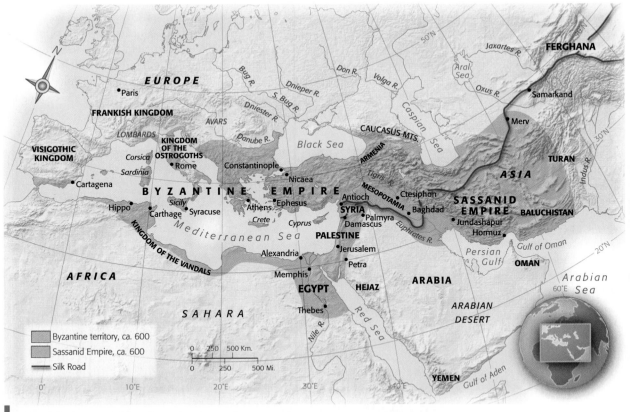

MAP 7.1   The Byzantine Empire, ca. 600

The strategic position of Constantinople on the waterway between the Black Sea and the Mediterranean was clear to Constantine when he chose the city as the capital of the Eastern Roman Empire, and it was also clear to later rulers and military leaders. Byzantine territories in Italy were acquired in Emperor Justinian's sixth-century wars and were held for several centuries.

The Law Code of Justinian

Byzantine emperors organized and preserved Roman law, making a lasting contribution to the medieval and modern worlds. Roman law had developed from many sources—decisions by judges, edicts of the emperors, legislation passed by the senate, and the opinions of jurists expert in the theory and practice of law. By the fourth century, it had become a huge, bewildering mass, and its sheer bulk made it almost unusable.

Sweeping and systematic codification took place under the emperor Justinian. He appointed a committee of eminent jurists to sort through and organize the laws. The result was the *Code*, which distilled the legal genius of the Romans into a coherent whole, eliminated outmoded laws and contradictions, and clarified the law itself. Not content with the *Code*, Justinian set about bringing order to the equally huge body of Roman *jurisprudence* (joor-is-PROOD-ins), the science or philosophy of law.

During the second and third centuries, the foremost Roman jurists had expressed varied learned opinions on complex legal problems. To harmonize this body of knowledge, Justinian directed his jurists to clear up disputed points and to issue definitive rulings. Accordingly, in 533 his lawyers published the *Digest*, which codified Roman legal thought. Finally, Justinian's lawyers compiled a handbook of civil law, the *Institutes*. These three works—the *Code*, the *Digest*, and the *Institutes*—are the backbone of the *corpus juris civilis* (KAWR-puhs JOOR-is si-VIL-is), the "body of civil law," which is the foundation of law for nearly every modern European nation.

Byzantine Intellectual Life

The Byzantines prized education; because of them many masterpieces of ancient Greek literature have survived to influence the intellectual life of the modern world. The literature of the Byzantine Empire was predominately Greek, although Latin was long spoken by top politicians, scholars, and lawyers. Among the large reading public, history was a favorite subject.

Justinian and His Attendants

This mosaic detail is composed of thousands of tiny cubes of colored glass or stone called *tessarae,* which are set in plaster against a blazing golden background. Some attempt has been made at naturalistic portraiture. (Scala/Art Resource, NY)

The most remarkable Byzantine historian was Procopius (ca. 500–ca. 562), who left a rousing account praising Justinian's reconquest of North Africa and Italy. Proof that the wit and venom of ancient Greek and Roman writers lived on in the Byzantine era can be found in Procopius's *Secret History*, a vicious and uproarious attack on Justinian and his wife, the empress Theodora. (See the feature "Individuals in Society: Theodora of Constantinople.")

Although the Byzantines discovered little that was new in mathematics and geometry, they passed Greco-Roman learning on to the Arabs, who made remarkable advances with it. In science, they faithfully learned what the ancients had to teach but made advances only in terms of military applications. For example, the best-known Byzantine scientific discovery was an explosive compound known as "Greek fire" that was heated and propelled by a pump through a bronze tube. As the liquid jet left the tube, it was ignited—somewhat like a modern flamethrower. Greek fire saved Constantinople from Arab assault in 678. In mechanics Byzantine scientists improved and modified artillery and siege machinery.

The Byzantines devoted a great deal of attention to medicine, and the general level of medical competence was far higher in the Byzantine Empire than in western Europe. Yet their physicians could not cope with the terrible disease, often called the "Justinian plague," that swept through the Byzantine Empire and parts of western Europe between 542 and about 560. Probably originating in northwestern India and carried to the Mediterranean region by ships, the disease was similar to modern forms of the bubonic plague. Characterized by high fever, chills, delirium, and enlarged lymph nodes (the buboes that gave bubonic plague its name), or by inflammation of the lungs that caused hemorrhages of black blood, the Justinian plague carried off tens of thousands of people. The epidemic had profound political as well as social consequences. It weakened Justinian's military resources, thus hampering his efforts to restore unity to the Mediterranean world.

By the ninth or tenth century, most major Greek cities had hospitals for the care of the sick. The hospitals might be divided into wards for different illnesses, and hospital staff had surgeons, practitioners, and aides with specialized responsibilities. The imperial Byzantine government bore the costs of these medical facilities.

The Growth of the Christian Church

What factors enabled the Christian church to expand and thrive?

As the Western Roman Empire disintegrated in the fourth and fifth centuries, the Christian church survived and grew, becoming the most important institution in Europe. The able administrators and highly creative thinkers of the church developed permanent institutions and complex philosophical concepts.

The Church and Its Leaders

Scriptural scholars tell us that the earliest use of the word *church* in the New Testament appears in Saint Paul's Letter to the Christians of Thessalonica (thes-uh-LON-ee-kuh) in northern Greece, written about 51 C.E. *Church* means assembly or congregation (in Greek, *ekklesia*); by *ekklesia* Paul meant the local community of Christian believers. In Paul's later letters the word refers to the entire Mediterranean-wide assembly of Jesus' followers. After the legalization of Christianity by the emperor Constantine (see page 128) and the growth of institutional offices and officials, the word *church* was sometimes applied to those officials—

Theodora of Constantinople

The most powerful woman in Byzantine history was the daughter of a bear trainer for the circus. Theodora (ca. 497–548) grew up in what her contemporaries regarded as an undignified and morally suspect atmosphere, and she worked as a dancer and burlesque actress, both dishonorable occupations in the Roman world. Despite her background, she caught the eye of Justinian, who was then a military leader and whose uncle (and adoptive father) Justin had himself risen from obscurity to become the emperor of the Byzantine Empire. Under Justinian's influence, Justin changed the law to allow an actress who had left her disreputable life to marry whom she liked, and Justinian and Theodora married in 525. When Justinian was proclaimed co-emperor with his uncle Justin on April 1, 527, Theodora received the rare title of *augusta*, empress. Thereafter her name was linked with Justinian's in the exercise of imperial power.

The empress Theodora shown with the halo, a symbol of power in Eastern art. (Scala/Art Resource, NY)

Most of our knowledge of Theodora's early life comes from the *Secret History*, a tell-all description of the vices of Justinian and his court, written by Procopius (proh-KOH-pee-uhs) (ca. 550), who was the official court historian and thus spent his days praising those same people. In the *Secret History*, he portrays Theodora and Justinian as demonic, greedy, and vicious, killing courtiers to steal their property. In scene after detailed scene, Procopius portrays Theodora as particularly evil, sexually insatiable, depraved, and cruel, a temptress who used sorcery to attract men, including the hapless Justinian.

In one of his official histories, *The History of the Wars of Justinian*, Procopius presents a very different Theodora. Riots between the supporters of two teams in chariot races—who formed associations somewhat like street gangs and somewhat like political parties—had turned deadly, and Justinian wavered in his handling of the per-

petrators. Both sides turned against the emperor, besieging the palace while Justinian was inside it. Shouting N-I-K-A (victory), the rioters swept through the city, burning and looting, and destroyed half of Constantinople. Justinian's counselors urged flight, but, according to Procopius, Theodora rose and declared:

> For one who has reigned, it is intolerable to be an exile. . . . If you wish, O Emperor, to save yourself, there is no difficulty: we have ample funds and there are the ships. Yet reflect whether, when you have once escaped to a place of security, you will not prefer death to safety. I agree with an old saying that the purple [that is, the color worn only by emperors] is a fair winding sheet to be buried in.

Justinian rallied, had the rioters driven into the hippodrome, and ordered between thirty and thirty-five thousand men and women executed. The revolt was crushed and Justinian's authority restored, an outcome approved by Procopius.

Other sources describe or suggest Theodora's influence on imperial policy. Justinian passed a number of laws that improved the legal status of women, such as allowing women to own property the same way that men could and to be guardians over their own children. He forbade the abandonment of unwanted infants, which happened more often to girls than to boys, as boys were valued more highly. Theodora presided at imperial receptions for Arab sheiks, Persian ambassadors, Germanic princesses from the West, and barbarian chieftains from southern Russia. When Justinian fell ill from the bubonic plague in 532, Theodora took over his duties, banning those who discussed his possible successor. Justinian is reputed to have consulted her every day about all aspects of state policy, including religious policy regarding the doctrinal disputes that continued throughout his reign. Theodora's favored interpretation of Christian doctrine about the nature of Christ was not accepted by the main body of theologians in Constantinople—nor by Justinian—but she urged protection of her fellow believers and in one case hid an aged scholar in the women's quarters of the palace for many years.

Theodora's influence over her husband and her power in the Byzantine state continued until she died, perhaps of cancer, twenty years before Justinian. Her influence may have even continued after death, for Justinian continued to pass reforms favoring women and, at the end of his life, accepted her interpretation of Christian doctrine. Institutions that she established, including hospitals, orphanages, houses for the rehabilitation of prostitutes, and churches, continued to be reminders of her charity and piety.

Theodora has been viewed as a symbol of the manipulation of beauty and cleverness to attain position and power, and also as a strong and capable co-ruler who held the empire together during riots, revolts, and deadly epidemics. Just as Procopius expressed both views, the debate continues today among writers of science fiction and fantasy as well as biographers and historians.

Questions for Analysis

1. How would you assess the complex legacy of Theodora?

2. Since the public and private views of Procopius are so different regarding the empress, should he be trusted at all as a historical source?

much as we use the terms *the college* or *the university* when referring to academic administrators.

In early Christian communities the local people elected their leaders, or bishops. Bishops were responsible for the community's goods and oversaw the distribution of those goods to the poor. They also were responsible for maintaining orthodox (established or correct) doctrine within the community and for preaching. Bishops alone could confirm believers in their faith and ordain men as priests.

The early Christian church benefited from the brilliant administrative abilities of some bishops. Bishop Ambrose, for example, the son of the Roman prefect of Gaul, was a trained lawyer and the governor of a province. He is typical of the Roman aristocrats who held high public office, were converted to Christianity, and subsequently became bishops. Such men later provided social continuity from Roman to Germanic rule. As bishop of Milan, Ambrose himself exercised responsibility in both the business and church affairs of northern Italy.

During the reign of Diocletian (284–305), the Roman Empire had been divided for administrative purposes into geographical units called dioceses. Gradually the church made use of this organizational structure. Christian bishops established their headquarters, or *sees*, in the urban centers of the old Roman dioceses. A bishop's jurisdiction extended throughout the diocese. The center of his authority was his cathedral (from the Latin *cathedra*, meaning "chair"). Thus, church leaders adapted the Roman imperial method of organization for ecclesiastical purposes.

The bishops of Rome—known as "popes," from the Latin word *papa*, meaning "father"—claimed to speak and act as the source of unity for all Christians. They based their claim to be the successors of Saint Peter and heirs to his authority as chief of the apostles on Jesus' words:

> *You are Peter, and on this rock I will build my church, and the jaws of death shall not prevail against it. I will entrust to you the keys of the kingdom of heaven. Whatever you declare bound on earth shall be bound in heaven; whatever you declare loosed on earth shall be loosed in heaven.*[1]

Petrine Doctrine The statement used by popes, bishops of Rome, based on Jesus' words, to substantiate their claim of being the successors of Saint Peter and heirs to his authority as chief of the apostles.

Theologians call this statement the **Petrine** (PEE-tryne) **Doctrine.**

After the capital and the emperor moved from Rome to Constantinople (see page 128), the bishop of Rome exercised considerable influence in the West because he had no real competitor there. He became known as the "Patriarch of the West." In the East, the bishops of Antioch, Alexandria, Jerusalem, and Constantinople, because of the special dignity of their sees, also gained the title of patriarch. Their jurisdictions extended over lands adjoining their sees; they consecrated bishops, investigated heresy, and heard judicial appeals.

In the fifth century the bishops of Rome began to stress their supremacy over other Christian communities and to urge other churches to appeal to Rome for the resolution of disputed doctrinal issues. While local churches often exercised their own authority and Rome was not yet as powerful as it would become, these arguments laid the groundwork for later appeals.

The Church and the Roman Emperors

The church benefited considerably from the emperors' support. Constantine had legalized the practice of Christianity in the empire in 312 and encouraged it throughout his reign. He freed the clergy from imperial taxation. At churchmen's request, he helped settle theological disputes and thus preserved doctrinal unity within the church. Constantine generously endowed the building of Christian churches, and one of his gifts—the Lateran (**LAT-er-uhn**) Palace in Rome—remained the official residence of the popes until the fourteenth century. Constantine also declared Sunday a public holiday, a day of rest for the service of God. Because of its favored position in the empire, Christianity slowly became the leading religion (see Map 7.2).

In the fourth century, theological disputes frequently and sharply divided the Christian community. Some disagreements had to do with the nature of Christ. For example, **Arianism** (**AIR-ree-uh-nizm**), which originated with Arius (ca. 250–336), a priest of Alexandria, held that Jesus was created by the will of the Father and thus was not co-eternal with the Father. Arius also reasoned that Jesus the Son must be inferior to God the Father because the Father was incapable of suffering and did not die. Orthodox theologians branded Arius's position a **heresy**—the denial of a basic doctrine of faith.

Arianism enjoyed such popularity and provoked such controversy that Constantine, to whom religious disagreement meant civil disorder, interceded. He summoned church leaders to a council in Nicaea (**neye-SEE-uh**) in Asia Minor and presided over it personally. The council produced the Nicene (**neye-SEEN**) Creed, which defined the orthodox position that Christ is "eternally begotten of

Arianism A theological belief that originated with Arius, a priest of Alexandria, denying that Christ was divine and co-eternal with God the Father.

heresy The denial of a basic doctrine of faith.

MAP 7.2   The Spread of Christianity
Originating in Judaea, the southern part of modern Israel and Jordan, Christianity first spread throughout the Roman world and then beyond it in all directions.

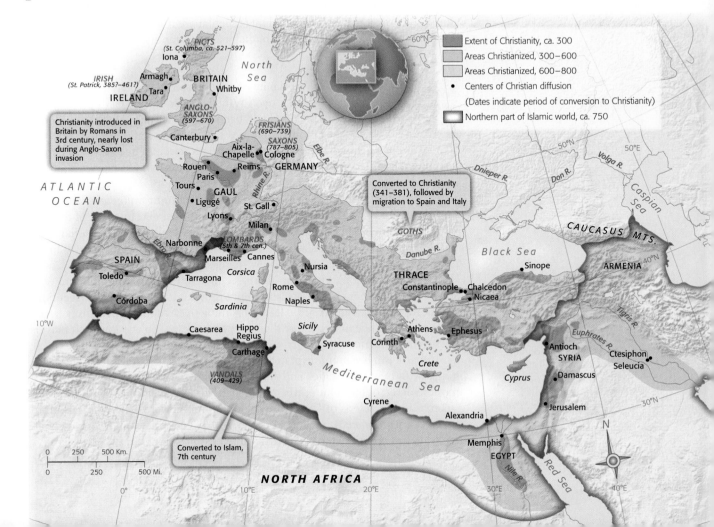

the Father" and of the same substance as the Father. Arius and those who refused to accept the creed were banished, the first case of civil punishment for heresy. This participation of the emperor in a theological dispute within the church paved the way for later emperors to do the same.

In 380 the emperor Theodosius made Christianity the official religion of the empire. Theodosius stripped Roman pagan temples of statues, made the practice of the old Roman state religion a treasonable offense, and persecuted Christians who dissented from orthodox doctrine. Most significant, he allowed the church to establish its own courts and to use its own body of law, called "canon law." These courts, not the Roman government, had jurisdiction over the clergy and ecclesiastical disputes. At the death of Theodosius, the Christian church was considerably independent of the Roman state. The foundation for later growth in church power had been laid.

Later Byzantine emperors continued the pattern of active involvement in church affairs. They appointed the highest officials of the church hierarchy and presided over ecumenical councils, where bishops would gather to make decisions on matters of faith and practice. The emperors also controlled some of the material resources of the church—land, rents, and indebted peasants. On the other hand, the emperors had minimal involvement in church services and rarely tried to impose their views in theological disputes. Greek churchmen vigorously defended the church's independence; some even asserted the superiority of the bishop's authority over the emperor's; and the church possessed such enormous economic wealth and influence over the population that it could block government decisions. The **Orthodox church,** the name generally given to the Eastern Christian church, was less independent of secular control than the Western Christian church, but it was not simply a branch of the Byzantine state.

Orthodox church Eastern orthodox church in the Byzantine empire.

The Development of Christian Monasticism

Christianity began and spread as a city religion. Since the first century, however, some especially pious Christians had felt that the only alternative to the decadence of urban life was complete separation from the world. All-consuming pursuit of material things, sexual promiscuity, and general political corruption disgusted them. They believed that the Christian life as set forth in the Gospel could not be lived in the midst of such immorality. They rejected the values of Roman society and were the first real nonconformists in the church.

This desire to withdraw from ordinary life led to the development of the monastic life. Some scholars believe that the monastic life of extreme material sacrifice appealed to Christians who wanted to make a total response to Christ's teachings; the monks became the new martyrs. Saint Anthony of Egypt (251?–356), the earliest monk for whom there is concrete evidence and the man later considered the father of monasticism, went to Alexandria during the persecutions of the Emperor Diocletian in the hope of gaining martyrdom. Christians believed that monks like the martyrs before them, could speak to God and that their prayers had special influence.

Monasticism began in Egypt in the third century. At first individuals and small groups withdrew from cities and from organized society to seek God through prayer in desert or mountain caves and shelters. Gradually large colonies of monks gathered in the deserts of Upper Egypt. These monks were called hermits, from the Greek word *eremos,* meaning "desert." Many devout women also were attracted to this **eremitical** (er-uh-MIT-ik-ul) type of monasticism.

eremitical A form of monasticism that began in Egypt in the third century where individuals and small groups withdrew from cities and organized society to seek God through prayer. The people who lived in caves and sought shelter in the desert and mountains were called hermits, from the Greek word *eremos.*

The Egyptian ascetic Pachomius (**puh-KOH-mee-uhs**) (290–346?) drew thousands of men and women to the monastic life at Tabennisi on the Upper Nile. There were too many for them to live as hermits, and Pachomius organized communities of men and women, creating a second type of monasticism, known as **coenobitic** (**seh-nuh-BIT-ik**) (communal). Saint Basil (329?–379), the scholarly bishop from Asia Minor, encouraged coenobitic monasticism, as he and the church hierarchy thought that communal living provided an environment for training the aspirant in the virtues of charity, poverty, and freedom from self-deception.

coenobitic monasticism Communal living in monasteries, encouraged by Saint Basil and the church because it provided an environment for training the aspirant in the virtues of charity, poverty, and freedom from self-deception.

Western and Eastern Monasticism

In the fourth, fifth, and sixth centuries, information about Egyptian monasticism came to the West, and both men and women sought the monastic life. Because of the difficulties and dangers of living alone in the forests of northern Europe, the eremitical form of monasticism did not take root. Most of the monasticism that developed in Gaul, Italy, Spain, England, and Ireland was coenobitic.

In 529 Benedict of Nursia (480–543), who had experimented with both the eremitical and the communal forms of monastic life, wrote a brief set of regulations for the monks who had gathered around him at Monte Cassino between Rome and Naples. Benedict's guide for monastic life, known as the *Rule of Saint Benedict*, slowly replaced all others. *The Rule of Saint Benedict* came to influence all forms of organized religious life in the Roman church. Men and women who lived in monastic houses all followed sets of rules, first those of Benedict and later those written by other individuals, and because of this came to be called **regular clergy**, from the Latin word *regulus* (rule). Priests and bishops who staffed churches in which people worshiped and who were not cut off from the world were called **secular clergy.** (According to official church doctrine, women are not members of the clergy, but this distinction was not clear to most medieval people.)

regular clergy Men and women who lived in monastic houses and followed sets of rules, first those of Benedict and later those written by other individuals.

secular clergy Priests and bishops who staffed churches where people worshiped and were not cut off from the world.

The Rule of Saint Benedict offered a simple code for ordinary men. It outlined a monastic life of regularity, discipline, and moderation in an atmosphere of silence. Each monk had ample food and adequate sleep. The monk spent part of each day in formal prayer, which Benedict called the *Opus Dei* (Work of God) and Christians later termed the *divine office*, the public prayer of the church. This consisted of chanting psalms and other prayers from the Bible in the part of the monastery church called the "choir." The rest of the day was passed in manual labor, study, and private prayer.

Why did the Benedictine form of monasticism eventually replace other forms of Western monasticism? The monastic life as conceived by Saint Benedict struck a balance between asceticism and activity. It thus provided opportunities for men of entirely different abilities and talents—from mechanics to gardeners to literary scholars. The Benedictine form of religious life also proved congenial to women. Five miles from Monte Cassino at Plombariola, Benedict's twin sister Scholastica (*skoh-LAS-tih-kuh*) (480–543) adapted the *Rule* for use by her community of nuns.

Benedictine monasticism also succeeded partly because it was so materially successful. In the seventh and eighth centuries monasteries pushed back forests and wastelands, drained swamps, and experimented with crop rotation. Benedictine houses made a significant contribution to the agricultural development of Europe. The communal nature of their organization, whereby property was held in common and profits were pooled and reinvested, made this contribution possible.

Finally, monasteries conducted schools for local young people. Some students learned about prescriptions and herbal remedies and went on to provide medical treatment in their localities. A few copied manuscripts and wrote books. Local and royal governments drew on the services of the literate men and able administrators the monasteries produced. This was not what Saint Benedict had intended, but perhaps the effectiveness of the institution he designed made it inevitable.

Monasticism in the Greek Orthodox world differed in fundamental ways from the monasticism that evolved in western Europe. First, while *The Rule of Saint Benedict* gradually became the universal guide for all western European monasteries, each individual house in the Byzantine world developed its own set of rules for organization and behavior, including rules about diet, clothing, liturgical functions, commemorative services for benefactors, the training of monks and nuns, and the election of officials. Second, education never became a central feature of the Greek houses. Monks and nuns had to be literate to perform the services of the choir, but no monastery assumed responsibility for the general training of the local young.

There were also similarities between Western and Eastern monasticism. As in the West, Eastern monasteries became wealthy, with fields, pastures, livestock, and buildings. Since bishops and patriarchs of the Greek church were recruited only from the monasteries, Greek houses also exercised cultural influence.

Christian Ideas and Practices

How did Christian thinkers adapt Greco-Roman ideas to Christian theology?

The evolution of Christianity was not simply a matter of institutions such as the papacy and monasteries, but also of ideas. Initially, Christians had believed that the end of the world was near and that they should dissociate themselves from the "filth" of Roman culture. The church father Tertullian (ter-TUHL-ee-uhn) (ca. 160–220) claimed: "We have no need for curiosity since Jesus Christ, nor for inquiry since the gospel." Gradually, however, Christians developed a culture of ideas that drew upon classical influences. The distinguished theologian Saint Jerome (340–419) translated the Old and New Testaments from Hebrew and Greek into vernacular Latin; his edition is known as the "Vulgate." The synthesis of Greco-Roman and Christian ideas found greatest expression in the writings of Saint Augustine, whose work had a profound influence on Christian theology.

Christian Notions of Gender and Sexuality

Christian attitudes toward gender and sexuality provide a good example of the ways early Christians both adopted and adapted the views of their contemporary world. In his plan of salvation, Jesus considered women the equal of men. He attributed no disreputable qualities to women and did not refer to them as inferior creatures. On the contrary, women were among his earliest and most faithful converts. He discussed his mission with them (John 4:21–25), and the first persons to whom he revealed himself after his resurrection were women (Matthew 28:9–10).

Women took an active role in the spread of Christianity, preaching, acting as missionaries, being martyred alongside men, and perhaps even baptizing believers. Because early Christians believed that the Second Coming of Christ was imminent, they devoted their energies to their new spiritual family of co-believers. Early Christians often met in people's homes and called one another brother and sister, a metaphorical use of family terms that was new to the Roman Empire.

Some women embraced the ideal of virginity and either singly or in monastic communities declared themselves "virgins in the service of Christ." All this made Christianity seem dangerous to many Romans, especially when becoming Christian actually led some young people to avoid marriage, which was viewed by Romans as the foundation of society and the proper patriarchal order.

Not all Christian teachings about gender were radical, however. In the first century C.E. male church leaders began to place restrictions on female believers. Paul and later writers forbade women to preach, and women were gradually excluded from holding official positions in Christianity other than in women's monasteries. In so limiting the activities of female believers Christianity was following classical Mediterranean culture, just as it patterned its official hierarchy after that of the Roman Empire.

Christian teachings about sexuality also built on classical culture. Many early church leaders, who are often called the church fathers, renounced marriage and sought to live chaste lives not only because they expected the Second Coming imminently, but also because they accepted the hostility toward the body that derived from certain strains of Hellenistic philosophy. Just as spirit was superior to matter, the mind was superior to the body. Though God had clearly sanctioned marriage, celibacy was the highest good. This emphasis on self-denial led to a strong streak of misogyny (hatred of women) in their writings, for they saw women and female sexuality as the chief obstacles to their preferred existence. They also saw intercourse as little more than animal lust, the triumph of the inferior body over the superior mind. Same-sex relations—which were generally acceptable in the Greco-Roman world, especially if they were between socially unequal individuals—were evil. The church fathers' misogyny and hostility toward sexuality had a greater influence on the formation of later attitudes than did the relatively egalitarian actions and words of Jesus.

Saint Augustine on Human Nature, Will, and Sin

The most influential church father in the West was Saint Augustine of Hippo (354–430). Saint Augustine was born into an urban family in what is now Algeria in North Africa. His father, a minor civil servant, was a pagan; his mother, Monica, a devout Christian. It was not until adulthood that he converted to his mother's religion. As bishop of the city of Hippo Regius, he was a renowned preacher, a vigorous defender of orthodox Christianity, and the author of more than ninety-three books and treatises.

Augustine's autobiography, *The Confessions*, is a literary masterpiece. Written in the rhetorical style and language of late Roman antiquity, it marks the synthesis of Greco-Roman forms and Christian thought. *The Confessions* describes Augustine's moral struggle, the conflict between his spiritual aspirations and his sensual self. Many Greek and Roman philosophers had taught that knowledge and virtue are the same: a person who knows what is right will do what is right. Augustine rejected this idea. People do not always act on the basis of rational knowledge.

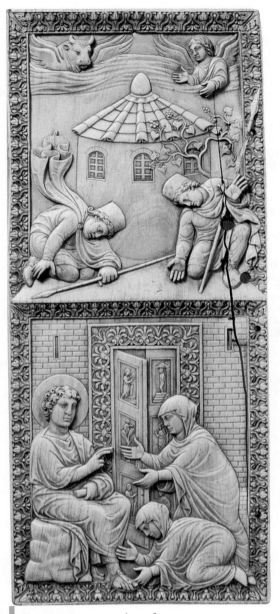

The Marys at Jesus' Tomb
This late-fourth-century ivory panel tells the story of Mary Magdalene and another Mary who went to Jesus' tomb to anoint the body (Matthew 28:1–7). At the top, guards collapse when an angel descends from Heaven, and at the bottom, the Marys listen to the angel telling them that Jesus had risen. Immediately after this, according to Matthew's Gospel, Jesus appears to the women. Here the artist uses Roman artistic styles to convey Christian subject matter, an example of the assimilation of classical form and Christian teaching. (Castello Sforzesco/Scala/Art Resource, NY)

sacraments Certain rituals defined by the church in which God bestows benefits on the believer through grace.

For example, Augustine regarded a life of chastity as the best possible life even before he became a Christian. As he notes in *The Confessions*, as a young man he prayed to God for "chastity and continency" and added "but not yet." His education had not made his will strong enough to avoid temptation; that would come only through God's power and grace.

Augustine's ideas on sin, grace, and redemption became the foundation of all subsequent Western Christian theology, Protestant as well as Catholic. He wrote that the basic or dynamic force in any individual is the will. When Adam ate the fruit forbidden by God in the Garden of Eden (Genesis 3:6), he committed the "original sin" and corrupted the will. Adam's sin was not simply his own, but was passed on to all later humans through sexual intercourse; even infants were tainted. Augustine viewed sexual desire as the result of Adam and Eve's disobedience, linking sexuality even more clearly with sin than had earlier church fathers. Because Adam disobeyed God, all human beings have an innate tendency to sin: their will is weak. But according to Augustine, God restores the strength of the will through grace, which is transmitted in certain rituals that the church defined as **sacraments.** Grace results from God's decisions, not from any merit on the part of the individual.

When the Visigothic (**viz-ee-GOTH-ic**) chieftain Alaric (**AL-er-ik**) conquered Rome in 410, horrified pagans blamed the disaster on the Christians. In response, Augustine wrote *City of God*. This original work contrasts Christianity with the secular society in which it existed. According to Augustine, history is the account of God acting in time. Human history reveals that there are two kinds of people: those who live the life of the flesh in the City of Babylon and those who live the life of the spirit in the City of God. The former will endure eternal hellfire; the latter will enjoy eternal bliss.

Augustine maintained that states came into existence as the result of people's inclination to sin. The state provides the peace, justice, and order that Christians need in order to pursue their pilgrimage to the City of God. The church, while not the equivalent of the City of God, is responsible for the salvation of all—including Christian rulers. Churches later used Augustine's theory to argue their superiority over secular authority. This remained the dominant political theory until the late thirteenth century.

Christian Missionaries and Conversion

What techniques did missionaries develop to convert barbarian peoples to Christianity?

The word *catholic* derives from a Greek word meaning "general," "universal," or "worldwide." Christ had said that his teaching was for all peoples, and Christians sought to make their faith catholic—that is, believed everywhere. This could be accomplished only through missionary activity. As Saint Paul had written to the Christian community at Colossae (**kuh-LOS-ee**) in Asia Minor, "there is no room for distinction between Greek and Jew, between the circumcised or the uncircumcised, or between barbarian or Scythian (**SITH-ee-uhn**), slave and free man. There is only Christ; he is everything and he is in everything."[2] Paul urged Christians to bring the "good news" of Christ to all peoples. The Mediterranean served as the highway over which Christianity spread to the cities of the Roman Empire. From there missionaries took Christian teachings to the countryside, and then to areas beyond the borders of the empire.

Missionaries on the Continent

Among the Germanic tribes of western Europe, religion was not a private or individual matter. It was a social affair, and the religion of the chieftain or king determined the religion of the people. Thus missionaries concentrated their initial efforts not on the people, but on kings or tribal chieftains. According to custom, kings negotiated with all foreign powers, including the gods. Because Christian missionaries represented a "foreign" power (the Christian God), the king dealt with them. Germanic kings accepted Christianity because they believed that the Christian God was more powerful than pagan gods and that the Christian God would deliver victory in battle, or because Christianity taught obedience to (kingly) authority, or because Christian priests possessed knowledge and a charisma that could be associated with kingly power. Kings who converted, such as Ethelbert of Kent and the Frankish chieftain Clovis (KLOH-vis), sometimes had Christian wives. Conversion may also have indicated that barbarian kings wanted to enjoy the cultural advantages that Christianity brought, such as literate assistants and an ideological basis for their rule.

In eastern Europe, missionaries traveled far beyond the boundaries of the Byzantine Empire. In 863 the emperor Michael III sent the brothers Cyril (826–869) and Methodius (815–885) (muh-THOH-dee-uhs) to preach Christianity in Moravia (a region of the modern central Czech Republic). Other missionaries succeeded in converting the Russians in the tenth century. Cyril invented a Slavic alphabet using Greek characters; this script, called the "Cyrillic (sih-RIL-ik) alphabet," is still in use today. Cyrillic script made possible the birth of Russian literature. Similarly, Byzantine art and architecture became the basis and inspiration of Russian forms. The Byzantines were so successful that the Russians claimed to be the successors of the Byzantine Empire. For a time Moscow was even known as the "Third Rome" (the second Rome being Constantinople).

Missionaries in the British Isles

Tradition identifies the conversion of the Celts of Ireland with Saint Patrick (ca. 385–461). After a vision urged him to Christianize Ireland, Patrick studied in Gaul and was consecrated a bishop in 432. He returned to Ireland, where he converted the Irish tribe by tribe, first baptizing the king. By the time of Patrick's death, the majority of the Irish people had received Christian baptism. In his missionary work, Patrick had the strong support of Bridget of Kildare (kil-DAIR) (ca. 450–ca. 528), daughter of a wealthy chieftain. Bridget defied parental pressure to marry and became a nun. She and the other nuns at Kildare instructed relatives and friends in basic Christian doctrine, made religious vestments for churches, copied books, taught children, and above all set a religious example by their lives of prayer. In Ireland and later in continental Europe, women shared in the process of conversion.

The Christianization of the English began in 597, when Pope Gregory I (590–604) sent a delegation of monks under the Roman Augustine to Britain. Augustine's approach, like Patrick's, was to concentrate on converting the king. When he succeeded in converting Ethelbert, king of Kent, the baptism of Ethelbert's people took place as a matter of course. Augustine established his headquarters, or see, at Canterbury, the capital of Kent.

Ardagh Silver Chalice

This chalice, crafted about 800 C.E. and used for wine in Christian ceremonies, formed part of the treasure of Ardagh Cathedral in County Limerick, Ireland. Made of several types of metal, it is decorated with Celtic patterns in the same way as Irish manuscripts from this era. Christianity was widespread in Ireland long before anywhere else in northern Europe, and Celtic traditions and practices differed significantly from those of Rome. (National Museum of Ireland)

In the course of the seventh century, two Christian forces competed for the conversion of the pagan Anglo-Saxons: Roman-oriented missionaries traveling north from Canterbury, and Celtic monks from Ireland and northwestern Britain. The Roman and Celtic church organization, types of monastic life, and methods of arriving at the date of the central feast of the Christian calendar (Easter) differed completely. Through the influence of King Oswiu of Northumbria (nawr-THUHM-bree-uh) and the energetic abbess Hilda of Whitby, the Synod (ecclesiastical council) held at Whitby in 664 opted to follow the Roman practices. The conversion of the English and the close attachment of the English church to Rome had far-reaching consequences because Britain later served as a base for the full-scale Christianization of the continent (see Map 7.2).

Conversion and Assimilation

Between the fifth and tenth centuries, the great majority of peoples living on the European continent and the nearby islands were baptized as Christians. When a ruler marched his people to the waters of baptism, though, the work of Christianization had only begun. Baptism meant either sprinkling the head or immersing the body in water. Conversion meant awareness and acceptance of the beliefs of Christianity, including those that seemed strange or radical, such as "love your enemies" or "do good to those that hate you."

How did missionaries and priests get masses of pagan and illiterate peoples to understand and live by Christian ideals and teachings? They did so through preaching, assimilation, and the penitential system. Preaching aimed at presenting the basic teachings of Christianity and strengthening the newly baptized in their faith through stories about the lives of Christ and the saints. But deeply ingrained pagan customs and practices could not be stamped out by words alone or even by imperial edicts. Christian missionaries often pursued a policy of assimila-

Procession to a New Church

In this sixth-century ivory carving, two men in a wagon, accompanied by a procession of people holding candles, carry a relic casket to a church under construction. Workers are putting tiles on the church roof. New churches often received holy items when they were dedicated, and processions were common ways in which people expressed community devotion. (Cathedral Treasury, Trier. Photo: Ann Muenchow)

tion, easing the conversion of pagan men and women by stressing similarities between their customs and beliefs and those of Christianity. In the same way that classically trained scholars such as Jerome and Augustine blended Greco-Roman and Christian ideas, missionaries and converts mixed pagan ideas and practices with Christian ones. Bogs and lakes sacred to Germanic gods became associated with saints, as did various aspects of ordinary life, such as traveling, planting crops, and worrying about a sick child. Aspects of existing midwinter celebrations, which often centered on the return of the sun as the days became longer, were incorporated into celebrations of Christmas. Spring rituals involving eggs and rabbits (both symbols of fertility) were added to Easter.

Also instrumental in converting pagans was the rite of reconciliation in which the sinner was able to receive God's forgiveness. The penitent knelt individually before the priest, who questioned the penitent about the sins he or she might have committed. A penance such as fasting on bread and water for a period of time or saying specific prayers was imposed as medicine for the soul. The priest and penitent were guided by manuals known as **penitentials** (pen-uh-TENT-shuls), which included lists of sins and the appropriate penance. Penitentials gave pagans a sense of expected behavior. The penitential system also encouraged the private examination of conscience and offered relief from the burden of sinful deeds.

Most religious observances continued to be community matters, however, as they had been in the ancient world. People joined with family members, friends, and neighbors to celebrate baptisms and funerals, presided over by a priest. They prayed to saints or to the Virgin Mary to intercede with God, or they simply asked the saints for protection and blessing. The entire village participated in processions marking saints' days or points in the agricultural year, often carrying images of saints or their **relics**—bones, articles of clothing, or other objects associated with the life of a saint—around the houses and fields.

penitentials Manuals for the examination of conscience.

relics Bones, articles of clothing, or other objects associated with the life of a saint.

Section Review

- St. Paul urged Christians to make their faith Catholic, meaning "universal" or "worldwide."

- Christian missionaries spread their faith throughout the Roman Empire and beyond.

- In western Europe missionaries gained influence by converting leaders; in eastern Europe Christianity spread to Moravia and Russia, bringing with it the Cyrillic alphabet and inspiring Russian literature.

- Saint Patrick brought Christianity to Ireland while the nun Bridget of Kildare and other women worked to spread it there.

- Roman and Celtic church organization differed in types of monastic life and dates of the Christian calendar, but after an ecclesiastical council in 664, the British followed the Roman practices, tying the English church to Rome.

- Christian missionaries accomplished conversion of pagans by preaching and by assimilating existing pagan customs.

- The rite of reconciliation forgave individual sins through penance and confession to a priest, yet religion continued to be mostly a community matter.

Migrating Peoples

What were some of the causes of the barbarian migrations and how did they affect the regions of Europe?

The migration of peoples from one area to another has been a dominant and continuing feature of Western history. Mass movements of Europeans occurred in the fourth through sixth centuries, in the ninth and tenth centuries, and in the twelfth and thirteenth centuries. From the sixteenth century to the present, such movements have been almost continuous, involving not just the European continent but the entire world. The causes of early migrations varied and are not thoroughly understood by scholars. But there is no question that the migrations profoundly affected both the regions to which peoples moved and the ones they left behind.

Celts, Germans, and Huns

In surveying the world around them, the ancient Greeks often conceptualized things in dichotomies, or sets of opposites: light/dark, hot/cold, wet/dry, mind/body, male/female, and so on. One of their key dichotomies was Greek/non-Greek, and the Greeks coined the word *barbaros* for those whose native language was not Greek, because they seemed to the Greeks to be speaking nonsense syllables—bar, bar, bar. ("Bar-bar" is the Greek equivalent to "blah-blah" or "yada-yada.") *Barbaros* originally meant simply not speaking Greek, but gradually it also implied unruly, savage, and more primitive than the advanced civilization of Greece. The word brought this meaning with it when it came into Latin and other European languages, with the Romans referring to those who lived beyond the northeastern boundary of Roman territory as **barbarians.** Migrating groups that the Romans labeled as barbarians had pressed along the Rhine-Danube frontier of the Roman Empire since about 150 C.E. (see page 109). In the third and fourth centuries, increasing pressures on the frontiers from the east and north placed greater demands on Roman military manpower, which plague and a declining birthrate had reduced. Therefore, Roman generals recruited barbarian refugees and tribes allied with the Romans to serve in the Roman army, and some rose to the highest ranks.

As Julius Caesar advanced through Gaul between 58 and 50 B.C.E. (see page 102), the largest barbarian groups he encountered were Celts (whom the Romans called Gauls) and Germans. Modern historians have tended to use the terms *German* and *Celt* in a racial sense, but recent research stresses that *Celt* and *German* are linguistic terms, a Celt being a person who spoke a Celtic language, an ancestor of the modern Gaelic or Breton language, and a German one who spoke a Germanic language, an ancestor of modern German, Dutch, Danish, Swedish, or Norwegian.

Celts and Germans were similar to one another in many ways. In the first century C.E., the Celts lived east of the Rhine River in an area bounded by the Main Valley and extending westward to the Somme (**sawm**) River. Germans were more numerous along the North and Baltic Seas. Both Germans and Celts used wheeled plows and a three-field system of crop rotation. Before the introduction of Christianity, both Celtic and Germanic peoples were polytheistic, with hundreds of gods and goddesses with specialized functions whose celebrations were often linked to points in the yearly agricultural cycle. Worship was often outdoors at sacred springs, groves, or lakes.

barbarians A name given by the Romans to all peoples living outside the frontiers of the Roman Empire (except the Persians).

Vandal Landowner

In this mosaic, a Vandal landowner rides out from his Roman-style house. His clothing—Roman short tunic, cloak, and sandals—reflects the way some Celtic and Germanic tribes accepted Roman lifestyles, though his beard is more typical of barbarian men's fashion.

(Courtesy of the Trustees of the British Museum)

The Celts had developed iron manufacturing, using shaft furnaces as sophisticated as those of the Romans to produce iron swords and spears. Celtic priests, called druids (DROO-idz), had legal and educational as well as religious functions, orally passing down laws and traditions from generation to generation. Bards singing poems and ballads also passed down stories of heroes and gods, which were written down much later. Celtic peoples conquered by the Romans often assimilated to Roman ways, adapting the Latin language and other aspects of Roman culture. By the fourth century C.E., under pressure from Germanic groups, the Celts had moved westward, settling in Brittany (modern northwestern France) and throughout the British Isles (England, Wales, Scotland, and Ireland). The Picts of Scotland as well as the Welsh, Britons, and Irish were peoples of Celtic descent. (See Map 7.3.)

MAPPING THE PAST

MAP 7.3 The Barbarian Migrations

This map shows the migrations of various barbarian groups in late antiquity and can be used to answer the following questions: **[1]** The map has no political boundaries. What does this suggest about the impact of barbarian migrations on political structures? **[2]** Human migration is caused by a combination of push factors (circumstances that lead people to leave a place) and pull factors (things that attract people to a new location). Based on the information in this and earlier chapters, what push and pull factors might have shaped the migration patterns you see on the map? **[3]** The movements of barbarian peoples used to be labeled "invasions" and are now usually described as "migrations." How do the dates on the map support the newer understanding of these movements?

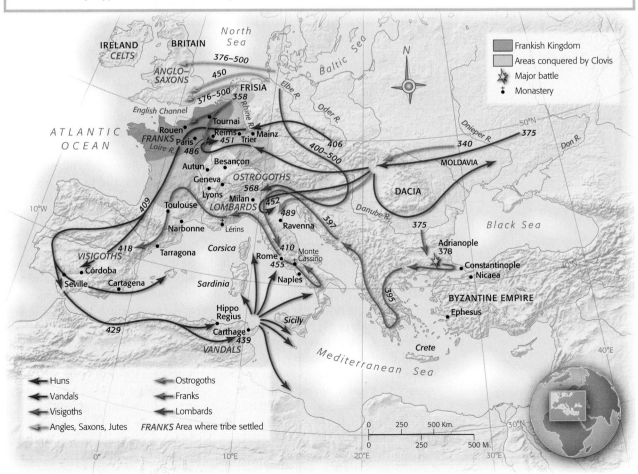

The migrations of the Germanic peoples were important in the political and social transformations of late antiquity. Many modern scholars have tried to explain who the Germans were and why they migrated. The present consensus, based on the study of linguistic and archaeological evidence, is that there was not one but rather many Germanic peoples with very different cultural traditions. The largest Germanic tribe, the Goths, was a polyethnic group of about one hundred thousand people, including perhaps fifteen thousand to twenty thousand warriors. The tribe was supplemented by slaves, who, because of their desperate situation under Roman rule, joined the Goths during their migrations.[3]

Why did the Germans migrate? Like the Celts, in part they were pushed by groups living farther eastward, especially by the Huns from central Asia in the fourth and fifth centuries. In part, they were searching for more regular supplies of food, better farmland, and a warmer climate. Conflicts within and among Germanic groups also led to war and disruption, which motivated groups to move. Franks fought Alemanni (al-uh-MAN-ahy) in Gaul; Visigoths fought Vandals in the Iberian Peninsula and across North Africa; and Angles and Saxons fought Celtic-speaking Britons in England.

All these factors can be seen in the movement of the Visigoths, one of the Germanic tribes, from an area north of the Black Sea southeastward into the Roman Empire. Pressured by defeat in battle, starvation, and the movement of the Huns, the Visigoths petitioned the emperor Valens to admit them to the empire. Seeing in the hordes of warriors the solution to his manpower problem, Valens agreed. Once the Visigoths were inside the empire, Roman authorities exploited their hunger by forcing them to sell their own people as slaves in exchange for dog flesh: "the going rate was one dog for one Goth." Still, the Visigoths sought peace. Fritigern offered himself as a friend and ally of Rome in exchange for the province of Thrace—land, crops, and livestock. Confident of victory over a considerably smaller army, Valens and his council chose to battle the Visigoths and lost.

Alaric I's invasion of Italy and sack of Rome in 410 represents the culmination of hostility between the Visigoths and the Romans. The Goths burned and looted the city for three days, which caused many Romans to wonder whether God had deserted them. This led the imperial government to pull its troops from the British Isles and many areas north of the Alps, leaving these northern areas more vulnerable and open to migrating groups. A year later Alaric died, and his successor led his people into southwestern Gaul.[4] Establishing their headquarters at Toulouse, they exercised a weak domination over Spain until a Muslim victory at Guadalete in 711 ended Visigothic rule.

One significant factor in Germanic migration was pressure from nomadic steppe peoples from central Asia. This included the Alans, Avars, Bulghars, Khazars, and most prominently the Huns, who attacked the Black Sea area and the Eastern Roman Empire beginning in the fourth century. Under the leadership of their warrior-king Attila, the Huns swept into central Europe in 451, attacking Roman settlements in the Balkans and Germanic settlements along the Danube and Rhine Rivers. After Attila turned his army southward and crossed the Alps into Italy, a papal delegation, including Pope Leo I himself, asked him not to attack Rome. Though papal diplomacy was later credited with stopping the advance of the Huns, a plague that spread among Hunnic troops and their dwindling food supplies were probably much more important. The Huns retreated from Italy, and within a year Attila was dead. Later leaders were not as effective, and the Huns were never again an important factor in European history. Their conquests had slowed down the movements of various Germanic groups, however, allowing barbarian peoples to absorb more of Roman culture as they picked the Western Roman Empire apart.

Germanic Kingdoms

Between 450 and 565, the Germans established a number of kingdoms, but none—other than the Frankish kingdom—lasted very long. The Germanic kingdoms did not have definite geographical boundaries, and their locations are approximate. The Vandals, whose destructive ways are commemorated in the word *vandal*, settled in North Africa. In northern and western Europe in the sixth century, the Burgundians (ber-GUHN-dee-uhns) ruled over lands roughly circumscribed by the old Roman army camps at Lyons, Besançon (buh-zahn-SAWN), Geneva, and Autun.

In northern Italy the Ostrogothic king Theodoric (r. 471–526) established his residence at Ravenna and gradually won control of all Italy, Sicily, and the territory north and east of the upper Adriatic. Although attached to the customs of his people, Theodoric pursued a policy of assimilation between Germans and Romans. He maintained close relations with the emperor at Constantinople and attracted able scholars such as Cassiodorus (kas-ee-uh-DAWR-uhs) (see page 212) to his administration. Theodoric's accomplishments were significant, but his administration fell apart after his death.

The kingdom established by the Franks in the sixth century, in spite of later civil wars, proved to be the most powerful and enduring of all the Germanic kingdoms. In the fourth and fifth centuries, they settled within the empire and allied with the Romans, some attaining high military and civil positions. In the sixth century one group, the Salian (SAY-lee-uhn) Franks, issued a law code called the **Salic (SAL-ik) Law,** the earliest description of Germanic customs. Chlodio (fifth century) is the first member of the Frankish dynasty for whom evidence survives. According to legend, Chlodio's wife went swimming, encountered a sea monster, and conceived Merowig. The Franks believed that Merowig, a man of supernatural origins, founded their ruling dynasty, which was thus called **Merovingian** (mer-uh-VIN-jee-uhn).

The reign of Clovis (ca. 481–511) marks the decisive period in the development of the Franks as a unified people. Through military campaigns, Clovis acquired the central provinces of Roman Gaul. Clovis's conversion to Christianity also brought him the crucial support of the papacy and of the bishops of Gaul. (See the feature "Listening to the Past: The Conversion of Clovis" on pages 160–161.) The next two centuries witnessed the steady assimilation of Franks and Gallo-Romans, as many Franks adopted the Latin language and Roman ways, and Gallo-Romans copied Frankish customs and Frankish personal names. These centuries also saw Frankish acquisition of the Burgundian kingdom and of territory held by the Goths in Provence.[5]

Salic Law A law code issued by Salian Franks that provides us with the earliest description of Germanic customs.

Merovingian The Frankish dynasty named after its founder, Merowig, a man of mythical origins.

Anglo-Saxon England

The island of Britain was populated by various Celtic-speaking tribes when it was conquered by Rome during the reign of Claudius. During the first four centuries C.E., it shared fully in the life of the Roman Empire. Towns were planned in the Roman fashion, with temples, public baths, theaters, and amphitheaters. In the countryside large manors controlled the surrounding lands. Roman merchants brought Eastern luxury goods and Eastern religions—including Christianity—into Britain. The Romans suppressed the Celtic chieftains, and a military aristocracy governed. In the course of the second and third centuries, many Celts assimilated to Roman culture, becoming Roman citizens and joining the Roman army.

When imperial troops withdrew from Britain in order to defend Rome from the Visigoths, the Picts from Scotland and the Scots from Ireland invaded British

Celtic territory. According to the eighth-century historian Bede (beed) (see page 181), the Celtic king Vortigern invited the Saxons from Denmark to help him against his rivals in Britain. Saxons and other Germanic tribes from modern-day Norway, Sweden, and Denmark turned from assistance to conquest, attacking in a hit-and-run fashion. Their goal was plunder, and at first their invasions led to no permanent settlements. As more Germanic peoples arrived, however, they took over the best lands and eventually conquered most of Britain. Some Britons fled to Wales and the westernmost parts of England, north toward Scotland, and across the English Channel to Brittany. Others remained and eventually intermarried with Germanic peoples.

Historians have labeled the period 500 to 1066, the years of the Norman Conquest, as the "Anglo-Saxon" period, after the two largest Germanic tribes, the Angles and the Saxons. The Germanic tribes destroyed Roman culture in Britain. Christianity disappeared, large urban buildings were allowed to fall apart, and tribal custom superseded Roman law.

Anglo-Saxon England was divided along ethnic and political lines. The Germanic kingdoms in the south, east, and center were opposed by the Britons in the west, who wanted to get rid of the invaders. The Anglo-Saxon kingdoms also fought among themselves, causing boundaries to shift constantly. Finally, in the ninth century, under pressure from the Viking invasions, the Celtic Britons and the Germanic Anglo-Saxons were molded together under the leadership of King Alfred of Wessex (WES-iks) (r. 871–899).

The Anglo-Saxon invasion gave rise to a rich body of Celtic mythology, particularly legends about the Celtic King Arthur, who first appeared in Welsh poetry in the sixth century and later in histories, epics, and saints' lives. Most scholars see Arthur as a composite figure who evolved over the centuries in songs and stories. According to these texts, Arthur was the illegitimate son of the king of Britain whose royal parentage was revealed when he successfully drew the invincible sword Excalibur from a stone. Arthur won recognition as king and used Excalibur to win many battles. His quests included a search for the Holy Grail, the dish supposedly used by Jesus at the Last Supper, which was said to have miraculous powers. Arthur held his court at Camelot, where his knights were seated at the Round Table, where all were equal. Those knights included Sir Tristan, Sir Galahad, Sir Percival (Parsifal), and Sir Lancelot; Lancelot's romance with Arthur's wife Guinevere (GWIN-uh-veer) led to the end of the Arthurian kingdom. In their earliest form as Welsh poems, the Arthurian legends may represent Celtic hostility to Anglo-Saxon invaders, but they later came to be more important as representations of the ideal of medieval knightly chivalry and as great stories whose retelling has continued to the present.

Barbarian Society

What patterns of social, political, and economic life characterized barbarian society?

Germanic and Celtic society had originated in the northern parts of central and western Europe and the southern regions of Scandinavia during the Iron Age (800–500 B.C.E.). After Germanic kingdoms replaced the Roman Empire as the primary political structure throughout much of Europe, barbarian customs and traditions formed the basis of European society for centuries.

Runic (ROO-nik) Inscriptions

This eighth-century chest made of whalebone depicts warriors, other human figures, and a horse, with a border of runic letters. This chest tells a story in both pictures and words. The runes are one of the varieties from the British Isles, from a time and place in which the Latin alphabet was known as well. Runes and Latin letters were used side-by-side in some parts of northern Europe for centuries. (Erich Lessing/Art Resource, NY)

runic alphabet Writings that help to give a more accurate picture of barbarian society; the oldest come from shortly after the time of Tacitus.

Kinship, Custom, and Class

Barbarians generally had no notion of the state as we use the term today; they thought in social, not political, terms. The basic social unit was the tribe, a group whose members believed that they were all descended from a common ancestor. Blood united them; kinship protected them. Law was custom—unwritten, preserved in the minds of the elders of the tribe, and handed down by word of mouth from generation to generation. Every tribe had its customs, and every member of the tribe knew what they were. Members were subject to their tribe's customary laws wherever they went, and friendly tribes respected one another's laws.

Barbarian tribes were led by tribal chieftains, who are often called kings, though this implies broader power than they actually had. The chief was the member recognized as the strongest and bravest in battle and was elected from among the male members of the strongest family. He led the tribe in war, settled disputes among its members, conducted negotiations with outside powers, and offered sacrifices to the gods. The period of migrations and conquests of the Western Roman Empire witnessed the strengthening of kingship among tribes.

Closely associated with the king in some southern tribes was the **comitatus**, or "war band." Writing at the end of the first century, Tacitus (**TAS-ee-tuhs**) described the war band as the bravest young men in the tribe. They swore loyalty to the chief, fought with him in battle, and were not supposed to leave the battlefield without him; to do so implied cowardice, disloyalty, and social disgrace. A social egalitarianism existed among members of the war band. The comitatus had importance for the later development of feudalism.

During the migrations of the third and fourth centuries, however, and as a result of constant warfare, the war band was transformed into a system of stratified

comitatus A war band, a group of young men who were closely associated with the king in some southern tribes and who swore loyalty to the chief, fought with him in battle, and were not supposed to leave the battlefield without him.

ranks. During the Ostrogothic conquest of Italy under Theodoric, warrior-nobles also sought to acquire land as both a mark of prestige and a means to power. As land and wealth came into the hands of a small elite class, social inequalities emerged and gradually grew stronger.[6] These inequalities help explain the origins of the European noble class (see pages 234).

Law

Early barbarian tribes had no written laws, but beginning in the late sixth century some tribal chieftains began to collect, write, and publish lists of their customs at the urging of Christian missionaries. The churchmen wanted to understand barbarian ways in order to assimilate the tribes into Christianity. Augustine of Canterbury, for example, persuaded King Ethelbert of Kent to have his folk laws written down; these *Dooms of Ethelbert* date from between 601 and 604, roughly five years after Augustine's arrival in Britain. Moreover, by the sixth century many barbarian kings needed regulations for the Romans under their jurisdiction as well as for their own people.

According to the code of the Salian Franks, every person had a particular monetary value to the tribe. This value was called the **wergeld** (**WUR-gild**), which literally means "man-money" or "money to buy off the spear." Men of fighting age had the highest wergeld, then women of childbearing age, children, and finally the aged. Everyone's value reflected his or her potential military worthiness. If a person accused of a crime agreed to pay the wergeld and if the victim and his or her family accepted the payment, there was peace. If the accused refused to pay the wergeld or if the victim's family refused to accept it, a blood feud ensued. Individuals depended on their kin for protection, and kinship served as a force of social control.

Some codes had specific clauses that protected the virtue of women. For example, the Salic Law of the Franks fined a man the large amount of 15 solidi (**SOL-ih-dee**) if he pressed the hand of a woman, and 35 if he touched her above the elbow. The very high fine of 600 solidi for the murder of a woman of childbearing years—the same value attached to military officers of the king, to priests, and to boys preparing to become warriors—suggests the importance of women in Frankish society, at least for their childbearing capacity.

At first, Romans had been subject to Roman law and Germans to Germanic custom. As German kings accepted Christianity and as Romans and barbarians increasingly intermarried, the distinction between the two laws blurred and, in the course of the seventh and eighth centuries, disappeared. The result would be the new feudal law, to which all who lived in certain areas were subject.

wergeld Man-money or money to buy off the spear; according to the code of Salian Franks, this is the particular monetary value that every person had in the tribe.

Social and Economic Structures

Barbarian groups usually resided in small villages, and climate and geography determined the basic patterns of agricultural and pastoral life. Many tribes lived in small settlements on the edges of clearings where they raised barley, wheat, oats, peas, and beans. Men and women tilled their fields with simple wooden scratch plows and harvested their grains with small iron sickles. The kernels of grain were eaten as porridge, ground up for flour, or fermented into strong, thick beer; the vast majority of people's caloric intake came from grain in some form.

Within the small villages, there were great differences in wealth and status. Free men and their families constituted the largest class. The number of cattle a man possessed indicated his wealth and determined his social status. Free men also shared in tribal warfare. Slaves (prisoners of war) worked as farm laborers, herdsmen, and household servants.

Did the barbarians produce goods for trade and exchange? Ironworking represented the most advanced craft; much of northern Europe had iron deposits, and the dense forests provided wood for charcoal. Most villages had an oven and smiths who produced agricultural tools and instruments of war—one-edged swords, arrowheads, and shields. In the first two centuries C.E., the quantity and quality of Germanic goods increased dramatically, and the first steel swords were superior to the weapons of Roman troops. These goods were produced for war and for the subsistence economy, not for trade. Goods were also used for gift giving, a major social custom. Gift giving conferred status on the giver, who, in giving, showed his higher (economic) status, cemented friendship, and placed the receiver in his debt.[7] Goods that could not be produced in the village were acquired by raiding and warfare rather than by commercial exchanges.

Barbarian tribes were understood to be made up of kin groups, and those kin groups were made up of families, the basic social unit in barbarian society. Families were responsible for the debts and actions of their members and for keeping the peace in general. Barbarian law codes set strict rules of inheritance based on position in the family and often set aside a portion of land that could not be sold or given away by any family member.

Germanic society was patriarchal: within each household the father had authority over his wife, children, and slaves. Some wealthy and powerful men had more than one wife, a pattern that continued even after they became Christian, but polygamy was not widespread among ordinary people. A woman was considered to be under the legal guardianship of a man, and she had fewer rights to own property than did Roman women in the late Empire. However, once they were widowed (and there must have been many widows in such a violent, warring society), women sometimes assumed their husbands' rights over family property and held the guardianship of their children.

Women found outlets for their talents in monasteries and convents as writers, copyists, artists, embroiderers, teachers, and estate managers. Some houses of religious women, such as Mauberge in northern Francia under Abbess Aldegund (ca. 661), produced important scholarship. The dowry required for entrance to a convent restricted admission as full sisters to upper-class women, but poorer women were taken in as lay sisters. Many women viewed the convent as a place of refuge from family pressures or tribal violence. The sixth-century Queen Radegund, for example, was forced to marry Chlotar I, the murderer of several of her relatives. Radegund later escaped her polygamous union and lived out her life in a convent.

Section Review

- Barbarian society was based on the tribe, led by a tribal chieftain (king) and a loyal and egalitarian comitatus (war band), though later it became stratified into ranks and landholding warrior-nobles eventually gained power.

- Barbarian tribes began to produce written collections of their laws and customs to rule better and for missionaries, who wanted to assimilate the tribes into Christianity.

- Franks protected themselves through Germanic customs and the Salic Law and eventually incorporated Roman law, as German kings became Christians and intermarried with Romans.

- Barbarians lived in kin groups of families from small agricultural villages with free men owning cattle and fighting, while slaves (prisoners of war) worked as laborers and servants.

- Barbarians worked with iron to produce steel swords and other tools for war but not for trade, relying on raiding and warfare to obtain goods they could not produce.

- Women had few rights but many found outlets for their creative talents and leadership abilities in convents.

Chapter Review

How was the Byzantine Empire able to survive for so long, and what were its most important achievements? (page 134)

Late antiquity was a period of rupture and transformation, but also of continuities and assimilation. Migrating barbarian groups broke the Western Roman Empire apart, creating much smaller states and more localized economies. As they encountered Roman culture and became Christian, their own ways of doing things were transformed, and the result was a blend of barbarian and Roman culture. In eastern Europe, the

Key Terms

Petrine Doctrine (p. 140)

Arianism (p. 141)

heresy (p. 141)

(continued)

Byzantine Empire thrived throughout late antiquity, maintaining Roman traditions. Throughout Europe, leaders in the Christian Church energetically developed more complex ideas and stronger institutional structures, transforming Christianity into the most powerful agent in the making of Europe. In the east, the Byzantine Empire withstood attacks from Germanic tribes and steppe peoples and remained a state until 1453, a thousand years longer than the Western Roman Empire. Byzantium preserved the philosophical and scientific texts of the ancient world—which later formed the basis for study in science and medicine in both Europe and the Arabic world—and produced a great synthesis of Roman law, the Justinian *Code*, which shapes legal structures in much of Europe and former European colonies to this day.

What factors enabled the Christian church to expand and thrive? (page 137)

Christianity gained the support of the fourth-century emperors and gradually adopted the Roman system of hierarchical organization. The church possessed able administrators and leaders whose skills were tested in the chaotic environment of the end of the Roman Empire in the West. Bishops expanded their activities, and in the fifth century the bishops of Rome began to stress their supremacy over other Christian communities. Monasteries offered opportunities for individuals to develop deeper spiritual devotion and also provided a model of Christian living, a pattern of agricultural development, and a place for education and learning.

How did Christian thinkers adapt Greco-Roman ideas to Christian theology? (page 144)

Christian thinkers reinterpreted the classics in a Christian sense, incorporating elements of Greek and Roman philosophy and of various pagan religious groups into Christian teachings. Prime among these were certain aspects of Greco-Roman notions of gender and sexuality. Most Christian thinkers accepted Greco-Roman ideas that men were superior to women, though they viewed sexuality and the body with greater suspicion than had ancient pagans and developed a strong sense that chastity and an ascetic life were superior to marriage and family life. Of these early thinkers, Augustine of Hippo was the most influential. His ideas about sin, free will, sexuality, and the role of government shaped western European thought from the fifth century on.

What techniques did missionaries develop to convert barbarian peoples to Christianity? (page 146)

Christianity had a dynamic missionary policy, and the church slowly succeeded in assimilating—that is, adapting—barbarian peoples into Christian teaching. Christian missionaries preached the Gospel to Germanic, Celtic, and Slavic peoples, instructed them in the basic tenets of the Christian faith, and used penitentials to give them a sense of expected behavior. Christianity refashioned the Germanic and classical legacies, creating new rituals and practices that were meaningful to people.

What were some of the causes of the barbarian migrations and how did they affect the regions of Europe? (page 149)

The migration of barbarian groups into Europe from the East affected both the regions into which peoples moved and the ones they left behind. Migrations were caused by many factors, including food shortages, disputes among groups, and pressure from outside, and they sometimes involved military actions, though not always. Barbarians are often divided into large linguistic groups, such as the Celtic and Germanic tribes, with ties to other tribes based on kinship and military alliances, not on loyalty to a particular government. Most barbarian states were weak and short-lived, though that of the Salian Franks was relatively more unified and powerful. Germanic-speaking Angles and Saxons invaded Celtic-speaking England and established a group of small kingdoms that slowly became more unified.

What patterns of social, political, and economic life characterized barbarian society? (page 154)

Though barbarian states were generally feeble politically, barbarian customs and traditions formed the basis of European society for centuries. Barbarian law codes, written down for the first time in the sixth century, set out social and gender distinctions and held the family responsible for the actions of an individual. Most people lived in family groups in villages, where men, women, and children shared in the agricultural labor that sustained society. Christianity and the barbarian states absorbed many aspects of Roman culture, and the Byzantine Empire continued to thrive, but western Europe was very different in 600 from how it had been in 350.

Notes

1. Matthew 16:18–19.
2. Colossians 3:9–11.
3. Wolfram, *History of the Goths* (Berkeley: University of California Press, 1988), pp. 6–10.
4. Ibid., pp. 125–131.
5. E. James, *The Franks* (New York: Basil Blackwell, 1988), pp. 3, 7–10, 58.
6. P. J. Geary, *Before France and Germany: The Creation and Transformation of the Merovingian World* (New York: Oxford University Press, 1988), pp. 108–112.
7. Ibid., p. 50.

To assess your mastery of this chapter, go to **bedfordstmartins.com/mckaywestbrief**

Listening to the Past

The Conversion of Clovis

Modern Christian doctrine holds that conversion is a gradual process of turning toward Jesus and his teachings. But in the early medieval world, conversion was perceived more as a one-time event determined by the tribal chieftain. This selection about the Frankish king Clovis is from The History of the Franks *by Gregory, bishop of Tours (ca. 504–594), written about a century after the events it describes.*

Queen Clotild continued to pray that her husband might recognize the true God and give up his idol-worship. Nothing could persuade him to accept Christianity. Finally war broke out against the Alamanni and in this conflict he was forced by necessity to accept what he had refused of his own free will. It so turned out that when the two armies met on the battlefield there was a great slaughter and the troops of Clovis were rapidly being annihilated. He raised his eyes to Heaven when he saw this, felt compunction in his heart and was moved to tears. "Jesus Christ," he said, "you who Clotild maintains to be the Son of the living God, you who deign to give help to those in travail and victory to those who trust in you, in faith I beg the glory of your help. If you will give me victory over my enemies, and if I may have evidence to that miraculous power which the people dedicated to your name say that they have experienced, then I will believe in you and I will be baptized in your name. I have called upon my own gods, but, as I see only too clearly, they have no intention of helping me. I therefore cannot believe that they possess any power for they do not come to the assistance of those who trust them. I now call upon you. I want to believe in you, but I must first be saved from my enemies." Even as he said this the Alamanni turned their backs and began to run away. As soon as they saw that their King was killed, they submitted to Clovis. "We beg you," they said, "to put an end to this slaughter. We are prepared to obey you." Clovis stopped the war. He made a speech in which he called for peace. Then he went home. He told the Queen how he had won a victory by calling on the name of Christ. This happened in the fifteenth year of his reign (496).

The Queen then ordered Saint Remigius, Bishop of the town of Rheims (**reemz**), to be summoned in secret. She begged him to impart the

Ninth-century ivory carving showing Clovis being baptized by Saint Remi. (Musée Condé, Chantilly/Laurie Platt Winfrey, Inc.)

word of salvation to the King. The Bishop asked Clovis to meet him in private and began to urge him to believe in the true God, Maker of Heaven and earth, and to forsake his idols, which were powerless to help him or anyone else. The King replied: "I have listened to you willingly, holy father. There remains one obstacle. The people under my command will not agree to forsake their gods. I will go and put to them what you have just said to me." He arranged a meeting with his people, but God in his power had preceded him, and before he could say a word all those present shouted in unison: "We will give up worshipping our mortal gods, pious King, and we are prepared to follow the immortal God about whom Remigius preaches." This news was reported to the Bishop. He was greatly pleased and he ordered the baptismal pool to be made ready.

Questions for Analysis

1. According to this account, why did Clovis ultimately accept Christianity?

2. For the Salian Franks, what was the best proof of divine power?

3. On the basis of this selection, do you consider *The History of the Franks* reliable history? Why?

Sources: L. Thorpe, trans., *The History of the Franks by Gregory of Tours* (Harmondsworth, England: Penguin, 1974), p. 159; P. J. Geary, ed., *Readings in Medieval History* (Peterborough, Ontario: Broadview Press, 1991), pp. 165–166.

CHAPTER 8

Europe in the Early Middle Ages

600–1000

Chapter Preview

The Spread of Islam
How did Islam take root in the Middle East and then spread to Europe?

The Frankish Kingdom
How did Frankish rulers govern their kingdoms?

The Empire of Charlemagne
How did Charlemagne gain control of a large part of Europe and how did power become decentralized after his death?

Early Medieval Scholarship and Culture
What were the significant intellectual and cultural changes in Charlemagne's era?

Invasions and Migrations
What effects did the assaults and migrations of the Vikings, Magyars, and Muslims have on the rest of Europe?

INDIVIDUALS IN SOCIETY: Ebo of Reims

LISTENING TO THE PAST: Feudal Homage and Fealty

Garden built by Muslim rulers in Seville, Spain. Tranquil gardens such as this one represented paradise in Islamic culture, perhaps because of the religion's desert origins. (Ric Ergenbright/Corbis)

In the fifteenth century writers and scholars in the growing cities of northern Italy began to think that they were living in a new era, one in which the glories of ancient Greece and Rome were being reborn. What separated their own time from classical antiquity, in their opinion, was a long period of darkness, to which a seventeenth-century professor gave the name "Middle Ages" (*Medium Aevum* in Latin). In this conceptualization, Western history was divided into three periods—ancient, medieval (a word derived from the Latin), and modern.

This three-part schema is still the primary way of organizing Western history. Exactly what marked the dividing lines between these periods was not very clear, however. For a long time the end of the Roman Empire in the West in 476 was seen as the division between the classical period and the Middle Ages, but as we saw in the last chapter, more recent historians have emphasized continuities as well as changes in the fifth and sixth centuries. The transition from ancient to medieval was a slow process, not a single event. The agents in this process included not only the Germanic tribes whose migrations broke the Roman Empire apart but also the new religion of Islam, Slavic and steppe (**step**) peoples in eastern Europe, and Christian officials and missionaries. The period from the end of antiquity to about 1000, conventionally know as the "Early Middle Ages," was a time of disorder and destruction, but also of the creation of a new type of society.

The Spread of Islam

How did Islam take root in the Middle East and then spread to Europe?

In the seventh century C.E. two empires dominated the area today called the Middle East: the Byzantine-Greek-Christian empire and the Sasanian-Persian-Zoroastrian empire. The Arabian peninsula lay between the two.

Around 610 in the Arabian city of Mecca, a merchant called Muhammad began to have religious visions. By the time he died in 632, all Arabia had accepted his creed. A century later his followers controlled Syria, Palestine, Egypt, North Africa, Spain, and part of France. This Arabic expansion profoundly affected the development of Western civilization as well as the history of Africa and Asia.

The Arabs

In Muhammad's time Arabia was inhabited by various tribes, most of them Bedouins (**BED-oo-inz**). These nomadic peoples grazed goats and sheep on the sparse patches of grass that dotted the vast semiarid peninsula. Other Arabs lived in the southern valleys and coastal towns along the Red Sea in Yemen, Mecca, Medina, and the northwestern region called "Hejaz" (**HEE-jaz**). The Hejazi supported themselves by agriculture and trade. Their caravan routes crisscrossed Arabia and carried goods to Byzantium, Persia, and Syria. The Hejazi had wide commercial dealings but avoided cultural contacts with their Jewish, Christian, and Persian neighbors. The wealth produced by their business transactions led to luxurious living in the towns.

Although the nomadic Bedouins condemned the urbanized lifestyle of the Hejazi as immoral and corrupt, Arabs of both types respected one another's local tribal customs. In addition, they had certain religious rules in common. For example, all Arabs kept three months of the year as sacred; during that time fighting stopped so that everyone could attend holy ceremonies in peace. The city of

Kaaba A sanctuary in Mecca where Arabs prayed.

Mecca in what is now Saudi Arabia was the religious center of the Arab world, and fighting was never tolerated there. All Arabs prayed at the **Kaaba** (KAH-buh), the sanctuary in Mecca. Within the Kaaba was a sacred black stone that Arabs revered because they believed it had fallen from heaven.

What eventually molded the diverse Arab tribes into a powerful political and social unity was the religion based on the teachings of Muhammad.

Qur'an The sacred book of Islam.

The Prophet Muhammad

Except for a few vague remarks in the **Qur'an** (kuh-RAHN), the sacred book of Islam, Muhammad (ca. 571–632) left no account of his life. Arab tradition accepts some of the sacred legends that developed about him as historically true, but those legends were not written down until about a century after his death. Orphaned at the age of six, Muhammad was brought up by his grandfather. When he was a young man, he became a merchant in the caravan trade. Later he entered the service of a wealthy widow, and their subsequent marriage brought him financial independence. The Qur'an reveals him to be an extremely devout man, ascetic, self-disciplined, and literate.

Since childhood Muhammad had been subject to seizures during which he lost consciousness and had visions. After 610 these visions apparently became more frequent. Unsure for a time about what he should do, Muhammad discovered his mission after a vision in which the angel Gabriel instructed him to preach.

Muhammad and the Earlier Prophets

Muhammad, with his head surrounded by fire representing religious fervor, leads Abraham, Moses, and Jesus in prayer. Islamic tradition holds that Judaism, Christianity, and Islam all derive from the pure religion of Abraham, but humankind has strayed from that faith. Therefore, Muhammad, as "the seal (last) of the prophets," had to transmit God's revelations to humankind. (Bibliothèque nationale de France)

Muhammad described his visions in a stylized and often rhyming prose and used this literary medium as his *Qur'an*, or "prayer recitation." Muhammad's revelations were written down by his followers during his lifetime and organized into chapters shortly after his death. In 651 Muhammad's third successor as religious leader, Othman, arranged to have an official version published. The Qur'an is regarded by Muslims as the direct words of God to his Prophet Muhammad and is therefore especially revered. (These revelations were in Arabic. When Muslims use translations in other languages, they do so alongside the original Arabic.) At the same time, other sayings and accounts of Muhammad, which gave advice on matters that went beyond the Qur'an, were collected into books termed *hadith* (hah-DEETH). Muslim tradition (Sunna) consists of both the Qur'an and the hadith.

Muhammad's visions ordered him to preach a message of a single God and to become God's prophet, which he began to do in his hometown of Mecca. He gathered followers slowly but also provoked a great deal of resistance, and in 622 he migrated with his followers to Medina, an event termed the *hijra* (HIJ-ruh) that marks the beginning of the Muslim calendar. At Medina Muhammad was much more successful, gaining converts and working out the basic principles of the faith. In 630 Muhammad returned to Mecca at the head of a large army, and by his death in 632 he had unified most of the Arabian peninsula into a religious/political community of Muslims, a word meaning those who comply with God's will. The religion itself came to be called Islam, which means "submission to God." The Kaaba was rededicated as a Muslim holy place, and Mecca became the most holy city in Islam. According to Muslim tradition, the Kaaba predates the creation of the world and represents the earthly counterpart of God's heavenly throne, to which "pilgrims come dishevelled and dusty on every kind of camel."[1]

CHRONOLOGY

ca. 571–632	Life of the Prophet Muhammad
700	Lindisfarne Gospel produced in Northumbria
711–720	Muslim conquest of Spain
ca. 720	Venerable Bede writes *Ecclesiastical History of the English People*
760s–840s	Carolingian Renaissance
768–814	Reign of Charlemagne
800–900	Free peasants in western Europe increasingly tied to the land as serfs
820	Muslim mathematician al-Khwarizmi writes first treatise on algebra
843	Treaty of Verdun divides Carolingian kingdom
850–1000	Most extensive Viking raids
ca. 900	Establishment of Kievan Rus
950	Muslim Córdoba is Europe's largest and most prosperous city
1001	Establishment of kingdom of Hungary

The Teachings of Islam

Muhammad's religion eventually attracted great numbers of people, partly because of the straightforward nature of its doctrines. The strictly monotheistic theology outlined in the Qur'an has only a few central tenets. Allah, the Arabic word for God, is all-powerful and all-knowing. Muhammad, Allah's prophet, preached his word and carried his message. Muhammad described himself as the successor both of the Jewish patriarch Abraham and of Christ, and he claimed that his teachings replaced theirs. He invited and won converts from Judaism and Christianity.

Because Allah is all-powerful, believers must submit themselves to him. All Muslims have the obligation of the *jihad* (jee-HAHD) (literally "self-exertion") to strive or struggle to lead a virtuous life and to spread God's rule and law. In some cases striving was individual against sin; in others it was social and communal and could involve armed conflict, though this was not an essential part of jihad. The Islamic belief of "striving in the path of God" is closely related to the central feature of Muslim doctrine, the coming Day of Judgment. Muslims need not be concerned about *when* judgment will occur, but they must believe with absolute and total conviction that the Day of Judgment *will* come. Consequently, all of a

Muslim's thoughts and actions should be oriented toward the Last Judgment and the rewards of Heaven.

To merit the rewards of heaven, a person must follow the strict code of moral behavior that Muhammad prescribed. The Muslim must recite a profession of faith in God and in Muhammad as God's prophet: "There is no god but God and Muhammad is his prophet." The believer must pray five times a day, fast and pray during the sacred month of Ramadan, and contribute alms to the poor and needy. If possible, the believer must make a pilgrimage to Mecca once during his or her lifetime. According to the Muslim *shari'a* (sha-REE-ah), or sacred law, these five practices—the profession of faith, prayer, fasting, giving alms to the poor, and pilgrimage to Mecca—constitute the **Five Pillars of Islam.**

The Qur'an forbids alcoholic beverages and gambling. It condemns business usury—that is, lending money at interest rates or taking advantage of market demand for products by charging high prices for them. A number of foods, such as pork, are also forbidden, a dietary regulation adopted from the Hebrews.

The Qur'an also sets forth an austere sexual morality. Muslim jurisprudence condemned licentious behavior on the part of men as well as women, which enhanced the status of women in Muslim society. So, too, did Muhammad's opposition to female infanticide. Polygyny, the practice of men having more than one wife, was common in Arab society, but the Qur'an restricted the number of wives to four—or even one, if the man could not treat all fairly. In a military society where there were apt to be many widows, polygyny provided women with a measure of security.

With respect to matters of property, Muslim women were more emancipated than Western women. For example, a Muslim woman retained complete jurisdiction over one-third of her property when she married and could dispose of it in any way she wished. Women in most European countries and the United States did not gain these rights until the nineteenth century.[2]

What did early Muslims think of Jesus? He is described in the Qur'an as a righteous prophet who was born of Mary the Virgin, performed miracles, and continued the work of Abraham and Moses, and he was a sign of the coming Day of Judgment. But Muslims held that Jesus was an apostle only, not God, and that those who called Jesus divine committed blasphemy (showing contempt for God). Muslims esteemed the Judeo-Christian Scriptures as part of God's revelation, although they believed that Christian communities had corrupted the Scriptures and that the Qur'an superseded them. The Christian doctrine of the Trinity—that there is one God in three persons (Father, Son, and Holy Spirit)—conflicts with the Muslim idea of monotheism.[3]

Five Pillars of Islam The five practices according to the Muslim shari'a, or sacred law, including the profession of faith, prayer, fasting, giving alms to the poor, and a pilgrimage to Mecca.

Expansion and Schism

By the time Muhammad died in 632, he had united the nomads of the desert and the merchants of the cities. The doctrines of Islam, instead of the ties of local custom, bound all Arabs. The crescent of Islam, the Muslim symbol, prevailed throughout the Arabian peninsula. During the next century one rich province of the old Roman Empire after another came under Muslim domination—first Syria, then Egypt, and then all of North Africa (see Map 8.1). Long and bitter wars (572–591, 606–630) between the Byzantine and Persian Empires left both so weak and exhausted that they easily fell to Muslim attack. The government headquarters of this vast new empire was established at Damascus in Syria by the ruling Umayyad (oo-MY-ad) family. By the early tenth century a Muslim proverb spoke of the Mediterranean Sea as a Muslim lake, though the Greeks at Constantinople

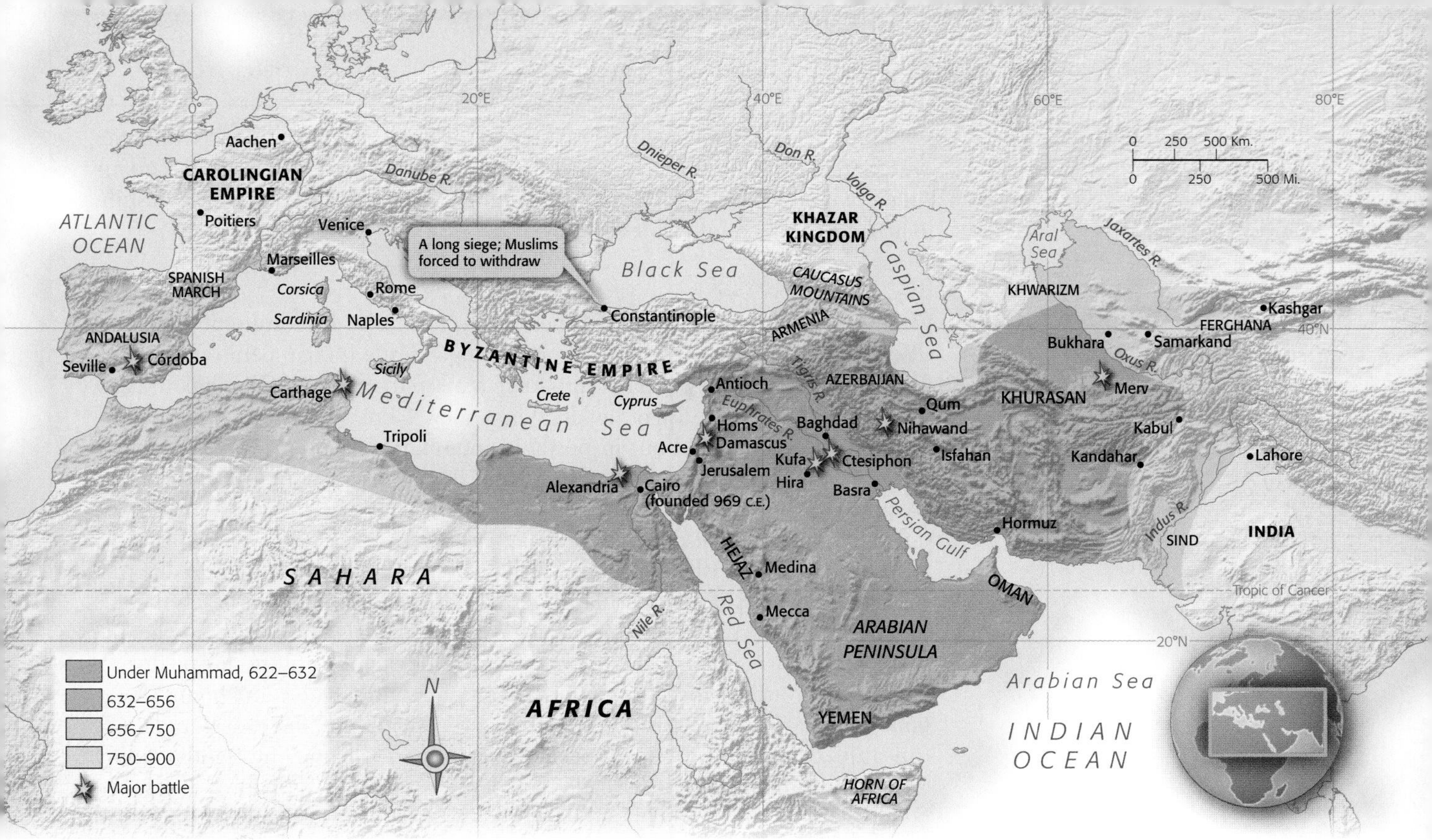
Aachen
CAROLINGIAN EMPIRE
Poitiers
ATLANTIC OCEAN
Venice
Marseilles
SPANISH MARCH
Corsica
Rome
Sardinia
Naples
ANDALUSIA
Seville
Córdoba
Carthage
Sicily
Crete
Cyprus
Tripoli
A long siege; Muslims forced to withdraw
Constantinople
Black Sea
BYZANTINE EMPIRE
Mediterranean Sea
Danube R.
Dnieper R.
Don R.
Volga R.
KHAZAR KINGDOM
CAUCASUS MOUNTAINS
ARMENIA
Caspian Sea
Aral Sea
Jaxartes R.
KHWARIZM
Kashgar
FERGHANA
Bukhara
Samarkand
Oxus R.
Merv
KHURASAN
AZERBAIJAN
Tigris R.
Euphrates R.
Antioch
Homs
Damascus
Acre
Jerusalem
Baghdad
Qum
Nihawand
Isfahan
Kufa
Hira
Ctesiphon
Basra
Kabul
Kandahar
Lahore
Alexandria
Cairo (founded 969 C.E.)
Persian Gulf
Hormuz
Indus R.
SIND
INDIA
HEJAZ
Medina
Mecca
SAHARA
Nile R.
Red Sea
ARABIAN PENINSULA
OMAN
Tropic of Cancer
Arabian Sea
INDIAN OCEAN
YEMEN
AFRICA
HORN OF AFRICA
Under Muhammad, 622–632
632–656
656–750
750–900
Major battle
0 250 500 Km.
0 250 500 Mi.

MAP 8.1 The Islamic World, ca. 900

The rapid expansion of Islam in a relatively short span of time testifies to the Arabs' superior fighting skills, religious zeal, and economic organization as well as to their enemies' weakness.

contested that notion. From the Arabian peninsula, Muslims carried their faith deep into Africa and across Asia all the way to India.

Despite the clarity and unifying force of Muslim doctrine, a schism soon developed within the Islamic faith. Neither the Qur'an nor the hadith gave clear guidance about how successors to Muhammad were to be chosen, but a group of Muhammad's closest followers elected Abu Bakr (a-BOO BAK-uhr), who was a close friend of the Prophet's and a member of a small tribe affiliated with the Prophet's tribe, as **caliph** (KEY-lif, KAL-if), a word meaning successor. This election set a precedent for the ratification of the subsequent patriarchal caliphs, though other Arab tribes unsuccessfully opposed it militarily.

caliph A successor, as chosen by a group of Muhammad's closest followers.

A more serious opposition developed later among supporters of the fourth caliph, Ali. Ali claimed the caliphate because of his blood ties with Muhammad—he was Muhammad's cousin and son-in-law—and because the Prophet had designated him as *imam* (ee-MAHM), or leader. Ali was assassinated shortly after becoming caliph, and some of his supporters began to assert that he should rightly have been the first caliph and that all subsequent caliphs were usurpers. These supporters of Ali—called ***Shi'ites*** (SHE-ites) or *Shi'a* (SHE-ah) from Arabic terms meaning "supporters" or "partisans" of Ali—saw Ali and subsequent imams as the divinely inspired leaders of the community. The larger body of Muslims who accepted the first elections—called ***Sunnis*** (SUN-nees), a word derived from *Sunna*, the traditional beliefs and practices of the community—saw the caliphs as political leaders. Since Islam did not have an organized church and priesthood, the caliphs had an additional function of safeguarding and enforcing the religious law *(shari'a)*

Shi'ites Muslims who regard Muhammad's cousin Ali as the rightful successor to the position as caliph.

Sunnis Muslims who regard the succession of leadership through Abu Bakr as legitimate.

with the advice of scholars *(ulama)*, particularly the jurists, judges, and scholastics who were knowledgeable about the Qur'an and hadith. Over the centuries, many different kinds of Shi'ites appeared, and enmity between Sunni and Shi'a Muslims sometimes erupted into violence.

Muslim Spain

In Europe, Muslim political and cultural influence was felt most strongly in the Iberian peninsula. In 711 a Muslim force crossed the Strait of Gibraltar and easily defeated the weak Visigothic kingdom. A few Christian princes supported by the Frankish rulers held out in northern mountain fortresses, but the Muslims took over most of Spain. A member of the Umayyad dynasty, Abd al-Rahman (AHB-d al-ruh-MAHN) (r. 756–788), established a kingdom in Spain with its capital at Córdoba (KAWR-doh-buh).

Throughout the Islamic world, Muslims used the term *al-Andalus* to describe the part of the Iberian Peninsula under Muslim control. The name al-Andalus probably derives from the Arabic for "land of the Vandals," the Germanic people who swept across Spain in the fifth century. In the eighth century, al-Andalus included the entire peninsula from Gibraltar in the south to the Cantabrian Mountains in the north (see Map 8.1). Today we often use the word *Andalusia* (an-duh-LOO-zhuh) to refer especially to southern Spain, but eighth-century Christians throughout Europe called the peninsula "Moorish Spain" because the people who invaded and conquered it were Moors—Berbers from northwest Africa. The ethnic term *Moorish* can be misleading, however, because the peninsula was home to sizable numbers of Jews and Christians as well as (Muslim) Moors. In business transactions and in much of daily life, all peoples used the Arabic language. With Muslims, Christians, and Jews trading with and learning from one another and occasionally intermarrying, Moorish Spain and Norman Sicily (see Chapter 9) were the only distinctly pluralistic societies in medieval Europe. Between roughly the eighth and twelfth centuries, Muslims, Christians, and Jews lived close together in Andalusia, and some scholars believe that the early part of this period was an era of remarkable interfaith harmony. Jews in Muslim Spain were generally treated well, and Córdoba became a center of Jewish as well as Muslim learning. Many Christians adopted Arabic patterns of speech and dress, gave up the practice of eating pork, and developed a special appreciation for Arabic music and poetry. Some Christian women of elite status chose the Muslim practice of veiling their faces in public. Records describe Muslim and Christian youths joining in celebrations and merrymaking.

From the sophisticated centers of Muslim culture in Baghdad, Damascus, and Cairo (founded 969), al-Andalus seemed a provincial backwater, a frontier outpost with little significance in the wide context of Islamic civilization. To European peoples, however, Spanish culture was dazzling. For example, the Saxon nun and writer Hroswita of Gandersheim (GAND-ershaym) called the city of Córdoba "the ornament of the world." It became Europe's largest and most prosperous city. With a population of about half a million; with well-paved and well-lighted streets and an abundance of

Harvesting Dates

This detail from an ivory casket given to a Córdoban prince reflects the importance of fruit cultivation in the Muslim-inspired agricultural expansion in southern Europe in the ninth and tenth centuries. (Louvre/Réunion des Musées Nationaux/Art Resource, NY)

fresh water; with 1,000 mosques, 900 public baths, 213,177 houses for ordinary people, and 60,000 mansions for officials and the wealthy; with 80,455 shops and 13,000 weavers producing silks, woolens, and brocades; with 27 free schools and a library containing 400,000 volumes (the largest library in northern Europe, at the Benedictine abbey of St. Gall in Switzerland, had 600 books), Córdoba was indeed an ornament, and the Western world had no comparable urban center. In Spain, as elsewhere in the Arab world, the Muslims had an enormous impact on agricultural development. They began the cultivation of rice, sugar cane, citrus fruits, dates, figs, eggplants, carrots, and, after the eleventh century, cotton. These crops, together with new methods of field irrigation, provided the urban population with food products unknown in the rest of Europe.

In about 950, Caliph Abd al-Rahman III (912–961) of the Umayyad dynasty of Córdoba ruled most of the Iberian Peninsula. Christian Spain consisted of the tiny kingdoms of Castile, León, Catalonia, Aragon, Navarre, and Portugal. However, civil wars among al-Rahman's descendents weakened the caliphate, and the small northern Christian kingdoms expanded southward.

Science and Medicine

The Islamic world, both in Spain and elsewhere, profoundly shaped Christian European culture. Toledo, for example, became an important center of learning through which Arab intellectual achievements entered and influenced western Europe. Arabic knowledge of science and mathematics, derived from the Chinese, Greeks, and Hindus, was highly sophisticated. The Muslim mathematician al-Khwarizmi (**al-KHWAHR-iz-mee**) (d. 830) wrote the important treatise *Algebra*, the first work in which the word *algebra* is used mathematically. Al-Khwarizmi adopted the Hindu system of numbers (1, 2, 3, 4), used it in his *Algebra*, and applied mathematics to problems of physics and astronomy. Scholars at Baghdad translated Euclid's *Elements*, the basic text for plane and solid geometry. Muslims also instructed Westerners in the use of the zero, which permitted the execution of complicated problems of multiplication and long division. Use of the zero represented an enormous advance over clumsy Roman numerals. (Since our system of numbers is actually Hindu in origin, the term *Arabic numerals*, coined about 1847, is a misnomer.)

Middle Eastern Arabs translated and codified the scientific and philosophical learning of Greek and Persian antiquity. In the ninth and tenth centuries that knowledge was brought to Spain, where between 1150 and 1250 it was translated into Latin. Europeans' knowledge of Aristotle changed the entire direction of European philosophy and theology (see page 60). Isaac Newton's discoveries in mathematics in the seventeenth century rested on ancient Greek theories translated in Spain.

In the transmission of Greek learning, one Muslim technological accomplishment played a most significant role—paper. Building on techniques invented by the Chinese, Muslims brought their papermaking method to the major hubs of their empire, and it eventually entered Spain. Even before the invention of printing (see page 317), papermaking had a revolutionary impact on the collection and diffusion of knowledge and thus on the transformation of society.[4]

Muslim medical knowledge far surpassed that of the West. By the ninth century Arab physicians had translated most of the treatises of Hippocrates, and later generations made their own advances in the diagnosis and treatment of illnesses and in surgical techniques. Arabic science reached its peak in the physician, philologist, philosopher, poet, and scientist ibn-Sina of Bukhara (980–1037), known in the West as Avicenna. His *al-Qanun* codified all Greco-Arabic medical thought, described the contagious nature of tuberculosis and the spreading of diseases, and listed 760 pharmaceutical drugs.

Unfortunately, many of these treatises came to the West as translations from Greek to Arabic and then to Latin and inevitably lost a great deal in translation. Nevertheless, in the ninth and tenth centuries Arabic knowledge and experience in anatomy and pharmaceutical prescriptions much enriched Western knowledge.

Muslim-Christian Relations

Beyond Andalusian Spain, mutual animosity restricted contact between Muslims and Christians. The Muslim expansion into Christian Europe in the eighth and ninth centuries left a legacy of bitter hostility. Christians felt threatened by a faith that denied the doctrine of the Trinity and Christ's divinity. Europeans' perception of Islam as a menace helped inspire the Crusades of the eleventh through thirteenth centuries (see pages 209–214).

By the thirteenth century Western literature sometimes displayed a sympathetic view of Islam. The Bavarian knight Wolfram von Eschenbach's (ESH-en-bak) *Parzival* (PAHR-tsi-fahl) and the Englishman William Langland's *Piers the Plowman*—two poems that survive in scores of manuscripts, suggesting that they circulated widely—reveal some broad mindedness and tolerance toward Muslims. Some travelers in the Middle East were impressed by the kindness and generosity of Muslims and with the strictness and devotion with which Muslims observed their faith.[5]

More frequently, however, Christian literature portrayed Muslims as the most dreadful of Europe's enemies, guilty of every kind of crime. In his *Inferno*, the great Florentine poet Dante placed the Muslim philosophers Avicenna (av-uh-SEN-uh) and Averroes (uh-VERR-oh-eez) with other virtuous "heathens," among them Socrates and Aristotle, in the first circle of hell, where they endured only moderate punishment. Muhammad, however, was consigned to the ninth circle, near Satan himself, where he was condemned as a spreader of discord and scandal.

Muslim views of Christians were also mixed, but here disinterest may have been more common than hostility. Muslim historical writing reflects strong knowledge of European geography but shows an almost total lack of interest in European languages, life, and culture. Commercially, from the Muslim perspective, Europe had very little to offer apart from woolens from the Frisian (FRIZH-uhn) Islands in the North Sea and some slaves from central and southeastern Europe.

Animosity began to develop between Muslims and Christians in Spain after the initial period of harmony. Muslim teachers feared that close contact between the two peoples would lead to Muslim contamination and become a threat to the Islamic faith. Christian bishops worried that knowledge of Islam would lead to ignorance of essential Christian doctrines.

Thus, beginning in the late tenth century, Muslim regulations increasingly defined what Christians and Muslims could do. A Christian, however much assimilated, remained an **infidel.** An infidel was an unbeliever, and the word carried a pejorative or disparaging connotation. Such divisions were enhanced in the twelfth century when al-Andalus was taken over by the Almohad dynasty, an extremist group from Morocco that outlawed Judaism and Christianity. When Christian forces conquered Muslim territory in subsequent centuries, Christian rulers regarded their Muslim and Jewish subjects as infidels and enacted similar restrictive measures.

infidel An unbeliever, a word carrying a pejorative or disparaging connotation.

Section Review

- Two tribes—the nomadic Bedouins and the city-dwelling Hejaz—respected each other's religious rules, sharing the city of Mecca as the religious center of the Arab world.

- Muhammad founded the religion of Islam, which unified the Arabian peninsula into a political and religious group known as Muslims, based on a belief that he was a prophet of God, and his visions were written down in the Qur'an and other teachings known as the hadith.

- Islam teaches the Five Pillars of Islam: the profession of faith (that there is only one God and Muhammad is his prophet), prayer, fasting, giving alms to the poor, and the pilgrimage to Mecca.

- Islam expanded rapidly, but upon Muhammad's death, a sometimes violent succession dispute developed, the Sunnis accepting an elected line of leadership and the Shi'ites following Muhammad's cousin and son-in-law, Ali.

- The region of Andalusia in the Spanish peninsula enjoyed a unique and peaceful blend of Muslims, Christians, and Jews, with a flourishing capital in Córdoba.

- After a period of peace, discord began to grow between Muslims and Christians when each thought of the other as infidels (unbelievers) who corrupted their respective faiths.

The Frankish Kingdom

How did Frankish rulers govern their kingdoms?

Several centuries before the Muslim conquest of Spain, the Frankish king Clovis converted to Roman Christianity and established a large kingdom in what had been Roman Gaul (see page 153). Though at the time the Frankish kingdom was established it was simply one barbarian kingdom among many, it became the most important state in Europe, expanding to become an empire. Rulers after Clovis used a variety of tactics to enhance their authority and create a stable system.

The Merovingians

Clovis established the Merovingian dynasty, named after a mythical founder Merowig. Before he died, Clovis arranged for his kingdom to be divided among his four sons, a decision that led to civil wars and chronic violence as Clovis's descendants fought among themselves. Still, the royal family and the royal court served as the focus around which conflicts arose, so that the dynasty itself was not threatened.[6]

A Merovingian ruler had multiple sources of income. These included revenues from the royal estates, which were especially large in the north, and the "gifts" of subject peoples, such as plunder and tribute paid by peoples east of the Rhine River. New lands might be conquered and confiscated in order to replenish revenues lost when the ruler endowed land to monasteries or other religious institutions. Fines imposed for criminal offenses and tolls and customs duties on roads, bridges, and waterways (and the goods transported over them) also yielded income. As with the Romans, the minting of coins was a royal monopoly, with drastic penalties for counterfeiting.

The responsibility for collecting royal revenues in a **civitas** (SIV-i-tas)—a city and surrounding territory—fell to a senior official or royal companion known as a **comites** (KOH-meh-tehs). A comites presided over the civitas and was also responsible for hearing lawsuits, enforcing justice, and raising troops. A military leader, known as a *dux* (dooks) or duke, commanded troops from several civitates and was responsible for both defending the kingdom and conquering new lands. The bishop of the civitas also played an important role in the community, and the king depended on him for local information. Merovingian, Carolingian (below), and later medieval rulers traveled constantly to check up on local administrators and peoples. Their hosts were required to provide for the king and his entourage of wives, children, servants, court officials, and warriors and their horses. These visits no doubt strained the local resources.

The court or household of Merovingian kings included scribes who kept records, legal advisors, and treasury agents responsible for aspects of royal finance. These officials could all read and write Latin. Over them all presided the mayor of the palace, the most important secular figure after the king in the kingdom. Usually a leader of one of the great aristocratic families, the mayor also governed in the king's absence.

Kings consulted regularly with the leaders of the aristocracy. This class represented a fusion of Franks and the old Gallo-Roman leadership. Its members possessed landed wealth—villas over which they exercised lordship and dispensed local customary, rather than royal, law—and they often had lavish lifestyles. When

civitas The city and surrounding territory that served as a basis of the administrative system in the Frankish kingdom.

comites A senior official or royal companion later called a count that presided over the civitas.

they were with the king, they constituted the royal court. If the king consulted them and they were in agreement, there was peace. Failure to consult could result in civil war.

The Rise of the Carolingians

From this aristocracy one family gradually emerged to replace the Merovingian dynasty. The rise of the Carolingians—whose name comes from the Latin *Carolus*, or Charles—rests on several factors. First, beginning with Pippin I (d. 640), the head of the Carolingian family acquired and held onto the powerful position of mayor of the palace. Second, a series of advantageous marriage alliances brought the family estates and influence in different parts of the Frankish world. The landed wealth and treasure acquired by Pippin II (d. 714), his son Charles Martel (r. 714–741), and Pippin III (r. 751–768) formed the basis of Carolingian power. Military victories over supporters of the Merovingians ensured their dominance.

Charles Martel's successful wars against the Saxons, Frisians, Alamanni, and Bavarians further enhanced the family's prestige. But it was his victory, in 732, over a Muslim force near Poitiers (**pwa-TYEY**) in central France that was most significant. For Christians, the Frankish victory was one of the great battles of history, halting Muslim expansion in Europe. (Muslims, however, viewed it as a minor skirmish.) Charles Martel and later Carolingians used it to portray themselves as defenders of Christendom against the Muslims.

The battle of Poitiers helped the Carolingians acquire the support of the church, perhaps their most important asset. Charles Martel and Pippin III further strengthened their ties to the church by supporting the work of missionaries who preached Christianity to pagan peoples, along with the Christian duty to obey secular authorities. The most famous of these missionaries was the Englishman Boniface (**BON-uh-feys**) (680–754), who had close ties to the Roman pope. Boniface ordered the oak of Thor, a tree sacred to many pagans, cut down and the wood used to build a church. When the god Thor did not respond by killing Boniface with his lightning bolts, Boniface won many converts.

As mayor of the palace, Charles Martel had exercised the power of king of the Franks. His son Pippin III aspired to have the title as well as its powers. His diplomats were able to convince an embattled Pope Zacharius to rule in his favor in exchange for military support against the Lombards. Chilperic, the last Merovingian ruler, was consigned to a monastery. An assembly of Frankish magnates elected Pippin king, and he was anointed by the missionary Boniface at Soissons.

Saint Boniface

The upper panel of this piece from an early-eleventh-century Fulda Mass book shows the great missionary to Germany baptizing, apparently by full immersion. The lower panel shows his death scene, with the saint protecting himself with a Gospel book. The fluttering robes are similar to those in earlier Anglo-Saxon books, probably modeled on illustrations in books that Boniface brought to Fulda Abbey from England. (Staatsbibliothek Bamberg, Ms. Lit. I, fol. 126v)

When, in 754, Lombard expansion again threatened the papacy, Pope Stephen II journeyed to the Frankish kingdom seeking help. On this occasion, he personally anointed Pippin with the sacred oils and gave him the title "Patrician of the Romans." Pippin promised restitution of the papal lands and later made a gift of estates in central Italy.

Prior to Pippin, only priests and bishops had received anointment. Pippin became the first monarch to be acknowledged as *rex et sacerdos* (reks et SAK-er-dose), meaning king and priest. Anointment, rather than royal blood, set the Christian king apart. By having himself anointed, Pippin cleverly eliminated possible threats to the Frankish throne coming from other claimants, and the pope promised him support in the future. When Pippin died, his son Charles succeeded him.

The Empire of Charlemagne

How did Charlemagne gain control of a large part of Europe and how did power become decentralized after his death?

Charles the Great (r. 768–814), generally known by the French version of his name, Charlemagne (SHAHR-leh-mane), built on the military and diplomatic foundations of his ancestors and on the administrative machinery of the Merovingian kings. He expanded the Frankish kingdom into what is now Germany and Italy and, late in his long reign, was crowned emperor by the pope.

Charlemagne's Personal Qualities and Marriage Strategies

Charlemagne's secretary and biographer, Einhard, wrote a lengthy idealization of this warrior-ruler. It is the earliest medieval biography of a layman, and historians consider it generally accurate:

> Charles was large and strong, and of lofty stature, though not disproportionately tall . . . the upper part of his head was round, his eyes very large and animated, nose a little long, hair fair, and face laughing and merry. Thus his appearance was always stately and dignified . . . although his neck was thick and somewhat short, and his belly rather prominent; but the symmetry of the rest of his body concealed these defects. His gait was firm, his whole carriage manly and his voice clear, but not so strong as his size led one to expect. His health was excellent, except during the four years preceding his death. . . .[7]

Though crude and brutal, Charlemagne was a man of enormous intelligence. He appreciated good literature, such as Saint Augustine's *City of God*, and Einhard considered him an unusually effective speaker.

The security and continuation of his dynasty and the need for diplomatic alliances governed Charlemagne's complicated marriage pattern. Charlemagne had a total of four legal wives and six concubines, and even after the age of sixty-five he continued to sire children. Though three sons reached adulthood, only one outlived him. Four surviving grandsons ensured perpetuation of the dynasty.

Territorial Expansion

Continuing the expansionist policies of his ancestors, Charlemagne fought more than fifty campaigns and became the greatest warrior of the early Middle Ages. He subdued all of the north of modern France, but his greatest successes were in today's Germany. In the course of a thirty-year war against the Saxons, he added

Section Review

- The Frankish king Clovis, a Roman Christian, established his Merovingian kingdom in what was Roman Gaul; while his four sons fought over it, the dynasty remained.

- Merovingian rulers amassed wealth as they collected revenues, conquered new land, imposed fines and tolls, and minted coins.

- In many Frankish territories, a **comites** (royal official) oversaw cities, a **dux** (duke) commanded the troops, and a bishop relayed local information to the king; the bishop also had religious and community duties.

- The Merovingian king's court included scribes, legal advisors, treasury agents, the mayor of the palace (who was second to the king), and the leaders of the aristocracy.

- Charles Martel, of the aristocratic Carolingian family, gained strength through wealth, advantageous land position, marriage, and most importantly the church; he put his son Pippin on the Frankish throne.

most of the northwestern German tribes to the Frankish kingdom. Charlemagne also achieved spectacular results in the south, incorporating Lombardy into the Frankish kingdom. He ended Bavarian independence and defeated the nomadic Avars, opening the Danubian plain for later settlement. He successfully fought the Byzantine Empire for Venetia (excluding the city of Venice itself), Istria, and Dalmatia, and temporarily annexed those areas to his kingdom.

Charlemagne's only defeat came at the hands of the Basques of northwestern Spain, as he was withdrawing after an unsuccessful siege of their territory. Although it was a forbidden topic during Charlemagne's lifetime, the ill-fated expedition inspired the great medieval epic, *The Song of Roland.* Based on legend and written in about 1100 at the beginning of the European crusading movement, the poem portrays the Frankish Count Roland as the ideal chivalric knight and Charlemagne as exercising a sacred kind of kingship. Although many of the epic's details differ from the historical evidence, *The Song of Roland* is important because it reveals the popular image of Charlemagne in later centuries.

By around 805 the Frankish kingdom included all of northwestern Europe except Scandinavia (see Map 8.2). Not since the third century C.E. had any ruler controlled so much of the Western world.

Reliquary Bust of Charlemagne

This splendid twelfth-century gothic idealization portrays the emperor of legend and myth rather than the squat, potbellied ruler described by his contemporary, Einhard. The jeweled helmet or crown is symbolic of Charlemagne's role as defender of church and people. (Photo: Ann Münchow, © Domkapitel Aachen)

The Government of the Carolingian Empire

Charlemagne ruled a vast rural world dotted with isolated estates and small villages and characterized by constant warfare. According to the chroniclers of the time, only seven years between 714 and 814 were peaceful. Charlemagne's empire was not a state as people today understand that term; it was a collection of peoples and tribes. Apart from a small class of warrior-aristocrats and clergy and a tiny minority of Jews, almost everyone engaged in agriculture. Towns served as the headquarters of bishops, as ecclesiastical centers.

The Carolingian rulers inherited the functions of both the king and the mayor of the palace. The scholar-adviser Alcuin (**AL-kwin**) (see page 183) wrote that "a king should be strong against his enemies, humble to Christians, feared by pagans, loved by the poor and judicious in counsel and maintaining justice."[8] Charlemagne worked to realize that ideal. By military expeditions that brought wealth—lands, booty, slaves, and tribute—and by peaceful travel, personal appearances, and the sheer force of his personality, Charlemagne sought to awe newly conquered peoples and rebellious domestic enemies.

The political power of the Carolingians rested on the cooperation of the dominant social class, the Frankish aristocracy. The lands and booty with which Charles Martel and Charlemagne rewarded their followers in these families enabled the nobles to improve their economic position, but it was only with noble help that the Carolingians were able to wage wars of expansion and suppress rebellions. In short, Carolingian success was a matter of reciprocal help and reward.[9]

For administrative purposes, Charlemagne divided his entire kingdom into *counties* based closely on the old Merovingian civitas (see page 171). Each of the approximately six hundred counties was governed by a count (or in his absence by a viscount) whose responsibilities were similar to those of a Merovingian comites. Counts were at first sent out from the royal court; later a person native to the region was appointed.

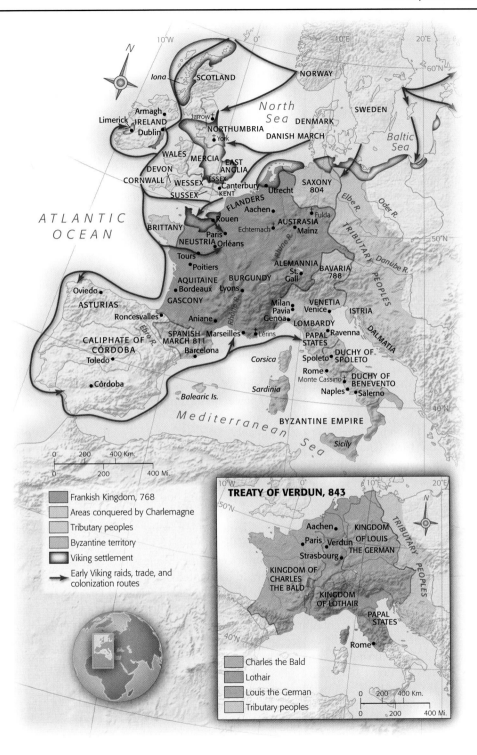

MAP 8.2 Charlemagne's Conquests

Though Charlemagne's hold on much of his territory was relatively weak, the size of his empire was not equaled again until the nineteenth-century conquests of Napoleon. (*Source:* Some data from Michael McCormick, *Origins of the European Economy: Communications and Commerce, A.D. 300–900* [Cambridge: Cambridge University Press, 2001], p. 762.)

As a link between local authorities and the central government, Charlemagne appointed officials called **missi dominici** (miss-ee doh-MEH-nee-chee), "agents of the lord king." Each year beginning in 802, two missi (singular: *missus*), usually a count and a bishop or abbot, visited assigned districts to check up on the local counts. They held courts; investigated the district's judicial, financial, and clerical

missi dominici Officials sent by Charlemagne to report on local districts.

activities; and organized commissions to regulate crime, moral conduct, the clergy, education, the poor, and many other matters.

The Imperial Coronation of Charlemagne

In autumn of the year 800, Charlemagne paid a momentous visit to Rome. Einhard gives this account of what happened:

His last journey there [to Rome] was due to another factor, namely that the Romans, having inflicted many injuries on Pope Leo—plucking out his eyes and tearing out his tongue, he had been compelled to beg the assistance of the king. Accordingly, coming to Rome in order that he might set in order those things which had exceedingly disturbed the condition of the Church, he remained there the whole winter. It was at the time that he accepted the name of Emperor and Augustus. At first he was so much opposed to this that he insisted that although that day was a great [Christian] feast, he would not have entered the Church if he had known beforehand the pope's intention. But he bore very patiently the jealousy of the Roman Emperors [that is, the Byzantine rulers] who were indignant when he received these titles. He overcame their arrogant haughtiness with magnanimity.[10]

For centuries scholars have debated the significance of the imperial coronation of Charlemagne. Did Charlemagne plan the ceremony in Saint Peter's on Christmas Day, or did he merely accept the title of emperor? If, as Einhard implies, the coronation displeased Charlemagne, was that because it put the pope in the superior position of conferring power on the emperor? What were Pope Leo's motives in arranging the coronation?

Though final answers will probably never be found, several things seem certain. First, Charlemagne gained the imperial title of Holy Roman emperor and the pope gained a military protector. Charlemagne considered himself a Christian king ruling a Christian people. Through his motto, *Renovatio romani imperi* (Revival of the Roman Empire), Charlemagne was consciously perpetuating old Roman imperial notions while at the same time identifying with the new Rome of the Christian church. Second, later German rulers were eager to gain the imperial title and to associate themselves with the legends of Charlemagne and ancient Rome. Finally, ecclesiastical authorities continually cited the event as proof that the dignity of the imperial crown could be granted only by the pope.

From Baghdad, Harun al Rashid (hah-ROON al-rah-SHEED), caliph of the Abbasid (ah-BASS-id) Empire (786–809), congratulated Charlemagne on his coronation with the gift of an elephant. But although the Muslim caliph recognized Charlemagne as a fellow sovereign, the Greeks regarded the papal acts as rebellious and Charlemagne as a usurper. The imperial coronation thus marks a decisive break between Rome and Constantinople. The coronation of Charlemagne, whether planned by the Carolingian court or by the papacy, was to have a profound effect on the course of German history and on the later history of Europe.

Decentralization and "Feudalism"

Charlemagne left his vast empire to his sole surviving son, Louis the Pious (r. 814–840), who attempted to keep the empire intact. This proved to be impossible. Members of the nobility engaged in plots and open warfare against the emperor, often allying themselves with one of Louis's three sons. (See the feature "Individuals in Society: Ebo of Reims.") In 843, shortly after Louis's death, those sons agreed to the **Treaty of Verdun** (ver-DUHN), which divided the empire into three parts: Charles the Bald received the western part, Lothair the middle part plus the title of emperor, and Louis the eastern part, from which he acquired the title "the German." Though of course no one knew it at the time, this treaty set the pattern for political boundaries in Europe that has been maintained until today. Other than brief periods under Napoleon and Hitler, Europe would never again see as large a unified state as it had under Charlemagne, which is one reason he has become a symbol of European unity in the twenty-first century.

The large-scale division of Charlemagne's empire was accompanied by a decentralization of power at the local level. Civil wars weakened the power and prestige of kings, who could do little about local violence. Likewise, the great invasions of the ninth century, especially the Viking invasions (see page 169), weakened royal authority. The western Frankish kings could do little to halt the invaders, and the local aristocracy had to assume responsibility for defense. Common people turned for protection to the strongest power, the local counts, whom they considered their rightful rulers. Thus, in the ninth and tenth centuries great aristocratic families increased their authority in the regions of their vested interests. They built private castles for defense and to live in, and they governed virtually independent territories in which distant and weak kings could not interfere.

The most powerful nobles were those able to gain the allegiance of warriors, often symbolized in an oath-swearing ceremony of homage and fealty that grew out of earlier Germanic oaths of loyalty. In this ceremony, a warrior (knight) swore his loyalty as a **vassal**—from a Celtic term meaning "servant"—to the more powerful individual, who became his lord. In return for the vassal's loyalty, aid, and military assistance, the lord promised him protection and material support. This support might be a place in the lord's household but was more likely land of the vassal's own, called a **fief** (feef). The fief might contain forests, churches, and towns. The fief theoretically still belonged to the lord, and the vassal only had the use of it. Peasants living on a fief produced the food and other goods necessary to maintain the knight.

Though historians debate this, fiefs appear to have been granted extensively first by Charles Martel and then by his successors, including Charlemagne and his grandsons. These fiefs went to their most powerful nobles, who often took the title of count. As the Carolingians' control of their territories weakened, the practice of granting fiefs moved to the local level, with lay lords, bishops, and abbots granting fiefs as well as kings.

This system, later named **feudalism**, was based on personal ties of loyalty cemented by grants of land rather than on allegiance to an abstract state or governmental system. In some parts of Europe, such as Ireland and the Baltic area, warrior-aristocrats or clan chieftains who controlled relatively small regions were the ultimate political authorities; they generally did not grant fiefs to secure loyalty but relied on strictly personal ties. Thus the word *feudal* does not properly apply to these areas.

Some historians argue, in fact, that the word *feudalism* should not be used at all, as it was unknown in the Middle Ages. In addition, the system that would later be called feudalism changed considerably in form and pattern between the ninth and fifteenth centuries, and differed from place to place. The feudalism of England in 1100, for example, differed greatly from that of France, scarcely fifty miles away, at the same time. The problem is that no one has come up with a better term for this loose arrangement of personal and property ties.

Whether one chooses to use the word *feudalism* or not, this system functioned as a way to organize political authority, particularly because vassals also owed

Treaty of Verdun Treaty signed in 843 by Louis's three sons, dividing the empire into three parts and setting the pattern for political boundaries in Europe that has been maintained until today.

vassal A warrior who swore loyalty to a noble in exchange for protection and support.

fief A piece of land granted by a feudal lord in return for service.

feudalism A political system in which a vassal was promised protection and material support by a lord in return for his loyalty, aid, and military assistance.

Individuals in Society

Ebo of Reims

The term *social mobility* came into broad use only in the twentieth century, but what it signifies—having the opportunity for an upward shift in status within society—is probably as old as organized society itself. "In all ages, service to the state and to men of power has raised some individuals and has enabled them to share in the social prestige that attaches to power."* In the Christian Middle Ages the Catholic Church provided the widest path for social advancement, and the archbishop symbolized political as well as religious prestige. Ebo of Reims (ca. 775–851) represents one such individual.

Ebo's father was a serf freed by Charlemagne; his mother, Himiltruda, was the nurse of Louis the Pious. Ebo's mother probably launched his career, for Ebo was brought up with Louis at the "palace school" at Aachen (**AH-kuhn**), where nobles and others were trained for administrative and judicial service to the emperor. A bond was forged between Ebo and Louis. When Louis became king of Aquitaine, he made Ebo his librarian; when Louis succeeded as emperor in 814, he secured for Ebo the important archiepiscopal see of Reims.

Ebo proved himself a very competent administrator. He began construction of a new cathedral, gaining imperial permission to use the city walls as building blocks. Ebo organized the cathedral chapter—the local clergy who handled routine business of the diocese under the bishop. He reformed the monasteries in his see, ending the diverse forms of religious life by enforcing the *Rule of Saint Benedict* in all houses. Ebo also patronized learning and the arts. He supported the production of manuscripts and the school long associated with the cathedral, and he commissioned the production of a book that bears his name, the *Ebo Gospels*.

Ebo served the emperor as *missus* in his province, where he worked to extend royal authority. Archbishop

Emperor Louis the Pious confers with bishops and lay magnates. (Bibliothèque nationale de France)

Ebo served both church and state when, acting on behalf of Pope Pascal I and Louis the Pious, he led a mission to King Harold of Denmark, whose goal was the conversion of the Danes to Christianity and peaceful relations with the Franks. When Harold and a large Danish entourage visited Louis in 826, the Danes were baptized, and Harold became Louis's vassal.

In 830 Louis was past fifty, an old man by contemporary standards. Louis had three adult sons. Adult sons often posed a test of medieval kingship. Sons wanted power on their own, resented paternal control, and often rebelled. In 833 Archbishop Ebo served as counselor to the sons of Louis the Pious in their plot to remove Louis and replace him with Lothar. Ebo headed a commission of bishops that drew up charges against the emperor, accusing him of failing in his imperial responsibilities, promoting discord among the Frankish people, and tolerating his (second) wife Judith's adultery, thereby bringing moral scandal to the kingdom. Louis was forced to renounce the throne and to do public penance. The charges proved false, and within months Louis regained his throne. A church council deposed Ebo, consigning him to a monastery. When Louis the Pious died, Lothar restored Ebo to Reims, but the pope refused to approve the appointment. Then a dispute with Lothar led Ebo to seek the support of Louis the German, who made him bishop of Hildesheim. Ebo died at Hildesheim.

Why did Ebo betray his boyhood friend and great benefactor? Was he resentful about some real or perceived slight and did he desire revenge? Was he willing to listen to dangerous advice? Did he wish to show himself the equal of any magnate who opposed the emperor? The *Annals of St.-Bertin*, the chief source of information about these events, describes Ebo as ungrateful, disobedient, disloyal, and cruel. What do you think?

Questions for Analysis

1. How does the career of Ebo of Reims illustrate social mobility?

2. What do Ebo's church appointments tell us about the Frankish state? What secular functions did bishops perform?

Sources: R. McKitterick, *The Frankish Kingdoms Under the Carolingians* (New York: Longman, 1983); J. L. Nelson, *Politics and Ritual in Early Medieval Europe* (London: Ronceverte, 1986).

* K. Bosl, "On Social Mobility in Medieval Society," in *Early Medieval Society*, ed. S. L. Thrupp (New York: Appleton-Century-Crofts, 1967).

obligations other than military service to the lord. They served as advisers and judges at the lord's court, provided lodging for the lord when he was traveling through their fief, gave him gifts at important family events, and might contribute ransom money if the lord was captured.

Along with granting fiefs to knights, lords gave fiefs to the clergy for spiritual services or promises of allegiance. In addition, the church held pieces of land on its own and granted fiefs to its own knightly vassals. Abbots and abbesses of monasteries, bishops, and archbishops were either lords or vassals in many feudal arrangements.

Women other than abbesses were generally not granted fiefs, but in most parts of Europe they could inherit them if their fathers had no sons. Occasionally, women did go through services swearing homage and fealty and swore to send fighters when the lord demanded them. More commonly, women acted as their husbands' surrogates when the men were away, defending the territory from attack and carrying out his administrative duties.

Feudalism existed at two social levels: at the higher level were the lords of great feudal principalities; below them were their knights, holding fiefs that may have been no larger than a small village with its surrounding land. In fact, some knights were landless and lived in the households of their lords. A wide and deep gap in social standing and political function separated these levels.

Manorialism, Serfdom, and the Slave Trade

The vast majority of people in medieval Europe were peasants who lived in family groups in villages or small towns, raising crops and animals. The village and the land surrounding it were called a *manor*, from the Latin word for "dwelling" or "homestead." Some fiefs might include only one manor, while great lords or kings might have hundreds of manors under their direct control. Residents of manors provided work for their lord in exchange for protection, a system that was later referred to as **manorialism**. Peasants surrendered themselves and their lands to the lord's jurisdiction. The land was returned to them to work, but the peasants became tied to the land by various kinds of payments and services. Like feudalism, manorialism involved an exchange. Because the economic power of the feudal lord and vassal rested on the work of peasants, feudalism and manorialism were inextricably linked.

In France, England, Germany, and Italy, local custom determined precisely what services peasants would provide to their lord, but certain practices became common everywhere. The peasant was obliged to give the lord a percentage of the annual harvest, usually in produce, sometimes in cash. The peasant paid a fee to marry someone from outside the lord's estate. To inherit property, the peasant paid a fine, often the best beast the person owned. Above all, the peasant became part of the lord's permanent labor force. With vast stretches of uncultivated virgin land and a tiny labor population, lords encouraged population growth and immigration. The most profitable form of capital was not land but laborers.

In entering into a relationship with a feudal lord, free farmers lost status. Their position became servile, and they became **serfs**. That is, they were bound to the land and could not leave it without the lord's permission. Serfdom was not the same as slavery in that lords did not own the person of the serf, but serfs were subject to the jurisdiction of the lord's court in any dispute over property and in any case of suspected criminal behavior.

The transition from freedom to serfdom was slow; its speed was closely related to the degree of political order in a given region. In the late eighth century there

manorialism A system in which residents of manors provided work for their lord in exchange for protection.

serfs Free farmers in the feudal relationship who lost status, therefore becoming servile and bound to the land.

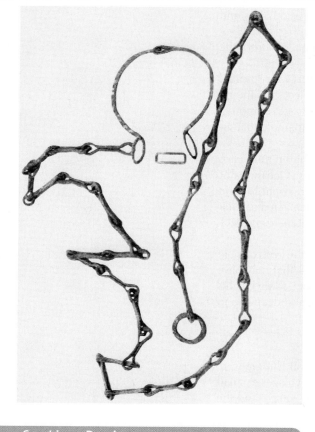

were still many free peasants. And within the legal category of serfdom there were many economic levels, ranging from the highly prosperous to the desperately poor. Nevertheless, a social and legal revolution was taking place. By the year 800 perhaps 60 percent of the population of western Europe—completely free a century before—had been reduced to serfdom. The ninth-century Viking assaults on Europe, discussed later in this chapter, created a vast climate of fear and led more people to accept serfdom in exchange for protection.

Persons captured in war often became actual slaves, who were then traded by merchants. Charlemagne's long wars against the Lombards, Avars, Saxons, and other groups produced thousands of prisoners who were exchanged for the Eastern luxury goods that nobles and the clergy desired. When Frankish conquests declined in the tenth century, slave merchants obtained people from the empire's eastern border who spoke Slavic languages; this was the origin of our word *slave*. Slaves sold across the Mediterranean fetched three or four times the amounts brought within the Carolingian Empire, so most slaves were sold to Muslims. For Europeans and Arabs alike, selling captives and other slaves was standard procedure. Christian moralists sometimes complained about the sale of Christians to non-Christians, but they did not object to slavery itself.

In general, the Carolingian period witnessed moderate population growth, as indicated by the steady reduction of forests and wasteland. The highest aristocrats and church officials lived well, with fine clothing and at least a few rooms heated by firewood. Male nobles hunted and managed their estates, while female nobles generally oversaw the education of their children and sometimes inherited and controlled land on their own. Craftsmen and craftswomen on manorial estates manufactured textiles, weapons, glass, and pottery, primarily for local consumption. Sometimes abbeys and manors served as markets; goods were shipped away to towns and fairs for sale; and a good deal of interregional commerce existed. In the towns, which were generally small, artisans and merchants produced and traded luxury goods for noble and clerical patrons. The modest economic expansion benefited townspeople and nobles, but it did not alter the lives of most people very much.

Section Review

- Charlemagne was a brutal but intelligent ruler who fought over fifty military campaigns and used diplomatic alliances so that by 805 the Frankish kingdom extended over all of northwestern Europe except Scandinavia.

- The Carolingian empire was primarily an agricultural society, divided into counties ruled by counts and regulated by missi dominici (agents of the king) who made regular inspection tours.

- The pope gained military protection from Charlemagne by granting him the imperial title Holy Roman Emperor, which the Muslims recognized but the Greeks resented, causing a rift between Rome and Constantinople.

- After Charlemagne's death, his grandsons divided his empire into three parts: Charles the Bald took the west, Lothair the middle with the title of emperor, and Louis the east and the title "the German."

- This division led to decentralization of power as the most powerful nobles gained the support of vassals (warriors) in return for fiefs (land that could contain forests, churches, and towns), in a system known today as feudalism.

- Under feudalism and manorialism, free farmers gained protection but lost ownership of their land and became serfs; in addition, many prisoners of war were sold and traded as slaves.

Early Medieval Scholarship and Culture

What were the significant intellectual and cultural changes in Charlemagne's era?

It is perhaps ironic that Charlemagne's most enduring legacy was the stimulus he gave to scholarship and learning. Barely literate himself, preoccupied with the control of vast territories, much more a warrior than an intellectual, he nevertheless set in motion a cultural revival that had widespread and long-lasting consequences.

Scholarship and Religious Life in Northumbria

The Anglo-Saxon kingdom of Northumbria in medieval England was the original source of the Carolingian intellectual revival. Northumbrian creativity owes a great deal to Saint Benet Biscop (ca. 628–689), who brought manuscripts and other treasures back from Italy. These formed the library on which much later study rested.

Northumbrian monasteries produced scores of books: *missals* (used for the celebration of the Mass), *psalters* (**SAL-ters**) (which contained the 150 psalms and other prayers used by the monks in their devotions), commentaries on the Scriptures, law codes, and collections of letters and sermons. The finest product of Northumbrian art is probably the illuminated manuscript of the Gospel produced at Lindisfarne (**LIN-duhs-farn**) around 700. The incredible expense involved in the publication of such a book—for vellum (calfskin or lambskin specially prepared for writing), coloring, and gold leaf—represents in part an aristocratic display of wealth. The illustrations have a strong Eastern quality, combining the abstract, nonrepresentational style of the Christian Middle East and the narrative (storytelling) approach of classical Roman art. Likewise, the use of geometrical decorative designs shows the influence of Syrian art. Many scribes and artists must have participated in the book's preparation.

In Gaul and Anglo-Saxon England, women shared with men the work of evangelization and the new Christian learning. Kings and nobles, seeking suitable occupations for daughters who did not or would not marry, founded monasteries for nuns, some of which were double monasteries. A **double monastery** housed men and women in two adjoining establishments and was governed by one superior, an *abbess*. Nuns looked after the children given to the monastery as *oblates* (**OB-laytz**) (offerings), the elderly who retired at the monastery, and travelers who needed hospitality. Monks provided protection, since an isolated house of women invited attack in a violent age. Monks also did the heavy work on the land.

double monastery A monastery that housed both men and women in two adjoining establishments and was governed by one superior, an abbess.

Perhaps the most famous abbess of the Anglo-Saxon period was Saint Hilda (614–680). A noblewoman of considerable learning and administrative ability, she ruled the double monastery of Whitby on the Northumbrian coast, advised kings and princes, hosted the famous synod of 664, and encouraged scholars and poets. Several generations after Hilda, Saint Boniface (see page 172) wrote many letters to Whitby and other houses of nuns pleading for copies of books; these letters attest to the nuns' intellectual reputations.[11]

The finest representative of Northumbrian—and indeed all Anglo-Saxon—scholarship is the Venerable Bede (ca. 673–735). When he was seven his parents gave him as an oblate to Benet Biscop's monastery at Wearmouth. Later he was

Nuns and Learning

In this tenth-century manuscript, the scholar Saint Aldhelm offers his book *In Praise of Holy Virgins* to a group of nuns, one of whom already holds a book. Early medieval nuns and monks spent much of their time copying manuscripts, preserving much of the learning of the classical world as well as Christian texts. (His Grace the Archbishop of Canterbury and the Trustees of Lambeth Palace Library. MS 200, fol. 68v)

sent to the new monastery at Jarrow five miles away. Surrounded by the books Benet Biscop had brought from Italy, Bede spent the rest of his life there.

Modern scholars praise Bede for his *Ecclesiastical History of the English People* (ca. 720), the chief source of information about early Britain. Bede searched far and wide for his information, discussed the validity of his evidence, compared various sources, and exercised rare critical judgment.

Bede popularized the system of dating events from the birth of Christ, rather than from the foundation of the city of Rome, as the Romans had done, or from the regnal years of kings, as the Germans did. He introduced the term *anno Domini*, "in the year of the Lord," abbreviated A.D. He fitted the entire history of the world into this new dating method. (The reverse dating system of B.C., "before Christ," does not seem to have been widely used before 1700.)

At about the time the monks at Lindisfarne were producing their Gospel book and Bede was writing his *History* at Jarrow, another Northumbrian monk was at work on a nonreligious epic poem that provides considerable information about the society that produced it. In contrast to the works of Bede, which were written in Latin, the poem *Beowulf* (BEY-uh-woolf) was written in the vernacular Anglo-Saxon. Although *Beowulf* is the only native English heroic epic, all the events take place in Denmark and Sweden, suggesting the close relationship between England and the continent in the eighth century. A classic of Western literature, *Beowulf* is the story of the hero's progress from valiant warrior to wise ruler.

Had they remained entirely insular, Northumbrian cultural achievements would have been of slight significance. But an Englishman from Northumbria—Alcuin—played a decisive role in the transmission of English learning to the Carolingian Empire and continental Europe.

The Carolingian Renaissance

In Roman Gaul through the fifth century, the general culture rested on an education that stressed grammar; the works of the Greco-Roman orators, poets, dramatists, and historians; and the legal and medical treatises of the Roman world. Beginning in the seventh and eighth centuries, a new cultural tradition common to Gaul, Italy, the British Isles, and to some extent Spain emerged. This culture was based primarily on Christian sources. Scholars have called this new Christian and ecclesiastical culture, and the educational foundation on which it was based, the "Carolingian Renaissance," because Charlemagne was its major patron.

Charlemagne directed that every monastery in his kingdom "should cultivate learning and educate the monks and secular clergy so that they might have a better understanding of the Christian writings." He also urged the establishment of cathedral and monastic schools where boys might learn to read and to pray properly. Thus the main purpose of this rebirth of learning was to promote an understanding of the Scriptures and of Christian writers.

At his court at Aachen, Charlemagne assembled learned men from all over Europe. The most important scholar and the leader of the palace school was the Northumbrian Alcuin (ca. 735–804). From 781 until his death, Alcuin was the emperor's chief adviser on religious and educational matters. An unusually prolific writer, he prepared some of the emperor's official documents and wrote many moral *exempla*, or "models," that set high standards for royal behavior and constitute a treatise on kingship. Alcuin's letters to Charlemagne set forth political theories on the authority, power, and responsibilities of a Christian ruler.

The scholars at Charlemagne's court also built up libraries, by hand copying books and manuscripts. They used the beautifully clear handwriting known as "caroline minuscule," from which modern Roman type is derived. Unlike the Merovingian majuscule, which had letters of equal size, minuscule had both uppercase and lowercase letters. Caroline minuscule improved the legibility of texts and meant that a sheet of vellum could contain more words and thus be used more efficiently. With the materials at hand, many more manuscripts could be copied. Book production on this scale represents a major manifestation of the revival of learning. Caroline minuscule illustrates the way a seemingly small technological change has broad cultural consequences.

Although scholars worked with Latin, the common people spoke local or vernacular languages. The Bretons, for example, retained their local dialect, and the Saxons and Bavarians could not understand each other. Some scholars believe that

Saint Luke from the Ada Gospels (late eighth to early ninth century)

In this lavishly illuminated painting from a manuscript of the four Gospels of the New Testament, a statuesque Saint Luke sits enthroned, his clothing falling in distinct folds reminiscent of Byzantine art. He is surrounded by an elaborate architectural framework, and above him is a winged ox, the symbol of Luke in early Christian art. The Ada school of painting was attached to the court of Charlemagne and gets its name from Ada, a sister of Charlemagne who commissioned some of the school's work. (Municipal Library, Trier, HS 22fol. 85r)

Latin words and phrases gradually penetrated the various vernacular languages, facilitating communication among diverse peoples.

Once basic literacy was established, monastic and other scholars went on to more difficult work. By the middle years of the ninth century, there was a great outpouring of more sophisticated books. Ecclesiastical writers imbued with the legal ideas of ancient Rome and the theocratic ideals of Saint Augustine instructed the rulers of the West. And it is no accident that medical study in the West began at Salerno in southern Italy in the late ninth century, *after* the Carolingian Renaissance.

Alcuin completed the work of his countryman Boniface—the Christianization of northern Europe. Latin Christian attitudes penetrated deeply into the consciousness of European peoples. By the tenth century the patterns of thought and the lifestyles of educated western Europeans were those of Rome and Latin Christianity.

Invasions and Migrations

What effects did the assaults and migrations of the Vikings, Magyars, and Muslims have on the rest of Europe?

After the Treaty of Verdun (843), continental Europe was fractured politically. All three kingdoms controlled by the sons of Louis the Pious were torn by domestic dissension and disorder. The frontier and coastal defenses erected by Charlemagne and maintained by Louis the Pious were neglected. No European political power was strong enough to put up effective resistance to external attacks. Three groups attacked Europe: Vikings from Scandinavia, representing the final wave of Germanic migrants; Muslims from the Mediterranean; and Magyars forced westward by other peoples (see Map 8.3).

Vikings in Western Europe

From the moors of Scotland to the mountains of Sicily, there arose in the ninth century the prayer, "Save us, O God, from the violence of the Northmen." The Northmen, also known as Vikings, were Germanic peoples from Norway, Sweden, and Denmark who had remained beyond the sway of the Christianizing influences of the Carolingian Empire. Some scholars believe that the name *Viking* derives from the old Norse word *vik*, meaning "creek." A Viking, then, was a pirate who waited in a creek or bay to attack passing vessels.

Viking boats were built for great speed and maneuverability. Propelled either by oars or by sails, deckless, and about sixty-five feet long, a Viking ship could carry between forty and sixty men—enough to harass an isolated monastery or village. These ships, navigated by thoroughly experienced and utterly fearless sailors, moved through the most complicated rivers, estuaries, and waterways in Europe. The Carolingian Empire, with no navy and no notion of the importance of sea power, was helpless. The Vikings moved swiftly, attacked, and escaped to return again.

Scholars disagree about the reasons for Viking attacks and migrations. Recent research asserts that a very unstable Danish kingship and disputes over the succession led to civil war and disorder, which drove warriors abroad in search of booty and supporters. Other writers insist that the Vikings were looking for trade and new commercial contacts. In that case, there were no better targets than the mercantile centers of Francia and Frisia.

Viking attacks were savage. The Vikings burned, looted, and did extensive short-term property damage, but there is little evidence that they caused long-term destruction—perhaps because, arriving in small bands, they lacked the manpower to do so. They seized magnates and high churchmen and held them for ransom; they also demanded tribute from kings. In 844–845 Charles the Bald had to raise seven thousand pounds of silver, and across the English Channel Anglo-Saxon

MAPPING THE PAST

MAP 8.3   Invasions and Migrations of the Ninth Century

This map shows the Viking, Magyar, and Arab invasions and migrations in the ninth century. Compare it with Map 7.3 (page 151) on the barbarian migrations of late antiquity to answer the following questions: **[1]** What similarities do you see in the patterns of migration in these two periods? What significant differences? **[2]** How is Viking expertise in shipbuilding and sailing reflected on this map? Based on the information in Map 7.3, what would you assume about the maritime skills of earlier Germanic tribes?

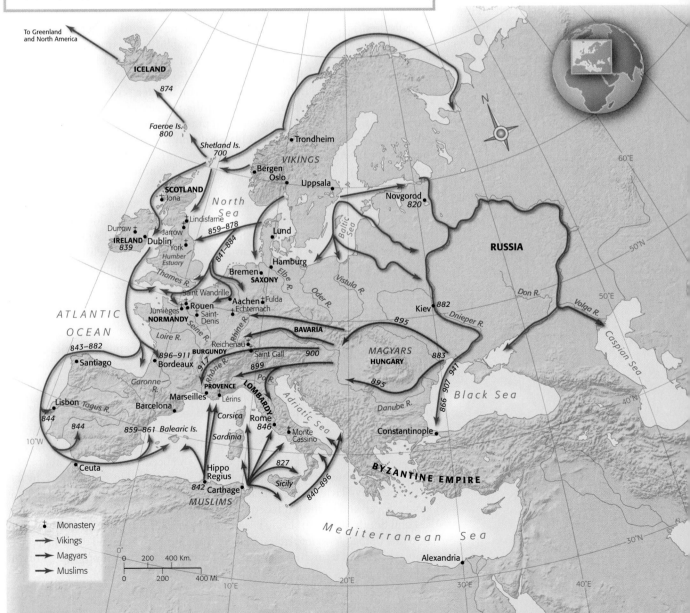

Animal Headpost from Viking Ship
Skilled woodcarvers produced ornamental headposts for ships, sledges, wagons, and bedsteads. The fearsome quality of many carvings suggests that they were intended to ward off evil spirits and to terrify. (© University Museum of Cultural Heritage, Oslo. Photographer: Eirik Irgens Johnsen)

rulers collected a land tax, the Danegeld, to buy off the Vikings. In the Seine and Loire Valleys the frequent presence of Viking war bands seems to have had economic consequences, stimulating the production of food and wine and possibly the manufacture (for sale) of weapons and the breeding of horses. In the early tenth century Danish Vikings besieged Paris with fleets of more than a hundred highly maneuverable ships, and the Frankish king Charles the Simple bought them off with a large part of northern France. The Vikings established the province of "Northmanland," or Normandy as it was later known, intermarrying with the local population and creating a distinctive Norman culture. From there they sailed around Spain and into the Mediterranean, eventually conquering Sicily from the Muslim Arabs in 1060–1090, while other Normans crossed the English Channel, defeating Anglo-Saxon forces in 1066.

Between 876 and 954 Viking control extended from Dublin across northern Britain to the Vikings' Scandinavian homelands. Norwegian Vikings moved farther west than any Europeans had before, establishing permanent settlements on Iceland and short-lived settlements in Greenland and Newfoundland, in what is now Canada.

In their initial attacks on isolated settlements, the Vikings took *thralls* (slaves) for the markets of Europe, and for trade with the Muslim world. The slave trade represented an important part of Viking commerce. The Icelander Hoskuld Dala-Kolsson paid three marks of silver, three times the price of a common concubine, for a pretty Irish girl; she was one of twelve offered by a Viking trader. No wonder many communities bought peace by paying tribute.

Along with destruction, the Vikings made positive contributions to the areas they settled. They carried their unrivaled knowledge of shipbuilding and seamanship everywhere. The northeastern and central parts of England where the Vikings settled became known as the Danelaw because Danish, not English, law and customs prevailed there. Scholars believe that some legal institutions, such as the ancestor of the modern grand jury, originated in the Danelaw. Thriving centers of Viking trade emerged in England and Ireland.

Slavs and Vikings in Eastern Europe

In antiquity the Slavs lived in central Europe, farming with iron technology, building fortified towns, and worshiping a variety of deities. With the start of the mass migrations of the late Roman Empire, the Slavs moved in different directions and split into what later historians identified as three groups: West, South, and East Slavs.

The group labeled the West Slavs included the Poles, Czechs, Slovaks, and Wends. The South Slavs, comprising peoples who became the Serbs, Croats, Slovenes, Macedonians, and Bosnians, migrated southward into the Balkans. In the seventh century Slavic peoples created the state of Moravia along the banks of the Danube River, and by the tenth century it was Roman Christian. Most of the other West and South Slavs also slowly became Roman Christian. The pattern was similar to that of the Germanic tribes: first the ruler was baptized, and then missionaries preached, built churches, and spread Christian teachings among the common people. The ruler of the Poland was able to convince the pope to establish an independent archbishopric there in 1000, the beginning of a long-lasting connection between Poland and the Roman church. In the Balkans the Serbs accepted Orthodox Christianity, while the Croats became Roman Christian, a division that has had a long impact; it was one of the factors in the civil war in this area in the late twentieth century.

Between the fifth and ninth centuries, the eastern Slavs moved into the practically uninhabited area of present-day European Russia and Ukraine. This enormous area consisted of an immense virgin forest to the north, where most of the eastern Slavs settled, and a vast prairie grassland to the south.

In the ninth century the Vikings appeared in the lands of the eastern Slavs. Called "Varangians" (va-RAN-gee-anz) in the old Russian chronicles, their initial raids for plunder gradually turned into trading missions. Moving up and down the rivers, they linked Scandinavia and northern Europe to the Black Sea and to the Byzantine Empire with its capital at Constantinople.

In order to increase and protect their international commerce, the Vikings declared themselves the rulers of the eastern Slavs. According to tradition, the semi-legendary chieftain Ruirik founded a princely dynasty about 860. In any event, the Varangian ruler Oleg (r. 878–912) established his residence at Kiev in modern-day Ukraine. He and his successors ruled over a loosely united confederation of Slavic territories known as Rus with its capital at Kiev until 1054. (The word *Russia* comes from *Rus*, though the origins of *Rus* are hotly debated, with some historians linking it with Swedish words and others with Slavic words.)

The Viking prince and his clansmen quickly became assimilated into the Slavic population, taking local wives and emerging as the noble class. Missionaries of the Byzantine Empire converted the Vikings and local Slavs to Eastern Orthodox Christianity, accelerating the unification of the two groups. Thus the rapidly Slavified Vikings left two important legacies for the future: they created a loose unification of Slavic territories under a single ruling prince and a single ruling dynasty, and they imposed a basic religious unity by accepting Orthodox Christianity (as opposed to Roman Catholicism) for themselves and the eastern Slavs.

Even at its height under Great Prince Iaroslav the Wise (r. 1019–1054), the unity of Kievan Rus was extremely tenuous. Trade, not government, was the main concern of the rulers. Moreover, the Slavified Vikings failed to find a way of peacefully transferring power from one generation to the next. In medieval western Europe, this fundamental problem of government was increasingly resolved by resorting to the principle of **primogeniture** (pry-muh-JEN-ee-choor): the king's eldest son received the crown as his rightful inheritance when his father died. Civil war was thus averted; order was preserved. In early Rus, however, there were apparently no fixed rules, and much strife accompanied each succession.

Possibly to avoid such chaos, Great Prince Iaroslav, before his death in 1054, divided Kievan Rus among his five sons, who in turn divided their properties when they died. Between 1054 and 1237, Kievan Rus disintegrated into more and more competing units, each ruled by a prince claiming to be a descendant of Ruirik.

The princes thought of their land as private property. A given prince owned a certain number of farms or landed estates and had them worked directly by his people, mainly slaves. Outside of these estates, which constituted the princely domain, the prince exercised only limited authority in his principality. Excluding the clergy, two kinds of people lived there: the noble boyars (BOY-arz) and the commoner peasants.

The **boyars** were descendants of the original Viking warriors, and they also held their lands as free and clear private property. Although the boyars normally

primogeniture A system in which the king's eldest son inherited the crown when his father died.

boyars Descendants of the original Viking warriors, they held their lands as free and clear private property.

fought in princely armies, the customary law declared that they could serve any prince they wished. The ordinary peasants were also truly free. They could move at will wherever opportunities were greatest. In the touching phrase of the times, theirs was "a clean road, without boundaries."[12] In short, fragmented princely power, private property, and personal freedom all went together.

Magyars and Muslims   Groups of central European steppe peoples known as Magyars also raided villages in the late ninth century, taking plunder and captives, and forcing leaders to pay tribute in an effort to prevent further looting and destruction. Moving westward, small bands of Magyars on horseback reached as far as Spain and the Atlantic coast. They subdued northern Italy, compelled Bavaria and Saxony to pay tribute, and even penetrated into the Rhineland and Burgundy. Magyar forces were defeated by a combined army of Frankish and other Germanic troops at the Battle of Lechfeld near Augsburg in southern Germany in 955, and the Magyars settled in the area that is now Hungary in eastern Europe.

Much as Clovis had centuries earlier, the Magyar ruler Géza (**GEE-za**) (r. 970–997), who had been a pagan, decided to become a Roman Christian. This gave him the support of the papacy and offered prospects for alliances with other Roman Christian rulers against the Byzantine Empire, Hungary's southern neighbor. Géza's son Stephen I (r. 997–1038) was officially crowned the king of Hungary by a papal representative on Christmas Day of 1001. He supported the building of churches and monasteries, built up royal power, and encouraged the use of Latin and the Roman alphabet. Hungary's alliance with the papacy shaped the later history of eastern Europe just as Charlemagne's alliance with the papacy shaped western European history. The Hungarians adopted settled agriculture, wrote law codes, and built towns, and Hungary became an important crossroads of trade for German and Muslim merchants.

The ninth century also saw invasions into western Europe from the south. Muslim fleets had attacked Sicily, which was part of the Byzantine Empire, beginning in the seventh century, and by the end of the ninth century they controlled most of the island. The Muslims drove northward and sacked Rome in 846. Expert seamen, they sailed around the Iberian Peninsula from North Africa and captured towns along the Adriatic coast nearly all the way to Venice. They attacked Mediterranean settlements along the coast of Provence and advanced on land as far as the Alps. In the tenth century Frankish, papal, and Byzantine forces were able to retake much territory, though the Muslims continued to hold Sicily. Disputes among the Muslim rulers on the island led one faction to ask the Normans for assistance, and between 1060 and 1090 the Normans gradually conquered all of Sicily.

What was the effect of these invasions on the structure of European society? From the perspective of those living in what had been Charlemagne's empire, Viking, Magyar, and Muslim attacks accelerated the fragmentation of political power. Lords capable of rallying fighting men, supporting them, and putting up resistance to the invaders did so. They also assumed political power in their territories. Weak and defenseless people sought the protection of local strongmen, and free peasants sank to the level of serfs. This period is thus often seen as one of terror and chaos.

People in other parts of Europe might have had a different opinion, however. In Muslim Spain, scholars worked in thriving cities, and new crops such as cotton

Section Review

- Three groups attacked Europe: Vikings from Scandinavia, Muslims from the Mediterranean, and Magyars from the east.

- With Europe fractured politically, the Vikings attacked the Carolingian empire in their highly maneuverable boats in search of booty and new commerce.

- The Vikings spread into what is now Normandy, Sicily, and England, moving north and west, trading in slaves, and displaying their vast maritime and naval skills.

- Vikings also moved eastward into lands populated by Slavic peoples, where they raided, traded, intermarried with Slavic peoples, and eventually assimilated.

- Magyars were central European steppe peoples who moved westward until Franks and Germans defeated them at Lechfeld in 955 in Germany; they settled in Hungary under the rule of Géza, who converted to Roman Christianity, gaining the support of the papacy.

- Muslim fleets attacked Sicily and moved northward as far as the Alps but were only able to hold on to Sicily, which later fell to the Normans.

and sugar enhanced ordinary people's lives. In eastern Europe, states such as Moravia and Hungary became strong kingdoms. A Viking point of view might be the most positive, for by 1100 descendents of the Vikings not only ruled their homelands in Denmark, Norway, and Sweden, but also ruled Normandy, England, Sicily, Iceland, and Kievan Rus, with an outpost in Greenland and occasional voyages to North America.

Chapter Review

How did Islam take root in the Middle East and then spread to Europe? (page 163)

In the seventh century the diverse Arab tribes were transformed into a powerful political and social force by the teachings of the Prophet Muhammad. They conquered much of the Middle East and North Africa, and in the eighth century they crossed into Europe, eventually gaining control of most of the Iberian Peninsula. Muslim-controlled Spain, known as al-Andalus, was the most advanced society in Europe in terms of agriculture, science, and medicine. Some Christian residents assimilated to Muslim practices, but hostility between the two groups was also evident as each increasingly regarded members of the other as infidels.

How did Frankish rulers govern their kingdoms? (page 171)

In western Europe, Frankish rulers of the Merovingian dynasty built on the foundations established by Clovis in the fifth century, dividing their territories into regions and sending out royal officials, later called counts, to administer the regions. Their authority was frequently challenged by civil wars and rebellions by nobles. One of these nobles, Charles Martel, held the important position of mayor of the palace, and in the eighth century he took power and established a new dynasty, the Carolingians. The Carolingians used both military victories and strategic marriage alliances to enhance their authority.

How did Charlemagne gain control of a large part of Europe and how did power become decentralized after his death? (page 173)

Carolingian government reached the peak of its development under Charles Martel's grandson, Charlemagne. Building on the military and diplomatic foundations of his ancestors, Charlemagne waged constant warfare to expand his kingdom, eventually coming to control most of central and western continental Europe except Muslim Spain. Christian missionary activity among the Germanic peoples continued, and strong ties were forged with the Roman papacy, which eventually resulted in Charlemagne's coronation as emperor. After his son's death, Charlemagne's empire was divided between his grandsons in the Treaty of Verdun (843). This division of Charlemagne's empire was accompanied by a decentralization of power at the local level, and a new political form involving mutual obligations, later called "feudalism," developed. The power of the local nobles in the feudal structure rested on landed estates worked by peasants in another system of mutual obligation termed "manorialism." An overwhelmingly agricultural economy supplied food for local needs, but there was some interregional trade in glass, pottery, and woolens and a sizable long-distance trade in slaves.

Key Terms

Kaaba (p. 164)
Qur'an (p. 164)
Five Pillars of Islam (p. 166)
caliph (p. 167)
Shi'ites (p. 167)
Sunnis (p. 167)
infidel (p. 170)
civitas (p. 171)
comites (p. 173)
missi dominici (p. 175)
Treaty of Verdun (p. 177)
vassal (p. 177)
fief (p. 177)
feudalism (p. 177)
manorialism (p. 179)
serfs (p. 179)
double monastery (p. 181)
primogeniture (p. 187)
boyars (p. 187)

What were the significant intellectual and cultural changes in Charlemagne's era? (page 181)

Charlemagne's support of education and learning proved his most enduring legacy. The revival of learning associated with Charlemagne and his court at Aachen, sometimes styled the "Carolingian Renaissance," drew its greatest inspiration from seventh- and eighth-century intellectual developments in the Anglo-Saxon kingdom of Northumbria in northern England. Here women and men in monasteries produced beautiful illustrated texts, and the Venerable Bede popularized the Christian dating system now in use in most of the world. After the Treaty of Verdun, continental Europe was fractured politically, with no European political power strong enough to put up effective resistance to external attack.

What effects did the assaults and migrations of the Vikings, Magyars, and Muslims have on the rest of Europe? (page 184)

Vikings from Scandinavia carried out raids for plunder along the coasts and rivers of western Europe and traveled as far as Iceland, Greenland, and North America. Eventually they settled in England and France, where they established the state of Normandy. In eastern Europe Vikings traded down the rivers as far as Constantinople and formed the state of Kievan Rus, assimilating to Slavic culture and converting to the Orthodox religion. Like the Vikings, the Magyars initially invaded Europe for plunder and then established a permanent state; their ruler Stephen I was crowned as king by a papal representative two hundred years after Charlemagne's coronation. Thus, in both western and eastern Europe, civil rulers and church leaders supported each other's goals and utilized each other's prestige and power, though their alliances and disputes had little effect on the daily life of most people in early medieval Europe.

Notes

1. F. E. Peters, *A Reader on Classical Islam* (Princeton, N.J.: Princeton University Press, 1994), pp. 208–209.
2. J. O'Faolain and L. Martines, eds., *Not in God's Image: Women in History from the Greeks to the Victorians* (New York: Harper & Row, 1973), pp. 108–114.
3. See Jane I. Smith, "Islam and Christendom: Historical, Cultural, and Religious Interaction from the Seventh to the Fifteenth Centuries," in *The Oxford History of Islam*, ed. John L. Esposito (New York: Oxford University Press, 1999), pp. 317–321.
4. J. M. Bloom, *Paper Before Print: The History and Impact of Paper in the Islamic World* (New Haven: Yale University Press, 2001), pp. 9–10, 17, 45, 85–89.
5. JoAnn Hoeppner Moran Cruz, "Western Views of Islam in Medieval Europe," in *Perceptions of Islam*, ed. D. Blanks and M. Frassetto (New York: St. Martin's Press, 1999), pp. 55–81.
6. I. Wood, *The Merovingian Kingdoms, 450–751* (New York: Longman, 1994), p. 101.
7. Einhard, *The Life of Charlemagne*, with a foreword by S. Painter (Ann Arbor: University of Michigan Press, 1960), pp. 50–51.
8. Quoted in R. McKitterick, *The Frankish Kingdoms Under the Carolingians, 751–987* (New York: Longman, 1983), p. 77.
9. See K. F. Werner, "Important Noble Families in the Kingdom of Charlemagne," in *The Medieval Nobility: Studies on the Ruling Class of France and Germany from the Sixth to the Twelfth Century*, ed. and trans. T. Reuter (New York: North-Holland, 1978), pp. 174–184.
10. Quoted in B. D. Hill, ed., *Church and State in the Middle Ages* (New York: John Wiley & Sons, 1970), pp. 46–47.
11. J. Nicholson, "Feminae Glorisae: Women in the Age of Bede," in *Medieval Women*, ed. D. Baker (Oxford: Basil Blackwell, 1978), pp. 15–31, esp. p. 19; and C. Fell, *Women in Anglo-Saxon England and the Impact of 1066* (Bloomington: Indiana University Press, 1984), p. 109.
12. Quoted in R. Pipes, *Russia Under the Old Regime* (New York: Charles Scribner's Sons, 1974), p. 48.

To assess your mastery of this chapter, go to **bedfordstmartins.com/mckaywestbrief**

Listening to the Past

Feudal Homage and Fealty

Feudalism developed in the ninth century during the disintegration of the Carolingian Empire because rulers needed fighting men and officials. A king, lay lord, bishop, or abbot would grant lands or estates to a noble or knight. In return, the recipient became the vassal of the lord and agreed to perform certain services. In a society that lacked an adequate government bureaucracy, a sophisticated method of taxation, or even the beginnings of national consciousness, personal ties provided some degree of cohesiveness. In the first document, a charter dated 876, the emperor Charles the Bald (r. 843–877), Charlemagne's grandson, grants a benefice, or fief. In the second document, dated 1127, the Flemish notary Galbert of Bruges describes homage and fealty before Count Charles the Good of Flanders (r. 1119–1127). The ceremony consists of three parts: the act of homage; the oath of fealty, intended to reinforce the act; and the investiture (apparently with property). Because all three parts are present, historians consider this evidence of a fully mature feudal system.

In the name of the holy and undivided Trinity. Charles by the mercy of Almighty God august emperor . . . let it be known to all the faithful of the holy church of God and to our now, present and to come, that one of our faithful subjects, by name of Hildebertus, has approached our throne and has beseeched our serenity that through this command of our authority we grant to him for all the days of his life and to his son after him, in right of usufruct and benefice, certain

estates which are . . . called Cavaliacus, in the county of Limoges (**lee-MOHZH**). Giving assent to his prayers for reason of his meritorious service, we have ordered this charter to be written, through which we grant to him the estates already mentioned, in all their entirety, with lands, vineyards, forests, meadows, pastures, and with the men living upon them, so that, without causing any damage through exchanges or diminishing or lessening the land, he for all the days of his life and his son after him, as we have said, may hold and possess them in right of benefice and usufruct. . . .

The hand of God blesses Charles the Bald as he receives the Bible, symbolic of his connection with Israelite kings David and Solomon. (Bibliothèque nationale de France)

On Thursday, the seventh of the ides of April [April 7, 1127], acts of homage were again made to the count, which were brought to a conclusion through this method of giving faith and assurance. First, they performed homage in this fashion: the count inquired if [the prospective vassal] wished completely to become his man. He replied, "I do wish it," and with his hands joined and covered by the hands of the count, the two were united by a kiss. Second, he who had done the homage gave faith to the representative of the count in these words: "I promise in my faith that I shall henceforth be faithful to Count William, and I shall fully observe the homage owed him against all men, in good faith and without deceit." Third, he took an oath on the relics of the saints. Then the count, with the rod which he had in his right hand, gave investiture to all those who by this promise had given assurance and due homage to the count, and had taken the oath.

Questions for Analysis

1. Why was the charter drawn up? Why did Charles grant the benefice?

2. Who were the "men living on it," and what economic functions did they perform?

3. What did the joined hands of the prospective vassal and the kiss symbolize?

4. In the oath of fealty, what was meant by the phrase "in my faith"? Why did the vassal swear on relics of the saints?

5. What does this ceremony tell us about the society that used it?

Source: The History of Feudalism by David Herlihy, ed. Copyright © 1970 by David Herlihy. Reprinted by permission of HarperCollins Publishers, Inc.

CHAPTER 9

State and Church in the High Middle Ages

1000–1300

In this thirteenth-century manuscript, knights of King Henry II stab Archbishop Thomas Becket in 1170 in Canterbury Cathedral, a dramatic example of church/state conflict. Becket was soon made a saint, and the spot where the murder occurred became a pilgrimage site; it is still a top tourist destination. (British Library, London)

Chapter Preview

Political Revival
How did medieval rulers create larger and more stable territories?

Law and Justice
How did the administration of law contribute to the development of national states?

The Papacy
How did the papacy attempt to reform the church, and what was the response from other powerful rulers?

The Crusades
How did the motives, course, and consequences of the Crusades reflect and shape developments in Europe?

INDIVIDUALS IN SOCIETY: The Jews of Speyer: A Collective Biography

LISTENING TO THE PAST: An Arab View of the Crusades

Beginning in the last half of the tenth century, the Viking, Muslim, and Magyar invasions that had contributed to the fragmentation of Europe gradually ended. Feudal rulers began to develop new institutions of government that enabled them to assert their power over lesser lords and the general population. Centralized states slowly crystallized, first in western Europe, and then in eastern and northern Europe as well. At the same time, energetic popes built their power within the Western Christian church and asserted their superiority over kings and emperors. A papal call to retake the holy city of Jerusalem led to nearly two centuries of warfare between Christians and Muslims. Christian warriors, clergy, and settlers moved out in all directions from western and central Europe, so that through conquest and colonization border regions were gradually incorporated into a more uniform European culture.

Political Revival

How did medieval rulers create larger and more stable territories?

The eleventh century witnessed the beginnings of new political stability. Rulers in France, England, and Germany worked to reduce private warfare and civil anarchy. Domestic disorder subsided, and external invasions gradually declined. In some parts of Europe, lords in control of large territories began to manipulate feudal institutions to build up their power even further, becoming kings over growing and slowly centralizing states.

As medieval rulers expanded their territories and extended their authority, they developed institutions to rule more effectively, including an enlarged bureaucracy of officials and larger armies. Officials and armies cost money, and rulers in various countries developed slightly different ways of acquiring more revenue and handling financial matters, some more successful than others.

Medieval Origins of the Modern State

Rome's great legacy to Western civilization had been the concepts of the state and the law, but for almost five hundred years after the disintegration of the Roman Empire in the West, the state as a reality did not exist. Political authority was completely decentralized. Power was spread among many lords who gave their localities such protection and security as their strength allowed. There existed many, frequently overlapping layers of authority—earls, counts, barons, knights—between a king and the ordinary people.

In these circumstances, medieval rulers had common goals. The rulers of England, France, and Germany wanted to strengthen and extend royal authority in their territories. They wanted to establish an effective means of communication with all peoples in order to increase public order. They wanted more revenue and efficient bureaucracies. The solutions they found to these problems laid the foundations for modern national states.

The modern state is an organized territory with definite geographical boundaries that are recognized by other states. It has a body of law and jurisdiction over many people. The modern national state counts on the loyalty of its citizens, or at least a majority of them. In return it provides order so that citizens can go about their daily work and other activities. It protects its citizens and their property. The state tries to prevent violence and to apprehend and punish those who commit it.

It supplies a currency or medium of exchange that permits financial and commercial transactions. It conducts relations with foreign governments. To accomplish these minimal functions, the state must have officials, bureaucracies, laws, courts of law, soldiers, information, and money. By the twelfth century medieval kingdoms and some lesser lordships possessed these attributes, at least to the extent that most modern states have them.

England

Before the Viking invasions, England had never been united under a single ruler. The victory of the remarkable Alfred, king of the West Saxons (or Wessex), over the Vikings in 878 inaugurated a great political revival. Alfred and his immediate successors built a system of local defenses and slowly extended royal rule beyond Wessex to other Anglo-Saxon peoples until one law, royal law, took precedence over local custom. England was divided into local units called "shires," or counties, each under the jurisdiction of a shire-reeve (a word that soon evolved into "sheriff") appointed by the king. Sheriffs were unpaid officials from well-off families responsible for collecting taxes, catching and trying criminals, and raising infantry.

The Bayeux (bay-YUH) Tapestry
William's conquest of England was recorded in thread on a narrative embroidery panel measuring 231 feet by 19 inches. In this scene, two nobles and a bishop acclaim Harold Godwinson as king of England. The nobles hold a sword, symbol of military power, and the bishop holds a stole, symbol of clerical power. Harold himself holds a scepter and an orb, both symbols of royal power. The embroidery provides an important historical source for the clothing, armor, and lifestyles of the Norman and Anglo-Saxon warrior class. It eventually ended up in Bayeux in northern France, where it is displayed in a museum today and is incorrectly called a "tapestry," which is a different kind of needlework. (Tapisserie de Bayeux et avec autorisation spéciale de la Ville de Bayeux)

Domesday Book A surviving record of a general inquiry ordered by William of Normandy; it serves as a source of social and economic information about medieval England.

Exchequer The bureau of finance established by Henry I, becoming the first institution of the governmental bureaucracy of England.

The Pipe Rolls

Twice yearly English medieval sheriffs appeared before the Barons of the Exchequer to account for the monies they had collected from the royal estates and from fines for civil and criminal offenses. Clerks recorded these revenues and royal expenditures on the pipe rolls, whose name derives from the pipelike form of the rolled parchments. A roll exists for 1129–1130, then continuously from 1156 to 1832, representing the largest series of English public records. (Crown copyright material in the Public Record Office is reproduced by permission of the Controller of the Britannic Majesty's Stationery Office [E40 1/1565])

The Viking invasions of England did not end, however, and the island eventually came under Viking rule. The Viking Canute (**kuh-NOOT**) made England the center of his empire while promoting a policy of assimilation and reconciliation between Anglo-Saxons and Vikings. When Canute's heir Edward died childless, there were a number of claimants to the throne of England—the Anglo-Saxon noble Harold Godwinson (ca. 1022–1066), who had been crowned by English nobles, the Norwegian king Harald III (r. 1045–1066), grandson of Canute, and Duke William of Normandy, who was the illegitimate son of Edward's cousin.

In 1066 William invaded England with his Norman vassals, met the exhausted forces of Harold Godwinson, and defeated them—an event now known as the Norman conquest. In both England and Normandy, William the Conqueror limited the power of his noble vassals and church officials and transformed the feudal system into a unified monarchy. In England he replaced Anglo-Saxon sheriffs with Normans. He retained another Anglo-Saxon device, the *writ*, through which the central government communicated with people at the local level, using the local tongue.

In addition to retaining Anglo-Saxon institutions that served his purposes, William also introduced a major innovation, the Norman inquest or general inquiry. William wanted to determine how much wealth there was in his new kingdom, who held what land, and what land had been disputed among his vassals since the Conquest of 1066. Groups of royal officials were sent to every part of the country. The resulting record, called the **Domesday Book** (**DOOMZ-day**) from the Anglo-Saxon word *doom*, meaning "judgment," still survives. It is an invaluable source of social and economic information about medieval England.

The *Domesday Book* provided William and his descendants with information vital for the exploitation and government of the country. Knowing the amount of wealth every area possessed, the king could tax accordingly. Knowing the amount of land his vassals had, he could allot knight service fairly. The book helped English kings regard their country as one unit.

William's son Henry I (r. 1100–1135) established a bureau of finance called the **Exchequer** (**EKS-chek-er**) (for the checkered cloth at which his officials collected and audited royal accounts), which became the first institution of the government bureaucracy of England. In addition to various taxes and annual gifts, Henry's income came from money paid to the crown for settling disputes and as penalties for crimes, as well as money due to Henry in his private position as feudal lord. The latter would include the fee paid by a vassal's son in order to inherit the father's properties and the fee paid by a knight who wished to avoid military service. Henry, like other medieval kings, made no distinction between his private income and state revenues, though the officials of the Exchequer began to keep careful records of the monies paid into and out of the royal treasury.

In 1128 William's granddaughter Matilda was married to Geoffrey of Anjou; their son became Henry II of England and inaugurated the Angevin (**AN-juh-vin**) (from Anjou, his father's county) dynasty. Henry inherited the French provinces of Anjou, Normandy, Maine, and Touraine in northwestern France, and then in 1152 he claimed lordship over Aquitaine, Poitou (**pwa-TOO**), and Gascony in southwestern France through his marriage to the great heiress Eleanor of Aquitaine (see Map 9.1). Each of the provinces in Henry's Angevin empire was separate and was only loosely linked to the others by dynastic law and personal oaths. The histories of England and France became closely intertwined, however, leading to disputes and conflicts down to the fifteenth century.

France

France also became increasingly unified in this era. Following the death of the last Carolingian ruler in 987, an assembly of nobles selected Hugh Capet (**ka-PAY**) as his successor. Soon after his own coronation, Hugh crowned his son Robert to ensure the succession and prevent disputes after his death and to weaken the feudal principle of elective kingship. The Capetian kings were weak, but they laid the foundation for later political stability.

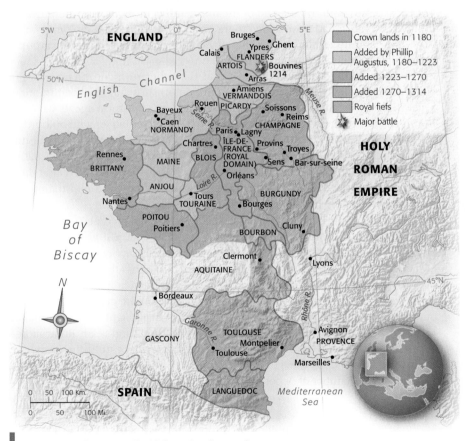

MAP 9.1 The Growth of the Kingdom of France

Some scholars believe that Philip II received the title "Augustus" (from a Latin word meaning "to increase") because he vastly expanded the territories of the kingdom of France. The province of Toulouse (**too-LOOZ**) in the south became part of France as a result of the crusade against the Albigensians (see page 212).

This stability came slowly. In the early twelfth century France still consisted of a number of virtually independent provinces. Each was governed by a local ruler; each had its own laws, customs, coinage, and dialect. Unlike the king of England, the king of France had jurisdiction over a very small area. Chroniclers called King Louis VI (r. 1108–1137) *roi de Saint-Denis* (wah duh san-duh-NEE), king of Saint-Denis, because the territory he controlled was limited to Paris and the Saint-Denis area surrounding the city (see Map 9.1). This region, called the *Île-de-France* (EEL-duh-franz), or royal domain, became the nucleus of the French state. The clear goal of the medieval French king was to increase the royal domain and extend his authority.

The work of unifying France began under Louis VI's grandson Philip II (r. 1180–1223). Rigord, Philip's biographer, gave him the title "Augustus" (from a Latin word meaning "to increase") because he vastly enlarged the territory of the kingdom of France. When King John of England, who was Philip's vassal for the rich province of Normandy, defaulted on his feudal obligation to come to the French court, Philip declared Normandy forfeit to the French crown. He enforced his declaration militarily, and in 1204 Normandy fell to the French. He gained other northern provinces as well, and by the end of his reign Philip was effectively master of northern France.

In the thirteenth century Philip Augustus's descendants acquired important holdings in the south. By the end of the thirteenth century most of the provinces of modern France had been added to the royal domain through diplomacy, marriage, war, and inheritance. The king of France was stronger than any group of nobles who might try to challenge his authority.

Philip Augustus devised a method of governing the provinces and providing for communication between the central government in Paris and local communities. Each province retained its own institutions and laws, but royal agents were sent from Paris into the provinces as the king's official representatives with authority to act for him. These agents were often middle-class lawyers who possessed full judicial, financial, and military jurisdiction in their districts. They were never natives of the provinces to which they were assigned, and they could not own land there. This policy reflected the fundamental principle of French administration that royal interests superseded local interests.

Medieval people believed that a good king lived on the income of his own land and taxed only in time of a grave emergency—that is, a just war. Because the church, and not the state, performed what we call social services—such as education and care of the sick, the aged, and orphaned children—there was no ordinary need for the government to tax. Taxation meant war financing. The French monarchy could not continually justify taxing the people on the grounds of the needs of war. Thus the French kings were slow to develop an efficient bureau of finance. French provincial laws and institutions—in contrast to England's early unification—also retarded the growth of a central financial agency. Not until the fourteenth century, as a result of the Hundred Years' War, did a state financial bureau emerge—the Chamber of Accounts.

Central Europe

In central Europe, the German king Otto I (r. 936–973) defeated many other lords to build up his power. To do this, Otto relied on the church, getting financial support and the bulk of his army from ecclesiastical lands. Otto asserted the right to control ecclesiastical appointments. Before receiving religious consecration and being invested with the staff and ring symbolic of their offices, bishops and abbots had to perform feudal homage for the lands that accompanied the church office. This practice, later known as "lay investiture," created a grave crisis in the eleventh century, as we will see later in this chapter.

Some of our knowledge of Otto derives from *The Deeds of Otto*, a history of his reign in heroic verse written by a nun, Hroswita of Gandersheim (ca. 935–ca. 1003). A learned poet, she also produced six verse plays, and she is considered the first dramatist writing in Europe after the fall of the Roman Empire.

In 955 Otto I inflicted a crushing defeat on the Magyars in the battle of Lechfeld (see page 188), which made Otto a great hero to the Germans. He used this victory to have himself crowned emperor in 962 by the pope in Aachen, which had been the capital of the Carolingian empire. He chose this site to symbolize his intention to continue the tradition of Charlemagne and to demonstrate papal support for his rule. It was not exactly clear what Otto was the emperor *of*, however, though by the eleventh century people were increasingly using the term **Holy Roman Empire** to refer to a loose confederation of principalities, duchies (DUTCH-eez), cities, bishoprics, and other types of regional governments stretching from Denmark to Rome and from Burgundy to Poland (see Map 9.2).

Holy Roman Empire The loose confederation of principalities, duchies, cities, bishoprics, and other types of regional governments stretching from Denmark to Rome and from Burgundy to Poland.

MAP 9.2   The Holy Roman Empire and the Kingdom of Sicily, ca. 1200

Frederick Barbarossa greatly expanded the size of the Holy Roman Empire, but it remained a loose collection of various types of governments. The kingdom of Sicily included mainland areas as well as the island in 1200, with an ethnically mixed population ruled by Norman kings.

Major battle

Boundary of the Holy Roman Empire

In this large area of central Europe, unified nation-states did not develop until the nineteenth century. The Holy Roman emperors shared power with princes, dukes, archbishops, counts, bishops, abbots, and cities. The office of emperor remained an elected one, though the electors included only seven men—four secular rulers of large territories within the empire and three archbishops.

Through most of the first half of the twelfth century, civil war wracked Germany. When Conrad III died in 1152, the resulting anarchy was so terrible that the electors decided the only alternative to continued chaos was the selection of a strong ruler. They chose Frederick Barbarossa of the house of Hohenstaufen (hoh-uhn-SHTOU-fen) (r. 1152–1190).

Like William the Conqueror in England and Philip in France, Frederick required vassals to take an oath of allegiance to him as emperor and appointed officials to exercise full imperial authority over local communities. He forbade private warfare and established sworn peace associations with the princes of various regions. These peace associations punished those who breached the peace and criminals, with penalties ranging from maiming to execution.

Frederick Barbarossa surrounded himself with men trained in Roman law (see page 203), and he used Roman law to justify his assertion of imperial rights over the towns of northern Italy. Between 1154 and 1188 Frederick made six expeditions into Italy. While he initially made significant conquests in the north, the brutality of his methods provoked revolts, and the Italian cities formed an alliance with the papacy. In 1176 Frederick suffered a defeat at Legnano (see Map 9.2). This battle marked the first time a feudal cavalry of armed knights was decisively defeated by bourgeois (boor-zwah) infantrymen. Frederick was forced to recognize the municipal autonomy of the northern Italian cities.

Sicily

The kingdom of Sicily is a good example of how a strong government could be built on a feudal base by determined rulers. Between 1061 and 1091 a bold Norman knight, Roger de Hauteville, and a small band of mercenaries defeated the Muslims and Greeks who controlled Sicily. Roger then governed a heterogeneous population of Sicilians, Italians, Greeks, Jews, Arabs, and Normans. Roger distributed scattered fiefs to his followers so no vassal would have a centralized power base. He took an inquest of royal property and rights and forbade private warfare. To these Norman practices, Roger fused Arabic and Greek governmental devices. For example, he retained the main financial agency of the previous Muslim rulers, the **diwān** (di-WAHN), a sophisticated bureau for record keeping and administration.

In the multicultural society of medieval Sicily, Muslims and Greeks, as well as Normans, staffed the diwān, as well as the army and judiciary. The diwān kept official documents in Greek, Latin, and Arabic. It supervised the royal estates in Sicily, collected revenues, managed the state monopoly of the sale of salt and lumber, and registered all income to the treasury. With revenues derived from those products, Roger hired mercenaries. He encouraged appeals from local courts to his royal court because such appeals implied respect for his authority.

In 1137 Roger's forces took the city of Naples and much of the surrounding territory in southern Italy. The entire area came to be known as the kingdom of Sicily (or sometimes the kingdom of the Two Sicilies), and was often caught up in conflicts between the pope, the Holy Roman emperor, and the kings of France and Spain over control of Italy.

Roger's grandson Frederick II (r. 1212–1250), who was also the grandson of Frederick Barbarossa of Germany, was crowned king of the Germans at Aachen

diwān A sophisticated Muslim bureau for record keeping and administration.

(1216) and Holy Roman emperor at Rome (1220). He concentrated his attention on Sicily and showed little interest in the northern part of the Holy Roman Empire. Frederick banned private warfare and placed all castles and towers under royal administration. He also replaced town officials with royal governors and subordinated feudal and ecclesiastical courts to the king's courts. Royal control of the nobility, of the towns, and of the judicial system added up to great centralization, which required a professional bureaucracy and sound state financing.

In 1224 Frederick founded the University of Naples to train officials for his bureaucracy. He too continued the use of Muslim institutions such as the diwān, and he tried to administer justice fairly to all his subjects, declaring, "We cannot in the least permit Jews and Saracens (Muslims) to be defrauded of the power of our protection and to be deprived of all other help, just because the difference of their religious practices makes them hateful to Christians,"[1] implying a degree of toleration exceedingly rare at the time.

Frederick's contemporaries called him the "Wonder of the World." He certainly transformed the kingdom of Sicily. But Sicily required constant attention, and Frederick's absences on crusades and on campaigns in mainland Italy took their toll. Shortly after he died, the unsupervised bureaucracy fell to pieces. The pope, as feudal overlord of Sicily, called in a French prince to rule. Frederick's reign had also weakened imperial power in the German parts of the empire, and in the later Middle Ages lay and ecclesiastical princes held sway in the Holy Roman Empire. Germany and Italy did not become unified states until the nineteenth century.

reconquista The Christian term for the conquest of Muslim territories in the Iberian peninsula by Christian forces.

The Iberian Peninsula

From the eleventh to the thirteenth centuries, power in the Iberian peninsula shifted from Muslim to Christian rulers. Castile, in the north-central part of the peninsula, became the strongest of the growing Christian kingdoms, and Aragon, in the northeast, the second most powerful. In 1085 King Alfonso VI of Castile and León captured Toledo in central Spain. Alfonso VIII (1158–1214), aided by the kings of Aragon, Navarre, and Portugal, crushed the Muslims at Las Navas de Tolosa in 1212, accelerating the Christian push southward. James the Conqueror of Aragon (r. 1213–1276) captured Valencia on the Mediterranean coast in 1233, and three years later Ferdinand of Castile and León captured the great Muslim city Córdoba in the heart of Andalusia. With the fall of Seville in 1248, Christians controlled the entire Iberian Peninsula, save for the small state of Granada (see Map 9.3).

Muslim Spain had had more cities than any other country in Europe, and Christian Spain became highly urbanized. The chief mosques in these cities became cathedrals and Muslim art was destroyed. Victorious Christian rulers expelled the Muslims and recruited immigrants from France and elsewhere in Iberia. The thirteenth century thus witnessed a huge migration of peoples from the north to the depopulated cities of the central and southern parts of the peninsula.

Fourteenth-century clerical propagandists called the movement to expel the Muslims the **reconquista** (reconquest)—a sacred and patriotic crusade to wrest the country from "alien" Muslim hands. This religious myth became part of Spanish political culture and of the

Section Review

- In 1066 William conquered England and transformed the feudal system into a monarchy, introducing the *Domesday Book* to record wealth and land; later bureaucratic innovations included the Exchequer, to audit royal accounts, and the pipe rolls, to audit the sheriffs.

- France became unified and expanded under Phillip II, who governed using royal agents assigned to provinces, giving priority to royal needs over local interests, but the limitation that taxation be used only for wars hindered royal growth.

- The German king Otto I became the Holy Roman Emperor after defeating the Magyars; later, following a series of civil wars in central Europe, Emperor Frederick Barbarossa forbade private warfare and required a sworn peace, using experts in Roman law to extend his dominion over northern Italy.

- In Sicily Roger de Hauteville gained political strength by distributing scattered fiefs to his followers, forbidding private warfare, and using Muslim bookkeeping methods, a policy his grandson Frederick II continued while also founding the University of Naples to train bureaucratic officials.

- The Christian conquest of Spain (the reconquista) linked the peninsula to Christian Europe and the Roman papacy, while introducing new immigrants to replace the expelled Muslims.

MAP 9.3   The Reconquista
The Christian conquest of Muslim Spain was followed by ecclesiastical reorganization, with the establishment of dioceses, monasteries, and the Latin liturgy, which gradually tied the peninsula to the heartland of Christian Europe and to the Roman papacy. (*Source:* Adapted from David Nicholas, *The Evolution of the Medieval World*. Copyright © 1992. Reprinted by permission of Pearson Education.)

national psychology. As a consequence of the reconquista, the Spanish and Portuguese learned how to administer vast tracts of newly acquired territory. Later, in the sixteenth and seventeenth centuries, they would impose these medieval methods on colonial Mexico, Brazil, Peru, Angola, and the Philippines.

Law and Justice

How did the administration of law contribute to the development of national states?

In the early Middle Ages society perceived of major crimes as acts against an individual, and a major crime was settled when the accused made a cash payment to the victim or his or her kindred. In the High Middle Ages suspects were pursued and punished for acting against the *public* interest. Throughout Europe, however, the form and application of laws depended on local and provincial custom and practice. In the twelfth and thirteenth centuries the law was a hodgepodge of Germanic customs, feudal rights, and provincial practices. Kings in France and

England wanted to blend these elements into a uniform system of rules acceptable and applicable to all of their peoples. Legal developments in continental countries like France were strongly influenced by Roman law, while England slowly built up a unique and unwritten common law.

The Customs of Aragon

This illumination, imitating the style of Parisian court art, shows King James of Aragon (r. 1213–1276) presiding over a law court. King James—called "the Conqueror" because of his victories over Catalonia, Valencia, and Majorca—ordered several codifications of law. The most important of these, the Customs of Aragon (1247), drew on Roman canonical practice for legal procedures. (Initial N: King James of Aragon Overseeing Court Law of Vidal Mayor, 83.MQ.165, folio 72v. © The J. Paul Getty Museum, Los Angeles)

France and the Holy Roman Empire

The French king Louis IX (r. 1226–1270) was famous in his time for his concern for justice. Each French province, even after being made part of the kingdom of France, retained its unique laws and procedures, but Louis IX created a royal judicial system. He established the Parlement of Paris, a kind of supreme court that welcomed appeals from local administrators and from the courts of feudal lords throughout France. By the very act of appealing the decisions of feudal courts to the Parlement of Paris, French people in far-flung provinces were recognizing the superiority of royal justice.

Louis was the first French monarch to publish laws for the entire kingdom. The Parlement of Paris registered (or announced) these laws, which forbade private warfare, judicial duels, gambling, blaspheming, and prostitution. Louis sought to identify justice with the kingship, and gradually royal justice touched all parts of the kingdom.

In the Holy Roman Empire, justice was administered at two levels. The manorial or seigneurial court, presided over by the lay or ecclesiastical lord, dealt with such common conflicts as damage to crops and fields, trespass, boundary disputes, and debt. The court of high justice, staffed by regional rather than local magistrates, dispensed justice in serious criminal cases involving theft, arson, assault with a weapon, rape, and homicide. The imposition of the death penalty by hanging was the distinctive feature of this court.

Henry II and Thomas Becket

Under Henry II (r. 1154–1189) England developed and extended a **common law**, a law that originated in, and was applied by, the king's court and that in the next two or three centuries became common to the entire country. England was unusual in developing one system of royal courts and one secular law. Henry I had occasionally sent out **circuit judges** (royal officials who traveled a given circuit or district) to hear civil and criminal cases. Every year royal judges left London and set up court in the counties. Wherever the king's judges sat, there sat the king's court.

Henry also improved procedure in criminal justice. In 1166 he instructed the sheriffs to summon local **juries** to conduct inquests and draw up lists of known or suspected criminals. These lists, or indictments, sworn to by the juries, were to be presented to the royal judges when they arrived in the community. This accusing jury is the ancestor of the modern grand jury.

Judges determined guilt or innocence in a number of ways. They heard testimony, sought witnesses, and read written evidence. If these were lacking and if a suspect had a bad public reputation, he or she might be submitted to trial by

common law A body of English law that originated in, and was applied by, King Henry II's court and in the next two or three centuries became common to the entire country.

circuit judges Royal officials who traveled a given circuit or district to hear civil and criminal cases.

jury Group of men in medieval England that conducted inquiries into criminal activities, similar to today's grand jury.

ordeal. An accused person could be tried by fire or water. In the latter case, the accused was tied hand and foot and dropped in a lake or river. People believed that water was a pure substance and would reject anything foul or unclean. Thus a person who sank was considered innocent; a person who floated was found guilty. Trial by ordeal was a ritual that appealed to the supernatural for judgment. God determined guilt or innocence, and thus a priest had to be present to bless the water.

Henry II disliked ordeal, and it was used less during his reign than it was on the continent. Gradually, in the course of the thirteenth century, the king's judges adopted the practice of calling on twelve people (other than the accusing jury) to consider the question of innocence or guilt. This became the jury of trial, but it was very slowly accepted because medieval people had more confidence in the judgment of God than in the judgment of twelve ordinary people.

One aspect of Henry's judicial reforms encountered stiff resistance from an unexpected source: the friend and former chief adviser whom Henry had made archbishop of Canterbury—Thomas Becket. In 1164 Henry II insisted that everyone, including clerics, be subject to the royal courts. Becket vigorously protested that church law required clerics to be subject to church courts. The disagreement between Henry II and Becket dragged on for years. Late in December 1170, in a fit of rage, Henry expressed the wish that Becket be destroyed. Four knights took the king at his word. They rode to Canterbury Cathedral and, as the archbishop was leaving evening services, slashed off the crown of his head and scattered his brains on the pavement.

What Thomas Becket could not achieve in life, he gained in death. The assassination of an archbishop turned public opinion in England and throughout western Europe against the king. Miracles were recorded at Becket's tomb; Becket was made a saint; and in a short time Canterbury Cathedral became a major pilgrimage and tourist site. Henry had to back down. He did public penance for the murder and gave up his attempts to bring clerics under the authority of the royal court.

Thieves Plunder Saint Edmund's Chapel
This eleventh-century painting shows thieves searching for jewelry and rich burial fabrics and even pulling the iron nails out of the wooden structure. They are also trying to dig up the coffin of Saint Edmund, the king of East Anglia (r. 841–869), who was defeated in battle and executed by Danish invaders and whose bones could be sold as relics. Crime and violence preoccupied secular and religious authorities alike. (Pierpont Morgan Library/Art Resource, NY)

King John and Magna Carta

Henry II's sons Richard I, known as Lion-Hearted (r. 1189–1199), and John (r. 1199–1216) lacked their father's interest in the work of government. Richard looked on England as a source of revenue for his military enterprises. Soon after his accession, he departed on crusade to the Holy Land. During his reign he spent only six months in England, and the government was run by ministers trained under Henry II.

John's basic problems were financial. King John inherited a heavy debt from his father and brother, and his efforts to squeeze money from knights, widows, and merchants created an atmosphere of resentment. In July 1214 John's cavalry suffered a severe defeat at the hands of Philip Augustus of France at Bouvines in Flanders. This battle ended English hopes for the recovery of territories from France and also strengthened the opposition to John. His ineptitude as a soldier in a society that idealized military glory was the final straw. Rebellion begun by northern barons eventually grew to involve many key members of the English nobility. After lengthy negotiations, John met the barons in 1215 at Runnymede and was forced to approve the peace treaty called **Magna Carta,** "Magna" (great or large) because it was so long and detailed.

For contemporaries, Magna Carta was intended to redress the grievances that particular groups—the barons, the clergy, the merchants of London—had against King John. Charters were not unusual: many kings and lords at the time issued them and then sometimes revoked them, as John did almost immediately. This revocation was largely ignored, however, and every English king until 1485 reissued Magna Carta as evidence of his promise to observe the law. Thus, this charter alone acquired enduring importance. It came to signify the principle that everyone, including the king and the government, must obey the law.

In the later Middle Ages references to Magna Carta underlined the old Augustinian theory that a government, to be legitimate, must promote law, order, and justice. An English king may not disregard or arbitrarily suspend the law to suit his convenience. The Magna Carta also contains the germ of the idea of "due process of law," meaning that a person has the right to be heard and defended in court and is entitled to the protection of the law. Because later generations referred to Magna Carta as a written statement of English liberties, it gradually came to have an almost sacred importance as a guarantee of law and justice.

The Papacy

How did the papacy attempt to reform the church, and what was the response from other powerful rulers?

Kings and emperors were not the only rulers consolidating their power in the High Middle Ages. Under the leadership of a series of reforming popes in the eleventh century, the church tried to assert control over the clergy and regain its spiritual and political strength. Church control had diminished during the ninth and tenth centuries when kings and feudal lords chose the priests and bishops in their territories, granting them fiefs and expecting loyalty and service in return. Church offices from village priest to pope brought with them the right to collect taxes and fees and often the profits from land under the officeholder's control. They were thus sometimes sold outright—a practice called **simony** (SY-muh-nee), after Simon Magus, a New Testament figure who wanted to buy his way into heaven. Not surprisingly, clergy at all levels who had bought their positions or had been granted them for political reasons were rarely effective moral or spiritual guides. Nonetheless, the popes' efforts to reform their institution were sometimes challenged by medieval kings.

The Gregorian Reforms

The papal reform movement of the eleventh century is frequently called the Gregorian reform movement, after Pope Gregory VII (1073–1085), its most prominent advocate. Serious efforts at reform actually began somewhat earlier, under Pope Leo IX (1049–1054).

During the ninth and tenth centuries the papacy provided little leadership to the Christian peoples of western Europe. Popes were appointed to advance the political ambitions of their families—the great aristocratic families of Rome—and not because of special spiritual qualifications. A combination of political machinations and sexual immorality damaged the papacy's moral prestige.

Magna Carta A long and detailed peace treaty intended to redress the grievances that particular groups had against King John.

Section Review

- In the early Middle Ages crime consisted of acts against an individual, but by the High Middle Ages crime also included acts against the public interest.

- In France, King Louis IX established public laws and set up a court of appeals system called the Parlement of Paris.

- In England, there was a system of royal courts and one of secular law with an accusing jury that sought out criminals and a trial jury of twelve ordinary men who decided a case.

- King Henry II wanted everyone, including clerics, to be subject to the royal courts but his friend, the archbishop Thomas Becket, defied him, arguing that clerics were only subject to church courts; Henry's knights went too far when they murdered Becket, enraging the public.

- King John was financially and militarily inept, inspiring a rebellion and lengthy negotiations that produced the Magna Carta, a treaty that concerned the interests of certain groups, but eventually came to have wider significance.

simony The sale of church offices.

At the local parish level, there were many married priests. Taking Christ as the model for the priestly life, the Roman church had always encouraged clerical celibacy, and celibacy had been an obligation for ordination since the fourth century. But in the tenth and eleventh centuries probably a majority of European priests were married or living with women, and in some cases they were handing down church positions and property to their children.

Pope Leo and his successors believed that lay control was largely responsible for the church's problems, so they proclaimed the church independent from secular rulers. The Lateran Council of 1059 decreed that the authority and power to elect the pope rested solely in the **college of cardinals,** a special group of priests from the major churches in and around Rome. The college retains that power today. In the Middle Ages the college of cardinals numbered around twenty-five or thirty, most of them from Italy. In 1586 the figure was set at seventy, though today it is much larger, with cardinals from around the world. When the office of pope was vacant, the cardinals were responsible for governing the church.

While reform began long before Gregory's pontificate and continued after it, Gregory VII was the first pope to emphasize the *political* authority of the papacy. His belief that kings had failed to promote reform in the church prompted him to claim an active role in the politics of Western Christendom. He believed that the pope, as the successor of Saint Peter, was the vicar of God on earth and that papal orders were the orders of God. Gregory was particularly opposed to **lay investiture**— the selection and appointment of church officials by secular authority, often symbolized by laymen giving bishops and abbots their symbols of office, such as a staff and ring. In February 1075 Pope Gregory held a council at Rome that decreed that clerics who accepted investiture from laymen were to be deposed, and laymen

college of cardinals A special group of high clergy that has the authority and power to elect the pope and who otherwise are responsible for governing the church when the office of the pope is vacant.

lay investiture The selection and appointment of church officials by secular authority.

Emperor Otto III Handing a Staff to Archbishop Adalbert of Prague (tenth century)
The staff, or crozier (KROH-zher), symbolized a bishop's spiritual authority. Receiving the staff from the emperor gave the appearance that the bishop gained his spiritual rights from the secular power. Pope Gregory VII vigorously objected to this practice. (Bildarchiv Marburg/Art Resource, NY)

who invested clerics were to be *excommunicated* (cut off from the sacraments and all Christian worship).

The church's penalty of **excommunication** relied for its effectiveness on public opinion. Gregory believed that the strong support he enjoyed for his *moral* reforms would carry over to his political ones; he thought that excommunication would compel rulers to abide by his changes. Immediately, however, Henry IV in the Holy Roman Empire, William the Conqueror in England (see page 196), and Philip I in France protested. Gregory's reforms would deprive them not only of church income but also of the right to choose which monks and clerics would help them administer their kingdoms. The tension between the papacy and the monarchy would have a major impact on both institutions and on society.

Meanwhile, the Gregorian reform movement built a strict hierarchical church structure with bishops and ordained priests higher in status than nuns, who could not be ordained. Church councils in the eleventh and twelfth centuries forbade monks and nuns to sing church services together and ordered priests to limit their visits to convents, heightening the sense that contact with nuns should be viewed with suspicion and avoided when possible. Church reformers put a greater emphasis on clerical celibacy and chastity. As part of these measures, Pope Boniface VIII's papal decree of 1298, *Periculoso*, ordered all female religious persons to be strictly **cloistered**. This meant that the nuns were to remain permanently inside the walls of the convent and that visits with those from outside the house, including family members, would be limited. *Periculoso* was not enforced everywhere, but it did mean that convents became more cut off from medieval society. People also gave more donations to male monastic houses where monks who had been ordained as priests could say memorial masses, and fewer to women's houses, many of which became impoverished.

excommunication A penalty used by the Catholic Church that meant being cut off from the sacraments and all Christian worship.

cloistered Cut off from the outside world.

Emperor versus Pope

The strongest reaction to Gregory's moves came from the Holy Roman Empire. Pope Gregory accused Henry of lack of respect for the papacy and insisted that disobedience to the pope was disobedience to God. Henry argued that Gregory's type of reform undermined royal authority and that the pope "was determined to rob me of my soul and my kingdom or die in the attempt."[2]

Within the empire, those who had the most to gain from the dispute quickly took advantage of it. In January 1076 many of the German bishops who had been invested by Henry withdrew their allegiance from the pope. Gregory replied by excommunicating them and suspending Henry from the emperorship. The lay nobility delighted in the bind the emperor had been put in: with Henry IV excommunicated and cast outside the Christian fold, they did not have to obey him and could advance their own interests. Powerful nobles invited the pope to come to Germany to settle their dispute with Henry. Gregory hastened to support them. The Christmas season of 1076 witnessed an ironic situation in Germany: the clergy supported the emperor, while the great nobility favored the pope.

Henry outwitted the pope. Crossing the Alps in January 1077, he approached the castle of Countess Matilda of Tuscany, where the pope was staying. According to legend, Henry stood for three days in the snow seeking forgiveness. As a priest, Pope Gregory was obliged to grant absolution and to readmit the emperor to the Christian community. When the sentence of excommunication was lifted, Henry regained the emperorship and authority over his rebellious subjects. Some historians claim that this incident marked the peak of papal power because the most powerful ruler in Europe, the emperor, had bowed before the pope.

Countess Matilda

A staunch supporter of the reforming ideals of the papacy, Countess Matilda (ca. 1046–1115) planned this dramatic meeting at her castle at Canossa in the Apennines (AP-uh-nines). The arrangement of the figures—King Henry kneeling, Abbot Hugh of Cluny lecturing, and Matilda persuading—suggests contemporary understanding of the scene in which Henry received absolution. Matilda's vast estates in northern Italy and her political contacts in Rome made her a person of considerable influence in the late eleventh century. (Biblioteca Apostolica Vaticana)

The battle between the pope and the emperor raged on, however. In 1080 Gregory VII again excommunicated and deposed the emperor. In return, Henry invaded Italy, captured Rome, and controlled the city when Gregory died in 1085. But Henry won no lasting victory. Gregory's successors encouraged Henry's sons to revolt against their father. With lay investiture the ostensible issue, the conflict between the papacy and the successors of Henry IV continued into the twelfth century.

Finally, in 1122 at a conference held at Worms, the issue was settled by compromise. Bishops were to be chosen according to canon law—that is, by the clergy—in the presence of the emperor or his delegate. The emperor surrendered the right of investing bishops with the ring and staff. But since lay rulers were permitted to be present at ecclesiastical elections and to accept or refuse feudal homage from the new prelates, they still possessed an effective veto over ecclesiastical appointments. Papal power was enhanced, but neither side won a clear victory.

The long controversy had tremendous social and political consequences in Germany. The lengthy struggle between papacy and emperor allowed emerging noble dynasties to enhance their position. To control their lands, the great lords built castles, symbolizing their increased power and growing independence. (In no European country do more castles survive today.) The German high aristocracy subordinated the knights, enhanced restrictions on peasants, and compelled Henry IV and Henry V to surrender certain rights and privileges. When the papal-imperial conflict ended in 1122, the nobility held the balance of power in Germany, and later German kings, such as Frederick Barbarossa (see page 200), would fail in their efforts to strengthen the monarchy against the princely families. For these reasons, particularism, localism, and feudal independence characterized the Holy Roman Empire in the High Middle Ages. The investiture controversy had a catastrophic effect there.

Innocent III and His Successors

The most powerful pope in history was Innocent III (1198–1216). During his pontificate the church in Rome declared itself to be supreme, united, and "catholic" (worldwide), responsible for the earthly well-being and eternal salvation of all citizens of **Christendom** (the Christian world). Innocent pushed the kings of France, Portugal, and England to do his will, compelling King Philip Augustus of France to take back his wife, Ingeborg of Denmark. He forced King John of England to accept as archbishop of Canterbury a man John did not want.

Innocent called the fourth Lateran Council in 1215, which affirmed the idea that ordained priests had the power to transform bread and wine during church ceremonies into the body and blood of Christ (a change termed "transubstantiation"). This power was possessed by no other group in society, not even kings. According to papal doctrine, priests now had the power to mediate for everyone with God, which set the spiritual hierarchy of the church above the secular hierarchies

Christendom The term used by early medieval writers to refer to the realm of Christianity.

of kings and other rulers. The council also affirmed that Christians should confess their sins to a priest at least once a year and ordered Jews and Muslims to wear special clothing that set them apart from Christians (see page 252).

Some of Innocent III's successors abused their prerogatives to such an extent that their moral impact was seriously weakened. Even worse, Innocent IV (1243–1254) used secular weapons, including military force, to maintain his leadership. These popes badly damaged papal prestige and influence. By the early fourteenth century cries for reform would be heard once again.

The Crusades

How did the motives, course, and consequences of the Crusades reflect and shape developments in Europe?

The **Crusades** of the eleventh and twelfth centuries were wars sponsored by the papacy for the recovery of the holy city of Jerusalem from the Muslim Turks. The word *crusade* was not actually used at the time and did not appear in English until the late sixteenth century. It means literally "taking the cross," from the cross that soldiers sewed on their garments as a Christian symbol. At the time, people going off to fight simply said they were taking "the way of the cross" or "the road to Jerusalem."

Though the reconquista in Spain (see page 201) did not directly inspire the Crusades to the Middle East, the pope did sponsor groups of soldiers in the Spanish campaign as well as in the Norman campaign against the Muslims in Sicily. In both campaigns Pope Gregory VII asserted that any land conquered from the Muslims belonged to the papacy because it had been a territory held by infidels. Thus these earlier wars set a pattern for the centuries-long Crusades.

Background

The Roman papacy had been involved in the bitter struggle over church reform and lay investiture with the German emperors. If the pope could muster a large army against the enemies of Christianity, his claim to be leader of Christian society in the West would be strengthened. Moreover, in 1054 a serious theological disagreement had split the Greek church of Byzantium and the Roman church of the West. The pope and the patriarch of Constantinople excommunicated each other and declared the beliefs of the other to be anathema (uh-NATH-uh-muh), that is, totally unacceptable for Christians. The pope believed that a crusade would lead to strong Roman influence in Greek territories and eventually the reunion of the two churches.

In 1071 Turkish soldiers defeated a Greek army at Manzikert in eastern Anatolia and occupied much of Asia Minor (see Map 9.4). The emperor at Constantinople appealed to the West for support. Shortly afterward the holy city of Jerusalem fell to the Turks. Pilgrimages to holy places in the Middle East became very dangerous, and the papacy claimed to be outraged that the holy city was in the hands of unbelievers. Because the Muslims had held Palestine since the eighth century, the papacy actually feared that the Seljuk (SEL-jook) Turks would be less accommodating to Christian pilgrims than the previous Muslim rulers had been.

In 1095 Pope Urban II called for a great Christian holy war against the infidels. He urged Christian knights who had been fighting one another to direct their energies against the true enemies of God, the Muslims. Urban proclaimed an

Crusades Holy wars sponsored by the papacy for the recovery of the Holy Land from the Muslims from the late eleventh to the late thirteenth century.

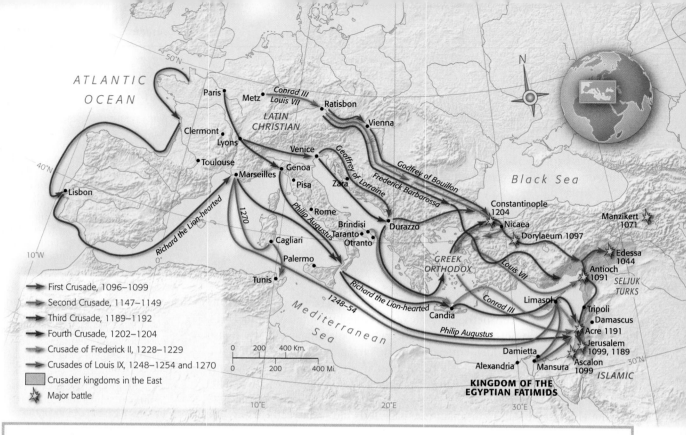

ATLANTIC OCEAN

LATIN CHRISTIAN

Black Sea

GREEK ORTHODOX

Mediterranean Sea

- First Crusade, 1096–1099
- Second Crusade, 1147–1149
- Third Crusade, 1189–1192
- Fourth Crusade, 1202–1204
- Crusade of Frederick II, 1228–1229
- Crusades of Louis IX, 1248–1254 and 1270
- Crusader kingdoms in the East
- Major battle

Paris · Metz · Conrad III / Louis VII · Ratisbon · Vienna
Clermont · Lyons · Venice · Geoffrey of Lorraine · Godfrey of Bouillon · Frederick Barbarossa
Toulouse · Genoa · Pisa · Zara · Constantinople 1204 · Nicaea · Manzikert 1071
Lisbon · Marseilles · Rome · Brindisi · Durazzo · Dorylaeum 1097 · Edessa 1044
Philip Augustus · Taranto · Otranto · Louis VII · Antioch 1091 · SELJUK TURKS
Richard the Lion-hearted · Cagliari · Palermo · Richard the Lion-hearted · Limasol · Tripoli · Damascus
Tunis · Candia · Conrad III · Acre 1191
1270 · 1248–54 · Philip Augustus · Damietta · Jerusalem 1099, 1189
Alexandria · Mansura · Ascalon 1099 · ISLAMIC
KINGDOM OF THE EGYPTIAN FATIMIDS

0 200 400 Km.
0 200 400 Mi.

10°W · 0° · 10°E · 20°E · 30°E
50°N · 40°N · 30°N

MAPPING THE PAST

Map 9.4   The Routes of the Crusades

This map shows the many different routes that Western Christians took over the centuries to reach Jerusalem. Use it and the information in the text to answer the following questions: **[1]** How were the results of the various Crusades shaped by the routes that the Crusaders took? **[2]** How did the routes offer opportunities for profit for Venetian and other Italian merchants? **[3]** Why might the Byzantines have worried about the Crusaders even before the Fourth Crusade?

indulgence Remission of the temporal penalties imposed by the church for sin.

indulgence, or a waiver from having to do penance for sin, to those who would fight for and regain the holy city of Jerusalem.

Thousands of people of all classes joined the crusade. Although most of the Crusaders were French, pilgrims from many regions streamed southward from the Rhineland, through Germany and the Balkans. Of all of the developments of the High Middle Ages, none better reveals Europeans' religious and emotional fervor and the influence of the reformed papacy than the extraordinary outpouring of support for the First Crusade.

Motives and Course of the Crusades

Many Crusaders were inspired by the possibility of foreign adventure as well as by religious fervor. Kings, who were trying to establish order and build states, saw the Crusades as an opportunity to get rid of troublemaking knights. Land-hungry younger sons seized upon the chance to acquire fiefs in the Middle East.

The First Crusade was successful, mostly because of the dynamic enthusiasm of the participants. The Crusaders had little more than religious zeal. They knew nothing about the geography or climate of the Middle East. Although there were several counts with military experience among the host, the Crusaders could never agree on a leader. Lines of supply were never set up. Starvation and disease wracked the army. Nevertheless, convinced that "God wills it," the war cry of the Crusaders, the army pressed on, defeating the Turks in several land battles and besieging a few larger towns. (See the feature "Listening to the Past: An Arab View of the Crusades" on pages 218–219.) Finally in 1099, after a three-year trek, they reached Jerusalem, and after a month-long siege they penetrated the city, where they slaughtered the Muslim defenders as well as civilian women and children.

With Jerusalem taken, many Crusaders set off for home again. Only the appearance of Egyptian troops convinced them that they needed to stay, and slowly institutions were set up to rule territories and the Muslim population. Four small "Crusader states"—Jerusalem, Edessa, Tripoli, and Antioch (AN-tee-ok)—were established; castles and fortified towns were built to defend against Muslim reconquest (see Map 9.4). Reinforcements arrived in the form of pilgrims and fighters from Europe, so that there was constant coming and going by land and more often by sea after the Crusaders conquered port cities such as Acre. Between 1096 and 1270 the crusading ideal was expressed in eight papally approved expeditions to the East, though none after the First Crusade accomplished very much. Despite this lack of success, for roughly two hundred years members of noble families in Europe went nearly every generation.

Women from all walks of life participated in the Crusades. In war zones some women concealed their sex by donning chain mail and helmets and fought with the knights. Others joined in the besieging of towns and castles. They assisted in filling the moats surrounding fortified places with earth so that ladders and war engines could be brought close. More typically, women provided water to fighting men, a service not to be underestimated in the hot, dry climate of the Middle East. They worked as washerwomen, foraged for food, and provided sexual services. There were many more European men than women, however, so there was a fair amount of intermarriage or at least sexual relations between Christian men and Muslim women.

The Muslim states in the Middle East were politically fragmented when the Crusaders first came, and it took about a century for them to reorganize. They did so dramatically under Saladin (Salah al-Din) (SAL-uh-din), who unified Egypt and Syria, and in 1187 the Muslims retook Jerusalem. Christians immediately attempted to take it back in what was later called the Third Crusade (1189–1192). Frederick Barbarossa of the Holy Roman Empire, Richard the Lion-Hearted of England, and Philip Augustus of France participated, and the Third Crusade was better financed than previous ones. But disputes among the leaders and strategic problems prevented any lasting results. The Crusaders were not successful in retaking Jerusalem, but they did keep their hold on port towns, and Saladin allowed pilgrims safe passage to Jerusalem. He also made an agreement with Christian rulers for keeping the peace. From that point on, the Crusader states were more important economically than politically or religiously, giving Italian and French merchants direct access to Eastern products such as perfumes and silk.

In 1202 Innocent III sent out preachers who called on Christian knights to retake Jerusalem. Those who responded—in what would become the Fourth Crusade—decided that going by sea would be better than going by land, and they stopped in Constantinople for supplies. The supplies never materialized, and in 1204 the Crusaders decided to capture and sack Constantinople instead, destroying its magnificent library and shipping gold, silver, and relics home. The Byzantine Empire, as a political unit, never recovered from this destruction. Although the Crusader Baldwin IX of Flanders was chosen emperor, the empire splintered into three parts and soon consisted of little more than the city of Constantinople.

Moreover, the assault by one Christian people on another—even though one of the goals of the Crusades was reunion of the Greek and Latin churches—made the split between the churches permanent. It also helped discredit the entire crusading movement.

In the late thirteenth century Turkish armies gradually conquered all other Muslim rulers and then turned against the Crusader states. In 1291 the last Crusader stronghold, the port of Acre, fell in a battle that was just as bloody as the first battle for Jerusalem two centuries earlier. Knights then needed a new battlefield for military actions, which some found in Spain, where the rulers of Aragon and Castile continued fighting Muslims until 1492.

Albigensians A heretical sect that rejected orthodox doctrine on the relationship of God and man, the sacraments, and clerical hierarchy.

Crusades Within Europe and the Expansion of Christendom

Crusades were also mounted against groups within Europe that were perceived as threats. In 1208 Pope Innocent III proclaimed a crusade against a group in southern France known either as the Cathars (from the Greek *katharos*, meaning "pure") or as the **Albigensians** (al-bi-JEN-see-uhns) (from the town of Albi in southern France). The Albigensians asserted that the material world was created not by the good God of the New Testament, but by a different evil God of the Old Testament. The good God had created spiritual things, and the evil God or the Devil had created material things; in this dualistic understanding, the soul was good and the body evil. Forces of good and evil battled constantly, and leading a perfect life meant being stripped of all physical and material things. To free oneself from the power of evil, a person had to lead a life of extreme asceticism. Albigensians were divided into the "perfect," who followed the principles strictly, and the "believers," who led ordinary lives until their deaths, when they repented and were saved. They used the teachings of Jesus about the evils of material goods to call for the church to give up its property, rejected the authority of the pope and the sacraments of the church, and began setting up their own bishoprics.

The Albigensians won many adherents in southern France. Faced with widespread defection, Pope Innocent III proclaimed a crusade against them. Fearing that religious division would lead to civil disorder, the French monarchy joined the crusade against the Albigensians. The French inflicted a savage defeat on the Albigensians in 1213. After more years of fighting, the leaders agreed to terms of peace, which left the French monarchy the primary beneficiary.

The end of the war did not mean an end to Albigensianism, but the papacy decided to combat heresy through education and individual punishment. The pope founded the University of Toulouse, which he hoped would promote knowledge of correct belief. In the 1230s and 1240s the papacy established the papal **Inquisition,** sending out inquisitors with the power to seek out suspected heretics, question them in private without revealing who had denounced them, and sentence them to punishments ranging from penance to life imprisonment. Heretics who did not repent were handed over to the secular government to be burned, and their property was confiscated. These measures were very successful, and the last Albigensian leaders were burned in the 1320s, though their beliefs did not die out completely.

Inquisition Court established by the papacy with power to investigate and try individuals for heresy and other religious crimes.

Fearful of encirclement by imperial territories, the popes also promoted crusades against Emperor Frederick II in 1227 and 1239. This use of force backfired, damaging papal credibility as the sponsor of peace.

Along with the papal Inquisition, the Crusades also inspired the establishment of new religious orders. For example, the Knights Templars, founded in 1118 with the strong backing of Saint Bernard of Clairvaux (klar-VOW) (see page 239), combined the monastic ideals of obedience and self-denial with the crusading practice of military aggression. Another order, the Teutonic (too-TON-ik) Knights, waged wars against the pagan Prussians in the Baltic region. After 1230, and from a base in Poland, they established a new territory, Christian Prussia, and gradually the entire eastern shore of the Baltic Sea came under their hegemony. Military orders served to unify Christian Europe.

Christianity also spread into northern and eastern Europe by more peaceful means. Latin Christian influences entered Scandinavian and Baltic regions primarily through the appointment of bishops and the establishment of dioceses. This took place in Denmark in the tenth and eleventh centuries, and the institutional church spread rather quickly due to the support offered by the strong throne. Dioceses were established in Norway and Sweden in the eleventh century, and in 1164 Uppsala, long the center of the pagan cults of Odin and Thor, became a Catholic archdiocese, though pagan and Christian practices existed side-by-side for centuries in more remote parts of Scandinavia.

Otto I (see page 198) planted a string of dioceses along his northern and eastern frontiers, hoping to pacify the newly conquered Slavs in eastern Europe. Frequent Slavic revolts illustrate the people's resentment of German lords and clerics and indicate that the church did not easily penetrate the region. In the same way that French knights had been used to crush the Albigensians, German nobles built castles and ruthlessly crushed revolts. The church also moved into central Europe, first in Bohemia in the tenth century and from there into Poland and Hungary in the eleventh. In the twelfth and thirteenth centuries, thousands of settlers poured into eastern Europe. New immigrants were German in descent, name, language, and law. Hundreds of small market towns populated by these newcomers supplied the needs of the rural countryside. Larger towns such as Cracow and Riga engaged in long-distance trade and gradually grew into large urban centers.

Consequences of the Crusades

The Crusades provided the means for what one scholar has called "the aristocratic diaspora," the movement of knights from their homes in France to areas then on the frontiers of Christian Europe.[3] Wars of foreign conquest had occurred before the Crusades, as the Norman Conquest of England in 1066 illustrates (see page 196), but for many knights migration began with the taking of the cross. Restless, ambitious knights, many of them younger sons with no prospects, left on crusade to the Holy Land, and some of them were able to carve out lordships in Palestine, Syria, and Greece. Along the Syrian and Palestinian coasts, the Crusaders set up a string of feudal states that managed to survive for about two centuries before the Muslims reconquered them; many of the castles they built still stand today.

The Crusades introduced some Europeans to Eastern luxury goods, but their immediate cultural impact on the West remains debatable. Strong economic and intellectual ties with the East had already been developed by the late eleventh century. The Crusades were a boon to Italian merchants, who profited from outfitting military expeditions, the opening of new trade routes, and the establishment of trading communities in the Crusader states. After those kingdoms collapsed, Muslim rulers still encouraged trade with European businessmen. Commerce with the West benefited both Muslims and Europeans, and it continued to flourish.

The Crusades proved to be a disaster for Jewish-Christian relations. In the eleventh century Jews played a major role in the international trade between the Muslim Middle East and the West. Jews also lent money to peasants, townspeople, and nobles. When the First Crusade was launched, many poor knights had to borrow from Jews to equip themselves for the expedition. Debt bred resentment.

The experience of the Rhenish Jews during the First Crusade (see the feature "Individuals in Society: The Jews of Speyer: A Collective Biography") was not unusual; later Crusades brought similar violence against Jewish communities. In addition to resenting Jewish business competition, Christians harbored the belief that Jews engaged in the ritual murder of Christians to use their blood in religious rituals. These accusations, termed the "blood libel," were condemned by Christian rulers and higher church officials, but were often spread through sermons preached by local priests. They also charged Jews with being "Christ killers" and of using the communion host for diabolical counter-rituals. Such accusations led to the killing of Jewish families and sometimes entire Jewish communities, sometimes by burning people alive in the synagogue or Jewish section of town.

Legal restrictions on Jews gradually increased. Jews were forbidden to have Christian servants or employees, to hold public office, to appear in public on Christian holy days, or to enter Christian parts of town without a badge marking them as Jews. Jews were prohibited from engaging in any trade with Christians except money-lending—which only fueled popular resentment—and in 1275 King Edward I of England prohibited that as well. In 1290 he expelled the Jews from England in return for a large parliamentary grant; it would be four centuries before they would be allowed back in. King Philip the Fair of France followed Edward's example in 1306, and many Jews went to the area of southern France known as Provence, which was not yet part of the French kingdom. In July 1315 the king's need for revenue led him to readmit the Jews to France in return for a huge lump sum and for an annual financial subsidy, but the returning Jews faced hostility and increasing pressure to convert.

The Crusades also left an inheritance of deep bitterness in Christian-Muslim relations. Each side dehumanized the other, viewing those who followed the other religion as unbelievers. Whereas Europeans perceived the Crusades as sacred religious movements, Muslims saw them as expansionist and imperialistic. The ideal of a sacred mission to conquer or convert Muslim peoples entered Europeans' consciousness and became a continuing goal. When in 1492 Christopher Columbus sailed west, hoping to reach India, he used the language of the Crusades in his diaries, which shows that he was preoccupied with the conquest of Jerusalem (see Chapter 15). Columbus wanted to establish a Christian base in India from which a new crusade against Islam could be launched.

The battles in the High Middle Ages between popes and kings, between Christians and Muslims, and between Christians and pagans were signs of how deeply Christianity had replaced tribal, political, and ethnic structures as the essence of Western culture. Christian Europeans identified themselves first and foremost as citizens of "Christendom," or even described themselves as belonging to "the Christian race."[4] Whether Europeans were Christian in their observance of the Gospels remains another matter.

Section Review

- In 1095 Pope Urban II offered an indulgence, or sin waiver, to any who would fight in a great crusade against "God's enemy" the Muslims, and thousands joined in.

- Jews who had moved into Speyer at the invitation of the bishop lived separately but were resented by Christians as economic competition and they became the victims of vicious attacks by Crusaders and burghers.

- The First Crusade was successful mostly due to religious enthusiasm, not skill, but the Crusaders pressed on, taking Jerusalem, slaughtering Muslims, and fortifying towns to prevent recapture.

- Saladin helped the Muslims reorganize and take back Jerusalem, but the Crusaders held the port towns; the Third Crusade failed and the Fourth Crusade never made it to the Holy Land, instead sacking Constantinople, splintering the Byzantine Empire.

- The papacy sent Crusaders against other groups within western Europe, such as the Albigensians, using inquisitors (the Inquisition) to seek out and punish heretics.

- The Crusades left deep animosity between Jews and Christians as well as between Muslims and Christians and contributed to Christianity's replacing tribal, political, or ethnic affiliation as the basis for Western culture.

Individuals in Society

The Jews of Speyer: A Collective Biography

In the winter of 1095–1096 news of Pope Urban II's call for a crusade spread. In the spring of 1096 the Jews of northern France, fearing that a crusade would arouse anti-Semitic hostility, sent a circular letter to the Rhineland's Jewish community seeking its prayers. Jewish leaders in Mainz responded, "All the (Jewish) communities have decreed a fast. . . . May God save us and save you from all distress and hardship. We are deeply fearful for you. We, however, have less reason to fear (for ourselves), for we have heard not even a rumor of the crusade."* Ironically, French Jewry survived almost unscathed, while the Rhenish Jewry suffered frightfully.

Beginning in the late tenth century Jews trickled into Speyer (SHPAHY-uhr)—partly through Jewish perception of opportunity and partly because of the direct invitation of the bishop of Speyer. The bishop's charter meant that Jews could openly practice their religion, could not be assaulted, and could buy and sell goods. But they could not proselytize their faith, as Christians could. Jews also extended credit on a small scale and, in an expanding economy with many coins circulating, determined the relative value of currencies. Unlike their Christian counterparts, many Jewish women were literate and acted as moneylenders. Jews also worked as skilled masons, carpenters, and jewelers. As the bishop had promised, the Jews of Speyer lived apart from Christians in a walled enclave where they exercised autonomy: they maintained law and order, raised taxes, and provided religious, social, and educational services for their community. (This organization lasted in Germany until the nineteenth century.) Jewish immigration to Speyer accelerated; everyday relations between Jews and Christians were peaceful.

But Christians resented Jews as newcomers, outsiders, and aliens; for enjoying the special protection of the bishop; and for providing economic competition. Anti-Semitic ideology had received enormous impetus from the virulent anti-Semitic writings of Christian apologists in the first six centuries C.E. Jews, they argued, were *deicides* (DAY-ah-sides) (Christ killers); worse, Jews could understand the truth of Christianity but deliberately rejected it; thus they were inhuman. By the late eleventh century anti-Semitism was an old and deeply rooted element in Western society.

Late in April 1096 Emich of Leisingen, a petty lord from the Rhineland who had the reputation of being a lawless thug, approached Speyer with a large band of Crusaders. Joined by a mob of burghers, they planned to surprise the Jews in their synagogue on Saturday morning, May 3, but the Jews prayed early and left before the attackers arrived. Furious, the mob randomly murdered eleven Jews. The bishop took the entire Jewish community into his castle, arrested some of the burghers, and cut off their hands. News of these events raced up the Rhine to Worms, creating confusion in the Jewish community. Some took refuge with Christian friends; others sought the bishop's protection.

A combination of Crusaders and burghers killed a large number of Jews, looted and burned synagogues, and desecrated the Torah and other books. Proceeding on to the old and prosperous city of Mainz, Crusaders continued attacking Jews. Facing overwhelming odds, eleven hundred Jews killed their families and themselves. Crusaders and burghers vented their hatred by inflicting barbaric tortures on the wounded and dying. The Jews were never passive; everywhere they resisted. If the Crusades had begun as opposition to Islam, after 1096 that hostility extended to all those who Christians saw as enemies of society, including heretics, Jews, and lepers. But Jews continued to move to the Rhineland and to make important economic and intellectual contributions. Crusader-burgher attacks served as harbingers of events to come in the later Middle Ages and well into modern times.

An engraving (18th century) of the mass suicide of the Jews of Worms in 1096, when they were overwhelmed by Crusaders (with shields). (Bildarchiv Preussischer Kulturbesitz/Art Resource, NY)

Questions for Analysis

1. How do you explain Christian attacks on the Jews of Speyer? Were they defenses of faith?
2. How did Christian views of the Jews as outsiders contribute to these events? Can you think of more recent examples of similar developments?

*Quoted in R. Chazan, *In the Year 1096: The First Crusade and the Jews* (Philadelphia: Jewish Publication Society, 1996), p. 28.

Chapter Review

How did medieval rulers create larger and more stable territories? (page 194)

The end of the great invasions signaled the beginning of profound changes in European society. As domestic disorder slowly subsided, feudal rulers began to develop new institutions of government that enabled them to assert their power over lesser lords and the general population. Centralized states slowly crystallized, first in England and France, where rulers such as William the Conqueror and Philip Augustus manipulated feudal institutions to build up their power. In central Europe the German king Otto had himself declared emperor and tried to follow a similar path, but unified nation-states did not develop until the nineteenth century. Emperors instead shared power with princes, dukes, archbishops, counts, bishops, abbots, and cities. In the Iberian peninsula Christian rulers of small states slowly expanded their territories, taking over land from Muslim rulers in the reconquista.

How did the administration of law contribute to the development of national states? (page 202)

As medieval rulers expanded territories and extended authority, they required more officials, larger armies, and more money with which to pay for them. They developed different sorts of financial institutions to provide taxes and other income. The most effective financial bureaucracies were those developed in England, including a bureau of finance called the Exchequer, and in Sicily, where Norman rulers retained the main financial agency that had been created by their Muslim predecessors. By contrast, the rulers of France and other continental states continued to rely primarily on the income from their own property to support their military endeavors, so their financial institutions were less sophisticated.

How did the papacy attempt to reform the church, and what was the response from other powerful rulers? (page 205)

In the twelfth and thirteenth centuries rulers in Europe sought to transform a hodgepodge of oral and written customs and rules into a uniform system of laws acceptable and applicable to all their peoples. In England such changes caused conflict with church officials, personified in the dispute between King Henry II and Thomas Becket, the archbishop of Canterbury. Fiscal and legal measures by Henry's son John led to opposition from the high nobles of England, who forced him to sign Magna Carta, agreeing to promise to observe the law. Magna Carta had little immediate impact, but it came to signify the principle that everyone, including the king and the government, must obey the law. At the same time that kings were creating more centralized realms, energetic popes built up their power within the Western Christian church and asserted their superiority over kings and emperors. The Gregorian reform movement led to a grave conflict with kings over lay investiture. The papacy achieved a technical success on the religious issue, but in Germany the greatly increased power of the nobility, at the expense of the emperor, represents the significant social consequence. Having put its own house in order, the Roman papacy built the first strong government bureaucracy in the twelfth and thirteenth centuries. In the High Middle Ages, the church exercised general leadership of European society.

Key Terms

Domesday Book (p. 196)
Exchequer (p. 196)
Holy Roman Empire (p. 199)
diwān (p. 200)
reconquista (p. 201)
common law (p. 203)
circuit judges (p. 203)
jury (p. 203)
Magna Carta (p. 205)
simony (p. 205)
college of cardinals (p. 206)
lay investiture (p. 206)
excommunication (p. 207)
cloistered (p. 207)
Christendom (p. 208)
Crusades (p. 209)
indulgence (p. 210)
Albigensians (p. 212)
Inquisition (p. 212)

How did the motives, course, and consequences of the Crusades reflect and shape developments in Europe? (page 209)

A papal call to retake the holy city of Jerusalem led to the Crusades, nearly two centuries of warfare between Christians and Muslims. The enormous popular response to papal calls for crusading reveals the influence of the reformed papacy and a new sense that war against the church's enemies was a duty of nobles. The Crusades were initially successful, and small Christian states were established in the Middle East. These did not last very long, however, and other effects of the Crusades were disastrous. Jewish communities in Europe were regularly attacked; relations between the Western and Eastern Christian churches were poisoned by the Crusaders' attack on Constantinople; and Christian-Muslim relations became more uniformly hostile than they had been earlier.

Notes

1. J. Johns, *Arabic Administration in Norman Sicily: The Royal Diwān* (New York: Cambridge University Press, 2002), p. 293.
2. I. S. Robinson, *The Papacy, 1073–1198: Continuity and Innovation* (New York: Cambridge University Press, 1990), p. 403.
3. Bartlett, *The Making of Europe: Conquest, Colonization and Cultural Change, 950–1350* (Princeton, N.J.: Princeton University Press, 1993), p. 24.
4. Ibid., pp. 250–255.

To assess your mastery of this chapter, go to **bedfordstmartins.com/mckaywestbrief**

Listening to the Past

An Arab View of the Crusades

To medieval Christians the Crusades were papally approved military expeditions for the recovery of the Holy Land; to the Arabs these campaigns were "Frankish wars" or "Frankish invasions" for the acquisition of territory. The Arab perspective is illustrated in a history of the First Crusade by Ibn Al-Athir (1160–1223). Al-Athir, a native of Mosul in northern Mesopotamia (modern Iraq), relied on Arab sources for the events he described. Here is his account of the Crusaders' capture of Antioch in Syria.

The power of the Franks first became apparent when in the year 478/1085–86* they invaded the territories of Islam and took Toledo and other parts of Andalusia. Then in 484/1091 they attacked and conquered the island of Sicily and turned their attention to the African coast. Certain of their conquests there were won back again but they had other successes, as you will see.

In 490/1097 the Franks attacked Syria. . . . When Yaghi Siyan, the ruler of Antioch, heard of their approach, he was not sure how the Christian people of the city would react, so he made the Muslims go outside the city on their own to dig trenches, and the next day sent the Christians out alone to continue the task. When they were ready to return home at the end of the day he refused to allow them. "Antioch is yours," he said, "but you will have to leave it to me until I see what happens between us and the Franks." "Who will protect our children and our wives?" they said. "I shall look after them for you." So they resigned themselves to their fate, and lived in the Frankish camp for nine months, while the city was under siege.

Yaghi Siyan showed unparalleled courage and wisdom, strength and judgment. If all the Franks who died had survived they would have overrun all the lands of Islam. He protected the families of the Christians in Antioch and would not allow a hair of their heads to be touched.

After the siege had been going on for a long time the Franks made a deal with . . . a cuirass [armor]-maker called Ruzbih whom they bribed with a fortune in money and lands. He worked in the tower that stood over the riverbed, where the

Miniature showing heavily armored knights fighting Muslims.
(Bibliothèque nationale de France)

*Muslims traditionally date events from Muhammad's hegira, or emigration, to Medina, which occurred in 622 according to the Christian calendar.

river flowed out of the city into the valley. The Franks sealed their pact with the cuirass-maker, God damn him! and made their way to the water-gate. They opened it and entered the city. Another gang of them climbed the tower with their ropes. At dawn, when more than 500 of them were in the city and the defenders were worn out after the night watch, they sounded their trumpets. . . . Panic seized Yaghi Siyan and he opened the city gates and fled in terror, with an escort of thirty pages. His army commander arrived, but when he discovered on enquiry that Yaghi Siyan had fled, he made his escape by another gate. This was of great help to the Franks, for if he had stood firm for an hour, they would have been wiped out. They entered the city by the gates and sacked it, slaughtering all the Muslims they found there. This happened in jumada I (491/April/May 1098). . . .

It was the discord between the Muslim princes . . . that enabled the Franks to overrun the country.

Questions for Analysis

1. From the Arab perspective, when did the Crusades begin?
2. Why did Antioch fall to the Crusaders?
3. The use of dialogue in historical narrative is a very old device dating from the Greek historian Thucydides (fifth century B.C.E.). Assess the value of Ibn Al-Athir's dialogues for the modern historian.

Sources: P. J. Geary, ed., *Readings in Medieval History* (Peterborough, Ontario: Broadview Press, 1991), pp. 443–444; E. J. Costello, trans., *Arab Historians of the Crusades* (Berkeley and Los Angeles: University of California Press, 1969).

CHAPTER 10

The Changing Life of the People in the High Middle Ages

Chapter Preview

In these scenes from a German manuscript, *Speculum Virginum,* ca. 1190, the artist shows men, women, and children harvesting, raking, sowing, and digging. All residents in a village engaged in agricultural tasks. (Rheinisches Landesmuseum, Bonn)

In a text produced at the court of Anglo-Saxon king Alfred, Christian society is described as composed of three **orders:** those who pray, those who fight, and those who work. This image of society became popular in the High Middle Ages, especially among people who were worried about the changes they saw around them. They asserted that the three orders had been established by God and that every person had been assigned a fixed place in the social order.

This tripartite model does not fully describe medieval society, however. There were degrees of wealth and status within each group. The model does not take townspeople and the emerging commercial classes (see pages 246–259) into consideration. It completely excludes those who were not Christian, such as Jews, Muslims, and pagans. Those who used the model, generally bishops and other church officials, ignored the fact that each of these groups was made up of both women and men; they spoke only of warriors, monks, and farmers. Despite—or perhaps because of—these limitations, the model of the three orders was a powerful mental construct. We can use it to organize our investigation of life in the High Middle Ages, though we can broaden our categories to include groups and issues that medieval authors did not.

Village Life

What was life like for the rural common people of medieval Europe?

The evolution of localized feudal systems into more centralized states had relatively little impact on the daily lives of peasants except when it involved warfare. While only nobles fought, their battles often destroyed the houses, barns, and fields of ordinary people, who might also be killed either directly or as a result of the famine and disease that often accompanied war. People might seek protection in the local castle during times of warfare, but typically they worked and lived without paying much attention to the political developments under way there.

This lack of attention went in the other direction as well. Since villagers did not perform what were considered "noble" deeds, the aristocratic monks and clerics who wrote the records that serve as historical sources did not spend time or precious writing materials on them. When common people were mentioned, it was usually with contempt or in terms of the services and obligations they owed. Usually—but not always. In the early twelfth century Honorius (hoh-NAWR-ee-uhs), a monk and teacher at the monastery of Autun, wrote: "What do you say about the agricultural classes? Most of them will be saved because they live simply and feed God's people by means of their sweat."[1]

Slavery, Serfdom, and Upward Mobility

Medieval theologians lumped everyone who worked the land into the category of "those who work," but in fact there were many levels of peasants, ranging from complete slaves to free and very rich farmers. The High Middle Ages was a period of considerable fluidity with significant social mobility.

The number of slaves who worked the land declined steadily in the High Middle Ages. Most rural people in western Europe during this period were serfs rather than slaves, though the distinction between slave and serf was not always clear. Both lacked freedom—the power to do as they wished—and both were subject to

orders Divisions of society in the High Middle Ages, including those who pray, those who fight, and those who work.

The Three Orders of Society (fourteenth century)
This book illustration shows the most common image of medieval society: those who fight, those who pray, and those who work. The group of clergy shown here includes a veiled nun; nuns were technically not members of the clergy, but most people considered them as such. (Copyright Royal Library of Belgium)

the arbitrary will of one person, the lord. Unlike a slave, however, a serf could not be bought and sold like an animal.

People's legal status was based on memory and traditions, not on written documents. The serf was required to perform labor services on the lord's land, usually three days a week except during the planting or harvest seasons, when it was more. Serfs frequently had to pay arbitrary levies. When a man married, he had to pay his lord a fee. When he died, his son or heir had to pay an inheritance tax to inherit his parcels of land. The precise amounts of tax paid to the lord on these important occasions depended on local custom and tradition. A free person had to pay rent to the lord but could move and live as he or she wished.

Serfdom was a hereditary condition. A person born a serf was likely to die a serf, though many serfs did secure their freedom. More than anything else, the economic revival that began in the eleventh century (see pages 255–259) advanced the cause of freedom for serfs. The revival saw the rise of towns, increased land productivity, the growth of long-distance trade, and the development of a money economy. With the advent of a money economy, serfs could save money and, through a third-person intermediary, use it to buy their freedom. Many energetic and hard-working serfs acquired their freedom through this method of manumission in the High Middle Ages.

Another opportunity for increased personal freedom came when lords organized groups of villagers to cut down forests or fill in swamps and marshes between villages to make more land available for farming. In some parts of Europe, peasants migrated to these new areas. The thirteenth century witnessed German peasant migrations into Brandenburg, Pomerania, Prussia, and the Baltic States, with Germans establishing new villages between existing Slavic villages or pushing the Slavs eastward. In the Iberian peninsula, Christian villagers followed after the Christian armies that were gaining areas from Muslims. In Scandinavia, farms were established in areas that had previously been used to harvest furs or lumber. This type of agricultural advancement frequently improved the peasants' social and legal condition. A serf could clear a patch of fen or forestland, make it productive, and, through prudent saving, buy more land and eventually purchase freedom.

Peasants who remained in the villages of their birth often benefited because landlords, threatened with the loss of serfs, relaxed ancient obligations and duties. While it would be unwise to exaggerate the social impact of the settling of new territories, frontier lands in the Middle Ages did provide opportunities for upward mobility.

The Manor

In the High Middle Ages most European peasants, free and unfree, lived in family groups in small villages. One or more villages, and the land surrounding them, made up a manor, controlled by a noble or a church official such as a bishop, abbot, or abbess. Sometimes a single village would be divided among several lords into small manors, for manors varied from several thousand to as few as one hundred acres. The manor was the basic unit of medieval rural organization and the center of rural life. All other generalizations about manors and manorial life have to be limited by variations in the quality of the soil, local climatic conditions, and methods of cultivation. The arable land of the manor was divided into two sections. The *demesne* (di-MAIN), or home farm, was cultivated for the lord. The other part was held by the peasantry. Usually the peasants' portion was larger and was held on condition that they cultivate the lord's demesne. All of the arable land, both the lord's and the peasants', was divided into strips that were scattered throughout the manor. If one strip yielded little, other strips (with better soil) might be more bountiful. All peasants cooperated in the cultivation of the land, working it as a group. This meant that all shared in any disaster as well as in any large harvest.

The peasants' work was typically divided according to gender. Men were responsible for clearing new land, plowing, and the care of large animals, and women were responsible for the care of small animals, spinning, and food preparation. Both sexes harvested and planted, though often there were gender-specific tasks within each of these major undertakings. Women and men worked in the vineyards and in the harvest and preparation of crops needed by the textile industry—flax and plants used for dyeing cloth. In fishing communities wives and daughters dried and salted fish for later use, while husbands and sons went out in boats.

In western and central Europe, villages were generally made up of small houses for individual families, with one married couple, their children (including stepchildren), and perhaps one or two other relatives—a grandmother, a cousin whose parents had died, an unmarried sister or brother of one of the spouses. The household thus contained primarily a **nuclear family** and some households contained only an unmarried person, a widow, or several unmarried people living together. Villages themselves were also *nucleated*—that is, the houses were clumped together, with the fields stretching out beyond the group of houses. In southern and eastern Europe, extended families were more likely to live in the same household or very near to one another. Father and son, or two married brothers, might share a house with the families of both, forming what demographers call a *stem*, or complex household.

A manor usually held pasture or meadowland for the grazing of cattle, sheep, and sometimes goats. Often the manor had some forestland as well. Forests were the source of wood for building and for fuel, resin for lighting, ash for candles, ash and lime for fertilizers and all sorts of sterilizing products, and bark for the manufacture of rope. From the forests came wood for the construction of barrels, vats, and all sorts of storage containers. Last but hardly least, the forests were used for feeding pigs, cattle, and domestic animals on nuts, roots, and wild berries. If the manor was intersected by a river, it had a welcome source of fish and eels.

The medieval village had no police as we know them, so villagers who saw a crime or infraction were expected to chase

909	Abbey of Cluny established
1050–1300	Steady rise in population
1080–1180	Period of milder climate
1098–1179	Life of Hildegard of Bingen
Early 1100s	Production of iron increases greatly
1100–1200	Rapid expansion of the Cistercian Order
1200	Notion of chivalry begins to develop
1215	Fourth Lateran Council accepts seven sacraments

nuclear family Family group consisting of parents and their children, but no other relatives.

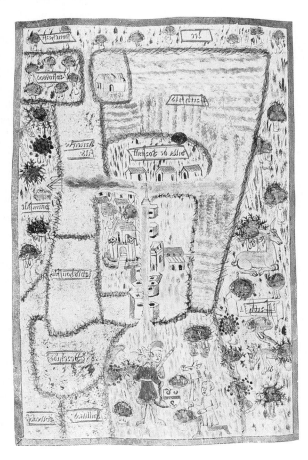

Boarstall Manor, Buckinghamshire
In 1440 Edmund Rede, lord of this estate, had a map made showing his ancestor receiving the title from King Edward I (*lower field*). Note the manor house, church, and peasants' cottages along the central road. In the common fields, divided by hedges, peasants cultivated on a three-year rotation cycle: winter wheat, spring oats, a year fallow. Peasants' pigs grazed freely in the woods, indicated by trees. We don't know whether peasants were allowed to hunt the deer. (Buckinghamshire Record Office, Aylesbury)

the perpetrator and yell to others to join in what was termed *raising the hue and cry*. Villages in many parts of Europe also developed institutions of self-government to handle issues such as crop rotation, and they chose additional officials such as constables and ale-tasters without the lord's interference. We do not know how these officials were chosen or elected in many cases, but we do know that they were always adult men and were generally heads of households. Women had no official voice in running the village, nor did slaves or servants (female or male), who often worked for and lived with wealthier village families. Women did buy, sell, and hold land independently and, especially as widows, headed households; when they did they were required to pay all rents and taxes. In areas of Europe where men were gone fishing or foresting for long periods of time, or where men left seasonally or more permanently in search of work elsewhere, women made decisions about the way village affairs were to be run, though they did not set up formal institutions to do this.

Manors do not represent the only form of medieval rural economy. In parts of Germany and the Netherlands, and in much of southern France, free independent farmers owned land outright, free of rents and services. These farms tended to be small and were surrounded by large estates that gradually swallowed them up. In Scandinavia the soil was so poor and the climate so harsh that people tended to live on widely scattered farms rather than in villages, but they still lived in relatively small family groups.

open-field system System in which the arable land of a manor was divided into two or three fields without hedges or fences to mark the individual holdings of the lord, serfs, and freemen.

Agricultural Methods and Improvements

Medieval farmers employed what historians term the **open-field system,** a pattern that differs sharply from modern farming practices. In the open-field system, the arable land of a manor was divided into two or three fields without hedges or fences to mark the individual holdings of the lord, serfs, and freemen. The village as a whole decided what would be planted in each field, rotating the crops according to tradition and need. Some fields would be planted in crops such as wheat, rye, peas, or barley for human consumption, some in oats or other crops for both animals and humans, and some would be left unworked or *fallow* to allow the soil to rejuvenate. The exact pattern of this rotation varied by location, but in most areas with open-field agriculture the holdings farmed by any one family did not consist of a whole field but, instead, of strips in many fields.

The milder climate of the Mediterranean area allowed for more frequent planting and a greater range of agricultural products; families tended to farm individual square plots rather than long strips. Milder climate also meant that more work (and play) could take place outdoors, which may have somewhat alleviated crowding in households with many family members.

While not approaching the temperatures of the Mediterrarean area, England, France, and Germany experienced exceptionally clement weather in the tenth and eleventh centuries. Meteorologists believe that a slow but steady retreat of polar ice occurred between the ninth and eleventh centuries. The mild winters and dry summers associated with this warming trend helped to increase agricultural output throughout Europe.

The tenth and eleventh centuries also witnessed a number of agricultural improvements, especially in the development of mechanisms that replaced or aided human labor. Water mills were one important part of this. In the ancient world, slaves ground the grain for bread; as slavery was replaced by serfdom, grinding became a woman's task. Water mills replaced human energy and increased productivity. A water mill unearthed near Monte Cassino in Italy could grind about

Windmill
The mill was constructed on a pivot so that it could turn in the direction of the wind. Used primarily to grind grain, as shown here with a man carrying a sack of grain to be ground into flour, windmills were also used to process cloth, brew beer, drive saws, and provide power for iron forges. (Bodleian Library, University of Oxford, MS Bodl. 264, fol. 81r)

1.5 tons of grain in ten hours, a quantity that would formerly have required the exertions of forty people.

Cloth production in medieval Europe grew because of water power. Women freed from the task of grinding grain could spend more time spinning yarn—the bottleneck in cloth production, as each weaver needed at least six spinners. Water mills were also well suited to the process known as *fulling*—scouring, cleansing, and thickening cloth—enabling men and women to full cloth at a much faster rate.

Next, medieval engineers harnessed wind power. Many windmills were erected in the flat areas of northern Europe, including Holland, that lacked fast-flowing streams.

In the early twelfth century the production of iron increased greatly. Iron was first used in agriculture for plowshares (the part of the plow that cuts the furrow and grinds up the earth), and then for pitchforks, spades, and axes. Harrows—cultivating instruments with heavy teeth that broke up and smoothed the soil—began to have iron instead of wooden teeth.

Plows and harrows were increasingly drawn by horses rather than oxen. The development of the padded horse collar that rested on the horse's shoulders and was attached to the load by shafts led to dramatic improvements. The horse collar meant that the animal could put its entire weight into the task of pulling. The use of horses spread in the twelfth century because horses' greater speed brought greater efficiency to farming and reduced the amount of human labor involved. Oxen were still used in areas where the soil was heavy and muddy.

The thirteenth century witnessed a tremendous spurt in the use of horses to haul carts to market. Consequently, goods reached market faster, and the number of markets to which the peasant had access increased. Peasants not only sold products, but also bought them as their opportunities for spending on at least a few nonagricultural goods multiplied.

By twenty-first-century standards, medieval agricultural yields were very low, but there was striking improvement over time. Increased agricultural output had a profound impact on society, improving Europeans' health, commerce, industry, and general lifestyle. A better diet had an enormous impact on women's lives: it meant increased body fat, which increased fertility; also, more iron in the diet meant that women were less anemic and less subject to opportunistic diseases. Some researchers believe that it was during the High Middle Ages that Western women began to outlive men. Improved opportunities also encouraged people to marry somewhat earlier, which meant larger families and further population growth.

Households, Work, and Food

Life for most people in medieval Europe meant country life. Most people rarely traveled more than twenty-five miles beyond their villages. Everyone's world was small, narrow, and provincial in the original sense of the word: limited by the boundaries of the province. This way of life did not have entirely unfortunate results. People had a strong sense of family and the certainty of its support and help in time of trouble. They had a sense of place, and pride in that place was reflected in adornment of the village church.

Life on the manor may have been stable, but it was dull. Medieval men and women often sought escape in heavy drinking. English judicial records of the thirteenth century reveal a surprisingly large number of "accidental" deaths. Strong, robust, commonsensible people do not ordinarily fall on their knives and stab themselves, or slip out of boats and drown, or get lost in the woods on a winter's night, or fall from horses and get trampled. The victims were probably drunk. Many of these accidents occurred, as the court records say, "coming from an ale." Brawls and violent fights were frequent at taverns.

The size and quality of peasants' houses varied according to their relative prosperity, and that prosperity usually depended on the amount of land held. Poorer

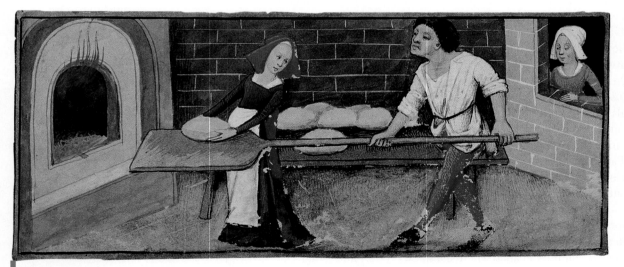

Baking Bread
Bread and beer or ale were the main manorial products for local consumption. While women dominated the making of ale and beer, men and women cooperated in the making and baking of bread—the staple of the diet. Most people did not have ovens in their own homes because of the danger of fire, but instead used the communal manorial oven, which, like a modern pizza oven, could bake several loaves at once. (Bibliothèque nationale de France)

peasants lived in windowless one-room cottages built of wood and clay or wattle (poles interwoven with branches or reeds) and thatched with straw. Prosperous peasants added rooms, and some wealthy peasants in the early fourteenth century had two-story houses with separate bedrooms for parents and children. For most people, however, living space—especially living space close enough to a fire to feel some warmth in cold weather—was cramped, dark, smoky, and smelly, with animals and people both sharing tight quarters, sometimes with each other.

Every house had a small garden and an outbuilding. Onions, garlic, turnips, and carrots were grown and stored through the winter in the main room of the dwelling or in the shed attached to it. Cabbage was shredded and salted for storage. Chickens and eggs were highly valued in the prudently managed household. Animals were too valuable to be used for food on a regular basis, but weaker animals were often slaughtered in the fall so that they did not need to be fed through the winter, and their meat was salted and eaten on great feast days such as Christmas and Easter. The rest of the household's needs—cloth, metal, leather goods, additional food, and copious quantities of ale—was purchased from village market stalls.

Health Care

Scholars are only beginning to explore questions of medieval health care, and there are still many aspects of public health that we know little about. The steady rise in population between the mid-eleventh and fourteenth centuries, usually attributed to warmer climate, increased food supply, and a reduction of violence with growing political stability, may also be ascribed partly to better health care. A recent study of skeletal remains in the village of Brandes in Burgundy showed that peasants enjoyed very good health: they were well built and had excellent teeth, and their bones revealed no signs of chronic disease. Obviously we cannot generalize about the health of all people on the basis of evidence from one village, but such research indicates that medieval adults were tough.

What care existed for the sick? As in the past, the sick everywhere depended above all on the private nursing care of relatives and friends. Beginning in the twelfth century in the British Isles, however, the royal family, the clergy, noble men and women, and newly rich merchants also established institutions to care for the sick or for those who for some reason could not take care of themselves. Within city walls they built hospitals, which were not hospitals in the modern sense, but rather places where those with chronic diseases that were not contagious, poor expectant mothers, the handicapped, people recovering from injuries, foundling children, and mentally retarded or psychologically disturbed children or adults went for care. Outside city walls they built leprosariums or small hospices for people with leprosy and other contagious diseases.

Such institutions might be staffed by members of religious orders, people who had less formally devoted themselves to lives of service, laymen and laywomen who were paid for their work, or a combination of the three. In the twelfth century medical personnel at hospitals were trained on the job, but by the thirteenth century some had been trained in faculties of medicine at Europe's new universities (see page 259). Outside of hospitals, people suffering from wounds, skin diseases, or broken bones turned to barber-surgeons who were trained in an apprenticeship system. For other internal ailments people used apothecaries—also trained through an apprenticeship system—to suggest and mix drugs, which combined herbs, salts, metals, and more fanciful ingredients such as "dragon's blood."

People also relied on men and women who had no official training at all, but who had learned healing techniques from their parents or other older people.

Monastic Entrance

In a world with few career opportunities for "superfluous children," monasteries served a valuable social function. Because a dowry was expected, monastic life was generally limited to the children of the affluent. Here a father—advising his son to be obedient and holding a bag of money for the monastery—hands his son over to the abbot. The boy does not look enthusiastic.

(The J. Paul Getty Museum, Los Angeles. Unknown illuminator, Initial Q: An Abbot Receiving a Child Decretum, ca. 1170–1180 [83.MQ.163.fol.63])

Their treatments were often mixtures of herbal remedies, sayings, specific foods, prayers, amulets, and ritual healing activities. Such combinations were also what people prescribed for themselves, for most treatment of illness was handled by home remedies handed down orally or perhaps through a cherished handwritten family herbal, cookbook, or household guide.

Childbirth and Child Abandonment

The most dangerous period of life for any person, peasant or noble, was infancy and early childhood. In normal years perhaps as many as one-third of all children died before age five, and in years with plagues, droughts, or famines this share climbed to more than half. Children often died from accidents as well as from malnutrition and illness, wandering into cooking fires, drowning in potholes in the road, or getting in the way of horses or cattle. Reaching adulthood meant that people had survived the most dangerous part of their lives, and many lived well into their fifties and sixties.

Childbirth was dangerous for mothers as well as for infants. Though mortality statistics are difficult to determine, every woman would have known someone who died in childbirth, and most would have seen such a death. Women developed prayers, rituals, and special sayings to ensure safe and speedy childbirth. Village women helped one another through childbirth, and women who were more capable acquired specialized midwifery skills. In larger towns and cities, such women gradually developed into professional midwives who were paid for their services and who trained younger women as apprentices, just as barber-surgeons and apothecaries trained their male apprentices. For most women, however, childbirth was handled by female friends and family, not by professionals.

The abandonment of infant children seems to have been the most favored form of family limitation and was widely practiced throughout the Middle Ages. Parents or guardians left children somewhere, sold them, or legally gave authority to some other person or institution. Sometimes parents believed that someone of greater means or status might find

Section Review

- The incidence of slavery was decreasing, as most of the slaves became serfs, an inherited condition, buying their freedom by saving money or migrating to new areas.

- The manor was the basic form of rural medieval life and contained land for the lord (the demesne) and additional land for the peasants, who farmed as a group, with separate jobs for men and women.

- In agriculture, production gradually increased as villages rotated crops in an open-field system, and improvements—such as water and windmills for grinding grain and processing cloth; the use of iron implements such as plows, pitchforks, and spades; and the increased use of horses—resulted in healthier lifestyles. Most people lived in the country in small, dark, smoky, smelly houses, often sharing space with animals, growing goods in small gardens, and purchasing things they could not produce at the market. The lifestyle was often dull, and heavy drinking was a common problem.

- Health care for most people was handled through home remedies given by friends and relatives, but a few hospitals and hospices provided care, and physicians, apothecaries, and barber-surgeons offered a variety of treatments to those who could afford them.

- Childbirth was dangerous for mothers and infants, and infancy and early childhood were the most dangerous times of life, as many children died from illness, famine, accidents, or abandonment, which was a common practice.

the child and bring it up in better circumstances than the natal parents could provide.

Disappointment in the sex of the child or its physical weakness or deformity might have also led parents to abandon it. Among Christians, superfluous children could be given to monasteries as **oblates.** The word *oblate* derives from the Latin *oblatio*, meaning "offering." Boys and girls were given to monasteries or convents as permanent gifts. But oblation also served social and economic functions. The monastery nurtured and educated the child in a familial atmosphere, and it provided career opportunities for the mature monk or nun whatever his or her origins. Oblation has justifiably been described as "in many ways the most humane form of abandonment ever devised in the West."[2] The abandonment of children remained socially acceptable, and church and state authorities never legislated against it.

oblates Children who were given to monasteries as offerings or permanent gifts.

Popular Religion

How did religious practices and attitudes permeate everyday life?

Apart from the land, the weather, and local legal and social conditions, religion had the greatest impact on the daily lives of ordinary people in the High Middle Ages. Religious practices varied widely from country to country and even from province to province. But nowhere was religion a one-hour-a-week affair. Most people in medieval Europe were Christian, but there were small Jewish communities scattered in many parts of Europe and Muslims in the Iberian peninsula, Sicily, other Mediterranean islands, and southeastern Europe.

Village Churches and Christian Symbols

For Christians the village church was the center of community life—social, political, and economic, as well as religious—with the parish priest in charge of a host of activities. Although church law placed the priest under the bishop's authority, the manorial lord appointed him and financed any education in Latin, Scriptures, and liturgy that he might receive. Parish priests were peasants and often were poor. Since they often worked in the fields with the people, they understood the people's labor, needs, and frustrations. The parish priest was also responsible for the upkeep of the church and for taking the lead in providing aid to the poorest of the village.

The center of the Christian religious life was the Mass, the re-enactment of Christ's sacrifice on the cross. Every Sunday and on holy days, the villagers stood at Mass or squatted on the floor (there were no chairs), breaking the painful routine of work. The feasts that accompanied baptisms, weddings, funerals, and other celebrations were commonly held in the churchyard. Medieval drama originated in the church. Mystery plays, based on biblical episodes, were performed first in the sanctuary, then on the church porch, which was often in front of the west door, and then at stations around the town.

From the church porch the priest read orders and messages from royal and ecclesiastical authorities to his parishioners. The west front of the church, with its scenes of the Last Judgment, was the background against which royal judges traveling on circuit disposed of civil and criminal cases. In busy mercantile centers such as London, business agreements and commercial exchanges were made in the aisles of the church itself, as at Saint Paul's.

Popular religion consisted largely of rituals heavy with symbolism. Before slicing a loaf of bread, the pious woman tapped the sign of the cross on it with her knife. Before planting, the village priest customarily went out and sprinkled the fields with water, symbolizing refreshment and life. Everyone participated in village processions. The entire calendar was designed with reference to Christmas, Easter, and Pentecost, events in the life of Jesus and his disciples. The varying colors of the vestments the priests wore at Mass gave villagers a sense of the changing seasons of the church's liturgical year. The signs and symbols of Christianity were visible everywhere.

saints Individuals thought to have lived particularly holy lives and regarded as having the power to work miracles.

Saints and Sacraments

Along with days marking events in the life of Jesus, the Christian calendar was filled with saints' days. **Saints** were individuals who had lived particularly holy lives and were honored locally or more widely for their connection with the divine. The cult of the saints, which developed in a rural and uneducated environment, represents a central feature of popular culture in the Middle Ages. People believed that the saints possessed supernatural powers that enabled them to perform miracles, and the saint became the special property of the locality in which his or her relics rested. Relics such as bones, articles of clothing, the saint's tears, saliva, and even the dust from the saint's tomb were enclosed in the church altar. In return for the saint's healing and support, peasants would offer the saint prayers, loyalty, and gifts. (See the feature "Listening to the Past: The Pilgrim's Guide to Santiago de Compostela" on pages 244–245.)

In the later Middle Ages popular hagiographies (**hag-ee-OG-ruh-fees**) (biographies of saints based on myths, legends, and popular stories) attributed specialized functions to the saints. Saint Elmo (ca. 300), who supposedly had preached unharmed during a thunder and lightning storm, became the patron of sailors. Saint Agatha (third century), whose breasts were torn with shears because she rejected the attentions of a powerful suitor, became the patron of wet nurses, women with breast difficulties, and bell ringers (because of the resemblance of breasts to bells).

Along with the veneration of saints, a new religious understanding developed in the High Middle Ages. Twelfth-century theologians expanded on Saint Augustine's understanding of sacraments—outward and visible signs regarded as instituted by Christ to give grace—and created an entire sacramental system. Only a priest could dispense a sacrament (except when someone was in danger of death), and the list of seven sacraments (baptism, penance, the Eucharist, confirmation, matrimony, ordination, anointment of the dying) was formally accepted by the Fourth Lateran Council in 1215.

Medieval Christians believed that these seven sacraments brought grace, the divine assistance or help needed to lead a good Christian life and to merit salvation. At the center of the sacramental system stood the Eucharist, the small piece of bread that through the words of priestly consecration at the Mass became the living body of Christ and, when worthily consumed, became a channel of Christ's grace. The ritual of consecration, repeated at every altar of Christendom,

The Eucharist
The Fourth Lateran Council of 1215 encouraged all Christians to receive the Eucharist at least once a year after confession and penance. Here a priest places the consecrated bread, called a *host,* on people's tongues. (Biblioteca Apostolica Vaticana)

became a unifying symbol in a complex world. The sacramental system, however, did not replace strong devotion to the saints.

Beliefs

Peasants had a strong sense of the presence of God. They believed that God rewarded the virtuous with peace, health, and material prosperity and punished sinners with disease, poor harvests, and war. Sin was caused by the Devil, who lurked everywhere and constantly incited people to evil deeds. Sin frequently took place in the dark. Thus evil and the Devil were connected in the peasant's mind with darkness or blackness. In some medieval literature, the Devil is portrayed as black, an identification that has had a profound and sorry impact on Western racial attitudes.

In the eleventh century theologians began to emphasize Mary's spiritual motherhood of all Christians. The huge outpouring of popular devotions to Mary concentrated on her special relationship to Christ as all-powerful intercessor with him. The most famous prayer, "Salve Regina," perfectly expresses medieval people's confidence in Mary, their advocate with Christ:

Hail, holy Queen, Mother of Mercy! Our life, our sweetness, and our hope. To thee we cry, poor banished children of Eve; to thee we send up our sighs, mourning and weeping in this valley of tears. Turn, then, most gracious advocate, thy merciful eyes upon us; and after this our exile show us the blessed fruit of thy womb, Jesus. O merciful, O loving, O sweet Virgin Mary!

The Mass was in Latin, but the priest delivered sermons in the vernacular. However, a common complaint was that priests did a poor job of preaching the Gospel. Nevertheless, people grasped the meaning of biblical stories and church doctrines from the paintings on the church walls or, in wealthy parishes, the scenes in stained-glass windows. Illiterate and uneducated, they certainly could not reason out the increasingly sophisticated propositions of clever theologians. Still, scriptural references and proverbs dotted everyone's language. The English *goodbye*, the French *adieu*, and the Spanish *adios* all derive from words meaning "God be with you." Christianity was the foundation of the common people's culture for most Europeans.

Muslims and Jews

The interpenetration of Christian ceremonies and daily life for most Europeans meant that those who did not participate or who had different religious rituals were clearly marked as outsiders. This included Muslims in the Iberian peninsula, where Christian rulers were establishing kingdoms in territory won through the *reconquista* (see page 201). Islam was outlawed in their territories, and some of the Muslims left Spain, leaving room for new settlers from elsewhere in Christian Europe. Other Muslims converted. In more isolated villages, people simply continued their Muslim rituals and practices, including abstaining from pork, reciting verses from the Qur'an, praying at specified times of the day, and observing Muslim holy days, though they might hide this from the local priest or visiting church or government officials.

Islam was geographically limited in medieval Europe, but by the late tenth century Jews could be found in many areas, often brought in from other parts of Europe as clients of rulers because of their skills as merchants. There were Jewish communities in Italian cities and in the cities along the Rhine such as Cologne,

Worms, Speyer, and Mainz. Jews migrated from there to England and France, where they generally lived in the growing towns, often separate from the larger Christian community.

Jewish dietary laws require meat to be handled in a specific way, so Jews had their own butchers; there were Jewish artisans in many other trades as well, though Jews were forbidden to join Christian guilds. Jews held weekly religious services on Saturday, the Sabbath holy day of rest, and celebrated an annual cycle of holidays, including the High Holidays of Rosh Hashanah and Yom Kippur in the fall and Passover in the spring. Each of these holidays involved special prayers, services, and often foods, and many of them commemorated specific events from Jewish history, including various times when Jews had been rescued from captivity.

The Crusades brought violence against Jews in many cities (see pages 209–214), and restrictions on Jews increased in much of Europe. When Jews were expelled from England and later from France, many of them went to Muslim and Christian areas of the Iberian peninsula. The rulers of both faiths initially welcomed them, though restrictions and violence gradually became more common there as well. Jews continued to live in the independent cities of the Holy Roman Empire and Italy, and some migrated eastward into new towns that were being established in Slavic areas.

Marriage and Children

In the Middle Ages, every major life transition was marked by a ceremony. The sacrament of marriage was followed by a wedding party that often included secular rituals. Some rituals symbolized the "proper" hierarchical relations between the spouses—such as placing the husband's shoe on the bedstead over the couple, symbolizing his authority—or worked to ensure the couple's fertility—such as untying all the knots in the household, for tying knots was one way that people reputed to have magical powers bound up the reproductive power of a man. All this came together in what was often the final event of a wedding, the priest blessing the couple in their marriage bed, often with family and friends standing around or banging on pans, yelling, or otherwise making as much noise as possible. The friends and family members had generally been part of the discussions, negotiations, and activities leading up to the marriage; marriage united two families and was far too important to leave up to two young people alone.

The involvement of family and friends in choosing one's spouse might lead to conflict, but more often the wishes of the young people and their parents, kin, and community were quite similar; all hoped for marriages that provided economic security, honorable standing, and a good number of healthy children. The best marriages offered companionship, emotional support, and even love, but these were understood to grow out of the marriage, not necessarily precede it. Breaking up a marriage meant breaking up the basic production and consumption unit, which was a very serious matter, so marital dissolution by any means other than the death of one spouse was rare.

Most brides hoped to be pregnant soon after their wedding, and if the rituals during the wedding had not been effective in bringing this about, there were other avenues to try. Christian women hoping for children said special prayers to the Virgin Mary or her mother Anne; wore amulets of amber, bone, or mistletoe, thought to increase fertility; repeated charms and verses they had learned from other women; or, in desperate cases, went on pilgrimages to make special supplications. Muslim and Jewish women wore small cases with sacred verses or asked for blessings from religious leaders. Women continued these prayers and rituals through pregnancy and childbirth, often combining religious traditions with folk beliefs handed down orally.

Religious ceremonies also welcomed children into the community. Among Christian families, infants were baptized soon after they were born, for without the sacrament of baptism they could not enter heaven. Thus midwives who delivered children who looked especially weak and sickly often baptized them in an emergency service. In normal baptisms, the women who had assisted the mother in the birth often carried the baby to church, where carefully chosen godparents vowed their support. Godparents were often close friends or relatives, but parents might also choose prominent villagers or even the local lord in the hope that he might later look favorably on the child and provide for it in some way.

Within Judaism, a boy was circumcised and given his name in a ceremony when he was in his eighth day of life. This *brit milah*, or "covenant of circumcision," was viewed as a reminder of the covenant between God and Abraham described in Hebrew Scripture. Muslims also circumcised boys in a special ritual, though the timing varied from a few days after birth to adolescence.

Death and the Afterlife

Death was similarly marked by religious ceremonies. Christians called for a priest to perform the sacrament of extreme unction when they thought the hour of death was near. The priest brought a number of objects and substances regarded as having power over death and the sin related to it. Holy water, holy oil, and a censer with incense all connected to rites that purified and blessed the dying. Lighted candles drove back the darkness both figuratively and literally. A crucifix served to remind the dying of Christ's own agony and the promise of salvation. Most important, the priest gave the dying person a last communion host.

Once the person had died, the body was washed and dressed in special clothing or a sack of plain cloth and buried within a day or two. Family and friends joined in a funeral procession, again with candles, holy water, incense, and a crucifix and marked by the ringing of church bells; sometimes extra women were hired so that the mourning and wailing were especially loud. The procession carried the body into the church, where there were psalms, prayers, and a funeral Mass, and then to a consecrated space for burial, the wealthy sometimes inside the church—in the walls, under the floor, or under the building itself in a crypt—but most often in the churchyard or a cemetery close by. Standing at the graveside, the priest asked for God's grace on the soul of the deceased and also asked that soul to "rest in peace."

This final request was made not only for the benefit of the dead, but also for that of the living. The souls of the dead were widely believed to return to earth: mothers who had died in childbed might come back seeking to take their children with them; executed criminals to gain revenge on those who had brought them to justice (for this reason they were buried at crossroads, permanently under the sign of the cross, or under the gallows itself); everyday people came seeking help from surviving family members in achieving their final salvation.

Jewish Cemetery
Tomb in Worms of a thirteenth-century German Jewish rabbi who was imprisoned by the emperor and died in prison. Jewish and Christian cemeteries were separated in medieval Europe, with Christian cemeteries generally next to churches and Jewish ones often outside town walls. (Erich Lessing/Art Resource, NY)

purgatory A place where souls on their way to heaven went after death to make amends for their earthly sins.

Section Review

- The village church was the center of life for the people, with priest-led Masses, feasts, dramas, and sometimes business exchanges, all of which provided distractions from daily toil.

- Medieval people worshiped saints, offering them prayers and gifts, and believed that the sacraments brought divine help and salvation.

- Peasants believed that God rewarded the just and punished evildoers, that sin was from the Devil, and that Christianity was the basis for common people's lives.

- Christians treated Muslims and Jews as outsiders, so Muslims practiced in secret while Jews lived with many restrictions and often experienced violence.

- Marriage was a celebration involving both families and divorce was a rarity. Couples welcomed children, Christians baptizing them soon after birth, while Jewish and Muslim parents circumcised their infant sons.

- After Christians died, rituals and symbols were thought to help them move through purgatory; Muslims fasted and said special prayers, and Jews observed specific mourning rites.

Priests were hired to say memorial masses on anniversaries of family deaths, especially one week, one month, and one year afterward; large churches had a number of side altars so that many masses could be going on at one time.

Learned theologians sometimes denied that souls actually returned, and during the twelfth century they increasingly emphasized the idea of **purgatory**, a place where souls on their way to heaven went after death to make amends for their earthly sins. (Those on their way to hell went straight there.) Souls safely in purgatory did not wander the earth, but they could still benefit from earthly activities; memorial masses, prayers, and donations made in their names could shorten their time in purgatory and hasten their way to heaven. So could indulgences, documents bearing the pope's name that released the souls from purgatory. (Indulgences, it was believed, also relieved the living of penalties imposed by the priest in confession for serious sins.) Indulgences could be secured for a small fee, and people came to believe that indulgences and pilgrimages to the shrines of saints could ensure a place in heaven for their deceased relatives (and also, perhaps, for themselves). Thus the bodies of the dead on earth and their souls in purgatory both required things from the living, for death did not sever family obligations and connections.

The living also had obligations to the dead among Muslims and Jews. In both groups, deceased people were to be buried quickly, and special prayers were to be said by mourners and family members. Muslims fasted on behalf of the dead and maintained a brief period of official mourning. The Qur'an promises an eternal paradise with flowing rivers to "those who believe and do good deeds" (Qur'an, 4:57) and a hell of eternal torment to those who do not.

Jews observed specified periods of mourning during which the normal activities of daily life were curtailed. Every day for eleven months after a death and every year after that on the anniversary of the death, a son of the deceased was to recite Kaddish, a special prayer of praise and glorification of God. Judaism emphasized this life more than an afterlife, so beliefs about what happens to the soul after death were more varied; the very righteous might go directly to a place of spiritual reward, but most souls went first to a place of punishment and purification generally referred to as *Gehinnom*. After a period that did not exceed twelve months, the soul ascended to the world to come. Those who were completely wicked during their lifetime might simply go out of existence or continue in an eternal state of remorse.

Nobles

How were the lives of nobles different from the lives of common people?

The **nobility**, though a small fraction of the total population, strongly influenced all aspects of medieval culture—political, economic, religious, educational, and artistic. Despite political, scientific, and industrial revolutions, the nobility continued to hold real political and social power in Europe into the nineteenth century. In order to account for this continuing influence, it is important to understand the development of the nobility in the High Middle Ages.

nobility A small group of people at the top of the medieval social structure, whose official role was fighting.

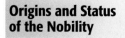
Origins and Status of the Nobility

In the early Middle Ages noble status was generally limited to very few families who were either descended from officials at the Carolingian court or leading families among Germanic tribes. Beginning in the eleventh century, knights in the service of higher nobles or kings began to claim noble status. The noble class grew larger and more diverse, ranging from poor knights who held tiny pieces of land (or sometimes none at all) to dukes and counts with vast territories.

Originally, most knights focused solely on military skills, but gradually a different ideal of knighthood emerged, usually termed **chivalry** (SHIV-uhl-ree). Chivalry was a code of conduct originally devised by the clergy to transform the crude and brutal behavior of the knightly class. It may have originated in oaths administered to Crusaders in which fighting was declared to have a sacred purpose and knights vowed loyalty to the church as well as to their lords. Other qualities gradually became part of chivalry: bravery, generosity, honor, graciousness, mercy, and eventually gallantry toward women. The chivalric ideal—and it was an ideal, not a standard pattern of behavior—created a new standard of masculinity for nobles, in which loyalty and honor remained the most important qualities, but graceful dancing and intelligent conversation were not considered unmanly.

chivalry Code of conduct originally devised by the clergy to transform the crude and brutal behavior of the knightly class.

Childhood

For children of aristocratic birth, the years from infancy to around the age of seven or eight were primarily years of play. Infants had rattles, as the twelfth-century monk Guibert of Nogent reports, and young children had special toys.

At about the age of seven, a boy of the noble class who was not intended for the church was placed in the household of one of his father's friends or relatives. There he became a servant to the lord and received formal training in arms. He was expected to serve the lord at the table, to assist him as a private valet, and, as he gained experience, to care for the lord's horses and equipment.

Training was in the arts of war. The boy learned to ride and to manage a horse. He had to acquire skill in wielding a sword, which sometimes weighed as much as twenty-five pounds. He had to be able to hurl a lance, shoot with a bow and arrow, and care for armor and other equipment. Increasingly, in the eleventh and twelfth centuries, noble youths learned to read and write some Latin. Still, on thousands of charters from that period, nobles signed with a cross (+) or some other mark. Literacy among the nobility became more common in the thirteenth century. Formal training was concluded around the age of twenty-one with the ceremony of knighthood. The custom of knighting, though never universal, seems to have been widespread in France and England but not in Germany.

Noble girls were also trained in preparation for their future tasks. They were often taught to read the local language and perhaps some Latin and to write and do enough arithmetic to keep household accounts. They also learned music, dancing, and embroidery and how to ride and hunt, both common noble pursuits. Much of this took place in the girl's own home, but, like boys, noble girls were often sent to the homes of relatives or higher nobles to act as servants or ladies in waiting. While her brothers cared for armor and horses, a noble girl looked after clothing and household goods and learned how to run a household. She often

Saint Maurice

Certain individuals were held up to young men as models of ideal chivalry. One of these was Saint Maurice (d. 287), a soldier apparently executed by the Romans for refusing to renounce his Christian faith. He first emerges in the Carolingian period, and later he was held up as a model knight and declared a patron of the Holy Roman Empire and protector of the imperial (German) army in wars against the pagan Slavs. Until 1240 he was portrayed as a white man, but after that he was usually represented as a black man, as in this sandstone statue from Magdeburg Cathedral (ca. 1250). We have no idea why this change happened. Who commissioned this statue? Who carved it? Did an actual person serve as the model, and if so what was he doing in Magdeburg? (Image of the Black Project, Harvard University/Hickey-Robertson, Houston)

learned from experience that she could expect to spend weeks, months, or even years running a castle and a manor on her own while her future husband was away fighting.

Youth and Marriage

The ceremony of knighthood was one of the most important in a man's life, but knighthood did not necessarily mean adulthood, power, and responsibility. Sons were completely dependent on their fathers for support. A young man remained a youth until he was in a financial position to marry—that is, until his father died. That might not happen until he was in his late thirties, and marriage at forty was not uncommon. Increasingly, families adopted primogeniture, with property passing to the oldest son. Younger sons might be forced into the clergy or simply forbidden to marry. One factor—the inheritance of land and the division of properties—determined the lifestyles of the aristocratic nobility. The result was tension, frustration, and sometimes violence.

Once knighted, the young man traveled for two to three years. His father selected a group of friends to accompany, guide, and protect him. The band's chief pursuit was fighting. They meddled in local conflicts, sometimes departed on crusades, hunted, and did the tournament circuit. The **tournament,** in which a number of men competed from horseback (in contrast to the **joust,** which involved only two competitors), gave the young knight experience in pitched battle. Since the horses and equipment of the vanquished were forfeited to the victors, the knight could also gain a reputation and a profit. Young knights took great delight in spending money on horses, armor, gambling, drinking, and women. Everywhere they went, they stirred up trouble, for chivalric ideals of honorable valor and gallant masculinity rarely served as a check on actual behavior.

Parents often wanted to settle daughters' futures as soon as possible. Men tended to prefer young brides. A woman in her late twenties or thirties would have fewer years of married fertility, limiting the number of children she could produce and thus threatening the family's continuation. Therefore, aristocratic girls in the High Middle Ages were married at around the age of sixteen, often to much older men. In the early Middle Ages the custom was for the groom to present a dowry to the bride and her family, but by the late twelfth century the process was reversed because men were in greater demand. Thereafter, the sizes of dowries offered by brides and their families rose higher and higher. Families engaged in complicated marriage strategies to balance the money they paid out to marry off daughters with the money they received in marrying off sons.

When society included so many married young women and unmarried young men, sexual tensions also arose. The young male noble, unable to marry for a long time, could satisfy his lust with peasant girls or prostitutes. But what was a young woman unhappily married to a much older man to do? Medieval literature is filled with stories of young bachelors in love with young married women and of cuckolded husbands who are not able to see what is going on in their households. Scholars disagree, however, about whether this reflected social realities or was simply wishful thinking.

Power and Responsibility

A male member of the nobility became an adult when he came into the possession of his property. He then acquired vast authority over lands and people. With it went responsibility. In the words of Honorius of Autun:

tournament An arena for knights to compete on horseback giving them valuable experience in pitched battle.

joust A competition between two knights on horseback.

Soldiers: You are the arm of the Church, because you should defend it against its enemies. Your duty is to aid the oppressed, to restrain yourself from rapine and fornication, to repress those who impugn the Church with evil acts, and to resist those who are rebels against priests. Performing such a service, you will obtain the most splendid of benefices from the greatest of Kings.[3]

The responsibilities of a nobleman in the High Middle Ages depended on the size and extent of his estates, the number of dependents, and his position in his territory relative to others of his class and to the king. As a vassal, he was required to fight for his lord or for the king when called on to do so. By the mid-twelfth century this service was limited to forty days a year in most parts of western Europe. The noble was obliged to attend his lord's court on important occasions when the lord wanted to put on great displays, such as at Easter, Pentecost, and Christmas. When the lord knighted his eldest son or married off his eldest daughter, he called his vassals to his court. The vassals were expected to attend and to present a contribution known as a "gracious aid."

Until the late thirteenth century, when royal authority intervened, a noble in France or England had great power over those on his estates. He maintained order among them and dispensed justice to them. Holding the manorial court, which punished criminal acts and settled disputes, was one of his gravest obligations. The quality of justice varied widely: some lords were vicious tyrants who exploited and persecuted their peasants; others were reasonable and even-handed. In any case, the quality of life on the manor and its productivity were related in no small way to the temperament and decency of the lord—and his lady.

Women played a large and important role in the functioning of the estate. They were responsible for the practical management of the household's "inner economy"—cooking, brewing, spinning, weaving, caring for yard animals. When the lord was away for long periods, the women frequently managed the herds, barns, granaries, and outlying fields as well. Often the responsibilities of the estate fell to them permanently, as the number of men slain in medieval warfare ran high.

Throughout the High Middle Ages, fighting remained the dominant feature of the noble lifestyle. The church's preaching and condemnations reduced but did not stop violence. Lateness of inheritance, depriving nobles of constructive outlets for their energy, together with the military ethos of their culture, encouraged petty warfare and disorder. The nobility thus represented a constant source of trouble for the monarchy. In the thirteenth century kings drew on the financial support of the middle classes to build the administrative machinery that gradually laid the foundations of strong royal government. The Crusades relieved the rulers of France, England, and the German Empire of some of their most dangerous elements. Complete royal control of the nobility, however, came only in modern times.

Elephant Ivory Mirror Case

The mirror case, forerunner of the modern woman's compact, protected a polished metal disk used by wealthy ladies as a looking glass. In this mid-fourteenth-century case, the French artist created a chivalric hunting scene. An aristocratic couple on horseback, holding falcons and accompanied by attendants, is portrayed in a forested landscape that is held in an eight-lobed frame with lions around the disk. Amazingly, the diameter of the case is less than four inches. Elephant ivory came from sub-Saharan Africa via the Mediterranean trade. (The Metropolitan Museum of Art, Gift of George M. Blumenthal, 1941 [41.100.160]. Photograph © 1995 The Metropolitan Museum of Art)

Section Review

- Originally, nobility was restricted to a few high aristocrats such as dukes and counts, but then it expanded to include knights, who aspired to follow the chivalric code of conduct with loyalty and honor, their most important virtues.

- Boys of the noble class began training for knighthood at about age seven, when they became pages to knights, managing their horses and acting as valets or servants, while girls received domestic training.

- The young noblemen were eligible to become full-fledged knights by age twenty-one, while daughters married starting around age sixteen, often paying dowries to the groom's family.

- Noble sons could not marry or inherit property until the death of their father, so they often had many years to travel, participate in tournaments, and cause trouble before they could settle down.

- A nobleman's power and responsibility were determined by the size of his estate, where he maintained order and dispensed justice to his peasants when he was not away fighting.

Monasteries and Convents

What roles did the men and women affiliated with religious orders play in medieval society?

Priests, bishops, monks, and nuns played significant roles in medieval society, both as individuals and as members of institutions. In the previous chapter we traced the evolution of the papacy and the church hierarchy in the High Middle Ages; here we focus on monks, nuns, and others who lived in religious houses.

In the fifth century Saints Benedict and Scholastica had written rules (*regulus* in Latin) for the men and women living in monasteries and convents (see page 148), who were known as regular clergy. In the early Middle Ages many religious houses followed the Benedictine Rule, while others developed their own patterns. In the High Middle Ages this diversity became more formalized, and **religious orders,** groups of monastic houses following a particular rule, were established. Historians term the foundation, strengthening, and reform of religious orders in the High Middle Ages the "monastic revival." They link it with the simultaneous expansion of papal power (see pages 205–209), because many of the same individuals were important in both.

religious orders Groups of monastic houses following a particular rule.

Medieval people believed that monks and nuns performed an important social service—prayer. In the Middle Ages prayer was looked on as a vital service, as crucial as the labor of peasants and the military might of nobles. Just as the knights protected and defended society with the sword and the peasants provided sustenance through their toil, so the monks and nuns worked to secure God's blessing for society with their prayers and chants.

Monastic Revival

In the early Middle Ages the best Benedictine monasteries had been centers of learning, copying and preserving manuscripts, maintaining schools, and setting high standards of monastic observance. Charlemagne had encouraged and supported these monastic activities, and the collapse of the Carolingian Empire had disastrous effects.

The Viking, Magyar, and Muslim invaders attacked and ransacked many monasteries across Europe. Some communities fled and dispersed. In the period of political disorder that followed the disintegration of the Carolingian Empire, many religious houses fell under the control and domination of local lords. Powerful laymen appointed themselves or their relatives as abbots, took the lands and goods of monasteries, and spent monastic revenues. The level of spiritual observance and intellectual activity in monasteries and convents declined.

The secular powers who selected church officials compelled them to become their vassals. Abbots, bishops, and archbishops thus had military responsibilities that required them to fight with their lords, or at least to send contingents of soldiers when called on to do so. As feudal lords themselves, ecclesiastical officials also had judicial authority over knights and peasants on their lands. The conflict between a prelate's religious duties on the one hand and his judicial and military obligations on the other posed a serious dilemma.

An opportunity for reform came in 909, when William the Pious, duke of Aquitaine, established the abbey of Cluny in Burgundy. Duke William declared that the monastery was to be free from any feudal responsibilities to him or any other lord, its members subordinate only to the pope.

The monastery at Cluny came to exert vast religious influence. The first two abbots of Cluny, Berno (910–927) and Odo (927–942), followed the Benedictine Rule closely and set very high standards of religious behavior. Cluny gradually came to stand for clerical celibacy and the suppression of simony (the sale of church offices). In the eleventh century Cluny was fortunate in having a series of highly able abbots who ruled for a long time. In a disorderly world, the monastery gradually came to represent stability. Therefore, laypersons placed lands under its custody and monastic priories (a priory is a religious house, usually smaller in number than an abbey, governed by a prior or prioress) under its jurisdiction for reform. Benefactors wanted to be associated with Cluniac piety, and monasteries under Cluny's jurisdiction enjoyed special protection, at least theoretically, from violence. In this way, hundreds of monasteries, primarily in France and Spain, came under Cluny's authority.

Deeply impressed laypeople showered gifts on monasteries with good reputations, such as Cluny and its many daughter houses. But as the monasteries became richer, the lifestyle of the monks grew increasingly luxurious. Monastic observance and spiritual fervor declined. Soon fresh demands for reform were heard, and the result was the founding of new religious orders in the late eleventh and early twelfth centuries.

The Cistercians (si-STUR-shuhns), because of their phenomenal expansion and the great economic, political, and spiritual influence they exerted, are the best representatives of the new reforming spirit. In 1098 a group of monks left the rich abbey of Molesmes in Burgundy and founded a new house in the swampy forest of Cîteaux (sit-OH). They planned to avoid all involvement with secular feudal society. They decided to accept only uncultivated lands far from regular habitation. They intended to refuse all gifts of mills, serfs, tithes, and ovens—the traditional manorial sources of income. The early Cistercians (the word is derived from Cîteaux) determined to avoid elaborate liturgy and ceremony and to keep their chant simple. Finally, they refused to allow the presence of powerful laypeople in their monasteries because such influence was usually harmful to careful observance.

Monastery of Saint Martin de Canigou
The Benedictine monastery of Saint Martin de Canigou was constructed in 1009 in the eastern Pyrenees (PIR-uh-neez) by a nobleman from one of the small Christian kingdoms in northern Spain. Like hundreds of other monasteries, it came under the influence of the abbey of Cluny (KLOO-nee). With its thick walls and strategic position, it served as a Christian defensive fortress against the Muslims in battles of the reconquista. (Editions Gaud)

The first monks at Cîteaux experienced sickness, a dearth of recruits, and terrible privations. But their obvious sincerity and high ideals eventually attracted attention. In 1112 a twenty-three-year-old nobleman called Bernard joined the community at Cîteaux, together with some of his brothers and other noblemen. Three years later Bernard was appointed founding abbot of Clairvaux (klare-VOH) in Champagne. From this position he conducted a vast correspondence, attacked the theological views of Peter Abelard (see page 261), intervened in the disputed papal election of 1130, drafted a constitution for the Knights Templars, and preached the Second Crusade. This reforming movement gained impetus. Cîteaux founded 525 new monasteries in the course of the twelfth century, and its influence on European society was profound. In England Saint Gilbert (1085?–1189) organized a community of nuns at Sempringham that followed the more rigorous Cistercian Rule "as far as the weakness of their sex allowed," as Gilbert put it. This convent established several daughter houses, and Gilbert asked the

Cistercians to take them all on as official female branches. They refused, saying that they did not want the burden of overseeing women, setting a pattern for other men's religious orders.

Unavoidably, however, Cistercian success brought wealth, and wealth brought power. By the later twelfth century economic prosperity and political power had begun to compromise the original Cistercian ideals.

Life in Convents and Monasteries

Throughout the Middle Ages social class also defined the kinds of religious life open to women. Kings and nobles usually established convents for their daughters, sisters, aunts, or aging mothers. Entrance was restricted to women of the founder's class. Like monks, many nuns came into the convent as children, and very often sisters, cousins, aunts, and nieces could all be found in the same place. Thus, though nuns were to some degree cut off from their families because they were cloistered, family relationships were maintained within the convent.

abbess/prioress Head of convent for women, usually a nun of considerable social standing.

The office of **abbess** or **prioress** was the most powerful position a woman could hold in medieval society (see the feature "Individuals in Society: Hildegard of Bingen"). Abbesses were part of the feudal structure in the same way that bishops and abbots were, with manors under their financial and legal control. They appointed tax collectors, bailiffs, judges, and often priests in the territory under their control; some abbesses in the Holy Roman Empire even had the right to name bishops and send representatives to the imperial assemblies. Abbesses also opened and supported hospitals, orphanages, and schools; they hired builders, sculptors, and painters to construct and decorate residences and churches.

abbot/prior Head of a monastery for men, who was generally a member of a noble family.

Monasteries for men were headed by an **abbot** or **prior**, who was generally a member of a noble family, often a younger brother in a family with several sons. The main body of monks, known as *choir monks*, were aristocrats and did not till the land themselves. In each house one monk, the *cellarer*, or general financial manager, was responsible for supervising the peasants or lay brothers who did the agricultural labor. **Lay brothers** were generally peasants and had simpler religious and intellectual obligations than did the choir monks. In women's houses, a nun acted as cellarer and was in charge of **lay sisters** who did the actual physical work. The *novice master* or *novice mistress* was responsible for the training of recruits, instructing them in the *Rule*, the chant, the Scriptures, and the history and traditions of the house. The efficient operation of a monastic house also required the services of cooks, laundresses, gardeners, seamstresses, mechanics, blacksmiths, pharmacists, and others whose essential work has left, unfortunately, no written trace.

lay brothers/lay sisters Peasants who did the agricultural labor for the monastery since choir monks were aristocrats and therefore could not till the land themselves.

The pattern of life within individual monasteries varied widely from house to house and from region to region. One central activity, however, was performed everywhere. Daily life centered on the *liturgy* or *Divine Office*, psalms and other prayers prescribed by Saint Benedict that monks and nuns prayed seven times a day and once during the night. Prayers were offered for peace, rain, good harvests, the civil authorities, the monks' families, and their benefactors. Monastic patrons in turn lavished gifts on the monasteries, which often became very wealthy.

Monks and nuns also performed social services. Monasteries often ran schools that gave primary education to young boys, while convents took in girls. Abbeys like Saint Albans, situated north of London on a busy thoroughfare, served as hotels and resting places for travelers. Monasteries frequently operated "hospitals" and leprosaria, which provided care and attention to the sick, the aged, and the afflicted—primitive care, it is true, but often all that was available. Monastaries and convents also fed the poor; at the French abbey of Saint-Requier in the eleventh

Individuals in Society

Hildegard of Bingen

The tenth child of a lesser noble family, Hildegard (1098–1179) (HIL-duh-gahrd), was given as an oblate to an abbey in the Rhineland when she was eight years old; there she learned Latin and received a good education. She spent most of her life in various women's religious communities, two of which she founded herself. When she was a child, she began having mystical visions, often of light in the sky, but told few people about them. In middle age, however, her visions became more dramatic: "And it came to pass . . . when I was 42 years and 7 months old, that the heavens were opened and a blinding light of exceptional brilliance flowed through my entire brain. And so it kindled my whole heart and breast like a flame, not burning but warming . . . and suddenly I understood of the meaning of expositions of the books."* She wanted the church to approve of her visions and wrote first to Saint Bernard of Clairvaux, who answered her briefly and dismissively, and then to Pope Eugenius, who encouraged her to write them down. Her first work was *Scivias* (Know the Ways of the Lord), a record of her mystical visions that incorporates vast theological learning.

Obviously possessed of leadership and administrative talents, Hildegard left her abbey in 1147 to found the convent of Rupertsberg near Bingen. There she produced *Physica* (On the Physical Elements) and *Causa et Curae* (Causes and Cures), scientific works on the curative properties of natural elements, poems, a mystery play, and several more works of mysticism. She carried on a huge correspondence with scholars, prelates, and ordinary people. When she was over fifty she left her community to preach to audiences of clergy and laity, and she was the only woman of her time whose opinions on religious matters were considered authoritative by the church.

* From *Scivias*, trans. Mother Columba Hart and Jane Bishop, *The Classics of Western Spirituality* (New York/Mahwah: Paulist Press, 1990).

Hildegard's visions have been explored by theologians and also by neurologists, who judge that they may have originated in migraine headaches, as she reported many of the same phenomena that migraine sufferers do: auras of light around objects, areas of blindness, feelings of intense doubt and intense euphoria. The interpretations that she developed come from her theological insight and learning, however, not illness. That same insight also emerged in her music, which is what she is best known for today. Eighty of her compositions survive—a huge number for a medieval composer—most of them written to be sung by the nuns in her convent, so they have strong lines for female voices.

In one of her visions, Hildegard saw the metaphorical figure Synagogue as a very tall woman who holds in her arms Moses with the stone tablets of the Ten Commandments. (Reinisches Bildarchiv, Koln, RBA-13 328)

Questions for Analysis

1. Why do you think Hildegard might have kept her visions secret? Why do you think she sought church approval for them?

2. In what ways might Hildegard's vision of Synagogue have been shaped by her own experiences? How does this vision compare with other ideas about the Jews that you have read about in this chapter?

Section Review

- In the High Middle Ages, monasteries and convents became affiliated with certain religious orders, which set the pattern of life for the men and women who lived in these religious houses.

- Monasteries gained wealth through donations, which often led to a decline in spiritual ideals; this in turn led to reform movements that sought to return the monasteries to stricter standards of poverty and separation from society.

- Convents were home to many women and were led by an abbess or prioress, one of the few positions of power for women in this age.

- Daily life in a convent or monastery centered on prayers said seven times a day or more, and on performing social services such as running schools and hospitals and feeding the poor.

- Hildegard of Bingen, the nun believed to have mystical powers, wrote books and composed music, becoming a woman of influence with a large following.

century, for example, 110 persons were given food daily. In short, monasteries and convents performed a variety of social services in an age when there was no "state" and no conception of social welfare as a public responsibility.

The agricultural recession of the fourteenth century (see pages 278–280) forced the lay nobility to reduce their endowment of monasteries. This development, combined with internal mismanagement, compelled many houses to restrict the number of recruits so that they could live within their incomes. Since the nobility continued to send their children to monasteries, there was no shortage of applicants for the limited number of places. Widespread relaxation in the observance of the Benedictine Rule and the weakening of community life, however, meant that the atmosphere in many monasteries resembled that of a comfortable and secure rooming house rather than an austere religious establishment.

Chapter Review

What was life like for the rural common people of medieval Europe? (page 221)

Generalizations about peasant life in the High Middle Ages must always be qualified according to manorial customs, the weather and geography, and the personalities of local lords. Everywhere, however, the performance of agricultural services and the payment of rents preoccupied peasants, with men, women, and children all working the land. Though peasants led hard lives, the reclamation of wastelands and forestlands, migration to frontier territory, or manumission offered means of social mobility. The warmer climate of the High Middle Ages and technological improvements such as water mills and horse-drawn plows increased the available food supply, though the mainstay of the peasant diet was still coarse bread. Death in childbirth of both infant and mother was a common occurrence, though there were some improvements in health care through the opening of hospitals.

How did religious practices and attitudes permeate everyday life? (page 229)

Religion provided strong emotional and spiritual solace for the majority of Europeans who were Christians as well as for Muslims and Jews. Within Christianity, the village church was the center of community life, where people attended services, honored the saints, and experienced the sacraments. People also carried out rituals full of religious meaning in their daily lives, and every major life transition—childbirth, weddings, death—was marked by a ceremony that included religious elements. This was true for Muslims and Jews as well as Christians, but the centrality of Christian ceremonies for most people meant that Muslims and Jews were increasingly marked as outsiders, and Christian persecution of Jews increased in the late eleventh century.

How were the lives of nobles different from the lives of common people? (page 234)

Nobles were a tiny fraction of the total population, but they exerted great power over all aspects of life. Aristocratic values and attitudes, often described as chivalry, shaded

Key Terms

orders (p. 221)

nuclear family (p. 223)

open-field system (p. 224)

oblates (p. 229)

saints (p. 230)

purgatory (p. 234)

nobility (p. 234)

chivalry (p. 235)

tournament (p. 236)

joust (p. 236)

religious orders (p. 238)

abbess/prioress (p. 240)

abbot/prior (p. 240)

lay brothers/lay sisters (p. 241)

all aspects of medieval culture. By 1100 the knightly class was united in its ability to fight on horseback, its insistence that each member was descended from a valorous ancestor, its privileges, and its position at the top of the social hierarchy. Noble children were trained for their later roles in life, with boys trained for war and women for marriage and running estates. Noblemen often devoted considerable time to fighting, and intergenerational squabbles were common. Yet noblemen, and sometimes noblewomen, also had heavy judicial, political, and economic responsibilities.

What roles did the men and women affiliated with religious orders play in medieval society? (page 238)

Monks and nuns exercised a profound influence on medieval society. In their prayers, monks and nuns battled for the Lord, just as the chivalrous knights did on the battlefield. In their chants and rich ceremonials and in their architecture and literary productions, monasteries and convents inspired Christian peoples. In the tenth century, under the leadership of the Abbey of Cluny, many monasteries shook off the dominance of local lords and became independent institutions. Cluny's success led people to donate land and goods, and it became wealthier, leading those who sought a more rigorous life to found a new religious order, the Cistercians. Monks and nuns were generally members of the upper classes and spent much of their days in group prayer and other religious activities, while lay brothers and sisters worked the lands owned by the monastery. Monasteries were an important part of the economy of medieval Europe, though sometimes the inhabitants lived beyond their means, which was also true of nobles and people who lived in Europe's growing towns.

Notes

1. Honorius of Autun, "Elucidarium sive Dialogus de Summa Totius Christianae Theologiae," in *Patrologia Latina*, ed. J. P. Migne (Paris: Garnier Brothers, 1854), vol. 172, col. 1149.
2. S. R. Scargill Bird, ed., *Custumals of Battle Abbey in the Reigns of Edward I and Edward II* (London: Camden Society, 1887), pp. 238–239.
3. Honorius of Autun, "Elucidarium sive Dialogus," vol. 172, col. 1148.

To assess your mastery of this chapter, go to **bedfordstmartins.com/mckaywestbrief**

Listening to the Past

The Pilgrim's Guide to Santiago de Compostela

Making pilgrimages to the shrines of holy persons is a common practice in many religions. Christian shrines often contained a body understood to be that of a saint or objects that had been in physical contact with the saint; thus believers perceived shrines as places where Heaven and earth met. A visit to a shrine and veneration of the saint's relics, Christians believed, would lead to the saint's intercession with God. After Jerusalem and Rome, the shrine of Saint James (Sant'Iago in Spanish) at Compostela in the Iberian peninsula became the most famous in the Christian world. Saint James was one of the twelve apostles and was said to have carried Christianity to Spain. Santiago de Compostela was situated in the kingdom of Galicia, close to the west coast of Spain.

In the twelfth century an unknown French author put together a sort of guidebook for the streams of pilgrims who travelled to Santiago from all over Europe. This excerpt from the Pilgrim's Guide details the characteristics of people one would meet on the way.

Pilgrims' badge from Santiago de Compostela. Enterprising smiths began making metal badges for pilgrims to buy as proof of their journey and evidence of their piety. The scallop shell became particularly associated with St. James and eventually with pilgrimages in general. Pilgrims who had visited many shrines would clink from the badges worn on their hats or capes, sometimes becoming objects of satire just as tourists laden with souvenirs are today. (Institut Amatller d'Art Hispanic)

After this valley is found the land of Navarre [nuh-VAHR], which abounds in bread and wine, milk and cattle. The Navarrese and Basques [baskz] are held to be exactly alike in their food, their clothing and their language, but the Basques are held to be of whiter complexion than the Navarrese. The Navarrese wear short black garments extending just down to the knee, like the Scots, and they wear sandals which they call *lavarcas* made of raw hide with the hair on and are bound around the foot with thongs, covering only the soles of the feet and leaving the upper foot bare. In truth, they wear black woollen hooded and fringed capes, reaching to their elbows, which they call *saias*. These people, in truth, are repulsively dressed, and they eat and drink repulsively. For in fact all those who dwell in the household of a Navarrese, servant as well as master, maid as well as mistress, are accustomed to eat all

Pilgrims' routes: monasteries in Cluny, Vézelay (vay-zuh-LAY), Saint-Gilles, and Moissac served as inns for pilgrims.

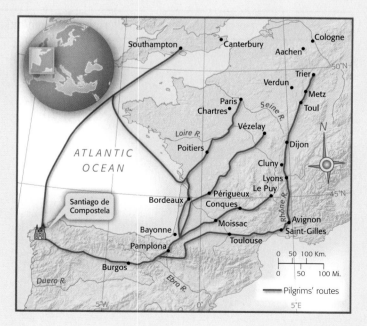

their food mixed together from one pot, not with spoons but with their own hands, and they drink with one cup. If you saw them eat you would think them dogs or pigs. If you heard them speak, you would be reminded of the barking of dogs. For their speech is utterly barbarous. . . .

This is a barbarous race unlike all other races in customs and in character, full of malice, swarthy in color, evil of face, depraved, perverse, perfidious, empty of faith and corrupt, libidinous, drunken, experienced in all violence, ferocious and wild, dishonest and reprobate, impious and harsh, cruel and contentious, unversed in anything good, well-trained in all vices and iniquities, like the Geats and Saracens in malice. . . .

However, they are considered good on the battlefield, bad at assaulting fortresses, regular in giving tithes, accustomed to making offerings for altars. For, each day, when the Navarrese goes to church, he makes God an offering of bread or wine or wheat or some other substance. . . .

Then comes Galicia [guh-LISH-ee-uh] . . . this is wooded and has rivers and is well-provided with meadows and excellent orchards, with equally good fruits and very clear springs; there are few cities, towns or cornfields. It is short of wheaten bread and wine, bountiful in rye bread and cider, well-stocked with cattle and horses, milk and honey, ocean fish both gigantic and small, and wealthy in gold, silver, fabrics, and furs of forest animals and other riches, as well as Saracen treasures. The Galicians, in truth, more than all the other uncultivated Spanish peoples, are those who most closely resemble our French race by their manners, but they are alleged to be irascible and very litigious. . . .

Questions for Analysis

1. How would you evaluate the author's opinion of the people of Navarre? of Galicia? How do these people compare with his own countrymen, the French?

2. Pilgrimages were in many ways the precursors of modern tourism. How would you compare the two in terms of economic effects and the expectations of the travelers?

Sources: From *The Pilgrim's Guide to Santiago de Compostela*, critical edition and annotated translation by Paula Gerson, Jeanne Krochalis, Annie Shaver-Crandell, and Alison Stones. Reprinted by permission of the authors. Data for map from Jonathan Sumption, *Pilgrimage: An Image of Medieval Religion* (Totowa, N.J.: Rowman and Littlefield, 1975).

CHAPTER 11

The Creativity and Challenges of Medieval Cities

Chapter Preview

Towns and Economic Revival
How did medieval cities originate, and what impact did they have on the economy and on culture?

Medieval Universities
How did universities evolve, and what needs of medieval society did they serve?

Arts and Architecture
How did the arts and architecture express the ideals, attitudes, and interests of medieval people?

Cities and the Church
Why did towns become the center of religious heresy, and what was the church's response?

INDIVIDUALS IN SOCIETY: Francesco Datini

IMAGES IN SOCIETY: From Romanesque to Gothic

LISTENING TO THE PAST: Courtly Love

This manuscript illumination shows a street scene of a medieval town, with a barber, cloth merchants, and an apothecary all offering their wares and services on the ground floor of their household-workshops. (Snark/Art Resource, NY)

The High Middle Ages witnessed some of the most remarkable achievements in the entire history of Western society. Europeans displayed tremendous creativity and vitality in many facets of culture. Relative security and an increasing food supply allowed for the growth and development of towns and a revival of long-distance trade. The university, a new—and very long-lasting—type of educational institution came into being, providing advanced training in theology, medicine, and law. Traditions and values were spread orally through stories and songs, some of which were written down as part of the development of vernacular literature. Gothic cathedrals manifested medieval people's deep Christian faith and their pride in their own cities, though the cities were also home to heretical movements that challenged church power.

Towns and Economic Revival

How did medieval cities originate, and what impact did they have on the economy and on culture?

The rise of towns and the growth of a new business and commercial class was a central part of Europe's recovery after the disorders of the tenth century. The growth of towns was made possible by some of the changes we have already traced: a rise in population; increased agricultural output, which provided an adequate food supply for new town dwellers; and a minimum of peace and political stability, which allowed merchants to transport and sell goods. The development of towns was to lay the foundations for Europe's transformation, centuries later, from a rural agricultural society into an urban industrial society—a change with global implications. In their backgrounds and abilities, townspeople represented diversity and change. Their occupations and their preoccupations were different from those of the feudal nobility and the laboring peasantry.

The Rise of Towns

Early medieval society was agricultural and rural. The emergence of a new class that was neither of these constituted a social revolution. Most of the members of the new class—artisans and merchants—came from the peasantry. The landless younger sons of large families were driven away by land shortage. Some were forced by war and famine to seek new possibilities. As in central Europe and Spain after the reconquista (see page 201), others were immigrants colonizing newly conquered lands. And some were unusually enterprising and adventurous, curious, and willing to take a chance.

Medieval towns began in many different ways. Some were fortifications erected during the ninth-century Viking invasions. Such towns were at first places of defense into which farmers from the surrounding countryside moved when their area was attacked. Later, merchants were attracted to the fortifications because they had something to sell and wanted to be where the customers were. They settled just outside the walls, in the *faubourgs* (foh-BOORS) or *suburbs*—both of which mean "outside" or "in the shelter of the walls." Other towns grew up around great cathedrals and monasteries whose schools drew students—potential customers—from far and wide. Many other towns grew from the sites of earlier Roman army camps. The restoration of order and political stability promoted rebirth and new development in these locations.

Carcassonne (kar-ka-SAWN**)**
This town in Languedoc (southern France) originated in pre-Roman times. Its thick double walls are an excellent example of the fortified medieval town. (Guido Alberto Rossi/TIPS Images)

Whether evolving from a newly fortified place or an old Roman army camp, from a cathedral site, a river junction, or a place where several overland routes met, medieval towns had a few common characteristics. Walls enclosed the town. (The terms *burgher* (BUR-ger) and *bourgeois* derive from the Old English and Old German words *burg, burgh, borg,* and *borough* for "a walled or fortified place." Thus a burgher or bourgeois was originally a person who lived or worked inside the walls.) The town had a marketplace. It often had a mint for the coining of money and a court to settle disputes.

As population increased, towns rebuilt their walls, expanding the living space to accommodate growing numbers. Through an archaeological investigation of the amount of land gradually enclosed by walls, historians have extrapolated rough estimates of medieval towns' populations. For example, the walled area of the German city of Cologne equaled 100 hectares in the tenth century (1 hectare = 2.471 acres), about 320 hectares in the twelfth, and 397 hectares in the fourteenth century. In the late twelfth century Cologne's population was at least 32,000; in the mid-fourteenth century it was perhaps 40,000. The concentration of the textile industry in the Low Countries brought into being the most populous cluster of cities in western Europe: Ghent, Bruges, Tournai, and Brussels. Venice, Florence, and Paris, each with about 110,000 people, and Milan with possibly 200,000, led all Europe in population.

Town Liberties and Merchant Guilds

The history of towns in the eleventh through thirteenth centuries consists largely of merchants' efforts to acquire liberties. In the Middle Ages *liberties* meant special privileges. **Town liberties** included the privilege of living and trading on the lord's land. The most important privilege a medieval townsperson could gain was

town liberties Privileges that included living and trading on the lord's land and, most importantly, personal freedom.

personal freedom. It gradually developed that an individual who lived in a town for a year and a day, and was accepted by the townspeople, was free of servile obligations and status. More than anything else, perhaps, the freedom that came with residence in a town contributed to the emancipation of the serfs in the High Middle Ages. Merchants joined together to form a **merchant guild** that prohibited nonmembers from trading in the town, and they often made up the earliest town government, serving as mayors and members of the city council, so that a town's economic policies were determined by its merchants' self-interest.

By the late eleventh century, especially in the towns of the Low Countries and northern Italy, the leaders of the merchant guilds were rich and powerful. They constituted an oligarchy in their towns, controlling economic life and bargaining with kings and lords for political independence. Full rights of self-government included the right to hold a town court that alone could judge members of the town, the right to select the mayor and other municipal officials, and the right to tax residents.

A charter that King Henry II of England granted to the merchants of Lincoln around 1157 nicely illustrates the town's rights. The quoted passages clearly suggest that the merchant guild had been the governing body in the city for almost a century and that anyone who lived in Lincoln for a year and a day was considered free:

> *Henry, by the grace of God, etc. . . . Know that I have granted to my citizens of Lincoln all their liberties and customs and laws which they had in the time of Edward [King Edward the Confessor] and William and Henry, kings of England. And I have granted them their gild-merchant, comprising men of the city and other merchants of the shire, as well and freely as they had it in the time of our aforesaid predecessors. . . . And all the men who live within the four divisions of the city and attend the market, shall stand in relation to gelds [taxes] and customs and the assizes [ordinances or laws] of the city as well as ever they stood in the time of Edward, William and Henry, kings of England. I also confirm to them that if anyone has lived in Lincoln for a year and a day without dispute from any claimant, and has paid the city taxes, and if the citizens can show by the laws and customs of the city that the claimant has remained in England during that period and has made no claim, then let the defendant remain in peace in my city of Lincoln as my citizen, without [having to defend his] right.[1]*

Feudal lords were reluctant to grant towns self-government, fearing loss of authority and revenue if they gave the merchant guilds full independence. When burghers bargained for a town's political independence, however, they offered sizable amounts of ready cash and sometimes promised payments for years to come. Consequently, feudal lords ultimately agreed to the burghers' requests.

Craft Guilds

While most towns were initially established as trading centers, they quickly became centers of production as well. Peasants left their villages—either with their lord's approval or without it—and moved to towns, providing both workers and customers. Some of them began to specialize in certain types of food and clothing production; others purchased and butchered cattle to sell meat and leather; others

CHRONOLOGY

1100–1200	Merchant guilds founded in many cities
1143	Founding of Lübeck, first city in the Hanseatic League
1180–1270	Height of construction of cathedrals in France
1200–1300	Craft guilds founded in many cities
ca. 1200	Founding of first universities
1216	Papal recognition of Dominican order
1221	Papal recognition of Franciscan order
1225–1274	Life of Thomas Aquinas; *Summa Theologica*
1233	Papacy creates new ecclesiastical court, the Inquisition
1302	Pope Boniface VIII declares all Christians subject to the pope in *Unam Sanctam*

merchant guild A band of merchants prohibiting nonmembers from trading in the town, and often serving as the earliest town government.

made metal arms, armor, and tableware. Wealthy merchants then bought these products for their own use, or they exported the finished products to other areas; certain cities became known for their fine fabrics, their reliable arms and armor, or their elegant gold and silver work.

Like merchants, producers recognized that organizing would bring benefits, and beginning in the twelfth century in many cities they developed **craft guilds.** These guilds set quality standards for their particular product, and they regulated the size of workshops, the training period, and the conduct of members. In most cities individual guilds, such as those of shoemakers or blacksmiths, achieved a monopoly in the production of one particular product, forbidding nonmembers to work. The craft guild then chose some of its members to act as inspectors and set up a court to hear disputes between members, though the city court remained the final arbiter.

Each guild set the pattern by which members were trained. A person who wanted to become a shoemaker, for instance, spent four to seven years as an apprentice, then at least that long as a journeyman, working in the shop of a master dyer, after which the person could theoretically make a "masterpiece." If the masterpiece—in the case of a shoemaker, of course, the masterpiece was a pair of shoes—was approved by the other master shoemakers and if they thought the market in their town was large enough to support another shoemaker, the person could then become a master and start a shop. Though the time required as an apprentice and as a journeyman varied slightly from guild to guild, all guilds fol-

craft guild A band of producers that regulated most aspects of production.

Spanish Apothecary

Town life meant variety—of peoples and products. Within the town walls, a Spanish pharmacist, seated outside his shop, describes the merits of his goods to a crowd of Christians and Muslims. (From the Cantigas of Alfonso X, ca. 1283. El Escorial/Laurie Platt Winfrey, Inc.)

lowed this same three-stage process. Guilds limited the amount of raw materials each master could have and the size of the workshop, thus assuring each master that his household-workshop would be able to support itself.

Many guilds required that masters be married, as they recognized the vital role of the master's wife. She assisted in running the shop, often selling the goods her husband had produced. Their children, both male and female, also worked alongside the apprentices and journeymen. The sons were sometimes formally apprenticed, but the daughters were generally not because many guilds limited formal membership to males. Most guilds did allow a master's widow to continue operating a shop for a set period of time after her husband's death, for they recognized that she had the necessary skills and experience. Such widows paid all guild dues, but they were not considered full members and could not vote or hold office in the guilds. The fact that women were not formally guild members did not mean that they did not work in guild shops, however, for alongside the master's wife and daughters female domestic servants often performed the lesser-skilled tasks. In addition, there were a few all-female guilds in several European cities, particularly in Cologne and Paris, in which girls were formally apprenticed in the same way boys were in regular craft guilds.

Both craft and merchant guilds provided their members with protection and social support. They took care of elderly masters who could no longer work, and they often supported masters' widows and orphans. They maintained an altar at a city church and provided for the funerals of members and baptisms of their children. Guild members marched together in city parades and reinforced their feelings of solidarity with one another by special ceremonies and distinctive dress.

City Life

Most streets in a medieval town were marketplaces as much as passages for transit. At the main marketplace just inside the city gates, poor people selling soap, candles, wooden dishes, and similar cheap products stood next to farmers from the surrounding countryside with eggs, chickens, or vegetables, people selling firewood or mushrooms they had gathered, and pawnbrokers selling used clothing and household goods. Because there was no way to preserve food easily, people—usually female family members or servants—had to shop every day, and the market was where they met their neighbors, exchanged information, and talked over recent events.

In some respects the entire city was a marketplace. A window or door in a craftsman's home opened onto the street and displayed the finished product made within to attract passersby. The family lived above the business on the second or third floor. As the business and the family expanded, additional stories were added.

Second and third stories were built jutting out over the ground floor and thus over the street. Since the streets were narrow to begin with, houses lacked fresh air and light. Initially, houses were made of wood and thatched with straw. Fire was a constant danger; because houses were built so close to one another, fires spread rapidly. Municipal governments consequently urged construction in stone or brick.

Most medieval cities developed with little town planning. As the population increased, space became more and more limited. Air and water pollution presented serious problems. Many families raised pigs for household consumption in sties next to the house. Horses and oxen, the chief means of transportation and power, dropped tons of dung on the streets every year. It was universal practice in the early towns to dump household waste, both animal and human, into the road in front of one's house. The stench must have been abominable.

livery Dress of distinctive colors worn by military men and servants who lived in noble households.

sumptuary laws Laws that regulated the value and style of clothing that various social groups could wear, and the amount they could spend on family celebrations.

People of all sorts, from beggars to fabulously wealthy merchants, regularly rubbed shoulders in the narrow streets and alleys of crowded medieval cities. This interaction did not mean that people were unaware of social differences, however, for clothing was a clear marker of social standing and sometimes of occupation. Monks, nuns, and friars wore black, white, or grey woolen clothing that marked them as members of a particular religious order, while priests and bishops wore layers of specialized clothing, especially when they were officiating at religious services. Military men and servants who lived in noble households wore dress with distinctive colors known as **livery** (LIV-uh-ree). Wealthier urban residents wore bright colors, imported silk or fine woolen fabrics, and fancy headgear, while poorer ones wore darker clothing made of rough linen or linen and wool blends. When universities developed in European cities, students wore clothing and headgear that marked their status. University graduates—lawyers, physicians, and university professors—often wore dark robes, trimmed with fur if they could afford it; the robes worn in contemporary academic ceremonies are descended from this medieval dress.

In the later Middle Ages many cities attempted to make clothing distinctions a matter of law as well as of habit. They passed **sumptuary laws** that regulated the value of clothing and jewelry that people of different social groups could wear. Only members of high social groups could wear velvet, satin, pearls, or fur, for example, or have clothing embroidered with gold thread or dyed in colors that were especially expensive to produce, such as the purple dye that came from mollusk shells. Along with enforcing social differences, sumptuary laws also attempted to impose moral standards by prohibiting plunging necklines on women or doublets that were too short on men and to protect local industries by restricting the use of imported fabrics or other materials. Some of these laws marked certain individuals as members of groups not fully acceptable in urban society—prostitutes might be required to wear red or yellow bands on their clothes that were supposed to represent the flames of hell, and Jews to wear yellow circles or stars to distinguish them from their Christian neighbors. (Many Jewish communities also developed their own sumptuary laws prohibiting extravagant or ostentatious dress.) In some cities, sumptuary laws were expanded to include restrictions on expenditures for parties and family celebrations, again set by social class. Weddings for members of the nobility or the urban elite could include imported wine, fancy food, musicians, and hundreds of guests, while those for the children of artisans could serve only local beer to several dozen guests.

Servants and the Poor

Many urban households hired domestic servants, with a less wealthy household employing one woman who assisted in all aspects of running the household and a wealthier one employing a large staff of male and female servants with specific duties. In Italian cities, household servants included slaves, usually young women brought in from areas outside of western Christianity, such as the Balkans. (Like Islam, Christianity favored slaves who were not believers.)

Along with permanent servants, many households hired additional workers to do specific tasks—laundering clothing and household linens, caring for children or invalids, repairing houses and walls, and carrying messages or packages around the city or the surrounding countryside. In contrast to rural peasants, who raised most of their own food, urban workers bought all their food, so they felt any increase in the price of ale or bread immediately. Their wages were generally low, and children from such families sought work at very young ages.

In cities with extensive cloth production, such as Florence or the towns of Flanders, the urban poor included workers who were paid by the piece. If prices dipped, merchants simply did not pay workers, who were left with thread or unfinished cloth that they technically did not own, and who had no wages with which to buy food.

The possibilities for legitimate employment were often very limited, and illegal activities offered another way for people to support themselves. They stole merchandise from houses, wagons, and storage facilities, fencing it to local pawnbrokers or taking it to the next town to sell. They stole goods or money directly from people, cutting the strings of their bags or purses. They sold sex for money — what later came to be called prostitution — standing on street corners or moving into houses that by the fifteenth century became official city brothels (see page 298). They made and sold mixtures of herbs and drugs offering to heal all sorts of ailments, perhaps combining this with a puppet show, trained animals, magic tricks, or music to draw customers. Or they did all these things, and also worked as laundresses, day laborers, porters, peddlers, or street vendors when they could. Cities also drew in orphans, blind people, and the elderly, who resorted to begging for food and money.

The Revival of Long-Distance Trade

The growth of towns went hand in hand with a remarkable revival of trade as artisans and craftsmen manufactured goods for local and foreign consumption (see Map 11.1). Most trade centered in towns and was controlled by professional traders. Long-distance trade was risky and required large investments of capital. Shipwrecks were common. Pirates infested the sea-lanes, and robbers and thieves roamed virtually all of the land routes. Since the risks were so great, merchants preferred to share them. A group of people would thus pool their capital to finance an expedition to a distant place. When the ship or caravan returned and the goods brought back were sold, the investors would share the profits. If disaster struck the caravan, an investor's loss was limited to the amount of that individual's investment.

Which towns took the lead in medieval "international" trade? In the late eleventh century the Italian cities, especially Venice, led the West in trade in general and completely dominated trade with the East. Lombard and Tuscan merchants exchanged those goods at the town markets and regional fairs of France, Flanders, and England. (Fairs were periodic gatherings that attracted buyers, sellers, and goods from all over Europe.) The towns of Bruges (BROOGH), Ghent, and Ypres (EE-pruh) in Flanders were also leaders in long-distance trade, and built up a vast industry in the manufacture of cloth.

Two circumstances help explain the lead Venice and the Flemish towns gained in long-distance trade. Both enjoyed a high degree of peace and political stability. Geographical factors were equally, if not more, important. Venice was ideally located at the northwestern end of the Adriatic Sea, with easy access to the transalpine land routes as well as the Adriatic and Mediterranean sea-lanes. The markets of North Africa, Byzantium, and Russia and the great fairs of Ghent in Flanders and Champagne in France provided commercial opportunities that Venice quickly seized. The geographical situation of Flanders also offered unusual possibilities: just across the channel from England, Flanders had easy access to English wool. Indeed, Flanders and England developed a very close economic relationship.

Wool was the cornerstone of the English medieval economy. Population growth in the twelfth century and the success of the Flemish and Italian textile industries created foreign demand for English wool. The production of English

Legend

- Textile and manufacturing areas
- Northern sea routes
- Venetian sea routes
- Genoese sea routes
- Other sea routes
- Overland routes

Aral Sea

Caspian Sea

Black Sea

Sea of Azov

Mediterranean Sea

Aegean Sea

Adriatic Sea

Baltic Sea

North Sea

ATLANTIC OCEAN

Bay of Biscay

Ireland

Corsica

Sardinia

Sicily

Crete

Cyprus

Rhodes

Balearic Is.

N

Bergen — Fish, Pitch

Oslo

Stockholm — Copper

Reval — Furs

Riga — Flax

Königsberg — Flax

Danzig

Gotland

Novgorod — Flax, Hemp, Wax, Pitch

Moscow — Furs, Honey

Furs

Kiev — Slave market

Rostov

Saffa — Fish, Slaves

Trebizond — Slave market

Sinope — Fruits+foodstuffs

Sivas — Cotton, Carpets+rugs

Ankara — Opium

Smyrna — Fruits+foodstuffs

Constantinople — Slave market

Antioch — Fruits+foodstuffs

Tripoli — Iron, Glassware

Damascus — Precious woods

Beirut

Sidon

Tyre — Silk, Horses

Jerusalem

Cairo — Indigo, Cotton, Slave market, Cotton

Alexandria — Fish

Baghdad

Copenhagen — Grain

Lübeck — Fish

Hamburg — Flax, Hemp

Bremen — Hemp

Amsterdam — Fish

Warsaw — Tar

Kraków — Pitch, Silver

Breslau — Iron

Frankfurt — Hemp

Leipzig — Silver

Magdeburg — Salt

Prague — Silver

Nuremberg — Paper, Wheat, Copper

Augsburg — Salt

Vienna — Iron

Buda

Pest — Wheat, Skins+hides

Belgrade — Horses, Silver

Ragusa — Slaves

Taranto — Olives

Cologne — Wine

Strasbourg — Iron

Basel — Salt

Geneva — Mfd. wares

Milan — Mfd. wares

Venice — Glass

Bologna

Florence — Mfd. wares

Genoa

Pisa — Timber, Pitch

Rome — Wine

Naples — Cotton, Olives

Palermo — Olives, Wine

Messina — Wine

Syracuse — Olives

Paris — Paper

London — Wool, Iron

Bruges

Brussels

Calais — Iron, Wine, Wheat

Rouen — Flax

Orléans

Lyons — Mfd. wares, Wine

Avignon — Wine

Marseilles

Clermont — Wine

Limoges

Tours — Wine

Nantes — Fish, Salt

Rennes

Bordeaux — Wine

Bayonne — Iron

Toulouse — Wool

Barcelona — Fruits+foodstuffs

Valencia — Metalwares, Paper, Horses

Cartagena — Olives

Almeira

Granada — Olives

Córdoba — Copper, Olives

León — Leather

Toledo

Santiago — Fruits+foodstuffs

Lisbon — Wine

Cork — Cotton

Seville — Silk

Ceuta — Slave market

Algiers — Slave market, Olives

Tunis — Fish

Tripoli — Slave market

Edinburgh

Carlisle

Durham — Lead

York

Chester — Wool

Bristol — Tin, Iron, Lead

Southampton — Fish

Wool

Slaves

Gold

Horses

Olives

Wine

Raisins

Currants

Fish

Skins+hides

Wool

Gold

Slaves

Dates

200 Mi. 400 Km.

0 200 0 200

10°W 0° 10°E 20°E 30°E 40°E 50°E

MAPPING THE PAST

MAP 11.1 Trade and Manufacturing in Medieval Europe

The development of towns and the reinvigoration of trade were directly related in medieval Europe. Using both of the maps in this chapter and the information in your text, answer the following questions: **[1]** What part of Europe had the highest density of towns? Why? **[2]** Which towns were the largest and most important centers of long-distance trade (see p. 253)? **[3]** What role did textile and other sorts of manufacturing play in the growth of towns? **[4]** Does the development of towns seem more closely related to that of universities, monastery schools, or cathedral schools? Why?

wool stimulated Flemish manufacturing, and the expansion of the Flemish cloth industry in turn spurred the production of English wool. The availability of raw wool also encouraged the development of domestic cloth manufacture in England.

Business Procedures   The growth of a money economy made possible the steadily expanding volume of international trade in the High Middle Ages. Beginning in the 1160s the opening of new silver mines in Germany, Bohemia, northern Italy, northern France, and western England led to the minting and circulation of vast quantities of silver coins. Demand for sugar (to replace honey), pepper, cloves, and Asian spices to season a bland diet; for fine wines from the Rhineland, Burgundy, and Bordeaux; for luxury woolens from Flanders and Tuscany; for furs from Ireland and Russia; for brocades and tapestries from Flanders and silks from Constantinople and even China; for household furnishings such as silver plate—not to mention the desire for products associated with a military aristocracy such as swords and armor— surged markedly.

To meet the greater volume, the work of merchants became specialized. Three separate types of merchants emerged: the sedentary merchant who ran the "home office," financing and organizing the firm's entire export-import trade; the carriers who transported goods by land and sea; and the company agents living abroad who, on the advice of the home office, looked after sales and procurements.

Business procedures changed radically. Commercial correspondence proliferated and regular courier service among commercial cities began. Commercial accounting became more complex when firms had to deal with shareholders, manufacturers, customers, branch offices, employees, and competing firms. Tolls on roads became high enough to finance what has been called a "road revolution," involving new surfaces, bridges, new passes through the Alps, and new inns and hospices for travelers. The growth of mutual confidence among merchants facilitated the growth of sales on credit.

In all these transformations, merchants of the Italian cities led the way. (See the feature "Individuals in Society: Francesco Datini.") They formalized their agreements with new types of contracts, including permanent partnerships termed *compagnie* (kahm-pa-NYEE) (literally "bread together," that is, sharing bread, and the root of the English word *company*). Many of these compagnie began as agreements between brothers or other relatives and in-laws, but quickly grew to include people who were not family members. In addition, they began to involve individuals— including a few women—who invested only their money, leaving the actual running of the business to the active partners.

Individuals in Society

Francesco Datini

In 1348, when he was a young teenager, Francesco Datini (1335–1410) lost his father, his mother, a brother, and a sister to the Black Death epidemic that swept through Europe (see pages 280–285). Leaving his hometown of Prato in northern Italy, he apprenticed himself to merchants in nearby Florence for several years to learn accounting and other business skills. At fifteen, he moved to the city of Avignon (ah-vee-NYON) in southern France. The popes were living in Avignon instead of Rome, and the city offered many opportunities for an energetic and enterprising young man. Datini first became involved in the weapons trade, which offered steady profits, and then handled spices, wool and silk cloth, and jewels. He was very successful, and when he was thirty-one he married the young daughter of another merchant in an elaborate wedding that was the talk of Avignon.

Statue of Franceso Datini outside the city hall in Prato. (© Peter Horree/Alamy)

In 1378 the papacy returned to Italy, and Datini soon followed, setting up trading companies in Prato, Pisa, Florence, and eventually other cities as well. He focused on cloth and leather and sought to control the trade in products used for preparation as well, especially the rare dyes that created the brilliant colors favored by wealthy noblemen and townspeople. He eventually had offices all over Europe and became one of the richest men of his day, opening a mercantile bank and a company that produced cloth, as well as his many branch offices.

Datini was more successful than most, but what makes him particularly stand out was his record-keeping. He kept careful account books and ledgers, all of them headed by the phrase "in the name of God and profit." He wrote to the managers of each of his offices every week, providing them with careful advice and blunt criticism: "You cannot see a crow in a bowl of milk." Taking on the son of a friend as an employee, he wrote to the young man: "Do your duty well, and you will acquire honor and profit, and you can count on me as if I were your own father. But if you do not, then do not count on me; it will be as if I had never known you."

When Datini was away from home, which was often, he wrote to his wife every day, and she sometimes responded in ways that were less deferential than we might expect of a woman who was many years younger. "I think it is not necessary," she wrote at one point, "to send me a message every Wednesday to say that you will be here on Sunday, for it seems to me that on every Friday you change your mind."

Datini's obsessive record-keeping lasted beyond his death, for someone put all of his records—hundreds of ledgers and contracts, eleven thousand business letters, and over a hundred thousand personal letters—in sacks in his opulent house in Prato, where they were found in the nineteenth century. They provide a detailed picture of medieval business practices and also reveal much about Datini as a person. Ambitious, calculating, luxury-loving, and a workaholic, Datini seems similar to a modern CEO. Like many of today's self-made super-rich people, at the end of his life Datini began to think a bit more about God and less about profit. In his will, he set up a foundation for the poor in Prato and a home for orphans in Florence, both of which are still in operation. In 1967 scholars established an institute for economic history in Prato, naming it in Datini's honor; the institute now manages the collection of Datini documents and gathers other relevant materials in its archives.

Questions for Analysis

1. How would you evaluate Datini's motto: as an honest statement of his aims, a hypocritical justification of greed, a blend of both, or something else?
2. Changes in business procedures in the Middle Ages have been described as a "commercial revolution." Do Datini's activities support this assessment? Why?

Source: Iris Origo, *The Merchant of Prato: Francesco di Marco Datini*, 1335–1410 (New York: Alfred A. Knopf Inc., 1957).

The ventures of the German Hanseatic League also illustrate these new business procedures. The **Hanseatic** (han-see-AT-ĭk) **League** was a mercantile association of towns. Initially the towns of Lübeck and Hamburg wanted mutual security, exclusive trading rights, and, where possible, a monopoly. During the next century, perhaps two hundred cities from Holland to Poland joined the league, but Lübeck always remained the dominant member. From the thirteenth to the sixteenth centuries, the Hanseatic League controlled the trade of northern Europe (see Map 11.1). In the fourteenth century the Hanseatics branched out into southern Germany and Italy by land and into French, Spanish, and Portuguese ports by sea.

At cities such as Bruges and London, Hanseatic merchants secured special trading concessions exempting them from all tolls and allowing them to trade at local fairs. Hanseatic merchants established foreign trading centers, called "factories," the most famous of which was the London Steelyard, a walled community with warehouses, offices, a church, and residential quarters for company representatives. By the late thirteenth century Hanseatic merchants had developed an important business technique, the business register. Merchants publicly recorded their debts and contracts and received a league guarantee for them.

The dramatic increase in trade ran into two serious difficulties in medieval Europe. One was the problem of money. Despite investment in mining operations to increase the production of metals, the amount of gold, silver, and copper available for coins was simply not adequate for the increased flow of commerce. Merchants developed paper letters of exchange, in which coins or goods in one location were exchanged for a sealed letter (much like a modern deposit statement), which could be used in place of metal coinage elsewhere. This made the long, slow, and very dangerous shipment of coins unnecessary. Begun in the late twelfth century, the bill of exchange was the normal method of making commercial payments by the early fourteenth century among the cities of western Europe, and it proved to be a decisive factor in the later development of credit and commerce in northern Europe.

The second problem was a moral and theological one. Church doctrine frowned on lending money at interest, termed **usury** (YOO-zhuh-ree). This restriction on Christians is one reason why Jews were frequently the moneylenders in early medieval society; it was one of the few occupations not forbidden them by Christian authorities. As money lending became more important to commercial ventures, the church relaxed its position. It declared that some interest was legitimate as a payment for the risk the investor was taking, and that only interest above a certain level would be considered usury. (This definition of usury has continued; modern governments generally set limits on the rate legitimate businesses may charge for loaning money.) The church itself then got into the money-lending business, opening pawnshops in cities and declaring that the shops were benefiting the poor by charging a lower rate of interest than that available from secular moneylenders. In rural areas, Cistercian monasteries loaned money at interest.

The stigma attached to lending money was in many ways attached to all the activities of a medieval merchant. Medieval people were uneasy about a person making a profit merely from the investment of money rather than labor, skill, and time. Merchants themselves shared these ideas to some degree, so they gave generous donations to the church and to charities. They also took pains not to flaunt their wealth through flashy dress and homes. By the end of the Middle Ages, society had begun to accept the role of the merchant.

Hanseatic League A mercantile association of towns that allowed for mutual protection and security.

usury Lending money at interest.

commercial revolution The transformation of the European economy as a result of changes in business procedures and growth in trade.

mercantile capitalism Capitalism primarily involving trade rather than production.

The Commercial Revolution

Changes in business procedures, combined with the growth in trade, led to a transformation of the European economy, often called the **commercial revolution** by historians, who see it as the beginning of the modern capitalist economy. Though you may be most familiar with using *revolution* to describe a violent political rebellion such as the American Revolution or the French Revolution, the word is also used more broadly to describe economic and intellectual changes such as the Industrial Revolution and the scientific revolution. These do not necessarily involve violence and may last much longer than political revolutions. What makes them revolutions is the extent of their effects on society. In calling this transformation the "commercial revolution," historians point not only to an increase in the sheer volume of trade and in the complexity and sophistication of business procedures, but also to the new attitude toward business and making money. Some even detect a "capitalist spirit" in which making a profit is regarded as a good thing in itself, regardless of the uses to which that profit is put.

Part of this capitalist spirit was a new attitude toward time. Country people needed only approximate times—dawn, noon, sunset—for their work. Monasteries needed much more precise times to call monks together for the recitation of the Divine Office. In the early Middle Ages monks used a combination of hourglasses, sundials, and water-clocks to determine the time, and then rang bells by hand. About 1280 new types of mechanical mechanisms seem to have been devised in which weights replaced falling water and bells were rung automatically. Records begin to use the word *clock* (from the Latin word for bell) for these machines, which sometimes figured the movement of astronomical bodies as well as the hours. The merchants who ran city councils quickly saw clocks as both useful and a symbol of their prosperity. Beautiful and elaborate mechanical clocks, usually installed on the cathedral or town church, were in general use in Italy by the 1320s, in Germany by the 1330s, in England by the 1370s, and in France by the 1380s. Buying and selling goods had initiated city people into the practice of quantification, and clocks contributed to the development of a mentality that conceived of the universe in quantitative terms.

Capitalism in the Middle Ages primarily involved trade rather than production, so it is termed **mercantile capitalism.** In a few places, such as Florence, cloth production was organized along capitalist lines, with a cloth merchant owning the raw materials, the finished product, and sometimes the tools, and with workers paid simply for their labor. Most production in the Middle Ages was carried out by craft guilds or by people working on their own, however.

Mechanical Clock

Slowly falling weights provide the force that pushes the hand on the face of this large, twenty-four-hour clock. Accurate time was important to monks such as the one seated here, although this clock appears to be in a public place, not a monastery, a reflection of the increasing importance of time-keeping to many social groups. (Bibliothèque royale Albert 1er, Brussels)

The commercial revolution created a great deal of new wealth, which did not escape the attention of kings and other rulers. Wealth could be taxed, and through taxation kings could create strong and centralized states. In the years to come, alliances with the middle classes enabled kings to defeat feudal powers and aristocratic interests and to build the states that came to be called "modern." The commercial revolution also provided the opportunity for thousands of serfs to improve their social position. The slow but steady transformation of European society from almost completely rural and isolated to relatively more sophisticated constituted the greatest effect of the commercial revolution that began in the eleventh century.

Even so, merchants and business people did not run medieval communities other than in central and northern Italy and in the county of Flanders. Most towns remained small, and urban residents were never more than 10 percent of the population. The castle, the manorial village, and the monastery dominated the landscape. The feudal nobility and churchmen determined the preponderant social attitudes, values, and patterns of thought and behavior. The commercial changes of the eleventh through thirteenth centuries did, however, lay the economic foundations for the development of urban life and culture.

Section Review

- Merchant guilds were organized groups of merchants within a town, controlling the economic life and working to gain political independence for their town in order to have their own court, mayor, officials, and taxes.
- Craft guilds developed in each trade, allowing members to set quality standards, open shops, offer apprenticeships, and provide care and protection to members and their families.
- Towns built up with little planning, resulting in crowded, unsanitary conditions where all members of society intermingled, while laws regulated what clothes you could wear, depending on your social class, profession, or ethnic group.
- Wealthy households hired servants, and poor people were paid by the day for their labor, but since wages were low, they sometimes also engaged in theft, begging, and prostitution.
- Trade offered the possibility of great wealth, but it was risky, making merchants frequently vulnerable to robbers and pirates.
- The largest trade centers were in Venice and the Flemish towns, where merchants specialized and formed more formalized partnerships called companies.
- Increased trade spurred a commercial revolution and the beginnings of modern capitalism as merchants developed new business procedures, paper letters of exchange to substitute for metal coins, and a new attitude toward wealth and time.

Medieval Universities

How did universities evolve, and what needs of medieval society did they serve?

Just as the first strong secular states emerged in the thirteenth century, so did the first universities. This was no coincidence. The new bureaucratic states and the church needed educated administrators, and universities were a response to this need. The word *university* derives from the Latin *universitas* (oo-nee-VERS-ee-tas), meaning "corporation" or "guild." Medieval universities were educational guilds that produced educated and trained individuals, and they continue to influence institutionalized learning in the Western world.

Origins In the early Middle Ages, outside of the aristocratic court or the monastery, anyone who received an education got it from a priest. Priests taught the rudiments of reading and writing as well as the Latin words of the Mass. Few boys acquired elementary literacy, however, and peasant girls did not obtain even that. The peasant father who wished to send his son to school had to secure the permission of his lord. Because the lord stood to lose the services of educated peasants, he limited the number of serfs sent to school.

Since the time of the Carolingian Empire, monasteries and cathedral schools had offered most of the available formal instruction, which focused on the Scriptures and the writings of the church fathers. Monasteries were unwilling to accept

Legend:
- ◆ University
- ✝ Monastery school
- 🏰 Cathedral school

MAP 11.2 Intellectual Centers of Medieval Europe

Universities provided more sophisticated instruction than did monastery and cathedral schools. What other factors distinguished the three kinds of intellectual centers?

large numbers of noisy lay students. In contrast, schools attached to cathedrals and run by the bishop and his clergy were frequently situated in bustling cities, and in the eleventh century in Italian cities like Bologna (boe-LOAN-yuh), wealthy businessmen had established municipal schools. In the course of the twelfth century, cathedral schools in France and municipal schools in Italy developed into educational institutions that attracted students from a wide area (see Map 11.2). These schools were called *studium generale* ("general center of study") or *universitas magistrorum et scholarium* ("universal society of teachers and students"), the origin of the English word *university*. The first European universities appeared in Italy in Bologna and Salerno.

The growth of the University of Bologna coincided with a revival of interest in Roman law during the investiture controversy. The study of Roman law as embodied in the Justinian *Code* had never completely died out in the West, but in the late eleventh century a complete manuscript of the *Code* was discovered in a library in Pisa. This discovery led scholars in nearby Bologna, beginning with Irnerius (ca. 1055–ca. 1130) (er-NEHR-ee-us), to study and teach Roman law intently again. His fame attracted students from all over Europe. Irnerius not only explained the Roman law of the Justinian *Code*, but he also applied it to difficult practical situations.

At Salerno in southern Italy interest in medicine had persisted for centuries. Medical practitioners—mostly men, but apparently also a few women—received training first through apprenticeship and then in an organized medical school. Individuals associated with Salerno, such as Constantine the African (fl. 1065–1085)—who was a convert from Islam and later a Benedictine monk—began to translate medical works out of Arabic. These translations included writings by the ancient Greek physicians and Muslim medical writers. Students of medicine poured into Salerno and soon attracted royal attention. In 1140, when King Roger II of Sicily took the practice of medicine under royal control, his ordinance stated:

> Who, from now on, wishes to practice medicine, has to present himself before our officials and examiners, in order to pass their judgment. Should he be bold enough to disregard this, he will be punished by imprisonment and confiscation of his entire property. In this way we are taking care that our subjects are not endangered by the inexperience of the physicians.[2]

In the first decades of the twelfth century, students converged on Paris. They crowded into the cathedral school of Notre Dame (noh-truh DAHM) and spilled over into the area later called the "Latin Quarter"—whose name reflects either the Italian origin of many of the students attracted to Paris by the surge of interest in the classics, logic, and theology, or the Latin language spoken in the area. The cathedral school's international reputation drew scholars from all over Europe to Paris.

Abelard and Heloise

One of the young men drawn to Paris was Peter Abelard (AB-uh-lahrd) (1079–1142), the son of a minor Breton knight. He was fascinated by logic, which he believed could be used to solve most problems. He had a brilliant mind and, though orthodox in his philosophical teaching, appeared to challenge ecclesiastical authorities. His book *Sic et Non* (seek et nohn) (Yes and No) was a list of apparently contradictory propositions drawn from the Bible and the writings of the church fathers. One such proposition, for example, stated that sin is pleasing to God and is not pleasing to God. Abelard used a method of systematic doubting in his writing and teaching. As he put it in the preface to *Sic et Non*, "By doubting we come to questioning, and by questioning we perceive the truth." While other scholars merely asserted theological principles, Abelard discussed and analyzed them. Through reasoning he even tried to describe the attributes of the three persons of the Trinity, the central mystery of the Christian faith. Abelard was severely censured by a church council, but his cleverness, boldness, and imagination made him a highly popular figure among students.

In a supposedly autobiographical statement, *A History of My Calamities*, Abelard described his academic career and his private life. He was hired by one of the

Law Lecture at Bologna
This beautifully carved marble sculpture, with the fluid drapery characteristic of late Gothic style, suggests the students' intellectual intensity. Medieval students often varied widely in age; here some have moustaches and some look like adolescents. (Museo Civico, Bologna/Scala/Art Resource, NY)

cathedral priests, Fulbert, to tutor his clever niece Heloise. The relationship between teacher and pupil passed beyond the intellectual. She became pregnant, and Fulbert pressured the couple to marry. Abelard insisted that the union be kept secret for the sake of his career, an arrangement Heloise much resented. Distrusting Abelard, Fulbert hired men to castrate him. Wounded in spirit as well as body, Abelard persuaded Heloise to enter a convent. He entered a monastery, and their baby, baptized Astrolabe (**AS-truh-layb**) for a recent Muslim navigational invention, was adopted by her family. The lovers were later buried together in a cemetery in Paris. Some scholars consider *A History of My Calamities* the most famous autobiography of the twelfth century, a fine example of the new self-awareness of the period's rebirth of learning. Other scholars believe the entire *History* a forgery, the source of a romantic legend with no basis in historical fact.[3]

Instruction and Curriculum

The influx of students eager for learning, together with dedicated and imaginative teachers, created the atmosphere in which universities grew. In northern Europe—at Paris and later at Oxford and Cambridge in England—associations or guilds of professors organized universities. They established the curriculum, set the length of time for study, and determined the form and content of examinations. By the end of the fifteenth century there were at least eighty universities in Europe. Some universities also offered younger students training in the liberal arts that could serve as a foundation for more specialized study in all areas.

Universities were all-male communities. The few women trained at Salerno during its early years of development were the last women in Europe to receive formal university training in any subject until the nineteenth century, although a handful of professor's daughters in one or two places were reputed to have listened to lectures from behind a curtain. (Most European universities did not admit or grant degrees to women until after World War I.) Though university classes were not especially expensive, the many years that university required meant that the sons of peasants or artisans could rarely attend, unless they could find wealthy patrons who would pay their expenses while they studied. Most students were the sons of urban merchants or lower-level nobles, especially the younger sons who would not inherit family lands.

University faculties grouped themselves according to academic disciplines—law, medicine, arts, and theology. The professors (a term first used in the fourteenth century) were known as "schoolmen" or **Scholastics.** They developed a method of thinking, reasoning, and writing in which questions were raised and authorities cited on both sides of the question. The goal of the Scholastic method was to arrive at definitive answers and to provide a rational explanation for what was believed on faith. Schoolmen held that reason and faith constituted two harmonious realms whose truths complemented each other.

Scholastics University professors who developed a method of thinking, reasoning, and writing in which questions were raised and authorities cited on both sides of the question.

The Scholastic approach rested on the recovery of classical philosophical texts. Ancient Greek and Arabic texts had entered Europe in the early twelfth century. Knowledge of Aristotle and other Greek philosophers came to Paris and Oxford by way of Islamic intellectual centers at Baghdad, Córdoba, and Toledo. These texts, which formed the basis of Western philosophical and theological speculation, were not the only Islamic gifts. The major contribution of Arabic culture to the new currents of Western thought rested in the stimulus Arabic philosophers and commentators gave to Europeans' reflection on the Greek texts. Aristotle had stressed the importance of the direct observation of nature, as well as the principles that theory must follow fact and that knowledge of a thing requires an explanation of its causes. The schoolmen reinterpreted Aristotelian texts in a Christian sense. But in their exploration of the natural world, they did not precisely follow Aristotle's axioms. Medieval scientists argued from authority, such as the Bible, the Justinian *Code*, or an ancient scientific treatise, rather than from direct observation and experimentation as modern scientists do. Thus the conclusions of medieval scientists were often wrong. Nevertheless, natural science gradually emerged as a discipline distinct from philosophy, and Scholastics laid the foundations for later scientific work.

At all universities the standard method of teaching was the *lecture*—that is, a reading. The syllabus consisted of a core of ancient texts. The professor read a passage from the Bible, the Justinian *Code*, or one of Aristotle's treatises. He then explained and interpreted the passage; his interpretation was called a *gloss*. Texts and glosses were sometimes collected and reproduced as textbooks. For example, the Italian Peter Lombard (d. 1160), a professor at Paris, wrote what became the standard textbook in theology, *Sententiae* (sen-TEN-shee-uh) (The Sentences), a compilation of basic theological principles.

Examinations were given after three, four, or five years of study, when the student applied for a degree. The professors determined the amount of material students had to know for each degree, and students frequently insisted that the professors specify precisely what that material was. Examinations were oral and very difficult. If the candidate passed, he was awarded a license to teach, which was the earliest form of academic degree. Initially these licenses granted the title of *master* or *doctor*, still in use today and both derived from Latin words meaning "teach." Bachelor's degrees came later. Most students, however, did not become teachers. They staffed the expanding diocesan, royal, and papal administrations.

Jewish scholars as well as Christian ones produced elaborate commentaries on law and religious tradition. Medieval universities were closed to Jews, but in some cities in the eleventh century special rabbinic academies opened that concentrated particularly on the study of the Talmud, a compilation of legal arguments, proverbs, sayings, and folklore that had been produced in the fifth century in Babylon (present-day Iraq). The Talmud was written in Aramaic, so that simply learning to read it required years of study, and medieval scholars began to produce commentaries on the Talmud to help facilitate this. The most famous of these was that of Rabbi Solomon bar Isaac, known as Rashi (1040–1105), who lived in Troyes, a city in France. Men seeking to become rabbis—highly respected figures within the Jewish community with authority over economic and social as well as religious matters—spent long periods of time studying the Talmud, which served as the basis for their legal decisions in all areas of life.

Thomas Aquinas and the Teaching of Theology

Thirteenth-century Scholastics devoted an enormous amount of time to collecting and organizing knowledge on all topics. These collections were published as **summa** (SOOM-uh), or reference books. There were summa on law, philosophy, vegetation, animal life, and theology. Saint Thomas Aquinas (1225–1274), a professor at Paris, produced the most famous collection, the *Summa Theologica*, which deals with a vast number of theological questions.

Aquinas drew an important distinction between faith and reason. He maintained that, although reason can demonstrate many basic Christian principles such as the existence of God, other fundamental teachings such as the Trinity and original sin cannot be proved by logic. That reason cannot establish them does not, however, mean they are contrary to reason. Rather, people understand such doctrines through revelation embodied in Scripture. Scripture cannot contradict reason, nor reason Scripture:

> *The light of faith that is freely infused into us does not destroy the light of natural knowledge [reason] implanted in us naturally. For although the natural light of the human mind is insufficient to show us these things made manifest by faith, it is nevertheless impossible that these things which the divine principle gives us by faith are contrary to these implanted in us by nature [reason]. Indeed, were that the case, one or the other would have to be false, and, since both are given to us by God, God would have to be the author of untruth, which is impossible. . . . [I]t is impossible that those things which are of philosophy can be contrary to those things which are of faith.*[4]

Aquinas also investigated the branch of philosophy called *epistemology* (ee-pis-tuh-MOL-uh-jee), which is concerned with how a person knows something. Aquinas stated that one knows, first, through sensory perception of the physical world—seeing, hearing, touching, and so on. He maintained that there can be nothing in the mind that is not first in the senses. Second, knowledge comes through reason, the mind exercising its natural abilities. Aquinas stressed the power of human reason to know, even to know God. His five proofs for God's existence exemplify the Scholastic method of knowing. His work later became the fundamental text of Roman Catholic doctrine.

---

summa Reference books created by Scholastics on the topics of law, philosophy, vegetation, animal life, and theology.

Section Review

- Universities became the primary centers of advanced learning, providing educated administrators for church and state.

- Peter Abelard was a brilliant scholar whose writings on logic fascinated students though they displeased the church; his autobiography describing his love affair with equally brilliant Heloise was widely read.

- Universities were all-male and grouped by disciplines such as law, medicine, the arts, and theology, each having their own distinct curriculum; upon graduation, students earned a license to teach. The scholastic method of teaching posed questions and then discussed both sides of the issue to provide a rational answer, combining lectures with readings, many of which became textbooks.

- Saint Thomas Aquinas was a professor whose works dealt with theological questions depicting the difference between faith and reason.

Arts and Architecture

How did the arts and architecture express the ideals, attitudes, and interests of medieval people?

The High Middle Ages saw the creation of new types of literature, architecture, and music. Technological advances in such areas as papermaking and stone masonry made innovations possible, but so did the growing wealth and sophistication of patrons. Artists and artisans flourished in the more secure environment of the High Middle Ages, producing works that celebrated the glories of love, war, and God.

Vernacular Literature and Entertainment

Latin was the language used in university education, scholarly writing, and works of literature; in short, it was the language of high culture. In contrast to Roman times, however, by the High Middle Ages no one spoke Latin as his or her original mother tongue. The barbarian invasions, the mixture of peoples, and evolution over time had resulted in a variety of local **dialects** that blended words and linguistic forms in various ways. These dialects were specific to one region, and as kings increased the size of their holdings they often ruled people who spoke many different dialects. In the early Middle Ages almost all written works continued to be in Latin, but in the High Middle Ages some authors began to write in their local dialect, that is, in the everyday language of their region, which linguistic historians call the vernacular. This new **vernacular literature** gradually transformed some local dialects into literary languages, such as French, German, Italian, and English, while other dialects remained (and remain to this day) simply means of oral communication. Most people in the High Middle Ages could no more read vernacular literature than they could read Latin, however, so oral transmission continued to be the most important way information was conveyed and traditions passed down.

By the thirteenth century, however, techniques of making paper from old linen cloth and rags began to spread from Spain, where they had been developed by the Arabs, providing a much cheaper material on which to write. People started to write down things that were more mundane and less serious—personal letters, lists, poems, songs, recipes, rules, instructions—in various vernacular dialects, using spellings that were often personal and idiosyncratic. The writings included fables, legends, stories, and myths that had circulated orally for generations, and slowly a body of written vernacular literature developed. Stories and songs in the vernacular were performed and composed at the courts of nobles and rulers. In Germany and most of northern Europe, they favored stories and songs recounting the great deeds of warrior heroes, such as the knight Roland who fought against the Muslims and Hildebrand who fought the Huns. These epics, known as *chansons de geste* (SHAN-suhn duh jest) ("songs of great deeds"), celebrate violence, slaughter, revenge, and physical power. In southern Europe, especially in the area of southern France known as Provence, poets who called themselves **troubadours** (TROO-bah-door) wrote and sang lyric verses celebrating love, desire, beauty, and gallantry. (See the feature "Listening to the Past: Courtly Love" on pages 275–276.) A troubadour was a poet who wrote lyric verse in Provençal (proh-vuhn-SAHL), the regional spoken language of southern France, and sang it at one of the noble courts. Troubadours included a few women, called *trobairitz*, most of whose exact identities are not known.

dialect A regional variety of a language, with differences in vocabulary, grammar, and pronunciation.

vernacular literature Writings in the author's local dialect, that is, in the everyday language of the region.

troubadours Poets who wrote and sang lyric verses celebrating love, desire, beauty, and gallantry.

Eleanor of Aquitaine may have taken troubadour poetry from France to England when she married Henry II. Since the songs of the troubadours were widely imitated in Italy, England, and Germany, they spurred the development of vernacular literature there as well. The romantic motifs of the troubadours also influenced the northern French *trouvères* (troo-VAIR), who wrote adventure-romances in the form of epic poems in a language we call Old French, the ancestor of modern French. At the court of his patron, Marie of Champagne, Chrétien de Troyes (krey-TYEN duh trwah) (ca. 1135–ca. 1190) used the legends of the fifth-century British king Arthur (see page 154) as the basis for innovative tales of battle and forbidden love. His most popular story is that of the noble Lancelot, whose love for Guinevere, the wife of King Arthur, his lord, became physical as well as spiritual. Most of the troubadours and trouvères came from and wrote for the aristocratic classes, and their poetry suggests the interests and values of noble culture. Their influence eventually extended to all social groups, however, for people who could not read heard the poems and stories from people who could, so that what had originally come from oral culture was recycled back into it every generation.

Drama, derived from the church's liturgy, emerged as a distinct art form during the High Middle Ages. Plays based on biblical themes and on the lives of the saints were performed in the towns. *Mystery* plays were financed and performed by "misteries," members of the craft guilds, and *miracle* plays were acted by amateurs or professional actors, not guild members.. By combining comical farce based on ordinary life with serious religious scenes, plays gave ordinary people an opportunity to identify with religious figures and think about the mysteries of their faith.

Games and sports were common forms of entertainment and relaxation. There were games akin to modern football, rugby, and soccer in which balls were kicked and thrown, wrestling matches, and dog fights. People played card and board games of all types, gambling on these and on games with dice. Dancing was part of religious and family celebrations.

Churches and Cathedrals

The visual arts, especially architecture, flourished as expressions of religious ideas as well. Tens of thousands of churches, chapels, abbeys, and, most spectacularly, **cathedrals** were built in the twelfth and thirteenth centuries. (A cathedral is the church of a bishop and the administrative headquarters of a diocese, a church district headed by a bishop. The word comes from the Greek word *kathedra*, meaning seat, because the bishop's throne, a symbol of the office, is located in the cathedral.)

Most of the churches in the early Middle Ages had been built primarily of wood, which meant they were very susceptible to fire. They were often small, with a flat roof, in a rectangular or slightly cross-shaped form called a *basilica* (buh-SIL-eh-kuh), based on earlier Roman public buildings. With the end of the Viking and Magyar invasions and the increasing political stability of the eleventh century, bishops and abbots supported the construction of larger and more fire-resistant churches made almost completely out of stone. These were based on the basilican style, but features were added that made the cross shape more pronounced. As the size of the church grew horizontally, it also grew vertically. Builders adapted Roman-style rounded barrel vaults made of stone for the ceiling; this use of Roman forms led this style to be labeled **Romanesque.**

The next architectural style was **Gothic,** so named by a later scholar who incorrectly attributed the style to Gothic tribes. In Gothic churches the solid stone barrel-vaulted roof was replaced by a roof made of stone ribs with plaster in be-

cathedral The church of a bishop and the administrative headquarters of a diocese.

Romanesque An architectural style, with rounded arches and small windows.

Gothic An architectural style typified by pointed arches and large, stained glass windows.

tween. This made the ceiling much lighter, so that the side pillars and walls did not need to carry so much weight. Solid walls could be replaced by windows, which let in great amounts of light. (See the feature "Images in Society: From Romanesque to Gothic.")

Begun in the Île-de-France, Gothic architecture spread throughout France with the expansion of royal power. From France the new style spread to England, Germany, Italy, Spain, and eastern Europe. In those countries, the Gothic style competed with strong indigenous architectural traditions and thus underwent transformations that changed it to fit local usage. French master masons (MAY-sens) were soon invited to design and supervise the construction of churches in other parts of Europe.

Extraordinary amounts of money were needed to build these houses of worship. Consider, for example, the expense and labor involved in quarrying and transporting the stone alone. More stone was quarried for churches in medieval France than had been mined in ancient Egypt, where the Great Pyramid alone consumed 40.5 million cubic feet of stone.

Money was not the only need. A great number of artisans had to be assembled: quarrymen, sculptors, stonecutters, masons, mortar makers, carpenters, blacksmiths, glassmakers, roofers. Each master craftsman had apprentices, and unskilled laborers had to be recruited for the heavy work. The construction of a large cathedral was rarely completed in a lifetime; many were never finished at all. Because generation after generation added to the building, many Gothic churches show the architectural influences of two or even three centuries. (These variations in style were one of the aspects of Gothic buildings hated by later Renaissance architects, who regarded unity of style as essential in an attractive building.)

Bishops and abbots sketched out what they wanted and set general guidelines, but they left practical needs and aesthetic considerations to the master mason. He held overall responsibility for supervision of the project. (Medieval chroniclers applied the term *architect* to the abbots and bishops who commissioned the projects or the lay patrons who financed them, not to the draftsmen who designed them.) **Master masons** were paid higher wages than other masons; their contracts usually ran for several years, and great care was taken in their selection. Being neither gentlemen, clerics, nor laborers, master masons fit uneasily into the social hierarchy.

Since cathedrals were symbols of civic pride, towns competed to build the largest and most splendid church. In northern France in the late twelfth and early thirteenth centuries, cathedrals grew progressively taller. In 1163 the citizens of Paris began Notre Dame Cathedral, planning it to reach the height of 114 feet. When reconstruction on Chartres Cathedral was begun in 1194, it was to be 119 feet. Many cathedrals well over 100 feet tall were built as each bishop and town sought to outdo the neighbors. Medieval people built cathedrals to glorify God—and if mortals were impressed, all the better.

master mason Man in charge of the design and construction of cathedrals and other major buildings.

Tree of Jesse

In Christian symbolism, a tree stands for either life or death. Glassmakers depicted the ancestors of Christ as a tree's branches, based on the prophecy of Isaiah (11:1–2)—"a shoot shall sprout from the stump of Jesse, and from his roots a bud shall blossom, the spirit of the Lord shall rest upon him"—and the genealogy of Jesus in Matthew (1:1–16). In this stained glass from the west façade of Chartres Cathedral (ca. 1150–1170), Jesse, David, and Solomon are shown from bottom to top; a fourth panel (not shown) depicts Mary holding the Christ child. (© Clive Hicks)

Images in Society

From Romanesque to Gothic

The word *church* has several meanings: assembly, congregation, sect. The Greek term from which it is derived means "a thing belonging to the Lord," and this concept was applied to the building where a congregation assembled. In the Middle Ages people understood the church building to be "the house of God and the gate to Heaven"; it served as an image or representation of supernatural reality (Heaven). A church symbolized faith. Christians revealed and exercised faith; they communicated with God through prayer—that is, by raising their minds and hearts to God. The church building seemed the ideal place for prayer: communal prayer built faith, and faith encouraged prayer.

Architecture became the dominant art form of the Middle Ages. Nineteenth-century architectural historians coined the term *Romanesque*, meaning "in the Roman manner," to describe church architecture in most of Europe between the tenth and twelfth centuries. The main features of the Romanesque style—solid walls, rounded arches, and masonry vaults—had been the characteristics of large Roman buildings. With the massive barrel vaulting of the roof, heavy walls were required to carry the weight (see Image 1). Romanesque churches had a massive quality, reflecting the increasing political and economic stability of the period and suggesting that they were places of refuge and security in times of attack. A Romanesque church was a "fortress of God."

Gothic churches, by contrast, were walls of light. Visitors and worshipers approached the west end of the building, noticing the carved statues in the *tympanum* (TIM-puh-nuhm) (space above the portal, or door), perhaps awestruck by the lancets and rose window over the portal. Inside, a long row of columns directed their gaze down the *nave* (center aisle), and they proceeded to the *transept* (cross aisle), which separated the sanctuary and the choir (reserved for the clergy) from the body

IMAGE 1   Saint-Savin-sur-Gartempe (Romanesque), Early Twelfth Century. (Editions Gaud)

of the church (the laypeople's area). See Image 2. So that the flow of pilgrims would not disturb the clergy in their chants, *ambulatories* (walkways) were constructed around the sanctuary. Off the ambulatories, radiating chapels surrounded the *apse* (aps), the semicircular domed projection at the east end of the building. Apsidal chapels, each dedicated to and containing the relics of a particular saint, were visible from the exterior, as were the *flying buttresses* that supported the outward thrusts of the interior vaults. Above the apse and the

IMAGE 2 Amiens Cathedral, Mid-Thirteenth Century. (Editions Gaud)

west, south, and north portals, circular windows emerged from the radiating stone tracery in the form of roses.

Compare the interior of the abbey church of Saint-Savin-sur-Gartempe (Image 1), a Romanesque church

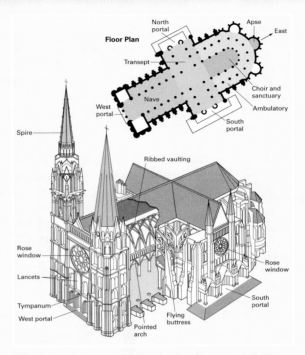

IMAGE 4 Elements of a Gothic Church (Chartres Cathedral).

IMAGE 3 Sainte-Chapelle, Paris, Mid-Thirteenth Century. (Scala/Art Resource, NY)

built in about 1100 in Poitou (pwa-TOO), France, and the interior of Amiens (AM-ee-uhnz) Cathedral (Image 2), a Gothic church built from 1220 to 1288. What are the most striking differences? What developments made the changes from Romanesque to Gothic structurally possible?

Architecture reveals the interests and values of a society, its goals and aspirations. What does Sainte-Chapelle (Image 4), built by King Louis IX of France to house relics—the crown of thorns placed on Jesus' head before the Crucifixion, a nail from the Crucifixion, a fragment of Jesus' cross—tell us about the values and aspirations of thirteenth-century French society?

A Gothic church represents more than a house of prayer or worship. Medieval people did not compartmentalize the various aspects of their lives as modern people tend to do. What civic, social, economic, and political functions did a church building serve?

Section Review

- All the arts, including literature, architecture, and music, flourished in the High Middle Ages through technological advances, increased wealth, and a more stable society.

- Latin was the language of high culture and education, but with advances in papermaking, a cheaper writing material was available, and literature from oral transmissions was written down gradually in vernacular or local dialects.

- Troubadours and female trobairitz were poets who wrote and sang lyric verse and provided a form of entertainment to the aristocratic classes along with dramas, games, and sports.

- Architecture provides the longest-lasting form of medieval art, most spectacularly in Romanesque cathedrals, which were massive "fortresses of God," and in Gothic cathedrals, which had many windows and were full of light.

- Cathedrals required huge amounts of money, skilled workers, and many years to complete, and were built to glorify God and to impress people.

- Stained glass windows along with elaborate tapestries were a focal point in Gothic churches, reflecting everyday life and scripture to enhance religious life and teachings.

Stained glass beautifully reflects the creative energy of the High Middle Ages. It is both an integral part of Gothic architecture and a distinct form of painting. As Gothic churches became more skeletal and had more windows, stained glass replaced manuscript illumination as the leading form of painting. At Chartres the craft and merchant guilds—drapers, furriers, haberdashers, tanners, butchers, bakers, fishmongers, and wine merchants—donated money and are memorialized in stained-glass windows. Thousands of scenes in the cathedral celebrate nature, country life, and the activities of ordinary people.

Tapestry making also came into its own in the fourteenth century. Heavy woolen tapestries were first made in the monasteries and convents as wall hangings for churches. Because they could be moved and lent an atmosphere of warmth, they replaced mural paintings. Early tapestries depicted religious scenes, but later hangings produced for the knightly class bore secular designs, especially romantic forests and hunting spectacles.

Once at least part of a Gothic cathedral had been built, the building began to be used for religious services. The Mass and other services became increasingly complex to fit with their new surroundings. Originally, services were chanted in unison, termed *plainsong* or *Gregorian chant*, but by the eleventh century additional voices singing on different pitches were added to create *polyphony* (puh-LIF-uh-nee). Certain parts of the service were broken off into stand-alone polyphonic pieces called *motets*, a style that composers soon adapted to secular music as well as ecclesiastical. Church leaders sometimes fumed that motets and polyphony made the text impossible to understand—Pope John XXII called this style an "avalanche of notes" in 1324—but, along with incense, candles, stained-glass windows, and the building itself, music made any service in a Gothic cathedral a rich experience.

Cities and the Church

Why did towns become the center of religious heresy, and what was the church's response?

The soaring towers of Gothic cathedrals were visible symbols of the Christian faith and civic pride of medieval urban residents, but many city people also felt that the church did not meet their spiritual needs. The bishops, usually drawn from the feudal nobility, did not understand urban culture and were suspicious of it. Christian theology, formulated for an earlier rural age, did not address the problems of the more sophisticated mercantile society. The new monastic orders of the twelfth century, such as the Cistercians, situated in remote, isolated areas had little relevance to the towns. Townspeople wanted a pious clergy capable of preaching the Gospel, and they disapproved of clerical ignorance and luxurious living. Critical of the clergy, neglected, and spiritually unfulfilled, townspeople turned to heretical sects.

Heretical Groups

Ironically, the eleventh-century Gregorian reform movement, which had worked to purify the church of disorder, led to some twelfth- and thirteenth-century heretical movements. Papal efforts to improve the sexual morality of the clergy, for example, had largely succeeded. When Gregory VII forbade married priests to celebrate church ceremonies, he expected public opinion to force priests to put aside their wives and concubines. But Gregory did not foresee the consequences of this order. Laypersons assumed they could, and indeed should, remove priests for any type of immorality or for not living according to standards that the parishioners judged appropriate.

In northern Italian towns, Arnold of Brescia (BREH-shee-uh), a vigorous advocate of strict clerical poverty, denounced clerical wealth. In France, Peter Waldo, a rich merchant of Lyons, gave his money to the poor and preached that only prayers, not sacraments, were needed for salvation. The **Waldensians** (wawl-DEN-see-uhnz)—as Peter's followers were called—bitterly attacked the sacraments and church hierarchy, and they carried these ideas across Europe. As we saw in Chapter 9, the Albigensians asserted that the material world was evil and that religious leaders should be those who rejected worldly things, not the wealthy bishops or the papacy (see page 212).

Waldensians The followers of Peter Waldo, a French merchant who gave his money to the poor and preached that only prayers were needed for salvation.

The Friars

In its continuing struggle against heresy, the church gained the support of two remarkable men, Saint Dominic (DOM-uh-nik) and Saint Francis, and of the orders they founded. Born in Castile, a province of Spain famous for its zealous Christianity, Domingo de Gúzman (1170?–1221) received a sound education and was ordained a priest. In 1206 he accompanied his bishop on an unsuccessful mission to win back the Albigensian heretics of Languedoc in France. Determined to succeed through ardent preaching, Dominic subsequently returned to France with a few followers. In 1216 the group—officially known as the "Preaching Friars" though often called **Dominicans** (DOM-mihn-uh-kuns)—won papal recognition as a new religious order.

Francesco di Bernardone (1181–1226), son of a wealthy Italian cloth merchant, was particularly inspired by two biblical texts: "If you seek perfection, go, sell your possessions, and give to the poor. You will have treasure in heaven. Afterward, come back and follow me." (Matthew 19:21); and Jesus' advice to his disciples as they went out to preach, "Take nothing for the journey, neither walking staff nor travelling bag, nor bread, nor money" (Luke 9:3). Francis's asceticism did not emphasize withdrawal from the world, but joyful devotion; in contrast to the Albigensians, who saw the material world as evil, Francis saw all creation as God-given and good. He wrote hymns to natural objects such as "brother moon" and was widely reported to perform miracles involving animals.

Dominicans The followers of Dominic, officially known as the "Preaching Friars."

The simplicity, humility, and joyful devotion with which Francis carried out his mission soon attracted companions. Although he resisted pressure to establish an order, his followers became so numerous that he was obliged to develop some formal structure. In 1221 the papacy approved the "Rule of the Little Brothers of Saint Francis," as the **Franciscans** (fran-SIS-kenz) were known.

The new Dominican and Franciscan orders differed significantly from older monastic orders such as the Benedictines and the Cistercians. First, the Dominicans and Franciscans were **friars,** not monks. Their lives and work focused on the cities and university towns, the busy centers of commercial and intellectual life, not the secluded and cloistered world of monks. They thought that *more* contact with ordinary Christians, not less, was a better spiritual path.

Franciscans The followers of Francis and his mission of simplicity, humility, and joyful devotion.

friars Men belonging to certain religious orders who did not live in monasteries but out in the world.

Second, the friars stressed apostolic poverty, a life based on the Gospel's teachings, in which they would own no property and depend on Christian people for their material needs. Hence they were called **mendicants** or mendicant orders, that is, begging friars. Benedictine and Cistercian abbeys, on the other hand, held land—not infrequently great tracts of land. Finally, the friars usually drew their

mendicants Begging friars.

members largely from the burgher class, from small property owners and shop-keepers. The monastic orders, by contrast, gathered their members (at least until the thirteenth century) overwhelmingly from the nobility.

The friars represented a response to the spiritual and intellectual needs of the thirteenth century. The Dominicans preferred that their friars be university graduates in order to better preach to a sophisticated urban society. The Dominicans soon held professorial chairs at leading universities, and they count Thomas Aquinas, probably the greatest medieval philosopher in Europe, as their most famous member. The Franciscans followed suit at the universities and also produced intellectual leaders. Women sought to develop similar orders devoted to active service out in the world. Clare of Assisi (1193–1253) sought to live in poverty and became a follower of Francis, who established a place for her to live in a nearby church. She was joined by other women, and they attempted to establish a rule for life in their community that would follow Francis's ideals of absolute poverty and allow them to serve the poor. Her rule was accepted by the papacy only after many decades, and then only because she agreed that the order, called the **Poor Clares,** would be enclosed.

Poor Clares A women's order established by Clare of Assisi, in devotion to active service out in the world.

In the growing cities of Europe, especially in the Netherlands, groups of women seeking to live a religious life came together as what later came to be known as **Beguines** (bih-GEENS). (The origins of the word are debated.) They lived communally in small houses called *beguinages*, combining a life of prayer with service to the needy. In a few cities these beguinages grew quite large, eventually incorporating churches and other buildings as well as housing for several hundred women. Beguine spirituality emphasized direct personal communication with God, sometimes through mystical experiences, rather than through the intercession of a saint or official church rituals. Many Beguines were also devoted to the church's sacraments, however, especially the Eucharist, and initially some church officials gave guarded approval of the movement. By the fourteenth century, however, they were declared heretical and much of their property was confiscated, for church officials were clearly uncomfortable with women who were neither married nor cloistered nuns.

Beguines Groups of women seeking to live a religious life in the growing cities of Europe.

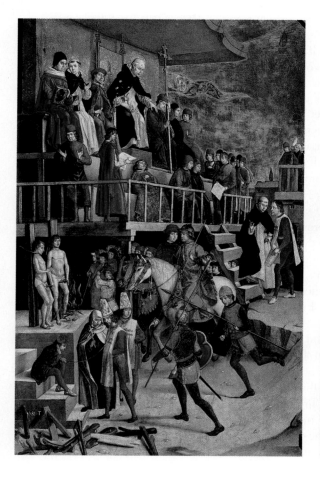

The Friars and Papal Power

Beginning in 1233 the papacy used the friars to staff its new ecclesiastical court, the Inquisition (see page 212). Popes selected the friars to direct the Inquisition because bishops proved unreliable and because special theological training was needed. *Inquisition* means "investigation," and the Franciscans and Dominicans developed ex-

Saint Dominic and the Inquisition

The fifteenth-century court painter to the Spanish rulers Ferdinand and Isabella, Pedro Berruguete here portrays an event from the life of Saint Dominic: Dominic presides at the trial of Count Raymond of Toulouse, who had supported the Albigensian heretics. Raymond, helmeted and on horseback, repented and was pardoned; his companions, who would not repent, were burned. Smoke from the fire has put one of the judges to sleep, and other officials, impervious to the human tragedy, chat among themselves. (Museo del Prado, Madrid/Institut Amatller d'Art Hispanic)

pert methods of rooting out unorthodox thought. Ironically, within a hundred years of Francis's death one of the Inquisition's targets was the Spiritual Franciscans, a breakaway group that wanted to follow Francis's original ideals of poverty and denied the pope's right to countermand that ideal.

Modern Americans consider the procedures of the Inquisition exceedingly unjust, and there was substantial criticism of it in the Middle Ages. The accused did not learn the evidence against them or see their accusers; they were subjected to lengthy interrogations often designed to trap them; and torture could be used to extract confessions. Medieval people, however, believed that heretics destroyed the souls of their neighbors. By attacking religion, it was also thought, heretics destroyed the very bonds of society. By the mid-thirteenth century secular governments steadily pressed for social conformity, and they had the resources to search out and punish heretics. So successful was the Inquisition as a tool of royal power that within a century heresy had been virtually extinguished.

Popes and kings jointly supported the Inquisition, but in the late thirteenth century the papacy came into a violent dispute with several of Europe's leading rulers. Pope Boniface VIII (1294–1303), arguing from precedent, insisted that King Edward I of England and Philip the Fair of France obtain his consent for taxes they had imposed on the clergy. Edward immediately denied the clergy the protection of the law, and Philip halted the shipment of all ecclesiastical revenue to Rome. Boniface had to back down.

The battle for power between the papacy and the French monarchy became a bitter war of propaganda. Finally, in 1302, in a letter titled *Unam Sanctam* (because its opening sentence spoke of one holy Catholic Church), Boniface insisted that all Christians—including kings—were subject to the pope. Philip maintained that he was completely sovereign in his kingdom and responsible to God alone. French mercenary troops assaulted and arrested the aged pope at Anagni in Italy. Although Boniface was soon freed, he died shortly afterward. The confrontation at Anagni foreshadowed serious difficulties in the Christian church, but religious struggle was only one of the crises that would face Western society in the fourteenth century.

Section Review

- People increasingly turned to heretical sects to meet their spiritual needs as traditional Christianity lost touch with laypeople.
- The Dominican and Franciscan friars sought to counteract heresy through vigorous preaching, services to laypeople, and devotion to poverty; they lived out in the world instead of in cloistered monasteries.
- The Beguines were groups of women who came together to live a life of prayer and service to the needy; though the church initially approved of them, it later declared them heretical.
- The Inquisition, the church's response to heresy, had the support of both popes and kings even though it used cruel and unjust methods to seek out and punish heretics.
- The struggle for power between the papacy and the monarchy was an ongoing problem.

Unam Sanctam An official letter issued by Pope Boniface VIII claiming that all Christians were subject to the pope.

Chapter Review

How did medieval cities originate, and what impact did they have on the economy and on culture? (page 247)

Medieval cities—whether beginning around the sites of cathedrals, fortifications, or market towns—recruited people from the countryside with the promise of greater freedom and new possibilities. Cities provided economic opportunity, which, together with the revival of long-distance trade and a new capitalistic spirit, led to greater wealth, a higher standard of living, and upward social mobility for many people. Merchants and artisans formed guilds to protect their means of livelihood. Not everyone in medieval cities shared in the prosperity, however; many residents lived hand-to-mouth on low wages.

How did universities evolve, and what needs of medieval society did they serve? (page 259)

The towns that became centers of trade and production in the High Middle Ages developed into cultural and intellectual centers. Trade brought in new ideas as well as

Key Terms
town liberties (p. 248)

merchant guild (p. 249)

craft guild (p. 250)

livery (p. 252)

sumptuary laws (p. 252)

Hanseatic League (p. 257)

usury (p. 257)

commercial revolution (p. 258)

mercantile capitalism (p. 258)

Scholastics (p. 263)

(continued)

merchandise, and in many cities a new type of educational institution—the university—emerged from cathedral and municipal schools. Universities developed theological, legal, and medical courses of study based on classical models and provided trained officials for the new government bureaucracies. University-trained professionals joined merchants and guild masters as well-off members of the urban elite, heading large households staffed with servants and charging high prices for their services.

> ### How did the arts and architecture express the ideals, attitudes, and interests of medieval people? (page 265)

University education was in Latin and was limited to men, but the High Middle Ages also saw the creation of new types of vernacular literature. Poems, songs, and stories, written down in local dialects, celebrated things of concern to ordinary people. In this, the troubadours of southern France led the way, using Arabic models to create romantic stories of heterosexual love. The ability to read the vernacular was still limited, however, so oral transmission continued as the most important way that information was conveyed and traditions passed down. The oral culture of medieval cities included plays with religious themes and also games, songs, and dancing.

Economic growth meant that merchants, nobles, and guild masters had disposable income they could spend on artistic products and more elaborate consumer goods. They supported the building of churches and cathedrals as visible symbols of their Christian faith and their civic pride; cathedrals in particular grew larger and more sumptuous, with high towers, stained-glass windows, and multiple altars. The sturdy Romanesque style was replaced by the soaring Gothic, in which sophisticated building techniques allowed windows to grow ever taller and wider. Cathedrals were places for socializing as well as worship, and increasingly complex music added to the experience.

> ### Why did towns become the center of religious heresy, and what was the church's response? (page 270)

Town residents demonstrated their deep religious faith in the construction of Gothic cathedrals, but many urban people thought that the church did not fulfill their spiritual needs. They turned instead to heresies, many of which taught that the church had grown too powerful and wealthy. Combating heresy became a principal task of new types of religious orders, most prominently the Dominicans and Franciscans, who preached, ministered to city dwellers, and also staffed the papal Inquisition, a special court designed to root out heresy. These efforts were largely successful, and the church continued to exercise leadership of Christian society in the High Middle Ages, though the clash between the papacy and the kings of France and England at the end of the thirteenth century seriously challenged papal power.

Notes

1. D. C. Douglas and G. W. Greenaway, *English Historical Documents*, vol. 2, pp. 969–970.
2. Quoted in H. E. Sigerist, *Civilization and Disease* (Chicago: University of Chicago Press, 1943), p. 102.
3. See John F. Benton, "Fraud, Fiction and Borrowing in the Correspondence of Abelard and Heloise," in *Culture, Power and Personality in Medieval France*, ed. T. N. Bisson (London and Rio Grande: The Hambledon Press, 1991), pp. 417–449, esp. pp. 430–443, which convincingly demonstrate that "the most personal parts of the correspondence are not genuine" and that the letters were probably written in the later thirteenth century; and the same scholar's "The Correspondence of Abelard and Heloise," in the same volume, pp. 487–512.
4. Quoted in J. H. Mundy, *Europe in the High Middle Ages, 1150–1309* (New York: Basic Books, 1973), pp. 474–475.

To assess your mastery of this chapter, go to **bedfordstmartins.com/mckaywestbrief**

Listening to the Past

Courtly Love

Whether female or male, the troubadour poets celebrated fin'amor, a Provençal word for the pure or perfect love a knight was supposed to feel for his lady, which has in English come to be called chivalry or "courtly love." In courtly love lyrics, the writer praises his or her love object, idealizing the beloved and promising loyalty and great deeds. Most of these songs are written by, or from the perspective of, a male lover who is socially beneath his female beloved; her higher status makes her unattainable, so the lover's devotion can remain chaste and pure, rewarded by her handkerchief, or perhaps a kiss, but nothing more. The noblemen and noblewomen who listened to these songs viewed such love as ennobling, and some authors even wrote courtly love lyrics directed to the Virgin Mary, the ultimate unattainable woman.

Scholars generally agree that poetry praising perfect love originated in the Muslim culture of the Iberian Peninsula, where heterosexual romantic love had long been the subject of poems and songs. Southern France was a border area where Christian and Muslim culture mixed; Spanish Muslim poets sang at the courts of Christian nobles, and Provençal poets picked up their romantic themes.

It is very difficult to know whether courtly love literature influenced the treatment of real women to any great extent—peasant women were certainly no less in danger of rape from knightly armies in the thirteenth century than they had been in the tenth—but it did introduce an ideal of heterosexual romance into Western literature that had not been there in the classical or early medieval period. The following excerpt is from a poem written by Arnaut Daniel, a thirteenth-century troubadour. Not much is known about him, but the songs that have survived capture courtly love conventions perfectly.

In this fourteenth-century painting, a lady puts the helmet on her beloved knight. (akg-images)

I only know the grief that comes to me,
  to my love-ridden heart, out of over-loving,
  since my will is so firm and whole
  that it never parted or grew distant from her
  whom I craved at first sight, and afterwards:
  and now, in her absence, I tell her burning words;
  then, when I see her, I don't know, so much I have
    to, what to say.

To the sight of other women I am blind, deaf to
    hearing them
  since her only I see, and hear and heed,
  and in that I am surely not a false slanderer,
  since heart desires her more than mouth may say;
  wherever I may roam through fields and valleys,
    plains and mountains
  I shan't find in a single person all those qualities
  which God wanted to select and place in her.

I have been in many a good court,
  but here by her I find much more to praise:
  measure and wit and other good virtues,
  beauty and youth, worthy deeds and fair disport;
  so well kindness taught and instructed her
  that it has rooted every ill manner out of her:
  I don't think she lacks anything good. . . .

Far fewer poems by female troubadours (trobair-itz) have survived than by male, but those that have express strong physical and emotional feelings. The

following excerpt is from the twelfth-century Count-
ess of Dia.

I've suffered great distress
From a knight whom I once owned.
Now, for all time, be it known:
I loved him—yes, to excess.
His jilting I've regretted,
Yet his love I never really returned.
Now for my sin I can only burn:
Dressed, or in my bed . . .

Lovely lover, gracious, kind,
When will I overcome your fight?
O if I could lie with you one night!
Feel those loving lips on mine!
Listen, one thing sets me afire:
Here in my husband's place I want you,
If you'll just keep your promise true:
Give me everything I desire.

Questions for Analysis

1. Both of these songs focus on a beloved who does not return the lover's affection. What similarities and differences do you see in them?

2. How does courtly love reinforce other aspects of medieval society? Are there aspects of medieval society it contradicts?

3. Can you find examples from current popular music that parallel the sentiments expressed in these two songs?

Sources: First poem: Leonardo Malcovati, *Prosody in England and Elsewhere: A Comparative Approach* (London: Gival Press, 2006), and online at http://www.trobar.org/troubadours/; second poem: quoted in J. J. Wilhelm, ed., *Lyrics of the Middle Ages: An Anthology* (New York: Garland Publishers, 1993), pp. 83–84.

CHAPTER 12

The Crisis of the Later Middle Ages

1300–1450

In this lavishly illustrated French chronicle, Wat Tyler, the leader of the English Peasant's Revolt, is stabbed during a meeting with the king. Tyler died soon afterward, and the revolt was ruthlessly crushed. (Bibliothèque nationale de France)

Chapter Preview

Prelude to Disaster
What were the demographic, social, and economic consequences of climate change?

The Black Death
How did the spread of the plague shape European society?

The Hundred Years' War
What were the causes of the Hundred Years' War, and how did the war affect European politics, economics, and cultural life?

Challenges to the Church
What were the causes of the Great Schism, and how did church leaders, intellectuals, and ordinary people respond?

Economic and Social Change
How did economic and social tensions contribute to revolts, crime, violence, and a growing sense of ethnic and national distinctions?

INDIVIDUALS IN SOCIETY: Jan Hus

LISTENING TO THE PAST: Christine de Pizan

During the later Middle Ages the last book of the New Testament, the Book of Revelation, inspired thousands of sermons and hundreds of religious tracts. The Book of Revelation deals with visions of the end of the world, with disease, war, famine, and death. It is no wonder this part of the Bible was so popular. Between 1300 and 1450 Europeans experienced a frightful series of shocks: climate change, economic dislocation, plague, war, social upheaval, and increased crime and violence. Death and preoccupation with death make the fourteenth century one of the most wrenching periods of Western civilization. Yet, in spite of the pessimism and crises, important institutions and cultural forms, including representative assemblies and national literatures, emerged. Even institutions that experienced severe crisis, such as the Christian church, saw new types of vitality.

Prelude to Disaster

What were the demographic, social, and economic consequences of climate change?

In the first half of the fourteenth century, Europe experienced a series of climate changes that led to lower levels of food production, which had dramatic and disastrous ripple effects. Political leaders attempted to find solutions, but were unable to deal with the economic and social problems that resulted.

The period from about 1000 to about 1300 saw a warmer than usual climate in Europe, which underlay all the changes and vitality of the High Middle Ages. About 1300 the climate changed, becoming colder and wetter. Historical geographers refer to the period from 1300 to 1450 as a "little ice age."

An unusual number of storms brought torrential rains, ruining the wheat, oat, and hay crops on which people and animals almost everywhere depended. Since long-distance transportation of food was expensive and difficult, most urban areas depended for bread and meat on areas no more than a day's journey away. Poor harvests—and one in four was likely to be poor—led to scarcity and starvation. Almost all of northern Europe suffered a **"Great Famine"** in the years 1315–1322, which contemporaries interpreted as a recurrence of the biblical "seven lean years" (Genesis 42). Even in non-famine years, the cost of grain, livestock, and dairy products rose sharply.

Great Famine A terrible famine that hit much of Europe after a period of climate change (1315–1322).

Reduced caloric intake meant increased susceptibility to disease, especially for infants, children, and the elderly. Workers on reduced diets had less energy, which in turn meant lower productivity, lower output, and higher grain prices.

Hardly had western Europe begun to recover from this disaster when another struck: an epidemic of typhoid fever carried away thousands. Then in 1318 disease hit cattle and sheep, drastically reducing the herds and flocks. Another bad harvest in 1321 brought famine and death.

The catastrophes of the fourteenth century had grave social consequences. In parts of the Low Countries and in the Scottish-English borderlands, entire villages were abandoned. In Flanders and East Anglia (eastern England), some peasants were forced to mortgage, sublease, or sell their holdings to richer farmers in order to buy food. Throughout the affected areas, young men and women sought work in the towns. Overall, the population declined because of the deaths caused by famine and disease; postponement of marriages may have also played a part.

Meanwhile, the international character of trade and commerce meant that a disaster in one country had serious implications elsewhere. For example, the infection that attacked English sheep in 1318 caused a sharp decline in wool exports in the following years. Without wool, Flemish weavers could not work, and thousands were laid off. Without woolen cloth, the businesses of Flemish, Hanseatic, and Italian merchants suffered. Unemployment encouraged people to turn to crime.

As the subsistence crisis deepened, popular discontent and paranoia increased. In France, starving people focused their anger on the rich, speculators, and the Jews, who were targeted as creditors fleecing the poor through pawnbroking. (Expelled from France in 1306, Jews were readmitted in 1315 and were granted the privilege of lending at high interest rates.) Rumors spread of a plot by Jews and their agents, the lepers, to kill Christians by poisoning the wells. Based on "evidence" collected by torture, many lepers and Jews were killed, beaten, or hit with heavy fines.

Government responses to these crises were ineffectual. The three sons of Philip the Fair who sat on the French throne between 1314 and 1328 condemned speculators, who held stocks of grain back until conditions were desperate and prices high; forbade the sale of grain abroad; and published legislation prohibiting fishing with traps that took large catches. These measures had few positive results.

CHRONOLOGY

1309–1376	Babylonian Captivity; papacy in Avignon
1310–1320	Dante, *Divine Comedy*
1315–1322	Famine in northern Europe
1324	Marsiglio of Padua, *Defensor Pacis*
1337–1453	Hundred Years' War
1348	Black Death arrives in mainland Europe
1358	Jacquerie peasant uprising in France
1378–1417	Great Schism
1381	Peasants' Revolt in England
1387–1400	Chaucer, *Canterbury Tales*
1405	Christine de Pizan, *The Treasure of the City of Ladies*
1415	English smash the French at Agincourt
1429	French victory at Orléans; Charles VII crowned king
1431	Joan of Arc declared a heretic and burned at the stake

Death from Famine

In this fifteenth-century painting, dead bodies lie in the middle of a path, while a funeral procession at the right includes a man with an adult's coffin and a woman with the coffin of an infant under her arm. People did not simply allow the dead to lie in the street in medieval Europe, though during famines and epidemics it was sometimes difficult to maintain normal burial procedures. (Erich Lessing/Art Resource, NY)

Black Death Bubonic plague that first struck Europe in 1347 and was spread mainly by rats and fleas. In less virulent forms, the disease reappeared many times until 1721.

In England, Edward I's incompetent son, Edward II (r. 1307–1327), also condemned speculators, after his attempts to set price controls on livestock and ale proved futile. He did try to buy grain abroad, but little was available: yields in the Baltic were low; the French crown, as we have seen, forbade exports; and the grain shipped from northern Spain was grabbed by pirates. Such grain as reached southern English ports was stolen by looters and sold on the black market. The Crown's efforts at famine relief failed.

The Black Death

How did the spread of the plague shape European society?

Royal attempts to provide food from abroad were unsuccessful, but they indicate the extent of long-distance shipping by the beginning of the fourteenth century. In 1291 Genoese (JEN-oh-eez) sailors had opened the Strait of Gibraltar to Italian shipping by defeating the Moroccans. Then, shortly after 1300, important advances were made in the design of Italian merchant ships. A square rig was added to the mainmast, and ships began to carry three masts instead of just one. Additional sails better utilized wind power to propel the ship. The improved design meant that cargo could now move quickly and regularly across great distances. So, however, could disease pathogens carried by the vermin that stowed away on these vessels. The most frightful of these diseases first emerged in western Europe in 1347 and was later called the **Black Death.** (Sometime in the fifteenth century, the Latin phrase *atra mors*, meaning "dreadful death," was translated as "black death," and the phrase stuck.)

Spread of the Disease

Most historians and almost all microbiologists identify the disease that spread in the fourteenth century as the bubonic (byoo-BON-ik) plague, caused by the bacillus *Yersinia pestis*. The disease normally afflicts rats. Fleas living on the infected rats drink their blood; the bacteria that cause the plague multiply in the flea's gut; and the flea passes them on to the next rat it bites by throwing up into the bite. Usually the disease is limited to rats and other rodents, but at certain points in history—perhaps when most rats have been killed off—the fleas have jumped from their rodent hosts to humans and other animals.

The classic symptom of the bubonic plague was a growth the size of a nut or an apple in the armpit, in the groin, or on the neck. This was the boil, or *bubo*, that gave the disease its name and caused agonizing pain. If the bubo was lanced and the pus thoroughly drained, the victim had a chance of recovery. The next stage was the appearance of black spots or blotches caused by bleeding under the skin. Finally, the victim began to cough violently and spit blood. This stage, indicating the presence of millions of bacilli in the bloodstream, signaled the end, and death followed in two or three days.

Plague symptoms were first described in 1331 in southwestern China, part of the Mongol Empire. Plague-infested rats accompanied Mongol armies and merchant caravans carrying silk, spices, and gold across central Asia in the 1330s. Then they stowed away on ships, carrying the disease to the ports of the Black Sea by the 1340s. Later stories told of more dramatic means of spreading the disease as well, reporting that Mongol armies besieging the city of Kaffa on the shores of the Black Sea catapulted plague-infected corpses over the walls to infect those inside.

The city's residents dumped the corpses into the sea as fast as they could, but they were already infected.

In October 1347 Genoese ships brought the plague from Kaffa to Messina, from which it spread across Sicily. Venice and Genoa were hit in January 1348, and from the port of Pisa (**PEE-zuh**) the disease spread south to Rome and east to Florence and all of Tuscany. By late spring southern Germany was attacked. Frightened French authorities chased a galley bearing the disease away from the port of Marseilles, but not before plague had infected the city, from which it spread to Languedoc (**lahng-DAWK**) and Spain. In June 1348 two ships entered the Bristol Channel and introduced it into England. All Europe felt the scourge of this horrible disease (see Map 12.1).

Although urban authorities from London to Paris to Rome had begun to try to achieve a primitive level of sanitation by the fourteenth century, urban conditions remained ideal for the spread of disease. Narrow streets filled with refuse and human excrement were as much cesspools as thoroughfares. Dead animals and sore-covered beggars greeted the traveler. Houses whose upper stories projected over

MAPPING THE PAST

MAP 12.1   The Course of the Black Death in Fourteenth-Century Europe

Use the map and the information in the text to answer the following questions: **[1]** How did the expansion of trade that resulted from the commercial revolution contribute to the spread of the Black Death? **[2]** When did the plague reach Paris? Why do you think it got to Paris before it spread to the rest of northern France or to southern Germany? **[3]** Which cities were spared? What might account for this? **[4]** Which regions were spared? Would the reasons for this be the same as those for cities, or might other causes have been operating in rural areas?

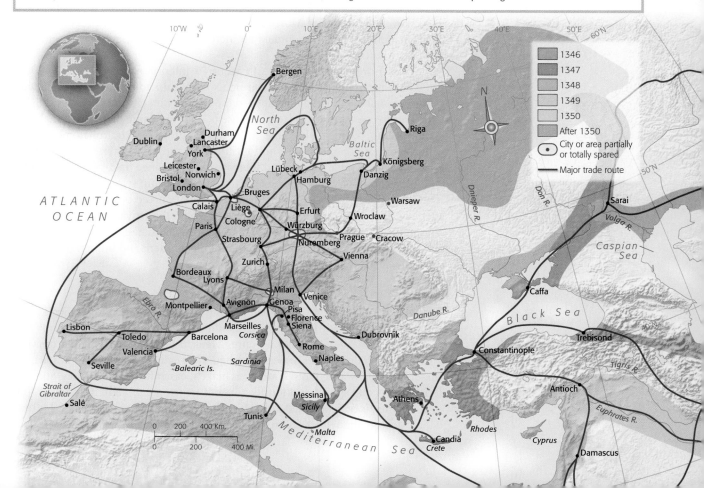

the lower ones blocked light and air. And extreme overcrowding was commonplace. When all members of an aristocratic family lived and slept in one room, it should not be surprising that six or eight persons in a middle-class or poor household slept in one bed—if they had one. Closeness, after all, provided warmth. Houses were beginning to be constructed of brick, but many wood, clay, and mud houses remained. A determined rat had little trouble entering such a house.

Standards of personal hygiene remained frightfully low. Fleas and body lice were universal afflictions: everyone from peasants to archbishops had them. One more bite did not cause much alarm. But if that nibble came from a bacillus-bearing flea, an entire household or area was doomed.

Mortality rates cannot be specified because population figures for the period before the arrival of the plague do not exist for most countries and cities. Of a total English population of perhaps 4.2 million, probably 1.4 million died of the Black Death in its several visits. Densely populated Italian cities endured incredible losses. Florence lost between one-half and two-thirds of its population when the plague visited in 1348. The most widely accepted estimate for western Europe is that the plague killed about one-third of the population in the first wave of infection.

Nor did central and eastern Europe escape the ravages of the disease. One chronicler records that, in the summer and autumn of 1349, between five hundred and six hundred died every day in Vienna. Styria, in what today is central Austria, was very hard hit, with cattle straying unattended in the fields.

As the Black Death took its toll on the German Empire, waves of emigrants fled to Poland, Bohemia, and Hungary. The situation there was better, though disease was not completely absent. The plague seems to have entered Poland through the Baltic seaports and spread from there. Still, population losses were lower than elsewhere in Europe. The plague spread from Poland to Russia, reaching Pskov, Novgorod, and Moscow. In Serbia, though, the plague left vast tracts of land unattended, which prompted an increase in Albanian immigration to meet the labor shortage.

Across Europe the Black Death recurred intermittently from the 1360s to 1400. It reappeared with reduced virulence from time to time over the following centuries, making its last appearance in the French port city of Marseilles in 1721. Survivors became more prudent. Because periods of famine had caused malnutrition, making people vulnerable to disease, Europeans controlled population growth so that population did not outstrip food supply. Western Europeans improved navigation techniques and increased long-distance trade, which permitted the importation of grain from sparsely populated Baltic regions (see page 281). They strictly enforced quarantine measures. They worked on the development of vaccines. But it was only in 1947, six centuries after the arrival of the plague in the West, that the American microbiologist Selman Waksman discovered an effective vaccine, streptomycin. Plague continues to infect rodent and human populations sporadically today.

Care

Fourteenth-century medical literature indicates that physicians could sometimes ease the pain, but they had no cure. Medical doctors observed that crowded cities had high death rates, especially when the weather was warm and moist. We understand that warm, moist conditions make it easier for germs, viruses, and bacteria to grow and spread, but fourteenth-century people thought in terms of "poisons" in the air or "corrupted air" rather than germs. The poisons caused illness, which doctors thought of as an imbalance in the fluids in the body, especially blood. Certain symptoms of the plague, especially bleeding and vomiting, were believed to be the body's natural reaction to too much fluid. Doctors frequently prescribed bloodletting—that is, taking blood from the body by applying leeches or making small cuts in veins—as standard treatment.

If the plague came from poisoned air, people reasoned, then strong-smelling herbs or other substances held in front of the nose or burned as incense might stop it. Perhaps loud sounds like ringing church bells or firing the newly invented cannon might help. Medicines made from plants that were bumpy or that oozed liquid might work, keeping the more dangerous swelling and oozing of the plague away. Magical letter and number combinations, called *cryptograms*, were especially popular in Muslim areas. They were often the first letters of words in prayers or religious sayings, and they gave people a sense of order when faced with the randomness with which the plague seemed to strike.

Wealthier people often fled cities for the countryside, though sometimes this simply spread the plague faster. Some cities tried shutting their gates to prevent infected people and animals from coming in, which worked in a few cities. They also walled up houses in which there was plague, trying to isolate those who were sick from those who were still healthy. Along with looking for medical causes and cures, people also searched for scapegoats, and savage cruelty sometimes resulted. Many people believed that the Jews had poisoned the wells of Christian communities and thereby infected the drinking water. This charge led to the murder of thousands of Jews across Europe.

Patients in a Hospital Ward, Fifteenth Century

In the thirteenth century, merchants donated some of their fortunes to establish hospitals, which filled past capacity when the plague struck. The practice of putting two or more adults in the same bed, as shown here, contributed to the spread of the disease. At the Hôtel-Dieu (oh-tel-DEW) in Paris, nurses complained of being forced to put eight to ten children in a single bed in which a patient had recently died. (Giraudon/The Bridgeman Art Library)

Many people did not see the plague as a medical issue, but instead interpreted it as the result of something within themselves. God must be punishing them for terrible sins, they thought, so the best remedies were religious ones: asking for forgiveness, prayer, trust in God, making donations to churches, and trying to live better lives. In Muslim areas, religious leaders urged virtuous living in the face of death: give to the poor, reconcile with your enemies, free your slaves, and say a proper goodbye to your friends and family.

Social, Economic, and Cultural Consequences

It is noteworthy that, in an age of mounting criticism of clerical wealth (see page 291), the behavior of the clergy during the plague was often exemplary. Priests, monks, and nuns cared for the sick and buried the dead. In places like Venice, from which even physicians fled, priests remained to give what ministrations they could. Consequently, their mortality rate was phenomenally high. The German clergy especially suffered a severe decline in personnel in the years after 1350.

Economic historians and demographers sharply dispute the impact of the plague on the economy in the late fourteenth century. The traditional view that the plague had a disastrous effect has been greatly modified. The clearest evidence comes from England, where by the early fifteenth century most landlords enjoyed the highest revenues of the medieval period. Why? The answer appears to lie in the fact that England and many parts of Europe suffered from overpopulation in the early fourteenth century. Population losses caused by the Black Death led to increased productivity by restoring a more efficient balance between labor, land, and capital.

What impact did visits of the plague have on urban populations? The rich evidence from a census of the city of Florence and its surrounding territory taken between 1427 and 1430 is fascinating. The region had suffered repeated epidemics since 1347. The census showed a high proportion of people who were age sixty or older, suggesting that the plague took the young rather than the mature. The high mortality rate of adults between the ages of twenty and fifty-nine led Florentine guilds to recruit many new members. It appears that economic organizations tried to keep their numbers constant, even though the size of the population, and its pool of potential guild members, was shrinking. Moreover, in contrast to the pre-1348 period, many new members of the guilds were not related to existing members. Thus the post-plague years represent an age of "new men."

The Black Death brought on a general European inflation. High mortality produced a fall in production, shortages of goods, and a general rise in prices. The price of wheat in most of Europe increased, as did the costs of meat, sausage, and cheese. This inflation continued to the end of the fourteenth century. But labor shortages meant that workers could demand better wages, and the broad mass of people enjoyed a higher standard of living. The greater demand for labor also meant greater mobility for peasants in rural areas and for industrial workers in the towns and cities.

The psychological consequences of the plague were profound. Imagine an entire society in the grip of the belief that it was at the mercy of a frightful affliction about which nothing could be done. It is not surprising that some sought release in wild living, while others turned to the severest forms of asceticism and frenzied religious fervor. Some extremists joined groups of **flagellants** (FLAJ-eh-lents), who whipped and scourged themselves as penance for their and society's sins in the belief that the Black Death was God's punishment for humanity's wickedness.

flagellants People who believed that the plague was God's punishment for sin and sought to do penance by flagellating (whipping) themselves.

Flagellants

In this manuscript illumination from 1349, shirtless flagellants scourge themselves with whips as they walk through the streets of the Flemish city of Tournai. The text notes that they are asking for God's grace to return to the city after it had been struck with the "most grave" illness. (Ann Ronan Picture Library, London/HIP/Art Resource, NY)

Groups of flagellants traveled from town to town, often provoking hysteria against Jews and growing into unruly mobs. Officials worried that they would provoke violence and riots, and ordered groups to disband or forbade them to enter cities.

Elaborate funeral services, which had provided comfort to the mourners as well as tribute to the dead, were abandoned in favor of hasty burials, sometimes in mass graves. Hospitality to travelers was replaced with hostility and suspicion, and European port cities began quarantining arriving ships to determine whether passengers brought the plague.

Popular endowments of educational institutions multiplied. The years of the Black Death witnessed the foundation of new colleges at old universities and of entirely new universities. The foundation charters specifically mention the shortage of priests and the decay of learning. Whereas universities such as those at Bologna and Paris had international student bodies, new institutions established in the wake of the Black Death had more national or local constituencies. Thus the international character of medieval culture weakened, paving the way for schism (SKIZ-uhm) in the Catholic Church even before the Reformation.

The literature and art of the fourteenth century reveal a terribly morbid concern with death. One highly popular artistic motif, the Dance of Death, depicted a dancing skeleton leading away a living person.

Section Review

- Improvements in ship design meant food and goods could now travel long distances, but rodents and fleas carrying the Black Death (bubonic plague) could also travel on these ships.

- The Black Death first appeared in China and then spread via Mongol armies and merchant caravans to ships across the Black Sea, Sicily, and into all of Europe.

- Crowded living conditions, poor sanitation, and low levels of personal hygiene helped the disease to spread, causing widespread population losses.

- Various attempted cures included bloodletting, herbal concoctions, quarantines, religious fervor to appease God, and victimizing Jews suspected of poisoning Christian wells.

- The population decrease meant new guild members, high inflation rates, and shortages of goods, but labor shortages resulted in better wages and greater mobility.

- New universities and colleges arose to resupply the shortage of priests and the learned, but the fear of outsiders who might bring the plague led to more national and local student bodies, weakening international bonds.

The Hundred Years' War

What were the causes of the Hundred Years' War, and how did the war affect European politics, economics, and cultural life?

The plague ravaged populations in Asia, North Africa, and Europe; in western Europe a long international war added further death and destruction. England and France had engaged in sporadic military hostilities from the time of the Norman Conquest in 1066, and in the middle of the fourteenth century these became more intense. From 1337 to 1453, the two countries intermittently fought one another in what was the longest war in European history, ultimately dubbed the Hundred Years' War though it actually lasted 116 years.

Causes

The Hundred Years' War had both distant and immediate causes. The distant cause was that in 1259, France and England had signed the Treaty of Paris, in which the English king agreed to become—for himself and his successors—vassal of the French crown for the duchy of Aquitaine (AK-wi-tain). The English claimed Aquitaine as an ancient inheritance. French policy, however, was strongly expansionist, and the French kings resolved to absorb the duchy into the kingdom of France so Aquitaine became disputed territory.

The immediate cause of the war was a dispute over who would inherit the French throne after Charles IV of France, the last surviving son of Philip the Fair, died childless in 1328. With him ended the Capetian (kuh-PEE-shuhn) dynasty of France. Charles IV did have a sister, however—Isabella—and her son was Edward III, king of England. An assembly of French barons, meaning to exclude Isabella and Edward from the French throne, proclaimed that "no woman nor her son could succeed to the [French] monarchy." The barons passed the crown to Philip VI of Valois (r. 1328–1350), a nephew of Philip the Fair.

In 1329 Edward III paid homage to Philip VI for Aquitaine. In 1337 Philip, eager to exercise full French jurisdiction in Aquitaine, confiscated the duchy. Edward III interpreted this action as a gross violation of the treaty of 1259 and as a cause for war. Moreover, Edward argued, as the eldest directly surviving male descendant of Philip the Fair, he

English Merchants in Flanders

In this 1387 illustration, an English merchant requests concessions from the count of Flanders to trade English wool at a favorable price. Flanders was officially on the French side during the Hundred Years' War, but Flemish cities depended heavily on English wool for their textile manufacturing. Hence the count of Flanders agreed to the establishment of the Merchant Staple, an English trading company with a monopoly on trade in wool.

(Copyright © British Library Board)

deserved the title of king of France. Edward III's dynastic argument upset the feudal order in France: to increase their independent power, French vassals of Philip VI used the excuse that they had to transfer their loyalty to a more legitimate overlord, Edward III. One reason the war lasted so long was that it became a French civil war, with some French barons supporting English monarchs in order to thwart the centralizing goals of the French crown.

The Popular Response

The governments of both England and France manipulated public opinion to support the war. The English public was convinced that the war was waged for one reason: to secure for King Edward the French crown he had been unjustly denied. Edward III issued letters to the sheriffs describing the evil deeds of the French in graphic terms and listing royal needs. Kings in both countries instructed the clergy to deliver sermons filled with patriotic sentiment. Philip VI sent agents to warn communities about the dangers of invasion and to stress the French crown's revenue needs to meet the attack. The English were led to believe that King Philip intended "to have seized and slaughtered the entire realm of England." Both sides developed a deep hatred of the other.

Most important of all, the Hundred Years' War was popular because it presented unusual opportunities for wealth and advancement. Poor knights and knights who were unemployed were promised regular wages. Criminals who enlisted were granted pardons. The great nobles expected to be rewarded with estates. Royal exhortations to the troops before battles repeatedly stressed that, if victorious, the men might keep whatever they seized. The French chronicler Jean Froissart (FROI-sahrt) wrote that, at the time of Edward III's expedition of 1359, men of all ranks flocked to the English king's banner. Some came to acquire honor, but many came "to loot and pillage the fair and plenteous land of France."[1]

The Course of the War to 1419

The war was fought almost entirely in France and the Low Countries (see Map 12.2). It consisted mainly of a series of random sieges and cavalry raids. In 1335 the French began ravaging the countryside in Aquitaine, sacking and burning coastal towns in southern England, and supporting Scottish incursions into northern England. Such tactics lent weight to Edward III's propaganda campaign. In fact, royal propaganda on both sides fostered a kind of early nationalism.

During the war's early stages, England was highly successful. At Crécy (KRES-ee) in northern France in 1346, English longbowmen scored a great victory over French knights and crossbowmen. Although the aim of the longbow was not very accurate, it allowed for rapid reloading, and an English archer could send off three arrows to the French crossbowman's one. The result was a blinding shower of arrows that unhorsed the French knights and caused mass confusion. The ring of cannon—probably the first use of artillery in the West—created further panic. Thereupon the English horsemen charged and butchered the French.

This was not war according to the chivalric rules that Edward III would have preferred. Nevertheless, his son, Edward the Black Prince, used the same tactics ten years later to smash the French at Poitiers, where he captured the French king and held him for ransom. Again, at **Agincourt** (AJ-in-kawrt) near Arras (AR-uhs) in 1415, the chivalric English soldier-king Henry V (r. 1413–1422) gained the field over vastly superior numbers. Henry followed up his triumph at Agincourt with the reconquest of Normandy. By 1419 the English had advanced to the walls

Agincourt The location near Arras in Flanders where an English victory in 1415 led to the reconquest of Normandy.

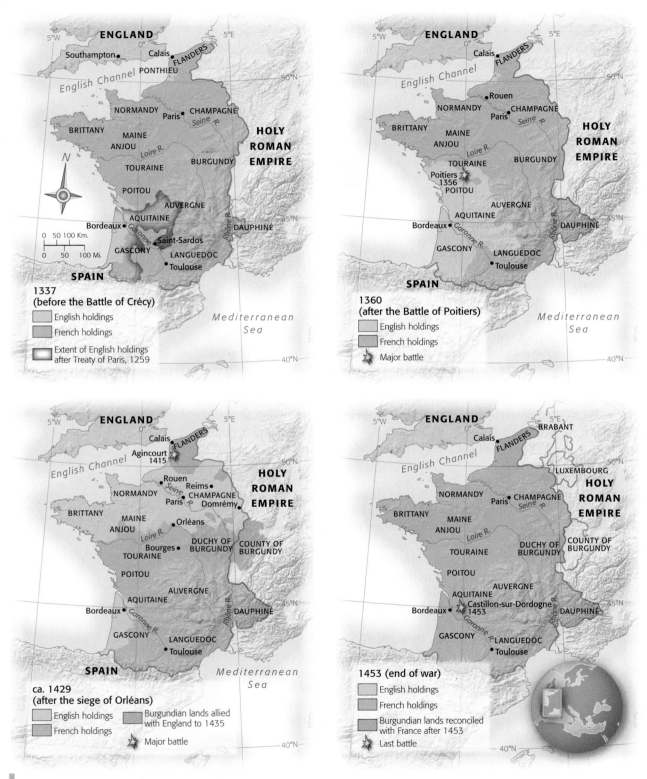

MAP 12.2 English Holdings in France During the Hundred Years' War

The year 1429 marked the greatest extent of English holdings in France.

of Paris (see Map 12.2). But the French cause was not lost. Though England had scored the initial victories, France won the war.

Joan of Arc and France's Victory

The ultimate French success rests heavily on the actions of an obscure French peasant girl, Joan of Arc, whose vision and work revived French fortunes and led to victory. A great deal of pious and popular legend surrounds Joan the Maid because of her peculiar appearance on the scene, her astonishing success, her martyrdom, and her canonization by the Catholic Church. The historical fact is that she saved the French monarchy, which was the embodiment of France.

Born in 1412 to well-to-do peasants in the village of Domrémy in Champagne, Joan of Arc grew up in a religious household. During adolescence she began to hear voices, which she later said belonged to Saint Michael, Saint Catherine, and Saint Margaret. In 1428 these voices spoke to her with great urgency, telling her that the dauphin (DAW-fin) (the uncrowned King Charles VII) had to be crowned and the English expelled from France. Joan went to the French court, persuaded the king to reject the rumor that he was illegitimate, and secured his support for her relief of the besieged city of Orléans (AWR-lee-uhn).

Joan arrived before Orléans on April 28, 1429. Seventeen years old, she knew little of warfare and believed that if she could keep the French troops from swearing and frequenting brothels, victory would be theirs. On May 8 the English, weakened by disease and lack of supplies, withdrew from Orléans. Ten days later Charles VII was crowned king at Reims. These two events marked the turning point in the war.

Joan's presence at Orléans, her strong belief in her mission, and the fact that she was wounded enhanced her reputation and strengthened the morale of the army. In 1430 England's allies, the Burgundians, captured Joan and sold her to the English. When the English handed her over to the ecclesiastical authorities for trial, the French court did not intervene. In 1431 the court condemned her as a heretic—her claim of direct inspiration from God, thereby denying the authority of church officials, constituted heresy—and burned her at the stake. The relief of Orléans stimulated French pride and rallied French resources. As the war dragged on, demands for an end increased in England. The clergy and intellectuals pressed for peace. Parliamentary opposition to additional war grants stiffened. Slowly the French reconquered Normandy and, finally, ejected the English from Aquitaine. At the war's end in 1453, only the town of Calais (KAL-lay) remained in English hands.

Costs and Consequences

In France thousands of soldiers and civilians had been slaughtered and hundreds of thousands of acres of rich farmland were ruined, leaving the rural economy of many parts of France a shambles. The war had disrupted trade and the great fairs, resulting in the drastic reduction of French participation in international commerce.

The war had wreaked havoc in England as well, even though only the southern coastal ports saw battle. England spent the huge sum of over £5 million on the war effort, and despite the money raised by some victories, the net result was an enormous financial loss. The government attempted to finance the war by raising taxes on the wool crop, which priced wool out of the export market. In addition,

representative assemblies
Deliberative meetings of lords and wealthy urban residents that flourished in many European countries between 1250 and 1450 and were the precursors to the English Parliament, German diets, and Spanish cortes.

nationalism A sense of unity among a people living in a particular area, based on language, shared customs, and culture, and often accompanied by hostility to outsiders.

Section Review

- Animosity arose between England and France involving the duchy of Aquitaine and the question of succession to the French Capetian dynasty in 1328; the resulting standoff led to the Hundred Years' War.

- Even though each side feared invasion and slaughter, they each believed their cause was just and many benefited from the war, gaining land, regular wages, or simply the spoils of looting and pillaging.

- The combatants fought most of the war in France, the English gaining an early lead using sieges and raids with longbow and cannon fire and advancing all the way to Paris, but eventually the French won.

- Joan of Arc saved the French monarchy and contributed to ending the war, but the English burned her at the stake as a heretic for claiming a direct connection with God.

- Economic costs of the war were high in both countries, with farms ruined and trade disrupted, but this period saw the beginning of the English parliament and the growth of nationalism and pride in both France and England.

the social order was disrupted as the knights who ordinarily served as sheriffs, coroners, jurymen, and justices of the peace were abroad. The war stimulated technological experimentation, especially with artillery. Cannon revolutionized warfare, making the stone castle no longer impregnable. Because only central governments, not private nobles, could afford cannon, they strengthened the military power of national states.

The long war also had a profound impact on the political and cultural lives of the two countries. Most notably, it stimulated the development of the English Parliament. Between 1250 and 1450, **representative assemblies** flourished in many European countries. In the English Parliament, German diets, and Spanish cortes, deliberative practices developed that laid the foundations for the representative institutions of modern liberal-democratic nations. While representative assemblies declined in most countries after the fifteenth century, the English Parliament endured. Edward III's constant need for money to pay for the war compelled him to summon not only the great barons and bishops, but knights of the shires and burgesses from the towns as well. Parliament met in thirty-seven of the fifty years of Edward's reign.[2]

The frequency of the meetings is significant. Representative assemblies were becoming a habit. Knights and wealthy urban residents—or the "Commons," as they came to be called—recognized their mutual interests and began to meet apart from the great lords. The Commons gradually realized that they held the country's purse strings, and a parliamentary statute of 1341 required that all nonfeudal levies have parliamentary approval. By signing the law, Edward III acknowledged that the king of England could not tax without Parliament's consent. During the course of the war, money grants were increasingly tied to royal redress of grievances: to raise money, the government had to correct the wrongs its subjects protested.

In England, theoretical consent to taxation and legislation was given in one assembly for the entire country. France had no such single assembly; instead, there were many regional or provincial assemblies. Why did a national representative assembly fail to develop in France? Linguistic, geographical, economic, legal, and political differences were very strong. People tended to think of themselves as Breton, Norman, Burgundian, or whatever, rather than French. Provincial assemblies, highly jealous of their independence, did not want a national assembly. The costs of sending delegates to it would be high, and the result was likely to be increased taxation. In addition, the initiative for convening assemblies rested with the king. But some monarchs lacked the power to call such an assembly, and others, including Charles VI, found the idea of representative assemblies thoroughly distasteful.

In both countries, however, the war did promote the growth of **nationalism**—the feeling of unity and identity that binds together a people. After victories, each country experienced a surge of pride in its military strength. Just as English patriotism ran strong after Crécy and Poitiers, so French national confidence rose after Orléans. French national feeling demanded the expulsion of the enemy not merely from Normandy and Aquitaine but from all French soil. Perhaps no one expressed this national consciousness better than Joan of Arc when she exulted that the enemy had been "driven out of *France*."

Challenges to the Church

What were the causes of the Great Schism, and how did church leaders, intellectuals, and ordinary people respond?

In times of crisis or disaster, people of all faiths have sought the consolation of religion. While local clergy eased the suffering of many, a dispute over who was the legitimate pope weakened the church as an institution. New ideas about church government took root.

The Babylonian Captivity and Great Schism

In order to control the church and its policies, Philip the Fair of France pressured Pope Clement V to settle permanently in Avignon in southeastern France, where the popes already had their summer residence (see Map 11.2). Clement, critically ill with cancer, lacked the will to resist Philip. The popes lived in Avignon from 1309 to 1376, a period in church history often called the **Babylonian Captivity** (referring to the seventy years the ancient Hebrews were held captive in Mesopotamian Babylon).

The Babylonian Captivity badly damaged papal prestige. The Avignon papacy reformed its financial administration and centralized its government. But the seven popes at Avignon concentrated on bureaucratic matters to the exclusion of spiritual objectives. Though some of the popes led austere lives, the general atmosphere was one of luxury and extravagance. The leadership of the church was cut off from its historic roots and the source of its ancient authority, the city of Rome. In 1377 Pope Gregory XI brought the papal court back to Rome. Unfortunately, he died shortly after the return. At Gregory's death, Roman citizens demanded an Italian pope who would remain in Rome. Between the time of Gregory's death and the opening of the conclave, great pressure was put on the cardinals to elect an Italian. At the time, none of them protested this pressure, and they chose a distinguished administrator, the archbishop of Bari, Bartolomeo Prignano, who took the name Urban VI.

Urban VI (1378–1389) had excellent intentions for church reform, but he went about this in a tactless and bullheaded manner. He attacked clerical luxury, denouncing individual cardinals by name, and even threatened to excommunicate certain cardinals.

The cardinals slipped away from Rome and met at Anagni. They declared Urban's election invalid because it had come about under threats from the Roman mob, and they asserted that Urban himself was excommunicated. The cardinals then elected Cardinal Robert of Geneva, the cousin of King Charles V of France, as pope. Cardinal Robert took the name Clement VII. There were thus two popes—Urban at Rome and Clement VII (1378–1394), who set himself up at Avignon in opposition to Urban. So began the **Great Schism,** which divided Western Christendom until 1417.

The powers of Europe aligned themselves with Urban or Clement along strictly political lines. France naturally recognized the French pope, Clement. England, France's historic enemy, recognized the Italian pope, Urban. Scotland, whose attacks on England were subsidized by France, followed the French and supported Clement. Aragon, Castile, and Portugal hesitated before deciding for Clement at Avignon. The German emperor, who bore ancient hostility to France,

Babylonian Captivity The period from 1309 to 1376 when the popes resided in Avignon, rather than in Rome. The phrase refers to the seventy years when the Hebrews were held captive in Babylon.

Great Schism The division, or split, in church leadership (1378–1417) when there were two, then three, popes.

recognized Urban. At first the Italian city-states recognized Urban; when he alienated them, they opted for Clement.

John of Spoleto, a professor at the law school at Bologna, eloquently summed up intellectual opinion of the schism, or division: "The longer this schism lasts, the more it appears to be costing, and the more harm it does; scandal, massacres, ruination, agitations, troubles and disturbances."[3] The common people, wracked by inflation, wars, and plague, were thoroughly confused about which pope was legitimate. The schism weakened the religious faith of many Christians and brought church leadership into serious disrepute. The schism also brought to the fore conciliar ideas about church government.

The Conciliar Movement

Theories about the nature of the Christian church and its government originated in the very early church, but the years of the Great Schism witnessed their maturity. **Conciliarists** believed that reform of the church could best be achieved through periodic assemblies, or general councils, representing all the Christian people. While acknowledging that the pope was head of the church, conciliarists favored a balanced or constitutional form of church government, with papal authority shared with a general council, in contrast to the monarchical one that prevailed.

conciliarists People who believed that the authority in the Roman church should rest in a general council composed of clergy, theologians, and laypeople, rather than in the pope alone.

The intellectual roots of the conciliar movement can be traced to the rector Marsiglio of Padua a half century earlier. In his *Defensor Pacis* (The Defender of the Peace), Marsiglio argued against the medieval idea of a society governed by both church and state, with church supreme. Instead, Marsiglio claimed, the state was the great unifying power in society and the church should be subordinate to it. Church leadership should rest in a general council, made up of laymen as well as priests, and superior to the pope. Marsiglio was excommunicated for these radical ideas and his work was condemned.

The English scholar and theologian John Wyclif (WIK-lif) (ca. 1330–1384) went even further than Marsiglio of Padua in his argument against medieval church structure. Wyclif wrote that Scripture alone should be the standard of Christian belief and practice, and papal claims of temporal power had no foundation in the Scriptures. He urged that the church be stripped of its property. He wanted Christians to read the Bible for themselves, and produced the first complete translation of the Bible into English.

Wyclif has been hailed as the precursor of the Reformation of the sixteenth century. Although his ideas were condemned by church leaders, they were spread by humble clerics and enjoyed great popularity in the early fifteenth century. His followers, known as Lollards, spread his ideas and

Spoon with Fox Preaching to Geese (southern Netherlands, ca. 1430)

Taking as his text a contemporary proverb, "When the fox preaches, beware your geese," the artist shows, in the bowl of a spoon, a fox dressed as a monk or friar, preaching with three dead geese in his hood, while another fox grabs one of the congregation. The preaching fox reads from a scroll bearing the word *pax* (peace), implying the perceived hypocrisy of the clergy. The object suggests the widespread criticism of churchmen in the later Middle Ages. (Painted enamel and gilding on silver; 17.6 x 4.9 x 2.6 cm, Museum of Fine Arts, Boston, Helen and Alice Colburn Fund, 51.2472)

made many copies of his Bible. Lollard teaching allowed women to preach, and they played a significant role in the movement. After Anne, sister of Wenceslaus (WEN-sis-laws), king of Germany and Bohemia, married Richard II of England, members of her household carried Lollard books back to Bohemia.

In response to continued calls throughout Europe for a council, the cardinals of Rome and Avignon summoned a council at Pisa in 1409. That gathering of prelates and theologians deposed both popes and selected another. Neither the Avignon pope nor the Roman pope would resign, however, and the appalling result was the creation of a threefold schism.

Finally, under pressure from the German emperor Sigismund (SEE-gis-muhnd), a great council met at the imperial city of Constance (KON-stuhns) (1414–1418). It had three objectives: to end the schism, to reform the church "in head and members" (from top to bottom), and to wipe out heresy. The council condemned the Czech reformer Jan Hus (yahn HOOS) (see the feature "Individuals in Society: Jan Hus"), and he was burned at the stake. The council eventually deposed both the Roman pope and the successor of the pope chosen at Pisa, and it isolated the Avignon antipope. A conclave elected a new leader, the Roman cardinal Colonna, who took the name Martin V (1417–1431).

Martin proceeded to dissolve the council. Nothing was done about reform. In the later fifteenth century the papacy concentrated on Italian problems to the exclusion of universal Christian interests. Though the church was reunited, the spiritual mystique of the clergy had weakened, and lay people were not willing to rely on the clergy or church hierarchy for their salvation. Pious men and women increasingly formed **confraternities** (kon-fruh-TUR-nih-teez), voluntary groups of lay people designed to express devotion through prayer, charitable giving, and devotional activities.

Economic and Social Change

How did economic and social tensions contribute to revolts, crime, violence, and a growing sense of ethnic and national distinctions?

In the fourteenth century economic and political difficulties, disease, and war profoundly affected the lives of European peoples. Decades of slaughter and destruction, punctuated by the decimating visits of the Black Death, made a grave economic situation virtually disastrous. In many parts of France and the Low Countries, fields lay in ruin or untilled for lack of labor power. In England, as taxes increased, criticisms of government policy and mismanagement multiplied. Crime and new forms of business organization aggravated economic troubles, and throughout Europe the frustrations of the common people erupted into widespread revolts.

Peasant Revolts

Nobles and clergy lived on the produce of peasant labor, thinking little of adding taxes to the burden of peasant life. While peasants had endured centuries of exploitation, the difficult conditions of the fourteenth and fifteenth centuries spurred a wave of **peasant revolts** across Europe. Peasants were sometimes joined by their urban counterparts on the social ladder, resulting in a wider revolution of poor against rich.

The first large-scale rebellion was in Flanders in the 1320s. In order to satisfy peace agreements, Flemish peasants were forced to pay taxes to the French, who

confraternities Voluntary lay groups organized by occupation, devotional preference, neighborhood, or charitable activity.

Section Review

- The so-called Babylonian Captivity was a period when the popes resided in Avignon instead of Rome, worked on bureaucratic reforms, lived in luxury, and lost their focus on spiritual objectives.

- The papacy relocated to Rome under Pope Gregory, but his death saw the beginning of the Great Schism (1378–1417) when two popes, Urban VI and Clement VII, competed to be the true pope.

- Conciliarists Rector Marsiglio, who advocated a general council to share power with the pope, and John Wyclif, who wrote that scripture was the basis of religion and translated the first Bible into English, both argued against medieval church structure.

- A third council (Pisa, 1409) calling for an end to the schism only resulted in a tri-fold schism, which ended when a fourth council at Constance (1414–1418) finally united the church, but the church's reputation was damaged and the faithful began to meet in small groups for devotional services.

- The priest Jan Hus denounced church abuses and papal authority, and when the church burned him at the stake in 1415, despite a promise of safe conduct, the nobility publicly made their first protest to ecclesiastical authority.

peasant revolts Revolts by peasants in the fourteenth and fifteenth centuries, often caused by social and economic conditions.

Individuals in Society

Jan Hus

In May 1990 the Czech Republic's parliament declared July 6, the date of Jan Hus's execution in 1415, a Czech national holiday. The son of free farmers, Hus (ca. 1369–1415) was born in Husinec in southern Bohemia, an area of heavy German settlement, and grew up conscious of the ethnic differences between Czechs and Germans. Most of his professors at Charles University in Prague were Germans. In 1396 he received a master's degree, and just before his ordination as a priest in 1400 he wrote that he would not be a "clerical careerist," implying that ambition for church offices motivated many of his peers.

The execution of Jan Hus. (University of Prague/The Art Archive)

The young priest lectured at the university and preached at the private Bethlehem Chapel. During his twelve years there Hus preached only in Czech. He denounced superstition, the sale of indulgences, and other abuses, but his remarks were thoroughly orthodox. He attracted attention among artisans and the small Czech middle class, but not Germans. His austere life and lack of ambition enhanced his reputation.

Around 1400 Czech students returning from study at Oxford introduced into Bohemia the reforming ideas of the English theologian John Wyclif. When German professors condemned Wyclif's ideas as heretical, Hus and the Czechs argued "academic freedom," the right to read and teach Wyclif's works regardless of their particular merits. When popular demonstrations against ecclesiastical abuses and German influence at the university erupted, King Vaclav (vah-SLAV) IV (1378–1419) placed control of the university in Czech hands. Hus was elected rector, the top administrative official.

The people of Prague, with perhaps the largest urban population in central Europe, 40 percent of it living below the poverty line and entirely dependent on casual labor, found Hus's denunciations of an overendowed church appealing. Hus considered the issues theological; his listeners saw them as socioeconomic.

Church officials in Prague were split about Hus's ideas, and popular unrest grew. The king forced Hus to leave the city, but he continued to preach and write. He disputed papal authority, denounced abuses, and argued that everyone should receive both bread and wine in the Eucharist (YOO-kuh-rist). (By this time, in standard Western Christian practice, the laity received only the bread; the priest received the wine *for* the laity, a mark of his distinctiveness.) Hus also defended transubstantiation (see page 341); insisted that church authority rested on Scripture, conscience, and tradition (in contrast to sixteenth-century Protestant reformers, who placed authority in Scripture alone); and made it clear that he had no intention of leaving the church or inciting a popular movement.

In 1413 the emperor Sigismund urged the calling of a general council to end the schism. Hus was invited, and, given the emperor's safe conduct (protection from attack or arrest), agreed to go. What he found was an atmosphere of inquisition. The safe conduct was disregarded, and Hus was arrested. Under questioning about his acceptance of Wyclif's ideas, Hus repeatedly replied, "I have not held; I do not hold." Council members were more interested in proving Hus a Wyclite than in his responses. They took away his priesthood, banned his teachings, burned his books, and burned Hus himself at the stake. He then belonged to the ages.

The ages have made good use of him. His death aggravated the divisions between the bishops at Constance and the Czech clerics and people. In September 1415, 452 nobles from all parts of Bohemia signed a letter saying that Hus had been unjustly executed and rejecting council rulings. This event marks the first time that an ecclesiastical decision was publicly defied. Revolution swept through Bohemia, with Hussites—Czech nobles and people—insisting on clerical poverty and both the bread and wine at the Eucharist, and with German citizens remaining loyal to the Roman church. In the sixteenth century reformers hailed Hus as the forerunner of Protestantism. In the eighteenth century Enlightenment philosophes evoked Hus as a defender of freedom of expression. In the nineteenth century central European nationalists used Hus's name to defend national sentiment against Habsburg rule. And in the twentieth century Hus's name was used against German fascist and Russian communist tyranny.

Questions for Analysis

1. Since Jan Hus lived and died insisting that his religious teaching was thoroughly orthodox, why has he been hailed as a reformer?

2. What political and cultural interests did the martyred Hus serve?

claimed fiscal rights over the county of Flanders. Monasteries also pressed peasants for additional money, above their customary tithes. In retaliation, peasants burned and pillaged castles and aristocratic country houses. A French army crushed peasant forces, and savage repression and the confiscation of peasant property followed in the 1330s.

Jacquerie A massive uprising by French peasants in 1358 protesting heavy taxation.

In 1358, when French taxation for the Hundred Years' War fell heavily on the poor, the frustrations of the French peasantry exploded in a massive uprising called the **Jacquerie** (zhahk-REE), after a mythical agricultural laborer, Jacques Bonhomme (Good Fellow). Peasants blamed the nobility for oppressive taxes, for the criminal brigandage of the countryside, for losses on the battlefield, and for the general misery. Crowds swept through the countryside, slashing the throats of nobles, burning their castles, raping their wives and daughters, and killing or maiming their horses and cattle. Artisans, small merchants, and parish priests joined the peasants. Urban and rural groups committed terrible destruction, and for several weeks the nobles were on the defensive. Then the upper class united to repress the revolt with merciless ferocity. Thousands of the "Jacques," innocent as well as guilty, were cut down. That forcible suppression of social rebellion, without any effort to alleviate its underlying causes, served to drive protest underground.

The Peasants' Revolt in England in 1381 involved thousands of people. Its causes were complex and varied from place to place. In general, though, the thirteenth century had witnessed the steady commutation of labor services for cash rents, and the Black Death had drastically cut the labor supply. As a result, peasants demanded higher wages and fewer manorial obligations. Their lords countered with a law freezing wages and binding workers to their manors. Unable to climb higher, the peasants sought release for their economic frustrations in revolt. Economic grievances combined with other factors. The south of England, where the revolt broke out, had been subjected to destructive French raids. The English government did little to protect the south, and villagers grew increasingly frightened and insecure. Moreover, decades of aristocratic violence against the weak peasantry had bred hostility and bitterness. Social and religious agitation by the popular preacher John Ball fanned the embers of discontent. Ball's famous couplet "When Adam delved and Eve span; Who was then the gentleman?" reflected real revolutionary sentiment.

The English revolt was ignited by the reimposition of a head tax on all adult males. Despite widespread opposition to the tax in 1380, the royal council ordered the sheriffs to collect it again in 1381 on penalty of a huge fine. Beginning with assaults on the tax collectors, the uprising in England followed a course similar to that of the Jacquerie in France. Castles and manors were sacked. Manorial records were destroyed. Many nobles, including the archbishop of Canterbury (KAN-ter-ber-ee), who had ordered the collection of the tax, were murdered.

The center of the revolt lay in the highly populated and economically advanced south and east, but sections of the north and the Midlands also witnessed rebellions. Violence took different forms in different places. Urban discontent merged with rural violence. In English towns where skilled Flemish craftsmen were employed, fear of competition led to their being attacked and murdered. Apprentices and journeymen, frustrated because the highest positions in the guilds were closed to them, rioted.

The boy-king Richard II (r. 1377–1399) met the leaders of the revolt, agreed to charters ensuring peasants' freedom, tricked them with false promises, and then crushed the uprising with terrible ferocity. The nobility tried to restore ancient duties of serfdom, but nearly a century of freedom had elapsed, and the commutation of manorial services continued. Rural serfdom disappeared in England by 1550.

Urban Conflicts

In Flanders, France, and England, peasant revolts often blended with conflicts involving workers in cities. Unrest also occurred in Italian, Spanish, and German cities.

These revolts typically flared up in urban centers where the conditions of work were changing for many people. In the thirteenth century craft guilds had organized the production of most goods, with masters, journeymen, and apprentices working side by side. In the fourteenth century a new system evolved to make products on a larger scale. Capitalist investors hired many households, with each household performing only one step of the process. Initially these investors were wealthy bankers and merchants, but eventually shop masters embraced the system. This promoted a greater division within guilds between wealthier masters and the poorer masters and journeymen they hired. Some masters became so wealthy that they no longer had to work in a shop themselves, nor did their wives and family members, though they still generally belonged to the craft guild.

While capitalism provided opportunities for some artisans to become investors and entrepreneurs, especially in cloth production, for many it led to a decrease in income and status. Guilds often responded to competition by limiting membership to existing guild families, which meant that journeymen who were not master's sons or who could not find a master's widow or daughter to marry could never become masters themselves. They remained journeymen their entire lives, losing their sense of solidarity with the masters of their craft. Resentment led to rebellion over economic issues.

Urban uprisings were also sparked by issues involving honor, such as employers' requiring workers to do tasks they regarded as beneath them. As their actual status and economic prospects declined and their work became basically wage labor, journeymen and poorer masters emphasized skill and honor as qualities that set them apart from less-skilled workers.

Guilds increasingly came to view the honor of their work as tied to an all-male workplace. When urban economies were expanding in the High Middle Ages, the master's wife and daughters worked alongside him, and female domestic servants also carried out productive tasks. (See the feature "Listening to the Past: Christine de Pizan" on pages 305–306.) Masters' widows ran shops after the death of their husbands. But in the fourteenth century, a woman's right to work slowly eroded. First, masters' widows were limited in the amount of time they could keep operating a shop or were prohibited from hiring journeymen; then female domestic servants were excluded from any productive tasks; then the number of daughters a master craftsman could employ was limited. When women were allowed to work, it was viewed as a substitute for charity.

Sex in the City

Peasant and urban revolts and riots had clear economic bases, but some historians have suggested that late medieval marital patterns may have also played a role in unrest. In northwestern Europe, people believed that couples should be economically independent before they married, so both spouses spent long periods as servants or workers in other households saving money and learning skills, or they waited until their own parents had died and the family property was distributed.

The most unusual feature of this pattern was the late age of marriage for women. Women entered marriage as adults and took charge of running a household immediately. They were thus not as dependent on their husbands or their mothers-in-law as were women who married at younger ages. They had fewer pregnancies than women who married earlier, though not necessarily fewer surviving children.

Men of all social groups were older when they married. In general, men were in their middle or late twenties at first marriage, with wealthier urban merchants often much older. Journeymen and apprentices were often explicitly prohibited from marrying, as were the students at universities, as they were understood to be in "minor orders" and thus like clergy, even if they were not intending on careers in the church.

The prohibitions on marriage for certain groups of men and the late age of marriage for most men meant that cities and villages were filled with large numbers of young adult men with no family responsibilities who often formed the core of riots and unrest. Not surprisingly, this situation also contributed to a steady market for sexual services outside of marriage, what in later centuries was termed prostitution. Research on the southern French province of Languedoc in the fourteenth and fifteenth centuries has revealed the establishment of legal houses of prostitution in many cities. Municipal authorities set up houses or red-light districts either outside the city walls or away from respectable neighborhoods. For example, authorities in Montpellier set aside Hot Street for prostitution, required public women to live there, and forbade anyone to molest them. Prostitution thus passed from being a private concern to a social matter requiring public supervision. The towns of Languedoc were not unique. Public authorities in Amiens, Dijon, Paris, Venice, Genoa, London, Florence, Rome, most of the larger German towns, and the English port of Sandwich set up brothels.

Visiting brothels was associated with achieving manhood in the eyes of young men, though for the women themselves their activities were work. Indeed, in some cases the women had no choice, for they had been traded to the brothel manager by their parents or other people in payment for debt, or had quickly become indebted to him (or, more rarely, her) for the clothes and other finery regarded as essential to their occupation. Poor women—and men—also sold sex illegally outside of city brothels, combining this with other sorts of part-time work such as laundering or sewing. Prostitution was an urban phenomenon because only populous towns had large numbers of unmarried young men, communities of transient merchants, and a culture accustomed to a cash exchange.

Though selling sex for money was legal in the Middle Ages, the position of women who did so was always marginal. In the late fifteenth century cities began to limit brothel residents' freedom of movement and choice of clothing, requiring them to wear distinctive head coverings or bands on their clothing so that they would not be mistaken for "honorable" women. The cities also began to impose harsher penalties on women who did not live in the designated house or section of town. A few prostitutes did earn enough to donate money to charity or buy property, but most were very poor.

Along with buying sex, young men also took it by force. Unmarried women often found it difficult to avoid sexual contact. Many of them worked as domestic servants, where their employers or employers' sons or male relatives could easily coerce them, or they worked in proximity to men. Notions of female honor kept upper-class women secluded in their homes, particularly in southern and eastern Europe, but there was little attempt anywhere to keep female servants or day laborers from the risk of seduction or rape. Rape was a capital crime in many parts of Europe, but the actual sentences handed out were more likely to be fines and brief

Prostitute Invites a Traveling Merchant
Poverty drove women into prostitution, which, though denounced by moralists, was accepted as a normal part of the medieval social fabric. In the cities and larger towns where prostitution flourished, public officials passed laws requiring prostitutes to wear a special mark on their clothing, regulated hours of business, forbade women to drag men into their houses, and denied business to women with the "burning sickness," gonorrhea. (Bodleian Library, Oxford, MS. Bodl. 264, fol. 245V)

imprisonment, with the severity of the sentence dependent on the social status of the victim and the perpetrator.

Same-sex relations—what in the late nineteenth century would be termed "homosexuality"—were another feature of medieval urban life (and of village life, though there are very few sources relating to sexual relations of any type in the rural context). Same-sex relations were of relatively little concern to church or state authorities in the early Middle Ages, but this attitude changed beginning in the late twelfth century. By 1300 most areas had defined such actions as "crimes against nature." Same-sex relations, usually termed "sodomy," became a capital crime in most of Europe, with adult offenders threatened with execution by fire. The Italian cities of Venice, Florence, and Lucca created special courts to deal with sodomy, which saw thousands of investigations.

Sodomy was not a marginal practice, which may account for the fact that, despite harsh laws and special courts, actual executions for sodomy were rare. Same-sex relations often developed within the context of all-male environments, such as the army, the craft shop, and the artistic workshop, and were part of the collective male experience. Homoerotic relationships played important roles in defining stages of life, expressing distinctions of status, and shaping masculine gender identity. Same-sex relations involving women almost never came to the attention of legal authorities, so it is difficult to find out how common they were. However, female-female desire was expressed in songs, plays, and stories, as was male-male desire, offering evidence of the way people understood same-sex relations.

Fur-Collar Crime The Hundred Years' War had provided employment and opportunity for thousands of idle and fortune-seeking knights. But during periods of truce and after the war finally ended, many nobles once again had little to do. Inflation hurt them. Although many were living on fixed incomes, their chivalric code demanded lavish generosity and an aristocratic lifestyle. Many nobles turned to crime as a way of raising money. The fourteenth and fifteenth centuries witnessed a great deal of "fur-collar crime," so called for the miniver fur nobles alone were allowed to wear on their collars.

Groups of noble brigands roamed the English countryside stealing from both rich and poor. Operating like modern urban racketeers, knightly gangs demanded that peasants pay "protection money" or else have their hovels burned and their fields destroyed. They seized wealthy travelers and held them for ransom.

When accused of wrongdoing, fur-collar criminals intimidated witnesses, threatened jurors, and used "pull" or cash to bribe judges. As a fourteenth-century English judge wrote to a young nobleman, "For the love of your father I have hindered charges being brought against you and have prevented execution of indictment actually made."[4] Criminal activity by nobles continued decade after decade because governments were too weak to stop it.

The ballads of Robin Hood, a collection of folk legends from late medieval England, describe the adventures of the outlaw hero and his merry men as they avenge the common people against fur-collar criminals—grasping landlords, wicked sheriffs, and mercenary churchmen. Robin Hood was a popular figure because he symbolized the deep resentment of aristocratic corruption and abuse; he represented the struggle against tyranny and oppression.

Ethnic Tensions and Restrictions

Large numbers of people in the twelfth and thirteenth centuries migrated from one part of Europe to another: the English into Scotland and Ireland; Germans, French, and Flemings into Poland, Bohemia, and Hungary; the French into Spain. The colonization of frontier regions meant that peoples of different ethnic backgrounds lived side by side. Everywhere in Europe, towns recruited people from the countryside (see page 249). In frontier regions, townspeople were usually long-distance immigrants and, in eastern Europe, Ireland, and Scotland, ethnically different from the surrounding rural population. In eastern Europe, German was the language of the towns; in Irish towns, French, the tongue of Norman or English settlers, predominated.

In the early periods of conquest and colonization, and in all regions with extensive migrations, a legal dualism existed: native peoples remained subject to their traditional laws; newcomers brought and were subject to the laws of the countries from which they came. On the Prussian and Polish frontier, for example, the law was that "men who come there . . . should be judged on account of any crime or contract engaged in there according to Polish custom if they are Poles and according to German custom if they are Germans."[5] Likewise, the conquered Muslim subjects of Christian kings in Spain had the right to be judged under Muslim law by Muslim judges.

The great exception to this broad pattern was Ireland. From the start, the English practiced an extreme form of discrimination toward the native Irish. The English distinguished between the free and the unfree, and the entire Irish population, simply by the fact of Irish birth, was unfree. When an English legal structure was established, the Irish were denied access to the common-law courts. In civil (property) disputes, an English defendant need not respond to his Irish plaintiff; no Irish person could make a will. In criminal procedures, the murder of an Irishman was not considered a felony. Other than in Ireland, although native peoples commonly held humbler positions, both immigrant and native townspeople prospered during the expanding economy of the thirteenth century. But when economic recession hit during the fourteenth century, ethnic tensions multiplied.

The later Middle Ages witnessed a movement away from legal pluralism or dualism and toward legal homogeneity and an emphasis on blood descent. The dominant ethnic group in an area tried to bar the other from positions of church leadership and guild membership. Marriage laws were instituted that attempted to maintain ethnic purity and some church leaders actively promoted ethnic discrimination.

The most extensive attempt to prevent intermarriage and protect ethnic purity is embodied in Ireland's **Statute of Kilkenny** (kil-KEN-ee) (1366), which states that "there were to be no marriages between those of immigrant and native stock; that the English inhabitants of Ireland must employ the English language and bear English names; that they must ride in the English way (i.e., with saddles) and have English apparel; that no Irishmen were to be granted ecclesiastical benefices or admitted to monasteries in the English parts of Ireland. . . ."[6]

Late medieval chroniclers used words such as *gens* (zhahn) (race or clan) and *natio* (NAHT-ee-oh) (species, stock, or kind) to refer to different groups. They held that peoples differed according to language, traditions, customs, and laws. None of these were unchangeable, however, and commentators increasingly also described ethnic differences in terms of "blood"—"German blood," "English blood," and so on—which made ethnicity heritable. Religious beliefs also came to be conceptualized as blood, with people regarded as having Jewish blood, Muslim blood, or Christian blood. The most dramatic expression of this was in Spain, where "purity of the blood"—having no Muslim or Jewish ancestors—became an obsession. Blood was also used as a way to talk about social differences, especially for nobles. Just as Irish and English were prohibited from marrying each other, those of "noble blood" were prohibited from marrying commoners in many parts of Europe. As Europeans increasingly came into contact with people from Africa and Asia, and particularly as they developed colonial empires, these notions of blood also became a way of conceptualizing racial categories (see page 325).

Statute of Kilkenny Laws issued in 1366 that discriminated against the Irish, forbidding marriage between the English and the Irish, requiring the use of the English language, and denying the Irish access to ecclesiastical offices.

Literacy and Vernacular Literature

The development of ethnic identities had many negative consequences, but a more positive effect was the increasing use of the vernacular. Two masterpieces of European culture, Dante's (DAHN-tay) *Divine Comedy* (1310–1320) and Chaucer's (CHAW-ser) *Canterbury Tales* (1387–1400), illustrate a sophisticated use of the rhythms and rhymes of the vernacular.

Dante Alighieri (ah-lee-ghee-AIR-ee) (1265–1321) called his work a "comedy" because he wrote it in Italian and in a different style from the "tragic" Latin; a later generation added the adjective *divine*, referring both to its sacred subject and to Dante's artistry. The *Divine Comedy* is an epic poem of one hundred cantos (verses) each of whose three equal parts (1 + 33 + 33 + 33) describes one of the realms of the next world: Hell, Purgatory, and Paradise. The Roman poet Virgil, representing reason, leads Dante through Hell, where Dante observes the torments of the damned and denounces the disorders of his own time, especially ecclesiastical ambition and corruption. Passing up into Purgatory, Virgil shows the poet how souls are purified of their disordered inclinations. From Purgatory, Beatrice (BEE-uh-triss), a woman Dante once loved and the symbol of divine revelation in the poem, leads him to Paradise. In Paradise, home of the angels and saints, Saint Bernard —representing mystic contemplation—leads Dante to the Virgin Mary. Through her intercession, he at last attains a vision of God.

The *Divine Comedy* portrays contemporary and historical figures, comments on secular and ecclesiastical affairs, and draws on Scholastic philosophy. Within the framework of a symbolic pilgrimage to the City of God, the *Divine Comedy* embodies the psychological tensions of the age. A profoundly Christian poem, it also contains bitter criticism of some church authorities. In its symmetrical structure and use of figures from the ancient world, such as Virgil, the poem perpetuates the classical tradition, but as the first major work of literature in the Italian vernacular, it is distinctly modern.

Geoffrey Chaucer (1342–1400) was an official in the administrations of the English kings Edward III and Richard II and wrote poetry as an avocation. Chaucer's *Canterbury Tales* is a collection of stories in lengthy rhymed narrative. On a pilgrimage to the shrine of Saint Thomas Becket at Canterbury (see page 203), thirty people of various social backgrounds tell tales. For example, the gross Miller tells a vulgar story about a deceived husband; the earthy Wife of Bath, who has buried five husbands, sketches a fable about the selection of a spouse; and the elegant Prioress, who violates her vows by wearing jewelry, delivers a homily on the Virgin. In depicting the interests and behavior of all types of people, Chaucer presents a rich panorama of English social life in the fourteenth century. Like the *Divine Comedy*, the *Canterbury Tales* reflects the cultural tensions of the times. Ostensibly Christian, many of the pilgrims are also materialistic, sensual, and worldly, suggesting the ambivalence of the broader society's concern for the next world and frank enjoyment of this one.

Beginning in the fourteenth century, a variety of evidence attests to the increasing literacy of laypeople. Wills and inventories reveal that many people, not just nobles, possessed books—mainly devotional, but also romances, manuals on manners and etiquette, histories, and sometimes legal and philosophical texts. In England the number of schools in the diocese of York quadrupled between 1350 and 1500. Information from Flemish and German towns is similar: children were sent to schools and were taught the fundamentals of reading, writing, and arithme-

Schoolmaster and Schoolmistress Teaching

Ambrosius Holbein (HOHL-bine), elder brother of the more famous Hans Holbein, produced this signboard for the Swiss educator Myconius; it is an excellent example of what we would call commercial art—art used to advertise, in this case Myconius's profession. The German script above promised that all who enrolled, girls and boys, would learn to read and write. Most schools were for boys only, but a few offered instruction for girls as well. By modern standards the classroom seems bleak: the windows have glass panes but they don't admit much light, and the schoolmaster is prepared to use the sticks if the boy makes a mistake. (Kunstmuseum Basel, Acc. No. 311/Martin Buhler, photographer)

tic. Laymen increasingly served as managers or stewards of estates and as clerks to guilds and town governments; such positions obviously required that they be able to keep administrative and financial records.

The penetration of laymen into the higher positions of governmental administration, long the preserve of clerics, also illustrates rising lay literacy. With growing frequency, the upper classes sent their daughters to convent schools, where, in addition to instruction in singing, religion, needlework, deportment, and household management, girls gained the rudiments of reading and sometimes writing.

The spread of literacy represents a response to the needs of an increasingly complex society. Trade, commerce, and expanding government bureaucracies required more and more literate people. Late medieval culture remained an oral culture in which most people received information by word of mouth. But by the mid-fifteenth century, even before the printing press was turning out large quantities of reading materials, the evolution toward a literary culture was already perceptible.

Section Review

- Peasant revolts due to increased taxes, economic frustration, and fear, resulted in widespread violence and destruction, leading to a backlash of repression by the nobility.
- Urban conflict occurred as capitalism magnified the disparity between rich and poor and caused limits on entry into guilds and on women's right to work in guild shops.
- Poor women were forced into prostitution in urban centers, and homosexuality and rape were common.
- After the Hundred Years' War, unemployed young nobles, called fur-collar criminals, roamed the countryside, stealing and causing trouble.
- The large migrations of different ethnicities brought with them the laws of their countries of origin, except in Ireland, where English law discriminated against the Irish.
- Ethnic identities increased the use of vernacular language, and great works of literature such as Dante's *Divine Comedy* and Chaucer's *Canterbury Tales* reflected the tensions of the era.
- With the advancements in trade, commerce, and government, literacy increased and more books became available.

Chapter Review

What were the demographic, social, and economic consequences of climate change? (page 278)

The crises of the fourteenth and fifteenth centuries were acids that burned deeply into the fabric of traditional medieval society. Bad weather brought poor harvests, which contributed to widespread famine and disease and an international economic depression. Political leaders attempted to find solutions, but were unable to deal with the economic and social problems that resulted.

How did the spread of the plague shape European society? (page 280)

In 1348 a new disease, most likely the bubonic plague, came to mainland Europe, carried from the Black Sea by ships. It spread quickly by land and sea and within two years may have killed as much as one-third of the European population. Contemporary medical explanations for the plague linked it to poisoned air or water, and treatments were ineffective. Many people regarded the plague as a divine punishment and sought remedies in religious practices such as prayer, pilgrimages, or donations to churches. Population losses caused by the Black Death led to inflation but in the long run may have contributed to more opportunities for the peasants and urban workers who survived the disease.

What were the causes of the Hundred Years' War, and how did the war affect European politics, economics, and cultural life? (page 286)

The miseries of the plague were enhanced in England and France by the Hundred Years' War, which was fought intermittently in France from 1337 to 1453. The war began as a dispute over the succession to the French crown, and royal propaganda on both sides fostered a kind of early nationalism. The English won most of the battles

Key Terms

Great Famine (p. 278)
Black Death (p. 280)
flagellants (p. 284)
Agincourt (p. 287)
representative assemblies (p. 290)
nationalism (p. 290)
Babylonian Captivity (p. 291)
Great Schism (p. 291)
conciliarists (p. 292)
confraternities (p. 293)
peasant revolts (p. 293)
Jacquerie (p. 296)
Statute of Kilkenny (p. 301)

and in 1419 advanced to the walls of Paris. The appearance of Joan of Arc rallied the French cause, and French troops eventually pushed English forces out of all of France except the port of Calais. The war served as a catalyst for the development of representative government in England. In France, on the other hand, the war stiffened opposition to national assemblies.

What were the causes of the Great Schism, and how did church leaders, intellectuals, and ordinary people respond? (page 291)

Religious beliefs offered people solace through these difficult times, but the Western Christian church was going through a particularly difficult period in the fourteenth and early fifteenth centuries. The papacy moved to Avignon in France, where it was dominated by the French monarchy. This led eventually to some cardinals electing a second, Roman pope, a division in the church called the Great Schism. The Avignon papacy and the Great Schism weakened the prestige of the church and people's faith in papal authority. The conciliar movement, by denying the church's universal sovereignty, strengthened the claims of secular governments to jurisdiction over all their peoples. As members of the clergy challenged the power of the pope, laypeople challenged the authority of the church itself. Women and men increasingly relied on direct approaches to God, often through mystical encounters, rather than on the institutional church. Some, including John Wyclif and Jan Hus, questioned basic church doctrines.

How did economic and social tensions contribute to revolts, crime, violence, and a growing sense of ethnic and national distinctions? (page 293)

The plague and the war both led to higher taxes and economic dislocations, which sparked peasant revolts in Flanders, France, and England. Peasant revolts often blended with conflicts involving workers in cities, where working conditions were changing to create a greater gap between wealthy merchant-producers and poor workers. Unrest in the countryside and cities may have been further exacerbated by marriage patterns that left large numbers of young men unmarried and rootless. The pattern of late marriage for men contributed to a growth in prostitution, which was an accepted feature of medieval urban society. Along with peasant revolts and urban crime and unrest, violence perpetrated by nobles was a common part of late medieval life. The economic and demographic crises of the fourteenth century also contributed to increasing ethnic tensions in the many parts of Europe where migration had brought different population groups together. A growing sense of ethnic and national identity led to restrictions and occasionally to violence, but also to the increasing use of vernacular languages for works of literature. The increasing number of schools that led to the growth of lay literacy represents another positive achievement of the later Middle Ages.

Notes

1. Quoted in J. Barnie, *War in Medieval English Society: Social Values and the Hundred Years' War* (Ithaca, N.Y.: Cornell University Press, 1974), p. 34.
2. See G. O. Sayles, *The King's Parliament of England* (New York: W. W. Norton, 1974), app., pp. 137–141.
3. Quoted in J. H. Smith, *The Great Schism, 1378: The Disintegration of the Medieval Papacy* (New York: Weybright & Talley, 1970), p. 15.
4. Quoted in B. A. Hanawalt, "Fur Collar Crime: The Pattern of Crime Among the Fourteenth-Century English Nobility," *Journal of Social History* 8 (Spring 1975): p. 7.
5. Quoted in R. Bartlett, *The Making of Europe: Conquest, Colonization and Cultural Change, 950–1350* (Princeton, N.J.: Princeton University Press, 1993), p. 205.
6. Quoted ibid., p. 239.

To assess your mastery of this chapter, go to **bedfordstmartins.com/mckaywestbrief**

Listening to the Past

Christine de Pizan

Christine de Pizan (duh PEE-zahn) (1364?–1430; earlier spelled "Pisan") was the well-educated daughter and wife of men who held positions at the court of the king of France. Widowed at twenty-five, Christine decided to support her family through writing. She began to write prose works and poetry, sending them to wealthy individuals in the hope of receiving their support. Her efforts resulted in commissions to write specific works, including a biography of the French king Charles V and a book of military tactics. She became the first woman in Europe to make her living as a writer, a difficult profession for anyone in this era before the printing press.

Among Christine's many works were several in which she considered women's nature and proper role in society, which had been a topic of debate since ancient times. The following selection is from The Treasure of the City of Ladies *(1405, also called* The Book of Three Virtues)*, which provides moral suggestions and practical advice on behavior and household management. Most of the book is directed toward princesses and court ladies (who would have been able to read it), but she also includes shorter sections for the wives of merchants and artisans, serving-women, female peasants, and even prostitutes. This is her advice to the wives of artisans, whose husbands were generally members of urban craft guilds.*

All wives of artisans should be very painstaking and diligent if they wish to have the necessities of life. They should encourage their husbands or their workmen to get to work early in the morning and work until late, for mark our words, there is no trade so good that if you neglect your work you will not have difficulty putting bread on the table. And besides encouraging the others, the wife herself should be involved in the work to the extent that she knows all about it, so that she may know how to oversee his workers if her husband is absent, and to reprove them if they do not do well. She ought to oversee them to keep them from idleness, for through careless workers the master is sometimes ruined. And when customers come to her husband and try to drive a hard bargain, she ought to warn him solicitously to take care that he does not make a bad deal. She should advise him to be chary of giving too much credit if he does not know precisely where and to whom it is going, for in this way many come to poverty, although sometimes the greed to earn more or to accept a tempting proposition makes them do it.

In addition, she ought to keep her husband's love as much as she can, to this end: that he will stay at home more willingly and that he may not have any reason to join the foolish crowds of other young men in taverns and indulge in unnecessary

Several manuscripts of Christine's works included illustrations showing her writing, which would have increased their appeal to the wealthy individuals who purchased them. (Copyright © British Library Board)

and extravagant expense, as many tradesmen do, especially in Paris. By treating him kindly she should protect him as well as she can from this. It is said that three things drive a man from his home: a quarrelsome wife, a smoking fireplace and a leaking roof. She too ought to stay at home gladly and not go every day traipsing hither and yon gossiping with the neighbours and visiting her chums to find out what everyone is doing. That is done by slovenly housewives roaming about the town in groups. Nor should she go off on these pilgrimages got up for no good reason and involving a lot of needless expense. Furthermore, she ought to remind her husband that they should live so frugally that their expenditure does not exceed their income, so that at the end of the year they do not find themselves in debt.

Questions

1. How would you describe Christine's view of the ideal artisan's wife?

2. The regulations of craft guilds often required that masters who ran workshops be married. What evidence does Christine's advice provide for why guilds would have stipulated this?

3. How are economic and moral virtues linked for Christine?

Source: Christine de Pisan, *The Treasure of the City of Ladies,* translated with an introduction by Sarah Lawson (Penguin Classics, 1985). Translation copyright © Sarah Lawson, 1985. Reproduced by permission of Penguin Books Ltd. For more on Christine, see: C. C. Willard, *Christine de Pisan: Her Life and Works* (1984), and S. Bell, *The Lost Tapestries of the City of Ladies: Christine de Pizan's Renaissance Legacy* (2004).

CHAPTER 13

European Society in the Age of the Renaissance

1350–1550

Michelangelo's frescoes in the Sistine Chapel in the Vatican, commissioned by the pope. The huge ceiling includes biblical scenes, and the far wall, painted much later, shows a dramatic and violent Last Judgment. (Vatican Museum)

Chapter Preview

Economic and Political Developments
What economic and political developments in Italy provided the setting for the Renaissance?

Intellectual Change
What were the key ideas of the Renaissance, and how were they different for men and women and for southern and northern Europeans?

Art and the Artist
How did changes in art both reflect and shape new ideas?

Social Hierarchies
What were the key social hierarchies in Renaissance Europe, and how did ideas about hierarchy shape people's lives?

Politics and the State in the Renaissance (ca. 1450–1521)
How did the nation-states of western Europe evolve in this period?

INDIVIDUALS IN SOCIETY: Leonardo da Vinci

LISTENING TO THE PAST: An Age of Gold

W̲hile the Four Horsemen of the Apocalypse seemed to be carrying war, plague, famine, and death across northern Europe, a new culture was emerging in southern Europe. The fourteenth century witnessed the beginnings of remarkable changes in many aspects of Italian intellectual, artistic, and cultural life. Artists and writers thought that they were living in a new golden age, but not until the sixteenth century was this change given the label we use today—the **Renaissance**, from the French version of a word meaning rebirth.

The word *Renaissance* was first used by the artist and art historian Giorgio Vasari (**vuh-ZAHR-ee**) (1511–1574) to describe the art of "rare men of genius," such as his contemporary, Michelangelo (**my-kuhl-AN-juh-low**). Through their works, Vasari judged, the glory of the classical past had been reborn—or perhaps even surpassed—after centuries of darkness. Vasari used *Renaissance* to describe painting, sculpture, and architecture, what he termed the "Major Arts." Gradually, however, the word was used to refer to many aspects of life at this time, first in Italy and then in the rest of Europe. This new attitude had a slow diffusion out of Italy, with the result that the Renaissance "happened" at different times in different parts of Europe: Italian art of the fourteenth through the early sixteenth centuries is described as "Renaissance," and so is English literature of the late sixteenth century, including Shakespeare's plays and poetry.

Although Vasari viewed the Renaissance as a sharp break with the Middle Ages, some contemporary historians have chosen to view the Renaissance as a bridge between the medieval and modern eras because it corresponded chronologically with the late medieval period and because there were many continuities along with the changes. Others have questioned whether the word *Renaissance* should be used at all to describe an era in which many social groups saw decline rather than advance. These debates remind us that these labels—medieval, Renaissance, modern—while offering a useful framework for viewing various periods, are also laden with value judgments.

Renaissance A French word, translated from the Italian *rinascita*, first used by art historian and critic Giorgio Vasari (1511–1574), meaning rebirth of the culture of classical antiquity; English-speaking students adopted the French term.

Economic and Political Developments

What economic and political developments in Italy provided the setting for the Renaissance?

The cultural achievements of the Renaissance rest on the economic and political developments of earlier centuries. Economic growth laid the material basis for the Italian Renaissance, and ambitious merchants gained political power to match their economic power. They then used their money and power to buy luxuries and hire talent.

Commercial Developments

Scholars tend to agree that the first artistic and literary manifestations of the Italian Renaissance appeared in Florence, which possessed enormous wealth because Florentine merchants and bankers had acquired control of papal banking toward the end of the thirteenth century. From their position as tax collectors for the papacy, Florentine mercantile families began to dominate European banking on both sides of the Alps, setting up offices in major European and North African cities. The profits from loans, investments, and money exchanges that poured back to Florence were pumped into urban industries. Such profits contributed to the city's economic vitality and allowed banking families to control the city's politics and culture.

By the first quarter of the fourteenth century, the economic foundations of Florence were so strong that even severe crises could not destroy the city. In 1344 King Edward III of England repudiated his huge debts to Florentine bankers and forced some of them into bankruptcy. Florence suffered frightfully from the Black Death, losing at least half its population. Serious labor unrest shook the political establishment. Nevertheless, the basic Florentine economic structure remained stable.

Communes and Republics

The northern Italian cities were **communes,** sworn associations of free men seeking complete political and economic independence from local nobles. The merchant guilds that formed the communes built and maintained the city walls, regulated trade, raised taxes, and kept civil order. The local nobles frequently moved into the cities, marrying into rich commercial families and starting their own businesses. This merger of the northern Italian feudal nobility and the commercial elite created a powerful oligarchy that ruled the city and surrounding countryside. Yet because of rivalries among different powerful families, Italian communes were often politically unstable.

Unrest coming from below exacerbated the instability. Merchant elites made citizenship in the communes dependent on a property qualification, years of residence within the city, and social connections. Only a tiny percentage of the male population possessed these qualifications and thus could hold office in the commune's political councils. The common people, called the **popolo,** were disenfranchised and heavily taxed, and they bitterly resented their exclusion from power. Throughout most of the thirteenth century, in city after city, the popolo used armed force and violence to take over the city governments. Republican governments—in which political power theoretically resides in the people and is exercised by their chosen representatives—were established in Bologna, Siena, Parma, Florence, Genoa, and other cities. The victory of the popolo proved temporary, however, because they could not establish civil order within their cities. Merchant oligarchies

communes Associations of merchants in Italian cities such as Milan, Florence, Genoa, and Pisa who sought political and economic independence from local nobles; members of communes wanted self-government.

popolo Disenfranchised, common people in Italian cities who resented their exclusion from power.

A Bank Scene, Florence
Originally a "bank" was just a counter; moneychangers who sat behind the counter became "bankers," exchanging different currencies and holding deposits for merchants and business-people. In this scene from fifteenth-century Florence, the bank is covered with an imported Ottoman geometric rug, one of many imported luxury items handled by Florentine merchants.
(Prato, San Francesco/Scala/Art Resource, NY)

condottieri Military leaders in Italian city-states who often took over political control as well.

signori Government by one-man rule in Italian cities such as Milan, in which the ruler handed power down to his son.

courts Magnificent households and palaces where the signori and the most powerful merchant oligarchs required political business to be conducted.

patrons Patrician merchants and bankers, popes and princes, who supported the arts as a means of glorifying themselves and their families.

reasserted their power and sometimes brought in powerful military leaders to establish order. These military leaders, called **condottieri** (kawn-duh-TYAIR-ey) (singular, condottiero), had their own mercenary armies, and in many cities they took over political power as well.

Many cities in Italy became **signori** (see-YOHR- ee), in which one man ruled and handed down the right to rule to his son. Some signori (the word is plural in Italian and is used both for persons and forms of government) kept the institutions of communal government in place, but these had no actual power.

In the fifteenth century the signori in many cities and the most powerful merchant oligarchs in others transformed their households into **courts**. They built magnificent palaces in the centers of cities and required all political business to be done there. They became **patrons** of the arts, hiring architects to design and build these palaces, artists to fill them with paintings and sculptures, and musicians and composers to fill them with music. They supported writers and philosophers, flaunting their patronage of learning and the arts. They used ceremonies connected with family births, baptisms, marriages, funerals, or triumphant entrances into the city as occasions for magnificent pageantry and elaborate ritual. Courtly culture afforded signori and oligarchs the opportunity to display and assert their wealth and power. The courts of the rulers of Milan, Florence, and other cities were models for those developed later by rulers of nation-states.

The Balance of Power Among the Italian City-States

In the fifteenth century five powers dominated the Italian peninsula: Venice, Milan, Florence, the Papal States, and the kingdom of Naples (see Map 13.1). Venice, with its enormous trade empire ranked as an international power. Though Venice was a republic in name, an oligarchy of merchant aristocrats actually ran the city. Milan was also called a republic, but the condottieri turned signori of the Sforza (SFAWRT-suh) family ruled harshly and dominated the smaller cities of the north. Likewise, in Florence the form of government was republican, with authority vested in several councils of state. In reality, between 1434 and 1494, power in Florence was held by the great Medici (MED-ih-chee) banking family. Though not public officers, Cosimo (1434–1464) and Lorenzo (1469–1492) ruled from behind the scenes. In central Italy Pope Alexander VI (1492–1503), aided militarily and politically by his son Cesare Borgia (CHE-zah-reh BAWR-zhuh), reasserted papal authority in the papal lands. South of the Papal States, the kingdom of Naples was under the control of Aragon.

The major Italian city-states controlled the smaller ones, such as Siena, Mantua, Ferrara, and Modena, and competed furiously among themselves for territory. The large cities used diplomacy, spies, paid informers, and any other available means to get information that could be used to advance their ambitions. While the states of northern Europe were moving toward centralization and consolidation, the world of Italian politics resembled a jungle where the powerful dominated the weak.

In one significant respect, however, the Italian city-states anticipated future relations among competing European states after 1500. Whenever one Italian state appeared to gain a predominant position within the peninsula, other states combined to establish a *balance of power* against the major threat. In the formation of these alliances, Renaissance Italians invented the machinery of modern diplomacy: permanent embassies with resident ambassadors in capitals where political relations and commercial ties needed continual monitoring. The resident ambassador was one of the great achievements of the Italian Renaissance.

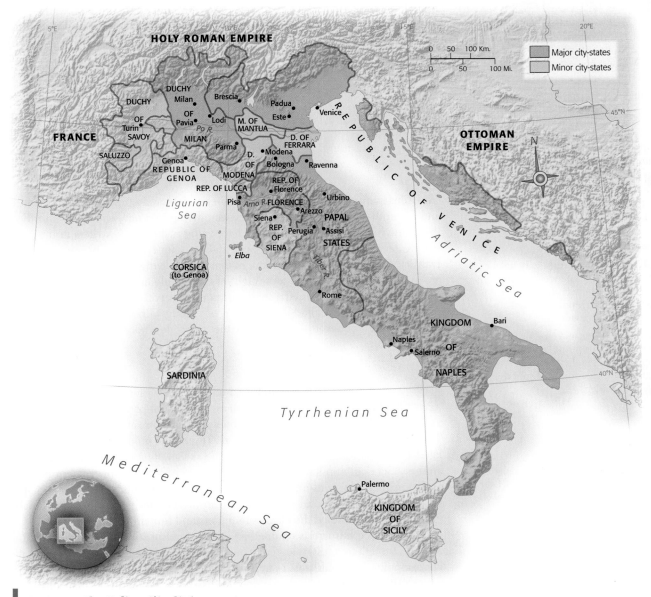

MAP 13.1   The Italian City-States, ca. 1494

In the fifteenth century the Italian city-states represented great wealth and cultural sophistication. The political divisions of the peninsula invited foreign intervention.

At the end of the fifteenth century Venice, Florence, Milan, and the papacy possessed great wealth and represented high cultural achievement. Wealthy and divided, however, they were also an inviting target for invasion. When Florence and Naples entered into an agreement to acquire Milanese territories, Milan called on France for support.

The invasion of Italy in 1494 by the French king Charles VIII (r. 1483–1498) inaugurated a new period in Italian and European power politics. Italy became the focus of international ambitions and the battleground of foreign armies, particularly those of France and the Holy Roman Empire in a series of conflicts called the Habsburg-Valois (HABZ-berg VAL-wah) Wars (named for the German and

humanism The new philosophy that emphasized the critical study of Latin and Greek literature with the goal of understanding human nature.

individualism A basic feature of the Italian Renaissance that stressed personality, uniqueness, genius, and self-consciousness.

French dynasties). The Italian cities suffered severely from continual warfare, especially in the frightful sack of Rome in 1527 by imperial forces under the emperor Charles V. Thus the failure of the city-states to form some federal system, to consolidate, or at least to establish a common foreign policy led to centuries of subjection by outside invaders. Italy was not to achieve unification until 1870.

Intellectual Change

What were the key ideas of the Renaissance, and how were they different for men and women and for southern and northern Europeans?

The Renaissance was characterized by self-conscious awareness among fourteenth- and fifteenth-century Italians that they were living in a new era. The realization that something new and unique was happening first came to writers in the fourteenth century, especially to the poet and humanist Francesco Petrarch (PEE-trahrk) (1304–1374). Petrarch thought that he was living at the start of a new age, a period of light following a long night of Gothic gloom. For Petrarch, the Germanic migrations had caused a sharp cultural break with the glories of Rome and inaugurated what he called the "Dark Ages." Along with many of his contemporaries, Petrarch believed that he was witnessing a new golden age of intellectual achievement.

Humanism

Petrarch and other poets, writers, and artists showed a deep interest in the ancient past, in both the physical remains of the Roman Empire and classical Latin texts. The study of Latin classics became known as the *studia humanitates*, usually translated as "liberal studies" or the "liberal arts." Like all programs of study, the liberal arts contained an implicit philosophy, which was generally known as **humanism.** Humanism emphasized human beings, their achievements, interests, and capabilities. Whereas medieval writers looked to the classics to reveal God, Renaissance humanists studied the classics to understand human nature.

Renaissance humanists retained a Christian perspective, however: men (and women, though to a lesser degree) were made in the image and likeness of God. For example, in a remarkable essay, *On the Dignity of Man* (1486), the Florentine writer Giovanni Pico della Mirandola (1463–1494) stressed that man possesses great dignity because he was made as Adam in the image of God before the Fall and as Christ after the Resurrection. According to Pico, man's place in the universe is somewhere between the beasts and the angels, but because of the divine image planted in him, there are no limits to what he can accomplish. Humanists generally rejected classical ideas that were opposed to Christianity, or they sought through reinterpretation an underlying harmony between the pagan and secular and the Christian faith.

Interest in human achievement led humanists to emphasize the importance of the individual. Groups such as families, guilds, and religious organizations continued to provide strong support for the individual and to exercise great social influence. Yet in the Renaissance, artists and intellectuals, unlike their counterparts in the Middle Ages, prized their own uniqueness. This attitude of **individualism** stressed the full development of one's special capabilities and talents. The idea of the "genius" who transcends traditions and rules is believed to have originated in this period. Thirst for fame and the quest for glory drove Italian creativity. (See the feature "Individuals in Society: Leonardo da Vinci.")

Individuals in Society

Leonardo da Vinci

What makes a genius? An infinite capacity for taking pains? A deep curiosity about an extensive variety of subjects? A divine spark as manifested by talents that far exceed the norm? Or is it just "one percent inspiration and ninety-nine percent perspiration," as Thomas Edison said? To most observers, Leonardo da Vinci was one of the greatest geniuses in the history of the Western world. In fact, Leonardo was one of the individuals that the Renaissance label "genius" was designed to describe: a special kind of human being with exceptional creative powers.

Leonardo (who, despite the title of a recent bestseller and movie, is always called by his first name) was born in Vinci, near Florence, the illegitimate son of Caterina, a local peasant girl, and Ser Piero da Vinci, a notary public. Caterina later married another native of Vinci. When Ser Piero's marriage to Donna Albrussia produced no children, he and his wife took in Leonardo. Ser Piero secured Leonardo's apprenticeship with the painter and sculptor Andrea del Verrocchio in Florence. In 1472, when Leonardo was just twenty years old, he was listed as a master in Florence's "Company of Artists."

Leonardo's most famous portrait, *Mona Lisa*, shows a woman with an enigmatic smile that Giorgio Vasari described as "so pleasing that it seemed divine rather than human." The portrait, probably of the young wife of a rich Florentine merchant (her exact identity is hotly debated), may actually be the best-known painting in the history of art. One of its competitors in that designation would be another work of Leonardo's, *The Last Supper*, which has been called "the most revered painting in the world."

Leonardo's reputation as a genius does not rest simply on his paintings, however, which are actually few in number, but rather on the breadth of his abilities and interests. In these, he is often understood to be the first "Renaissance man," a phrase we still use for a multi-talented individual. He wanted to reproduce what the eye can see, and he drew everything he saw around him, including executed criminals hanging on gallows as well as the beauties of nature. Trying to understand how the human body worked, Leonardo studied live and dead bodies, doing autopsies and dissections to investigate muscles and circulation. He carefully analyzed the effects of light, using his analysis to paint strong contrasts of light and shadow, and he experimented with perspective.

Leonardo used his drawings as the basis for his paintings and also as a tool of scientific investigation. He drew plans for hundreds of inventions, many of which would become reality centuries later, such as the helicopter, tank, machine gun, and parachute. He was hired by one of the powerful new rulers in Italy, Duke Ludovico Sforza of Milan, to design practical things that the duke needed, including weapons, fortresses, and water systems, as well as to produce works of art. Leonardo left Milan when Sforza was overthrown in war and spent the last years of his life painting, drawing, and designing for the pope and the French king.

Leonardo experimented with new materials for painting and sculpture, some of which worked and some of which did not. The experimental method he used to paint *The Last Supper* caused the picture to deteriorate rapidly, and it began to flake off the wall as soon as it was finished. Leonardo actually regarded it as never quite completed, for he could not find a model for the face of Christ that would evoke the spiritual depth he felt it deserved. His gigantic equestrian statue in honor of Ludovico's father, Duke Francesco Sforza, was never made. The clay model collapsed, and only notes survived. He planned to write books on many subjects but never finished any of them, leaving only notebooks. Leonardo once said that "a painter is not admirable unless he is universal." The patrons who supported him—and he was supported very well—perhaps wished that his inspirations would have been a bit less universal in scope, or at least accompanied by more perspiration.

Leonardo da Vinci, *Lady with an Ermine*. The enigmatic smile and smoky quality of this portrait can be found in many of Leonardo's works. (Czartoryski Museum, Krakow/The Bridgeman Art Library)

Questions for Analysis

1. In what ways do the notion of a "genius" and of a "Renaissance man" support one another? In what ways do they contradict one another? Which seems a better description of Leonardo?

2. Has the idea of artistic genius changed since the Renaissance? How?

Sources: Giorgio Vasari, *Lives of the Artists*, vol. 1, trans. G. Bull (London: Penguin Books, 1965); S. B. Nuland, *Leonardo da Vinci* (New York: Lipper/Viking, 2000).

Education

One of the central preoccupations of the humanists was education and moral behavior. Humanists poured out treatises, often in the form of letters, on the structure and goals of education and the training of rulers. They taught that a life active in the world should be the aim of all educated individuals and that education was not simply for private or religious purposes, but benefited the public good.

Humanists put their ideas into practice. They opened schools and academies in Italian cities and courts in which pupils began with Latin grammar and rhetoric, went on to study Roman history and political philosophy, and then learned Greek in order to study Greek literature and philosophy. These classics, humanists taught, would provide models of how to write clearly, argue effectively, and speak persuasively, important skills for future diplomats, lawyers, military leaders, businessmen, and politicians. Gradually, humanist education became the basis for intermediate and advanced education for a large share of the males of the middle and upper classes.

Humanists were ambivalent about education for women. While they saw the value of exposing women to classical models of moral behavior and reasoning, they also thought that a program of study that emphasized eloquence and action was not proper for women, whose sphere was private and domestic. Humanists never established schools for girls, though a few women of very high social status did gain a humanist education from private tutors. The ideal Renaissance woman looked a great deal more like her medieval counterpart than did the Renaissance man.

No book on education had broader influence than Baldassare Castiglione's (ball-duh-SAH-ree kah-stee-lee-OW-nee) *The Courtier* (1528). This treatise sought to train, discipline, and fashion the young man into the courtly ideal, the gentleman. According to Castiglione, who himself was a courtier serving several different rulers, the educated man of the upper class should have a broad background in many academic subjects, and his spiritual and physical as well as intellectual capabilities should be trained. Castiglione envisioned a man who could compose a sonnet, wrestle, sing a song and accompany himself on an instrument, ride expertly, solve difficult mathematical problems, and, above all, speak and write eloquently. Castiglione also included discussion of the perfect court lady, who, like the courtier, was to be well educated and able to play a musical instrument, to paint, and to dance. Physical beauty, delicacy, affability, and modesty were also important qualities for court ladies.

The Prince A treatise by Machiavelli on ways to gain, keep, and expand power; because of its subsequent impact it is probably the most important literary work of the Renaissance.

Political Thought

No Renaissance book on any topic has been more widely read than the short political treatise ***The Prince*** by Niccolò Machiavelli (NICK-oh-loh mak-ee-uh-VEL-ee) (1469–1527). The subject of *The Prince* (1513) is

Raphael: Portrait of Castiglione

In this portrait by Raphael, the most sought-after portrait painter of the Renaissance, Castiglione is shown dressed exactly as he advised courtiers to dress, in elegant, but subdued clothing that would enhance the splendor of the court, but never outshine the ruler. (Scala/Art Resource, NY)

political power: how the ruler should gain, maintain, and increase it. Its hero is Cesare Borgia, who ruthlessly conquered the Papal States and exacted total obedience from them (see page 310). As a good humanist, Machiavelli explores the problems of human nature and concludes that human beings are selfish and out to advance their own interests. This pessimistic view of humanity led him to maintain that the prince might have to manipulate the people in any way he finds necessary:

> For a man who, in all respects, will carry out only his professions of good, will be apt to be ruined amongst so many who are evil. A prince therefore who desires to maintain himself must learn to be not always good, but to be so or not as necessity may require.[1]

The prince should combine the cunning of a fox with the ferocity of a lion to achieve his goals. Asking rhetorically whether it is better for a ruler to be loved or feared, Machiavelli writes, "It will naturally be answered that it would be desirable to be both the one and the other; but as it is difficult to be both at the same time, it is much more safe to be feared than to be loved, when you have to choose between the two."[2]

Unlike medieval political theorists, Machiavelli maintained that the ruler should be concerned with the way things actually are rather than aiming for an ethical ideal. The sole test of a "good" government is whether it is effective, whether the ruler increases his power. Machiavelli did not advocate amoral behavior, but he believed that political action cannot be restricted by moral considerations. Nevertheless, on the basis of a crude interpretation of *The Prince*, the word *Machiavellian* entered the language as a synonym for the politically devious, corrupt, and crafty, indicating actions in which the end justifies the means. The ultimate significance of Machiavelli rests on two ideas: first, that one permanent social order reflecting God's will cannot be established, and second, that politics has its own laws, based on expediency, not morality.

Secular Spirit

Machiavelli's *The Prince* is often seen as a prime example of another aspect of the Renaissance, secularism. **Secularism** involves a basic concern with the material world instead of with the eternal world of spirit. A secular way of thinking tends to find the ultimate explanation of everything and the final end of human beings within the limits of what the senses can discover. Even though medieval business people ruthlessly pursued profits and medieval monks fought fiercely over property, the dominant ideals focused on the otherworldly, on life after death. Renaissance people often had strong and deep spiritual interests, but in their increasingly secular society, attention was concentrated on the here and now. Wealth allowed greater material pleasures, a more comfortable life, and the leisure time to appreciate and patronize the arts. The rich, social-climbing residents of Venice, Florence, Genoa, and Rome came to see life more as an opportunity to be enjoyed than as a painful pilgrimage to the City of God.

In *On Pleasure*, humanist Lorenzo Valla (VAHL-lah) (1406–1457) defends the pleasures of the senses as the highest good. Scholars praise Valla as a father of modern historical criticism. His study *On the False Donation of Constantine* (1444) demonstrates by careful textual examination that an anonymous eighth-century document supposedly giving the papacy jurisdiction over vast territories in western Europe was a forgery. Medieval people had accepted the Donation of Constantine as a reality, and the proof that it was an invention weakened the foundations of

secularism A way of thinking that tends to find the ultimate explanation of everything and the final end of human beings in what reason and the senses can discover, rather than in any spiritual or transcendental belief.

Bennozzo Gozzoli: Procession of the Magi, 1461
This segment of a huge fresco covering three walls of a chapel in the Medici Palace in Florence shows members of the Medici family and other contemporary individuals in a procession accompanying the biblical three wise men as they brought gifts to the infant Jesus. Reflecting the self-confidence of his patrons, Gozzoli places the elderly Cosimo and Piero at the head of the procession, accompanied by their grooms.
(Scala/Art Resource, NY)

papal claims to temporal authority. Lorenzo Valla's work exemplifies the application of critical scholarship to old and almost sacred writings as well as the new secular spirit of the Renaissance.

The tales in *The Decameron* (1350–1353), by the Florentine Giovanni Boccaccio (**jo-VAH-nee boh-KAH-chee-oh**) (1313–1375), which describe ambitious merchants, lecherous friars, and cuckolded husbands, portray a frankly acquisitive, sensual, and worldly society. Although Boccaccio's figures were stock literary characters, *The Decameron* contains none of the "contempt of the world" theme so pervasive in medieval literature. Renaissance writers justified the accumulation and enjoyment of wealth with references to ancient authors.

Nor did church leaders do much to combat the new secular spirit. In the fifteenth and early sixteenth centuries, the papal court and the households of the cardinals were just as worldly as those of great urban patricians. Of course, most of the popes and higher church officials had come from the bourgeois aristocracy. Renaissance popes beautified the city of Rome, patronized artists and men of letters, and expended enormous enthusiasm and huge sums of money. Pope Julius II (1503–1513) tore down the old Saint Peter's Basilica and began work on the present structure in 1506. Michelangelo's dome for Saint Peter's is still considered his greatest architectural work.

Despite their interest in secular matters, however, few people (including Machiavelli) questioned the basic tenets of the Christian religion. The thousands of pious paintings, sculptures, processions, and pilgrimages of the Renaissance period prove that strong religious feeling persisted.

Christian Humanism

In the last quarter of the fifteenth century, students from the Low Countries, France, Germany, and England flocked to Italy, imbibed the "new learning," and carried it back to their own countries. Northern humanists, often called **Christian humanists**, interpreted Italian ideas about and attitudes toward classical antiquity, individualism, and humanism in terms of their own traditions. They developed a program for broad social reform based on Christian ideals.

Christian humanists were interested in an ethical way of life. To achieve it, they believed that the best elements of classical and Christian cultures should be combined. For example, the classical ideals of calmness, stoical patience, and

Christian humanists Northern humanists who interpreted Italian ideas about and attitudes toward classical antiquity, individualism, and humanism in terms of their own traditions.

broad-mindedness should be joined in human conduct with the Christian virtues of love, faith, and hope. Northern humanists also stressed the use of reason, rather than acceptance of dogma, as the foundation for an ethical way of life. They believed that, although human nature had been corrupted by sin, it was fundamentally good and capable of improvement through education.

The Englishman Thomas More (1478–1535) envisioned a society that would bring out this inherent goodness in his revolutionary book *Utopia* (1516). *Utopia*, whose title means both "a good place" and "nowhere," describes an ideal community on an island somewhere off the mainland of the New World. All children receive a good education, primarily in the Greco-Roman classics, and learning does not cease with maturity, for the goal of all education is to develop rational faculties. Adults divide their days between manual labor or business pursuits and intellectual activities. Because profits from business and property are held in common, there is absolute social equality. Citizens of Utopia lead an ideal, nearly perfect existence because they live by reason; their institutions are perfect.

Contrary to the long-prevailing view that vice and violence existed because people were basically corrupt, More maintained that acquisitiveness and private property promoted all sorts of vices and civil disorders. Since society protected private property, society's flawed institutions were responsible for corruption and war. According to More, the key to improvement and reform of the individual was reform of the social institutions that molded the individual. His ideas were profoundly original in the sixteenth century.

Better known by contemporaries than Thomas More was the Dutch humanist Desiderius Erasmus (**dez-ih-DARE-ee-us uh-RAZ-muhs**) (1466?–1536) of Rotterdam. His fame rested largely on his exceptional knowledge of Greek and the Bible. Erasmus's long list of publications includes *The Education of a Christian Prince* (1504), a book combining idealistic and practical suggestions for the formation of a ruler's character through the careful study of Plutarch, Aristotle, Cicero, and Plato; *The Praise of Folly* (1509), a satire of worldly wisdom and a plea for the simple and spontaneous Christian faith of children; and, most important, a critical edition of the Greek New Testament (1516). In the preface to the New Testament, Erasmus explained the purpose of his great work:

> *I wish that even the weakest woman should read the Gospel—should read the epistles of Paul. And I wish these were translated into all languages, so that they might be read and understood, not only by Scots and Irishmen, but also by Turks and Saracens.*[3]

Two fundamental themes run through all of Erasmus's work. First, education is the means to reform, the key to moral and intellectual improvement. The core of education ought to be study of the Bible and the classics. (See the feature "Listening to the Past: An Age of Gold" on pages 335–336.) Second, the essence of Erasmus's thought is, in his own phrase, "the philosophy of Christ." By this Erasmus meant that Christianity is an inner attitude of the heart or spirit. Christianity is not formalism, special ceremonies, or law; Christianity is Christ—his life and what he said and did, not what theologians have written.

The Printed Word

The fourteenth-century humanist Petrarch and the sixteenth-century humanist Erasmus had similar ideas about many things, but the immediate impact of their ideas was very different because of one thing: the printing press with movable metal type. The ideas of Petrarch were spread slowly from person to person by

The Print Shop

This sixteenth-century engraving captures the busy world of a print shop. On the left, men set pieces of type, and an individual wearing glasses checks a copy. At the rear, another applies ink to the type, while a man carries in fresh paper on his head. At the right, the master printer operates the press, while a boy removes the printed pages and sets them to dry. The well-dressed figure in the right foreground may be the patron checking to see whether his job is done. (Giraudon/Art Resource, NY)

hand copying. The ideas of Erasmus were spread quickly through print, in which hundreds or thousands of identical copies could be made in a short time. Print shops were gathering places for those interested in new ideas. Though printers were trained through apprenticeships just like blacksmiths or butchers, they had connections to the world of politics, art, and scholarship that other craftsmen did not.

Printing with movable metal type developed in Germany in the middle of the fifteenth century as a combination of existing technologies. Several metalsmiths, most prominently Johan Gutenberg, recognized that the metal stamps used to mark signs on jewelry could be covered with ink and used to mark symbols onto a surface, in the same way that other craftsmen were using carved wood stamps to print books. (This woodblock printing technique originated in China and Korea centuries earlier.) Gutenberg and his assistants made stamps—later called *type*—for every letter of the alphabet and built racks that held the type in rows. This type could be rearranged for every page and so used over and over. The printing revolution was also enabled by the ready availability of paper, which was also made using techniques that had originated in China.

Gutenberg's invention involved no special secret technology or materials, and he was not the only one to recognize the huge market for books. Other craftsmen made their own type, built their own presses, and bought their own paper, setting themselves up in business (see Map 13.2). Historians estimate that somewhere between 8 million and 20 million books were printed in this manner in Europe before 1500, many more than the number of books produced in all of Western history up to that point.

The effects of the invention of movable-type printing were not felt overnight. Nevertheless, within a half century of the publication of Gutenberg's Bible of 1456, movable type had brought about radical changes. Printing transformed both the private and the public lives of Europeans. It gave hundreds or even thousands of people identical books, so that they could more easily discuss the ideas that the

MAPPING THE PAST

MAP 13.2　The Growth of Printing in Europe

The speed with which artisans spread printing technology across Europe provides strong evidence for the existing market in reading material. Presses in the Ottoman Empire were first established by Jewish immigrants who printed works in Hebrew, Greek, and Spanish. Use this map and those in other chapters to answer the following questions: **[1]** What part of Europe had the greatest number of printing presses by 1550? Why might this be? **[2]** Printing was developed in response to a market for reading materials. Use Maps 11.1 and 11.2 (pages 254 and 260) to help explain why printing spread the way it did. **[3]** Many historians also see printing as an important factor in the spread of the Protestant Reformation. Use Map 14.2 (page 358) to test this assertion.

books contained with one another in person or through letters. Printed materials reached an invisible public, allowing silent individuals to join causes and groups of individuals widely separated by geography to form a common identity; this new group consciousness could compete with older, localized loyalties.

　　Government and church leaders both used and worried about printing. They printed laws, declarations of war, battle accounts, and propaganda, and they also attempted to censor books and authors whose ideas they thought were wrong. Officials developed lists of prohibited books and authors, enforcing their prohibitions

Section Review

- Humanist artists sought to understand human nature by using the idea of genius to develop their talents.

- Humanists worked for the common good, setting up schools to enhance human mental, spiritual, and physical capabilities.

- Machiavelli's *The Prince* concludes that humans are selfish and a Godly social order cannot exist, thus acknowledging that politics is power, not morality.

- Secularism marked a shift from concern with the spiritual to an interest in pleasure, as expressed in Valla's *On Pleasure* and Boccaccio's *The Decameron*.

- Christian humanists believed that Christian virtues (faith, hope, love) and humanist ideals (education and reason) together were the means to reform social institutions.

- Movable-type printing and a ready supply of paper meant the easy distribution and reading aloud of books, enhancing the exchange of ideas between the literate and the nonliterate.

by confiscating books, arresting printers and booksellers, or destroying the presses of printers who disobeyed. None of this was very effective, and books were printed secretly, with fake title pages, authors, and places of publication, and smuggled all over Europe.

Printing also stimulated the literacy of laypeople and eventually came to have a deep effect on their private lives. Although most of the earliest books and pamphlets dealt with religious subjects, printers produced anything that would sell. They printed professional reference sets for lawyers, doctors, and students, and historical romances, biographies, and how-to manuals for the general public. They discovered that illustrations increased a book's sales, so they published both history and pornography full of woodcuts and engravings. Single-page broadsides and fly-sheets allowed great public events and "wonders" such as comets or two-headed calves to be experienced vicariously by a stay-at-home readership. Since books and other printed materials were read aloud to illiterate listeners, print bridged the gap between the written and oral cultures.

Art and the Artist

How did changes in art both reflect and shape new ideas?

No feature of the Renaissance evokes greater admiration than its artistic masterpieces. The 1400s (*quattrocento*) and 1500s (*cinquecento*) bore witness to dazzling creativity in painting, architecture, and sculpture. In all the arts, the city of Florence led the way. But Florence was not the only artistic center, for Rome and Venice also became important, and northern Europeans perfected their own styles.

Art and Power

In early Renaissance Italy, powerful urban groups commissioned works of art. The Florentine cloth merchants, for example, delegated Filippo Brunelleschi (Fill-EEP-oh broon-el-ES-kee) to build the magnificent dome on the cathedral of Florence and selected Lorenzo Ghiberti (law-REN-tsow gee-BER-tee) to design the bronze doors of the Baptistery. These works represented the merchants' dominant influence in the community.

Increasingly in the later fifteenth century, individuals and oligarchs, rather than corporate groups, sponsored works of art. Patrician merchants and bankers and popes and princes spent vast sums on the arts as a means of glorifying themselves and their families. Patrons varied in their level of involvement as a work progressed; some simply ordered a specific subject or scene, while others oversaw the work of the artist or architect very closely, suggesting themes and styles and demanding changes while the work was in progress.

In addition to power, art reveals changing patterns of consumption in Renaissance Italy. In the rural world of the Middle Ages, society had been organized for war and men of wealth spent their money on military gear. As Italian nobles settled in towns (see page 248), they adjusted to an urban culture. Rather than employing knights for warfare, cities hired mercenaries. Expenditure on military hardware declined. For the rich merchant or the noble recently arrived from the countryside, a grand urban palace represented the greatest outlay of cash. Wealthy individuals and families ordered gold dishes, embroidered tablecloths, wall tapestries, paintings on canvas (an innovation), and sculptural decorations to adorn their homes. By the late sixteenth century the Strozzi banking family of Florence spent more on household goods than on anything else except food; the value of those furnishings was three times that of their silver and jewelry.

After the palace itself, the private chapel within the palace symbolized the largest expenditure for the wealthy of the sixteenth century. Decorated with religious scenes and equipped with ecclesiastical furniture, the chapel served as the center of the household's religious life and its cult of remembrance of the dead.

Subjects and Style

The content and style of Renaissance art were often different from those of the Middle Ages. The individual portrait emerged as a distinct artistic genre. In the fifteenth century members of the newly rich middle class often had themselves painted in scenes of romantic chivalry or courtly society. Rather than reflecting a spiritual ideal, as medieval painting and sculpture tended to do, Renaissance portraits showed human ideals, often portrayed in a more realistic style. The Florentine painter Giotto (JAW-toh) (1276–1337) led the way in the use of realism; his treatment of the human body and face replaced the formal stiffness and artificiality that had long characterized representation of the human body. Piero della Francesca (1420–1492) and Andrea Mantegna (1430/31–1506) seem to have pioneered *perspective* in painting, the linear representation of distance and space on a flat surface. The sculptor Donatello (1386–1466) revived the classical figure, with its balance and self-awareness. In architecture, Filippo Brunelleschi (1377–1446) looked to the classical past for inspiration, designing a hospital for orphans and

Botticelli: Primavera, or Spring (ca. 1482)

Venus, the Roman goddess of love, is flanked on her left by Flora, goddess of flowers and fertility, and on her right by the Three Graces, goddesses of banquets, dance, and social occasions. Above, Venus's son Cupid, the god of love, shoots darts of desire, while at the far right the wind god Zephyrus chases the nymph Chloris. Botticelli captured the ideal for female beauty in the Renaissance: slender, with pale skin, a high forehead, red-blond hair, and sloping shoulders. (Digital image © The Museum of Modern Art/Licensed by Scala/Art Resource, NY)

Rogier van der Weyden: Deposition
Taking as his subject the suffering and death of Jesus, a popular theme of Netherlandish piety, van der Weyden describes
(in an inverted T) Christ's descent from the cross, surrounded by nine sorrowing figures. An appreciation of human anatomy,
the rich fabrics of the clothes, and the pierced and bloody hands of Jesus were all intended to touch the viewers'
emotions. (Museo del Prado/Scala/Art Resource, NY)

foundlings in which all proportions—of the windows, height, floor plan, and covered walkway with a series of rounded arches—were carefully thought out to achieve a sense of balance and harmony. As the fifteenth century advanced, classical themes and motifs, such as the lives and loves of pagan gods and goddesses, figured increasingly in painting and sculpture. Religious topics, such as the Annunciation of the Virgin and the Nativity, remained popular among both patrons and artists, but frequently the patron had himself and his family portrayed in the scene.

Art produced in northern Europe in the fourteenth and fifteenth centuries tended to be more religious in orientation than that produced in Italy. Some Flemish painters, notably Rogier van der Weyden (1399/1400–1464) and Jan van Eyck (1366–1441), were considered the artistic equals of Italian painters and were much admired in Italy. Van Eyck, one of the earliest artists to use oil-based paints successfully, shows the Flemish love for detail in paintings such as *Ghent Altarpiece* and the portrait *Giovanni Arnolfini and His Bride*; the effect is great realism and remarkable attention to human personality. Northern architecture was little influenced by the classical revival so obvious in Renaissance Italy.

In the fifteenth century the center of the new art shifted to Rome, where wealthy cardinals and popes wanted visual expression of the church's and their own families' power and piety. Michelangelo, a Florentine who had spent his young adulthood at the court of Lorenzo de' Medici, went to Rome in about 1500 and began the series of statues, paintings, and architectural projects from which he gained an international reputation: the Pieta, Moses, the redesigning of the Capitoline Hill in central Rome, and, most famously, the ceiling and altar wall of the Sistine Chapel. Pope Julius II, who commissioned the Sistine Chapel, demanded that Michelangelo work as fast as he could and frequently visited the artist at his work with suggestions and criticisms. Michelangelo complained in person and by letter about the pope's meddling, but his reputation did not match the power of the pope, and he kept working.

Raphael Sanzio (rah-fahy-EL) (1483–1520), another Florentine, got the commission for frescoes in the papal apartments, and in his relatively short life he painted hundreds of portraits and devotional images, becoming the most sought-after artist in Europe. Raphael also oversaw a large workshop with many collaborators and apprentices—who assisted on the less difficult sections of some paintings—and wrote treatises on his philosophy of art in which he emphasized the importance of imitating nature and developing an orderly sequence of design and proportion.

Venice became another artistic center in the sixteenth century. Titian (TISH-uhn) (1490–1576) produced portraits, religious subjects, and mythological scenes, developing techniques of painting in oil without doing elaborate drawings first, which speeded up the process and pleased patrons eager to display their acquisition. Titian and other sixteenth-century painters developed an artistic style known in English as "mannerism" (from *maniera* or "style" in Italian) in which artists sometimes distorted figures, exaggerated musculature, and heightened color to express emotion and drama more intently. (This is the style in which Michelangelo painted the Last Judgment in the Sistine Chapel, shown in the frontispiece to this chapter.)

Whether in Italy or northern Europe, most Renaissance artists trained in the workshops of older artists; Botticelli, Raphael, Titian, and at times even Michelangelo were known for their large, well-run, and prolific workshops. Though they might be "men of genius," artists were still expected to be well trained in proper artistic techniques and stylistic conventions, for the notion that artistic genius could show up in the work of an untrained artist did not emerge until the twentieth century. Beginning artists spent years copying drawings and paintings, learning how to prepare paint and other artistic materials, and, by the sixteenth century, reading books about design and composition. Younger artists gathered together in the evenings for further drawing practice; by the later sixteenth century some of these informal groups had turned into more formal artistic "academies," the first of which was begun in 1563 in Florence by Vasari under the patronage of the Medicis.

The types of art in which more women were active, such as textiles, needlework, and painting on porcelain, were not regarded as "major arts," but only as "minor" or "decorative" arts. Like painting, embroidery changed in the Renaissance to become more classical in its subject matter, naturalistic, and visually complex. Embroiderers were not trained to view their work as products of individual genius, however, so they rarely included their names on their works, and there is no way to discover who they were.

Several women did become well known as painters in their day. Stylistically, their works are different from one another, but their careers show many similarities. The majority of female painters were the daughters of painters or of minor noblemen with ties to artistic circles. Many were eldest daughters or came from families in which there were no sons, so their fathers took unusual interest in their

Artemisia Gentileschi: Esther Before Ahasuerus (ca. 1630)

In this oil painting, Gentileschi (**jen-tee-LES-kee**) shows an Old Testament scene of the Jewish woman Esther who saved her people from being killed by her husband, King Ahasuerus. This deliverance is celebrated in the Jewish holiday of Purim. Both figures are in the elaborate dress worn in Renaissance courts. Typical of a female painter, Artemisia Gentileschi was trained by her father. She mastered the dramatic style favored in the early seventeenth century and became known especially for her portraits of strong biblical and mythological heroines. (Image copyright © The Metropolitan Museum of Art/Art Resource, NY)

Section Review

- Individuals and oligarchs spent elaborate sums on works of art to display their wealth and power.

- Art began to be more realistic and show human ideals, often portraying individuals or families.

- Rome and Venice gained international fame as art centers, producing artists such as Michelangelo, Raphael Sanzio, and the "mannerism" painter, Titian.

- Leonardo da Vinci epitomized the "Renaissance man" as a painter, scientist, and inventor.

- Young artists became apprentices, creating formal groups called "academies" that excluded women.

careers. Many women began their careers before they were twenty and produced far fewer paintings after they married, or stopped painting entirely. Women were not allowed to study the male nude, which was viewed as essential if one wanted to paint large history paintings with many figures. Women could also not learn the technique of fresco, in which colors are applied directly to wet plaster walls, because such works had to be done out in public, which was judged inappropriate for women. Joining a group of male artists for informal practice was also seen as improper, and the artistic academies that were established were for men only. Like universities, humanist academies, and most craft guild shops, artistic workshops were male-only settings in which men of different ages came together for training and created bonds of friendship, influence, patronage, and sometimes intimacy.

Women were not alone in being excluded from the institutions of Renaissance culture. Though a few "rare men of genius" such as Leonardo or Michelangelo emerged from artisanal backgrounds, most scholars and artists came from families with at least some money. Renaissance culture did not influence the lives of most people in cities and did not affect life in the villages at all. A small, highly educated minority of literary humanists and artists created the culture of and for an exclusive elite. The Renaissance maintained, or indeed enhanced, a gulf between the learned minority and the uneducated multitude that has survived for many centuries.

Social Hierarchies

What were the key social hierarchies in Renaissance Europe, and how did ideas about hierarchy shape people's lives?

The division between educated and uneducated people was only one of many social hierarchies evident in the Renaissance. Every society has social hierarchies; in ancient Rome, for example, there were patricians and plebeians (see page 89).

Such hierarchies are to some degree descriptions of social reality, but they are also idealizations—that is, they describe how people *imagined* their society to be, without all the messy reality of social-climbing plebeians or groups that did not fit the standard categories. Social hierarchies in the Renaissance built on those of the Middle Ages but also developed new features that contributed to modern social hierarchies.

Race

Renaissance people did not use the word *race* the way we do, but often used "race," "people," and "nation" interchangeably for ethnic, national, and religious groups—the French race, the Jewish nation, the Irish people, and so on. They did make distinctions based on skin color that provide some of the background for later conceptualizations of race, but these distinctions were interwoven with other characteristics when people thought about human differences.

Ever since the time of the Roman republic, a few black Africans had lived in western Europe. They had come, along with white slaves, as the spoils of war. Even after the collapse of the Roman Empire, Muslim and Christian merchants continued to import them. Unstable political conditions in many parts of Africa enabled enterprising merchants to seize people and sell them into slavery. Local authorities afforded them no protection. Long tradition, moreover, sanctioned the practice of slavery. The evidence of medieval art attests to the continued presence of Africans in Europe throughout the Middle Ages and to Europeans' awareness of them.

Beginning in the fifteenth century sizable numbers of black slaves entered Europe. Portuguese sailors brought perhaps a thousand Africans a year to the markets of Seville, Barcelona, Marseilles (mahr-SAY), and Genoa. In the late fifteenth century this flow increased, with thousands of people leaving the west African coast. By 1530 between four thousand and five thousand were being sold to the Portuguese each year. By the mid-sixteenth century blacks, slave and free,

Carpaccio: Black Laborers on the Venetian Docks (detail)

Enslaved and free blacks, besides working as gondoliers on the Venetian canals, served on the docks: here, seven black men careen—clean, caulk, and repair—a ship. Carpaccio's (kahr-PAH-choh) reputation as one of Venice's outstanding painters rests on his eye for details of everyday life. (Gallerie dell'Accademia, Venice/Scala/Art Resource, NY)

constituted about 10 percent of the population of the Portuguese cities of Lisbon and Évora and roughly 3 percent of the Portuguese population. In the Iberian peninsula, African slaves intermingled with the people they lived among and sometimes intermarried. Cities such as Lisbon had significant numbers of people of mixed African and European descent.

Although blacks were concentrated in the Iberian Peninsula, there must have been some Africans in northern Europe as well. In the 1580s, for example, Queen Elizabeth I of England complained that there were too many "blackamoores" competing with needy English people for places as domestic servants.[4] Black servants were much sought after; the medieval interest in curiosities, the exotic, and the marvelous continued in the Renaissance. Italian aristocrats had their portraits painted with their black pageboys to indicate their wealth (see the illustration on page 316, in which Gozzoli's depiction of Cosimo de' Medici shows him with a black groom). Blacks were so greatly in demand at the Renaissance courts of northern Italy, in fact, that the Venetians defied papal threats of excommunication to secure them. In 1491 Isabella of Este, duchess of Mantua, instructed her agent to secure a black girl between four and eight years old, "shapely and as black as possible." The duchess saw the child as a source of entertainment: "We shall make her very happy and shall have great fun with her." She hoped the girl would become "the best buffoon in the world,"[5] as the cruel ancient practice of a noble household's retaining a professional "fool" for the family's amusement persisted through the Renaissance—and down to the twentieth century. Tradition, stretching back at least as far as the thirteenth century, connected blacks with music and dance. In Renaissance Spain and Italy, blacks performed as dancers, as actors and actresses in courtly dramas, and as musicians, sometimes making up full orchestras.

Africans were not simply amusements at court. In Portugal, Spain, and Italy, slaves supplemented the labor force in virtually all occupations—as servants, agricultural laborers, craftsmen, and as seamen on ships going to Lisbon and Africa. Agriculture in Europe did not involve large plantations, so large-scale agricultural slavery did not develop there; African slaves formed the primary work force on the sugar plantations set up by Europeans on the Atlantic islands in the late fifteenth century, however (see page 386).

Until the voyages down the African coast in the late fifteenth century, Europeans had little concrete knowledge of Africans and their cultures. They perceived Africa as a remote place, the home of strange people isolated by heresy and Islam from superior European civilization. Africans' contact, even as slaves, with Christian Europeans could only "improve" the blacks, they thought. The expanding slave trade only reinforced negative preconceptions about the inferiority of black Africans.

Class

The notion of class—working class, middle class, upper class—did not exist in the Renaissance. By the thirteenth century, however, and even more so by the fifteenth, the idea of a changeable hierarchy based on wealth, what would later come to be termed "social class," was emerging alongside the medieval concept of orders (see page 221). This was particularly true in towns. Most residents of towns were technically members of the "third estate," that is "those who work" rather than "those who fight" and "those who pray." However, this group now included wealthy merchants who oversaw vast trading empires and lived in splendor that rivaled the richest nobles. As we saw earlier, in many cities these merchants had

Italian City Scene

In this detail from a fresco by the Italian painter Lorenzo Lotto, the artist captures the mixing of social groups in a Renaissance Italian city. The crowd of men in the right foreground includes wealthy merchants in elaborate hats and colorful coats. Two mercenary soldiers (carrying a sword and a pike), probably in hire to a condottiero, wear short doublets and tight hose stylishly slit to reveal colored undergarments, while boys play with toy weapons at their feet. Clothing like that of the soldiers, which emphasized the masculine form, was frequently the target of sumptuary laws both for its expense and its "indecency." At the left, women sell vegetables and bread, which would have been a common sight at any city marketplace. (Scala/Art Resource, NY)

gained political power to match their economic might, becoming merchant oligarchs who ruled through city councils.

The development of a hierarchy of wealth did not mean an end to the hierarchy of orders, however, and even poorer nobility still had higher status. If this had not been the case, wealthy Italian merchants would not have bothered to buy noble titles and country villas as they began doing in the fifteenth century, nor would wealthy English or Spanish merchants have been eager to marry their daughters and sons into often impoverished noble families. The nobility maintained its status in most parts of Europe not by maintaining rigid boundaries, but by taking in and integrating the new social elite of wealth.

Along with being tied to the hierarchy of orders, social status was also linked with considerations of honor. Among the nobility, for example, certain weapons and battle tactics were favored because they were viewed as more honorable. Among urban dwellers, certain occupations, such as city executioner or manager of the municipal brothel, might be well paid but were understood to be "dishonorable" and so of low status.

Gender

Renaissance people would not have understood the word *gender* to refer to categories of people, but they would have easily grasped the concept. Toward the end of the fourteenth century, learned men (and a few women) began what was termed the "**debate about women**" (*querelle des femmes*), a debate about women's character and nature that would last for centuries. Misogynist (mi-SOJ-uh-nist) critiques of women from both clerical and secular authors denounced females as devious, domineering, and demanding. In answer, several authors compiled long lists of famous and praiseworthy women exemplary for their loyalty, bravery, and morality. Christine de Pizan was among those writers who were not only interested in defending women, but also in exploring the reasons behind women's secondary status—that is, why the great philosophers, statesmen, and poets had generally been men. In this they were anticipating recent discussions about the "social construction of gender" by six hundred years. (See the feature "Listening to the Past: Christine de Pizan" in Chapter 12 on pages 305–306.)

debate about women Debate among writers and thinkers about women's qualities and proper role in society.

With the development of the printing press, popular interest in the debate about women grew, and works were translated, reprinted, and shared around Europe. Prints that juxtaposed female virtues and vices were also very popular, with the virtuous women depicted as those of the classical or biblical past and the vice-ridden dressed in contemporary clothes. The favorite metaphor for the virtuous wife was either the snail or the tortoise, both animals that never leave their "houses" and are totally silent, although such images were never as widespread as those depicting wives beating their husbands or hiding their lovers from them.

Beginning in the sixteenth century, the debate about women also became one about female rulers, sparked primarily by dynastic accidents in many countries, including Spain, England, France, and Scotland, which led to women serving as advisers to child kings or ruling in their own right (see pages 330 and 353). The questions were vigorously and at times viciously disputed. They directly concerned the social construction of gender: could a woman's being born into a royal family and educated to rule allow her to overcome the limitations of her sex? Should it? Or stated another way: which was (or should be) the stronger determinant of character and social role, gender or rank? There were no successful rebellions against female rulers simply because they were women, but in part this was because female rulers, especially Queen Elizabeth I of England, emphasized qualities regarded as masculine—physical bravery, stamina, wisdom, duty—whenever they appeared in public.

Ideas about women's and men's proper roles determined the actions of ordinary men and women even more forcefully. The dominant notion of the "true" man was that of the married head of household, so men whose class and age would have normally conferred political power but who remained unmarried did not participate to the same level as their married brothers. Unmarried men in Venice, for example, could not be part of the ruling council. Women were also understood as "married or to be married," even if the actual marriage patterns in Europe left many women (and men) unmarried until quite late in life (see page 298). This meant that women's work was not viewed as supporting a family—even if it did—and was valued less than men's. If they worked for wages, and many women did, women earned about half to two-thirds of what men did even for the same work. Of all the ways in which Renaissance society was hierarchically arranged—class, age, level of education, rank, race, occupation—gender was regarded as the most "natural" and therefore the most important to defend.

Section Review

- Social hierarchies of the Renaissance were based on how people imagined their societies to be, not on how society actually worked.

- Black Africans first came to Europe in Roman times as spoils of war, but were not present in great numbers until the Renaissance and the onset of the slave trade.

- Free and enslaved blacks worked in all occupations, but the wealthy sought them as exotic household novelties.

- The nobility maintained its status by integrating the newly economically and politically powerful merchant class.

- Female rulers maintained their power by assuming masculine qualities but debates emerged about women's secondary status.

Politics and the State in the Renaissance (ca. 1450–1521)

How did the nation-states of western Europe evolve in this period?

The High Middle Ages had witnessed the origins of many of the basic institutions of the modern state. Sheriffs, inquests, juries, circuit judges, professional bureaucracies, and representative assemblies all trace their origins to the twelfth and thirteenth centuries. The linchpin for the development of states, however, was strong monarchy, and during the period of the Hundred Years' War, no ruler in western Europe was able to provide effective leadership. The resurgent power of feudal nobilities weakened the centralizing work begun earlier.

Beginning in the fifteenth century, rulers utilized aggressive methods to rebuild their governments. First in Italy, then in France, England, and Spain, rulers began the work of reducing violence, curbing unruly nobles, and establishing domestic order. They emphasized royal majesty and royal sovereignty and insisted on the respect and loyalty of all subjects.

France

The Hundred Years' War left France drastically depopulated, commercially ruined, and agriculturally weak. Nonetheless, the ruler whom Joan of Arc had seen crowned at Reims, Charles VII (r. 1422–1461), revived the monarchy and France. He seemed an unlikely person to do so. Frail, indecisive, and burdened with questions about his paternity (his father had been deranged; his mother, notoriously promiscuous), Charles VII nevertheless began France's long recovery.

Charles reconciled the Burgundians and Armagnacs (ahr-muhn-YAKZ), who had been waging civil war for thirty years. By 1453 French armies had expelled the English from French soil except in Calais. Charles reorganized the royal council, giving increased influence to middle-class men, and strengthened royal finances through such taxes as the *gabelle* (guh-BEL) (on salt) and the *taille* (teyl) (land tax). These taxes remained the Crown's chief sources of income until the Revolution of 1789.

By establishing regular companies of cavalry and archers—recruited, paid, and inspected by the state—Charles created the first permanent royal army. His son Louis XI (r. 1461–1483), called the "Spider King" because of his treacherous character, improved upon Charles's army and used it to stop aristocratic brigandage and to curb urban independence. The army was also employed in 1477, when Louis conquered Burgundy upon the death of its ruler Charles the Bold. Three years later, the extinction of the house of Anjou (AN-joo) brought Louis the counties of Anjou, Bar, Maine, and Provence.

Two further developments strengthened the French monarchy. The marriage of Louis XII (r. 1498–1515) and Anne of Brittany added the large western duchy of Brittany to the state. Then the French king Francis I and Pope Leo X reached a mutually satisfactory agreement about church and state powers in 1516. The new treaty, the Concordat of Bologna, approved the pope's right to receive the first year's income of new bishops and abbots. In return, Leo X recognized the French ruler's right to select French bishops and abbots. French kings thereafter effectively controlled the appointment and thus the policies of church officials in the kingdom.

England

English society suffered severely from the disorders of the fifteenth century. The aristocracy dominated the government of Henry IV (r. 1399–1413) and indulged in mischievous violence at the local level. Population, decimated by the Black Death, continued to decline. Between 1455 and 1471 adherents of the ducal houses of York and Lancaster waged civil war, commonly called the **Wars of the Roses** because the symbol of the Yorkists was a white rose and that of the Lancastrians a red one. The chronic disorder hurt trade, agriculture, and domestic industry. Under the pious but mentally disturbed Henry VI (r. 1422–1461), the authority of the monarchy sank lower than it had been in centuries.

Wars of the Roses Civil war in England over who would become the next king.

The Yorkist Edward IV (r. 1461–1483) began establishing domestic tranquility. He succeeded in defeating the Lancastrian forces and after 1471 began to reconstruct the monarchy. Edward, his brother Richard III (r. 1483–1485), and Henry VII (r. 1485–1509) of the Welsh house of Tudor worked to restore royal prestige, to crush the power of the nobility, and to establish order and law at the local level. All three rulers used methods that Machiavelli himself would have praised—ruthlessness, efficiency, and secrecy.

Edward IV and subsequently the Tudors, excepting Henry VIII, conducted foreign policy on the basis of diplomacy, avoiding expensive wars. Thus the English monarchy did not depend on Parliament for money, and the Crown undercut that source of aristocratic influence.

royal council The body of men who represented the center of royal authority; Renaissance princes tended to prefer middle-class councilors to noble ones.

Henry VII did summon several meetings of Parliament in the early years of his reign, primarily to confirm laws, but the center of royal authority was the **royal council,** which governed at the national level. There Henry VII revealed his distrust of the nobility: though not completely excluded, very few great lords were among the king's closest advisers. Regular representatives on the council numbered between twelve and fifteen men, and while many gained high ecclesiastical rank, their origins were in the lesser landowning class, and their education was in law. They were, in a sense, middle class.

The royal council handled any business the king put before it—executive, legislative, and judicial. For example, the council conducted negotiations with foreign governments and secured international recognition of the Tudor dynasty through the marriage in 1501 of Henry VII's eldest son Arthur to Catherine of Aragon, the daughter of Ferdinand and Isabella of Spain. The council dealt with real or potential aristocratic threats through a judicial offshoot, the **court of Star Chamber,** so called because of the stars painted on the ceiling of the room. The court applied principles of Roman law, and its methods were sometimes terrifying: accused persons were not entitled to see evidence against them; sessions were secret; torture could be applied to extract confessions; and juries were not called. These procedures ran directly counter to English common-law precedents, but they effectively reduced aristocratic troublemaking. Because the government halted the long period of anarchy, it won the key support of the merchant and agricultural upper middle class.

court of Star Chamber A division of the English royal council, a court that used Roman legal procedures to curb real or potential threats from the nobility, so named because of the stars painted on the ceiling of the chamber in which the court sat.

Secretive, cautious, and thrifty, Henry VII rebuilt the monarchy. He encouraged the cloth industry and built up the English merchant marine. English exports of wool and the royal export tax on that wool steadily increased. Henry crushed an invasion from Ireland and secured peace with Scotland through the marriage of his daughter Margaret to the Scottish king. When Henry VII died in 1509, he left a country at peace both domestically and internationally, a substantially augmented treasury, and the dignity and role of the royal majesty much enhanced.

Spain

While England and France laid the foundations of unified nation-states during the Renaissance, Spain remained a conglomerate of independent kingdoms. By the middle of the fifteenth century, the kingdoms of Castile and Aragon dominated the weaker Navarre, Portugal, and Granada, and the Iberian Peninsula, with the exception of Granada, had been won for Christianity. But even the wedding in 1469 of the dynamic and aggressive Isabella of Castile and the crafty and persistent Ferdinand of Aragon did not bring about administrative unity. Rather, their marriage constituted a dynastic union of two royal houses, not the political union of two peoples. Although Ferdinand and Isabella (r. 1474–1516) pursued a common foreign policy, until about 1700 Spain existed as a loose confederation of separate kingdoms, each maintaining its own *cortes* (parliament), laws, courts, and systems of coinage and taxation. Ferdinand and Isabella were able to exert their authority in ways similar to the rulers of France and England, however. They curbed aristocratic power by excluding aristocrats and great territorial magnates from the royal council, which had full executive, judicial, and legislative powers under the monarchy. Instead they appointed only people of middle-class background to the council. The council and various government boards recruited men trained in Roman law, which exalted the power of the Crown. They also secured from the Spanish pope Alexander VI the right to appoint bishops in Spain and in the Hispanic territories in America, enabling them to establish the equivalent of a national church. And with the revenues from ecclesiastical estates, they were able to expand their territories to include the remaining land held by Arabs in southern Spain. The victorious entry of Ferdinand and Isabella into Granada on January 6, 1492, signaled the conclusion of the reconquista (see Map 9.3 on page 202). Granada in the south was incorporated into the Spanish kingdom, and in 1512 Ferdinand conquered Navarre in the north.

There still remained a sizable and, in the view of the majority of the Spanish people, potentially dangerous minority, the Jews. When the kings of France and England had expelled the Jews from their kingdoms (see page 214), many had sought refuge in Spain. During the long centuries of the reconquista, Christian kings had renewed Jewish rights and privileges; in fact, Jewish industry, intelligence, and money had supported royal power. While Christians of all classes borrowed from Jewish moneylenders and while all who could afford them sought Jewish physicians, a strong undercurrent of resentment of Jewish influence and wealth festered.

In the fourteenth century anti-Semitism in Spain was aggravated by fiery anti-Jewish preaching, by economic dislocation, and by the search for a scapegoat during the Black Death. Anti-Semitic pogroms swept the towns of Spain; one scholar estimates that 40 percent of the Jewish population was killed or forced to convert.[6] Those converted were called *conversos* (kon-VER-sowz) or **New Christians.** Conversos were often well educated and held prominent positions in government, the church, medicine, law, and business. Numbering perhaps two hundred thousand in a total Spanish population of about 7.5 million, New Christians and Jews exercised influence disproportionate to their numbers.

New Christians A term applied to Jews who accepted Christianity, but since many were from families who had become Christian centuries earlier, the word *new* is not accurate.

Such successes bred resentment. Aristocratic grandees resented their financial dependence; the poor hated the converso tax collectors; and churchmen doubted the sincerity of their conversions. Queen Isabella shared these suspicions, and she and Ferdinand received permission from Pope Sixtus IV to establish an Inquisition to "search out and punish converts from Judaism who had transgressed against Christianity by secretly adhering to Jewish beliefs and performing rites of the Jews."[7] Investigations and trials began immediately, as officials of the Inquisition looked for conversos who showed any sign of incomplete conversion, such as not eating pork.

Recent scholarship has carefully analyzed documents of the Inquisition. Most conversos identified themselves as sincere Christians; many came from families that had received baptism generations before. In response, officials of the Inquisition developed a new type of anti-Semitism. A person's status as a Jew, they argued, could not be changed by religious conversion, but was in their blood and was heritable, so Jews could never be true Christians. In what were known as "purity of the blood" laws, having pure Christian blood became a requirement for noble status. Ideas about Jews developed in Spain were important components in European concepts of race, and discussions of "Jewish blood" later expanded into notions of the "Jewish race."

Felipe Bigarny: Ferdinand and Isabella

In these wooden sculptures, the Burgundian artist Felipe Bigarny portrays Ferdinand and Isabella as paragons of Christian piety, kneeling at prayer. Ferdinand is shown in armor, a symbol of his military accomplishments and masculinity. Isabella wears a simple white head-covering rather than something more elaborate to indicate her modesty, a key virtue for women, though her actions and writings indicate that she was more determined and forceful than Ferdinand. (Capilla Real, Granada/Laurie Platt Winfrey, Inc.)

Section Review

- Charles VII reorganized France by creating the first permanent royal army, with later kings adding strength by coming to terms with the pope over church and state power.

- The Wars of the Roses in England damaged English trade, agriculture, and industry.

- Edward VII strengthened the monarchy and brought domestic and international peace.

- Ferdinand and Isabella in Spain decreased aristocratic power, strengthened the monarchy, and gained favor with the pope to expand their territories.

- The financial success of the Spanish Jews who converted to Christianity for protection against anti-Semitism incurred jealousy, so Ferdinand and Isabella ordered an Inquisition to eliminate these Jews, leading to the notion that being Jewish was by "blood," so a Jew could never truly convert to Christianity.

Shortly after the conquest of Granada, Isabella and Ferdinand issued an edict expelling all practicing Jews from Spain. Of the community of perhaps 200,000 Jews, 150,000 fled. Absolute religious orthodoxy and purity of blood ("untainted" by Jews or Muslims) served as the theoretical foundation of the Spanish national state.

The diplomacy of the Catholic rulers of Spain achieved a success they never anticipated. In 1496 Ferdinand and Isabella married their second daughter Joanna, heiress to Castile, to the archduke Philip, heir to the Burgundian Netherlands and the Holy Roman Empire. Philip and Joanna's son, Charles V (r. 1519–1556) thus succeeded to a vast patrimony. When Charles's son Philip II joined Portugal to the Spanish crown in 1580, the Iberian Peninsula was at last politically united.

Chapter Review

What economic and political developments in Italy provided the setting for the Renaissance? (page 308)

The Italian Renaissance rested on the phenomenal economic growth of the High Middle Ages. In the period from about 1050 to 1300, a new economy emerged based on Venetian and Genoese shipping and long-distance trade and on Florentine banking. These commercial activities, combined with the struggle of urban communes for political independence from surrounding feudal lords, led to the appearance of a new ruling group in Italian cities—merchant oligarchs. Unrest in some cities led to their being taken over by single rulers, but however Italian cities were governed, they jockeyed for power with one another and prevented the establishment of a single Italian nation-state.

What were the key ideas of the Renaissance, and how were they different for men and women and for southern and northern Europeans? (page 312)

The Renaissance was characterized by self-conscious awareness among fourteenth- and fifteenth-century Italians, particularly scholars and writers known as humanists, that they were living in a new era. Key to this attitude was a serious interest in the Latin classics, a belief in individual potential, and a more secular attitude toward life. All these are evident in political theory developed during the Renaissance, particularly that of Machiavelli. Humanists opened schools for boys and young men to train them for an active life of public service, but they had doubts about whether humanist education was appropriate for women. As humanism spread to northern Europe, religious concerns became more pronounced, and Christian humanists set out plans for the reform of church and society. Their ideas were spread to a much wider audience than those of early humanists because of the development of the printing press with movable metal type, which revolutionized communication.

How did changes in art both reflect and shape new ideas? (page 320)

Interest in the classical past and in the individual also shaped Renaissance art in terms of style and subject matter. Painting became more naturalistic, and the individual portrait emerged as a distinct artistic genre. Wealthy merchants, cultured rulers, and powerful popes all hired painters, sculptors, and architects to design and ornament public and private buildings. Art in Italy became more secular and classical, while that in northern Europe retained a more religious tone. Artists began to understand themselves as having a special creative genius, though they continued to produce works on order for patrons, who often determined the content and form.

What were the key social hierarchies in Renaissance Europe, and how did ideas about hierarchy shape people's lives? (page 324)

Social hierarchies in the Renaissance built on those of the Middle Ages, but new features also developed that contributed to the modern social hierarchies of race, class, and gender. Black Africans entered Europe in sizable numbers for the first time since the collapse of the Roman Empire, and Europeans fit them into changing understandings of ethnicity and race. The medieval hierarchy of orders based on function in society intermingled with a new hierarchy based on wealth, with new types of elites becoming more powerful. The Renaissance debate about women led many to discuss

Key Terms

Renaissance (p. 308)

communes (p. 309)

popolo (p. 309)

condottieri (p. 310)

signori (p. 310)

courts (p. 310)

patrons (p. 310)

humanism (p. 312)

individualism (p. 312)

The Prince (p. 314)

secularism (p. 315)

Christian humanists (p. 316)

debate about women (p. 327)

Wars of the Roses (p. 329)

royal council (p. 330)

court of Star Chamber (p. 330)

New Christians (p. 331)

women's nature and proper role in society, a discussion sharpened by the presence of a number of ruling queens in this era.

How did the nation-states of western Europe evolve in this period? (page 328)

With taxes provided by business people, kings in western Europe established greater peace and order, both essential for trade. Feudal monarchies gradually evolved in the direction of nation-states. In Spain, France, and England, rulers also emphasized royal dignity and authority, and they utilized Machiavellian ideas to ensure the preservation and continuation of their governments. Like the merchant oligarchs and signori of Italian city-states, Renaissance monarchs manipulated culture to enhance their power.

Notes

1. C. E. Detmold, trans., *The Historical, Political and Diplomatic Writings of Niccolò Machiavelli* (Boston: J. R. Osgood, 1882), pp. 51–52.
2. Ibid., pp. 54–55.
3. Quoted in F. Seebohm, *The Oxford Reformers* (London: J. M. Dent & Sons, 1867), p. 256.
4. J. Hale, *The Civilization of Europe in the Renaissance* (New York: Atheneum, 1994), p. 44.
5. Quoted in J. Devisse and M. Mollat, *The Image of the Black in Western Art*, vol. 2, trans. W. G. Ryan (New York: William Morrow, 1979), pt. 2, pp. 187–188.
6. See B. F. Reilly, *The Medieval Spains* (New York: Cambridge University Press, 1993), pp. 198–203.
7. B. Netanyahu, *The Origins of the Inquisition in Fifteenth Century Spain* (New York: Random House, 1995), p. 921.

To assess your mastery of this chapter, go to **bedfordstmartins.com/mckaywestbrief**

Listening to the Past

An Age of Gold

As the foremost scholar of the early sixteenth century and a writer with international contacts, Desiderius Erasmus (1466?–1536) maintained a vast correspondence. In the following letter to Wolfgang Capito (1478?–1541), a German scholar and professor of theology at the University of Basel, he explains his belief that Europe was entering a golden age. The letter also reflects the spiritual ideals of northern European humanists.

To Capito

It is no part of my nature, most learned Wolfgang, to be excessively fond of life; whether it is that I have, to my own mind, lived nearly long enough, having entered my fifty-first year, or that I see nothing in this life so splendid or delightful that it should be desired by one who is convinced by the Christian faith that a happier life awaits those who in this world earnestly attach themselves to piety. But at the present moment I could almost wish to be young again, for no other reason but this, that I anticipate the near approach of a golden age, so clearly do we see the minds of princes, as if changed by inspiration, devoting all their energies to the pursuit of peace. The chief movers in this matter are Pope Leo and Francis, King of France.

There is nothing this king does not do or does not suffer in his desire to avert war and consolidate peace . . . and exhibiting in this, as in everything else, a magnanimous and truly royal character. Therefore, when I see that the highest sovereigns of Europe—Francis of France, Charles the King Catholic, Henry [VIII] of England, and the Emperor Maximilian—have set all their warlike preparations aside and established peace upon solid and, as I trust, adamantine foundations, I am led to a confident hope that not only morality and Christian piety, but also a genuine and purer literature, may come to renewed life or greater splendour; especially as this object is pursued with equal zeal in various regions of the world. . . . To the piety of these princes it is due, that we see everywhere, as if

Hans Holbein the Younger, *Erasmus* (ca. 1521). Holbein persuaded his close friend Erasmus to sit for this portrait and portrayed him at his characteristic work, writing. (Louvre/Scala/Art Resource, NY)

upon a given signal, men of genius are arising and conspiring together to restore the best literature.

Polite letters, which were almost extinct, are now cultivated and embraced by Scots, by Danes, and by Irishmen. Medicine has a host of champions. . . . The Imperial Law is restored at Paris by William Budé, in Germany by Udalric Zasy; and mathematics at Basel by Henry of Glaris. In the theological sphere there was no little to be done, because this science has been hitherto mainly professed by those who are most pertinacious in their abhorrence of the better literature,* and are the more successful in defending their own ignorance as they do it under pretext of piety, the unlearned

* Latin, Greek, and Hebrew.

vulgar being induced to believe that violence is offered to religion if anyone begins an assault upon their barbarism. . . . But even here I am confident of success if the knowledge of the three languages continues to be received in schools, as it has now begun. . . .

But one doubt still possesses my mind. I am afraid that, under cover of a revival of ancient literature, paganism may attempt to rear its head—as there are some among Christians that acknowledge Christ in name but breathe inwardly a heathen spirit—or, on the other hand, that the restoration of Hebrew learning may give occasion to a revival of Judaism. This would be a plague as much opposed to the doctrine of Christ as anything that could happen. . . . I know that your sincere piety will have regard to nothing but Christ, to whom all your studies are devoted. . . .

Questions for Analysis

1. What does Erasmus mean by a "golden age"?

2. Do education and learning ensure improvement in the human condition, in his opinion? Do you agree?

3. What would you say are the essential differences between Erasmus's educational goals and those of modern society?

Source: Epistles 522 and 530, from *The Epistles of Erasmus,* trans. F. M. Nichols (London: Longmans, Green & Co., 1901).

CHAPTER 14

Reformations and Religious Wars

1500–1600

Giorgio Vasari: *Massacre of Coligny and the Huguenots* (1573). This fresco shows the Saint Bartholomew's Day massacre in Paris, one of many bloody events in the religious wars that accompanied the Reformation. (Vatican Palace/Scala/Art Resource, NY)

Chapter Preview

The Early Reformation
What were the central ideas of the reformers, and why were they appealing to different social groups?

The Reformation and German Politics
How did the political situation in Germany shape the course of the Reformation?

The Spread of the Protestant Reformation
How did Protestant ideas and institutions spread beyond German-speaking lands?

The Catholic Reformation
How did the Catholic Church respond to the new religious situation?

Religious Violence
What were the causes and consequences of religious violence, including riots, wars, and witch hunts?

INDIVIDUALS IN SOCIETY: Teresa of Ávila

IMAGES IN SOCIETY: Art in the Reformation

LISTENING TO THE PAST: Martin Luther, *On Christian Liberty*

In 1500 there was one Christian church in western Europe to which all Christians at least nominally belonged. Fifty years later there were many, as a result of a religious reform movement that gained wide acceptance and caused Christianity to break into many divisions.

Along with the Renaissance, the Reformation is often seen as a key element in the creation of the "modern" world. This radical change contained many elements of continuity, however. Sixteenth-century reformers looked back to the early Christian church for their inspiration, and many of their reforming ideas had been advocated for centuries.

The Early Reformation

What were the central ideas of the reformers, and why were they appealing to different social groups?

Calls for reform in the church came from many quarters in early-sixteenth-century Europe—from educated laypeople such as Christian humanists and urban residents, from villagers and artisans, and from church officials themselves. This dissatisfaction helps explain why the ideas of Martin Luther, an obscure professor from a new and not very prestigious German university, found a ready audience. Within a decade of his first publishing his ideas (using the new technology of the printing press), much of central Europe and Scandinavia had broken with the Catholic Church and even more radical concepts of the Christian message were being developed and linked to calls for social change.

The Christian Church in the Early Sixteenth Century

Sixteenth-century Europeans of all social classes devoted an enormous amount of their time and income to religious causes and foundations. Despite—or perhaps because of—the depth of their piety, many people were also highly critical of the Roman Catholic Church and its clergy. The papal conflict with the German emperor Frederick II in the thirteenth century, followed by the Babylonian Captivity and then the Great Schism, badly damaged the prestige of church leaders. Humanists denounced corruption in the church. In *The Praise of Folly*, Erasmus condemned the superstitions of the parish clergy and the excessive rituals of the monks. Many ordinary people agreed. Court records, bishop's visitations of parishes, and even popular songs and printed images show widespread **anticlericalism,** or opposition to the clergy.

In the early sixteenth century critics of the church concentrated their attacks on three disorders—clerical immorality, clerical ignorance, and clerical pluralism, with the related problem of absenteeism. Charges of clerical immorality were aimed at a number of priests who were drunkards, neglected the rule of celibacy, gambled, or indulged in fancy dress. Charges of clerical ignorance applied to barely literate priests who delivered sermons of poor quality and who were obviously ignorant of the Latin words of the Mass.

In regard to absenteeism and **pluralism,** many clerics, especially higher ecclesiastics, held several *benefices* (**BEN-ah-fiss-es**) (or offices) simultaneously but seldom visited the benefices, let alone performed the spiritual responsibilities those offices entailed. Instead, they collected revenues from all of them and hired a poor priest, paying him just a fraction of the income to fulfill the spiritual duties of a

anticlericalism Opposition to the clergy.

pluralism The clerical practice of holding more than one church benefice (or office) at the same time and enjoying the income from each.

particular local church. Many Italian officials in the papal curia held benefices in England, Spain, and Germany. Revenues from those countries paid the Italian priests' salaries, provoking not only charges of absenteeism but also nationalistic resentment.

There was also local resentment of clerical privileges and immunities. Priests, monks, and nuns were exempt from civic responsibilities, such as defending the city and paying taxes. Yet religious orders frequently held large amounts of urban property, in some cities as much as one-third. City governments were increasingly determined to integrate the clergy into civic life. This brought city leaders into opposition with bishops and the papacy, which for centuries had stressed the independence of the church from lay control and the distinction between members of the clergy and laypeople.

Martin Luther

By itself, widespread criticism of the church did not lead to the dramatic changes of the sixteenth century. Those resulted from the personal religious struggle of a German university professor, Martin Luther (1483–1546), who was also a priest. Martin Luther was born at Eisleben in Saxony. At considerable sacrifice, his father sent him to school and then to the University of Erfurt, where he earned a master's degree with distinction. Luther was to proceed to the study of law and a legal career, which for centuries had been the stepping-stone to public office and material success. Instead, however, a sense of religious calling led him to join the Augustinian friars, an order whose members often preached, taught, and assisted the poor. Luther was ordained a priest in 1507 and after additional study earned a doctorate of theology. From 1512 until his death in 1546, he served as professor of the Scriptures at the new University of Wittenberg. Throughout his life, he frequently cited his professorship as justification for his reforming work.

Martin Luther was a very conscientious friar. His scrupulous observance of the religious routine, frequent confessions, and fasting, however, gave him only temporary relief from anxieties about sin and his ability to meet God's demands. Through his study of Saint Paul's letters in the New Testament, he gradually arrived at a new understanding of Christian doctrine. His understanding is often summarized as "faith alone, grace alone, Scripture alone." He believed that salvation and justification come through faith. Faith is a free gift of God, not the result of human effort. God's word is revealed only in Scripture, not in the traditions of the church.

At the same time that Luther was engaged in scholarly reflections and professorial lecturing, Pope Leo X authorized the sale of a special St. Peter's indulgence to finance his building plans in Rome. An **indulgence** was a document, signed by the pope or another church official, that substituted for penance. The archbishop who controlled the area in which Wittenberg was located, Albert of Mainz, was an enthusiastic promoter of this indulgence sale. He received a share of the profits in order to pay off a debt from a wealthy banking family, a debt he had incurred in order to purchase a papal dispensation allowing him to become the bishop of

indulgence A papal statement (a document addressed to an individual) granting remission of priest-imposed penalty for sin (no one knew what penalty God would impose after death). Popular belief, however, held that an indulgence secured complete remission of all penalties for sin, before and after death.

The Folly of Indulgences

In this woodcut from the early Reformation, the church's sale of indulgences is viciously satirized. With one claw in holy water, another resting on the coins paid for indulgences, and a third stretched out for offerings, the church, in the form of a rapacious bird, writes out an indulgence with excrement. The creature's head and gaping mouth represent Hell, with foolish Christians inside, others being cooked in a pot above, and a demon delivering the pope in a three-tiered crown and holding the keys to Heaven, a symbol of papal authority. Illustrations such as this, often printed as single-sheet broadsides and sold very cheaply, clearly conveyed criticism of the church to people who could not read. (Kunstsammlungen der Veste Coburg)

several other territories as well. Albert's indulgence sale, run by a Dominican friar who mounted an advertising blitz, promised that the purchase of indulgences would bring full forgiveness for one's own sins or release from purgatory for a loved one. One of the slogans—"As soon as coin in coffer rings, the soul from purgatory springs"—brought phenomenal success.

Luther was severely troubled that many people believed they had no further need for repentance once they had purchased indulgences. He wrote a letter to Archbishop Albert on the subject and enclosed in Latin his "Ninety-five Theses on the Power of Indulgences." His argument was that indulgences undermined the seriousness of the sacrament of penance, competed with the preaching of the Gospel, and downplayed the importance of charity in Christian life. After Luther's death, biographies reported that the theses were also posted on the door of the church at Wittenberg Castle on October 31, 1517. Such an act would have been very strange—they were in Latin and written for those learned in theology, not for normal churchgoers—but it has become a standard part of Luther lore. In any case, Luther intended the theses for academic debate, but by December 1517 they had been translated into German and were read throughout the Holy Roman Empire.

Luther was ordered to come to Rome, which he was able to avoid because of the political situation in the empire, but he did engage in formal scholarly debate with a representative of the church, Johann Eck, at Leipzig in 1519. He denied both the authority of the pope and the infallibility of a general council. The Council of Constance, he said, had erred when it had condemned Jan Hus (see page 294).

The papacy responded with a letter condemning some of Luther's propositions, ordering that his books be burned, and giving him two months to recant or be excommunicated. Luther retaliated by publicly burning the letter. By January 3, 1521, when the excommunication was supposed to become final, the controversy involved more than theological issues. The papal legate wrote, "All Germany is in revolution. Nine-tenths shout 'Luther' as their war cry; and the other tenth cares nothing about Luther, and cries 'Death to the court of Rome.'"[1] In this highly charged atmosphere, the twenty-one-year-old emperor Charles V held his first diet (assembly of the Estates of the empire) in the German city of Worms. Charles summoned Luther to appear before the **Diet of Worms.** When ordered to recant, Luther replied in language that rang all over Europe:

> *Unless I am convinced by the evidence of Scripture or by plain reason—for I do not accept the authority of the Pope or the councils alone, since it is established that they have often erred and contradicted themselves—I am bound by the Scriptures I have cited and my conscience is captive to the Word of God. I cannot and will not recant anything, for it is neither safe nor right to go against conscience. God help me. Amen.*[2]

Diet of Worms An assembly held by Charles V (1521) in the German city of Worms where Luther defended his doctrines before the emperor, refusing to recant.

Protestant Thought

As he developed his ideas, Luther gathered followers, who came to be called Protestants. The word **Protestant** derives from the protest drawn up by a small group of reforming German princes at the Diet of Speyer in 1529. The princes "protested" the decisions of the Catholic majority. At first Protestant meant "Lutheran," but with the appearance of many protesting sects, it became a general term applied to all non-Catholic western European Christians.

Protestant The name originally given to Lutherans, after a group of reforming princes protested decisions of the Catholic princes at the Diet of Speyer (1529); as other reforming groups appeared, the term came to mean all non-Catholic western Christian groups.

The most important early reformer other than Luther was the Swiss humanist, priest, and admirer of Erasmus, Ulrich Zwingli (ZWING-glee) (1484–1531). Zwingli announced in 1519 that he would preach not from the church's prescribed readings but, relying on Erasmus's New Testament, go right through the New Testament "from A to Z," that is, from Matthew to Revelation. Zwingli was convinced that Christian life rested on the Scriptures, which were the pure words of God and the sole basis of religious truth. He went on to attack indulgences, the Mass, the institution of monasticism, and clerical celibacy. In his gradual reform of the church in Zurich, he had the strong support of the city authorities, who had long resented the privileges of the clergy.

Luther, Zwingli, and other Protestants agreed on many things. First, how is a person to be saved? Traditional Catholic teaching held that salvation is achieved by both faith and good works. Protestants held that salvation comes by faith alone, irrespective of good works or the sacraments. God, not people, initiates salvation. (See the feature "Listening to the Past: Martin Luther, *On Christian Liberty*" on pages 368–369.) Second, where does religious authority reside? Christian doctrine had long maintained that authority rests both in the Bible and in the traditional teaching of the church. For Protestants, authority rested in the Bible alone. For a doctrine or issue to be valid, it had to have a scriptural basis. Because of this, most Protestants rejected Catholic teachings about the sacraments (see page 368), holding that only baptism and the Eucharist have scriptural support. Third, what is the church? Protestants held that the church is a spiritual *priesthood of all believers*, an invisible fellowship not fixed in any place or person, which differed markedly from the Roman Catholic practice of a clerical, hierarchical institution headed by the pope in Rome. Fourth, what is the highest form of Christian life? The medieval church had stressed the superiority of the monastic and religious life over the secular. Luther disagreed and argued that every person should serve God in his or her individual calling.

Protestants did not agree on everything. One important area of dispute was the ritual of the Eucharist (also called communion, or the Lord's Supper). Catholicism holds the dogma of **transubstantiation:** by the consecrating words of the priest during the Mass, the bread and wine become the actual body and blood of Christ, who is then fully present in the bread and wine. In opposition, Luther believed that Christ is really present in the consecrated bread and wine, but this is

transubstantiation Catholic doctrine of the Eucharist, that when the bread and wine are consecrated by the priest at Mass, they are transformed into the actual body and blood of Christ.

Lucas Cranach the Elder: The Ten Commandments, 1516
Cranach, who was the court painter for the Elector of Saxony from 1505 to 1553, painted this giant illustration of the Ten Commandments (more than 5 feet by 11 feet) for the city hall in Wittenberg just at the point when Luther was beginning to question Catholic doctrine. Cranach became an early supporter of Luther, and many of his later works depict the reformer and his ideas. This close association, and the fact that the painting captures the Protestant emphasis on biblical texts very well, led it to be moved to the Luther House in Wittenberg, the largest museum of the Protestant Reformation in the world. Paintings were used by both Protestants and Catholics to teach religious ideas.   (Lutherhalle, Wittenberg/The Bridgeman Art Library)

the result of God's mystery, not the actions of a priest. Zwingli understood the Lord's Supper as a *memorial*, in which Christ was present in spirit among the faithful, but not in the bread and wine. The Colloquy of Marburg, summoned in 1529 to unite Protestants, failed to resolve these differences, though Protestants reached agreement on almost everything else.

The Appeal of Protestant Ideas

Pulpits and printing presses spread Luther's message all over Germany. By the time of his death, people of all social classes had become Lutheran. What was the immense appeal of Luther's religious ideas and those of other Protestants?

Educated people and humanists were much attracted by Luther's ideas. He advocated a simpler personal religion based on faith, a return to the spirit of the early church, the centrality of the Scriptures in the liturgy and in Christian life, and the abolition of elaborate ceremonies—precisely the reforms the Christian humanists had been calling for. His insistence that everyone should read and reflect on the Scriptures attracted the literate and thoughtful middle classes partly because Luther appealed to their intelligence. This included many priests and monks, who became clergy in the new Protestant churches. Luther's ideas also appealed to townspeople who envied the church's wealth and resented paying for it. After Zurich became Protestant, the city council taxed the clergy and placed them under the jurisdiction of civil courts.

Scholars in many disciplines have attributed Luther's fame and success to the invention of the printing press, which rapidly reproduced and made known his ideas. Many printed works included woodcuts and other illustrations, so that even those who could not read could grasp the main ideas. (See the feature "Images in Society: Art in the Reformation" on pages 344–345.) Equally important was Luther's incredible skill with language, as seen in his two catechisms (1529), compendiums of basic religious knowledge. Hymns such as "A Mighty Fortress Is Our God" (which Luther wrote) were also important means of conveying central points of doctrine. Luther's linguistic skill, together with his translation of the New Testament into German in 1523, led to the acceptance of his dialect of German as the standard version of the German language.

Both Luther and Zwingli recognized that if reforms were going to be permanent, political authorities as well as concerned individuals and religious leaders would have to accept them. Zwingli worked closely with the city council of Zurich, and in other cities and towns of Switzerland and south Germany city councils similarly took the lead. They appointed pastors that they knew had accepted Protestant ideas, required them to swear an oath of loyalty to the council, and oversaw their preaching and teaching.

Luther lived in a territory ruled by a noble—the Elector of Saxony—and he also worked closely with political authorities, viewing them as fully justified in asserting control over the church in their territories. Indeed, he demanded that German rulers reform the papacy and ecclesiastical institutions, and he instructed all Christians to obey their secular rulers, whom he saw as divinely ordained to maintain order. Individuals may have been convinced of the truth of Protestant teachings by hearing sermons, listening to hymns, or reading pamphlets, but a territory became Protestant when its ruler, whether a noble or a city council, brought in a reformer or two to reeducate the territory's clergy, sponsored public sermons, and confiscated church property. This happened in many of the states of the empire during the 1520s and then moved beyond the empire to Denmark-Norway and Sweden.

The Radical Reformation

Some individuals and groups rejected the idea that church and state needed to be united, and sought to create a voluntary community of believers as they understood it to have existed in New Testament times. In terms of theology and spiritual practices, these individuals and groups varied widely, though they are generally termed "radicals" for their insistence on a more extensive break with the past. Some adopted the baptism of believers—for which they were given the title of "Anabaptists" or rebaptizers by their enemies—while others saw all outward sacraments or rituals as misguided. Some groups attempted communal ownership of property, living very simply and rejecting anything they thought unbiblical. Some reacted harshly to members who deviated, but others argued for complete religious toleration and individualism.

Religious radicals were met with fanatical hatred and bitter persecution. Protestants and Catholics alike saw—quite correctly—that the radicals' call for the separation of church and state would lead ultimately to the secularization of society. In Saxony, in Strasbourg, and in the Swiss cities, radicals were either banished or cruelly executed by burning, beating, or drowning. Their community spirit and the edifying example of their lives, however, contributed to the survival of radical ideas. Later, the Quakers, with their gentle pacifism; the Baptists, with their emphasis on inner spiritual light; the Congregationalists, with their democratic church organization; and in 1787 the authors of the U.S. Constitution, with their opposition to the "establishment of religion" (state churches), would all trace their origins, in part, to the radicals of the sixteenth century.

Images in Society

Art in the Reformation

In the Reformation era, controversy raged over the purpose and function of art. Protestants and Catholics disagreed, and Protestant groups disagreed with one another. The Bible specifically prohibits making images of anything "in the heavens above or the earth below or the waters beneath the earth" (Exodus 20:4–6 and Deuteronomy 5:8–10). Based on this, some Protestant leaders, including Ulrich Zwingli, stressed that "the Word of God" should be the only instrument used in the work of evangelization. Martin Luther disagreed, saying he was not "of the opinion that the Gospel should blight and destroy all the arts." Luther believed that painting and sculpture had value in spreading the Gospel message because "children and simple folk are more apt to retain the divine stories when taught by pictures and parables than merely by words or instruction." Similar debates involved music, with Luther supporting and even writing hymns, and Swiss Protestants removing organs from their churches.

Lucas Cranach the Elder (1472–1553), a close friend of Luther's, is the finest representative of Protestant Reformation artists. He and Luther collaborated on the production of woodcuts and paintings, such as *The Ten Commandments* (see page 342), that spread the new evangelical theology. Each square in Cranach's painting represents one of the Ten Commandments.

Lucas Cranach the Younger (1515–1586) continued his father's work of spreading Luther's message. His woodcut *The True and False Churches* (Image 1) contains blatant and more subtle messages. At the center Luther stands in a pulpit, preaching the word of God from an open Bible. At the right, a flaming open mouth symbolizing the jaws of Hell engulfs the pope, cardinals, and friars, one kind of "false church." The scene at the left actually suggests another kind of "false church," however. Cranach shows a crucified Christ emerging out of the "lamb of God" on the altar as people are receiving communion. This image represents the Lutheran understanding of the Lord's Supper, in which Christ is really present in the bread and wine, in contrast to other Protestants who saw the ceremony as a memorial (see page 342). The woodcut thus could be understood on different levels by different viewers, which is true of much effective religious art.

For John Calvin, the utter transcendence of God made impossible any attempt to bring God down to human level through visual portraiture; to domesticate or to humanize God would deprive him of his glory. In houses of worship Calvin emphasized the centrality of the divine word, allowing wall inscriptions from the Bible. In later life, Calvin tolerated narrative biblical scenes as long as they did not include pictures of God or Jesus Christ. In the Netherlands, which adopted a Calvinist version of Protestantism, many formerly Catholic churches were stripped of all statues, images, and decoration and were redesigned with a stark, bare simplicity that mirrored the Calvinist ideal. Notice the interior of the church of Saint Bavo in Haarlem (Image 2).

IMAGE 1 Lucas Cranach the Younger: The True and False Churches (Staatliche Kunstsammlungen Dresden)

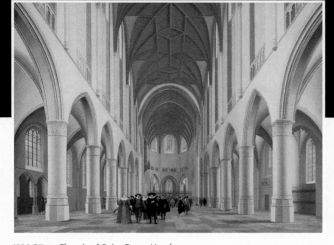

IMAGE 2 Church of Saint Bavo, Haarlem (Pieter Jansz. Saenredam, S. Bavo in Haarlem. John G. Johnson Collection, Philadelphia Museum of Art)

IMAGE 3 Jesuit Priest Distributing Holy Pictures (From Pierre Chenu, *The Reformation* [New York: St. Martin's Press, 1986])

The Catholic Church officially addressed the subject of art at the Council of Trent in December 1563. The church declared that honor and veneration should be given to likenesses of Christ, the Virgin Mary, and the saints; that images would remind people of the saints' virtues, which should be imitated; and that pictorial art would promote piety and the love of God. Examine the painting *Jesuit Priest Distributing Holy Pictures* (Image 3). Such pictures and images of saints were often given to children to help educate them on matters of doctrine. How do these pictures serve the same function as the Protestant *Ten Commandments* shown on page 342?

Both Protestants and Catholics used religious art for propaganda purposes, to oppose religious heterodoxy, and to arouse piety in laypeople. Catholic Reformation art came into full flowering with the style later known as baroque (buh-ROKE) (see page 415). Baroque art originated in Rome and reflected the dynamic and proselytizing spirit of the Counter-Reformation. The church encouraged artists to appeal to the senses, to touch the souls and kindle the faith of ordinary people while proclaiming the power and confidence of the reformed Catholic Church.

In addition to this underlying religious emotionalism, the baroque drew from the Catholic Reformation a sense of drama, motion, and ceaseless striving. The interior of the Jesuit church of Jesus—the Gesù (JAY-soo)—combined all these characteristics in its lavish, shimmering, wildly active decorations and frescoes

(Image 4). This triumphant, elaborate, and flamboyant church celebrates both the Catholic baroque and Rome as the artistic capital of Europe. How would you compare the Gesù with the Saint Bavo church (Image 2)?

IMAGE 4 Ceiling of the Gesù (Scala/Art Resource, NY)

The German Peasants' War

In the early sixteenth century the economic condition of the peasantry varied from place to place but was generally worse than it had been in the fifteenth century and was deteriorating. Crop failures in 1523 and 1524 aggravated an explosive situation. Nobles had aggrieved peasants by seizing village common lands, imposing new rents and requiring additional services, and by taking the peasants' best horses or cows in payment for death duties. The peasants made demands that they believed conformed to the Scriptures, and they cited Luther as a theologian who could prove that they did.

Luther wanted to prevent rebellion. Initially he sided with the peasants, blasting the lords for robbing their subjects. But when rebellion broke out, the peasants who expected Luther's support were soon disillusioned. Freedom for Luther meant independence from the authority of the Roman church; it did *not* mean opposition to legally established secular powers. Firmly convinced that rebellion would hasten the end of civilized society, he wrote the tract *Against the Murderous, Thieving Hordes of the Peasants*: "Let everyone who can smite, slay, and stab [the peasants], secretly and openly, remembering that nothing can be more poisonous, hurtful or devilish than a rebel."[3] The nobility ferociously crushed the revolt. Historians estimate that more than seventy-five thousand peasants were killed in 1525.

The German Peasants' War of 1525 greatly strengthened the authority of lay rulers. Not surprisingly, the Reformation lost much of its popular appeal after 1525, though peasants and urban rebels sometimes found a place for their social and religious ideas in radical groups. Peasants' economic conditions did moderately improve, however. For example, in many parts of Germany, enclosed fields, meadows, and forests were returned to common use.

The Reformation and Marriage

Luther and Zwingli both believed that a priest or nun's vows of celibacy went against human nature and God's commandments. Luther married a former nun, Katharina von Bora (1499–1532), and Zwingli married a Zurich widow, Anna Reinhart (1491–1538). Both women quickly had several children. Most other Protestant reformers also married, and their wives had to create a new and respectable role for themselves—pastor's wife—to overcome being viewed as simply a new type of priest's concubine. They were living demonstrations of their husband's convictions about the superiority of marriage to celibacy, and they were expected to be models of wifely obedience and Christian charity.

Protestants did not break with medieval scholastic theologians in their idea that women were to be subject to men. Women were advised to be cheerful rather than grudging in their obedience, for in doing so they demonstrated their willingness to follow God's plan. Men were urged to treat their wives kindly and considerately, but also to enforce their authority, through physical coercion if necessary. Both continental and English marriage manuals use the metaphor of breaking a horse for teaching a wife obedience, though laws did set limits on the husband's power to do so. A few women took Luther's idea about the priesthood of all believers to heart and wrote religious pamphlets and hymns, but no sixteenth-century Protestants officially allowed women to hold positions of religious authority. Monarchs such as Elizabeth I of England and female territorial rulers of the states of the Holy Roman Empire did determine religious policies, however.

Catholics viewed marriage as a sacramental union that, if validly entered into, could not be dissolved. Protestants saw marriage as a contract in which each part-

Lucas Cranach the Elder: Martin Luther and Katharina von Bora

Cranach painted this double marriage portrait to celebrate Luther's wedding in 1525 to Katharina von Bora, a former nun. The artist was one of the witnesses at the wedding and, in fact, had presented Luther's marriage proposal to Katharina. Using a go-between for proposals was very common, as was having a double wedding portrait painted. This particular couple quickly became a model of the ideal marriage, and many churches wanted their portraits. More than sixty similar paintings, with slight variations, were produced by Cranach's workshop and hung in churches and wealthy homes.

(Uffizi, Florence/Scala/Art Resource, NY)

ner promised the other support, companionship, and the sharing of mutual goods. Because, in Protestant eyes, marriage was created by God as a remedy for human weakness, marriages in which spouses did not comfort or support one another physically, materially, or emotionally endangered their own souls and the surrounding community. The only solution might be divorce and remarriage, which most Protestants came to allow, although divorce remained rare everywhere in Europe as marriage was such an important social and economic institution.

The Reformation generally brought the closing of monasteries and convents, and marriage became virtually the only occupation for upper-class Protestant women. Women in some convents recognized this and fought the Reformation, or argued that they could still be pious Protestants within convent walls. Most nuns left, however, and we do not know what happened to them. The Protestant emphasis on marriage made unmarried women (and men) suspect, for they did not belong to the type of household regarded as the cornerstone of a proper, godly society.

Section Review

- Many people were discontented with the Catholic Church and charged that the clergy were immoral, uneducated, and concerned more with wealth than fulfilling their spiritual duties.

- Martin Luther was a priest and theology professor who initially wanted to reform abuses in the Catholic Church, but came to break with the church; leading a movement later termed the Protestant Reformation.

- Both Luther and the Swiss reformer Ulrich Zwingli advocated that salvation was from God, that the Scripture and not the popes held all truth, that the church was what the people believed and not a physical place, and opposed the hierarchy of the priests over believers.

- Disputes arose over the proper role of the arts in religion, with Luther allowing music, painting, and sculpture, while Zwingli and the stricter Calvinists banned religious images.

- The printing press greatly boosted the spread of Protestant ideas and both Luther and Zwingli targeted political rulers to ensure the success of their reforms.

- Radical groups such as the Anabaptists, wanting communal living and complete separation of church and state, experienced harsh persecution, although their ideas survived.

- German peasants lost interest in the Reformation when Luther failed to back their demands for better conditions and the nobility viciously crushed their rebellion during the German Peasants' War of 1525.

- Protestants thought celibacy was against human nature and God and allowed church leaders to marry, but still believed women were inferior to men.

The Reformation and German Politics

How did the political situation in Germany shape the course of the Reformation?

Criticism of the church was widespread in Europe in the early sixteenth century, and calls for reform came from many areas. Yet such movements could be more easily squelched by the strong central governments of Spain, France, and England. The Holy Roman Empire, in contrast, included hundreds of largely independent states. Against this background of decentralization and strong local power, Martin Luther had launched a movement to reform the church. Two years after Luther published the "Ninety-five Theses," the electors chose as emperor a nineteen-year-old Habsburg prince who ruled as Charles V. The course of the Reformation was shaped by this election and by the political relationships surrounding it.

The Rise of the Habsburg Dynasty

War and diplomacy were important ways that states increased their power in sixteenth-century Europe, but so was marriage. The benefits of an advantageous marriage stretched across generations, a process that can be seen most dramatically with the Habsburgs. The Holy Roman emperor Frederick III, a Habsburg who was the ruler of most of Austria, acquired only a small amount of territory—but a great deal of money—with his marriage to Princess Eleonore of Portugal in 1452. He arranged for his son Maximilian to marry Europe's most prominent heiress, Mary of Burgundy, in 1477; she inherited the Netherlands, Luxembourg, and the County of Burgundy in what is now eastern France. Through this union with the rich and powerful duchy of Burgundy, the Austrian house of Habsburg, already the strongest ruling family in the empire, became an international power. The marriage of Maximilian and Mary angered the French, however, who considered Burgundy French territory, and inaugurated centuries of conflict between the Austrian house of Habsburg and the kings of France.

Maximilian learned the lesson of marital politics well, marrying his son and daughter to the children of Ferdinand and Isabella, the rulers of Spain, much of southern Italy, and eventually the Spanish New World empire. His grandson Charles V (1500–1558) fell heir to a vast and incredibly diverse collection of states and peoples, each governed in a different manner and held together only by the person of the emperor (see Map 14.1 on page 349). Charles's Italian adviser, the grand chancellor Gattinara, told the young ruler, "God has set you on the path toward world monarchy." Charles not only believed this but also was convinced that it was his duty to maintain the political and religious unity of Western Christendom.

The Political Impact of the Protestant Reformation

In the sixteenth century the practice of religion remained a public matter. Rulers determined the official form of religious practice in his (or occasionally her) jurisdiction. Almost everyone believed that the presence of a faith different from that of the majority represented a political threat to the security of the state. Few believed in religious liberty.

Luther's ideas appealed to German rulers for a variety of reasons. Though Germany was not a nation, people did have an understanding of being German because of their language and traditions. Luther frequently used the phrase "we

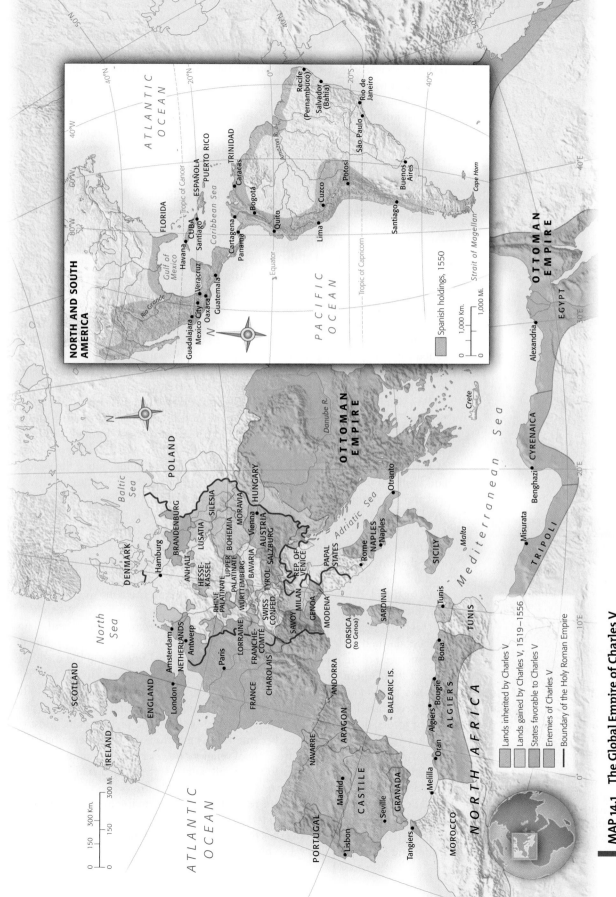

MAP 14.1   The Global Empire of Charles V

Charles V exercised theoretical jurisdiction over more European territory than anyone since Charlemagne. He also claimed authority over large parts of North and South America, though actual Spanish control was weak in much of this area.

NORTH AND SOUTH AMERICA

Spanish holdings, 1550

OTTOMAN EMPIRE

NORTH AFRICA

Germans" in his attacks on the papacy. Luther's appeal to national feeling influenced many rulers otherwise confused by or indifferent to the complexities of the religious issues. Some German rulers were sincerely attracted to Lutheran ideas, but material considerations swayed many others to embrace the new faith. The rejection of Roman Catholicism and adoption of Protestantism would mean the legal confiscation of lush farmlands, rich monasteries, and wealthy shrines. Thus many political authorities in the empire used the religious issue to extend their financial and political power and to enhance their independence from the emperor.

Charles V was a vigorous defender of Catholicism, however, so it is not surprising that the Reformation led to religious wars. The first battleground was Switzerland, which was officially part of the Holy Roman Empire, though it was really a loose confederation of thirteen largely autonomous territories called "cantons." Some cantons remained Catholic, and some became Protestant, and in the late 1520s the two sides went to war. Zwingli was killed on the battlefield in 1531, and both sides quickly decided that a treaty was preferable to further fighting. The treaty basically allowed each canton to determine its own religion and ordered each side to give up its foreign alliances, a policy of neutrality that has been characteristic of modern Switzerland.

Trying to halt the spread of religious division, Charles V called an Imperial Diet in 1530, to meet at Augsburg. The Lutherans developed a statement of faith, later called the Augsburg Confession, and the Protestant princes presented this to the emperor. (The Augsburg Confession remained an authoritative statement of belief for many Lutheran churches for centuries.) Charles refused to accept it and ordered all Protestants to return to the Catholic Church and give up any confiscated church property. This demand backfired, and Protestant territories in the empire—mostly northern German principalities and southern German cities—formed a military alliance. The emperor could not respond militarily, as he was in the midst of a series of wars with the French: the Habsburg-Valois wars, fought in Italy along the eastern and southern borders of France and eventually in Germany. The Ottoman Turks had also taken much of Hungary and in 1529 were besieging Vienna.

The 1530s and early 1540s saw complicated political maneuvering among many of the powers of Europe. Various attempts were made to heal the religious split with a church council, but intransigence on both sides made it increasingly clear that this would not be possible and that war was inevitable. Charles V realized that he was fighting not only for religious unity, but also for a more unified state, against territorial rulers who wanted to maintain their independence. He was thus defending both church and empire.

Fighting began in 1546, and initially the emperor was very successful. This success alarmed both France and the pope, however, who did not want Charles to become even more powerful. The pope withdrew papal troops, and the Catholic king of France sent money and troops to the Lutheran princes. Finally, in 1555 Charles agreed to the Peace of Augsburg, which, in accepting the status quo, officially recognized Lutheranism. The political authority in each territory was permitted to decide whether the territory would be Catholic or Lutheran. Most of northern and central Germany became Lutheran, while the south remained Roman Catholic. There was no freedom of religion, however. Princes or town councils established state churches to which all subjects of the area had to belong. Dissidents had to convert or leave.

The Peace of Augsburg ended religious war in Germany for many decades. His hope of uniting his empire under a single church dashed, Charles V abdicated in 1556, transferring power over his Spanish and Netherlandish holdings to his son Philip and his imperial power to his brother Ferdinand.

Section Review

- The strong central governments of Spain, France, and England initially crushed calls for reform, but in the decentralized independent states of the Holy Roman Empire, Luther found the right conditions for reform.

- Through politically advantageous marriages, the House of Habsburg acquired much land and money, becoming an international power.

- In the sixteenth century, religion continued to be a public matter more than a personal choice, and the Reformation led to religious wars.

- As a result of the religious wars, the ruler of each territory chose whether it would be Catholic or Lutheran; there was no personal religious freedom within each area, so dissenters had to convert or leave.

The Spread of the Protestant Reformation

How did Protestant ideas and institutions spread beyond German-speaking lands?

States within the Holy Roman Empire and the kingdom of Denmark-Norway were the earliest territories to accept the Protestant Reformation, but by the later 1520s religious change came to England, France, and eastern Europe. In all of these areas, a second generation of reformers built on Lutheran and Zwinglian ideas to develop their own theology and plans for institutional change. The most important of the second-generation reformers was John Calvin, whose ideas would profoundly influence the social thought and attitudes of European and English-speaking peoples all over the world, especially in Canada and the United States.

The Reformation in England and Ireland

As on the continent, the Reformation in England had economic as well as religious causes. However, the impetus for England's break with Rome was the ruler's desire for a new wife.

King Henry VIII (r. 1509–1547) was married to Catherine of Aragon, the daughter of Ferdinand and Isabella and widow of his older brother Arthur. Marriage to a brother's widow went against canon law, and Henry had been required to obtain a special papal dispensation to marry Catherine. The marriage had produced only one living heir, a daughter, Mary. By 1527 Henry decided that God was showing his displeasure with the marriage by denying him a son, and he appealed to the pope to have the marriage annulled. He was also in love with a court lady-in-waiting, Anne Boleyn, and assumed that she would give him the son he wanted. Normally an annulment would not have been a problem, but the troops of Emperor Charles V were in Rome at that point, and Pope Clement VII was essentially their prisoner. Charles V was the nephew of Catherine of Aragon and thus was vigorously opposed to an annulment, which would have declared his aunt a fornicator and his cousin Mary a bastard. The pope stalled.

Since Rome appeared to be thwarting Henry's matrimonial plans, he decided to remove the English church from papal jurisdiction. Henry used Parliament to legalize the Reformation in England and to make himself the supreme head of the Church of England. Some opposed the king and were beheaded, among them Thomas More, the king's chancellor and author of *Utopia* (see page 317). When Anne Boleyn failed twice to produce a male child, Henry VIII charged her with adulterous incest and in 1536 had her beheaded. His third wife, Jane Seymour, gave Henry the desired son, Edward, but she died in childbirth. Henry went on to three more wives. Between 1535 and 1539, under the influence of his chief minister, Thomas Cromwell, Henry decided to dissolve the English monasteries because he wanted their wealth. The king ended nine hundred years of English monastic life, dispersing the monks and nuns and confiscating their lands. Hundreds of properties were sold to the middle and upper classes and the proceeds enriched the Exchequer. The dissolution of the monasteries did not achieve a more equitable distribution of land and wealth. Rather, the redistribution of land strengthened the upper classes and tied them to the Tudor dynasty.

Henry's motives combined personal, political, social, and economic elements. Theologically, he retained such traditional Catholic practices and doctrines as confession, clerical celibacy, and transubstantiation. Meanwhile, Protestant literature

Allegory of the Tudor Dynasty

The unknown creator of this work intended to glorify the virtues of the Protestant succession; the painting has no historical reality. Enthroned Henry VIII (r. 1509–1547) hands the sword of justice to his Protestant son Edward VI (r. 1547–1553). The Catholic Queen Mary (r. 1553–1558) and her husband Philip of Spain are followed by Mars, god of war, signifying violence and civil disorder. At right the figures of Peace and Plenty accompany the Protestant Elizabeth I (r. 1558–1603), symbolizing England's happy fate under her rule. (Yale Center for British Art, Paul Mellon Collection/The Bridgeman Art Library)

circulated, and Henry approved the selection of men of Protestant sympathies as tutors for his son.

Most clergy and officials accepted Henry's moves, but all did not quietly acquiesce. In 1536 popular opposition in the north to the religious changes led to the Pilgrimage of Grace, a massive multiclass rebellion that proved the largest in English history. The "pilgrims" accepted a truce, but their leaders were arrested, tried, and executed. Recent scholarship points out that people rarely "converted" from Catholicism to Protestantism overnight. People responded to an action of the crown that was played out in their own neighborhood—the closing of a monastery, the ending of masses for the dead—with a combination of resistance, acceptance, and collaboration.

Loyalty to the Catholic Church was particularly strong in Ireland. Ireland had been claimed by English kings since the twelfth century, but in reality the English had firm control of only the area around Dublin, known as the Pale. In 1536, on orders from London, the Irish parliament, which represented only the English landlords and the people of the Pale, approved the English laws severing the church from Rome. The Church of Ireland was established on the English pattern, and the (English) ruling class adopted the new reformed faith. Most of the Irish people remained Roman Catholic, thus adding religious antagonism to the ethnic hostility that had been a feature of English policy toward Ireland for centuries (see page 300). Irish armed opposition to the Reformation led to harsh repression by the English. Catholic property was confiscated and sold, and the profits were shipped to England. With the Roman church driven underground, Catholic clergy acted as national as well as religious leaders.

The nationalization of the church and the dissolution of the monasteries led to important changes in government administration in both England and Ireland. Vast tracts of formerly monastic land came temporarily under the Crown's jurisdiction, and new bureaucratic machinery had to be developed to manage those properties. Cromwell reformed and centralized the king's household, the council, the secretariats, and the Exchequer. New departments of state were set up. Surplus funds from all departments went into a liquid fund to be applied to areas where there were deficits. This balancing resulted in greater efficiency and economy. Henry VIII's reign saw the growth of the modern centralized bureaucratic state.

In the short reign of Henry's sickly son, Edward VI (r. 1547–1553), strongly Protestant ideas exerted a significant influence on the religious life of the country. Archbishop Thomas Cranmer simplified the liturgy, invited Protestant theologians to England, and prepared the first **Book of Common Prayer** (1549). In stately and dignified English, the *Book of Common Prayer* included, together with the Psalter, the order for all services of the Church of England.

The equally brief reign of Mary Tudor (r. 1553–1558) witnessed a sharp move back to Catholicism. The devoutly Catholic daughter of Catherine of Aragon, Mary rescinded the Reformation legislation of her father's reign and restored Roman Catholicism. Mary's marriage to her cousin Philip of Spain, son of the emperor Charles V, proved highly unpopular in England, and her execution of several hundred Protestants further alienated her subjects. During her reign, many Protestants fled to the continent. Mary's death raised to the throne her sister Elizabeth (r. 1558–1603) and inaugurated the beginnings of religious stability.

Elizabeth, Henry's daughter with Anne Boleyn, had been raised a Protestant, but at the start of her reign sharp differences existed in England. On the one hand, Catholics wanted a Roman Catholic ruler. On the other hand, a vocal number of returning exiles wanted all Catholic elements in the Church of England eliminated. The latter, because they wanted to "purify" the church, were called "Puritans."

Shrewdly, Elizabeth chose a middle course between Catholic and Puritan extremes. She referred to herself as the "supreme governor of the Church of England," which allowed Catholics to remain loyal to her without denying the pope. She required her subjects to attend church or risk a fine, but did not interfere with their privately held beliefs. The Anglican Church, as the Church of England was called, moved in a moderately Protestant direction. Services were conducted in English, monasteries were not re-established, and clergymen were (grudgingly) allowed to marry. But the episcopate was not abolished, and the bishops remained as church officials, and church services were quite traditional.

Elizabeth's reign was threatened by European powers attempting to re-establish Catholicism. In 1586 Elizabeth's cousin and heir to the crown, Mary, Queen of Scots, became implicated in a plot to assassinate Elizabeth. Hoping to reunite England with Catholic Europe through Mary, Philip of Spain (Philip II) gave the conspiracy his full backing. When the English executed Mary, the Catholic pope urged Philip to retaliate.

Philip prepared a vast fleet to sail from Lisbon to Flanders, where a large army of Spanish troops were stationed, and then escort barges carrying the troops across the English Channel. On May 9, 1588, *la felícissima armada*—"the most fortunate fleet," as it was ironically called in official documents—sailed from Lisbon harbor composed of more than 130 vessels. The **Spanish Armada** met an English

Book of Common Prayer The official (parliament-approved) prayer book of the Church of England, containing the prayers for all services, the forms for administration of the sacraments, and a manual for the ordination of deacons, priests, and bishops.

Spanish Armada The fleet sent by Philip II of Spain in 1588 against England as a religious crusade against Protestantism. Weather and the English fleet defeated it.

fleet in the channel before it reached Flanders. The English ships were smaller, faster, and more maneuverable, and many of them had greater firing power than their Spanish counterparts. A combination of storms and squalls, spoiled food and rank water, inadequate Spanish ammunition, and, to a lesser extent, English fire ships that caused the Spanish to scatter, gave England the victory. On the journey home many Spanish ships went down around Ireland; perhaps 65 managed to reach home ports.

The battle in the English Channel has frequently been described as one of the decisive battles in world history. In fact, it had mixed consequences. Spain soon rebuilt its navy, and after 1588 the quality of the Spanish fleet improved. The war between England and Spain dragged on for years. Yet the defeat of the Spanish Armada prevented Philip II from reimposing Catholicism on England by force. In England the victory contributed to a David and Goliath legend that enhanced English national sentiment.

Calvinism

In 1509, while Luther was preparing for a doctorate at Wittenberg, John Calvin (1509–1564) was born in Noyon in northwestern France. As a young man he studied law, which had a decisive impact on his mind and later his thought. In 1533 he experienced a religious crisis, as a result of which he converted to Protestantism.

Calvin believed that God had specifically selected him to reform the church. Accordingly, he accepted an invitation to assist in the reformation of the city of Geneva. There, beginning in 1541, Calvin worked assiduously to establish a Christian society ruled by God through civil magistrates and reformed ministers. Geneva, "a city that was a church," became the model of a Christian community for sixteenth-century Protestant reformers.

The Institutes of the Christian Religion Calvin's formulation of Christian doctrine, which became a systematic theology for Protestantism.

To understand Calvin's Geneva, it is necessary to understand Calvin's ideas. These he embodied in *The Institutes of the Christian Religion,* first published in 1536 and definitively issued in 1559. The cornerstone of Calvin's theology was his belief in the absolute sovereignty and omnipotence of God and the total weakness of humanity. Before the infinite power of God, he asserted, men and women are as insignificant as grains of sand.

Calvin did not ascribe free will to human beings because that would detract from the sovereignty of God. Men and women cannot actively work to achieve salvation; rather, God in his infinite wisdom decided at the beginning of time who would be saved and who damned. This viewpoint constitutes the theological principle called **predestination.**

predestination The teaching that God has determined the salvation or damnation of individuals based on His will and purpose, not on their merit of works.

Many people consider the doctrine of predestination, which dates back to Saint Augustine and Saint Paul, to be a pessimistic view of the nature of God. But "this terrible decree," as even Calvin called it, did not lead to pessimism or fatalism. Rather, the Calvinist believed in the redemptive work of Christ and was confident that God had elected (saved) him or her. Predestination served as an energizing dynamic, forcing a person to undergo hardships in the constant struggle against evil.

Calvin aroused Genevans to a high standard of morality. He had two remarkable assets: complete mastery of the Scriptures and exceptional eloquence. In the reformation of the city, the Genevan Consistory also exercised a powerful role. This body of laymen and pastors was assembled "to keep watch over every man's life [and] to admonish amiably those whom they see leading a disorderly life."[4]

Although all municipal governments in early modern Europe regulated citizens' conduct, none did so with the severity of Geneva's Consistory under Calvin's leadership. Absence from sermons, criticism of ministers, dancing, card playing, family quarrels, and heavy drinking were all investigated and punished by the Consistory. Serious crimes and heresy were handled by the civil authorities, which, with the Consistory's approval, sometimes used torture to extract confessions. Between 1542 and 1546 alone seventy-six persons were banished from Geneva and fifty-eight executed for heresy, adultery, blasphemy, and witchcraft. Among them was the Spanish humanist Michael Servetus, who was burned at the stake for denying the scriptural basis for the Trinity, rejecting child baptism, and insisting that a person under twenty cannot commit a mortal sin. This last idea was considered especially dangerous to public morality.

Religious refugees from France, England, Spain, Scotland, and Italy visited Calvin's Geneva. Subsequently, the Reformed church of Calvin served as the model for the Presbyterian church in Scotland, the Huguenot church in France, and the Puritan churches in England and New England.

Calvinism became the compelling force in international Protestantism. The Calvinist ethic of the "calling" dignified all work with a religious aspect. Hard work, well done, was pleasing to God. This doctrine encouraged an aggressive, vigorous activism. These factors, together with the social and economic applications of Calvin's theology, made Calvinism the most dynamic force in sixteenth- and seventeenth-century Protestantism.

Young John Calvin
Even in youth, Calvin's face showed the strength and determination that were later to characterize his religious zeal. (Bibliothèque de Genève, Département Iconographique)

The Establishment of the Church of Scotland

Calvinism found a ready audience in Scotland, where the Scottish nobles supported reform. One man, John Knox (1505?–1572), dominated the reform movement, which led to the establishment of a state church.

Knox was determined to structure the Scottish church after the model of Geneva, where he had studied and worked with Calvin. The Presbyterian Church of Scotland was strictly Calvinist in doctrine, adopted a simple and dignified service of worship, and laid great emphasis on preaching. Its name describes its governance by *presbyters*, or ministers, instead of bishops. Knox's *Book of Common Order* (1564) became the liturgical directory for the church.

The Reformation in Eastern Europe

While political and economic issues determined the course of the Reformation in western and northern Europe, ethnic factors often proved decisive in eastern Europe, where people of diverse backgrounds had settled in the later Middle Ages.

In Bohemia in the fifteenth century, a Czech majority was ruled by Germans. Most Czechs had adopted the ideas of Jan Hus, and the emperor had been forced to recognize a separate Hussite church. Yet Lutheranism appealed to Germans in Bohemia in the 1520s and 1530s, and the nobility embraced Lutheranism in opposition to the Catholic Habsburgs. The forces of the Catholic Reformation (see page 357) promoted a Catholic spiritual revival in Bohemia, and some areas reconverted. This complicated situation would be one of the causes of the Thirty Years' War (see pages 435–437).

By 1500 Poland and the Grand Duchy of Lithuania were jointly governed by king, senate, and diet (parliament), but the two territories retained separate officials, judicial systems, armies, and forms of citizenship. The combined realms covered about 440,150 square miles, making Poland-Lithuania the largest European polity. A population of only about 7.5 million people was very thinly scattered over that land.

The population of Poland-Lithuania was also very diverse; Germans, Italians, Tartars, and Jews lived with Poles and Lithuanians. Such peoples had come as merchants, invited by medieval rulers because of their wealth or to make agricultural improvements. Each group spoke its native language, though all educated people spoke Latin. Luther's ideas took root in Germanized towns but were opposed by King Sigismund I (r. 1506-1548) as well as by ordinary Poles who held strong anti-German feeling. The Reformed tradition of John Calvin, with its stress on the power of church elders, appealed to the Polish nobility, however. The fact that Calvinism originated in France, not in Germany, also made it more attractive than Lutheranism. But doctrinal differences among Calvinists, Lutherans, and other groups prevented united opposition to Catholicism, and a Counter-Reformation gained momentum. By 1650, due to the efforts of Stanislaus Hosius (1505–1579) and those of the Jesuits (see page 359), the identification of Poland and Roman Catholicism was well established.

Hungary's experience with the Reformation was even more complex. Lutheranism was spread by Hungarian students who had studied at Wittenberg, but the Catholic hierarchy and Hungarian magnates threatened to execute all Lutherans.

However, a military event on August 26, 1526, had profound consequences for both the Hungarian state and the Protestant Reformation there. On the plain of Mohács in southern Hungary, the Ottoman sultan Suleiman the Magnificent (see page 439) inflicted a crushing defeat on the Hungarians, killing King Louis II, many of the magnates, and more than sixteen thousand ordinary soldiers. The Hungarian kingdom was then divided into three parts: the Ottoman Turks absorbed the great plains, including the capital, Buda; the Habsburgs ruled the north and west; and Ottoman-supported Janos Zapolya held eastern Hungary and Transylvania.

The Turks were indifferent to the religious conflicts of the infidels. Many Magyar (Hungarian) magnates accepted Lutheranism; Lutheran schools and parishes headed by men educated at Wittenberg multiplied; and peasants welcomed the new faith. The majority of people were Protestant until the late seventeenth century, when Hungarian nobles recognized Habsburg (Catholic) rule and Ottoman Turkish withdrawal in 1699 led to Catholic restoration.

Section Review

- John Calvin and others who developed their own theology led the spread of the Protestant Reformation beyond Germany to England, France, and eastern Europe.
- In England, King Henry VIII broke with Rome over his desire to divorce his wife Catherine of Aragon, using Parliament to legalize the Reformation and make himself the head of the Church of England.
- Following Henry's death, England returned to Catholicism briefly while his daughter Mary was queen, then adopted moderate Protestantism under his daughter Elizabeth.
- In Geneva, John Calvin emphasized the absolute power of God and demanded high standards of morality; Calvinism encouraged hard work and dynamic activism.
- Calvinism was the model for the Presbyterian Church of Scotland established by John Knox who advocated a simple service, an emphasis on preaching, and governance by ministers instead of bishops.

The Catholic Reformation

How did the Catholic Church respond to the new religious situation?

Between 1517 and 1547 Protestantism made remarkable advances. Nevertheless, the Roman Catholic Church made a significant comeback. After about 1540 no new large areas of Europe, other than the Netherlands, accepted Protestant beliefs (see Map 14.2). Many historians see the developments within the Catholic Church after the Protestant Reformation as two interrelated movements, one a drive for internal reform linked to earlier reform efforts, and the other a Counter-Reformation that opposed Protestants intellectually, politically, militarily, and institutionally. In both movements, the papacy, new religious orders, and the Council of Trent that met from 1545 to 1563 were important agents.

The Reformed Papacy

Renaissance popes and advisers were not blind to the need for church reforms, but they resisted calls for a general council representing the entire church, fearing loss of power, revenue, and prestige. This changed beginning with Pope Paul III (1534–1549), and the papal court became the center of the reform movement rather than its chief opponent. The lives of the pope and his reform-minded cardinals, abbots, and bishops were models of decorum and piety.

In 1542 Pope Paul III established the Sacred Congregation of the **Holy Office,** with jurisdiction over the Roman Inquisition, a powerful instrument of the Catholic Reformation. The Inquisition was a committee of six cardinals with judicial authority over all Catholics and the power to arrest, imprison, and execute. Within the Papal States, the Inquisition effectively destroyed heresy (and some heretics).

Holy Office The official Roman Catholic agency founded in 1542 to combat international doctrinal heresy and to promote sound doctrine on faith and morals.

The Council of Trent

Pope Paul III also called an ecumenical council, which met intermittently from 1545 to 1563 at Trent, an imperial city close to Italy. It was called not only to reform the church but also to secure reconciliation with the Protestants. Lutherans and Calvinists were invited to participate, but their insistence that the Scriptures be the sole basis for discussion made reconciliation impossible.

Nonetheless, the decrees of the Council of Trent laid a solid basis for the spiritual renewal of the Catholic Church. It gave equal validity to the Scriptures and to tradition as sources of religious truth and authority. It reaffirmed the seven sacraments and the traditional Catholic teaching on transubstantiation. It tackled the disciplinary matters that had disillusioned the faithful, requiring bishops to reside in their own dioceses, suppressing pluralism and simony, and forbidding the sale of indulgences. Clerics who kept concubines were to give them up. In a highly original decree, the council required every diocese to establish a seminary for the education and training of the clergy. Seminary professors were to determine whether candidates for ordination had *vocations*, genuine callings to the priesthood. This was a novel idea, since from the time of the early church, parents had determined their sons' (and daughters') religious careers. Finally, great emphasis was laid on preaching and instructing the laity, especially the uneducated.

One decision had especially important social consequences for laypeople. The Council of Trent stipulated that for a marriage to be valid, consent (the essence of marriage) as given in the vows had to be made publicly before witnesses, one of

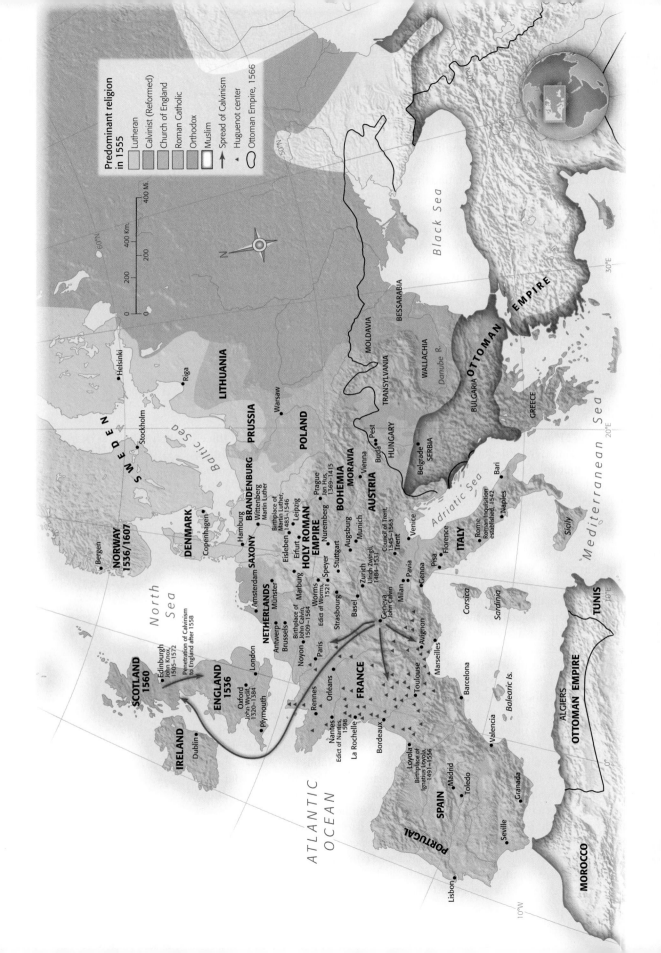

Predominant religion
in 1555
Lutheran
Calvinist (Reformed)
Church of England
Roman Catholic
Orthodox
Muslim
Spread of Calvinism
Huguenot center
Ottoman Empire, 1566

N

400 Mi.
400 Km.
200
200
0
0

ATLANTIC
OCEAN

North
Sea

Baltic Sea

Black Sea

Mediterranean Sea

Adriatic Sea

NORWAY
1536/1607

SWEDEN

DENMARK

LITHUANIA

PRUSSIA

BRANDENBURG

SAXONY

POLAND

BOHEMIA

MORAVIA

AUSTRIA

HUNGARY

TRANSYLVANIA

MOLDAVIA

BESSARABIA

WALLACHIA

BULGARIA

SERBIA

GREECE

OTTOMAN   EMPIRE

HOLY ROMAN
EMPIRE

NETHERLANDS

SCOTLAND
1560

IRELAND

ENGLAND
1536

FRANCE

SPAIN

PORTUGAL

ITALY

TUNIS

ALGIERS
OTTOMAN EMPIRE

MOROCCO

Corsica

Sardinia

Sicily

Balearic Is.

Danube R.

Bergen

Helsinki

Riga

Stockholm

Copenhagen

Warsaw

Hamburg

Wittenberg
Birthplace of
Martin Luther

Leipzig

Eisleben
Birthplace of
Martin Luther,
1483–1546

Erfurt

Prague
Jan Hus,
1369–1415

Nuremberg

Augsburg

Munich

Vienna

Buda
Pest

Belgrade

Amsterdam

Münster

Brussels

Antwerp

Marburg

Worms
Edict of Worms,
1521

Speyer

Stuttgart

Strasbourg

Basel

Zurich
Ulrich Zwingli,
1484–1531

Geneva
John Calvin

Milan

Pavia

Genoa

Venice

Trent
Council of Trent,
1545–1563

Florence

Pisa

Rome
Roman Inquisition
established, 1542

Naples

Bari

Edinburgh
John Knox,
1505–1572

Penetration of Calvinism
to England after 1558

London

Oxford
John Wyclif,
1320–1384

Plymouth

Dublin

Rennes

Orléans

Paris

Noyon
Birthplace of
John Calvin,
1509–1564

Nantes
Edict of Nantes,
1598

La Rochelle

Bordeaux

Toulouse

Avignon

Marseilles

Barcelona

Valencia

Loyola
Birthplace of
Ignatius Loyola,
1491–1556

Madrid

Toledo

Granada

Seville

Lisbon

whom had to be the parish priest. Trent thereby ended the widespread practice of secret marriages in Catholic countries. The decrees of the Council of Trent laid a solid basis for the spiritual renewal of the church. For four centuries the doctrinal and disciplinary legislation of Trent served as the basis for Roman Catholic faith, organization, and practice.

New Religious Orders

The establishment of new religious orders within the church reveals a central feature of the Catholic Reformation. Most of these new orders developed in response to one crying need: to raise the moral and intellectual level of the clergy and people. (See the feature "Individuals in Society: Teresa of Ávila.") Education was a major goal of the two most famous orders.

The Ursuline order of nuns, founded by Angela Merici (1474–1540), attained enormous prestige for the education of women. The daughter of a country gentleman, Angela Merici worked for many years among the poor, sick, and uneducated around her native Brescia in northern Italy. In 1535 she established the first women's religious order concentrating exclusively on teaching young girls, with the goal of re-Christianizing society by training future wives and mothers. After receiving papal approval in 1565, the Ursulines rapidly spread to France and the New World.

The Society of Jesus, or **Jesuits,** founded by Ignatius Loyola (1491–1556), played a powerful international role in strengthening Catholicism in Europe and spreading the faith around the world. While recuperating from a severe battle wound in his legs, Loyola studied a life of Christ and other religious books and decided to give up his military career and become a soldier of Christ. The first Jesuits, whom Loyola recruited primarily from the wealthy merchant and professional classes, saw the Reformation as a pastoral problem, its causes and cures related not to doctrinal issues but to people's spiritual condition. Reform of the church, as Luther and Calvin understood that term, played no role in the future the Jesuits planned for themselves. Their goal was "to help souls."

The Society of Jesus developed into a highly centralized, tightly knit organization. In addition to the traditional vows of poverty, chastity, and obedience, professed members vowed to go anywhere the pope said they were needed. They attracted many recruits and achieved phenomenal success for the papacy and the reformed Catholic Church, carrying Christianity to India and Japan before 1550 and to Brazil, North America, and the Congo in the seventeenth century. Within Europe the Jesuits brought southern Germany and much of eastern Europe back

Jesuits Members of the Society of Jesus, founded by Ignatius Loyola and approved by the papacy in 1540, whose goal was the spread of the Roman Catholic faith through humanistic schools and missionary activity.

Section Review

- The Council at Trent (1545–1563) failed to reconcile Protestants and Catholics but succeeded in renewing the spirituality of the Catholic Church.

- The reforms of Trent included establishing seminaries to train young clergy, determining "callings" or church vocations, and reforming marriage laws, which ended secret marriages.

- The mystical Carmelite nun Teresa of Ávila reformed her order, stressing poverty, enclosure, obedience, and social equality.

- The Ursuline nuns were the first order solely dedicated to the education of young women.

- The Jesuits contributed to the spread of Catholicism and strengthened the papacy by travelling throughout much of the world preaching and teaching.

Individuals in Society

Teresa of Ávila

Her family derived from Toledo, center of the Moorish, Jewish, and Christian cultures in medieval Spain. Her grandfather, Juan Sanchez, made a fortune in the cloth trade. A "New Christian" (see pages 330–332), he was accused of secretly practicing Judaism. Although he endured the humiliation of a public repentance, he moved his family south to Ávila. Beginning again, he recouped his wealth and, aspiring to the prestige of an "Old Christian," bought noble status. Juan's son Alzonzo Sanchez de Cepeda married a woman of thoroughly Christian background, giving his family an aura of impeccable orthodoxy. The third of their nine children, Teresa, became a saint and in 1970 was the first woman declared a Doctor of the Church, a title given to a theologian of outstanding merit.

Seventeenth-century cloisonné enamelwork illustrating Teresa of Ávila's famous vision of an angel piercing her heart. (By gracious permission of Catherine Hamilton Kappauf)

At age twenty, inspired more by the fear of Hell than the love of God, Teresa (1515–1582) entered the Carmelite Convent of the Incarnation in Ávila. Most of the nuns were daughters of Ávila's leading citizens; they had entered the convent because of a family decision about which daughters would marry and which would become nuns. Their lives were much like those of female family members outside the convent walls, with good food, comfortable surroundings, and frequent visits from family and friends. Teresa was frequently ill, but she lived quietly in the convent for many years. In her late thirties, she began to read devotional literature intensely and had profound mystical experiences—visions and voices in which Christ chastised her for her frivolous life and friends. She described one such experience in 1560:

> It pleased the Lord that I should see an angel. . . .
> Short, and very beautiful, his face was so aflame that
> he appeared to be one of the highest types of angels. . . .
> In his hands I saw a long golden spear and at the end
> of an iron tip I seemed to see a point of fire. With this
> he seemed to pierce my heart several times so that it

> penetrated to my entrails. When he drew it out . . . he
> left me completely afire with the great love of God.*

Teresa responded with a new sense of purpose: although she encountered stiff opposition, she resolved to found a reformed house. Four basic principles were to guide the new convent. First, poverty was to be fully observed, symbolized by the nuns' being barefoot, hence *discalced*. Charity and the nuns' own work must support the community. Second, the convent must keep strict enclosure; the visits of powerful benefactors with material demands were forbidden. Third, Teresa intended an egalitarian atmosphere in which class distinctions were forbidden. She had always rejected the emphasis on "purity of blood," a distinctive and racist feature of Spanish society that was especially out of place in the cloister. All sisters, including those of aristocratic background, must share the manual chores. Finally, like Ignatius Loyola and the Jesuits, Teresa placed great emphasis on obedience, especially to one's confessor.

Between 1562 and Teresa's death in 1582, she founded or reformed fourteen other houses of nuns, traveling widely to do so. Though Teresa did not advocate institutionalized roles for women outside the convent, she did chafe at the restrictions placed on her because of her sex, and she thought of the new religious houses she founded as answers to the Protestant takeover of Catholic churches elsewhere in Europe. From her brother, who had obtained wealth in the Spanish colonies, Teresa learned about conditions in Peru and instructed her nuns "to pray unceasingly for the missionaries working among the heathens." Through prayer, Teresa wrote, her nuns could share in the exciting tasks of evangelization and missionary work otherwise closed to women. Her books, along with her five hundred extant letters, show her as a practical and down-to-earth woman as well as a mystic and a creative theologian.

Questions for Analysis

1. How did sixteenth-century convent life reflect the values of Spanish society?
2. How is the life of Teresa of Ávila typical of developments in the Catholic Reformation? How is her life unusual?

* *The Autobiography of St. Teresa of Ávila,* trans. and ed. E. A. Peers (New York: Doubleday, 1960, pp. 273–274).

to Catholicism. Jesuit schools adopted the modern humanist curricula and methods, educating the sons of the nobility as well as the poor. As confessors and spiritual directors to kings, Jesuits exerted great political influence.

Religious Violence

What were the causes and consequences of religious violence, including riots, wars, and witch hunts?

In 1559 France and Spain signed the Treaty of Cateau-Cambrésis (cah-toh-kam-BRIE-sees), which ended the long conflict known as the Habsburg-Valois Wars. Spain was the victor. France, exhausted by the struggle, had to acknowledge Spanish dominance in Italy, where much of the fighting had taken place. However, over the next century religious differences led to riots, civil wars, and international conflicts. Especially in France and the Netherlands, Protestants and Catholics used violent actions as well as preaching and teaching against each other, for each side regarded the other as a poison in the community that would provoke the wrath of God. Catholics continued to believe that Calvinists and Lutherans could be reconverted; Protestants persisted in thinking that the Roman church should be destroyed. Catholics and Protestants alike feared people of other faiths, who they often saw as agents of Satan. Even more, they feared those who were explicitly identified with Satan: witches living in their midst. This era was the time of the most virulent witch persecutions in European history, as both Protestants and Catholics tried to make their cities and states more godly.

French Religious Wars   The costs of the Habsburg-Valois Wars, waged intermittently through the first half of the sixteenth century, forced the French to increase taxes and borrow heavily. King Francis I (r. 1515–1547) also tried two new devices to raise revenue: the sale of public offices and a treaty with the papacy. The former proved to be only a temporary source of money: once a man bought an office he and his heirs were exempt from taxation. But the latter, known as the Concordat of Bologna (see page 329), gave the French crown the right to appoint all French bishops and abbots, ensuring a rich supplement of money and offices. Because French rulers possessed control over appointments and had a vested financial interest in Catholicism, they had no need to revolt against Rome.

Significant numbers of those ruled, however, were attracted to the "reformed religion," as Calvinism was called. Initially, Calvinism drew converts from among reform-minded members of the Catholic clergy, the industrious middle classes, and artisan groups. Most French Calvinists (called **Huguenots**) lived in major cities, such as Paris, Lyons, and Rouen. When Henry II died in 1559, perhaps one-tenth of the population had become Calvinist.

Huguenots Originally a pejorative term for French Calvinists, later the official title for members of this group.

The feebleness of the French monarchy was the seed from which the weeds of civil violence sprang. The three weak sons of Henry II who occupied the throne could not provide the necessary leadership, and they were often dominated by their mother, Catherine de' Medici. The French nobility took advantage of this monarchical weakness. Just as German princes in the Holy Roman Empire had adopted Lutheranism as a means of opposition to Emperor Charles V, so French nobles frequently adopted the reformed religion as a religious cloak for their independence. Armed clashes between Catholic royalist lords and Calvinist antimonarchical lords occurred in many parts of France. Both Calvinists and Catholics believed that the others' books, services, and ministers polluted the community. Preachers incited violence, and religious ceremonies such as baptisms, marriages, and funerals triggered it.

Calvinist teachings called the power of sacred images into question, and mobs in many cities took down and smashed statues, stained-glass windows, and paintings. Though it was often inspired by fiery Protestant sermons, this **iconoclasm** is an example of men and women carrying out the Reformation themselves, rethinking the church's system of meaning and the relationship between the unseen and the seen. Catholic mobs responded by defending images, and crowds on both sides killed their opponents, often in gruesome ways.

iconoclasm Ridicule and destruction of religious images.

A savage Catholic attack on Calvinists in Paris on August 24, 1572 (Saint Bartholomew's Day), followed the usual pattern. The occasion was the marriage ceremony of the king's sister Margaret of Valois to the Protestant Henry of Navarre, which was intended to help reconcile Catholics and Huguenots. Instead, Huguenot wedding guests in Paris were massacred, and other Protestants were slaughtered by mobs. Religious violence spread to the provinces, where thousands were killed. This **Saint Bartholomew's Day massacre** led to a civil war that dragged on for fifteen years. Agriculture in many areas was destroyed; commercial life declined severely; and starvation and death haunted the land.

Saint Bartholomew's Day massacre Massacre of thousands of Protestants in Paris and other cities by Catholics, beginning on Saint Bartholomew's Day (August 24) 1572.

What ultimately saved France was a small group of moderates of both faiths, called **politiques,** who believed that only the restoration of strong monarchy could reverse the trend toward collapse. The politiques also favored accepting the Huguenots as an officially recognized and organized pressure group. The death of Catherine de' Medici, followed by the assassination of King Henry III, paved the way for the accession of Henry of Navarre (the unfortunate bridegroom of the St. Bartholomew's Day massacre), a politique who became Henry IV (r. 1589–1610).

politiques Moderates of both religious faiths who held that only a strong monarchy could save France from total collapse.

Henry's willingness to sacrifice religious principles to political necessity saved France. He converted to Catholicism but also issued the **Edict of Nantes,** which granted liberty of conscience and liberty of public worship to Huguenots in 150 fortified towns. The reign of Henry IV and the Edict of Nantes prepared the way for French absolutism in the seventeenth century by helping restore internal peace in France.

Edict of Nantes A document issued by Henry IV of France in 1598, granting liberty of conscience and of public worship to Calvinists in 150 towns; it helped restore peace in France.

The Netherlands Under Charles V

In the Netherlands, what began as a movement for the reformation of the church developed into a struggle for Dutch independence. Emperor Charles V had inherited the seventeen provinces that compose present-day Belgium and the Netherlands (see page 348). Each was self-governing and enjoyed the right to make its own laws and collect its own taxes. They were united politically only in recognition of a common ruler, the emperor. The cities of the Netherlands made their living by trade and industry.

In the Low Countries as elsewhere, corruption in the Roman church and the critical spirit of the Renaissance provoked pressure for reform, and Lutheran ideas took root. Charles V had grown up in the Netherlands, however, and he was able to limit their impact. But Charles V abdicated in 1556 and transferred power over the Netherlands to his son Philip, who had grown up in Spain. Protestant ideas spread.

By the 1560s Protestants in the Netherlands were primarily Calvinists. Calvinism's intellectual seriousness, moral gravity, and emphasis on any form of labor well done appealed to middle-class merchants and financiers and working-class

Iconoclasm in the Netherlands

Calvinist men and women break stained-glass windows, remove statues, and carry off devotional altarpieces. Iconoclasm, or the destruction of religious images, is often described as a "riot," but here the participants seem very purposeful. Calvinist Protestants regarded pictures and statues as sacrilegious and saw removing them as a way to purify the church. (The Fotomas Index/The Bridgeman Art Library)

people. Whereas Lutherans taught respect for the powers that be, Calvinism tended to encourage opposition to "illegal" civil authorities.

In the 1560s Spanish authorities attempted to suppress Calvinist worship and raised taxes, which sparked riots. Thirty churches in Antwerp were sacked and the religious images in them destroyed in a wave of iconoclasm. From Antwerp the destruction spread. Philip II sent twenty thousand Spanish troops under the duke of Alva to pacify the Low Countries. Alva interpreted "pacification" to mean the ruthless extermination of religious and political dissidents. On top of the Inquisition, he opened his own tribunal, soon called the "Council of Blood." On March 3, 1568, fifteen hundred men were executed.

For ten years, civil war raged in the Netherlands between Catholics and Protestants and between the seventeen provinces and Spain. Eventually the ten southern provinces, the Spanish Netherlands (the future Belgium), came under the control of the Spanish Habsburg forces. The seven northern provinces, led by Holland, formed the **Union of Utrecht** and in 1581 declared their independence from Spain. The north was Protestant; the south remained Catholic. Philip did not accept this, and war continued. England was even drawn into the conflict, supplying money and troops to the northern United Provinces. (Spain launched an unsuccessful invasion of England in response; see pages 353–354.) Hostilities ended in 1609 when Spain agreed to a truce that recognized the independence of the United Provinces.

Union of Utrecht The alliance of seven northern provinces (led by Holland) that declared its independence from Spain and formed the United Provinces of the Netherlands.

The Great European Witch Hunt

The relationship between the Reformation and the upsurge in trials for witchcraft that occurred at roughly the same time is complex. Increasing persecution for witchcraft actually began before the Reformation in the 1480s, but it became especially common about 1560. Religious reformers' extreme notions of the Devil's powers and the insecurity created by the religious wars contributed to this increase. Both Protestants and Catholics tried and executed witches, with church officials and secular authorities acting together.

The heightened sense of God's power and divine wrath in the Reformation era was an important factor in the witch hunts, but other factors were also significant. One of these was a change in the idea of what a witch was. Nearly all premodern societies believe in witchcraft and make some attempts to control witches, who are

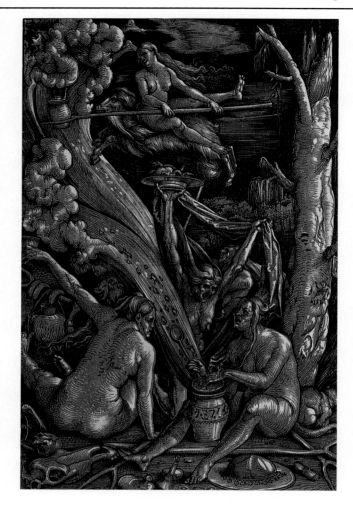

Hans Baldung Grien: Witches' Sabbat (1510)
In this woodcut, Grien combines learned and popular beliefs about witches: they traveled at night, met at sabbats (or assemblies), feasted on infants (in dish held high), concocted strange potions, and had animal "familiars" that were really demons (here, a cat). Grien also highlights the sexual nature of witchcraft by portraying the women naked and showing them with goats, which were common symbols of sexuality. (Germanisches Nationalmuseum Nürnberg)

understood to be people who use magical forces. In the later Middle Ages, however, many educated Christian theologians, canon lawyers, and officials added a demonological component to this notion of what a witch was. For them, the essence of witchcraft was making a pact with the Devil that required the witch to do the Devil's bidding. Witches were no longer simply people who used magical power to get what they wanted, but rather people used by the Devil to do what *he* wanted. Some demonological theorists also claimed that witches were organized in an international conspiracy to overthrow Christianity. Witchcraft was thus spiritualized, and witches became the ultimate heretics, enemies of God.

Trials involving this new notion of witchcraft as diabolical heresy began in Switzerland and southern Germany in the late fifteenth century, became less numerous in the early decades of the Reformation when Protestants and Catholics were busy fighting each other, and then picked up again in about 1560. Scholars estimate that during the sixteenth and seventeenth centuries somewhere between 100,000 and 200,000 people were officially tried for witchcraft and between 40,000 and 60,000 were executed. While the trials were secret, executions were not, and the lists of charges were read out for all to hear.

Though the gender balance varied widely in different parts of Europe, between 75 and 85 percent of those tried and executed were women. Ideas about women, and the roles women actually played in society, were thus important factors shaping the witch hunts. Some demonologists expressed virulent **misogyny**, or hatred of women, and particularly emphasized women's powerful sexual desire, which could be satisfied only by a demonic lover. Most people viewed women as weaker and so more likely to give in to any kind of offer by the Devil, including better food or nicer clothing. Women were associated with nature, disorder, and the body, all of which were linked with the demonic.

Most witch trials began with a single accusation in a village or town. Individuals accused someone they knew of using magic to spoil food, make children ill, kill animals, raise a hailstorm, or do other types of harm. Tensions within families, households, and neighborhoods often played a role in these accusations. Women number very prominently among accusers and witnesses as well as among those accused of witchcraft because the actions witches were initially charged with, such as harming children or curdling milk, were generally part of women's sphere. A woman also gained economic and social security by conforming to the standard of the good wife and mother and by confronting women who deviated from it.

misogyny Hatred of women.

Once a charge was made, judges began to question other neighbors and acquaintances, building up a list of suspicious incidents that might have taken place over decades. Historians have pointed out that one of the reasons those accused of witchcraft were often older was that it took years to build up a reputation as a witch. At this point, the suspect was brought in for questioning by legal authorities. Judges and inquisitors sought the exact details of a witch's demonic contacts, including sexual ones. Suspects were generally stripped and shaved in a search for a "witch's mark," or "pricked" to find a spot insensitive to pain, and then tortured.

Once the initial suspect had been questioned, and particularly if he or she had been tortured, the people who had been implicated were brought in for questioning. This might lead to a small hunt, involving from five to ten victims, and it sometimes grew into a much larger hunt, what historians have called a "witch panic." Panics were most common in the part of Europe that saw the most witch accusations in general—the Holy Roman Empire, Switzerland, and parts of France. Most of this area consisted of very small governmental units, which were jealous of each other and after the Reformation were divided by religion. The rulers of these small territories often felt more threatened than did the monarchs of western Europe, and they saw persecuting witches as a way to demonstrate their piety and concern for order.

Sometimes witch panics were the result of legal authorities' rounding up a group of suspects together. Such panics often occurred after some type of climatic disaster, such as an unusually cold and wet summer, and they came in waves. In large-scale panics a wider variety of suspects were taken in—wealthier people, children, a greater proportion of men. Mass panics tended to end when it became clear to legal authorities, or to the community itself, that the people being questioned or executed were not what they understood witches to be, or that the scope of accusations was beyond belief. Some from their community might be in league with Satan, they thought, but not this type of person and not as many as this.

Similar skepticism led to the gradual end of witch hunts in Europe. Even in the sixteenth century a few individuals questioned whether witches could ever do harm, make a pact with the Devil, or engage in the wild activities attributed to them. Doubts about whether secret denunciations were valid or torture would ever yield a truthful confession gradually spread among the same type of religious and legal authorities who had so vigorously persecuted witches. Prosecutions for witchcraft became less common and were gradually outlawed. The last official execution for witchcraft in England was in 1682, though the last one in the Holy Roman Empire was not until 1775.

Section Review

- The religious differences between Catholics and Protestants led to conflict and violence, each side viewing the other as wrong.

- The French Calvinist Huguenots clashed with the Catholic majority in bloody riots and massacres, ending only when moderates of both faiths aided in securing official recognition for the minority.

- Protestant ideas spread to the Netherlands, where civil war raged for years between the Dutch and Spain, ending when Spain recognized the independence of the United Provinces.

- Witch hunts intensified with the belief that witches did the bidding of the Devil, and all were in danger of experiencing God's wrath as a result of their acts.

- Witch hunts began with an accusation (usually of a woman), then an investigation, often under torture, and sometimes grew to a "witch panic" involving more people, until the whole witch hunt movement gradually faded with the growth of scepticism.

Chapter Review

What were the central ideas of the reformers, and why were they appealing to different social groups? (page 338)

The Catholic Church in the early sixteenth century had serious problems, and many individuals and groups had long called for reform. This background of discontent helps explain why Martin Luther's ideas found such a ready audience. Luther and other Protestants developed a new understanding of Christian doctrine that emphasized faith, the power of God's grace, and the centrality of the Bible. Protestant ideas were attractive to educated people and urban residents, and they spread rapidly through preaching, hymns, and the printing press. By 1530 many parts of the Holy Roman

Key Terms

anticlericalism (p. 338)

pluralism (p. 338)

indulgence (p. 339)

Diet of Worms (p. 341)

(continued)

Empire and Scandinavia had broken with the Catholic Church. Some reformers developed more radical ideas about infant baptism, the ownership of property, and separation between church and state. Both Protestants and Catholics regarded these as dangerous, and radicals were banished or executed. The German Peasants' War, in which Luther's ideas were linked to calls for social and economic reform, was similarly put down harshly. The Protestant reformers did not break with medieval ideas about the proper gender hierarchy, though they did elevate the status of marriage and viewed orderly households as the key building blocks of society.

How did the political situation in Germany shape the course of the Reformation? (page 348)

The progress of the Reformation was shaped by the political situation in the Holy Roman Empire. The Habsburg emperor, Charles V, ruled almost half of Europe along with Spain's overseas colonies. Within the empire his authority was limited, however, and local princes, nobles, and cities actually held most power. This decentralization allowed the Reformation to spread. Charles remained firmly Catholic, and in the 1530s religious wars began in Germany. These were brought to an end with the Peace of Augsburg in 1555, which allowed rulers in each territory to choose whether their territory would be Catholic or Lutheran.

How did Protestant ideas and institutions spread beyond German-speaking lands? (page 351)

In England, Henry VIII's desire for a son who would succeed to his throne triggered the break with Rome, and a Protestant church was established. Protestant ideas also spread into France and eastern Europe. In all these areas, a second generation of reformers built on Lutheran and Zwinglian ideas to develop their own theology and plans for institutional change. The most important of the second-generation reformers was John Calvin, whose ideas would come to shape Christianity over a much wider area than did Luther's.

How did the Catholic Church respond to the new religious situation? (page 357)

The Roman Catholic Church responded slowly to the Protestant challenge, but by the 1530s the papacy was leading a movement for reform within the church instead of blocking it. Catholic doctrine was reaffirmed at the Council of Trent, and reform measures such as the opening of seminaries for priests and a ban on holding multiple church offices were introduced. New religious orders such as the Jesuits and the Ursulines spread Catholic ideas through teaching, and in the case of the Jesuits through missionary work.

What were the causes and consequences of religious violence, including riots, wars, and witch hunts? (page 361)

Religious differences led to riots, civil wars, and international conflicts in the later sixteenth century. In France and the Netherlands, Calvinist Protestants and Catholics used violent actions against one another, and religious differences mixed with political and economic grievances. Long civil wars resulted, which in the case of the Netherlands became an international conflict. War ended in France with the Edict of Nantes in which Protestants were given some civil rights, and in the Netherlands with a division of the country into a Protestant north and Catholic south. The era of religious wars was also the time of the most extensive witch persecutions in European history, as

Protestant (p. 341)

transubstantiation (p. 341)

Book of Common Prayer (p. 353)

Spanish Armada (p. 353)

The Institutes of the Christian Religion (p. 354)

predestination (p. 354)

Holy Office (p. 357)

Jesuits (p. 359)

Huguenots (p. 361)

iconoclasm (p. 362)

Saint Bartholomew's Day massacre (p. 362)

politiques (p. 362)

Edict of Nantes (p. 362)

Union of Utrecht (p. 363)

misogyny (p. 364)

both Protestants and Catholics tried to rid their cities and states of people they regarded as linked to the Devil.

Notes

1. Quoted in O. Chadwick, *The Reformation* (Baltimore: Penguin Books, 1976), p. 55.
2. Quoted in E. H. Harbison, *The Age of Reformation* (Ithaca, N.Y.: Cornell University Press, 1963), p. 52.
3. Quoted in S. E. Ozment, *The Age of Reform, 1250–1550: An Intellectual and Religious History of Late Medieval and Reformation Europe* (New Haven, Conn.: Yale University Press, 1980), p. 284.
4. E. W. Monter, *Calvin's Geneva* (New York: John Wiley & Sons, 1967), p. 137.

To assess your mastery of this chapter, go to **bedfordstmartins.com/mckaywestbrief**

Listening to the Past

Martin Luther, *On Christian Liberty*

The idea of liberty or freedom has played a powerful role in the history of Western society and culture, but the meaning and understanding of liberty has undergone continual change and interpretation. In the Roman world, where slavery was a basic institution, liberty meant the condition of being a free man, independent of obligations to a master. In the Middle Ages possessing liberty meant having special privileges or rights that other persons or institutions did not have.

The idea of liberty also has a religious dimension, and the reformer Martin Luther formulated a classic interpretation of liberty in his treatise On Christian Liberty (sometimes translated On the Freedom of a Christian). Luther writes that Christians were freed from sin and death through Christ, not through their own actions.

On effective preaching, especially to the uneducated, Luther urged the minister "to keep it simple for the simple." (Church of St. Marien, Wittenberg/The Bridgeman Art Library)

A Christian man is the most free lord of all, and subject to none; a Christian man is the most dutiful servant of all, and subject to everyone.

Although these statements appear contradictory, yet, when they are found to agree together, they will do excellently for my purpose. They are both the statements of Paul himself, who says, "Though I be free from all men, yet have I made myself a servant unto all" (I Cor. 9:19), and "Owe no man anything but to love one another" (Rom. 13:8). Now love is by its own nature dutiful and obedient to the beloved object. Thus even Christ, though Lord of all things, was yet made of a woman; made under the law; at once free and a servant; at once in the form of God and in the form of a servant.

Let us examine the subject on a deeper and less simple principle. Man is composed of a twofold nature, a spiritual and a bodily. As regards the spiritual nature, which they name the soul, he is called the spiritual, inward, new man; as regards the bodily nature, which they name the flesh, he is called the fleshly, outward, old man. The Apostle speaks of this: "Though our outward man perish, yet the inward man is renewed day by day" (II Cor. 4:16). The result of this diversity is that in the Scriptures opposing statements are made concerning the same man, the fact being that in the same man these two men are opposed to one another; the flesh lusting against the spirit, and the spirit against the flesh (Gal. 5:17).

We first approach the subject of the inward man, that we may see by what means a man becomes justified, free, and a true Christian; that is, a spiritual, new, and inward man. It is certain that absolutely none among outward things, under whatever name they may be reckoned, has any influence in producing Christian righteousness or liberty, nor, on the other hand, unrighteousness or slavery. This can be shown by an easy argument.

What can it profit to the soul that the body should be in good condition, free, and full of life, that it should eat, drink, and act according to its pleasure, when even the most impious slaves of every kind of vice are prosperous in these matters? Again, what harm can ill health, bondage, hunger, thirst, or any other outward evil, do to the soul, when even the most pious of men, and the freest in the purity of their conscience, are harassed by these things? Neither of these states of things has to do with the liberty or the slavery of the soul.

. . . [A]nd since it [faith] alone justifies, it is evident that by no outward work or labour can the inward man be at all justified, made free, and saved; and that no works whatever have any relation to him. . . . Therefore the first care of every Christian ought to be to lay aside all reliance on works, and strengthen his faith alone more and more, and by it grow in knowledge, not of works, but of Christ Jesus, who has suffered and risen again for him, as Peter teaches (I Peter 5).

Questions for Analysis

1. What did Luther mean by liberty?
2. What aspects of Luther's message might especially appeal to the poor and powerless?

Source: Luther's Primary Works, ed. H. Wace and C. A. Buchheim (London: Holder and Stoughton, 1896). Reprinted in *The Portable Renaissance Reader*, ed. James Bruce Ross and Mary Martin McLaughlin (New York: Penguin Books, 1981), pp. 721–726.

CHAPTER 15

European Exploration and Conquest

1450–1650

Chapter Preview

World Contacts Before Columbus
What was the Afro-Eurasian trading world before Columbus?

The European Voyages of Discovery
How and why did Europeans undertake ambitious voyages of expansion that would usher in a new era of global contact?

Europe and the World After Columbus
What effect did overseas expansion have on the conquered societies, on enslaved Africans, and on world trade?

Changing Attitudes and Beliefs
How did culture and art in this period respond to social and cultural transformation?

INDIVIDUALS IN SOCIETY: Juan de Pareja

LISTENING TO THE PAST: Columbus Describes His First Voyage

A detail from an early-seventeenth-century Flemish painting depicting maps, illustrated travel books, a globe, a compass, and an astrolabe. (Reproduced by courtesy of the Trustees, The National Gallery, London)

Prior to 1400 Europeans were relatively marginal players in a centuries-old trading system that linked Africa, Asia, and Europe. Elite classes everywhere prized Chinese porcelains and silks, while wealthy members of the Celestial Kingdom, as China called itself, wanted ivory and black slaves from East Africa, and exotic goods and peacocks from India. African people wanted textiles from India and cowrie shells from the Maldive Islands. Europeans craved spices and silks, but they had few desirable goods to offer their trading partners.

The European search for better access to Southeast Asian trade led to a new overseas empire in the Indian Ocean and the accidental discovery of the Western Hemisphere. Within a short time, South and North America had joined a worldwide web. Europeans came to dominate trading networks and political empires of truly global proportions. The era of "globalization" had begun.

Global contacts created new forms of cultural exchange, assimilation, conversion, and resistance. Europeans sought to impose their cultural values on the people they encountered and struggled to comprehend the peoples and societies they found. New forms of racial prejudice emerged in this period, but so did new openness and curiosity about different ways of life. Together with the developments of the Renaissance and the Reformation, the Age of Discovery laid the foundations for the modern world as we know it today.

World Contacts Before Columbus

What was the Afro-Eurasian trading world before Columbus?

Columbus did not sail west on a whim. To understand his and other Europeans' explorations, we must first understand late medieval trade networks. Historians now recognize important ties between Europe and other parts of the world prior to Columbus's voyages, arguing that a type of "world economy" linked the products and people of Europe, Asia, and Africa in the fifteenth century. The West was not the dominant player in 1492, and the European voyages derived from the possibilities and constraints of this system.

The Trade World of the Indian Ocean   The center of the pre-Columbian world trade network was the Indian Ocean. Its location made it a crossroads for commercial and cultural exchange between China (always the biggest market for Southeast Asian goods), India, the Middle East, Africa, and Europe. From the seventh through the thirteenth centuries, the volume of this trade steadily increased. After a period of decline resulting from the Black Death, demand for Southeast Asian goods accelerated once more in the late fourteenth century.

Merchants congregated in a series of multicultural, cosmopolitan port cities strung around the Indian Ocean. Most of these cities had some form of autonomous self-government. Mutual self-interest had largely limited violence and attempts to monopolize trade. As one historian stated, "before the arrival of the Portuguese . . . in 1498 there had been no organised attempt by any political power to control the sea-lanes and the long-distance trade of Asia. . . . The Indian Ocean as a whole and its different seas were not dominated by any particular nations or empires."[1]

The most developed area of this commercial web lay to the east on the South China Sea. In the fifteenth century the port of Malacca (muh-LAH-kuh) became a great commercial entrepôt (ON-truh-poh), to which goods were shipped for temporary storage while awaiting redistribution to other places. To Malacca came Chinese porcelains, silks, and camphor (used in the manufacture of many medications, including those to reduce fevers); pepper, cloves, nutmeg, and raw materials such as sappanwood and sandalwood from the Moluccas; sugar from the Philippines; and Indian printed cotton and woven tapestries, copper weapons, incense, dyes, and opium.

The Mongol emperors opened the doors of China to the West, encouraging European traders like Marco Polo to do business there. Marco Polo's tales of his travels from 1271 to 1295 and his encounter with the Great Khan fueled Western fantasies about the exotic Orient. Unbeknownst to the West, the Mongols fell to the new Ming Dynasty in 1368. During the Ming Dynasty (1368–1644), China entered a period of agricultural and commercial expansion, population growth, and urbanization. Historians agree that it had the most advanced economy in the world and played a key role in the fifteenth-century revival of Indian Ocean trade.

China also took the lead in naval expeditions, sending Admiral Zheng He's fleet of 317 ships far along the trade web, voyaging as far west as Egypt. Court

The Port of Banten in Western Java
Influenced by Muslim traders and emerging in the early sixteenth century as a Muslim kingdom, Banten evolved into a thriving entrepôt. The city stood on the trade route to China and, as this Dutch engraving suggests, in the seventeenth century the Dutch East India Company used Banten as an important collection point for spices purchased for sale in Europe. (Archives Charmet/The Bridgeman Art Library)

conflicts and the need to defend against renewed Mongol encroachment led to the abandonment of the expeditions and ship-building after the deaths of Zheng He and the emperor. Despite the Chinese decision not to pursue overseas voyages, trade continued in the South China Sea.

Another center of trade in the Indian Ocean was India, the crucial link between the Persian Gulf and the Southeast Asian and East Asian trade networks. The need for stopovers along the sea voyage led to the development of trading posts along the southern coast of the subcontinent, and these trading posts evolved into thriving commercial centers. India itself was an important contributor of goods to the world trading system. Most of the world's pepper was grown in India, and Indian cotton and silk textiles were highly prized.

Africa

Africa also played an important role in the world trade system before Columbus. Around 1450 Africa had a few large and developed empires along with hundreds of smaller polities. Cairo, the capital of the powerful Mameluke (MAM-look) Egyptian empire, was a hub for Indian Ocean trade goods. Sharing in the newfound Red Sea prosperity was the African highland state of Ethiopia, which in 1270 saw the rise of a new dynasty claiming descent from the biblical King Solomon and the Queen of Sheba. Trading hubs flourished as well on the east coast of Africa, where Swahili-speaking city-states were peopled by confident and urbane merchants known for their prosperity and culture.

Another important African contribution to world trade was gold. In the fifteenth century most of the gold that reached Europe came from Sudan in West Africa and from the Akan (AH-kahn) peoples living near present-day Ghana (GAH-nuh). Transported across the Sahara by Arab and African traders on camels, the gold was sold in the ports of North Africa. Other trading routes led to the Egyptian cities of Alexandria and Cairo, where the Venetians held commercial privileges.

Nations in the inland savannah that sat astride the north-south caravan routes grew wealthy from this trade. In the mid-thirteenth century Sundiata Keita (soon-JAH-tuh KEY-tah) founded the powerful kingdom of Mali. His famous successor, Mansa Musa, reportedly discussed sending vessels to explore the Atlantic Ocean, which suggests that not only the Europeans envisaged westward naval exploration. By the time the Portuguese arrived, however, the Malian empire was fading, to be replaced by the Songhay (song-GAH-ee), who themselves fell to Moroccan invasion at the end of the sixteenth century. The Portuguese diversion of gold away from the trans-Sahara routes weakened this area politically and economically.

Gold was one important object of trade; slaves were another. Slavery was practiced in Africa, as virtually everywhere else in the world, before the arrival of Europeans. Arabic and African merchants took West African slaves to the Mediterranean to be sold in European, Egyptian, or Middle Eastern markets and also brought eastern Europeans—a major element of European slavery—to West Africa as slaves. In addition, Indian and Arabic merchants traded slaves in the coastal regions of East Africa. European contact would revolutionize the magnitude and character of African slavery (see page 389).

Africa—or legends about Africa—played an important role in Europeans' imagination of the outside world. They long cherished the belief in a Christian

CHRONOLOGY

1443	Portuguese establish first African trading post at Arguim
1450–1650	Age of Discovery
1492	Columbus lands on San Salvador
1511	Portuguese capture Malacca from Muslims
1518	Atlantic slave trade begins
1519–1522	Magellan's expedition circumnavigates the world
1521	Last Aztec emperor surrenders to Spanish
1532-33	Pizarro arrives in Peru and defeats Inca Empire
1547	Oviedo, *General History of the Indies*
1570–1630	Worldwide commercial boom
1602	Dutch East India Company established

nation in Africa ruled by a mythical king, Prester John, thought to be a descendant of one of the three kings who visited Jesus after his birth.

The Ottoman and Persian Empires

The Middle East was crucial to the late medieval world trade system, serving as an intermediary for trade from all points of the compass. In addition, the Middle East was an important supplier of goods for foreign exchange, especially silk and cotton. Two great rival empires, the Persian Safavids (sah-FAH-vidz) and the Turkish Ottomans, dominated this region. Persian merchants could be found in trading communities as far away as the Indian Ocean. Persia was also a major producer and exporter of silk. Although both were Muslim states, the Persians' Shi'ite faith clashed with the Ottomans' adherence to Sunnism. Economically, the two competed for control over western trade routes to the East. Under a succession of brilliant military leaders, however, the Ottomans were ultimately able to monopolize these routes.

Under Sultan Mohammed II (r. 1451–1481), the Ottomans captured Europe's largest city, Constantinople, in May 1453. Renamed Istanbul, the city became the capital of the Ottoman Empire. The emperor Suleiman I (SOO-lay-man) (1494–1566) completed the conquest of Anatolia in 1461 and pressed northwest into the Balkans. By the early sixteenth century the Ottomans controlled the sea trade on the eastern Mediterranean. Steadily expanding, they conquered Syria, Palestine, Egypt, and the rest of North Africa. They worked westward into Europe, gathering parts of the Hungarian kingdom. Their advance was halted by Habsburg forces, and Vienna stood as the westward limit of their expansion into Europe.

Turkish expansion badly frightened Europeans. Ottoman armies seemed nearly invincible and the empire's desire for expansion limitless. In France in the sixteenth century, twice as many books were printed about the Turkish threat as about the American discoveries. The strength of the Ottomans helps explain some of the missionary fervor Christians brought to new territories. It also raised economic concerns. With trade routes to the east in the hands of the Ottomans, Europeans were convinced that they needed new trade routes.

The Taking of Constantinople by the Turks
The Ottoman conquest of the capital of the Byzantine Empire in 1453 sent waves of shock and despair through Europe. Capitalizing on the city's strategic and commercial importance, the Ottomans made it the center of their empire. (Bibliothèque nationale de France)

Genoese and Venetian Middlemen

Europe was the western terminus of the world trading system. In the late Middle Ages, the Italian city-states of Venice and Genoa controlled the European luxury trade with the East.

In 1304, Venice etablished formal relations with the sultan of Mameluke Egypt, opening offices in Cairo, the gateway to Asian trade. The city's merchants specialized in expensive luxury goods like spices, silks, and carpets. They did not, as later Europeans did, explore new routes to get to the sources of supply of these goods. Instead, they obtained them from middlemen in the Eastern Mediterranean or Asia Minor. A little went a long way. Venetians purchased no more than 500 tons of spices a year around 1400, but with a profit of about 40 percent.

The Venetians exchanged Eastern luxury goods for European products they could trade abroad, including Spanish and English wool, German metal goods, Flemish textiles, and silk cloth made in their own manufactures with imported raw materials. The demand for such goods in the East, however, was low. To make up the difference, the Venetians earned currency in the shipping industry and through trade in firearms and slaves, mostly Christians taken from the Balkans. At least half of what they traded with the East took the form of precious metal, much of it acquired in Egypt and North Africa. When the Portuguese arrived in Asia, they found Venetian coins everywhere.

Venice's ancient rival was Genoa. In the wake of the Crusades, Genoa dominated the northern route to Asia through the Black Sea. Expansion in the thirteenth and fourteenth centuries took the Genoese as far as Persia and the Far East. In 1291 they sponsored an expedition by the Vivaldi brothers into the Atlantic in search of "parts of India." The ships were lost, and their exact destination and motivations remain unknown. However, the voyage underlines the long history of Genoese aspirations for Atlantic exploration.

In the fifteenth century Genoa made a bold change of direction. With Venice claiming victory over the spice trade, the Genoese shifted focus from trade to finance and from the Black Sea to the western Mediterranean. Given its location on the northwestern coast of Italy, Genoa had always been active in the western Mediterranean, trading with North African ports, southern France, Spain, and even England and Flanders through the Strait of Gibraltar. When new voyages took place in the western Atlantic, Genoese merchants, navigators, and financiers provided their skills to the Iberian monarchs, whose own subjects had much less commercial experience. The Genoese, for example, ran many of the sugar plantations established on the Atlantic islands colonized by the Portuguese. From their settlement in Seville, Genoese merchants financed Spanish colonization of the New World and conducted profitable trade with its colonies.

After the loss of the Black Sea—and thus the source of slaves—to the Ottomans, the Genoese sought new supplies of slaves in the West, taking the Guanches (indigenous peoples from the Canary Islands), Muslim prisoners and Jewish refugees from Spain, and by the early 1500s both black and Berber Africans. With the growth of Spanish colonies in the New World, Genoese and Venetian merchants became important players in the Atlantic slave trade.

Italian experience in colonial administration, slaving, and international trade and finance served as crucial models for the Iberian states as they pushed European expansion to new heights. Mariners, merchants, and financiers from Venice and Genoa—most notably Christopher Columbus—played a crucial role in bringing the fruits of this experience to the Iberian peninsula.

Section Review

- The pre-Columbian trading world centered on the cosmopolitan port cities of the Indian Ocean, which conducted brisk commerce with China and India.

- Africa was a center of world trade in gold and slaves and its east coast city-states played an important role in Indian Ocean trade.

- The rival Ottoman and Persian empires were intermediaries for trade between east and west; Ottoman expansion badly frightened Europeans and closed trading opportunities in the Eastern Mediterranean.

- In the late Middle Ages, Venice and Genoa controlled European luxury trade with the east, losing prominence with the rise of the Ottomans.

- Italian mariners and merchants drew on their long trading experience to assist and finance Spanish and Portuguese voyages, colonization, and slave-trading in the New World.

The European Voyages of Discovery

How and why did Europeans undertake ambitious voyages of expansion that would usher in a new era of global contact?

As we have seen, Europe was by no means isolated before the voyages of exploration and the "discovery" of the New World. But because they did not produce many products desired by Eastern elites, Europeans were relatively modest players in the Afro-Eurasian trading world. Yet the demand for Eastern goods grew as the population recovered from the Black Death, and Europeans sought an expanded role. New European players entered the scene, eager to undo Italian and Ottoman dominance of trade with the East. A century after the plague, Iberian explorers began the overseas voyages that helped create the modern world, with staggering consequences for their own continent and the rest of the planet.

Causes of European Expansion

European expansion had multiple causes. By the middle of the fifteenth century, the European market was eager for luxury goods from the East and for spices in particular. These spices not only added flavor to the monotonous European diet, but they also served as perfumes, medicines, and dyes. Apart from a desire for trade goods, religious fervor was another important catalyst for expansion. The passion and energy ignited by the Iberian reconquista encouraged the Portuguese and Spanish to continue the Christian crusade. Since organized Muslim polities such as the Ottoman Empire were too strong to defeat, Iberians turned their attention to non-Christian peoples elsewhere.

Individual explorers combined these motivations in unique ways. Christopher Columbus was a devout Christian who was increasingly haunted by messianic obsessions in the last years of his life. As Bartholomew Diaz put it, his own motives were "to serve God and His Majesty, to give light to those who were in darkness and to grow rich as all men desire to do." When Vasco da Gama reached the port of Calicut, India, in 1498 and a native asked what the Portuguese wanted, he replied, "Christians and spices."[2] The bluntest of the Spanish conquistadors, Hernando Cortés, announced as he prepared to conquer Mexico, "I have come to win gold, not to plow the fields like a peasant."[3]

Eagerness for exploration could be heightened by a lack of opportunity at home. After the reconquista, young men of the Spanish upper classes found their economic and political opportunities greatly limited. The ambitious turned to the Americas to seek their fortunes.[4] A desire for glory and the urge to explore motivated many as well. Whatever the reasons, the voyages were made possible by the growth of government power. Individuals did not possess the massive sums needed to explore mysterious oceans and control remote continents. The Spanish monarchy was stronger than before and in a position to support foreign ventures. In Portugal explorers looked to Prince Henry the Navigator (1394–1460) for financial support and encouragement. Like voyagers, monarchs shared a mix of motivations, from desire to please God to desire to win glory and profit from trade.

Ordinary sailors were ill paid, and life at sea meant danger, overcrowding, unbearable stench, and hunger. For months at a time, 100 to 120 people lived and worked in a space of between 150 and 180 square meters. Horses, cows, pigs, chickens, rats, and lice accompanied them on the voyages. As one scholar concluded, "traveling on a ship must have been one of the most uncomfortable and oppressive experiences in the world."[5]

Why did men choose to join these miserable crews? They did so to escape poverty at home, to continue a family trade, to win a few crumbs of the great riches of empire, or to find a better life as illegal immigrants in the colonies. Moreover, many orphans and poor boys were placed on board as young pages and had little say in the decision. Women also paid a price for the voyages of exploration. Left alone for months or years at a time, and frequently widowed, sailors' wives struggled to feed their families. The widow of a sailor lost on Magellan's 1519 voyage had to wait until 1547 to collect her husband's salary from the Crown.[6]

The people who stayed at home had a powerful impact on the process. Court coteries and factions influenced a monarch's decisions and could lavishly reward individuals or cut them out of the spoils of empire. Then there was the public: the small number of people who could read were a rapt audience for tales of fantastic places and unknown peoples. Scholars have frequently described the European discoveries as a manifestation of Renaissance curiosity about the physical universe — the desire to know more about the geography and peoples of the world. Fernández de Oviedo's (oh-VYE-do) *General History of the Indies* (1547), a detailed eyewitness account of plants, animals, and peoples, was widely read. Indeed, the elite's desire for the exotic goods brought by overseas trade helped stimulate the whole process of expansion.

Technological Stimuli to Exploration

Technological developments in shipbuilding, weaponry, and navigation provided another impetus for European expansion. Since ancient times, most seagoing vessels had been narrow, open boats called *galleys*, propelled largely by slaves or convicts manning the oars. Though well suited to the placid waters of the Mediterranean, galleys could not withstand the rough winds and uncharted shoals of the Atlantic. The need for sturdier craft, as well as population losses caused by the Black Death, forced the development of a new style of ship that would not require much manpower to sail.

In the course of the fifteenth century, the Portuguese developed the **caravel,** a small, light, three-masted sailing ship. Though somewhat slower than the galley, the caravel held more cargo. Its triangular lateen sails and sternpost rudder also made the caravel a much more maneuverable vessel. When fitted with cannon, it could dominate larger vessels.

Great strides in cartography and navigational aids were also made during this period. Around 1410 Arab scholars reintroduced Europeans to **Ptolemy's *Geography.*** Written in the second century C.E. by a Hellenized Egyptian, the work synthesized the geographical knowledge of the classical world. It also treated the idea of latitude and longitude that, when plotted using an astrolabe, allowed mariners to map their location. The magnetic compass also enabled sailors to determine their direction and position at sea. Although it showed the world as round, Ptolemy's work also contained crucial errors. Unaware of the Americas, he showed the world as much smaller than it is, so that Asia appeared not very distant from Europe to the west. Based on this work, cartographers fashioned new maps that combined classical knowledge with the latest information from mariners. First the Genoese and Venetians, and then the Portuguese and Spanish, took the lead in these advances.[7]

Much of the new technology that Europeans used on their voyages was borrowed from the East. For example, gunpowder, the compass, and the sternpost rudder were all Chinese inventions. The lateen sail, which allowed European ships to tack against the wind, was a product of the Indian Ocean trade world and was brought to the

General History of the Indies A fifty-volume first-hand description of the natural plants, animals, and peoples of Spanish America. Its author, Fernández de Oviedo, was a former colonial administrator who was named Historian of the Indies by the King of Spain in 1532.

caravel A small, maneuverable, three-mast sailing ship developed by the Portuguese in the fifteenth century. The caravel gave the Portuguese a distinct advantage in exploration and trade.

Ptolemy's *Geography* A second century C.E. work that synthesized the classical knowledge of geography and treated the concepts of longitude and latitude. The work was reintroduced to Europeans in 1410 by Arab scholars and provided a template for later geographical scholarship.

Nocturnal
An instrument for determining the hour of night at sea by finding the progress of certain stars around the polestar (center aperture). (National Maritime Museum, London)

Mediterranean on Arab ships. Navigational aids, such as the astrolabe, were also acquired from others, and advances in cartography drew on the rich tradition of Judeo-Arabic mathematical and astronomical learning in Iberia.

The Portuguese Overseas Empire

At the end of the fourteenth century Portugal was a small and poor nation on the margins of European life whose principal activities were fishing and subsistence farming. It would have been hard for a European to predict Portugal's phenomenal success overseas in the next two centuries. Yet Portugal had a long history of seafaring and navigation. Blocked from access to western Europe by Spain, the Portuguese turned to the Atlantic and North Africa, whose waters they knew better than other Europeans. Nature favored the Portuguese: winds blowing along their coast offered passage to Africa, its Atlantic islands, and, ultimately, Brazil.

In the early phases of Portuguese exploration, Prince Henry, a younger son of the king, played a leading role. A nineteenth-century scholar dubbed Henry "the Navigator" because of his support for the study of geography and navigation and for the annual expeditions he sponsored down the western coast of Africa. Although he never personally participated in voyages of exploration, Henry's involvement ensured that Portugal did not abandon the effort despite early disappointments.

The objectives of Portuguese policy included aristocratic desires for martial glory, the historic Iberian crusade to Christianize Muslims, and the quest to find gold, slaves, an overseas route to the spice markets of India, and the mythical king Prester John. Portugal's conquest of Ceuta, an Arab city in northern Morocco, in 1415 marked the beginning of European exploration and control of overseas territory. In the 1420s, under Henry's direction, the Portuguese began to settle the Atlantic islands of Madeira (ca. 1420) and the Azores (1427). In 1443 the Portuguese founded their first African commercial settlement at Arguim in present-day Mauritania (mawr-ee-TAY-nee-uh). By the time of Henry's death in 1460, his support for exploration was vindicated by thriving sugar plantations on the Atlantic islands and new access to gold.

Under King John II (r. 1481–1495) the Portuguese established trading posts and forts on the gold-rich Guinea coast and penetrated into the African continent all the way to Timbuktu (see Map 15.1). Portuguese ships transported gold to Lisbon, and by 1500 Portugal controlled the flow of African gold to Europe. The golden century of Portuguese prosperity had begun.

Still the Portuguese pushed farther south down the west coast of Africa. In 1487 Bartholomew Diaz rounded the Cape of Good Hope at the southern tip, but storms and a threatened mutiny forced him to turn back. On a later expedition in

MAPPING THE PAST

MAP 15.1   Overseas Exploration and Conquest, Fifteenth and Sixteenth Centuries

The voyages of discovery marked a dramatic new phase in the centuries-old migrations of European peoples. This map depicts the voyages of Ferdinand Magellan, Christopher Columbus, and Vasco da Gama. **[1]** What was the contemporary significance of each of these voyages? **[2]** Was the importance of the voyages primarily economic, political, or cultural? **[3]** Which voyage had the most impact, and why?

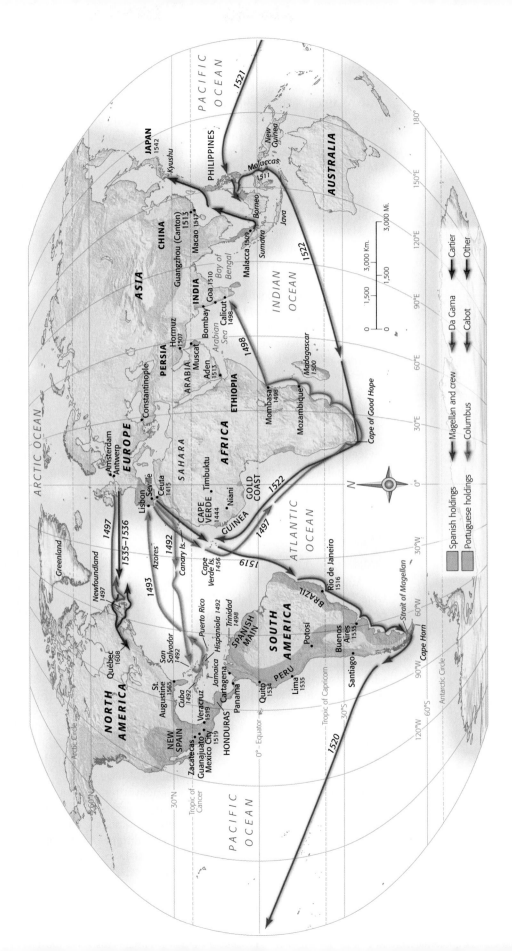

1497 Vasco da Gama commanded a fleet of four ships in search of a sea route to the Indian Ocean trade. Da Gama's ships rounded the Cape and sailed up the east coast of Africa. With the help of an Indian guide, da Gama sailed across the Arabian Sea to the port of Calicut in India. Overcoming local hostility, he returned to Lisbon loaded with spices and samples of Indian cloth. He had failed to forge any trading alliances with local powers, and Portuguese arrogance ensured the future hostility of Muslim merchants who dominated the trading system. Nonetheless, he had proved the possibility of lucrative trade with the East via the Cape route.

King Manuel (r. 1495–1521) promptly dispatched thirteen ships under the command of Pedro Alvares Cabral, assisted by Diaz, to set up trading posts in India. Half the fleet was lost on the return voyage, but the six spice-laden vessels that dropped anchor in Lisbon harbor in July 1501 more than paid for the entire expedition. Thereafter, a Portuguese convoy set out for passage around the Cape every March. Lisbon became the entrance port for Asian goods into Europe—but this was not accomplished without a fight.

As we have seen, port city-states had controlled the rich spice trade of the Indian Ocean, and they did not surrender it willingly. Portuguese cannons blasted open the ports of Malacca, Calicut, Ormuz, and Goa, the vital centers of Muslim domination of South Asian trade. This bombardment laid the foundation for Portuguese imperialism in the sixteenth and seventeenth centuries—a strange way to bring Christianity to "those who were in darkness." As one scholar wrote about the opening of China to the West, "while Buddha came to China on white elephants, Christ was borne on cannon balls."[8]

In March 1493, between the voyages of Diaz and da Gama, Spanish ships under a triumphant Genoese mariner named Christopher Columbus (1451–1506), in the service of the Spanish crown, entered Lisbon harbor. Spain also had begun the quest for an empire.

The Problem of Christopher Columbus   Christopher Columbus is a controversial figure in history—glorified by some as the brave discoverer of America, vilified by others as a cruel exploiter of Native Americans. It is important to put him into the context of his own time. First, what kind of man was Columbus, and what forces or influences shaped him? Second, in sailing westward from Europe, what were his goals? Third, did he achieve his goals, and what did he make of his discoveries?

In his dream of a westward passage to the Indies, Columbus embodied a long-standing Genoese ambition to circumvent Venetian domination of eastward trade, which was now being claimed by the Portuguese. Columbus was also very knowledgeable about the sea. He had worked as a mapmaker, and he was familiar with such fifteenth-century Portuguese navigational developments as *portolans*—written descriptions of the courses along which ships sailed, showing bays, coves, capes, and ports, and the distances between these places—and the use of the compass as a nautical instrument. As he implied in his *Journal*, he had acquired not only theoretical but also practical experience: "I have spent twenty-three years at sea and have not left it for any length of time worth mentioning, and I have seen everything from east to west [meaning he had been to England] and I have been to Guinea [north and west Africa]."[9] Although some of Columbus's geographical information, such as his measurement of the distance from Portugal to Japan as 2,760 miles when it is actually 12,000, proved inaccurate, his successful thirty-three-day voyage to the Caribbean owed a great deal to his seamanship.

Columbus was also a deeply religious man. He had witnessed the Spanish reconquest of Granada and shared fully in the religious and nationalistic fervor surrounding that event. Like the Spanish rulers and most Europeans of his age, Columbus understood Christianity as a missionary religion that should be carried to places where it did not exist. He viewed himself as a divine agent: "God made me the messenger of the new heaven and the new earth of which he spoke in the Apocalypse of St. John . . . and he showed me the post where to find it."[10]

What was the object of this first voyage? Columbus wanted to find a direct ocean trading route to Asia. Rejected by the Portuguese in 1483 and by Ferdinand and Isabella of Spain in 1486, the project finally won the backing of the Spanish monarchy in 1492. Inspired by the stories of Marco Polo, Columbus dreamed of reaching the court of the Mongol emperor, the Great Khan (not realizing that the Ming Dynasty had overthrown the Mongols in 1368). Based on Ptolemy's *Geography* and other texts, he expected to pass the islands of Japan and then land on the east coast of China.

How did Columbus interpret what he had found, and in his mind did he achieve what he had set out to do? He landed in the Bahamas, which he christened San Salvador, on October 12. Columbus believed he had found some small islands off the east coast of Cipangu (Japan). On encountering natives of the islands, he gave them some beads and "many other trifles of small value," pronouncing them delighted with these gifts and eager to trade. In a letter he wrote to Ferdinand and Isabella on his return to Spain, Columbus described the natives as handsome, peaceful, and primitive people whose body painting reminded him of the Canary Islands natives. He concluded that they would make good slaves and could quickly be converted to Christianity. (See the feature "Listening to the Past: Columbus Describes His First Voyage" on pages 398–399.)

Columbus received reassuring reports—via hand gestures and mime—of the presence of gold and of a great king in the vicinity. From San Salvador, Columbus sailed southwest, believing that this course would take him to Japan or the coast of China. He landed on Cuba on October 28. Deciding that he must be on the mainland near the coastal city of Quinsay (Hangzhou) (**hahng-jo**), he sent a small embassy inland with letters from Ferdinand and Isabella and instructions to locate the grand city. The expedition included an Arabic-speaking member to serve as interpreter with the khan.

The landing party, however, found only small villages. Confronted with this disappointment, Columbus apparently gave up on his aim to meet the Great Khan. Instead, he focused on trying to find gold or other valuables among the peoples he had discovered. In January, confident that gold would later be found, he headed back to Spain. News of his voyage spread rapidly across Europe.[11]

Over the next decades, the Spanish confirmed Columbus's change of course by adopting the model of conquest and colonization they had already introduced

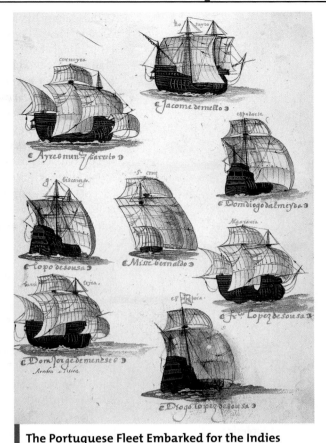

The Portuguese Fleet Embarked for the Indies

This image shows a Portuguese trading fleet in the late fifteenth century, bound for the riches of the Indies. Between 1500 and 1635, over nine hundred ships sailed from Portugal to ports on the Indian Ocean, in annual fleets composed of five to ten ships. (British Museum/HarperCollins Publishers/The Art Archive)

in the Canary Islands rather than one of exchange with equals (as envisaged for the Mongol khan). On his second voyage, Columbus forcibly subjugated the island of Hispaniola, enslaved its indigenous peoples, and laid the basis for a system of land grants tied to their labor service. Columbus himself, however, had little interest in or capacity for governing. Revolt soon broke out against him and his brother on Hispaniola. A royal expedition sent to investigate returned the brothers to Spain in chains. Columbus was quickly cleared of wrongdoing, but he did not recover his authority over the territories. Instead, they came under royal control.

Columbus was very much a man of his times. To the end of his life in 1506, he believed that he had found small islands off the coast of Asia. He never realized the scope of his achievement: to have found a vast continent unknown to Europeans, except for a fleeting Viking presence centuries earlier. He could not know that the scale of his discoveries would revolutionize world power, raising issues of trade, settlement, government bureaucracy, and the rights of native and African peoples.

Later Explorers

The Florentine navigator Amerigo Vespucci (**ve-SPOO-chee**) (1454–1512) realized what Columbus had not. Writing about his discoveries on the coast of modern-day Venezuela, Vespucci stated: "Those new regions which we found and explored with the fleet . . . we may rightly call a New World." This letter, titled *Mundus Novus* (The New World), was the first document to describe America as a continent separate from Asia. In recognition of Amerigo's bold claim, the continent was named for him. (When later cartographers realized that Columbus had made the discovery first, it was too late to change the maps.)

To settle competing claims to the Atlantic discoveries, Spain and Portugal turned to Pope Alexander VI. The **Treaty of Tordesillas** (**tor-duh-SEE-yuhs**) (1494) gave Spain everything to the west of an imaginary line drawn down the Atlantic and Portugal everything to the east. This arbitrary division worked in Portugal's favor when in 1500 an expedition led by Pedro Alvares Cabral landed on the coast of Brazil, which Cabral claimed as Portuguese territory. The country's name derives from the brazilwood trees found there, an important source of red dye.

Treaty of Tordesillas The 1494 agreement giving Spain everything to the west of an imaginary line drawn down the Atlantic and giving Portugal everything to the east.

The search for profits determined the direction of Spanish exploration and expansion into South America. When it became apparent that the Portuguese were reaping enormous riches in Asian trade while the Caribbean yield of gold was insubstantial, new routes to the East and new sources of gold and silver were sought. In 1519 the Spanish ruler Charles V commissioned the Portuguese mariner Ferdinand Magellan (1480–1521) to find a direct route to the spices of the Moluccas off the southeast coast of Asia. Magellan sailed southwest across the Atlantic to Brazil, and after a long search along the coast he located the treacherous straits that now bear his name (see Map 15.1). The new ocean he sailed into after a rough passage through the straits seemed so peaceful that Magellan dubbed it the Pacific. He was soon to realize his mistake. His fleet sailed north up the west coast of South America and then headed west into the immense expanse of the Pacific toward the Malay Archipelago. (Some of these islands were conquered in the 1560s and named the "Philippines" for Philip II of Spain.)

Terrible storms, disease, starvation, and violence haunted the expedition. Magellan had set out with a fleet of five ships and around 270 men. Sailors on two of the ships attempted mutiny on the South American coast; one ship was lost, and another ship deserted and returned to Spain before even traversing the straits. The trip across the Pacific took ninety-eight days, and the men survived on rats and sawdust. Magellan himself was killed in a skirmish in the Philippines. The expedi-

World Map of Diogo Ribeiro, 1529

This map integrates the wealth of new information provided by European explorers in the decades after Columbus's 1492 voyage. Working on commission for the Spanish king Charles V, the mapmaker has incorporated new details on Africa, South America, India, the Malay Archipelago, and China. Note the inaccuracy in his placement of the Moluccas or Spice Islands, which are much too far east. This "mistake" was intended to serve Spain's interests in trade negotiations with the Portuguese. (Biblioteca Apostolica Vaticana)

tion had enough survivors to man only two ships, and one of them was captured by the Portuguese. One ship with eighteen men returned to Spain from the east by way of the Indian Ocean, the Cape of Good Hope, and the Atlantic in 1522. The voyage had taken almost exactly three years.

Despite the losses, this voyage revolutionized Europeans' understanding of the world by demonstrating the vastness of the Pacific. The earth was clearly much larger than Columbus had believed. The voyage actually made a small profit in spices, but Magellan had proved the westward passage to the Indies to be too long and dangerous for commercial purposes. Spain abandoned the attempt to oust Portugal from the Eastern spice trade and concentrated on exploiting her New World territories.

The English and French also set sail across the Atlantic during the early days of exploration. In 1497 John Cabot, a Genoese merchant living in London, aimed for Brazil but discovered Newfoundland. The next year he returned and explored the New England coast, perhaps going as far south as Delaware. Since these expeditions found no spices or gold, Henry VII lost interest in exploration. Between 1534 and 1541 Frenchman Jacques Cartier made several voyages and explored the St. Lawrence region of Canada. The first permanent French settlement, at Quebec, was founded in 1608.

New World Conquest

In 1519, the year Magellan departed on his worldwide expedition, a brash and determined Spanish **conquistador** (kon-KEY-stuh-dor) ("conqueror") named Hernando Cortés (1485–1547) crossed from Hispaniola in the West Indies to mainland Mexico in search of gold. Accompanied by six hundred men, seventeen horses, and ten cannon, Cortés was to launch the conquest of Aztec Mexico.

Cortés landed at Vera Cruz in February 1519. From there he led a march to Tenochtitlán (teh-noch-tit-LAN) (now Mexico City), capital of the sophisticated

conquistador Spanish for "conqueror," the term refers to Spanish soldier-explorers, such as Hernando Cortés and Francisco Pizarro, who sought to conquer the New World for the Spanish crown.

Aztec Empire A Native American civilization that possessed advanced mathematical, astronomical, and engineering technology. Its capital, Tenochtitlán (now the site of Mexico City), was larger than any contemporary European city. Conquered by Cortés in 1520.

Aztec Empire ruled by Montezuma II (r. 1502–1520). Larger than any European city of the time, the capital was the heart of a civilization with advanced mathematics, astronomy, and engineering, with a complex social system, and with oral poetry and historical traditions.

The Spaniards arrived in the capital when the Aztecs were preoccupied with harvesting their crops. According to a later Spanish account, the timing was ideal. A series of natural phenomena, signs, and portents seemed to augur disaster for the Aztecs. A comet was seen in daytime, and two temples were suddenly destroyed, one by lightning unaccompanied by thunder. These and other apparently inexplicable events had an unnerving and demoralizing effect on Montezuma.

Even more important was the empire's internal weakness. The Aztec state religion, the sacred cult of Huitzilopochtli (wheat-zeel-oh-POSHT-lee), necessitated constant warfare against neighboring peoples to secure captives for religious sacrifice and laborers for agricultural and infrastructural work. When Cortés landed, recently defeated tribes were not yet fully integrated into the empire. Increases in tribute provoked revolt, which led to reconquest, retribution, and demands for higher tribute, which in turn sparked greater resentment and fresh revolt. When the Spaniards appeared, the Totonac people greeted them as liberators, and other subject peoples joined them against the Aztecs.[12]

Montezuma himself refrained from attacking the Spaniards as they advanced toward his capital and welcomed Cortés and his men into Tenochtitlán. Historians have often condemned the Aztec ruler for vacillation and weakness. But he relied on the advice of his state council, itself divided, and on the dubious loyalty of tributary communities. When Cortés—with incredible boldness—took Montezuma hostage, the emperor's influence over his people crumbled.

Doña Marina Translating for Hernando Cortés During His Meeting with Montezuma

In April of 1519 Doña Marina (or La Malinche as she is known in Mexico) was among twenty women given to the Spanish as slaves. Fluent in Nahuatl (NAH-what-el) and Yucatec (YOO-kuh-tek) Mayan (spoken by a Spanish priest accompanying Cortés), she acted as an interpreter and diplomatic guide for the Spanish. She had a close personal relationship with Cortés and bore his son Don Martín Cortés in 1522. Doña Marina has been seen as a traitor to her people, as a victim of Spanish conquest, and as the founder of the Mexican people. She highlights the complex interaction between native peoples and the Spanish and the particular role women often played as cultural mediators between the two sides. (The Granger Collection, New York)

Later, in retaliation for a revolt by the entire population of Tenochtitlán that killed many Spaniards, Montezuma was executed. Afterwards, the Spaniards escaped from the city and defeated the Aztec army at Otumba near Lake Texcoco. On August 13, 1520, the last Aztec emperor surrendered to the Spanish.

More amazing than the defeat of the Aztecs was the fall of the remote **Inca Empire** perched at 9,800 to 13,000 feet above sea level. (The word *Inca* refers both to the people who lived in the valleys of the Andes Mountains in present-day Peru and to their ruler.) The borders of this vast and sophisticated empire were well fortified, but the Inca neither expected foreign invaders nor knew of the fate of the Aztec empire to the north. The imperial government, based in the capital city of Cuzco (KOOS-koh), commanded loyalty from the people, but at the time of the Spanish invasion it had been embroiled in a civil war over succession. The Inca Huascar (WAHS-kahr) had been fighting his half-brother Atahualpa (ah-tah-WAHL-pa) for five years over the crown.

Francisco Pizarro (ca. 1475–1541), a conquistador of modest Spanish origins, landed on the northern coast of Peru on May 13, 1532, the very day Atahualpa won the decisive battle. The Spaniard soon learned about the war and its outcome. As Pizarro advanced across the steep Andes toward Cuzco, Atahualpa was proceeding to the capital for his coronation. Like Montezuma in Mexico, Atahualpa was kept fully informed of the Spaniards' movements and accepted Pizarro's invitation to meet in the provincial town of Cajamarca. Intending to extend a peaceful welcome to the newcomers, Atahualpa and his followers were unarmed. The Spaniards captured him and collected an enormous ransom in gold. Instead of freeing the new emperor, however, they executed him in 1533 on trumped-up charges.

Decades of violence ensued, marked by Incan resistance and internal struggles among Spanish forces for the spoils of empire. By the 1570s the Spanish crown had succeeded in imposing control. With Spanish conquest, a new chapter opened in European relations with the New World.

Europe and the World After Columbus

What effect did overseas expansion have on the conquered societies, on enslaved Africans, and on world trade?

Europeans had maintained commercial relations with Asia and sub-Saharan Africa since Roman times. In the Carolingian era the slave trade had linked northern Europe and the Islamic Middle East. The High Middle Ages had witnessed a great expansion of trade with Africa and Asia. But with the American discoveries, for the first time commercial and other relations became worldwide, involving all the continents except Australia. European involvement in the Americas led to the acceleration of global contacts. In time, these contacts had a profound influence on European society and culture.

Spanish Settlement and Indigenous Population Decline

In the sixteenth century perhaps two hundred thousand Spaniards immigrated to the New World. Mostly ex-soldiers and adventurers unable to find employment in Spain, they came for profits. After assisting in the conquest of the Aztecs and the subjugation of the Incas, these men carved out vast estates in temperate grazing areas and imported Spanish sheep, cattle, and horses

---

Inca Empire The vast and sophisticated Peruvian empire, centered at the capital city of Cusco, that was at its peak from 1438 until 1532.

Section Review

- The desire for trade goods, religious zeal for new converts, a chance for power and glory, and simple curiosity motivated European exploration, made possible by the financial support of strong monarchs and sailors willing to endure the danger of sea travel to escape poverty.

- Technological advances in shipbuilding, navigation, and weaponry borrowed from the East made exploration more feasible.

- Portuguese seafaring skills, with financial backing by the royal family, led to exploration and conquest in Africa and the Atlantic islands, and the establishment of trading posts in India.

- The Spanish monarchy financed the seasoned mariner Columbus, who set out to find a direct ocean trading route to Asia, although he landed in the Bahamas and Cuba, leading to European conquest and colonization in the New World.

- Cabral of Portugal and Magellan of Spain also sought a trade route to Asia, but proved that the westward passage to India was too long and dangerous.

- Cortés, in search of gold, sailed to Mexico, where he discovered and conquered the rich Aztec Empire, while the Incas fell to Pizarro.

for the kinds of ranching with which they were familiar. In coastal tropical areas unsuited for grazing the Spanish erected huge plantations to supply sugar for the European market. Around 1550 silver was discovered in present-day Bolivia and Mexico. How were the cattle ranches, sugar plantations, and silver mines to be worked? The conquistadors first turned to the Amerindians.

encomienda system The Spanish system whereby the Crown granted the conquerors the right to employ groups of Amerindians in a town or area as agricultural or mining laborers or as tribute payers; it was a disguised form of slavery.

The Spanish quickly established the **encomienda system** (in-co-mee-EN-dah), in which the Crown granted the conquerors the right to employ groups of Amerindians as agricultural or mining laborers or as tribute payers. Theoretically, the Spanish were forbidden to enslave the natives; in actuality, the encomiendas were a legalized form of slavery. Laboring in the blistering heat of tropical cane fields or in the dark, dank, and dangerous mines, the Amerindians died in staggering numbers.

Students of the history of medicine have suggested another crucial explanation for indigenous population losses: disease. Having little or no resistance to diseases brought from the Old World, the inhabitants of the highlands of Mexico and Peru, especially, fell victim to smallpox, typhus, influenza, and other diseases. According to one expert, smallpox caused "in all likelihood the most severe single loss of aboriginal population that ever occurred."[13] (The old belief that syphilis was a New World disease imported to Europe by Columbus's sailors has been discredited by the discovery of pre-Columbian skeletons in Europe bearing signs of the disease.)

Although disease was a leading cause of death, there were many others, including malnutrition and starvation as people were forced to neglect their own fields. Many indigenous peoples also died through outright violence.[14] According to the Franciscan missionary Bartolomé de Las Casas (1474–1566), the Spanish maliciously murdered thousands:

> To these quiet Lambs . . . came the Spaniards like most c(r)uel Tygres, Wolves and Lions, enrag'd with a sharp and tedious hunger; for these forty years past, minding nothing else but the slaughter of these unfortunate wretches, whom with divers kinds of torments neither seen nor heard of before, they have so cruelly and inhumanely butchered, that of three millions of people which Hispaniola itself did contain, there are left remaining alive scarce three hundred persons.[15]

Las Casas's remarks concentrate on the Caribbean islands, but the death rate elsewhere was also overwhelming. The Franciscan, Dominican, and Jesuit missionaries who accompanied the conquistadors and settlers played an important role in converting the Amerindians to Christianity, teaching them European methods of agriculture, and inculcating loyalty to the Spanish crown. In terms of numbers of people baptized, missionaries enjoyed phenomenal success, though the depth of the Amerindians' understanding of Christianity remains debatable. Missionaries, especially Las Casas, asserted that the Amerindians had human rights, and through Las Casas's persistent pressure the emperor Charles V abolished the worst abuses of the encomienda system in 1531.

For colonial administrators the main problem posed by the astronomically high death rate was the loss of a subjugated labor force. As early as 1511 King Ferdinand of Spain observed that the Amerindians seemed to be "very frail" and that "one black could do the work of four Indians."[16] Thus was born an absurd myth and the new tragedy of the Atlantic slave trade.

Sugar and Slavery

Throughout the Middle Ages slavery was deeply entrenched in the Mediterranean. The bubonic plague, famines, and other epidemics created a severe shortage of agricultural and domestic workers throughout Europe, encouraging Italian

A New World Sugar Refinery, Brazil

Sugar, a luxury in great demand in Europe, was the most important and most profitable plantation crop in the New World. This image shows the processing and refinement of sugar on a Brazilian plantation. Sugar cane was grown, harvested, and processed by African slaves who labored under brutal and ruthless conditions to generate enormous profits for plantation owners. (The Bridgeman Art Library/ Getty Images)

merchants to buy slaves from the Black Sea region and the Balkans. Renaissance merchants continued the slave trade despite papal threats of excommunication. The Genoese set up colonial stations in the Crimea and along the Black Sea, and according to an international authority on slavery, these outposts were "virtual laboratories" for the development of slave plantation agriculture in the New World.[17] This form of slavery had nothing to do with race; almost all slaves were white. How, then, did black African slavery enter the European picture and take root in South and then North America?

In 1453 the Ottoman capture of Constantinople halted the flow of white slaves. Mediterranean Europe, cut off from its traditional source of slaves, then turned to sub-Saharan Africa, which had a long history of slave trading. (See the feature "Individuals in Society: Juan de Pareja.")

Native to the South Pacific, sugar was taken in ancient times to India, where farmers learned to preserve cane juice as granules that could be stored and shipped. From there, sugar cane growing traveled to China and the Mediterranean, where islands like Crete, Sicily, and Cyprus had the necessary warm and wet climate. When Genoese and other Italians colonized the Canary Islands and the Portuguese settled on the Madeira Islands, sugar plantations came to the Atlantic. In this stage of European expansion, "the history of slavery became inextricably tied up with the history of sugar."[18] Originally sugar was an expensive luxury that only the very affluent could afford, but population increases and monetary expansion in the fifteenth century led to an increasing demand for it.

Resourceful Italians provided the capital, cane, and technology for sugar cultivation on plantations in southern Portugal, Madeira, and the Canary Islands.

Individuals in Society

Juan de Pareja (pa-REH-ha)

A marginal person is one who lives outside the mainstream of the dominant society, who is not fully assimilated into or accepted by that society. Apart from revealing little-known aspects of past cultures, marginalized people teach us much about the values and ideals of the dominant society. Such a person was the Spanish religious and portrait painter Juan de Pareja.

Pareja was born in Antequera, an agricultural region and the old center of Muslim culture near Seville in southern Spain. Of his parents we know nothing. Because a rare surviving document calls him a "mulatto," one of his parents must have been white and the other must have had some African blood. In 1630 Pareja applied to the mayor of Seville for permission to travel to Madrid to visit his brother and "to perfect his art." The document lists his occupation as "a painter in Seville." Since it mentions no other name, it is reasonable to assume that Pareja arrived in Madrid a free man. Sometime between 1630 and 1648, however, he came into the possession of the artist Diego Velázquez (1599–1660); Pareja became a slave.

During the long wars of the reconquista, Muslims and Christians captured each other in battle and used the defeated as slaves. The fifteenth and sixteenth centuries had seen a steady flow of sub-Saharan Africans into the Iberian Peninsula. Thus early modern Spain was a slaveholding society.

How did Velázquez acquire Pareja? By purchase? As a gift? Had Pareja fallen into debt or committed some crime and thereby lost his freedom? We do not know. Velázquez, the greatest Spanish painter of the seventeenth century, had a large studio with many assistants. Pareja was set to grinding powders to make colors and to preparing canvases. He must have demonstrated ability because, when Velázquez went to Rome in 1648, he chose Pareja to accompany him.

In 1650, as practice for a portrait of Pope Innocent X, Velázquez painted Pareja. That same year, Velázquez signed the document that gave Pareja his freedom, to become effective in 1654. Pareja lived out the rest of his life as an independent painter.

What does the public career of this seventeenth-century marginal person tell us about the man and his world? Pareja's career suggests that a person of talent and ability could rise in Spanish society despite the social and religious barriers that existed at the time. Jonathan Brown, the leading authority on Velázquez, describes Pareja's appearance in Velázquez's portrait as "self-confident." A more enthusiastic student writes, "The man was technically a slave. . . . However, we can see from Velázquez's painting that the two were undeniably equals. That steady look of self-controlled power can even make us wonder which of the two had a higher opinion of himself."

Questions for Analysis

1. Since slavery was an established institution in Spain, speculate on Velázquez's possible reasons for giving Pareja his freedom.
2. What issues of cultural diversity might Pareja have faced in seventeenth-century Spain?

Sources: Jonathan Brown, *Velázquez: Painter and Courtier* (New Haven, Conn.: Yale University Press, 1986); *Grove Dictionary of Art* (New York: Macmillan, 2000); Sister Wendy Beckett, *Sister Wendy's American Collection* (New York: Harper Collins Publishers, 2000), p. 15.

Velázquez, Juan de Pareja (1650). (The Metropolitan Museum of Art, Fletcher Fund, Rogers Fund, and Bequest of Miss Adelaide Milton de Groot (1876–1967), by exchange, supplemented by gifts from friends of the Museum, 1971. [1971.86]. Photograph © 1986 The Metropolitan Museum of Art)

Meanwhile, in the period 1490 to 1530, Portuguese traders brought between three hundred and two thousand black slaves to Lisbon each year (see Map 15.2), where they performed most of the manual labor and constituted 10 percent of the city's population. From there slaves were transported to the sugar plantations of Madeira, the Azores, and the Cape Verde Islands. Sugar and these small Atlantic island colonies gave New World slavery its distinctive shape. Columbus himself, who spent a decade in Madeira, brought sugar plants on his voyages to "the Indies."

In Africa, where slavery was entrenched (as it was in the Islamic world, southern Europe, and China), African kings and dealers sold black slaves to European merchants who participated in the transatlantic trade. The Portuguese brought the first slaves to Brazil; by 1600 four thousand were being imported annually. After its founding in 1621, the Dutch West India Company, with the full support of the government of the United Provinces, transported thousands of Africans to Brazil and the Caribbean, mostly to work on sugar plantations. In the late seventeenth century, with the chartering of the Royal African Company, the English got involved. In total, scholars estimate that European traders from all these nations brought over eleven million African slaves to the West Indies and North America, with the peak of the trade occuring in the eighteenth century.

European sailors found the Atlantic passage cramped and uncomfortable, but conditions for African slaves were lethal. Before 1700, when slavers decided it was better business to improve conditions, some 20 percent of slaves died on the voyage.[19] The most common cause of death was from dysentery induced by poor-quality food and water, intense crowding, and lack of sanitation. Men were often kept in irons during the passage, while women and girls were fair game for sailors. To increase profits, slave traders packed several hundred captives on each ship. One slaver explained that he removed his boots before entering the slave hold because he had to crawl over their packed bodies.[20]

By 1790 there were 757,181 blacks in a total U.S. population of 3,929,625. In Brazil during the same decade, blacks numbered about 2 million in a total population of 3.25 million. African slaves ultimately worked in an infinite variety of occupations: as miners, soldiers, sailors, servants, and artisans and in the production of cotton, rum, indigo, tobacco, wheat and corn. Sugar remained a predominant slave-produced crop, leading to boycotts by European abolitionists in the late eighteenth century.

The Columbian Exchange

The Age of Discovery led to the migration of peoples, which in turn led to an exchange of fauna and flora—of animals, plants, and disease, a complex process known as the **Columbian exchange.** Spanish and Portuguese immigrants to the Americas wanted the diet with which they were familiar, so they searched for climatic zones favorable to those crops. Everywhere they settled they brought and raised wheat—in the highlands of Mexico, the Rio de la Plata, New Granada (in northern South America), and Chile. By 1535 Mexico was exporting wheat. Grapes did well in parts of Peru and Chile. It took the Spanish longer to discover areas where suitable soil and adequate rainfall would nourish olive trees, but by the 1560s the coastal valleys of Peru and Chile were dotted with olive groves. Columbus had brought sugar plants on his second voyage; Spaniards also introduced rice and bananas from the Canary Islands, and the Portuguese carried these items to Brazil. Not all plants arrived intentionally. In clumps of mud on shoes and in the folds of textiles came the seeds of immigrant grasses.

Columbian exchange The exchange of animals, plants, and diseases between the Old and the New Worlds.

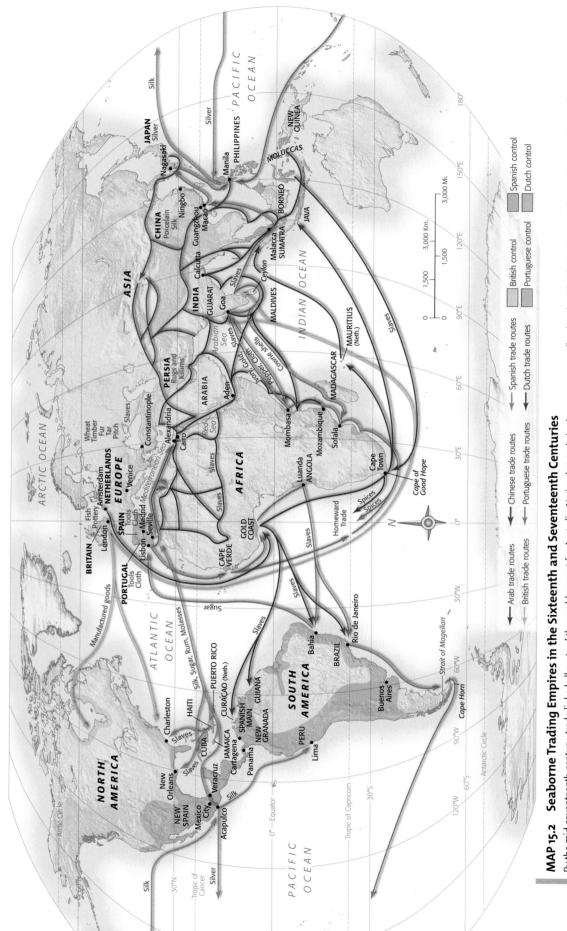

MAP 15.2 Seaborne Trading Empires in the Sixteenth and Seventeenth Centuries
By the mid-seventeenth century, trade linked all parts of the world, except for Australia. Notice that trade in slaves was not confined to the Atlantic but involved almost all parts of the world.

Spanish control
Dutch control
British control
Portuguese control

Spanish trade routes
Dutch trade routes
Chinese trade routes
Portuguese trade routes
Arab trade routes
British trade routes

Apart from wild turkeys and game, Native Americans had no animals for food; apart from alpacas and llamas, they had no animals for travel or to use as beasts of burden. On his second voyage in 1493 Columbus introduced horses, cattle, sheep, dogs, pigs, chickens, and goats. The multiplication of these animals proved spectacular. The horse enabled the Spanish conquerors and the Amerindians to travel faster and farther and to transport heavy loads.

The Spanish and Portuguese returned to Europe with maize (corn), white potatoes, and many varieties of beans, squash, pumpkins, avocados, and tomatoes. Because maize grows in climates too dry for rice and too wet for wheat, gives a high yield per unit of land, and has a short growing season, it proved an especially important crop for Europeans. So too did the nutritious white potato, which slowly spread from west to east—to Ireland, England, and France in the seventeenth century; and to Germany, Poland, Hungary, and Russia in the eighteenth. Ironically, the white potato reached New England from old England in 1718.

Colonial Administration

Columbus, Cortés, and Pizarro had claimed the lands they had "discovered" for the Spanish crown. How were these lands governed? In the sixteenth century the Crown divided its New World territories into four **viceroyalties** or administrative divisions: New Spain, which consisted of Mexico, Central America, and present-day California, Arizona, New Mexico, and Texas, with the capital at Mexico City; Peru, originally all the lands in continental South America, later reduced to the territory of modern Peru, Chile, Bolivia, and Ecuador, with the viceregal seat at Lima; New Granada, including present-day Venezuela, Colombia, Panama, and, after 1739, Ecuador, with Bogotá as its administrative center; and La Plata, consisting of Argentina, Uruguay, and Paraguay, with Buenos Aires as the capital.

> **viceroyalties** The name for the four administrative units of Spanish possessions in the Americas: New Spain, Peru, New Granada, and La Plata.

Within each territory, the viceroy, or imperial governor, exercised broad military and civil authority as the direct representative of the sovereign in Madrid. The viceroy presided over the *audiencia* (ow-dee-ENS-ee-ah), a board of twelve to fifteen judges that served as his advisory council and the highest judicial body. The reform-minded Spanish king Charles III (r. 1759–1788) introduced the system of *intendants*, pioneered by the Bourbon kings of France, to the New World territories. These royal officials possessed broad military, administrative, and financial authority within their *intendancies* and were responsible not to the viceroy but to the monarchy in Madrid.

> **audiencia** Presided over by the viceroy, the twelve to fifteen judges who served as an advisory council and as the highest judicial body.

The Portuguese governed their colony of Brazil in a similar manner. After the union of the crowns of Portugal and Spain in 1580, Spanish administrative forms were introduced. Local officials called *corregidores* (kuh-REG-i-dawr-eez) held judicial and military powers. Mercantilist policies placed severe restrictions on Brazilian industries that might compete with those of Portugal. In the seventeenth century the use of black slave labor made possible the cultivation of coffee and cotton, and in the eighteenth century Brazil produced around one-tenth of the world's sugar. The unique feature of colonial Brazil's culture and society was its thoroughgoing intermixture of Indians, whites, and blacks.

Silver and the Economic Effects of Spain's Discoveries

The sixteenth century has often been called Spain's golden century, but silver mined in the Americas was the true source of Spain's incredible wealth. In 1545, at an altitude of fifteen thousand feet, the Spanish discovered an incredible source of silver at Potosí (poh-toh-SEE) (in present-day Bolivia) in territory conquered from the Inca Empire. The frigid place where nothing grew had been unsettled. A half-century later, 160,000 people lived there, making it about the size of the city of London. In the second half of the sixteenth century Potosí yielded perhaps 60 percent of all the silver mined in the world. From Potosí and the mines at Zacatecas (sah-kah-TE-kahs) and Guanajuato (gwah-nah-HWAH-taw) in Mexico, huge quantities of precious metals poured forth, destined for the port of Seville in Spain.

The mining of gold and silver became the most important industry in the colonies. The Crown claimed the **quinto,** one-fifth of all precious metals mined in South America. Gold and silver yielded the Spanish monarchy 25 percent of its total income.

In many ways, it was not Spain but China that controlled the world trade in silver. The Chinese demanded silver for its products and for the payment of imperial taxes. China was thus the main buyer of world silver, serving as a "sink" for half the world's production. The silver market drove world trade, with the Americas and Japan being mainstays on the supply side and China dominating the demand side.

quinto One-fifth of all precious metals mined in the Americas that the Crown claimed as its own.

The Birth of the Global Economy

With the Europeans' discovery of the Americas and their exploration of the Pacific, the entire world was linked for the first time in history by seaborne trade. That trade brought into being three successive commercial empires: the Portuguese, the Spanish, and the Dutch.

The Portuguese were the first worldwide traders, and Portuguese was the language of the Asian maritime trade. In the sixteenth century they controlled the sea route to India (see Map 15.2). From their fortified bases at Goa on the Arabian Sea and at Malacca on the Malay Peninsula, ships carried goods to the Portuguese settlement at Macao in the South China Sea. From Macao Portuguese ships loaded with Chinese silks and porcelains sailed to the Japanese port of Nagasaki and to the Philippine port of Manila, where Chinese goods were exchanged for Spanish (that is, Latin American) silver. Throughout Asia the Portuguese traded in slaves—black Africans, Chinese, and Japanese. The Portuguese exported to India horses from Mesopotamia and copper from Arabia; from India they exported hawks and peacocks for the Chinese and Japanese markets. Back to Portugal they brought Asian spices that had been purchased with textiles produced in India and with gold and ivory from East Africa. They also shipped back sugar from their colony in Brazil, produced by African slaves whom they had transported across the Atlantic.

Spanish possessions in the New World constituted basically a land empire, and in the sixteenth century the Spaniards devised a method of governing that empire (see page 391). But across the Pacific the Spaniards also built a seaborne empire centered at Manila in the Philippines, which had been "discovered" by Ferdinand Magellan in 1521 and later conquered by the Spanish navigator Miguel Lopez de Legazpi. The city of Manila served as

Chinese Porcelain

This porcelain from a seventeenth-century Chinese ship's cargo, recovered from the sea, was intended for European luxury markets. (Christie's Images)

the transpacific bridge between Spanish America and the extreme Eastern trade. In Manila, Spanish traders used silver from American mines to purchase Chinese silk for European markets. The European demand for silk was so huge that in 1597, for example, 12 million pesos of silver, almost the total value of the transatlantic trade, moved from Acapulco to Manila (see Map 15.2). After about 1640 the Spanish silk trade declined because it could not compete with Dutch imports.

In the latter half of the seventeenth century the worldwide Dutch seaborne trade predominated. The Dutch Empire was built on spices. In 1599 a Dutch fleet returned to Amsterdam carrying 600,000 pounds of pepper and 250,000 pounds of cloves and nutmeg. Those who had invested in the expedition received a 100 percent profit. The voyage led to the establishment in 1602 of the Dutch East India Company, founded with the stated intention of capturing the spice trade from the Portuguese.

The Dutch fleet, sailing from the Cape of Good Hope in Africa and avoiding the Portuguese forts in India, steered directly for the Sunda Strait in Indonesia (see Map 15.2). The Dutch wanted direct access to and control of the Indonesian sources of spices. In return for assisting Indonesian princes in local squabbles and disputes with the Portuguese, the Dutch won broad commercial concessions. Through agreements, seizures, and outright war, they gained control of the western access to the Indonesian archipelago. Gradually, they acquired political domination over the archipelago itself. The Dutch managed to expel the Portuguese from Ceylon and other East Indian islands. By 1650 the Dutch West India Company had successfully intruded on the Spanish possessions in the Americas, in the process gaining control of much of the African and American trade.

Changing Attitudes and Beliefs

How did culture and art in this period respond to social and cultural transformation?

The age of overseas expansion was characterized by an extraordinary degree of intellectual and artistic ferment. This effervescence can be seen in the development of the essay as a distinct literary genre, in other prose, in poetry, in drama, in art, and in music. In many ways, literature, the visual arts, music, and the drama of the period mirrored the social and cultural conditions that gave rise to them. An important theme running through the culture of this time was the encounter with radically new places and peoples.

New Ideas About Race

Ancient Greeks and Romans were in close contact with Africa and they also practiced slavery, but they did not associate one with the other. Slavery, which was endemic in the ancient world, stemmed from either capture in war or debt. Although generations could be born in captivity, no particular ethnic or racial associations were involved. How did slavery come to be so closely associated with race in the Age of Discovery?

Settlers brought to the Americas the racial attitudes they had absorbed in Europe. In the sixteenth and seventeenth centuries in England, for example, slavers' accounts of their travels depicted Africans as savages because of their eating habits, morals, clothing, and social customs; as barbarians because of their language and methods of war; and as heathens because they were not Christian (nearly the

Section Review

- The Spanish set up the encomienda system of labor, forcing the Amerindians to work in plantations, causing great suffering from malnutrition, disease, and violence that killed large numbers.

- Europeans originally turned to Africa for slaves as Europe had a labor shortage and a diminishing supply of white slaves in the Mediterranean.

- The plantation model of slavery developed for sugar production on Atlantic islands was brought to the New World, along with great numbers of African slaves; the history of sugar and slavery were inextricably linked.

- The Columbian Exchange included the plants, animals, and diseases that accompanied people as they migrated to the New World and those they took back with them.

- The Spanish set up viceroys, or governors, to rule their new territories with military and civic authority.

- The majority of silver mined in Bolivia and Mexico was traded to China for luxury goods desired by Europeans.

- Europeans established trade routes that linked the world by sea for the first time, giving birth to a global economy.

identical language with which the English described the Irish—see page 301). Africans were believed to possess a potent sexuality; African women were considered sexually aggressive, with a "temper hot and lascivious."[21] Medieval Arabs had also depicted Africans as primitive people ideally suited to enslavement.

The racial biases that the Portuguese, Spanish, Dutch, and English brought to the New World also derived from Christian theological speculation. As Europeans turned to Africa for new sources of slaves, they used ideas about Africans' primitiveness and barbarity to defend slavery and even argue that enslavement benefited Africans by bringing the light of Christianity to heathen peoples. Thus, the institution of slavery contributed to the dissemination of more rigid notions of racial inferiority. From rather vague assumptions and prejudices, Europeans developed more elaborate ideological notions of racial superiority and inferiority to safeguard the ever-increasing profits gained from plantation slavery.

Michel de Montaigne and Cultural Curiosity

Racism was not the only possible reaction to the new worlds emerging in the sixteenth century. Decades of religious fanaticism, bringing civil anarchy and war, led both Catholics and Protestants to doubt that any one faith contained absolute truth. Added to these doubts was the discovery of peoples in the New World who had radically different ways of life. These shocks helped produce ideas of skepticism and cultural relativism in the sixteenth and seventeenth centuries. Skepticism is a school of thought founded on doubt that total certainty or definitive knowledge is ever attainable. The skeptic is cautious and critical and suspends judgment. Cultural relativism suggests that one culture is not necessarily superior to another, just different. Both notions found expression in the work of Frenchman Michel de Montaigne (1533–1592) (duh mon-TEN).

Montaigne developed a new literary genre, the essay—from the French *essayer*, meaning "to test or try"—to express his thoughts and ideas. Montaigne's *Essays* provides insight into the mind of a remarkably civilized man. From the ancient authors, especially the Roman Stoic Seneca, Montaigne acquired a sense of calm, patience, tolerance, and broad-mindedness.

Montaigne's essay "On Cannibals" reveals the impact of overseas discoveries on one European's consciousness. His tolerant mind rejected the notion that one culture is superior to another:

> I long had a man in my house that lived ten or twelve years in the New World, discovered in these latter days, and in that part of it where Villegaignon landed [Brazil]. . . .
>
> I find that there is nothing barbarous and savage in [that] nation, . . . excepting, that every one gives the title of barbarism to everything that is not in use in his own country. As, indeed, we have no other level of truth and reason, than the example and idea of the opinions and customs of the place wherein we live.[22]

In his own time and throughout the seventeenth century, few would have agreed with Montaigne. The publication of his ideas, however, anticipated a basic shift in attitudes. Montaigne inaugurated an era of doubt. "Wonder," he said, "is the foundation of all philosophy, research is the means of all learning, and ignorance is the end."[23]

Elizabethan and Jacobean Literature

In addition to the essay as a literary genre, the period fostered remarkable creativity in other branches of literature. England—especially in the latter part of Elizabeth's reign and in the first years of her successor, James I (r. 1603–1625)—witnessed remarkable literary expression. The terms *Elizabethan* and *Jacobean* (referring to the reign of James) are used to designate the English music, poetry, prose, and drama of this period.

The undisputed master of this period is the dramatist William Shakespeare, whose genius lay in the originality of his characterizations, the diversity of his plots, his understanding of human psychology, and his unexcelled gift for language. Shakespeare was a Renaissance man in his deep appreciation of classical culture, individualism, and humanism. Such plays as *Julius Caesar, Pericles,* and *Antony and Cleopatra* deal with classical subjects and figures. Several of his comedies have Italian Renaissance settings. The nine history plays, including *Richard II, Richard III,* and *Henry IV,* express English national consciousness. Shakespeare's later tragedies, including *Hamlet, Othello,* and *Macbeth,* explore an enormous range of human problems and are open to an almost infinite variety of interpretations.

Another great masterpiece of the Jacobean period was the Authorized Bible. So called because it was produced under the royal sponsorship of James I (it had no official ecclesiastical endorsement), the Authorized Bible represented the Anglican and Puritan desire to encourage laypeople to read the Scriptures. It quickly achieved great popularity and displaced all earlier versions. British settlers carried this Bible to the North American colonies, where it became known as the King James Bible.

Section Review

- A flowering of artistic expression in poetry, prose, drama, art, and music accompanied the age of overseas expansion.

- Europeans developed prejudicial racial attitudes from Christian theology and beliefs about the alleged primitiveness and barbarity of Africans that they used to justify slavery.

- The Frenchman Michel de Montaigne discussed skepticism, the philosophy based on doubt that absolute certainty or definitive knowledge is ever attainable, and cultural relativism, which suggests that one culture is not necessarily superior to another.

- The dramatic works of William Shakespeare during the reign of Elizabeth crowned a period of remarkable creativity in English music, poetry, prose, and drama, that later saw the creation of another masterpiece—the King James Bible.

Chapter Review

What was the Afro-Eurasian trading world before Columbus? (page 371)

Prior to Columbus's voyages, well-developed trade routes linked the peoples and products of Africa, Asia, and Europe. The Indian Ocean was the center of the Afro-Eurasian trade world, ringed by cosmopolitan commercial cities such as Mombasa, Malacca, and Macao. Venetian and Genoese merchants brought sophisticated luxury goods, like silks and spices, into western Europe from the East. Overall, though, Europeans played a minor role in the Afro-Eurasian trading world, since they did not produce many products desired by Eastern elites.

How and why did Europeans undertake ambitious voyages of expansion that would usher in a new era of global contact? (page 375)

In the sixteenth and seventeenth centuries Europeans gained access to large parts of the globe for the first time. European peoples had the intellectual curiosity, driving ambition, religious zeal, and material incentive to challenge their marginal role in the pre-existing trade world. The revived monarchies of the sixteenth century now possessed sufficient resources to back ambitious seafarers like Christopher Columbus and Vasco da Gama. Exploration and exploitation contributed to a more sophisticated standard of living, in the form of spices and Asian luxury goods.

Key Terms

General History of the Indies (p. 377)

caravel (p. 377)

Ptolemy's *Geography* (p. 377)

Treaty of Tordesillas (p. 382)

conquistador (p. 383)

Aztec Empire (p. 384)

Inca Empire (p. 385)

encomienda system (p. 386)

Columbian exchange (p. 389)

viceroyalties (p. 391)

audiencia (p. 391)

quinto (p. 392)

> **What effect did overseas expansion have on the conquered societies, on enslaved Africans, and on world trade? (page 385)**

Other consequences of European expansion had global proportions. Indian Ocean trade, long dominated by Muslim merchants operating from autonomous city-ports, increasingly fell under the control of Portuguese merchants sponsored by their Crown. Later these would shift to the Dutch East India Company. In the New World, Europeans discovered territories wholly unknown to them and forcibly established new colonies. The resulting Columbian exchange contributed to the decimation of native populations by disease and fostered the exchange of a myriad of plant, animal, and viral species. The slave trade took on new proportions of scale and intensity, as many millions of Africans were transported to labor in horrific conditions in the mines and plantations of the New World.

> **How did culture and art in this period respond to social and cultural transformation? (page 393)**

Cultural attitudes were challenged as well. While most Europeans did not question the superiority of Western traditions and beliefs, new currents of religious skepticism and new ideas about race were harbingers of developments to come. The essays of Montaigne, the plays of Shakespeare, and the King James Bible remain classic achievements of the Western cultural heritage. They both reflected dominant cultural values and projected new ideas into the future.

Notes

1. K. N. Chaudhuri, *Trade and Civilisation in the Indian Ocean: An Economic History from the Rise of Islam to 1750* (Cambridge: Cambridge University Press, 1985), p. 14.
2. Quoted in C. M. Cipolla, *Guns, Sails, and Empires: Technological Innovation and the Early Phases of European Expansion, 1400–1700* (New York: Minerva Press, 1965), p. 132.
3. Quoted in F. H. Littell, *The Macmillan Atlas: History of Christianity* (New York: Macmillan, 1976), p. 75.
4. See C. R. Phillips, *Ciudad Real, 1500–1750: Growth, Crisis, and Readjustment in the Spanish Economy* (Cambridge, Mass.: Harvard University Press, 1979), pp. 103–104, 115.
5. Pablo E. Pérez-Mallaína, *Spain's Men of the Sea: Daily Life on the Indies Fleet in the Sixteenth Century* (Baltimore: Johns Hopkins University Press, 1998), p. 133.
6. Ibid., p. 19.
7. G. V. Scammell, *The World Encompassed: The First European Maritime Empires, c. 800-1650* (Berkeley: University of California Press, 1981), p. 207.
8. Quoted in Cipolla, *Guns, Sails, and Empires*, pp. 115–116.
9. Quoted in F. Maddison, "Tradition and Innovation: Columbus' First Voyage and Portuguese Navigation in the Fifteenth Century," in *Circa 1492: Art in the Age of Exploration*, ed. J. A. Levenson (Washington, D.C.: National Gallery of Art, 1991), p. 69.
10. Quoted in R. L. Kagan, "The Spain of Ferdinand and Isabella," in *Circa 1492: Art in the Age of Exploration*, ed. J. A. Levenson (Washington, D.C.: National Gallery of Art, 1991), p. 60.
11. Peter Hulme, *Colonial Encounters: Europe and the Native Caribbean, 1492–1797* (London and New York: Methuan, 1986). 22–31.
12. G. W. Conrad and A. A. Demarest, *Religion and Empire: The Dynamics of Aztec and Inca Expansionism* (New York: Cambridge University Press, 1993), pp. 67–69.
13. Quoted in Crosby, *The Columbian Exchange: Biological and Cultural Consequences of 1492* (Westport, Conn.: Greenwood, 1972), p. 39.
14. Ibid., pp. 35–59.
15. Quoted in C. Gibson, ed., *The Black Legend: Anti-Spanish Attitudes in the Old World and the New* (New York: Knopf, 1971), pp. 74–75.
16. Quoted in L. B. Rout, Jr., *The African Experience in Spanish America* (New York: Cambridge University Press, 1976), p. 23.
17. C. Verlinden, *The Beginnings of Modern Colonization*, trans. Y. Freccero (Ithaca, N.Y.: Cornell University Press, 1970), pp. 5–6, 80–97.

18. This section leans heavily on D. B. Davis, *Slavery and Human Progress* (New York: Oxford University Press, 1984), pp. 54–62; the quotation is on p. 58.

19. Herbert S. Klein, "Profits and the Causes of Mortality," in David Northrup, ed., *The Atlantic Slave Trade* (Lexington, Mass.: D. C. Heath and Co., 1994), p. 116.

20. Malcolm Cowley and Daniel P. Mannix, "The Middle Passage," in David Northrup, ed., *The Atlantic Slave Trade* (Lexington, Mass.: D. C. Heath and Co., 1994), p. 101.

21. Quoted in D .P. Mannix, with M. Cowley, *Black Cargoes: A History of the Atlantic Slave Trade* (New York: Viking Press, 1968), p. 19.

22. C. Cotton, trans., *The Essays of Michel de Montaigne* (New York: A. L. Burt, 1893), pp. 207, 210.

23. Ibid., p. 523.

To assess your mastery of this chapter, go to **bedfordstmartins.com/mckaywestbrief**

Listening to the Past

Columbus Describes His First Voyage

On his return voyage to Spain in January 1493, Christopher Columbus composed a letter intended for wide circulation and had copies of it sent ahead to Isabella and Ferdinand and others when the ship docked at Lisbon. Because the letter sums up Columbus's understanding of his achievements, it is considered the most important document of his first voyage. Remember that his knowledge of Asia rested heavily on Marco Polo's Travels, *published around 1298.*

Christopher Columbus, by Ridolpho Ghirlandio. Friend of Raphael and teacher of Michelangelo, Ghirlandio (1483–1561) enjoyed distinction as a portrait painter, and so we can assume that this is a good likeness of the older Columbus. (Scala/Art Resource, NY)

Since I know that you will be pleased at the great success with which the Lord has crowned my voyage, I write to inform you how in thirty-three days I crossed from the Canary Islands to the Indies, with the fleet which our most illustrious sovereigns gave me. I found very many islands with large populations and took possession of them all for their Highnesses; this I did by proclamation and unfurled the royal standard. No opposition was offered.

I named the first island that I found "San Salvador," in honour of our Lord and Saviour who has granted me this miracle.... When I reached Cuba, I followed its north coast westwards, and found it so extensive that I thought this must be the mainland, the province of Cathay.* . . . From there I saw another island eighteen leagues eastwards which I then named "Hispaniola."†

Hispaniola is a wonder. The mountains and hills, the plains and meadow lands are both fertile and beautiful. They are most suitable for planting crops and for raising cattle of all kinds, and there are good sites for building towns and villages. The harbours are incredibly fine and there are many great rivers with broad channels and the majority

contain gold.‡ The trees, fruits and plants are very different from those of Cuba. In Hispaniola there are many spices and large mines of gold and other metals. . . .§

I hoped to win them to the love and service of their Highnesses and of the whole Spanish nation and to persuade them to collect and give us of the things which they possessed in abundance and which we needed. They have no religion and are not idolaters; but all believe that power and goodness dwell in the sky and they are firmly convinced that I have come from the sky with these ships and people. In this belief they gave me a good reception everywhere, once they had overcome their fear; and this is not because they are stupid—far from it, they are men of great intelligence, for they navigate

---

* Cathay is the old name for China. In the log-book and later in this letter Columbus accepts the native story that Cuba is an island that they can circumnavigate in something more than twenty-one days, yet he insists here and later, during the second voyage, that it is in fact part of the Asiatic mainland.
† Hispaniola is the second largest island of the West Indies; Haiti occupies the western third of the island, the Dominican Republic the rest.

‡ This did not prove to be true.
§ These statements are also inaccurate.

all those seas, and give a marvellously good account of everything—but because they have never before seen men clothed or ships like these. . . .

In conclusion, to speak only of the results of this very hasty voyage, their Highnesses can see that I will give them as much gold as they require, if they will render me some very slight assistance; also I will give them all the spices and cotton they want. . . . I will also bring them as much aloes as they ask and as many slaves, who will be taken from the idolaters. I believe also that I have found rhubarb and cinnamon and there will be countless other things in addition. . . .

So all Christendom will be delighted that our Redeemer has given victory to our most illustrious King and Queen and their renowned kingdoms, in this great matter. They should hold great celebrations and render solemn thanks to the Holy Trinity with many solemn prayers, for the great triumph which they will have, by the conversion of so many peoples to our holy faith and for the temporal benefits which will follow, for not only Spain, but all Christendom will receive encouragement and profit.

This is a brief account of the facts. Written in the caravel off the Canary Islands.||

15 February 1493

At your orders
THE ADMIRAL

Questions for Analysis

1. How did Columbus explain the success of his voyage?

2. What was Columbus's view of the Native Americans he met?

3. Evaluate his statements that the Caribbean islands possessed gold, cotton, and spices.

4. Why did Columbus cling to the idea that he had reached Asia?

Source: From *The Four Voyages of Christopher Columbus*, edited and translated by J. M. Cohen (Penguin Classics, 1969). Copyright © J. M. Cohen, 1969. Reproduced by permission of Penguin Books, Ltd.

|| Actually, Columbus was off Santa Maria in the Azores.

CHAPTER 16

Absolutism and Constitutionalism in Western Europe

ca. 1589–1715

Hyacinthe Rigaud, *Louis XIV, King of France and Navarre* (1701). Louis XIV is surrounded by the symbols of his power: the sword of justice, the scepter of power, and the crown. The vigor and strength of the king's stocking-covered legs contrast with the age and wisdom of his lined face. (Scala/Art Resource, NY)

Chapter Preview

Seventeenth-Century Crisis and Rebuilding
What were the common crises and achievements of seventeenth-century states?

Absolutism in France and Spain
To what extent did French and Spanish monarchs succeed in creating absolute monarchies?

The Culture of Absolutism
What cultural forms flourished under absolutist governments?

Constitutionalism
What is constitutionalism, and how did this form of government emerge in England and the Dutch Republic?

INDIVIDUALS IN SOCIETY: Glückel of Hameln

LISTENING TO THE PAST: The Court at Versailles

The seventeenth century was a period of crisis and transformation. Agricultural and manufacturing slumps meant that many people struggled to feed themselves and their families. After a long period of growth in the sixteenth century, population rates stagnated or even fell. Religious and dynastic conflicts led to almost constant war, visiting violence and destruction on ordinary people.

The demands of war reshaped European states. Armies grew larger than they had been since the time of the Roman Empire. To pay for these armies, governments greatly increased taxes. They also created new bureaucracies to collect the taxes and to foster economic activity that might increase state revenue. Despite numerous obstacles, European states succeeded in gathering more power during this period. What one historian described as the long European "struggle for stability" that originated with the Reformation in the early sixteenth century was largely resolved by 1680.[1]

Important differences existed, however, in terms of *which* authority within the state possessed sovereignty—the Crown or privileged groups. Between roughly 1589 and 1715 two basic patterns of government emerged in Europe: absolute monarchy and the constitutional state. Almost all subsequent European governments have been modeled on one of these patterns.

Seventeenth-Century Crisis and Rebuilding

What were the common crises and achievements of seventeenth-century states?

Historians often refer to the seventeenth century as an "age of crisis." After the economic and demographic growth of the sixteenth century, Europe faltered into stagnation and retrenchment. This was partially due to climate changes beyond anyone's control, but it also resulted from the bitterness of religious divides, the increased pressures exerted by governments, and the violence and dislocation of war. Overburdened peasants and city dwellers took action to defend themselves, sometimes profiting from elite conflicts to obtain redress of their grievances. In the long run, however, governments proved increasingly able to impose their will on the populace. This period witnessed a spectacular growth in army size as well as new forms of taxation, government bureaucracies, and increased state sovereignty.

Economic and Demographic Crisis

In the seventeenth century the vast majority of western Europeans lived in villages centered on a church and a manor. A small number of peasants in each village owned enough land to feed themselves and the livestock necessary to work their land. These independent farmers were leaders of the peasant village. They employed the landless poor, rented out livestock and tools, and served as agents for the noble lord. Below them were small landowners and tenant farmers who did not have enough land to be self-sufficient. These families sold their best produce on the market to earn cash for taxes, rent, and food. At the bottom were the rural proletariat who worked as dependent laborers and servants.

Rich or poor, bread was the primary element of the diet. Peasants paid stiff fees to the local miller for grinding grain into flour and sometimes to the lord for the right to bake bread in his oven. Bread was most often accompanied with a soup made of roots, herbs, beans, and perhaps a small piece of salt pork. One of the biggest annual festivals in the rural village was the killing of the family pig. The whole family gathered to help, sharing a rare abundance of meat with neighbors and carefully salting the extra and putting down the lard.

Rural society lived on the edge of subsistence. Because of the crude technology and low crop yield, peasants were constantly threatened by scarcity and famine. In the seventeenth century a period of colder and wetter climate, dubbed by historians as a "little ice age," meant a shorter farming season. A bad harvest created dearth; a series of bad harvests could lead to famine. Recurrent famines significantly reduced the population of early modern Europe. Most people did not die of outright starvation, but rather of diseases brought on by malnutrition and exhaustion. Facilitated by the weakened population, outbreaks of bubonic plague continued in Europe until the 1720s.

Industry also suffered. While the evidence does not permit broad generalizations, it appears that the output of woolen textiles, one of the most important European manufactures, declined sharply in the first half of the seventeenth century. Food prices were high, wages stagnated, and unemployment soared. This economic crisis was not universal: it struck various regions at different times and to different degrees. In the middle decades of the century, Spain, France, Germany, and England all experienced great economic difficulties; but these years were the golden age of the Netherlands.

The urban poor and peasants were the hardest hit. When the price of bread rose beyond their capacity to pay, they frequently took action. In towns they invaded the bakers' shop to seize bread and resell it at a "just price." In rural areas they attacked convoys taking grain away to the cities and also redistributed it. Women often led these actions, since their role as mothers gave them some impunity in authorities' eyes. Historians have labeled this vision of a world in which community needs predominate over competition and profit a **moral economy**.

1589–1610	Henry IV in France
1598	Edict of Nantes
1602	Dutch East India Company founded
1605–1715	Food riots common across Europe
1618–1648	Thirty Years' War
1635	Birth of French Academy
1640–1680	Golden age of Dutch art (Vermeer, Van Steen, Rembrandt)
1642–1649	English civil war ends with execution of Charles I
1643–1715	Louis XIV in France
1648–1653	The Fronde
1653–1658	Military rule in England under Oliver Cromwell
1659	Treaty of the Pyrenees marks end of Spanish imperial dominance
1660	Restoration of English monarchy under Charles II
1665–1683	Jean-Baptiste Colbert applies mercantilism to France
1685	Edict of Nantes revoked
1688–1689	Glorious Revolution in England
1701–1713	War of the Spanish Succession
1713	Peace of Utrecht

moral economy A historian's term for an economic perspective in which the needs of a community take precedence over competition and profit.

Seventeenth-Century State-Building: Common Obstacles and Achievements

In this context of economic and demographic depression, monarchs began to make new demands on their people. Traditionally, historians have distinguished sharply between the "absolutist" governments of France, Spain, Central Europe, and Russia and the constitutional monarchies of England and the Dutch Republic. Whereas absolutist monarchs gathered all power under their personal control, constitutional monarchs were obliged to respect laws passed by representative institutions. More recently, historians have emphasized commonalities among these powers. Despite their political differences, absolutist and constitutional monarchs shared common projects of protecting and expanding their frontiers, raising new taxes, and consolidating state control.

Rulers who wished to increase their authority encountered formidable obstacles. Some obstacles were purely material. Without paved roads, telephones, or

An English Food Riot

Nothing infuriated ordinary women and men more than the idea that merchants and landowners were withholding grain from the market in order to push high prices even higher. In this cartoon an angry crowd hands out rough justice to a rich farmer accused of hoarding. (Courtesy of the Trustees of the British Museum)

other modern technology, it took weeks to convey orders from the central government to the provinces. Rulers also suffered from a lack of information about their realms, due to the limited size of their bureaucracies. Without accurate knowledge of the number of inhabitants and the wealth they possessed, it was impossible to police and tax the population effectively. Cultural and linguistic differences presented their own obstacles. In some kingdoms the people spoke a language different from the Crown's, diminishing their willingness to obey its commands.

Local power structures presented another serious obstacle to a monarch's attempts to centralize power. Across Europe, nobles retained great legal, military, political, and financial powers, in addition to their traditional social prestige. Moreover, the church, legislative corps, town councils, guilds, and other bodies had acquired autonomy during the course of the Middle Ages. In some countries whole provinces held separate privileges granted when they became part of the kingdom.

While some monarchs succeeded in breaking the power of these institutions and others were forced to concede political power to elected representatives, the situation was nuanced. Absolutist monarchs did not crush the power of nobles and other groups but rather had to compromise with them. Louis XIV, the model of absolutist power, succeeded because he co-opted and convinced nobles. And in England and the Netherlands constitutional government did not mean democracy, the rule of the people.

Both absolutist and constitutional monarchs were able to overcome obstacles and achieve new levels of central control. They exercised greater power in four areas in particular: greater taxation, growth in armed forces, larger and more efficient bureaucracies, and the increased ability to compel obedience from their subjects. Over time, centralized power added up to something close to **sovereignty.** A state may be termed sovereign when it possesses a monopoly over the instruments of justice and the use of force within clearly defined boundaries. In a sovereign state, no system of courts, such as ecclesiastical tribunals, competes with state courts in the dispensation of justice; and private armies, such as those of feudal lords, present no threat to central authority because the state's army is stronger. State law touches all persons in the country. While seventeenth-century states did not acquire total sovereignty, they made important strides toward that goal.

sovereignty The supreme authority in a political community; a modern state is said to be sovereign when it controls the instruments of justice (the courts) and the use of force (military and police powers) within geographical boundaries recognized by other states.

Popular Political Action

In the seventeenth century bread riots turned into **popular revolts** in England, France, Spain, Portugal, and Italy.[2] In 1640 Philip IV of Spain faced revolt on three fronts simultaneously: Catalonia, the economic center of his realm; Portugal; and the northern provinces of the Netherlands. In 1647 the city of Palermo, in Spanish-occupied Sicily, exploded in protest over food shortages caused by a series of bad harvests. The city government responded by subsidizing the price of bread, but Madrid ordered an end to subsidies. Local women led a bread riot, shouting, "Long live the king and down with the taxes and the bad government!" Apart from affordable food, rebels demanded the suppression of extraordinary taxes, participation in municipal government, and the end to noble tax exemptions. Lacking unity and strong leadership, the revolt was squelched.[3] The Spanish were equally successful in the Netherlands, at first; by the early 1570s, however, a new wave of revolt broke out, resulting in the independent Dutch Republic (see page 424).

In France, uprisings became "a distinctive feature of life"[4] in the cities, where resentment at taxes fostered violence. Major insurrections occurred at Dijon in 1630 and 1668, at Bordeaux (bor-DOH) in 1635 and 1675, at Montpellier in 1645, at Lyons from 1667 through 1668 and again in 1692, and at Amiens in 1685, 1695, 1704, and 1711. All were characterized by deep popular anger, a vocabulary of violence, and what a recent historian calls "the culture of retribution"—that is, the punishment of royal "outsiders," officials who attempted to announce or collect taxes.[5] Royal officials were sometimes seized, beaten, and hacked to death. The limitations of royal authority gave some leverage to rebels. Royal edicts were sometimes suspended, prisoners released, and discussions initiated. By the end of the seventeenth century, this leverage had largely disappeared. Municipal governments were better integrated into the national structure, and local authorities had prompt military support from the central government. People who publicly opposed royal policies and taxes received swift and severe punishment.[6]

popular revolts Uprisings that were extremely common in the seventeenth century across Europe, due to the increasing pressures of taxation and warfare.

Absolutism in France and Spain

To what extent did French and Spanish monarchs succeed in creating absolute monarchies?

In the Middle Ages monarchs were said to rule "by the grace of God." Law was given by God; kings discovered or "found" the law and acknowledged that they must respect and obey it. In the seventeenth century absolutist state, kings amplified these claims, asserting that, because they were chosen by God, they were responsible to God alone. They claimed exclusive power to make and enforce laws, denying any other institution or group the authority to check their power.

Philosophers and theologians supported the kings' position with arguments for the necessity of absolute power for the public good. In *Leviathan* (li-VYE-uh-thuhn) (1651), the English philosopher Thomas Hobbes argued that any limits on or divisions of government power would lead only to paralysis or civil war. At the court of Louis XIV the French theologian Bossuet (baw-SWAY) proclaimed that without "absolute authority the king could neither do good nor repress evil."

The Foundations of Absolutism: Henry IV, Sully, and Richelieu

Louis XIV's absolutism had long roots. In 1589 his grandfather Henry IV (r. 1589–1610), the founder of the Bourbon dynasty, acquired a devastated country. As we saw in Chapter 14, civil wars between Protestants and Catholics wracked France in the last decades of the sixteenth century. Catastrophically poor harvests meant that peasants across France lived on the verge of starvation. Commercial activity had fallen to one-third its 1580 level. Nobles, officials, merchants, and peasants wanted peace, order, and stability. "Henri le Grand" (Henry the Great), as the king was called, promised "a chicken in every pot" and inaugurated a remarkable recovery. He was beloved because of the belief that he cared about the people; his was the only royal statue the Paris crowd did not tear down two hundred years later in the French Revolution.

Aside from a short war in 1601, Henry kept France at peace. He had converted to Catholicism but also issued the Edict of Nantes (see page 362), allowing Protestants the right to worship in 150 traditionally Protestant towns throughout France. Along with his able chief minister, the Protestant Maximilien de Béthune (mak-suh-MIL-yuhn duh bay-TOON), duke of Sully, Henry IV laid the foundations for the growth of state power. He sharply lowered direct taxes on the overburdened peasants and focused instead on increasing income from indirect taxes on salt, sales, and transit. He also instituted an annual fee on royal officials to guarantee heredity in their offices. (Although effective at the time, the long-term effect of this tax was to reduce royal control over officeholders.)

Alongside fiscal reform, Henry sponsored new industries and trade and improved the infrastructure of the country, building new roads, bridges, and canals to repair the ravages of years of civil war. In only twelve years he significantly raised royal revenues and restored public order.[7] Yet despite his efforts at peace, Henry was murdered in 1610 by François Ravaillac, a Catholic zealot, setting off a national crisis.

After the death of Henry IV his wife, the queen-regent Marie de' Medici (MED-ih-chee), headed the government for the child-king Louis XIII (r. 1610–1643). In 1624 Marie de' Medici secured the appointment of Armand Jean du Plessis—Cardinal Richelieu (ree-shuh-LYOO) (1585–1642)—to the council of ministers. Richelieu's maneuvers would allow the monarchy to maintain power within Europe and within its own borders despite the turmoil of the Thirty Years' War (see pages 435–436).

Richelieu's goal was to subordinate competing groups and institutions to the French monarchy. The nobility constituted the foremost threat. Nobles sat in royal councils, ran the army, controlled large provinces of France, and were immune from direct taxation. Richelieu sought to curb their power. In 1624 he succeeded in reshuffling the royal council, eliminating nobles who were potential power brokers and dominating the council as its president. In 1628 he became the first minister of the French crown.

Cardinal Richelieu's political genius is best reflected in the administrative system he established to strengthen royal control. He extended the use of **intendants,** commissioners for each of France's thirty-two districts who were appointed directly by the monarch, to whom they were solely responsible. Intendants could not be natives of the districts where they held authority; thus they had no vested interest in their localities. They recruited men for the army, supervised the collection of taxes, presided over the administration of local law, checked up on the local nobility, and regulated economic activities—commerce, trade, the guilds, marketplaces—in their districts. They were to use their power for three related purposes: to inform the central government about their districts, to enforce royal orders, and to undermine the influence of the regional nobility. As the intendants' power increased under Richelieu, so did the power of the centralized French state.

intendants Royal commissioners. Appointed by and answering directly to the monarch, they were key elements in Richelieu's plan to centralize the French state.

Under Richelieu the French monarchy also reasserted the principle of one people united by one faith. In 1627 Louis XIII decided to end Protestant military and political independence because, he said, it constituted "a state within a state." According to Louis, Huguenots were politically disobedient because they did not allow Catholics to worship in their cities.[8] Attention focused on La Rochelle, fourth largest of the French Atlantic ports and a major commercial center with strong ties to the northern Protestant states of Holland and England. Louis personally supervised the siege of La Rochelle. After the city fell in October 1628, its municipal government was suppressed and its walled fortifications were destroyed. Although Protestants retained the right of public worship, the king reinstated the Catholic liturgy, and Cardinal Richelieu himself celebrated the first Mass. The fall of La Rochelle weakened the influence of aristocratic Huguenots and was one step in the removal of Protestantism as a strong force in French life. Richelieu did not aim to wipe out Protestantism in the rest of Europe, however. His main foreign policy goal was to destroy the Catholic Habsburgs' grip on territories that surrounded France. Consequently, Richelieu supported the Habsburgs' enemies, including Protestants. In 1631 he signed a treaty with the Lutheran king Gustavus Adolphus promising French support against the Habsburgs in what has been called the Swedish phase of the Thirty Years' War (see page 436). French influence became an important factor in the political future of the German Empire. Richelieu acquired for France extensive rights in Alsace in the east and Arras in the north.

In building the French state, Richelieu knew that his approach sometimes seemed to contradict traditional Christian teaching. As a priest and bishop, how did he justify his policies? He developed his own *raison d'état* (reason of state): "Where the interests of the state are concerned, God absolves actions which, if privately committed, would be a crime."[9] Richelieu's successor as chief minister for the next boy-king, Louis XIV, was Cardinal Jules Mazarin (1602–1661). Along with the regent, Queen Mother Anne of Austria, Mazarin continued Richelieu's centralizing policies. His struggle to increase royal revenues to meet the costs of war with Spain led to the uprisings of 1648–1653 known as the **Fronde.** A *frondeur* was originally a street urchin who threw mud at the passing carriages of the rich, but the word came to be applied to the many individuals and groups who opposed the policies of the government. The most influential of these groups were the robe nobility—court judges—and the sword nobility—the aristocracy—both of whom resented growing centralized control. During the first of several riots, the queen mother fled Paris with Louis XIV. As the rebellion continued, civil order broke down completely. In 1651 Anne's regency ended with the declaration of Louis as king in his own right. Much of the rebellion died away, and its leaders came to terms with the government.

Fronde A series of violent uprisings during the minority of Louis XIV triggered by oppressive taxation and growing royal authority; the last attempt of the French nobility to resist the king by arms.

The conflicts of the Fronde had significant results for the future. The twin evils of noble factionalism and popular riots left the French wishing for peace and for a strong monarch to re-impose order. This was the legacy that Louis XIV inherited when he assumed personal rule in 1661. Humiliated by his flight from Paris, he was determined to avoid any recurrence of rebellion.

Louis XIV and Absolutism

The reign of Louis XIV (r. 1643–1715) was the longest in European history, and the French monarchy reached the peak of absolutist development. In the magnificence of his court and the brilliance of the culture that he presided over, the "Sun King" dominated his age.

divine right of kings The belief that God had established kings as his rulers on earth and that they were answerable ultimately to God alone.

Religion, Anne, and Mazarin all taught Louis the doctrine of the **divine right of kings:** God had established kings as his rulers on earth, and they were answerable ultimately to God alone. Though kings were divinely anointed and shared in the sacred nature of divinity, they could not simply do as they pleased. They had to obey God's laws and rule for the good of the people.

Louis worked very hard at the business of governing. He ruled his realm through several councils of state, and insisted on taking a personal role in many of the councils' decisions. He selected councilors from the recently ennobled or the upper middle class because he wanted "people to know by the rank of the men who served him that he had no intention of sharing power with them."[10] Despite increasing financial problems, Louis never called a meeting of the Estates General. The nobility therefore had no means of united expression or action. Nor did Louis have a first minister; he kept himself free from worry about the inordinate power of a Richelieu. Louis also used spying and terror—a secret police force, a system of informers, and the practice of opening private letters—to eliminate potential threats.

Religion was also a tool of national unity under Louis. In 1685 he revoked the Edict of Nantes, by which his grandfather Henry IV had granted liberty of conscience to French Huguenots. The new law ordered the destruction of Huguenot churches, the closing of schools, the Catholic baptism of Huguenots, and the exile of Huguenot pastors who refused to renounce their faith. The result was the departure of some of his most loyal and industrially skilled subjects.

Richelieu had already deprived French Calvinists of political rights and many had converted to Catholicism. Why, then, did Louis XIV undertake such an apparently unnecessary, cruel, and self-destructive measure? First, Louis considered religion primarily a political question. Although he was personally tolerant, he hated division within the realm and insisted that religious unity was essential to his royal dignity and to the security of the state. Second, aristocrats had long petitioned Louis to crack down on Protestants. His decision to do so won him enormous praise.

absolute monarchy A form of government in which sovereignty is vested in a single person, the king or queen; absolute monarchs in the sixteenth and seventeenth centuries based their authority on the theory of the divine right of kings.

Louis's personal hold on power, his exclusion of great nobles from his councils, and his ruthless pursuit of religious unity persuaded many earlier historians that his reign witnessed the creation of an **absolute monarchy.** Louis supposedly crushed the political pretensions of the nobility, leaving them with social grandeur and court posing but no real power. A later generation of historians has revised that view, showing the multiple constraints on Louis's power and his need to cooperate with the nobles. Louis may have declared his absolute power, but in practice he governed through collaboration with nobles, who maintained tremendous prestige and authority in their ancestral lands. Scholars also underline the traditional nature of Louis's motivations. Like his predecessors, Louis XIV sought to enhance

Rubens: The Death of Henri IV and The Proclamation of the Regency (1622–1625)
In 1622 the regent Marie de' Medici commissioned Peter Paul Rubens to paint a cycle of paintings depicting her life. This one portrays two distinct moments: the assassination of Henry IV (shown on the left ascending to Heaven), and Marie's subsequent proclamation as regent. The other twenty-three canvasses in the cycle similarly glorify Marie, a tricky undertaking given her unhappy marriage to Henry IV and her tumultuous relationship with her son Louis XIII, who removed her from the regency in 1617. As in this image, Rubens frequently resorted to allegory and classical imagery to elevate the events of Marie's life. (Réunion des Musées Nationaux/ Art Resource, NY)

the glory of his dynasty and his country, mostly through war. The creation of a new state apparatus was a means to that goal, not an end in itself.

| **Financial and Economic Management Under Louis XIV: Colbert** |

France's ability to build armies and fight wars depended on a strong economy. The king named Jean-Baptiste Colbert (1619–1683), the son of a wealthy merchant-financier of Reims, as controller general of finances. Colbert came to manage the entire royal administration and proved himself a financial genius. His central principle was that the wealth and the economy of France should serve the state. He did not invent the system called "mercantilism," but he rigorously applied it to France.

Mercantilism is a collection of governmental policies for the regulation of economic activities, especially commercial activities, by and for the state. In seventeenth- and eighteenth-century economic theory, a nation's international power was thought to be based on its wealth, specifically its gold supply. Because resources were limited, mercantilist theory held, state intervention was needed to secure the largest part of a limited resource. To accumulate gold, a country always had to sell more goods abroad than it bought. Colbert thus insisted that France should be self-sufficient, able to produce within its borders everything French subjects needed. Consequently, the outflow of gold would be halted; debtor states would pay in bullion; unemployment and poverty would greatly diminish; and with the wealth of the nation increased, its power and prestige would be enhanced.

mercantilism A system of economic regulations aimed at increasing the power of the state.

Colbert supported old industries and created new ones so that France would be self-sufficient. He focused especially on textiles, the most important sector of the economy, reinforcing the system of state inspection and regulation and forming guilds. Colbert encouraged foreign craftsmen to immigrate to France by giving them special privileges, and he worked to bring more female workers into the labor force. To encourage the people to buy French goods, he abolished many domestic tariffs and raised tariffs on foreign products. One of Colbert's most ambitious projects was the creation of a merchant marine to transport French goods. In 1661 France possessed 18 unseaworthy vessels; by 1681 it had 276 working ships manned by trained sailors. In 1664 Colbert founded the Company of the East Indies with (unfulfilled) hopes of competing with the Dutch for Asian trade.

Colbert also hoped to make Canada—rich in untapped minerals and some of the best agricultural land in the world—part of a vast French empire. He sent four thousand peasants from western France to the province of Quebec. (In 1608, one year after the English arrived at Jamestown, Virginia, Sully had established the city of Quebec, which became the capital of French Canada.) Subsequently, the Jesuit Jacques Marquette and the merchant Louis Joliet sailed down the Mississippi River and claimed possession of the land on both sides as far south as present-day Arkansas. In 1684 the French explorer Robert La Salle continued down the Mississippi to its mouth and claimed vast territories and the rich delta for Louis XIV. The area was called, naturally, "Louisiana."

During Colbert's tenure as controller general, Louis was able to pursue his goals without massive tax increases and without creating a stream of new offices. Colbert managed to raise revenues significantly by cracking down on inefficiences and corruption in the tax collection system. The constant pressure of warfare after Colbert's death, however, undid many of his economic achievements.

Louis XIV's Wars

Louis XIV wrote that "the character of a conqueror is regarded as the noblest and highest of titles." In pursuit of the title of conqueror, he kept France at war for thirty-three of the fifty-four years of his personal rule. In 1666 Louis appointed François le Tellier (later, marquis de Louvois) as secretary of state for war. Under the king's watchful eye, Louvois created a professional army that was modern in the sense that the French state, rather than private nobles, employed the soldiers. Louvois utilized several methods in recruiting troops: dragooning, in which press gangs seized men off the streets; conscription; and, after 1688, lottery. With these techniques, the French army grew from roughly 125,000 men in the Thirty Years' War (1618–1648) to 250,000 during the Dutch War (1672–1678) and 340,000 during the War of the League of Augsburg (1688–1697).[11] Uniforms and weapons were standardized and rational systems of training and promotion devised. Many historians believe that the new loyalty, professionalism, and size of the French army is the best case for the success of absolutism under Louis XIV. Whatever his compromises elsewhere, the French monarch had firm control of his armed forces. As in so many other matters, Louis's model was followed across Europe.

Louis's supreme goal was to expand France to what he considered its "natural" borders and to secure those lands from any threat of invasion. His armies managed to expand French borders to include important commercial centers in the Spanish Netherlands and Flanders, as well as all of Franche-Comté between 1667 and 1678. In 1681 Louis seized the city of Strasbourg, and three years later he sent armies into the province of Lorraine. At that moment the king seemed invincible.

In fact, Louis had reached the limit of his expansion. The wars of the 1680s and 1690s brought no additional territories.

Louis understood his wars largely as defensive undertakings, but his neighbors naturally viewed French expansion with great alarm. Louis's wars inspired the formation of Europe-wide coalitions against him. As a result, he was obliged to support a huge army in several different theaters of war. This task placed unbearable strains on French resources, especially given the inequitable system of taxation.

Colbert's successors as minister of finance resorted to the devaluation of the currency and the old device of selling offices and tax exemptions. They also created new direct taxes in 1695 and 1710, which nobles and clergymen had to pay for the first time. In exchange for this money, the king reaffirmed the traditional social hierarchies by granting honors, pensions, and titles to the nobility. Commoners had to pay the new taxes as well as the old ones.

A series of bad harvests between 1688 and 1694 added social to fiscal catastrophe. The price of wheat skyrocketed. The result was widespread starvation, and in many provinces the death rate rose to several times the normal figure. Parish registers reveal that France buried at least one-tenth of its population in those years, perhaps 2 million in 1693 and 1694 alone. Rising grain prices, new taxes for war, a slump in manufacturing, and the constant nuisance of pillaging troops all meant great suffering for the French people. France wanted peace at any price and won a respite for five years, which was shattered by the War of the Spanish Succession (1701–1713).

In 1700 the childless Spanish king Charles II (r. 1665–1700) died, opening a struggle for control of Spain and its colonies. His will bequeathed the Spanish crown and its empire to Philip of Anjou, Louis XIV's grandson (Louis's wife, Maria-Theresa, had been Charles's sister). This testament violated a prior treaty by which the European powers had agreed to divide the Spanish possessions between the king of France and the Holy Roman emperor, both brothers-in-law of Charles II. Claiming that he was following both Spanish and French national interests, Louis broke with the treaty and accepted the will.

In 1701 the English, Dutch, Austrians, and Prussians formed the Grand Alliance against Louis XIV. The allied powers united to prevent France from becoming too strong in Europe and to check France's expanding commercial power in North America, Asia, and Africa. The war dragged on until 1713. The **Peace of Utrecht,** which ended the war, applied the principle of partition. Louis's grandson Philip remained the first Bourbon king of Spain on the understanding that the French and Spanish crowns would never be united. France surrendered Newfoundland, Nova Scotia, and the Hudson Bay territory to England, which also acquired Gibraltar, Minorca, and control of the African slave trade from Spain. The Dutch gained little because Austria received the former Spanish Netherlands (see Map 16.1).

Peace of Utrecht A series of treaties, from 1713 to 1715, that ended the War of the Spanish Succession, ended French expansion in Europe, and marked the rise of the British Empire.

The Peace of Utrecht had important international consequences. It represented the balance-of-power principle in operation, setting limits on the extent to which any one power—in this case, France—could expand. The treaty completed the decline of Spain as a great power. It vastly expanded the British Empire, and it gave European powers experience in international cooperation. The Peace of Utrecht also marked the end of French expansion. Thirty-five years of war had brought rights to all of Alsace and the gain of important cities in the north such as Lille, as well as Strasbourg. But at what price? In 1714 an exhausted France hovered on the brink of bankruptcy. It is no wonder that when Louis XIV died on September 1, 1715, many subjects felt as much relief as they did sorrow.

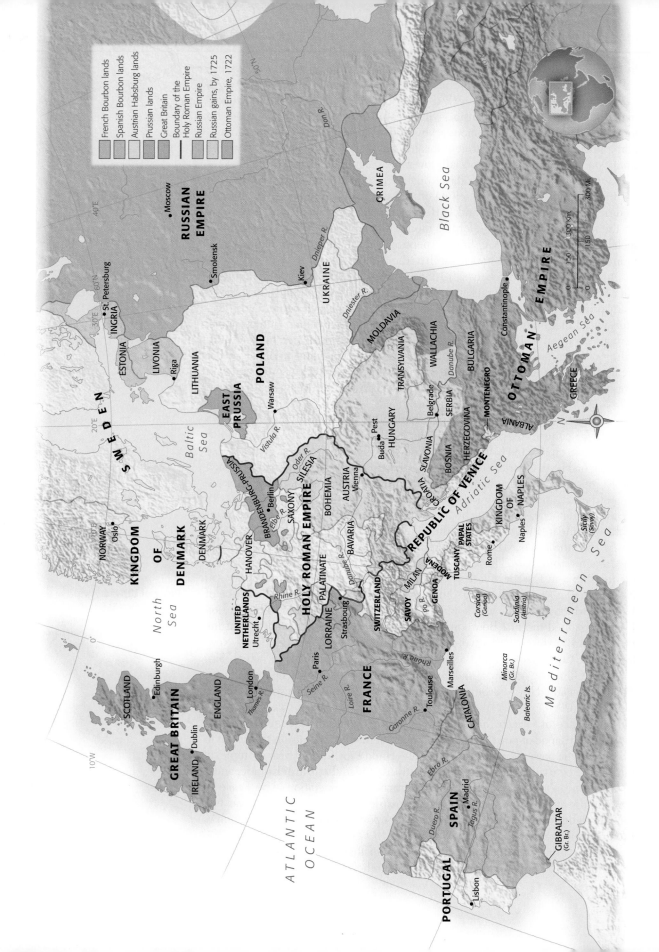

Legend

- French Bourbon lands
- Spanish Bourbon lands
- Austrian Habsburg lands
- Prussian lands
- Great Britain
- Boundary of the Holy Roman Empire
- Russian Empire
- Russian gains, by 1725
- Ottoman Empire, 1722

RUSSIAN EMPIRE

- Moscow
- St. Petersburg
- Smolensk
- Kiev

INGRIA
ESTONIA
LIVONIA
- Riga
LITHUANIA

POLAND
- Warsaw

SWEDEN

EAST PRUSSIA

KINGDOM OF DENMARK

- Oslo
NORWAY
DENMARK

Baltic Sea

North Sea

BRANDENBURG-PRUSSIA
- Berlin
HANOVER

UNITED NETHERLANDS
- Utrecht

SILESIA
SAXONY
BOHEMIA
HOLY ROMAN EMPIRE
AUSTRIA
- Vienna
BAVARIA
PALATINATE
LORRAINE
- Strasbourg
SWITZERLAND
SAVOY
MILAN
MODENA
GENOA
TUSCANY

Buda
- Pest
HUNGARY

MOLDAVIA
TRANSYLVANIA
WALLACHIA
CROATIA
SLAVONIA
REPUBLIC OF VENICE
BOSNIA
HERZEGOVINA
SERBIA
- Belgrade
BULGARIA
MONTENEGRO
ALBANIA

OTTOMAN EMPIRE
- Constantinople
GREECE

CRIMEA
UKRAINE

Black Sea
Aegean Sea
Adriatic Sea

PAPAL STATES
- Rome
KINGDOM OF NAPLES
- Naples

Corsica (Genoa)
Sardinia (Austria)
Sicily (Savoy)

Mediterranean Sea

FRANCE
- Paris
- Toulouse
- Marseilles
CATALONIA
Minorca (Gr. Br.)
Balearic Is.

GREAT BRITAIN
- Edinburgh
SCOTLAND
ENGLAND
- London
IRELAND
- Dublin

ATLANTIC OCEAN

SPAIN
- Madrid
PORTUGAL
- Lisbon
GIBRALTAR (Gr. Br.)

Rivers: Don R., Dnieper R., Dniester R., Danube R., Vistula R., Oder R., Elbe R., Rhine R., Seine R., Loire R., Garonne R., Rhône R., Po R., Ebro R., Duero R., Tagus R., Thames R.

300 Mi.
300 Km.
150
0

50°N
60°N
40°E
30°E
20°E
10°E
0°
10°W

MAPPING THE PAST

MAP 16.1   Europe in 1715

The series of treaties commonly called the Peace of Utrecht (April 1713–November 1715) ended the War of the Spanish Succession and redrew the map of Europe. A French Bourbon king succeeded to the Spanish throne. France surrendered to Austria the Spanish Netherlands (later Belgium), then in French hands, and France recognized the Hohenzollern (HOH-uhn-zol-urn) rulers of Prussia. Spain ceded Gibraltar to Great Britain, for which it has been a strategic naval station ever since. Spain also granted to Britain the *asiento,* the contract for supplying African slaves to America. **[1]** Identify the areas on the map that changed hands as a result of the Peace of Utrecht. How did these changes affect the balance of power in Europe? **[2]** How and why did so many European countries possess scattered or discontiguous territories? What does this suggest about European politics in this period? **[3]** Does this map suggest potential for future conflict?

The Decline of Absolutist Spain in the Seventeenth Century

As French power was growing, Spanish power was diminishing. By the early seventeenth century the seeds of disaster were sprouting. Between 1610 and 1650 Spanish trade with the colonies fell 60 percent, due to competition from local industries in the colonies and from Dutch and English traders. At the same time, the native Indians and African slaves who toiled in the South American silver mines suffered frightful epidemics of disease. Ultimately, the lodes started to run dry, and the quantity of metal produced steadily declined after 1620.

In Madrid, however, royal expenditures constantly exceeded income. To meet mountainous state debt and declining revenues, the Crown repeatedly devalued the coinage and declared bankruptcy. In 1596, 1607, 1627, 1647, and 1680, Spanish kings found no solution to the problem of an empty treasury other than to cancel the national debt. Given the frequency of cancellation, national credit plummeted.

Seventeenth-century Spain was the victim of its past. It could not forget the grandeur of the sixteenth century and respond to changing circumstances. Although Spain lacked the finances to fight expensive wars, the imperial tradition demanded the revival of war with the Dutch at the expiration of a twelve-year truce in 1622 and a long war with France over Mantua (1628–1659). Spain thus became embroiled in the Thirty Years' War. These conflicts, on top of an empty treasury, brought disaster.

In 1640 Spain faced serious revolts in Catalonia and Portugal. The Portuguese succeeded in regaining independence from Habsburg rule under their new king, John IV (r. 1640–1656). In 1643 the French inflicted a crushing defeat on a Spanish army at Rocroi in what is now Belgium. By the Treaty of the Pyrenees of 1659, which ended the French-Spanish conflict, Spain was compelled to surrender extensive territories to France. This treaty marked the decline of Spain as a great military power.

Spain's decline can also be traced to a failure to invest in productive enterprises. In contrast to the other countries of western Europe, Spain had only a tiny middle class. Public opinion, taking its cue from the aristocracy, condemned moneymaking as vulgar and undignified. Thousands entered economically unproductive professions: there were said to be nine thousand monasteries in the province of Castile alone. Some three hundred thousand people who had once been Muslims were expelled by Philip III in 1609, significantly reducing the pool

Peeter Snayers: Spanish Troops (detail)
The long wars that Spain fought over Dutch independence, in support of Habsburg interests in Germany, and against France left the country militarily exhausted and financially drained by the mid-1600s. Here, Spanish troops—thin, emaciated, and probably unpaid—straggle away from battle. (Museo Nacional del Prado, Madrid. Photo: José Baztan y Alberto Otero)

of skilled workers and merchants. Those working in the textile industry were forced out of business when the flood of gold and silver produced severe inflation, pushing their production costs to the point where they could not compete in colonial and international markets. Other businessmen found so many obstacles in the way of profitable enterprise that they simply gave up.[12] Spanish aristocrats, attempting to maintain an extravagant lifestyle they could no longer afford, increased the rents on their estates. High rents and heavy taxes in turn drove the peasants from the land. Agricultural production suffered, and peasants departed for the large cities, where they swelled the ranks of unemployed beggars.

Spanish leaders seemed to lack the will to reform. If one can discern personality from pictures, the portraits of Philip III (r. 1598–1622), Philip IV (r. 1622–1665), and Charles II (r. 1665–1700) hanging in the Prado, the Spanish national museum in Madrid, reflect the increasing weakness of the dynasty. Pessimism and fatalism permeated national life. In the reign of Philip IV, a royal council was appointed to plan the construction of a canal linking the Tagus and Manzanares Rivers in Spain. After interminable debate, the committee decided that "if God had intended the rivers to be navigable, He would have made them so." Spain ignored new scientific methods because they came from heretical nations, Holland and England.

In the brilliant novel ***Don Quixote*** (dohn kee-HOH-tee), Spanish writer Miguel de Cervantes (1547–1616) produced one of the great masterpieces of world literature. The main character, Don Quixote, lives in a world of dreams, traveling about the countryside seeking military glory. From the title of the book, the English language has borrowed the word *quixotic*. Meaning "idealistic but

Don Quixote A novel authored by Miguel de Cervantes that is perhaps the greatest work of Spanish literature. It is a survey of the entire fabric of Spanish society that can be read on several levels: as a burlesque of chivalric romances and as an exploration of conflicting views (idealistic vs. realistic) of life and of the world.

impractical," the term characterizes seventeenth-century Spain. As a leading scholar has written, "The Spaniard convinced himself that reality was what he felt, believed, imagined. He filled the world with heroic reverberations. Don Quixote was born and grew."[13]

The Culture of Absolutism

What cultural forms flourished under absolutist governments?

Under absolutist monarchs, culture became an instrument of state power. The **baroque style** in art and music flourished in Spain, Italy, and Central Europe. Baroque masters like Rubens painted portraits celebrating the glory of European monarchs. Architecture became an important tool for the French monarch Louis XIV, who made the magnificent palace of Versailles (vehr-SIGH) the center of his kingdom, inspiring imitators across Europe (see Chapter 17). Even language reflected the growing power of the French crown. Within France Richelieu established an academy to oversee French literature and language. Outside its borders French became the common language of the European elite.

Baroque Art and Music

Rome and the revitalized Catholic church of the later sixteenth century played an important role in the early development of the baroque. As we have seen (pages 539–540), the papacy and the Jesuits encouraged the growth of an intensely emotional, exuberant art aimed at kindling the faith of ordinary churchgoers. In addition to this underlying religious emotionalism, the baroque drew its sense of drama, motion, and ceaseless striving from the art and architecture of the Catholic Reformation. Yet baroque art was more than just "Catholic art" in the seventeenth century and the first half of the eighteenth. True, neither Protestant England nor the Netherlands ever came fully under the spell of the baroque, but neither did Catholic France. And Protestants accounted for some of the finest examples of baroque style, especially in music. The baroque style spread partly because its tension and bombast spoke to an agitated age that was experiencing great violence and controversy in politics and religion.

In painting, the baroque reached maturity early with the painter Peter Paul Rubens (1577–1640). Rubens studied the masters of the High Renaissance such as Michelangelo but developed his own style, which was characterized by animated figures, melodramatic contrasts, and monumental size. Rubens excelled in glorifying monarchs such as Queen Mother Marie de' Medici of France (see the painting on page 409). He was also a devout Catholic; nearly half of his pictures treat Christian subjects. Yet one of Rubens's trademarks was fleshy, sensual nudes who populate his canvases as Roman goddesses, water nymphs, and remarkably voluptuous saints and angels.

In music, the baroque style reached its culmination almost a century later in the dynamic, soaring lines of Johann Sebastian Bach (1685–1750), an organist and choirmaster of several Lutheran churches across Germany. Bach's organ music combined the baroque spirit of invention, tension, and emotion in both secular concertos and sublime religious cantatas. Unlike Rubens, Bach was not fully appreciated in his lifetime, but since the early nineteenth century his reputation has grown steadily.

baroque style An intensely emotional and exuberant style of art, practiced by artists such as Rubens and associated with the late-sixteenth-century Catholic Reformation; in music, it reached maturity almost a century later with the compositions of Bach.

Juan de Pareja: The Calling of Saint Matthew
Using rich but subdued colors, Pareja depicts the biblical text (Mark 2:13–17), with Jesus in traditional first-century dress and the other figures, arranged around a table covered with an oriental carpet, in seventeenth-century apparel. Matthew, at Jesus's right hand, seems surprised by the "call." Pareja, following a long tradition, includes himself (*standing, far left*).
(Museo Nacional del Prado, Madrid/The Bridgeman Art Library)

Court Culture

In 1682 Louis formally established his court at Versailles, which became the center of the kingdom: a model of rational order and the perfect symbol of the king's power. The art and architecture of Versailles were tools of Louis's policy, used to overawe his subjects and foreign visitors. The Russian tsar Peter the Great imitated Versailles in the construction of his palace, Peterhof, as did the Prussian emperor Frederick the Great in his palace at Potsdam outside Berlin and the Habsburgs at Schonbrunn outside Vienna. (See the feature "Images in Society: Absolutist Palace Building" on pages 440–441.)

The palace was the summit of political, social, and cultural life. The king required all great nobles to spend at least part of the year in attendance on him at Versailles. Between three thousand and ten thousand people occupied the palace each day. Given the demand for space, even high nobles had to make do with cramped and uncomfortable living quarters. The palace gardens, and the palace itself on some occasions, were open to the public, allowing even local peasants a glimpse of their sovereign. More than a royal residence or administrative center, Versailles was a mirror of French greatness to the world.

Much has been made of the "domestication" of the nobility at Versailles. Nobles had to follow a tortuous system of court etiquette, and they vied for the honor of serving the monarch, with the highest in rank claiming the privilege to hand the king his shirt when he dressed. These rituals were far from meaningless or trivial. The king controlled immense resources and privileges; access to him meant favored treatment for pensions, military and religious posts, honorary titles, and a host of other benefits. Courtiers sought these rewards for themselves and for their family members and followers. As in ancient Rome, a patronage system—in which higher-ranked individuals protected lower-ranked ones in return for loyalty and services—dominated political life. Patronage flowed from the court to the provinces; it was the mechanism through which Louis gained cooperation from social elites.

Although they were denied public offices and posts, women played a central role in the patronage system. At court, the king's wife, mistresses, and other female relatives used their high rank to establish their own patronage relations. They recommended individuals for honors, advocated policy decisions, and brokered alliances between noble factions. Noblewomen played a similar role, bringing their family connections to marriage to form powerful social networks. Onlookers sometimes resented the influence of powerful women at court. The Duke of Saint-Simon said of Madame de Maintenon, Louis XIV's mistress and secret second wife:

> *The power of Madame de Maintenon was, as may be imagined, immense. She had everybody in her hands, from the highest and most favored ministers to the meanest subject of the realm. Many people have been ruined by her, without having been able to discover the author of the ruin, search as they might.*

French Classicism

To this day, culture is a central element of French national pride and identity. French emphasis on culture dates back to Cardinal Richelieu, whose efforts at state centralization embraced cultural activities. In 1635 he gave official recognition to a group of scholars interested in grammar and rhetoric. Thus was born the French Academy, which prepared a dictionary to standardize the French language; the dictionary was completed in 1694 and has been updated in many successive editions. The Academy survives today as a prestigious society and retains authority over correct usage in the French language.

Scholars characterize the art and literature of the age of Louis XIV as **French classicism.** By this they mean that the artists and writers of the late seventeenth century imitated the subject matter and style of classical antiquity, that their work resembled that of Renaissance Italy, and that French art possessed the classical qualities of discipline, balance, and restraint. This was a movement away from the perceived excesses of baroque style.

French classicism A style of French art, architecture, and literature (ca. 1600–1750), based on admiration and imitation of Greek and Roman models but with greater exuberance and complexity.

Louis XIV was an enthusiastic patron of the arts. Music and theater frequently served as backdrops for court ceremonials. Louis favored Jean-Baptiste Lully (1632–1687), whose orchestral works combined lively animation with the restrained austerity typical of French classicism. Louis also supported François Couperin (1668–1733), whose harpsichord and organ works possessed the regal grandeur the king loved, and Marc-Antoine Charpentier (1634–1704), whose solemn religious music entertained him at meals.

Louis XIV loved the stage, and in the plays of Molière (mohl-YAIR) (1622–1673) and Racine (ra-SEEN) (1639–1699) his court witnessed the finest achievements in the history of the French theater. As playwright, stage manager, director, and actor, Molière (born Jean-Baptiste Poquelin) produced comedies that exposed the hypocrisies and follies of polite society through brilliant caricature. *Tartuffe* (tahr-TOOF) satirized the religious hypocrite; his plays *Le Bourgeois Gentilhomme* (The Bourgeois Gentleman) and *Les Précieuses ridicules* (The Pretentious Young Ladies) mocked the social pretensions of the bourgeoisie, stopping short of criticizing the high nobility.

- The baroque style, practiced by artists such as Rubens, was intensely emotional and exuberant; it was particularly associated with the late sixteenth century Catholic Reformation, but appeared in both religious and secular themes and in Protestant artists.

- Baroque composers such as Bach combined invention, tension, and emotion in their music, much of which was organ music played in church.

- The palace at Versailles was the showpiece and center of the French kingdom, crowded with nobles vying for the king's favor and patronage

- French classicism, a movement reviving classical antiquity in art and literature, was popular during the reign of Louis XIV; theater also gained popularity with playwrights such as the comic Molière and the tragedian Racine.

- The French language was adopted by elites across Europe for diplomacy, scholarship, and polite conversation.

constitutionalism A form of government in which power is limited by law and balanced between the authority and power of the government on the one hand, and the rights and liberties of the subject or citizen on the other hand.

Molière's contemporary Jean Racine based his tragic dramas on Greek and Roman legends. His persistent theme was the conflict of good and evil. Several plays—*Andromaque* (ahn-dro-MAK), Bérénice (bear-ay-NEES), Iphigénie (if-ee-jay-NEE), and *Phèdre* (FAY-druh)—bear the names of women and deal with the power of female passion. For simplicity of language, symmetrical structure, and calm restraint, the plays of Racine represent the finest examples of French classicism.

Louis XIV's reign inaugurated the use of French as the language of polite society, international diplomacy, and, gradually, scholarship and learning. The royal courts of Sweden, Russia, Poland, and Germany all spoke French. France inspired a cosmopolitan European culture in the late seventeenth century, which looked to Versailles as its center.

Constitutionalism

What is constitutionalism, and how did this form of government emerge in England and the Dutch Republic?

While France and later Prussia, Russia, and Austria (see Chapter 17) developed the absolutist state, England and Holland evolved toward **constitutionalism**, which is the limitation of government by law. Constitutionalism also implies a balance between the authority and power of the government, on the one hand, and the rights and liberties of the subjects, on the other.

A nation's constitution may be written or unwritten. It may be embodied in one basic document, occasionally revised by amendment, like the Constitution of the United States. Or it may be only partly formalized and include parliamentary statutes, judicial decisions, and a body of traditional procedures and practices, like the English and Dutch constitutions. Whether written or unwritten, a constitution gets its binding force from the government's acknowledgment that it must respect that constitution—that is, that the state must govern according to the laws.

Absolutist Claims in England (1603–1649)

In 1588 Queen Elizabeth I of England exercised very great personal power; by 1689 the English monarchy was severely circumscribed. Change in England was anything but orderly. Seventeenth-century England executed one king and experienced a bloody civil war; experimented with military dictatorship, then restored the son of the murdered king; and finally, after a bloodless revolution, established constitutional monarchy. Political stability came only in the 1690s. After such a violent and tumultuous century, how did England produce a constitutional monarchy?

A rare and politically astute female monarch, Elizabeth was able to maintain control over her realm in part by refusing to marry and submit to a husband. The problem with this strategy was that it left the queen with no immediate heir to continue her legacy.

In 1603 Elizabeth's Scottish cousin James Stuart succeeded her as James I (r. 1603–1625). King James was well educated and had thirty-five years' experience as king of Scotland. But he was not as interested in displaying the majesty of monarchy as Elizabeth had been. Urged to wave at the crowds who waited to greet their new ruler, James complained that he was tired and threatened to drop his breeches "so they can cheer at my arse." Moreover, in contrast to Elizabeth, James was a poor judge of character, and in a society already hostile to the Scots, James's

Scottish accent was a disadvantage.[14] James's greatest problem, however, stemmed from his belief that a monarch has a divine (or God-given) right to his authority and is responsible only to God. James went so far as to lecture the House of Commons: "There are no privileges and immunities which can stand against a divinely appointed King." This notion, implying total royal jurisdiction over the liberties, persons, and properties of English men and women, formed the basis of the Stuart concept of absolutism. Such a view ran directly counter to the long-standing English idea that a person's property could not be taken away without due process of law. James's expression of such views before the English House of Commons was a grave political mistake, especially given the royal debt that he had inherited from Elizabeth. The House of Commons guarded the state's pocketbook.

In England, unlike France, there was no social stigma attached to paying taxes. Members of the wealthy House of Commons were willing to assess and pay taxes to ease the royal debt provided they had some say in the formulation of state policies. James I and his son Charles I, however, considered such ambitions intolerable and a threat to their divine-right prerogative. Consequently, at every Parliament between 1603 and 1640, bitter squabbles erupted between the Crown and the articulate and legally minded Commons. Charles I's attempt to govern without Parliament (1629–1640) and to finance his government by arbitrary nonparliamentary levies brought the country to a crisis.

Religious Divides   Religious issues also embittered relations between the king and the House of Commons. In the early seventeenth century increasing numbers of English people felt dissatisfied with the Church of England established by Henry VIII and reformed by Elizabeth. Many **Puritans** believed that the Reformation had not gone far enough. They wanted to "purify" the Anglican church of Roman Catholic elements—elaborate vestments and ceremonials, bishops, and even the giving and wearing of wedding rings.

It is difficult to establish what proportion of the English population was Puritan. According to present scholarly consensus, the dominant religious groups in the early seventeenth century were Calvinist; their more zealous members were Puritans. It also seems clear that many English people were attracted by Calvinism's emphasis on hard work, sobriety, thrift, competition, and postponement of pleasure. These values, which have frequently been called the "Protestant ethic" or "capitalist ethic," fit in precisely with the economic approaches and practices of many successful business people and farmers. While it is hazardous to identify capitalism with Protestantism—there were many successful Catholic capitalists, for example—the "Protestant virtues" represented the prevailing values of members of the House of Commons.

Puritans wanted to abolish bishops in the Church of England, and when James I said, "No bishop, no king," he meant that the bishops were among the chief supporters of the throne. Under Charles I, people believed that the country was being led back to Roman Catholicism. Not only did he marry a French Catholic princess, but he also supported the policies of the Archbishop of Canterbury William Laud (1573–1645), who tried to impose elaborate ritual on all churches.

In 1637 Laud attempted to impose two new elements on church organization in Scotland: a new prayer book, modeled on the Anglican *Book of Common Prayer*, and bishoprics, which the Presbyterian Scots firmly rejected. The Scots therefore revolted. To finance an army to put down the Scots, King Charles was compelled to summon Parliament in November 1640.

Puritans Members of a sixteenth- and seventeenth-century reform movement within the Church of England that advocated "purifying" it of Roman Catholic elements, such as bishops, elaborate ceremonials, and the wedding ring.

a Confectioner   a Smith   a Sho=maker   a Taylor

a Sadler   a Porter   a Box-maker   a Sope-boyler

a Glover   a Meal-man   a Chick en-man   a Button-maker

Puritan Occupations

These twelve engravings depict typical Puritan occupations and show that the Puritans came primarily from the artisan and lower middle classes. The governing classes and peasants adhered to the traditions of the Church of England. (Visual Connection Archive)

Charles I was an intelligent man, but contemporaries found him deceitful and treacherous. After quarreling with Parliament over his right to collect customs duties on wine and wool and over what the Commons perceived as religious innovations, Charles had dissolved Parliament in 1629. From 1629 to 1640, he ruled without Parliament, financing his government through extraordinary stopgap levies considered illegal by most English people. For example, the king revived a medieval law requiring coastal districts to help pay the cost of ships for defense, but he levied the tax, called "ship money," on inland as well as coastal counties. Most members of Parliament believed that such taxation without consent amounted to despotism. Consequently, they were not willing to trust the king with an army. Moreover, many supported the Scots' resistance to Charles's religious innovations and had little wish for military action against them. Accordingly, this Parliament, called the "Long Parliament" because it sat from 1640 to 1660, enacted legislation that limited the power of the monarch and made arbitrary government impossible.

In 1641 the Commons passed the Triennial Act, which compelled the king to summon Parliament every three years. The Commons impeached Archbishop Laud and then went further and threatened to abolish bishops. King Charles, fearful of a Scottish invasion—the original reason for summoning Parliament—accepted these measures. Understanding and peace were not achieved, however, partly because radical members of the Commons pushed increasingly revolutionary propositions, and partly because Charles maneuvered to rescind those he had already approved.

The next act in the conflict was precipitated by the outbreak of rebellion in Ireland, where English governors and landlords had long exploited the people. In 1641 the Catholic gentry of Ireland led an uprising in response to a feared invasion by anti-Catholic forces of the British Long Parliament.

Without an army, Charles I could neither come to terms with the Scots nor respond to the Irish rebellion. After a failed attempt to arrest parliamentary leaders who remained unwilling to grant him an army, Charles left London for the north of England. There, he recruited an army drawn from the nobility and its cavalry staff, the rural gentry, and mercenaries. The parliamentary army was composed of the militia of the city of London, country squires with business connections, and men with a firm belief in the spiritual duty of serving.

The English civil war (1642–1649) pitted the power of the king against that of the Parliament. After three years of fighting, Parliament's **New Model Army** defeated the king's armies at the battles of Naseby and Langport in the summer of 1645. Charles, though, refused to concede defeat and accept restrictions on royal authority and church reform. Both sides jockeyed for position, waiting for a decisive event. This arrived in the form of the army under the leadership of Oliver Cromwell, a member of the House of Commons. In 1647 Cromwell's forces captured the king and dismissed members of the Parliament who opposed his actions. In 1649 the remaining representatives, known as the "Rump Parliament," put Charles on trial for high treason, a severe blow to the theory of divine-right monarchy. Charles was found guilty and beheaded on January 30, 1649, an act that sent shock waves around Europe.

New Model Army The parliamentary army, under the command of Oliver Cromwell, that fought the army of Charles I in the English civil war.

Puritanical Absolutism in England: Cromwell and the Protectorate

With the execution of Charles, kingship was abolished. A *commonwealth*, or republican government, was proclaimed. Theoretically, legislative power rested in the surviving members of Parliament, and executive power was lodged in a council of state. In fact, the army that had defeated the king controlled the government, and Oliver Cromwell controlled the army. Though called the **Protectorate**, the rule of Cromwell (1653–1658) constituted military dictatorship.

The army prepared a constitution, the Instrument of Government (1653), that invested executive power in a lord protector (Cromwell) and a council of state. The instrument provided for triennial parliaments and gave Parliament the sole power to raise taxes. But after repeated disputes, Cromwell dismissed Parliament in 1655 and the instrument was never formally endorsed. Cromwell continued the standing army and proclaimed quasi-martial law. He divided England into twelve military districts, each governed by a major general. Reflecting Puritan ideas of morality, Cromwell's state forbade sports, kept the theaters closed, and rigorously censored the press.

On the issue of religion, Cromwell favored some degree of toleration, and the Instrument of Government gave all Christians except Roman Catholics the right to practice their faith. Cromwell had long associated Catholicism in Ireland with sedition and heresy. In September of the year that his army came to power, it crushed a rebellion at Drogheda and massacred the garrison. Another massacre followed in October. These brutal acts left a legacy of Irish hatred for England. After Cromwell's departure for England, the atrocities worsened. The English banned Catholicism in Ireland, executed priests, and confiscated land from Catholics for English and Scottish settlers.

Cromwell adopted mercantilist policies similar to those of absolutist France. He enforced a Navigation Act (1651) requiring that English goods be transported on English ships. The Navigation Act was a great boost to the development of an English merchant marine and brought about a short but successful war with the commercially threatened Dutch. Cromwell also welcomed the immigration of Jews because of their skills, and they began to return to England after four centuries of absence.

The Protectorate collapsed when Cromwell died in 1658 and his ineffectual son, Richard, succeeded him. Having lost support of the army, Richard was forced to abdicate. Fed up with military rule, the English longed for a return to civilian government and, with it, common law and social stability. By 1660 they were ready to restore the monarchy.

Protectorate The military dictatorship established by Oliver Cromwell following the execution of Charles I in 1649.

Cartoon of 1649: "The Royall Oake of Brittayne"

Chopping down this tree signifies the end of royal authority, stability, Magna Carta (see page 205), and the rule of law. As pigs graze (representing the unconcerned common people), being fattened for slaughter, Oliver Cromwell, with his feet in Hell, quotes Scripture. This is a royalist view of the collapse of Charles I's government and the rule of Cromwell. (Courtesy of the Trustees of the British Museum)

Test Act Written in 1673, this act stated that those who refused to receive the Eucharist of the Church of England could not vote, hold public office, preach, teach, attend the universities, or even assemble for meetings.

The Restoration of the English Monarchy

The Restoration of 1660 brought Charles II (r. 1660–1685) to the throne at the invitation of a special session of Parliament called for that purpose. He was the eldest son of Charles I and had been living on the European continent. Both houses of Parliament were also restored, together with the established Anglican church, the courts of law, and the system of local government through justices of the peace. The Restoration failed to resolve two serious problems, however. What was to be the attitude of the state toward Puritans, Catholics, and dissenters from the established church? And what was to be the relationship between the king and Parliament?

Charles II, an easygoing and sensual man, was not interested in imposing religious uniformity on the English, but members of Parliament were. They enacted the **Test Act** of 1673 against those who refused to receive the Eucharist of the Church of England, denying them the right to vote, hold public office, preach, teach, attend the universities, or even assemble for meetings. But these restrictions could not be enforced. When the Quaker William Penn held a meeting of his Friends and was arrested, the jury refused to convict him.

In politics Charles II was determined "not to set out in his travels again," which meant that he intended to avoid exile by working well with Parliament. Therefore he appointed a council of five men to serve both as his major advisers and as members of Parliament, thus acting as liaison agents between the executive and the legislature. This body—known as the "Cabal" from the names of its five members (Clifford, Arlington, Buckingham, Ashley-Cooper, and Lauderdale)—was an ancestor of the later cabinet system. It gradually came to be accepted that the Cabal was answerable in Parliament for the decisions of the king. This development gave rise to the concept of ministerial responsibility: royal ministers must answer to the Commons.

Harmony between the Crown and Parliament was upset in 1670, however. When Parliament did not grant Charles an adequate income, he entered into a secret agreement with his cousin Louis XIV. The French king would give Charles two hundred thousand pounds annually, and in return Charles would relax the laws against Catholics, gradually re-Catholicize England, support French policy against the Dutch, and convert to Catholicism himself. When the details of this treaty leaked out, a great wave of anti-Catholic fear swept England. This fear was compounded by a crucial fact: with no legitimate heir, Charles would be succeeded by his Catholic brother, James, duke of York. A combination of hatred for French absolutism and hostility to Catholicism produced virtual hysteria. The Commons passed an exclusion bill denying the succession to a Roman Catholic, but Charles quickly dissolved Parliament, and the bill never became law.

When James II (r. 1685–1688) succeeded his brother, the worst English anti-Catholic fears, already aroused by Louis XIV's revocation of the Edict of Nantes, were realized. In violation of the Test Act, James appointed Roman Catholics to positions in the army, the universities, and local government. When these actions were challenged in the courts, the judges, whom James had appointed, decided for the king. The king was suspending the law at will and appeared to be reviving the absolutism of his father and grandfather. He went further. Attempting to broaden his base of support with Protestant dissenters and nonconformists, James issued a declaration of indulgence granting religious freedom to all.

Two events gave the signals for revolution. First, seven bishops of the Church of England were imprisoned in the Tower of London for protesting the declaration of indulgence but were subsequently acquitted amid great public enthusiasm. Second, in June 1688 James's second wife produced a male heir. The fear of a Roman Catholic dynasty supported by France and ruling outside the law prompted a group of eminent persons to offer the English throne to James's Protestant daughter Mary and her Dutch husband, Prince William of Orange. In December 1688 James II, his queen, and their infant son fled to France and became pensioners of Louis XIV. Early in 1689 William and Mary were crowned king and queen of England.

The Triumph of England's Parliament: Constitutional Monarchy and Cabinet Government

The English call the events of 1688 and 1689 the "Glorious Revolution" because it replaced one king with another with a minimum of bloodshed. It also represented the destruction, once and for all, of the idea of divine-right monarchy. William and Mary accepted the English throne from Parliament and in so doing explicitly recognized the supremacy of Parliament. The revolution of 1688 established the principle that sovereignty, the ultimate power in the state, was divided between king and Parliament and that the king ruled with the consent of the governed.

The men who brought about the revolution quickly framed their intentions in the Bill of Rights, the cornerstone of the modern British constitution. The principles of the Bill of Rights were formulated in direct response to Stuart absolutism. Law was to be made in Parliament; once made, it could not be suspended by the Crown. Parliament had to be called at least once every three years. Both elections to and debate in Parliament were to be free in the sense that the Crown was not to interfere in them (this aspect of the bill was widely disregarded in the eighteenth century). The independence of the judiciary was established, and there was to be no standing army in peacetime. And while Protestants could possess arms, the feared Catholic minority could not. Additional legislation granted freedom of worship to Protestant dissenters and nonconformists and required that the English monarch always be Protestant.

Second Treatise of Civil Government A work of political philosophy published by John Locke in 1690 that argued government's only purpose was to defend the natural rights of life, liberty, and property. A justification of the Glorious Revolution of 1688 to 1689.

The Glorious Revolution and the concept of representative government found its best defense in political philosopher John Locke's *Second Treatise of Civil Government* (1690). Locke (1632–1704) maintained that a government that oversteps its proper function—protecting the natural rights of life, liberty, and property—becomes a tyranny. By "natural" rights Locke meant rights basic to all men because all have the ability to reason. Under a tyrannical government, the people have the natural right to rebellion. Such rebellion can be avoided if the government carefully respects the rights of citizens and if people zealously defend their liberty. Locke linked economic liberty and private property with political freedom. On the basis of this link, he justified limiting the vote to property owners.

The events of 1688 and 1689 did not constitute a *democratic* revolution. The revolution placed sovereignty in Parliament, and Parliament represented the upper classes. The great majority of English people acquired no say in their government. The English revolution established a constitutional monarchy; it also inaugurated an age of aristocratic government that lasted at least until 1832 and in many ways until 1928, when women received full voting rights.

The Dutch Republic in the Seventeenth Century

In the late sixteenth century the seven northern provinces of the Netherlands fought for and won their independence from Spain. The independence of the Republic of the United Provinces of the Netherlands was recognized in 1648, in the treaty that ended the Thirty Years' War. The seventeenth century witnessed an unparalleled flowering of Dutch scientific, artistic, and literary achievement. In this period, often called the "golden age of the Netherlands," Dutch ideas and attitudes played a profound role in shaping a new and modern worldview. At the same time, the United Provinces was another model of the development of the modern constitutional state.

The government of the United Provinces had none of the standard categories of seventeenth-century political organization. The Dutch were not monarchical but rather fiercely republican. Within each province, an oligarchy of wealthy merchants and financiers called "regents" handled domestic affairs in the local Estates (assemblies). The provincial Estates held virtually all the power. A federal assembly, or **States General,** handled matters of foreign affairs, such as war. But the States General did not possess sovereign authority; all issues had to be referred back to the local Estates for approval. In each province, the Estate appointed an executive officer, known as the **stadtholder** (STAT-hohl-der), who carried out ceremonial functions and was responsible for military defense. Although in theory freely chosen by the Estates and answerable to them, in practice the Princes of Orange were almost always chosen as stadtholders. Tensions persisted between supporters of the staunchly republican Estates and those of the aristocratic House of Orange. Holland, which had the largest navy and the most wealth, dominated the seven provinces of the republic and the States General.

States General The national assembly of the United Provinces of the Netherlands; because many issues had to be refereed back to the provinces, the United Provinces was a confederation, or weak union of strong states.

stadtholder The chief executive officer in each province of the United Provinces; in the seventeenth century these positions were often held by the princes of the House of Orange.

The political success of the Dutch rested on the phenomenal commercial prosperity of the Netherlands. The moral and ethical bases of that commercial wealth were thrift, frugality, and religious toleration. As long as business people conducted their religion in private, the government did not interfere with them. Although there is scattered evidence of anti-Semitism, Jews enjoyed a level of acceptance and assimilation in Dutch business and general culture unique in early modern Europe. (See the feature "Individuals in Society: Glückel of Hameln.") For example, Benedict Spinoza (1632–1677), a descendant of Spanish Jews who fled the Inquisition, passed his entire life in Amsterdam, supporting himself as a

Individuals in Society

Glückel of Hameln

In 1690 a Jewish widow in the small German town of Hameln* in Lower Saxony sat down to write her autobiography. She wanted to distract her mind from the terrible grief she felt over the death of her husband and to provide her twelve children with a record "so you will know from what sort of people you have sprung, lest today or tomorrow your beloved children or grand-children came and know naught of their family." Out of her pain and heightened consciousness, Glückel (1646–1724) produced an invaluable source for scholars.

She was born in Hamburg two years before the end of the Thirty Years' War. In 1649 the merchants of Hamburg expelled the Jews, who moved to nearby Altona, then under Danish rule. When the Swedes overran Altona (1657–1658), the Jews returned to Hamburg "purely at the mercy of the Town Council." Glückel's narrative proceeds against a background of the constant harassment to which Jews were subjected—special papers, permits, bribes—and in Hameln she wrote, "And so it has been to this day and, I fear, will continue in like fashion."

When Glückel was "barely twelve," her father betrothed her to Chayim Hameln (**HI-um HAH-muhln**). She married at age fourteen. She describes him as "the perfect pattern of the pious Jew," a man who stopped his work every day for study and prayer, fasted, and was scrupulously honest in his business dealings. Only a few years older than Glückel, Chayim earned his living dealing in precious metals and in making small loans on pledges (articles held on security). This work required his constant travel to larger cities, markets, and fairs, often in bad weather, always over dangerous roads. Chayim consulted his wife about all his business dealings. As he lay dying, a friend asked if he had any last wishes. "None," he replied. "My wife knows everything. She shall do as she has always done." For thirty years Glückel had been his friend, full business partner, and wife. They had thirteen children, twelve of whom survived their father, eight then unmarried. As Chayim had foretold, Glückel succeeded in launching the boys in careers and in providing dowries for the girls.

Glückel's world was her family, the Jewish community of Hameln, and the Jewish communities into which her children married. Social and business activities took her to Amsterdam, Baiersdorf, Bamberg, Berlin, Cleves, Danzig, Metz, and Vienna, so her world was not narrow or provincial. She took great pride that Prince Frederick of Cleves, later the king of Prussia, danced at the wedding of her eldest daughter. The rising prosperity of Chayim's businesses allowed the couple to maintain up to six servants.

Gentleness and deep mutual devotion seem to pervade Rembrandt's *The Jewish Bride*. (Rijksmuseum-Stichting Amsterdam)

Glückel was deeply religious, and her culture was steeped in Jewish literature, legends, and mystical and secular works. Above all, she relied on the Bible. Her language, heavily sprinkled with scriptural references, testifies to a rare familiarity with the basic book of Western civilization. The Scriptures were her consolation, the source of her great strength in a hostile world.

Students who would learn about business practices, the importance of the dowry in marriage, childbirth, the ceremony of bris, birthrates, family celebrations, and even the meaning of life can gain a good deal from the memoirs of this extraordinary woman who was, in the words of one of her descendants, the poet Heinrich Heine, "the gift of a world to me."

Questions for Analysis

1. Consider the ways in which Glückel of Hameln was both an ordinary and an extraordinary woman of her times. Would you call her a marginal or a central person in her society?

2. How was Glückel's life affected by the broad events and issues of the seventeenth century?

Source: The Memoirs of Glückel of Hameln (New York: Schocken Books, 1977).

---

* A town immortalized by the Brothers Grimm. In 1284 the town contracted with the Pied Piper to rid it of rats and mice; he lured them away by playing his flute. When the citizens refused to pay, he charmed away their children in revenge.

Jan Steen: The Christening Feast

As the mother, surrounded by midwives, rests in bed *(rear left)* and the father proudly displays the swaddled child, thirteen other people, united by gestures and gazes, prepare the celebratory meal. Very prolific, Steen was a master of warm-hearted domestic scenes. In contrast to the order and cleanliness of many seventeenth-century Dutch genre paintings, Steen's more disorderly portrayals gave rise to the epithet "a Jan Steen household," meaning an untidy house. (Wallace Collection, London/The Bridgeman Art Library)

lens grinder while producing important philosophical treatises. In the Dutch Republic, toleration paid off: it attracted a great deal of foreign capital and investment. People of all races and creeds traded in Amsterdam, at whose docks on the Amstel River five thousand ships were berthed.

The Dutch came to dominate the shipping business by putting profits from their original industry—herring fishing—into shipbuilding. They boasted the lowest shipping rates and largest merchant marine in Europe. Their shipping power allowed them to control the Baltic grain trade, buying entire crops in Poland, eastern Prussia, and Swedish Pomerania. Because the Dutch dealt in bulk, nobody could undersell them. Foreign merchants coming to Amsterdam could buy anything from precision lenses for the microscope (recently invented by Dutchman Anton van Leeuwenhoek) to muskets for an army of five thousand. Although Dutch cities became famous for their exports—diamonds and linens from Haarlem, pottery from Delft—Dutch wealth depended less on exports than on transport.

In 1602 leaders of the Estate of Holland formed the **Dutch East India Company,** a joint stock company. The investors each received a percentage of the profits proportional to the amount of money they had put in. Within half a century the Dutch East India Company had cut heavily into Portuguese trading in East Asia. The Dutch seized the Cape of Good Hope, Ceylon, and Malacca and established trading posts in each place. In the 1630s the Dutch East India Company was paying its investors about a 35 percent annual return on their investments. The Dutch West India Company, founded in 1621, traded extensively with Latin America and Africa (see Map 16.2). Ultimately both companies would move beyond trading to imperialist exploitation.

Trade and commerce brought the Dutch the highest standard of living in Europe, and perhaps in the world. Salaries were high for all workers except women, but even women's wages were high when compared with those of women in other parts of Europe. All classes of society, including unskilled laborers, ate well. Massive granaries held surplus supplies so that the price of bread remained low. A higher

Dutch East India Company A joint stock company chartered by the States General of the Netherlands to expand trade and promote relations between the Dutch government and its colonial ventures. It established a colony at the Cape of Good Hope (1652), and in the 1630s it paid a return of 35 percent on investments.

percentage of the worker's income could therefore be spent on fish, cheese, butter, vegetables, and even meat. A scholar has described the Netherlands as "an island of plenty in a sea of want." Consequently, the Netherlands experienced very few of the food riots that characterized the rest of Europe.[15] The Dutch republic was not a federation but a confederation—that is, a weak union of strong provinces. Wealthy and lacking a monarch, the provinces were a temptation to other European powers. Nonetheless, the Dutch resisted the long Spanish effort at reconquest and withstood both French and English attacks in the second half of the century. They were severely weakened, however, by the long War of the Spanish Succession, which was a costly drain on Dutch labor and financial resources. The peace signed in 1713 to end the war brought the republic few gains to compensate for its expenses and marked the beginning of Dutch economic decline.

Section Review

- In England, King James I's belief that he was subject only to God led to tension with the House of Commons as he tried to govern without Parliament.

- Financial and religious disputes between King Charles I and the House of Commons led to civil war, and even though the king allied himself with northern nobles, Parliament won out, tried Charles for treason, and beheaded him in 1649.

- After Charles's death, Cromwell came to power, proclaiming a commonwealth that was actually a military dictatorship, holding Puritanical ideals of morality, earning the ire of the Irish by outlawing Catholicism in Ireland, but also boosting the English sea trade and allowing Jewish immigration.

- After Cromwell's death, the 1660 Restoration brought Charles to the throne, who alienated the English by favoring Catholics; Protestant fears intensified when the Catholic James II succeeded his brother, ending in the Glorious Revolution of 1688, whereby James was exiled to France while his Protestant daughter Mary and her Dutch husband William of Orange were crowned as the monarchs.

- The government of William and Mary was a constitutional monarchy that provided freedom of religion, but economic and political liberty came only with property ownership, so the masses still had no political rights.

- The Dutch republic in the seventeenth century found political success and prosperity by providing religious tolerance, attracting foreign capital, and promoting trade.

MAP 16.2 Seventeenth-Century Dutch Commerce

Dutch wealth rested on commerce, and commerce depended on the huge Dutch merchant marine, manned by perhaps forty-eight thousand sailors. The fleet carried goods from all parts of the globe to the port of Amsterdam.

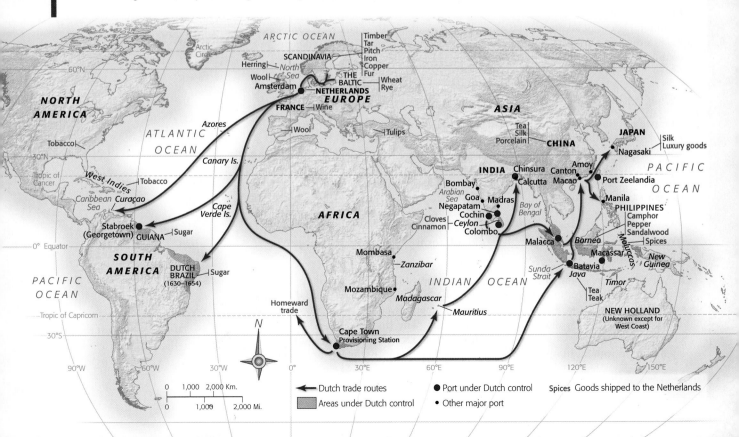

Chapter Review

What were the common crises and achievements of seventeenth-century states? (page 402)

Most parts of Europe experienced the seventeenth century as a period of severe economic, social, and military crisis. Across the continent, rulers faced popular rebellions from their desperate subjects, who were pushed to the brink by poor harvests, high taxes, and decades of war. Many forces, including powerful noblemen, the church, and regional and local loyalties, constrained the state's authority. Despite these obstacles, most European states emerged from the seventeenth century with increased powers and more centralized control. Whether they ruled through monarchical fiat or parliamentary negotiation, European governments strengthened their bureaucracies, raised more taxes, and significantly expanded their armies.

According to Thomas Hobbes, the central drive in every human is "a perpetual and restless desire of Power, after Power, that ceaseth only in Death." The seventeenth century solved the problem of sovereign power in two fundamental ways: absolutism and constitutionalism.

To what extent did French and Spanish monarchs succeed in creating absolute monarchies? (page 405)

Under Louis XIV France witnessed the high point of absolutist ambition in western Europe. The king saw himself as the representative of God on earth, and it has been said that "to the seventeenth century imagination God was a sort of image of Louis XIV."[16] Under Louis's rule, France developed a centralized bureaucracy, a professional army, and a state-directed economy, all of which he personally supervised.

Despite his claims to absolute power, Louis XIV ruled, in practice, by securing the collaboration of high nobles. In exchange for confirmation of their ancient privileges, the nobles were willing to cooperate with the expansion of state power. This was a common pattern in attempts at absolutism across Europe. In Spain, where monarchs made similar claims to absolute power, the seventeenth century witnessed economic catastrophe and a decline in royal capacities.

What cultural forms flourished under absolutist governments? (page 415)

France's dominant political role in Europe elevated its cultural influence as well. French became the common language of the European elite, as all heads turned to Versailles and the radiant aristocratic culture emanating from it. Within France, the Bourbon monarchy pursued culture as one more aspect of absolutist policy, creating cultural academies, sponsoring playwrights and musicians, and repressing Protestantism with a bloody hand.

What is constitutionalism, and how did this form of government emerge in England and the Dutch Republic? (page 418)

As Louis XIV personified absolutist ambitions, so Stuart England exemplified the evolution of the constitutional state. The conflicts between Parliament and the first two Stuart rulers, James I and Charles I, tested where sovereign power would reside. The resulting civil war did not solve the problem. The Instrument of Government provided for a balance of government authority and recognition of popular rights; as such, the Instrument has been called the first modern constitution. Unfortunately, it

Key Terms

moral economy (p. 403)

sovereignty (p. 405)

popular revolts (p. 405)

intendants (p. 407)

Fronde (p. 407)

divine right of kings (p. 408)

absolute monarchy (p. 408)

mercantilism (p. 409)

Peace of Utrecht (p. 411)

Don Quixote (p. 414)

baroque style (p. 415)

French classicism (p. 417)

constitutionalism (p. 418)

Puritans (p. 419)

New Model Army (p. 421)

Protectorate (p. 421)

Test Act (p. 422)

Second Treatise of Civil Government (p. 424)

States General (p. 424)

stadtholder (p. 424)

Dutch East India Company (p. 426)

did not survive the Protectorate. James II's absolutist tendencies brought on the Glorious Revolution of 1688 and 1689, and the people who made that revolution settled three basic issues: sovereign power was divided between king and Parliament, with Parliament enjoying the greater share; government was to be based on the rule of law; and the liberties of English people were made explicit in written form in the Bill of Rights.

Having won independence from Spain, the United Provinces of the Netherlands provided another model of constitutional government, one dominated by wealthy urban merchants rather than the landed gentry who controlled the English system. The federal constitution of the Netherlands invested power in the Estates General, but diluted their authority by giving veto power to provincial assemblies. Dominated by Holland, the Netherlands provided a shining example of industriousness, prosperity, and relative tolerance for the rest of Europe.

Notes

1. The classic study is by Theodore K. Rabb, *The Struggle for Stability in Early Modern Europe* (Oxford: Oxford University Press, 1975).
2. G. Parker and L. M. Smith, "Introduction," and N. Steensgaard, "The Seventeenth Century Crisis," in *The General Crisis of the Seventeenth Century*, ed. G. Parker and L. M. Smith (London: Routledge & Kegan Paul, 1985), pp. 1–53, esp. p. 12.
3. H. G. Koenigsberger, "The Revolt of Palermo in 1647," *Cambridge Historical Journal* 8 (1944–1946): 129–144.
4. See W. Beik, *Urban Protest in Seventeenth-Century France: The Culture of Retribution* (New York: Cambridge University Press, 1997), p. 1.
5. Ibid.
6. See ibid., chaps. 1, 2, 3, and 11.
7. Ibid., pp. 22–26.
8. See M. Turchetti, "The Edict of Nantes," in *The Oxford Encyclopedia of the Reformation*, ed. H. J. Hillerbrand, vol. 3 (New York: Oxford University Press, 1996), pp. 126–128.
9. Quoted in J. H. Elliott, *Richelieu and Olivares* (Cambridge: Cambridge University Press, 1984), p. 135; and in W. F. Church, *Richelieu and Reason of State* (Princeton, N.J.: Princeton University Press, 1972), p. 507.
10. Quoted in J. Wolf, *Louis XIV* (New York: W. W. Norton, 1968), p. 146.
11. John A. Lynn, "Recalculating French Army Growth," in *The Military Revolution Debate: Readings on the Military Transformation of Early Modern Europe*, ed. Clifford J. Rogers (Boulder, Colo.: Westview Press, 1995), p. 125.
12. J. H. Elliott, *Imperial Spain, 1469–1716* (New York: Mentor Books, 1963), pp. 306–308.
13. B. Bennassar, *The Spanish Character: Attitudes and Mentalities from the Sixteenth to the Nineteenth Century*, trans. B. Keen (Berkeley: University of California Press, 1979), p. 125.
14. For a revisionist interpretation, see J. Wormald, "James VI and I: Two Kings or One?" *History* 62 (June 1983): 187–209.
15. S. Schama, *The Embarrassment of Riches: An Interpretation of Dutch Culture in the Golden Age* (New York: Alfred A. Knopf, 1987), pp. 165–170; quotation is on p. 167.
16. C. J. Friedrich and C. Blitzer, *The Age of Power* (Ithaca, N.Y.: Cornell University Press, 1957), p. 112.

To assess your mastery of this chapter, go to **bedfordstmartins.com/mckaywestbrief**

Listening to the Past

The Court at Versailles

Although the Duc de Saint-Simon (1675–1755) was a soldier, courtier, and diplomat, his enduring reputation rests on The Memoirs (1788), his eyewitness account of the personality and court of Louis XIV. A nobleman of extremely high status, Saint-Simon resented Louis's high-handed treatment of the ancient nobility and his promotion of newer nobles and the bourgeoisie. The Memoirs, excerpted here, remains a monument of French literature and an indispensable historical source, partly for its portrait of the court at Versailles.

Very early in the reign of Louis XIV the Court was removed from Paris, never to return. The troubles of the minority had given him a dislike to that city; his enforced and surreptitious flight from it still rankled in his memory; he did not consider himself safe there, and thought cabals would be more easily detected if the Court was in the country, where the movements and temporary absences of any of its members would be more easily noticed. . . . No doubt that he was also influenced by the feeling that he would be regarded with greater awe and veneration when no longer exposed every day to the gaze of the multitude.

He availed himself of the frequent festivities at Versailles, and his excursions to other places, as a means of making the courtiers assiduous in their attendance and anxious to please him; for he nominated beforehand those who were to take part in them, and could thus gratify some and inflict a snub on others. He was conscious that the substantial favours he had to bestow were not nearly sufficient to produce a continual effect; he had therefore to invent imaginary ones, and no one was so clever in devising petty distinctions and preferences which aroused jealousy and emulation. . . .

Not only did he expect all persons of distinction to be in continual attendance at Court, but he was quick to notice the absence of those of inferior degree; at his *lever* (**LEV-ay**) [formal rising from bed in the morning], his *coucher* (**KOO-shay**) [preparations for going to bed], his meals, in the gardens of Versailles (the only place where the courtiers in general were allowed to follow him), he used to cast his eyes to right and left; nothing escaped him, he saw everybody. If any one habitually living at Court absented himself he insisted on knowing the reason; those who came there only for flying visits had also to give a satisfactory explanation; any one who seldom or never appeared there was certain to incur his displeasure. If asked to bestow a favour on

Louis XIV was extremely proud of the gardens at Versailles and personally led ambassadors and other highly ranked visitors on tours of the extensive palace grounds. (Erich Lessing/Art Resource, NY)

430

such persons he would reply haughtily: "I do not know him"; of such as rarely presented themselves he would say, "He is a man I never see"; and from these judgements there was no appeal.

He loved splendour, magnificence, and profusion in all things, and encouraged similar tastes in his Court; to spend money freely on equipages [horse carriages] and buildings, on feasting and at cards, was a sure way to gain his favour, perhaps to obtain the honour of a word from him. Motives of policy had something to do with this; by making expensive habits the fashion, and, for people in a certain position, a necessity, he compelled his courtiers to live beyond their income, and gradually reduced them to depend on his bounty for the means of subsistence. This was a plague which, once introduced, became a scourge to the whole country, for it did not take long to spread to Paris, and thence to the armies and the provinces; so that a man of any position is now estimated entirely according to his expenditure on his table and other luxuries. This folly, sustained by pride and ostenta-tion, has already produced widespread confusion; it threatens to end in nothing short of ruin and a general overthrow.

Questions for Analysis

1. What was the role of etiquette and ceremony at the court of Versailles? How could Louis XIV use them in everyday life at court to influence and control nobles?

2. How important do you think Louis's individual character and personality were to his style of governing? What challenges might this present to his successors?

3. Consider the role of ceremony in some modern governments, such as the U.S. government. How does it compare to Louis XIV's use of ceremony as portrayed by Saint-Simon?

4. Do you think Saint-Simon is an objective and trustworthy recorder of life at court? Why?

Source: "The Court at Versailles" from *The Memoirs of the Duke de Saint Simon*, ed. F. Arkwright (New York: Brentano's, n.d.), Vol. V, pp. 271–274, 276–278.

CHAPTER 17

Absolutism in Central and Eastern Europe

to 1740

Chapter Preview

Warfare and Social Change in Central and Eastern Europe
What social and economic changes affected central and eastern Europe from 1400 to 1650?

The Rise of Austria and Prussia
How did the rulers of Austria and Prussia manage to build powerful absolute monarchies?

The Development of Russia and the Ottoman Empire
What were the distinctive features of Russian and Ottoman absolutism in this period?

Peter the Great's magnificent new crown, created for his joint coronation in 1682 with his half-brother Ivan. (State Museum of the Kremlin, Moscow)

The crises of the seventeenth century—religious division, economic depression, and war—were not limited to western Europe. Central and eastern Europe experienced even more catastrophic dislocation, with German lands serving as the battleground of the Thirty Years' War and borders constantly vulnerable to attack from the east. In Prussia and Habsburg Austria absolutist states emerged in the aftermath of this conflict.

Russia and the Ottoman Turks also developed absolutist governments. These empires seemed foreign and exotic to western Europeans, who saw them as the antithesis of their political, religious, and cultural values. To Western eyes, their own monarchs respected law—either divine or constitutional—while Eastern despots ruled with an iron fist. In this view, the Ottoman Muslim state was home to fanaticism and heresy, and even Russian Orthodoxy had rituals and traditions, if not core beliefs, that differed sharply from either Catholicism or Protestantism. Beneath the surface, however, these Eastern governments shared many similarities with Western ones.

The most successful Eastern empires lasted until 1918, far longer than monarchical rule endured in France, the model of absolutism under Louis XIV. Eastern monarchs had a powerful impact on architecture and the arts, encouraging new monumental construction to reflect their glory. Questions about the relationship between East and West remain potent today, as evidenced by the debate surrounding Turkey's bid for membership in the European Union.

Warfare and Social Change in Central and Eastern Europe

What social and economic changes affected central and eastern Europe from 1400 to 1650?

When absolute monarchy emerged in the seventeenth century, it built on social and economic foundations laid between roughly 1400 and 1650. In those years the elites of eastern Europe rolled back the gains made by the peasantry during the High Middle Ages and reimposed a harsh serfdom on the rural masses. The nobility also reduced the importance of the towns and the middle classes. This process differed from developments in western Europe, where peasants won greater freedom and the urban middle class continued its rise. The Thirty Years' War represented the culmination of these changes. Decades of war in central Europe led to depopulation and economic depression, which allowed lords to impose ever-harsher controls on the peasantry.

The Consolidation of Serfdom

The period from 1050 to 1300 was a time of general economic expansion in eastern Europe characterized by the growth of trade, towns, and population. The rulers of eastern Europe attracted settlers to the frontier beyond the Elbe River with economic and legal incentives and the offer of greater personal freedom. These benefits were also gradually extended to the local Slavic populations, even those of central Russia. Thus, by 1300 **serfdom** had all but disappeared in eastern Europe.

After the Black Death (1348), however, as Europe's population and economy declined grievously, lords sought to solve their economic problems by more heavily

serfdom A system used by nobles and rulers in which peasants were bound to the land they worked and to the lords they served.

Estonia in the 1660s
The Estonians were conquered by German military nobility in the Middle Ages and reduced to serfdom. The German-speaking nobles ruled the Estonian peasants with an iron hand, and Peter the Great reaffirmed their domination when Russia annexed Estonia (see Map 17.3 on page 445). (Mansell Collection/Time Life Pictures/Getty Images)

exploiting the peasantry. This reaction generally failed in the West, where by 1500 almost all peasants were free or had their serf obligations greatly reduced. East of the Elbe, however, the landlords won. They pushed for laws restricting or eliminating the peasants' right to move wherever they wished. They also took more of their peasants' land and imposed heavier labor obligations. Instead of being independent farmers paying freely negotiated rents, peasants became forced laborers on the lords' estates. By the early 1500s, lords in many territories could command their peasants to work without pay as many as six days a week. The peasants had no recourse through the courts to fight these injustices. The local lord was also the prosecutor, judge, and jailer.

Between 1500 and 1650 the social, legal, and economic conditions of peasants in eastern Europe continued to decline, and free peasants became serfs. Polish nobles gained complete control over their peasants in 1574, after which they could legally inflict the death penalty whenever they wished. In Prussia in 1653 peasants were assumed to be tied to their lords in hereditary subjugation—bound to their lords and the land from one generation to the next. In Russia a peasant's right to move from an estate was permanently abolished in 1603. In 1649 the tsar lifted the nine-year time limit on the recovery of runaways and eliminated all limits on lords' authority over their peasants.

Political factors were crucial to the re-emergence of serfdom in eastern Europe. In the late Middle Ages central and eastern Europe experienced innumerable wars and general political chaos, which allowed noble landlords to increase their power. There were, for example, many disputed royal successions, so that weak kings were forced to grant political favors to win the nobility's support. Thus while strong monarchs and effective central government were rising in Spain, France, and England, kings were generally losing power in the East and could not resist the demands of lords regarding peasants.

Moreover, most Eastern monarchs did not oppose the growth of serfdom. The typical king was only first among noble equals. He, too, wanted to squeeze his peasants. The Western concept of sovereignty, as embodied in a king who protected the interests of all his people, was not well developed in eastern Europe before 1650.

Not only the peasants suffered. Also with the approval of kings, landlords systematically undermined the medieval privileges of the towns and the power of the urban classes. Instead of selling products to local merchants, landlords sold directly to foreigners. For example, Dutch ships sailed up the rivers of Poland and eastern Germany to the loading docks of the great estates, completely bypassing the local towns. Moreover, "town air" no longer "made people free," for the Eastern towns had lost their medieval right of refuge and were now compelled to return runaways to their lords. The population of the towns and the importance of the urban middle classes declined greatly.

The Thirty Years' War

The Holy Roman Empire was a confederation of hundreds of principalities, independent cities, duchies, and other polities loosely united under an elected emperor. An uneasy truce had prevailed in the Holy Roman Empire since the Peace of Augsburg (AWGZ-burg) of 1555 (see page 350). According to the settlement, the faith of the prince determined the religion of his subjects. Later in the century, however, Catholics and Lutherans grew alarmed as the faiths of various areas shifted. Calvinists and Jesuits had converted some Lutheran princes; Lutherans had acquired Catholic bishoprics. Lutheran princes felt compelled to form the Protestant Union (1608), and Catholics retaliated with the Catholic League (1609). Each alliance was determined that the other should make no religious or territorial advance. Dynastic interests were also involved; the Spanish Habsburgs strongly supported the goals of their Austrian relatives—the unity of the empire and the preservation of Catholicism within it.

The immediate catalyst of violence was the closure of some Protestant churches by Ferdinand of Styria, the new Catholic king in Bohemia (boh-HEE-mee-uh) in 1617. On May 23, 1618, Protestants hurled two of Ferdinand's officials from a castle window in Prague. They fell seventy feet but survived: Catholics claimed that angels had caught them; Protestants said that the officials had fallen on a heap of soft horse manure. Called the "defenestration of Prague," this event marked the beginning of the Thirty Years' War (1618–1648).

The war is traditionally divided into four phases. The first, or Bohemian, phase (1618–1625) was characterized by civil war in Bohemia between the Catholic League, led by Ferdinand, and the Protestant Union, headed by Frederick, the elector of the Palatinate of the Rhine, one of the states of the Holy Roman Empire. The Protestant Union fought for religious liberty and independence from Habsburg rule. In 1620 Catholic forces defeated Frederick at the Battle of the White Mountain.

The second, or Danish, phase of the war (1625–1629)—so called because of the leadership of the Protestant king Christian IV of Denmark (r. 1588–1648)—witnessed additional Catholic victories. The Catholic imperial army led by Albert of Wallenstein swept through Silesia, north to the Baltic, and east into Pomerania, scoring smashing victories. Wallenstein, an unscrupulous opportunist who used his vast riches to build an army loyal only to himself, seemed more interested in carving out his own empire than in aiding the Catholic cause. He quarreled with the Catholic League, and soon the Catholic forces were divided. Religion was eclipsed as a basic issue of the war.

Habsburg power peaked in 1629. The emperor issued the Edict of Restitution, whereby all Catholic properties lost to Protestantism since 1552 were restored, and only Catholics and Lutherans were allowed to practice their faiths. When Wallenstein began ruthless enforcement, Protestants throughout Europe feared the collapse of the balance of power in north-central Europe.

CHRONOLOGY

ca. 1400–1650	Re-emergence of serfdom in eastern Europe
1462–1505	Reign of Ivan III in Russia
1533–1584	Reign of Ivan the Terrible in Russia
1618–1648	Thirty Years' War
1620	Habsburgs crush Protestantism in Bohemia
1620–1740	Growth of absolutism in Austria and Prussia
1640–1688	Reign of Frederick William in Prussia
1652	Nikon reforms Russian Orthodox Church
1670–1671	Cossack revolt led by Razin
ca. 1680–1750	Construction of palaces by absolutist rulers
1683–1718	Habsburgs defend Vienna; win war with Ottoman Turks
1702	Peter the Great founds St. Petersburg
1713–1740	Growth of Prussian military

The third, or Swedish, phase of the war (1630–1635) began with the arrival in Germany of the Swedish king Gustavus Adolphus (goo-STAV-us ah-DOLF-us) (r. 1594–1632). The ablest administrator of his day and a devout Lutheran, he intervened to support the empire's oppressed Protestants. The French chief minister, Cardinal Richelieu, subsidized the Swedes, hoping to weaken Habsburg power in Europe. Gustavus Adolphus won two important battles but was fatally wounded in combat. The Swedish victories ended the Habsburg ambition to unite the German states under imperial authority.

The last, or French, phase of the war (1635–1648) was prompted by Richelieu's concern that the Habsburgs would regain their strength after the death of Gustavus Adolphus. Richelieu declared war on Spain and sent military as well as financial assistance to the Swedes and the Protestant princes fighting in Germany. The war dragged on. The French, Dutch, and Swedes, supported by Scots, Finns, and German mercenaries, burned, looted, and destroyed German agriculture and commerce. Finally, in October 1648 peace was achieved.

Peace of Westphalia A series of treaties that concluded the Thirty Years' War, recognized the sovereign authority of over three hundred German princes, acknowledged the independence of the United Provinces, made Calvinism a permissible creed within Germany, and reduced the role of the Roman Catholic Church in European politics.

Consequences of the Thirty Years' War

The 1648 **Peace of Westphalia** (west-FEY-lee-uh) that ended the Thirty Years' War marked a turning point in European history. Conflicts fought over religious faith ended. The treaties recognized the sovereign, independent authority of more than three hundred German princes (see Map 17.1). Since the time of Holy Roman Emperor Frederick II (1194–1250), Germany had followed a pattern of state-building different from that of France and England: the emperor shared authority with the princes. After the Peace of Westphalia, the emperor's power continued to be severely limited, and the Holy Roman Empire remained a loosely knit federation.

The peace agreement acknowledged the independence of the United Provinces of the Netherlands. France acquired the province of Alsace along with the advantages of the weakened status of the empire. Sweden received a large cash indemnity and jurisdiction over German territories along the Baltic Sea, leaving it as a major threat to the future kingdom of Brandenburg-Prussia (BRAN-duhn-burg PRUHSH-uh). The papacy lost the right to participate in central European religious affairs and the Augsburg agreement of 1555 became permanent, adding Calvinism to Catholicism and Lutheranism as legally permissible creeds. The north German states remained Protestant; the south German states, Catholic.

The Thirty Years' War was probably the most destructive event for the central European economy and society prior to the twentieth century. Perhaps one-third of urban residents and two-fifths of the rural population died. Entire areas were depopulated by warfare, by the flight of refugees, and by disease. The trade of southern German cities such as Augsburg, already hard hit by the shift in transportation routes from the Mediterranean to the Atlantic, was virtually destroyed. All of Europe was experiencing severe inflation due to the influx of Spanish silver, but the destruction of land and foodstuffs made the price rise worse in central Europe than anywhere else. Agricultural areas suffered catastrophically. Many small farmers lacked the revenue to rework their holdings and had to become day laborers. In parts of central Europe, especially in areas east of the Elbe River, loss of land contributed to the consolidation of serfdom.[1]

Some people prospered, however. Nobles and landlords who controlled agricultural estates profited from rising food prices. They bought or seized the land of failed small farmers and then demanded more unpaid labor on those enlarged estates. Surpluses in wheat and timber were sold to foreign merchants, who exported them to the growing cities of the West.

Section Review

- The great decline in population and economy from the Black Death (1348), as well as many wars and political instability, led eastern European landlords to reimpose harsh serfdom on peasants and undermine the privileges of urban dwellers, a tactic that failed in western Europe, where by 1500 most peasants were free.

- Conflict between Lutheran and Catholic princes within the Holy Roman Empire broke the peace of Augsburg (1555), resulting in the outbreak of the Thirty Years' War (1618–1648).

- The Thirty Years' War erupted in Prague in 1618 and continued through four phases: Bohemian, Danish, Swedish, and French.

- Consequences of the Thirty Years' War included an end to conflicts over religious faith, legal inclusion of Calvinism, greater independence of princes in the Holy Roman Empire, severe inflation, the loss of small farms, and the destruction of a third of the population.

NORWAY
SWEDEN
FINLAND
ESTONIA
LIVONIA
RUSSIA
SCOTLAND
Edinburgh
IRELAND
Dublin
ENGLAND
North Sea
See Inset
DENMARK
Copenhagen
Baltic Sea
Vilna
Danzig
PRUSSIA
UNITED PROVINCES
London
Amsterdam
Elbe R.
Berlin
Magdeburg
Vistula R.
Warsaw
POLAND-LITHUANIA
ATLANTIC OCEAN
Antwerp
Essen
SPANISH NETHERLANDS
Cologne
Rhine R.
SAXONY
SILESIA
Seine R.
Paris
Prague
LOWER PALATINATE
UPPER PALATINATE
BOHEMIA
MORAVIA
Metz
Nantes
Loire R.
BAVARIA
Vienna
Augsburg
AUSTRIA
Salzburg
FRANCHE-COMTÉ
FRANCE
Zurich
SWITZERLAND
TYROL
Geneva
Trent
CARINTHIA
STYRIA
Buda
Pest
HUNGARY
TRANSYLVANIA
MOLDAVIA
JEDISAN
BESSARABIA
SAVOY
PIEDMONT
MILAN
REPUBLIC OF VENICE
Venice
CARNIOLA
CROATIA
SLAVONIA
Rhône R.
GENOA
Belgrade
WALLACHIA
Ebro R.
BOSNIA
SERBIA
Danube R.
Black Sea
SPAIN
Tagus R.
TUSCANY
PAPAL STATES
Adriatic Sea
HERZEGOVINA
MONTENEGRO
BULGARIA
Corsica (to Genoa)
Rome
NAPLES
Naples
Constantinople
OTTOMAN EMPIRE
Sardinia
Balearic Is.
Aegean Sea
Palermo
Sicily
GREECE
Athens
Mediterranean Sea
Crete (to Rep. Of Venice)
North Sea
SWEDEN
JUTLAND
Copenhagen
DENMARK
Baltic Sea
SCHLESWIG
WISMAR
Lübeck
Hamburg
POMERANIA
BREMEN
MECKLENBURG
VERDEN
Elbe R.
BRANDENBURG
Austrian Habsburg lands
Spanish Habsburg lands
Other German states
Swedish lands by 1648
Ottoman Empire and tributary states
Boundary of the Holy Roman Empire
0 150 300 Km.
0 150 300 Mi.

MAP 17.1 Europe After the Thirty Years' War

Which country emerged from the Thirty Years' War as the strongest European power? What dynastic house was that country's major rival in the early modern period?

The Rise of Austria and Prussia

How did the rulers of Austria and Prussia manage to build powerful absolute monarchies?

The monarchs of central and eastern Europe gradually gained political power in three key areas. First, they imposed permanent taxes without consent. Second, they maintained permanent standing armies to police the country and fight abroad. Third, they conducted relations with other states as they pleased. They were able to gain these powers by allowing the nobles greater control over serfs and by providing protection from outside invaders.

As with all general historical developments, there were important variations on the absolutist theme in eastern Europe. Royal absolutism in Prussia was stronger and more effective than in Austria. This would give Prussia a thin edge in the struggle for power in east-central Europe in the eighteenth century. Prussian-style absolutism had great long-term political significance, for it was a rising Prussia that unified the German people in the nineteenth century and imposed on them a militaristic stamp.

The Austrian Habsburgs

Like all of central Europe, the Habsburgs emerged from the Thirty Years' War impoverished and exhausted. Their efforts to destroy Protestantism in the German lands and to turn the weak Holy Roman Empire into a real state had failed. Although the Habsburgs remained the hereditary emperors, real power lay in the hands of a bewildering variety of separate political jurisdictions, including independent cities, small principalities, medium-sized states such as Bavaria and Saxony, and some of the territories of Prussia and the Habsburgs.

Defeat in central Europe encouraged the Habsburgs to turn away from a quest for imperial dominance and to focus inward and eastward in an attempt to unify their diverse holdings. If they could not impose Catholicism in the empire, at least they could do so in their own domains.

The Habsburg victory over Bohemia during the Thirty Years' War was an important step in this direction. The victorious king, Ferdinand II (r. 1619–1637), had drastically reduced the power of the **Bohemian Estates,** which was the largely Protestant representative assembly. He also confiscated the landholdings of many Protestant nobles and gave them to a few loyal Catholic nobles and to the foreign aristocratic mercenaries who led his armies. After 1650 a large portion of the Bohemian nobility was of recent origin and owed everything to the Habsburgs.

With the help of this new nobility, the Habsburgs established direct rule over Bohemia. The condition of the enserfed peasantry worsened substantially: three days per week of unpaid labor—the *robot*—became the norm, and a quarter of the serfs worked for their lords every day but Sundays and religious holidays. Protestantism was also stamped out. The reorganization of Bohemia was a giant step toward creating absolutist rule. As in France in the same years, the pursuit of religious unity was an essential element of absolutism.

Ferdinand III (r. 1637–1657) continued to build state power. He centralized the government in the hereditary German-speaking provinces, which formed the core Habsburg holdings. For the first time, a permanent standing army was ready to put down any internal opposition.

Bohemian Estates The largely Protestant representative body of the different estates in Bohemia. Significantly reduced in power by Ferdinand II.

Austrian Rule in Hungary

The Habsburg monarchy then turned east toward the plains of Hungary, which had been divided between the Ottomans and the Habsburgs in the early sixteenth century (see page 356). Between 1683 and 1699 the Habsburgs pushed the Ottomans from most of Hungary and Transylvania. The recovery of all of the former kingdom of Hungary was completed in 1718.

The Hungarian nobility, despite its reduced strength, effectively thwarted the full development of Habsburg absolutism. Throughout the seventeenth century Hungarian nobles—the most numerous in Europe—rose in revolt against attempts to impose absolute rule. They never triumphed decisively, but neither were they crushed the way the Czech nobility had been in 1620.

The Hungarians resisted because many of them remained Protestants, especially in areas formerly ruled by the Turks. In some of these regions, the Ottomans acted as military allies to the nobles, against the Habsburgs. Finally, the Hungarian nobility, and even part of the peasantry, became attached to a national ideal long before most of the other peoples of eastern Europe. Hungarian nobles were determined to maintain as much independence and local control as possible. In 1703, with the Habsburgs bogged down in the War of the Spanish Succession (see page 411), the Hungarians rose in one last patriotic rebellion under Prince Francis Rákóczy.

Rákóczy and his forces were eventually defeated, but the Habsburgs had to accept a compromise. Charles VI (r. 1711–1740) restored many of the traditional privileges of the aristocracy in return for Hungarian acceptance of hereditary Habsburg rule. Thus Hungary, unlike Austria and Bohemia, was never fully integrated into a centralized, absolute Habsburg state.

Despite checks on their ambitions in Hungary, the Habsburgs made significant achievements in state-building overall by forging consensus with the church and the nobility. A sense of common identity and loyalty to the monarchy grew among elites in Habsburg lands, even to a certain extent in Hungary. The best evidence for this consensus is the spectacular sums approved by the Estates for the growth of the army. German became the language of the common culture and zealous Catholicism also helped fuse a collective identity. Vienna became the political and cultural center of the empire. By 1700 it was a thriving city with a population of one hundred thousand, with its own version of Versailles, the royal palace of Schönbrunn. (SHUN-broon) (See the feature "Images in Society: Absolutist Palace Building" on pages 440–441.)

Prussia in the Seventeenth Century

In the fifteenth and sixteenth centuries, the Hohenzollern family had ruled parts of eastern Germany as the imperial electors of Brandenburg and the dukes of Prussia, but they had little real power. The **elector of Brandenburg** had the right to help choose the Holy Roman emperor, which bestowed prestige, but the elector had no military strength of his own. Nothing suggested that the Hohenzollern family and its territories would come to play as important a role in European affairs as they did.

The elector of Brandenburg was a helpless spectator in the Thirty Years' War, his territories alternately ravaged by Swedish and Habsburg armies. Yet foreign armies also dramatically weakened the political power of the Estates, which helped the elector Frederick William (r. 1640–1688) make significant progress toward royal absolutism. This constitutional struggle was the most crucial in Prussian history until that of the 1860s.

elector of Brandenburg One of the electors of the Holy Roman Empire, with the right to help choose the emperor, hereditarily held by the Hohenzollern family. Frederick William, "the Great Elector," was able to use and expand the office, ultimately resulting in the consolidation of the Prussian state under his successors.

Images in Society

Absolutist Palace Building

By 1700 palace building had become a veritable obsession for the rulers of central and eastern Europe. Their dramatic palaces symbolized the age of absolutist power, just as soaring Gothic cathedrals had expressed the idealized spirit of the High Middle Ages. With its classically harmonious, symmetrical, and geometric design, Versailles, shown in Image 1, served as the model for the wave of palace building that began in the last decade of the seventeenth century.

Located ten miles southwest of Paris, Versailles began as a modest hunting lodge built by Louis XIII in 1623. His son, Louis XIV, loved the site so much that he spent decades enlarging and decorating the original chateau. Between 1668 and 1670, his architect Louis Le Vau (**LOO-ee luh VOH**) enveloped the old building within a much larger second structure that still exists today. In 1682 the new palace became the official residence of the Sun King and his court, although construction continued until 1710, when the royal chapel was completed. At any one time, several thousand people lived in the bustling and crowded palace. The awesome splendor of the eighty-yard Hall of Mirrors, replete with floor to ceiling mirrors and ceiling murals illustrating the king's triumphs, contrasted with the strong odors from the courtiers who commonly relieved themselves in discreet corners. Royal palaces like Versailles were intended to overawe the people and proclaim their owners' authority and power.

In 1693 Charles XI of Sweden, having reduced the power of the aristocracy, ordered the construction of his Royal Palace, which dominates the center of Stockholm to this day. Another such palace was Schönbrunn, an enormous Viennese Versailles begun in 1695 by Emperor Leopold to celebrate Austrian military victories and Habsburg might. Image 2 shows architect Joseph Bernhard Fischer von Erlach's ambitious plan for

IMAGE 1 Pierre-Denis Martin: View of the Chateau de Versailles, 1722 (Châteaux de Versailles et de Trianon, Versailles/Réunion des Musées Nationaux/Art Resource, NY)

Schönbrunn palace. Erlach's plan emphasizes the palace's vast size and its role as a site for military demonstrations. Ultimately financial constraints resulted in a more modest building.

Petty German princes contributed mightily to the palace-building mania. Frederick the Great of Prussia noted that every descendant of a princely family "imagines himself to be something like Louis XIV. He builds his Versailles, has his mistresses, and maintains his army."* The elector-archbishop of Mainz, the ruling prince of that city, confessed apologetically that "building is a craze which costs much, but every fool likes his own hat."†

In central and eastern Europe, the favorite noble servants of royalty became extremely rich and powerful,

* Quoted in R. Ergang, *The Potsdam Fuhrer: Frederick William I, Father of Prussian Militarism* (New York: Octagon Books, 1972), p. 13.
† Quoted in J. Summerson, in *The Eighteenth Century: Europe in the Age of Enlightenment*, ed. A. Cobban (New York: McGraw-Hill, 1969), p. 80.

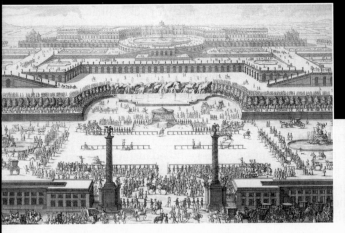

IMAGE 2 Project for the Palace at Schönbrunn (ca. 1700) (Austrian National Library, Vienna)

IMAGE 4 View of the Petit Parc at Versailles from the Canal (Bibliothèque nationale de France)

IMAGE 3 Prince Eugene's Summer Palace, Vienna (Erich Lessing/Art Resource, NY)

and they too built grandiose palaces in the capital cities. These palaces were in part an extension of the monarch, for they surpassed the buildings of less-favored nobles and showed all the high road to fame and fortune. Take, for example, the palaces of Prince Eugene of Savoy, a French nobleman who became Austria's most famous military hero. It was Eugene who led the Austrian army, smashed the Turks, fought Louis XIV to a standstill, and generally guided the triumph of absolutism in Austria. Rewarded with great wealth by his grateful king, Eugene called on the leading architects of the day, J. B. Fischer von Erlach and Johann Lukas von Hildebrandt, to consecrate his glory in stone and fresco. Fischer built Eugene's Winter (or Town) Palace in Vienna, and he and Hildebrandt collaborated on the prince's Summer Palace on the city's outskirts, shown in Image 3. The

prince's summer residence featured two baroque gems, the Lower Belvedere and the lovely Upper Belvedere, completed in 1722 and shown here. The building's interior is equally stunning, with crouching giants serving as pillars and a magnificent great staircase.

Palace gardens were an extension of the architecture. The rational orderliness and symmetry of a garden showed that the ruler's force extended even to nature, which offered its subjugated pleasures to the delight of sovereign and courtiers. The terraces and waterworks of these gardens served as showcases for the latest techniques in military and civil engineering. Exotic plants and elaborate designs testified to the sovereign's global trading networks and elevated taste.

The gardens at Versailles, shown in Image 4, exemplify absolutist palace gardens. In the foreground of this image we see a mock naval campaign being enacted on the canal for the edification of courtiers. For diplomatic occasions, Louis XIV himself wrote lengthy guides for viewing the gardens of Versailles. Modern visitors can still follow his itineraries. The themes of the sculptures in the Versailles gardens also hailed Louis's power, with images of Apollo, the sun god, and Neptune, the sea god, making frequent appearances.

Compare the image of Prince Eugene's summer palace with the plans for Schönbrunn and the palace of Versailles. What did concrete objects and the manipulation of space accomplish for these rulers that mere words could not? What disadvantages might stem from using architecture in this way? Is the use of space and monumental construction still a political tool in today's world?

When he came to power in 1640, the twenty-year-old Frederick William, later known as the "Great Elector," was determined to unify his three provinces and enlarge them by diplomacy and war. These provinces were Brandenburg; Prussia, inherited in 1618; and scattered holdings along the Rhine, inherited in 1614 (see Map 17.2). Each was inhabited by German-speaking people, but each had its own Estates. Although the Estates had not met regularly during the chaotic Thirty Years' War, taxes could not be levied without their consent. The Estates of Brandenburg and Prussia were dominated by the nobility and the landowning classes, known as the **Junkers** (YOONG-kuhrs).

To pay for the permanent standing army he first established in 1660, Frederick William forced the Estates to accept the introduction of permanent taxation without consent. The Estates' power declined rapidly thereafter, for the Great Elector had both financial independence and superior force. The state's total revenue tripled during his reign, and the size of the army leaped by ten. In 1688 a population of one million was supporting a peacetime standing army of thirty thousand.

Two factors were central to the Great Elector's triumph. First, as in the formation of every absolutist state, war was a decisive factor. The ongoing struggle between Sweden and Poland for control of the Baltic after 1648 and the wars of Louis XIV in western Europe created an atmosphere of permanent crisis. The nomadic Tatars (TAY-terz) of the Crimea in southern Russia swept through Prussia in the winter of 1656–1657, killing and carrying off thousands as slaves. This invasion softened up the Estates and strengthened the urgency of the Great Elector's demands for more military funding.

Second, the nobility proved willing to accept Frederick William's new claims in exchange for reconfirmation of their own privileges, including authority over

Junkers The nobility of Brandenburg and Prussia. Reluctant allies of Frederick William in his consolidation of the Prussian state.

MAP 17.2   The Growth of Austria and Brandenburg-Prussia to 1748

Austria expanded to the southwest into Hungary and Transylvania at the expense of the Ottoman Empire. It was unable to hold the rich German province of Silesia, however, which was conquered by Brandenburg-Prussia.

Austrian territory at end of Thirty Years' War (1648)
Austrian acquisitions by end of Turkish Wars (1699)
Austrian acquisitions after decisive victory over Ottoman Empire (1718)
Prussian territory at Great Elector's accession (1640)
Prussian acquisitions by Great Elector's death (1688)
Prussian acquisitions by end of War of the Austrian Succession (1748)
—— Boundary of the Holy Roman Empire

the serfs. The Junkers chose not to join representatives of the towns in a common front against the elector. Instead, they accepted new taxes that fell primarily on towns. The elector used naked force to break the liberties of the towns; the main leader of urban opposition in the key city of Königsberg (**KUHN-nigz-burg**), for example, was arrested and imprisoned for life without trial.

Like Louis XIV, the Great Elector built his absolutist state in collaboration with traditional elites, reaffirming their privileges in return for loyal service and revenue. He also created a larger centralized government bureaucracy to oversee his realm and to collect the new taxes. Pre-existing representative institutions were bypassed. The Diet of Brandenburg did not meet again after 1652. In 1701 the elector's son, Frederick I (1701–1713), received the elevated title of king of Prussia (instead of elector) as a reward for aiding the Holy Roman emperor in the War of the Spanish Succession.

The Consolidation of Prussian Absolutism

Frederick William I, "the Soldiers' King" (r. 1713–1740), completed his grandfather's work. He created a strong centralized bureaucracy and eliminated the last traces of parliamentary estates and local self-government. He truly established Prussian absolutism and transformed Prussia into a military state. King Frederick William was intensely attached to military life. He always wore an army uniform, and he lived the highly disciplined life of the professional soldier. He began his work by five or six in the morning; at ten he almost always went to the parade ground to drill or inspect his troops. Years later he summed up his life's philosophy in his instructions to his son: "A formidable army and a war chest large enough to make this army mobile in times of need can create great respect for you in the world, so that you can speak a word like the other powers."[2]

The king's power grab brought him into considerable conflict with the Junkers. In his early years he even threatened to destroy them; yet, in the end, the Prussian nobility was not destroyed but enlisted—into the army. Responding to a combination of threats and opportunities, the Junkers became the officer caste. A new compromise was worked out whereby the proud nobility imperiously commanded the peasantry in the army as well as on the estates.

Through penny-pinching and hard work, Frederick William achieved results. Prussia, twelfth in Europe in population, had the fourth largest army by 1740. Moreover, soldier for soldier, the Prussian army was the best in Europe, astonishing foreign observers with its precision, skill, and discipline. For the next two hundred years Prussia and then Prussianized Germany would win many crucial military battles.

Frederick William and his ministers also built an exceptionally honest and conscientious bureaucracy to administer the country and foster economic

A Prussian Giant Grenadier

Frederick William I wanted tall, handsome soldiers. He dressed them in tight bright uniforms to distinguish them from the peasant population from which most soldiers came. He also ordered several portraits of his favorites from his court painter, J. C. Merk. Grenadiers (**gren-AH-deers**) wore the miter cap instead of an ordinary hat so that they could hurl their heavy grenades unimpeded by a broad brim. (The Royal Collection © 2008, Her Majesty Queen Elizabeth II)

Section Review

- In the aftermath of the Thirty Years' War, monarchs of central and eastern Europe gained new power through increased taxation, the creation of permanent standing armies, and exercising a free hand in foreign policy.

- The Austrian Habsburgs gained control over Bohemia by reducing the power of the Estates and creating a new and loyal nobility, but were less successful in Hungary, where they were forced to compromise with a fiercely independent Protestant nobility.

- In Prussia, the elector of Brandenburg, Frederick William Hohenzollern, the "Great Elector," set out to unify his provinces under absolutist rule by restoring privileges to the Junker nobility and by using the threat of war to build the best army in Europe.

- His grandson, King Frederick William I, transformed Prussia into a military state, centralized government, eliminated parliament and local self-government, and incorporated the nobility within his army to enforce obedience.

- Palace building modeled on Versailles near Paris and Schönbrunn in Vienna spread through central and eastern Europe, as princes competed for power and aristocrats showcased the riches won through service to the monarchy.

Mongol Yoke The two-hundred-year rule of the Mongol khan over the former territories of Kievan Rus'; this period is considered a prelude to the rise of absolutist Russia.

development. And like the miser he was known to be, the king loved his "blue boys" so much that he hated to "spend" them. This most militaristic of kings was, paradoxically, almost always at peace.

Nevertheless, Prussians paid a heavy and lasting price for the obsessions of their royal drillmaster. Civil society became rigid and highly disciplined, and Prussia became the "Sparta of the North"; unquestioning obedience was the highest virtue. As a Prussian minister later summed up: "To keep quiet is the first civic duty."[3] Thus the policies of Frederick William I combined with harsh peasant bondage and Junker tyranny to lay the foundations for a highly militaristic country.

The Development of Russia and the Ottoman Empire

What were the distinctive features of Russian and Ottoman absolutism in this period?

A favorite parlor game of nineteenth-century intellectuals was debating whether Russia was a Western (European) or non-Western (Asian) society. This question was particularly fascinating because it was unanswerable. To this day, Russia differs from the West in some fundamental ways, though its history has paralleled that of the West in other aspects.

There was no question in the mind of Europeans, however, that the Ottomans were outsiders. Even absolutist rulers disdained Ottoman sultans as cruel and tyrannical despots. Despite stereotypes, the Ottomans were in many ways more tolerant than Westerners, providing protection and security to other religions while steadfastly maintaining their Muslim faith. The Ottoman state combined the Byzantine heritage of the territory they conquered with Persian and Arab traditions. Flexibility and openness to other ideas and practices were sources of strength for the empire.

The Mongol Yoke and the Rise of Moscow

In the thirteenth century the Kievan principality (see page 445) was conquered by the Mongols, a group of nomadic tribes from present-day Mongolia who had come together under Chinggis Khan (1162–1227). At its height, the Mongol empire stretched from Korea to eastern Europe, and the portion that encompassed Russia was known as the Golden Horde. The two-hundred-year period of rule under the Mongol khan (king), known as the **Mongol Yoke,** set the stage for the rise of absolutist Russia.

The Mongols forced the Slavic princes to submit to their rule and to give them tribute and slaves. Although the Mongols conquered, they were quite willing to use local princes as obedient servants and tax collectors. Thus, they did not abolish the title of "great prince," bestowing it instead on the prince who served them best and paid them most handsomely. Beginning with Alexander Nevsky in 1252, the princes of Moscow became particularly adept at serving the Mongols. They loyally put down popular uprisings and collected the khan's taxes. As reward, the princes of Moscow emerged as hereditary great princes. Eventually the Muscovite princes were able to destroy the other princes who were their rivals for power. Ivan III (r. 1462–1505) consolidated power around Moscow and won Novgorod (NOV-guh-rod), almost reaching the Baltic Sea (see Map 17.3).

By 1480 Ivan III felt strong enough to stop acknowledging the khan as his supreme ruler and cease tribute payments to the Mongols. To legitimize their new

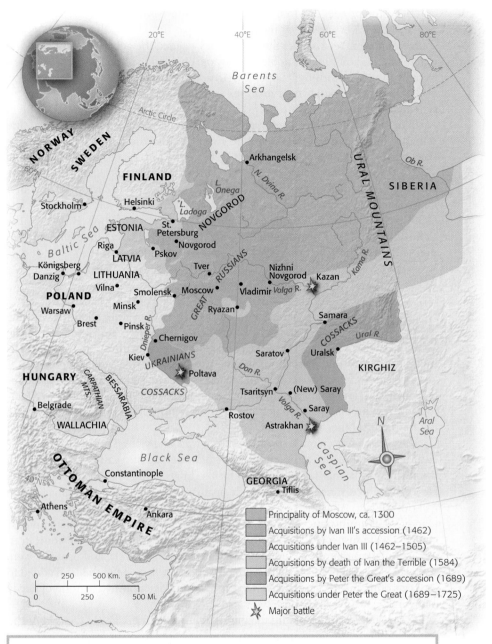

Principality of Moscow, ca. 1300
Acquisitions by Ivan III's accession (1462)
Acquisitions under Ivan III (1462–1505)
Acquisitions by death of Ivan the Terrible (1584)
Acquisitions by Peter the Great's accession (1689)
Acquisitions under Peter the Great (1689–1725)
Major battle

MAPPING THE PAST

MAP 17.3 The Expansion of Russia to 1725

After the disintegration of the Kievan (KEE-ef-ahn) state and the Mongol conquest, the princes of Moscow and their descendants gradually extended their rule over an enormous territory. **[1]** Compare this map with Map 17.4, which shows Ottoman expansion from 1300. What explains the fantastic success of both the Russians and the Ottomans in expanding their territories? Why was the sixteenth century such an important period for expansion? **[2]** How do you explain the geographic direction that expansion followed in each case? **[3]** What happened after the periods shown on these maps? Did the territorial development of the two states diverge from each other or follow the same trajectory?

boyars The highest-ranking nobles in Russia.

tsar A title first taken by Ivan IV, it is a contraction of the word *caesar*.

service nobility A newly emerging class of nobles who held some of the tsar's land on the explicit condition that they serve in the tsar's army.

Cossacks Free groups and outlaw armies living on the steppes bordering Russia, whose numbers were increased by runaway peasants during the time of Ivan the Terrible.

authority, the princes of Moscow drew on two sources of authority. First, they declared themselves *autocrats*, meaning that, like the khans, they were the sole source of power. Yet also like the khans, they needed the cooperation of the local elites. The highest-ranking nobles, or **boyars,** enabled the tsars to rule with an extremely limited government apparatus. In addition to political authority, Moscow also took over Mongol tribute relations and borrowed institutions such as the tax system, postal routes, and the census.

The second source of legitimacy lay in Moscow's claim to the political and religious inheritance of the Byzantine Empire. After the fall of Constantinople (kon-stan-tun-OH-puhl) to the Turks in 1453, the princes of Moscow saw themselves as the heirs of both the caesars and Orthodox Christianity, the one true faith. The title **tsar,** first taken by Ivan IV in 1547, is a contraction of *caesar*. All the other kings of Europe were heretics; only the Russians were rightful and holy rulers. The idea was promoted by Orthodox churchmen, who spoke of "holy Russia" as the "Third Rome." Ivan's marriage to the daughter of the last Byzantine emperor further enhanced the aura of Moscow's imperial inheritance.

Tsar and People to 1689

Developments in Russia took a chaotic turn with the reign of Ivan IV (r. 1533–1584), the famous "Ivan the Terrible," who ascended to the throne at age three. His mother died, possibly poisoned, when he was eight, leaving Ivan to suffer insults and neglect from the boyars at court. At age sixteen he suddenly pushed aside his hated advisers, and in an awe-inspiring ceremony, complete with gold coins pouring down on his head, Ivan majestically crowned himself, taking the august title of tsar for the first time.

Ivan's reign was characterized by endless wars and violent purges. He was successful in defeating the remnants of Mongol power, adding vast new territories to the realm and laying the foundations for the huge, multiethnic Russian empire. He engaged in a much longer struggle against the large Polish-Lithuanian state, without success. After the sudden death of his beloved wife Anastasia [of the Romanov (ROH-muh-nawf) family], the increasingly demented Ivan jailed and executed any he suspected of opposing him. Many were intimates of the court from the leading boyar families, and their families, friends, servants, and peasants were also executed. Their large estates were broken up, with some of the land added to the tsar's domain and the rest given to the lower **service nobility,** a group of newly made nobles who served in the tsar's army.

Ivan also took strides toward making all commoners servants of the tsar. As the service nobles demanded more from those peasants who survived the wars and persecutions, growing numbers fled toward wild, recently conquered territories to the east and south. There they joined free groups and outlaw armies known as **Cossacks** (KOS-akz) and maintained a precarious independence. The solution to the problem of peasant flight was to tie peasants ever more firmly to the land and to the noble landholders, who in turn served the tsar.

Simultaneously, urban traders and artisans were also bound to their towns and jobs so that the tsar could tax them more heavily. Ivan assumed that the tsar owned Russia's trade and industry, just as he owned all the land. The urban classes had no security in their work or property, and even the wealthiest merchants were dependent agents of the tsar. These restrictions checked the growth of the Russian middle classes and stood in sharp contrast to developments in western Europe, where the middle classes were gaining security in their private property.

Saint Basil's Cathedral, Moscow

With its sloping roofs and colorful onion-shaped domes, Saint Basil's is a striking example of powerful Byzantine influences on Russian culture. According to tradition, an enchanted Ivan the Terrible blinded the cathedral's architects to ensure that they would never duplicate their fantastic achievement, which still dazzles the beholder in today's Red Square. (George Holton/Photo Researchers)

After the death of Ivan and his successor, Russia entered a chaotic period known as the "Time of Troubles" (1598–1618). While Ivan's relatives struggled for power, the Cossacks and peasants rebelled against nobles and officials, demanding fairer treatment. This social explosion from below brought the nobles, big and small, together. They crushed the Cossack rebellion at the gates of Moscow and elected Ivan's sixteen-year-old grandnephew, Michael Romanov, the new hereditary tsar (r. 1613–1645). Michael's election was represented as a restoration of tsarist autocracy. (See the feature "Listening to the Past: A Foreign Traveler in Russia" on pages 456–457.)

Although the new tsar successfully reconsolidated central authority, social and religious uprisings continued through the seventeenth century. One of the largest rebellions was led by the Cossack Stenka Razin, who attracted a great army of urban poor and peasants, killing landlords and government officials, and proclaiming freedom from oppression. Eventually this rebellion was defeated.

Despite the turbulence of the period, the Romanov tsars made several important achievements during the second half of the seventeenth century. After a long war, Russia gained a large mass of Ukraine from weak and decentralized Poland in 1667 (see Map 17.3) and completed the conquest of Siberia by the end of the century. Territorial expansion was accompanied by growth of the bureaucracy and the army. Foreign experts were employed to help build and reform the Russian army. The great profits from Siberia's natural resources, especially furs, funded the Romanov's bid for great power status.

The Reforms of Peter the Great

Heir to the first efforts at state-building, Peter the Great (r. 1682–1725) embarked on a tremendous campaign to accelerate and complete these processes. A giant for his time, at six feet seven inches, and possessing enormous energy and willpower, Peter was determined to build and improve the army. He was equally determined to continue the tsarist tradition of territorial expansion. After 1689 Peter ruled independently for thirty-six years, only one of which was peaceful.

Fascinated by weapons and foreign technology, the tsar led a group of two hundred fifty Russian officials and young nobles on an eighteen-month tour of western European capitals. Traveling unofficially to avoid lengthy diplomatic ceremonies, Peter worked with his hands at various crafts and met with foreign kings and experts. He was particularly impressed with the growing power of the Dutch and the English, and he considered how Russia could profit from their example.

Returning to Russia, Peter entered into a secret alliance with Denmark and Poland to wage a sudden war of aggression against Sweden, with the goal of securing access to the Baltic Sea and opportunities for westward expansion. Peter and his allies believed that their combined forces could win easy victories because Sweden was in the hands of a new and inexperienced king.

Eighteen-year-old Charles XII of Sweden (1697–1718) surprised Peter. He defeated Denmark quickly in 1700, then turned on Russia. In a blinding snowstorm, his well-trained professional army attacked and routed unsuspecting Russians besieging the Swedish fortress of Narva (NAHR-vuh) on the Baltic coast. Peter and the survivors fled in panic to Moscow. It was, for the Russians, a grim beginning to the long and brutal Great Northern War, which lasted from 1700 to 1721.

Suffering defeat and faced with a military crisis, Peter responded with measures designed to increase state power, strengthen his armies, and gain victory. He required every nobleman, great or small, to serve in the army or in the civil administration—for life. Since a more modern army and government required skilled technicians and experts, Peter created schools and universities to produce them. One of his most hated reforms was requiring a five-year education away from home for every young nobleman. Peter established an interlocking military-

Gustaf Cederstrom: The Swedish Victory at Narva (1701)
This poignant re-creation focuses on the contrast between the Swedish officers in handsome dress uniforms and the battered Russian soldiers laying down their standards in surrender. Charles XII of Sweden scored brilliant, rapid-fire victories over Denmark, Saxony, and Russia, but he failed to make peace with Peter while he was ahead and eventually lost Sweden's holdings on the Baltic coast. (The National Museum of Fine Arts, Stockholm)

civilian bureaucracy with fourteen ranks, and he decreed that all had to start at the bottom and work toward the top. Some people of non-noble origins rose to high positions in this embryonic meritocracy. Drawing on his experience abroad, Peter searched out talented foreigners and placed them in his service. These measures gradually combined to make the army and government more powerful and efficient.

Peter also greatly increased the service requirements of commoners. In the wake of the Narva disaster, he established a regular standing army of more than two hundred thousand peasant-soldiers commanded by officers from the nobility. In addition, special forces of Cossacks and foreigners numbered more than one hundred thousand. Taxes on peasants increased threefold during Peter's reign. Serfs were arbitrarily assigned to work in the growing number of factories and mines that supplied the military.

Peter's new war machine was able to crush the small army of Sweden in Ukraine at Poltava (**pol-TAH-vah**) in 1709, one of the most significant battles in Russian history. Russia's victory was conclusive in 1721, and Estonia and present-day Latvia (see Map 17.3) came under Russian rule for the first time. The cost was high—warfare consumed eighty to eighty-five percent of all revenues. But Russia became the dominant power in the Baltic and very much a European Great Power.

After his victory at Poltava, Peter channeled enormous resources into building a new Western-style capital on the Baltic to rival the great cities of Europe. Originally a desolate and swampy Swedish outpost, the magnificent city of St. Petersburg was designed to reflect modern urban planning, with wide, straight avenues; buildings set in a uniform line; and large parks.

Peter the Great dictated that all in society realize his vision. Just as the government drafted the peasants for the armies, so it drafted twenty-five thousand to forty thousand men each summer to labor in St. Petersburg without pay. Many peasant construction workers died from hunger, sickness, and accidents. Nobles were ordered to build costly stone houses and palaces in St. Petersburg and to live in them most of the year. Merchants and artisans were also commanded to settle and build in the new capital. These nobles and merchants were then required to pay for the city's infrastructure. The building of St. Petersburg was, in truth, an enormous direct tax levied on the wealthy, with the peasantry forced to do the manual labor.

There were other important consequences of Peter's reign. For Peter, modernization meant Westernization, and both Westerners and Western ideas flowed into Russia for the first time. He required nobles to shave their heavy beards and wear Western clothing, previously banned in Russia. He required them to attend parties where young men and women would mix together and freely choose their own spouses. He forced a warrior elite to accept administrative service as an honorable occupation. From these efforts a new class of Western-oriented Russians began to emerge.

At the same time, vast numbers of Russians hated Peter's massive changes. For nobles, one of Peter's most detested reforms was the imposition of unigeniture—inheritance of land by one son alone—cutting daughters and other sons from

Peter the Great in 1723

This compelling portrait by Grigory Musikiysky captures the strength and determination of the warrior tsar after more than three decades of personal rule. In his hand Peter holds the scepter, symbol of royal sovereignty, and across his breastplate is draped an ermine fur, a mark of honor. In the background are the battleships of Russia's new Baltic fleet and the famous St. Peter and St. Paul Fortress that Peter built in St. Petersburg. (Kremlin Museums, Moscow/The Bridgeman Art Library)

family property. For peasants, the reign of the reforming tsar saw a significant increase in the bonds of serfdom. The gulf between the enserfed peasantry and the educated nobility increased, even though all were caught up in the tsar's demands.

Thus Peter built on the service obligations of old Muscovy (MUHS-kuh-vee). His monarchical absolutism was the culmination of the long development of a unique Russian civilization. Yet the creation of a more modern army and state introduced much that was new and Western to Russia. This development paved the way for Russia to move somewhat closer to the European mainstream in its thought and institutions during the Enlightenment, especially under Catherine the Great.

The Growth of the Ottoman Empire

Most Christian Europeans perceived the Ottomans as the antithesis of their own values and traditions and viewed the empire as driven by an insatiable lust for warfare and conquest. In their view the fall of Constantinople was a catastrophe and the taking of the Balkans a despotic imprisonment of those territories. From the perspective of the Ottomans, the world looked very different. The siege of Constantinople liberated a glorious city from its long decline under the Byzantines. Rather than being a despoiled captive, the Balkans became a haven for refugees fleeing the growing intolerance of Western Christian powers. The Ottoman Empire provided Jews, Muslims, and even some Christians safety from the Inquisition and religious war.

The Ottomans came out of Central Asia as conquering warriors, settled in Anatolia (present-day Turkey), and, at their peak in the mid-sixteenth century, they ruled one of the most powerful empires in the world. Their possessions stretched from western Persia across North Africa and into the heart of central Europe (see Map 17.4).

When the Ottomans captured Constantinople in 1453 they fulfilled a long-held Islamic dream. Under Suleiman the Magnificent (r. 1520–1566), they made great inroads into eastern Europe, capturing Bosnia, Croatia, Romania, Ukraine, and part of Hungary at the battle of Mohács in 1526. For the next hundred and fifty years, the Ottomans ruled the many different ethnic groups living in southeastern Europe and the eastern Mediterranean. In 1529 their European expansion was halted with a failed siege of the Habsburg capital, Vienna. The Ottoman loss at the battle of Lepanto (leh-PAN-toh) in 1571, against the Christian Holy League, confirmed the limits of their ambitions in Europe.

The Ottoman Empire was originally built on a unique model of state and society. There was an almost complete absence of private landed property. Agricultural land was the personal hereditary property of the **sultan** (SUHL-tun), and peasants paid taxes to use the land. There was therefore no security of landholding and no hereditary nobility.

The Ottomans also employed a distinctive form of government administration. The top ranks of the bureaucracy were staffed by the sultan's slave corps. Because Muslim law prohibited enslaving other Muslims, the sultan's agents purchased slaves along the borders of the empire. Within the realm, the sultan levied a "tax" of one thousand to three thousand male children on the conquered Christian populations in the Balkans every year. Young slaves were raised in Turkey as Muslims and were trained to fight and to administer. The most talented rose to the top of the bureaucracy, where they might acquire wealth and power; the less fortunate formed the brave and skillful core of the sultan's army, the **janissary** (JAN-uh-ser-ee) corps. These highly organized and efficient troops gave the Ottomans a formidable advantage in war with western Europeans. By 1683, service in the janissary

sultan The ruler of the Ottoman Empire; he owned all the agricultural land of the empire and was served by an army and bureaucracy composed of highly trained slaves.

janissary corps The core of the sultan's army, composed of conscripts from non-Muslim parts of the empire until 1683.

corps had become so prestigious that the sultan ceased recruitment by force and it became a volunteer force open to Christians and Muslims.

The Ottomans divided their subjects into religious communities, and each *millet*, or "nation," enjoyed autonomous self-government under its religious leaders. (The Ottoman Empire recognized Orthodox Christians, Jews, Armenian Christians, and Muslims as distinct millets.) The **millet** (MIL-it) **system** created a powerful bond between the Ottoman ruling class and the different religious leaders, who supported the sultan's rule in return for extensive authority over their own communities. Each millet collected taxes for the state, regulated group behavior, and maintained law courts, schools, synagogues, and hospitals for its people.

After 1453 Constantinople—renamed Istanbul (is-tahn-BOOL)—became the capital of the empire. The "old palace" was for the sultan's female family members, who lived in isolation under the care of eunuchs. The newly constructed Topkapi palace was where officials worked and young slaves trained for future administrative or military careers. To prevent wives from bringing foreign influence

millet system A system used by the Ottomans whereby subjects were divided into religious communities with each millet (nation) enjoying autonomous self-government under its religious leaders.

MAP 17.4   The Ottoman Empire at Its Height, 1566

The Ottomans, like their great rivals the Habsburgs, rose to rule a vast dynastic empire encompassing many different peoples and ethnic groups. The army and the bureaucracy served to unite the disparate territories into a single state under an absolutist ruler.

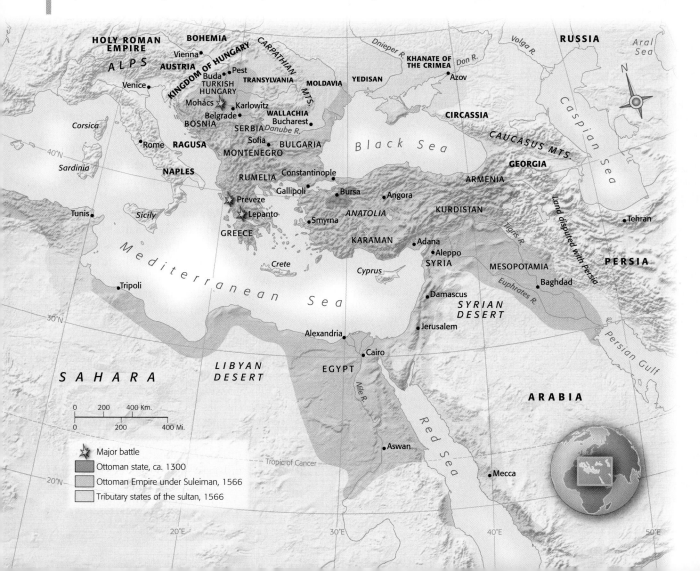

Major battle
Ottoman state, ca. 1300
Ottoman Empire under Suleiman, 1566
Tributary states of the sultan, 1566

The Sultan's Harem at Topkapi Palace, Istanbul
Sultan Suleiman I created separate quarters at the Topkapi Palace for his wife Hürrem and her ladies-in-waiting. His successors transferred all of their wives, concubines, and female family members to the harem (HAIR-uhm) at Topkapi, carefully situated out of sight of the staterooms and courtyards where public affairs took place. The harem was the object of intense curiosity and fascination in the West. (Vanni/Art Resource, NY)

into government—a constant concern in the West—sultans procreated only with their concubines and not with official wives. They also adopted a policy of allowing each concubine to produce only one male heir. At a young age, each son went to govern a province of the empire under his mother's supervision. These practices were intended to stabilize power and prevent a recurrence of the civil wars of the late fourteenth and early fifteenth centuries.

Sultan Suleiman undid these policies when he boldly married his concubine and had several children with her. He established a wing in the Topkapi palace for his own female family members and his brothers' families. Starting with Suleiman, imperial wives begin to take on more power. Marriages were arranged between sultans' daughters and high-ranking servants, creating powerful new members of the imperial household. Over time, the sultan's exclusive authority waned in favor of a more bureaucratic administration. These changes brought the Ottoman court closer to the European model of factionalism, intrigue, and informal female power. (See the feature "Individuals in Society: Hürrem.")

The Ottoman Empire experienced the same economic and social crises that affected the rest of Europe in this period. In the 1580s and 1590s rebellions broke out among many different groups in the vast empire: frustrated students, underpaid janissaries, and ambitious provincial governors. Revolts continued during the seventeenth century as the janissaries formed alliances with court factions that resulted in the overthrow or execution of several Ottoman sultans.

In the late seventeenth century the Ottomans succeeded in marshaling their forces for one last attack on the Habsburgs, and a huge Turkish army laid siege to Vienna in 1683. Not only did they fail to hold the city, but their retreat became a rout. As Russian and Venetian allies attacked on

Section Review

- The Mongols under Chinggis Khan added the Kievan principality in Russia to the Mongol Empire stretching from Korea to Eastern Europe, ruling the area as the Golden Horde for the next two hundred years through the Russian princes, who collected taxes and maintained order.

- By 1480 the prince of Moscow, Ivan III, defied the khan (Mongol ruler) and seized power to begin the dynasty of the tsars.

- The reign of Ivan IV "the Terrible" featured constant war, violent purges, peasant and outlaw army (Cossack) uprisings, and the addition of vast new territories.

- Following Ivan's death, a period of chaos known as the "Time of Troubles" (1598–1618) ensued, ending with the coronation of Ivan's grandnephew, Michael, the first Romanov tsar.

- Despite ongoing rebellions, the seventeenth-century Romanov tsars succeeded in consolidating royal authority, increasing the bureaucracy and army, and acquiring Siberia and parts of Ukraine.

- Peter the Great (r. 1682–1725) transformed Russian society and the Russian landscape by drafting citizens for military or civil service, enabling him to create a powerful war machine, enlarge the empire, and build the modern, Westernized capital city of St. Petersburg on Baltic coastal land conquered from Sweden.

- Despite Christian stereotypes, the Ottoman empire was tolerant of religious diversity and protected Jews and other religious refugees.

- The Ottomans captured Constantinople in 1453 and renamed it Istanbul, then conquered much of southeastern Europe until their expansion was halted with the failed siege of Vienna in 1529.

- Highly trained slaves staffed the elite of the sultan's administration and army; while the millet system allowed autonomous self-government to religious minority groups; all land in the empire belonged to the sultan.

- Starting with Sultan Suleiman, wives began to exercise more power and the sultan's exclusive authority gave way to more bureaucratic administration.

Individuals in Society

Hürrem

In Muslim culture *harem* means a sacred place or a sanctuary, which is forbidden to profane outsiders. The term was applied to the part of the household occupied by women and children and forbidden to men outside the family. The most famous member of the Ottoman sultan's harem was Hürrem, wife of Suleiman the Magnificent.

Hürrem (1505?–1558) came to the harem as a slave-concubine. Like many of the sultan's concubines, Hürrem was of foreign birth. Tradition holds that she was born Aleksandra Lisowska in what was then the kingdom of Poland and today is Ukraine. She was captured during a Tartar raid and enslaved. Between 1517 and 1520, when she was about fifteen years old, she entered the imperial harem. Venetian ambassadors' reports insist that she was not outstandingly beautiful but was possessed of wonderful grace, charm, and good humor. These qualities gained her the Turkish nickname Hürrem, or "joyful one." After her arrival in the harem, Hürrem quickly became the imperial favorite.

Suleiman's love for Hürrem led him to break all precedents for the role of a concubine, including the rule that concubines must cease having children once they gave birth to a male heir. By 1531 Hürrem had given birth to one daughter and five sons. In 1533 or 1534 Suleiman entered formal marriage with his consort—an unprecedented honor for a concubine. He reportedly gave his exclusive attention to his wife and also defied convention by allowing Hürrem to remain in the palace throughout her life instead of accompanying her son to a provincial governorship as other concubines had done.

Contemporaries were shocked by Hürrem's influence over the sultan and resentful of the apparent role she played in politics and diplomacy. The Venetian ambassador Bassano wrote that "the Janissaries and the entire court hate her and her children likewise, but because the Sultan loves her, no one dares to speak."* She was suspected of using witchcraft to control the sultan and accused of or-

dering the death of the sultan's first-born son (with another mother) in 1553. These stories were based on court gossip and rumor. The correspondence between Suleiman and Hürrem, unavailable until the nineteenth century, along with Suleiman's own diaries, confirms her status as the sultan's most trusted confidant and adviser. During his frequent absences, the pair exchanged passionate love letters. Hürrem included information about the political situation and warnings about any potential uprisings. She also intervened in affairs between the empire and her former home. She wrote to Polish king Sigismund Augustus and seems to have helped Poland attain its privileged diplomatic status.

Hürrem and her ladies in the harem.
(Bibliothèque nationale de France)

She brought a particularly feminine touch to diplomatic relations, sending the Persian shah and the Polish king personally embroidered articles.

Hürrem used her enormous pension to contribute a mosque, two schools, a hospital, a fountain, and two public baths to Istanbul. In Jerusalem, Mecca, and Istanbul, she provided soup kitchens and hospices for pilgrims and the poor. She died in 1558. When her husband died in 1566, their son Selim II (r. 1566–1574) inherited the throne.

Drawing from reports of contemporary Western observers, historians depicted Hürrem as a manipulative and power-hungry social climber. They saw her career as the beginning of a "sultanate of women" in which strong imperial leadership gave way to court intrigue and dissipation. More recent historians have emphasized the intelligence and courage Hürrem demonstrated in navigating the ruthlessly competitive world of the harem.

Hürrem's journey from Ukrainian maiden to harem slave girl to sultan's wife captured enormous

* Cited in Galina Yermolenko, "Roxolana: The Greatest Empresse of the East," in *The Muslim World* 95, 2 (2005).

public attention. She is the subject of numerous paintings, plays, and novels as well as an opera, a ballet, and a symphony by the composer Haydn. Interest in and suspicion of Hürrem continues. In 2003 a Turkish miniseries once more depicted her as a scheming intriguer.

Questions for Analysis

1. Compare Hürrem to other powerful early modern women such as Isabella of Castile, Elizabeth I of England, and Catherine de' Medici of France.

2. What can an exceptional woman like Hürrem reveal about the broader political and social world in which she lived?

Source: Leslie P. Pierce, *The Imperial Harem: Women and Sovereignty in the Ottoman Empire* (New York: Oxford University Press, 1993).

other fronts, the Habsburgs conquered almost all of Hungary and Transylvania by 1699 (see Map 17.4). The Habsburgs completed their victory in 1718, with the Treaty of Passarowitz. From this point on, a weakened Ottoman empire ceased to pose a threat to Western Europe.

Chapter Review

What social and economic changes affected central and eastern Europe from 1400 to 1650? (page 433)

From about 1400 to 1650 social and economic developments in eastern Europe diverged from those in western Europe. In the East, after enjoying relative freedom in the Middle Ages, peasants and townspeople lost freedom and fell under the economic, social, and legal authority of the nobles, who increased their power and prestige.

How did the rulers of Austria and Prussia manage to build powerful absolute monarchies? (page 438)

Within this framework of resurgent serfdom and entrenched nobility, Austrian and Prussian monarchs fashioned absolutist states in the seventeenth and early eighteenth centuries. These monarchs won absolutist control over standing armies, taxation, and representative bodies, but they did not question underlying social and economic relationships. Indeed, they enhanced the privileges of the nobles, who filled enlarged armies and growing state bureaucracies. In exchange for entrenched privileges over their peasants, nobles thus cooperated with the growth of state power.

Triumphant absolutism interacted spectacularly with the arts. Central and eastern European rulers built grandiose palaces, and even whole cities, like Saint Petersburg, to glorify their power and majesty.

What were the distinctive features of Russian and Ottoman absolutism in this period? (page 444)

In Russia the social and economic trends were similar, but the timing of political absolutism was different. Mongol conquest and rule were a crucial experience, and a harsh indigenous tsarist autocracy was firmly in place by the reign of Ivan the Terrible in the sixteenth century. More than a century later Peter the Great succeeded in modernizing Russia's traditional absolutism by reforming the army and the bureaucracy. Farther to the east, the Ottoman sultans developed a distinctive political and economic system in which all land theoretically belonged to the sultan, who was served by a slave corps of administrators and soldiers. The Ottoman Empire was relatively tolerant on religious matters and served as a haven for Jews and other marginalized religious groups.

Key Terms

serfdom (p. 433)
hereditary subjugation (p. 434)
Peace of Westphalia (p. 436)
Bohemian Estates (p. 438)
elector of Brandenburg (p. 439)
Junkers (p. 442)
Mongol Yoke (p. 444)
boyars (p. 446)
tsar (p. 446)
service nobility (p. 446)
Cossacks (p. 446)
sultan (p. 450)
millet system (p. 451)
janissary corps (p. 453)

Notes

1. H. Kamen, "The Economic and Social Consequences of the Thirty Years' War," *Past and Present* 39 (April 1968): 44–61.
2. H. Rosenberg, *Bureaucracy, Aristocracy, and Autocracy: The Prussian Experience, 1660–1815* (Boston: Beacon Press, 1966), p. 43.
3. Quoted in Rosenberg, *Bureaucracy, Aristocracy, and Autocracy*, p. 40.

To assess your mastery of this chapter, go to **bedfordstmartins.com/mckaywestbrief**

Listening to the Past

A Foreign Traveler in Russia

*Seventeenth-century Russia remained a remote and mysterious land for western and even central Europeans, who had few direct contacts with the tsar's dominion. Knowledge of Russia came mainly from occasional travelers who had visited Muscovy and sometimes wrote accounts of what they saw. The most famous of these accounts—*Travels in Muscovy—*was by the German Adam Olearius (ca. 1599–1671), who was sent to Moscow by the duke of Holstein on three diplomatic missions in the 1630s. Published in German in 1647 and soon translated into several languages (but not Russian), Olearius's unflattering study played a major role in shaping European ideas about Russia.*

The government of the Russians is what political theorists call a "dominating and despotic monarchy," where the sovereign, that is, the tsar or the grand prince who has obtained the crown by right of succession, rules the entire land alone, and all the people are his subjects, and where the nobles and princes no less than the common folk—townspeople and peasants—are his serfs and slaves, whom he rules and treats as a master treats his servants. . . .

If the Russians be considered in respect to their character, customs, and way of life, they are justly to be counted among the barbarians. . . . The vice of drunkenness is so common in this nation, among people of every station, clergy and laity, high and low, men and women, old and young, that when they are seen now and then lying about in the streets, wallowing in the mud, no attention is paid to it, as something habitual. If a cart driver comes upon such a drunken pig whom he happens to know, he shoves him onto his cart and drives him home, where he is paid his fare. No one ever refuses an opportunity to drink and to get drunk, at any time and in any place, and usually it is done with vodka. . . .

The Russians being naturally tough and born, as it were, for slavery, they must be kept under a harsh and strict yoke and must be driven to do their work with clubs and whips, which they suffer without impatience, because such is their station, and they are accustomed to it. Young and half-grown fellows sometimes come together on certain days and train themselves in fisticuffs, to accustom themselves to receiving blows, and, since habit is second nature, this makes blows given as punishment easier to bear. Each and all, they are slaves and serfs. . . .

Although the Russians, especially the common populace, living as slaves under a harsh yoke, can bear and endure a great deal out of love for their masters, yet if the pressure is beyond measure, then it can be said of them: "Patience, often wounded, finally turned into fury." A dangerous indignation

The brutality of serfdom is shown in this illustration from Olearius's *Travels in Muscovy.* (University of Illinois Library, Champaign)

results, turned not so much against their sovereign as against the lower authorities, especially if the people have been much oppressed by them and by their supporters and have not been protected by the higher authorities. And once they are aroused and enraged, it is not easy to appease them. Then, disregarding all dangers that may ensue, they resort to every kind of violence and behave like madmen. . . . They own little; most of them have no feather beds; they lie on cushions, straw, mats, or their clothes; they sleep on benches and, in winter, like the non-Germans [natives] in Livonia, upon the oven, which serves them for cooking and is flat on the top; here husband, wife, children, servants, and maids huddle together. In some houses in the countryside we saw chickens and pigs under the benches and the ovens.

Questions for Analysis

1. In what ways were all social groups in Russia similar, according to Olearius?

2. How did Olearius characterize the Russians in general? What supporting evidence did he offer for his judgment?

3. Does Olearius's account help explain Stenka Razin's rebellion? In what ways?

4. On the basis of these representative passages, why do you think Olearius's book was so popular and influential in central and western Europe?

Source: G. Vernadsky and R. T. Fisher, Jr., eds., *A Source Book for Russian History from Early Times to 1917*, 3 vols., vol. 1, pp. 249–251. Copyright © 1972. Reprinted by permission of the publisher, Yale University Press.

Index